PALESTINE IN LATE ANTIQUITY

Palestine
in
Late Antiquity

HAGITH SIVAN

OXFORD
UNIVERSITY PRESS

OXFORD
UNIVERSITY PRESS

Great Clarendon Street, Oxford ox2 6DP

Oxford University Press is a department of the University of Oxford.
It furthers the University's objective of excellence in research, scholarship,
and education by publishing worldwide in

Oxford New York

Auckland Cape Town Dar es Salaam Hong Kong Karachi
Kuala Lumpur Madrid Melbourne Mexico City Nairobi
New Delhi Shanghai Taipei Toronto

With offices in

Argentina Austria Brazil Chile Czech Republic France Greece
Guatemala Hungary Italy Japan Poland Portugal Singapore
South Korea Switzerland Thailand Turkey Ukraine Vietnam

Oxford is a registered trade mark of Oxford University Press
in the UK and in certain other countries

Published in the United States
by Oxford University Press Inc., New York

British Library Cataloguing in Publication Data
Data available

Library of Congress Cataloging in Publication Data
Data available

Typeset by SPI Publisher Services, Pondicherry, India
Printed in Great Britain
on acid-free paper by the
MPG Books Group, Bodmin and King's Lynn

ISBN 978–0–19–928417–7

To
Lellia Cracco Ruggini
The Diva

Acknowledgements

In 2003–4 I had the privilege of holding a Senior Fulbright Hays Fellowship. My gratitude goes in the first place to the Fulbright Hays committee which selected my application. I spent that year in Israel, fortunate to benefit from the hospitality of the Hebrew University's Institute for Advanced Study and its director, Professor Benjamin Kedar and staff. My time at the Institute coincided with the presence of two research groups, one focusing on the study of Arab dialects, the other on Sanskrit poetry. I owe to members of both the pleasure of unplanned broadening of my research horizons. It was also a privilege while in Jerusalem to have been associated with the Albright Institute of Archaeology and its director, Dr Sy Gitin and staff. The excursions organized by Dr Benjamin Seidel at the Albright for fellows provided valuable insights into a host of archaeological excavations throughout Israel. A Newberry Library–British Academy fellowship enabled me to spend a few weeks in London in summer 2005 at the Palestine Exploration Fund where I greatly enjoyed the cheerful hospitality of its chief librarian, Dr Rupert Chapman. I am always grateful for the professional assistance of Pam Lerow at the University of Kansas' Word Processing Center. My thanks to Brandon Minster who helped with the maps. Thanks are also due to the University of Kansas' Graduate Research Fund for summer assistance. A month at the Rockfeller Center at Bellagio gave me an opportunity for reflection in incomparable surroundings.

While in Israel I benefited from conversations with many colleagues including Gideon Avni, Doron Bar, Shimon Dar, Lea Di Segni, Esti and Hanan Eshel, Pau Figueras, Yochanan Friedman, Tali Gini, Moti Hayman, Oded Irshai, Menahem Kister, Ian Retso, Ben Saidel, David Stern, Yoram Tsafrir, and Yossi Yahalom, as well as a host of archaeological enthusiasts who are capable of enlivening even the muted stones of the Golan and the Negev. I also owe a great deal to Ken Holum for two delightful seasons of digging in Caesarea. My friends in Jerusalem, Ada and Amitai Spitzer, and Sonia Grober and Aliza Rodnitzky in Tel Aviv made this year one of the happiest.

No study of Palestine in Late Antiquity can ignore the major contributions of Michael Avi Yonah, Yaron Dan, and Claudine Dauphin. I stand indebted.

This is a book for anyone interested in the Middle East, then and now, and for anyone willing to plunge into the complexities and diversities of one corner of this region in an age of transition. It is emphatically not intended either solely for Judaica experts or for those interested only in Christian Palestine or just in Samaritans. Rather, it brings to bear the best in the fields of scholarship which I deemed relevant to my study and which are now taught in separate academic departments, namely history, archaeology, Jewish studies, religious studies, classical literature and art. I refer to only a selected number of publications subsequent to when the bulk of the research for this book was done in 2003–4. If, amidst embracing so many disciplines I neglected a reference to an important study, I hereby tender my apologies.

Contents

List of Maps

Abbreviations

AASS	Acta Sanctorum
AB	*Analecta Bollandiana*
ACO	*Acta Conciliorum Oecumenicorum*
AHC	*Annuarium Historiae Conciliorum*
AJS Review	*Association of Jewish Studies Review*
ANRW	*Aufstieg und Niedergang der römischen Welt*
AS	*Acta Sanctorum*, 3rd edn. (Brussels 1863 ff.)
BA	*Biblical Archaeologist*
BASOR	*Bulletin of the American Schools of Oriental Research*
BF	*Byzantinische Forschungen*
BHG	*Bibliotheca Hagiographica Graeca*, 3 vols., ed. F. Halkin (Subsidia Hagiographica 8)
BJRL	*Bulletin of the John Rylands Library*, Manchester
BSOAS	*Bulletin of the School of Oriental and African Studies*
BT	Babylonian Talmud
Byz.	*Byzantion*
BZ	*Byzantinische Zeitschrift*
CBQ	*Catholic Biblical Quarterly*
CCSL	Corpus Christianorum, Series Latina
CJ	*Classical Journal*
CJ	Codex Justinianus
CPG	*Clavis Patrum Graecorum*, ed. M. Geerard, 5 vols. (Turnhout 1974–87)
CQ	*Classical Quarterly*
CSCO	Corpus Scriptorum Christianorum Orientalium
CSEL	Corpus Scriptorum Ecclesiasticorum Latinorum
CTh.	Codex Theodosianus
DACL	*Dictionnaire d'Archéologie Chrétienne et de Liturgie*
DOP	*Dumbarton Oaks Papers*

EJ	*Encyclopedia Judaica*
EO	*Échos d'Orient. Revue d'histoire, de géographie et de liturgie orientales*
Ep.	*Epistula*
ETL	*Ephemerides Theologicae Lovanienses*
FC	*Fathers of the Church* (Washington: Catholic University of America Press)
GCS	*Die griechischen christlichen Schriftsteller der ersten drei Jahrhunderte*
GRBS	*Greek, Roman and Byzantine Studies*
HAR	*Hebrew Annual Review*
HB	Hebrew Bible
HE	*Historia Ecclesiastica* (title of works by several ancient writers)
HTR	*Harvard Theological Review*
HUCA	*Hebrew Union College Annual*
IEJ	*Israel Exploration Journal*
JANES	*Journal of the Ancient Near Eastern Society*
JBL	*Journal of Biblical Literature*
JECS	*Journal of Early Christian Studies*
JEH	*Journal of Ecclesiastical History*
JJA	*Journal of Jewish Art*
JJS	*Journal of Jewish Studies*
JPOS	*Journal of the Palestine Oriental Society*
JQR	*Jewish Quarterly Review*
JRA	*Journal of Roman Archaeology*
JRS	*Journal of Roman Studies*
JSJ	*Journal for the Study of Judaism in the Persian, Hellenistic and Roman Period*
JTS	*Journal of Theological Studies*
LA	*Liber Annuus*
LXX	Septuagint version
M	Mishnah
Mansi	J. Mansi, *Sacrorum conciliorum nova et amplissima collectio*

NEAEHL	*The New Encyclopedia of Archaeological Excavations in the Holy Land*, ed. E. Stern (Jerusalem 1993)
NPNF	Nicene and Post Nicene Fathers (Edinburgh: T. & T. Clark, repr. 1988)
OC	*Oriens Christianus*
OCA	*Orientalia Christiana Analecta*
OCP	*Orientalia Christiana Periodica*
PAAJR	*Proceedings. American Academy of Jewish Research*
PEQ	*Palestine Exploration Quarterly*
PEFQS	*Palestine Exploration Fund. Quarterly Statement*
PG	*Patrologia Graeca*, ed. J.-P. Migne
PL	*Patrologia Latina*, ed. J.-P. Migne
PLRE	*Prosopography of the Later Roman Empire*, 3 vols. (Cambridge 1971–92)
PO	Patrologia Orientalis
POC	*Proche-Orient Chrétien*
PPTS	Palestine Pilgrims Text Society
PT	Palestinian Talmud
RB	*Revue Biblique*
REArm.	*Revue des Études Arméniennes*
REB	*Revue des Études Byzantines*
REG	*Revue des études grecques*
REJ	*Revue des Études Juives*
ROC	*Revue de l'Orient Chrétien*
SC	Sources chrétiennes (Paris: Éditions du Cerf)
SCI	*Scripta Classica Israelica*
SP	*Studia Patristica*
T	Tosefta
TIR. J-P	*Tabula Imperii Romani. Iudaea-Palaestina. Maps and Gazetteer*, Y. Tsafrir, L. Di Segni, J. Green (Jerusalem 1994)
TM	*Travaux et Mémoires*
TTH	Translated Texts for Historians (Liverpool)
TZ	*Theologische Zeitschrift*

VC	*Vigiliae Christianae*
ZAW	*Zeitschrift für die alttestamentliche Wissenschaft*
ZDPV	*Zeitschrift des Deutschen Palästina Vereins*
ZPE	*Zeitschrift für Papyrologie und Epigraphik*
ZSS.RA	*Zeitschrift der Savigny Stiftung für Rechtsgechichte. Romanistische Abteilung*

Greek patristic texts are cited according to the abbreviations listed in G. W. H. Lampe (ed.), *A Patristic Greek Lexicon* (Oxford 1961).

Latin patristic texts follow the abbreviations of A. Blaise and H. Chirat, *Dictionnaire latin-français des auteurs chrétiens* (Paris 1954).

Biblical and rabbinic texts follow the abbreviations listed in *JBL* 107 (1988), 579–96, and in Stemberger, *Introduction to the Talmud and Midrash* (1991), 401–3.

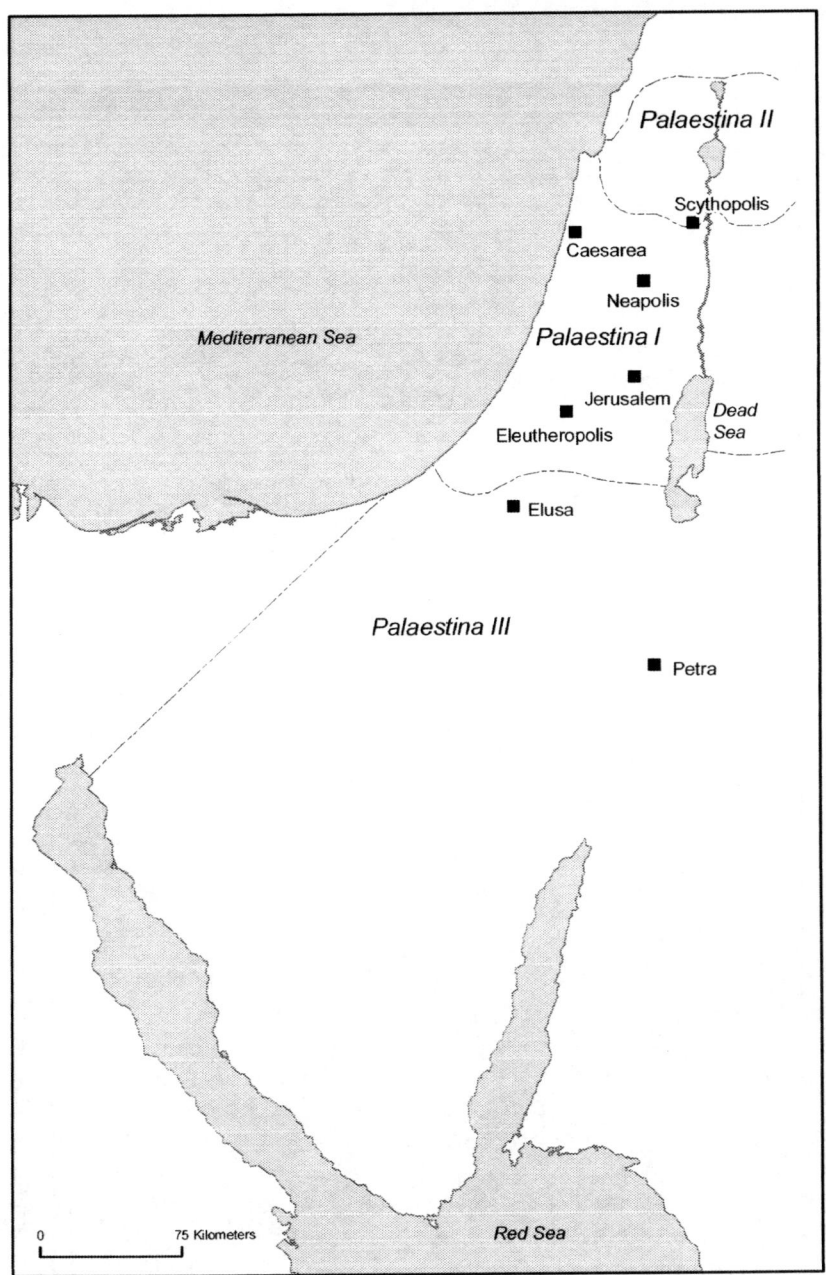

Map 1. Palaestina (overall view of the Palestinian provinces)

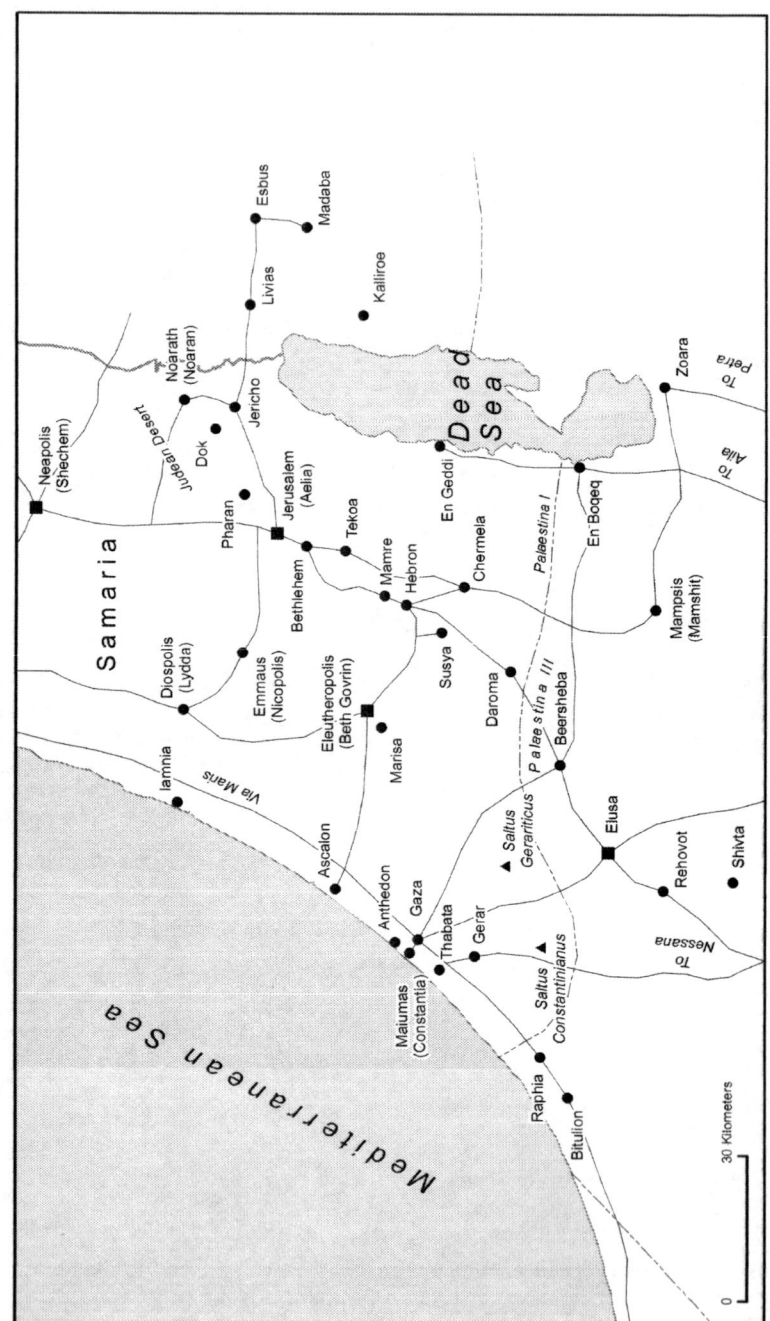

Map 2. Palaestina I (Shephela, Daroma, Gaza region, Jerusalem region)

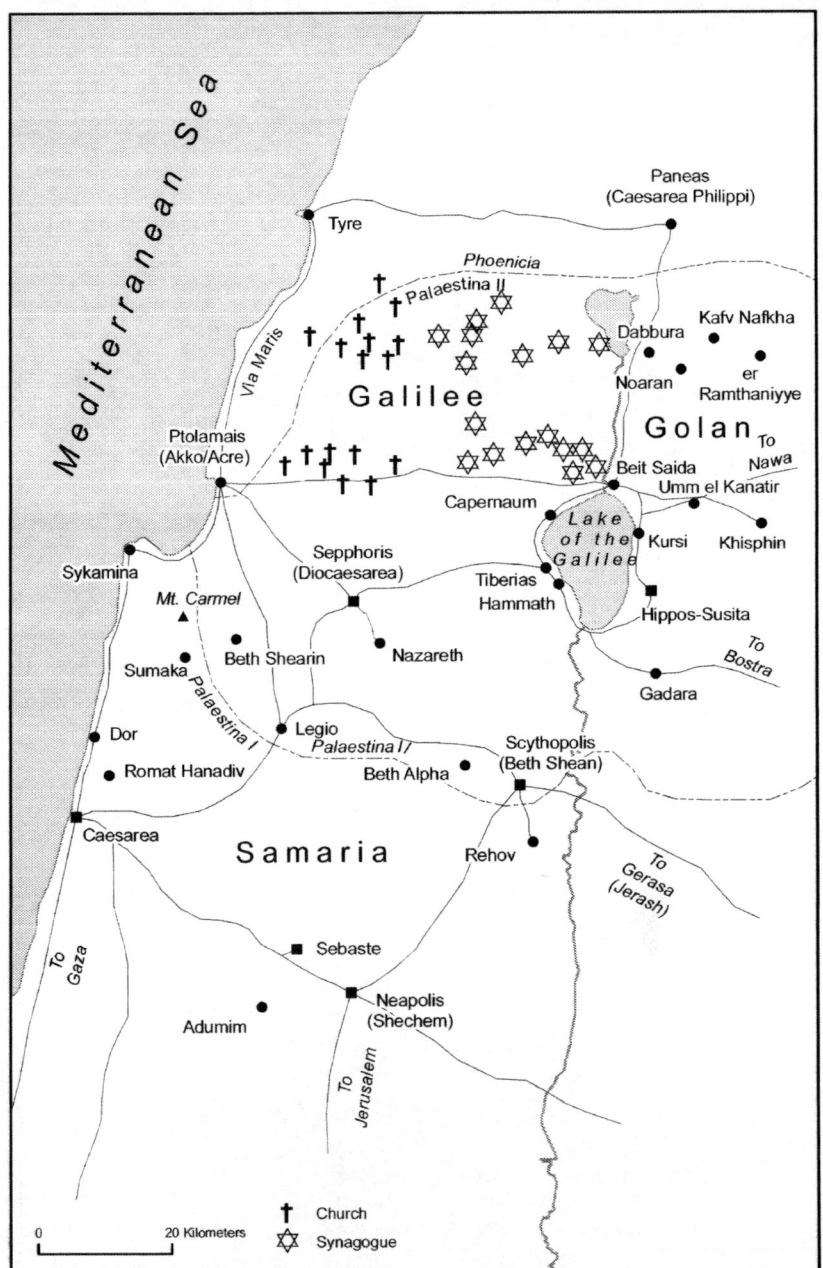

Map 3. Palaestina II (Galilee and Samaria)

Map 4. Palaestina III (Negev, Sinai, Transjordan)

Introduction

1. ANTHROPOLOGY OF A REGION

For decades the 'Orient' has exerted its magic over westerners. Not a little of its allure was (and is) due to the mixture of spices and uncivilized violence, the smells of the *souq* (market) and the sweating crowds, the veiled women and the men whose eyes never leave the bare flesh of unveiled women. This is an orient of wild contrasts, colourful and attractive yet also menacing and unfamiliar. To understand this territory, and primarily the Middle East, which continually captures the headlines, a 'trip' into its past is a must. One such is the guided 'tour' offered in this book which focuses on a period when the fortunes of the 'east' and the 'west' were intimately linked, when thousands of westerners in the guise of pilgrims, pious monks, soldiers, and civilians flocked to what became a Christian holy land. This is the period, roughly between CE 300 and 600, that witnessed the transformation of Jerusalem from a sleepy Roman town (Aelia Capitolina), itself on the ruins of the spectacular Herodian Jerusalem, into an international centre of Christianity and ultimately into a centre of Islamic worship. This is the period that accompanied the unparalleled prosperity of frontier zones, once the territory of clever nomads like the Nabataeans, and in late antiquity the scenes of numerous villages and towns whose inhabitants cultivated, against all odds, vineyards and olive groves. And this is the period in which religious experts, rabbis, Christian theologians, Samaritan reformers were actively engaged in guiding their communities while contesting the right of each other to the Bible and its interpretation.

Palestinian politics in late antiquity reveal a mixture of realism and idealism which often proved paradoxical. To begin with, there is no one 'history' of the land, or even a unified concept of 'Palestine'. For the Jews of Palestine the territory of the 'Land of Israel' (*Eretz Israel*) did not coincide with the official frontiers of the province.[1] In rabbinic collective imagination, as recorded in the Palestinian Talmud and in midrashic literature, imperial politics had scant place.[2] For Christians, likewise oblivious of conventional frontiers, the biblical past shaped the land and its history, enveloping both in intertwining circles which embraced the secular and the sacred. Even the imperial court experimented with repeated divisions of the province, thus infusing amorphous theological concepts with a concrete sense of shifting frontiers.[3]

Left to itself Palestine would have remained a provincial backwater known to Romans in late antiquity for nothing more exciting than its linen factories, to Diaspora Jews for its sanctity and its sages, and to Christians for its biblical connotations. But Palestine proved a particular challenge. Claimed by Christians as the cradle of their creed, Palestinian pre-existing monotheism, whether Jewish or Samaritan, presented a budding monotheistic emperor with theocratic histories in which divine will operated in the world of men entirely devoted to one God. The culture of Palestine, unlike that of any other province in the empire, had burgeoning historiographies that hinged on epiphanies. It rendered impossible banal presentations which deprived the enemy of the prize of a victory won with the aid of a single divinity. And it was improbable that any but a mind, like Eusebius', which had been nurtured in Palestine, would have been able to inscribe Constantine into a historiography that lifted him

---

[1] See Ch. 6.

[2] The redactional date of the Palestinian Talmud (=Yerushalmi) has been assigned to either the second half of the 4th cent. or the early 5th; the redactions of some of the *midrashim* have been assigned to the 5th. G. Stemberger, *Introduction to the Talmud and Midrash*, 2nd edn. (Edinburgh 1991), *passim*. On Talmudic reticence regarding contemporary rulers and events and its implication, M. Goodman, 'Palestinian Rabbis and the Conversion of Constantine to Christianity', in P. Schäfer and C. Hezser (eds.), *The Talmud Yerushalmi and Graeco-Roman Culture*, ii (Tübingen 2000), 1–9. On Jewish-Palestinian sources used in this study see Appendix.

[3] See Chs. 2 and 6.

from the temporality of a catalogue of human exploits to the level of mythical logic.[4]

All, yet none, were 'making history'. Palestinian-Christian history annexed to its own advantage certain events belonging to a common imperial history, transforming them into milestones of its own history. Jewish-Palestinian history developed its own rhythm occasionally and subtly arranged likewise around echoes of imperial policies. When Eusebius of Caesarea congratulated Constantine on his thirtieth anniversary he cast Christianity and Constantine as twin buffers of Jewish aggression.[5] From a Jewish point of view this same combination, namely a zealous imperial court and a fervent creed, had an increasingly detrimental effect on freedom of worship. Palestinian polytheists and Samaritans entered a phase of their history from which one never emerged and the other just barely.

In their Jewish subjects the emperors had a group that etched its own map and traditions on the land. No other minority in late antiquity was so dispersed throughout the provinces of both Rome and Persia. No other Diaspora enabled its historical centre to retain its prestigious standing and to maintain such far-flung associations.[6] In their Palestinian-pagan subjects the emperors had dwellers of flourishing cities, loyal taxpayers and helpless spectators, and often victims, of militant Christian missions. The third group, the Samaritans, adhered to long-standing traditions like the Jews from whom they had split in a mythic past. In late antiquity the Samaritans began to feature in imperial decrees as a twin sect of Judaism, both ancient monotheistic creeds of Palestine cast as representatives of illegitimate conflicts. The fourth important element of Palestinian population in late antiquity, the Christians, were negligible in size at the dawn of the fourth century. Recent victims of imperial persecutions, Christian thinkers proved exceptionally adapt at using figures of subversion as the basis of an ultimate formulation of a winning creed. From a

---

[4] In general, Av. Cameron and S. G. Hall, *Eusebius' Life of Constantine* (Oxford 1999).

[5] *Tricennial Oration* 16 (Eng. trans. NPNF, 606).

[6] F. Millar, *The Roman Near East 31 BC–AD 337* (Cambridge, Mass., 1993), *passim*. This study does not concern itself with the Jewish Diaspora of late antiquity or with its relations with Palestinian Jewry, both subjects worthy of separate studies. On the impossibility of writing the history of the Jews between 70 and 640, S. Schwartz, 'Historiography on the Jews in the "Talmudic Period"', in M. Goodman (ed.), *The Oxford Handbook of Jewish Studies* (Oxford 2002), 79–114.

collective Palestinian point of view late ancient Palestine was a periphery which was not a periphery, a space opened up by a displacement of the centre.

It is difficult to discern with precision dates which lend themselves to conventional chronology as dramatic turning points in the continuous history of the area which lies between the River Jordan and the Mediterranean.[7] There are many ways of bracketing the events, personalities, and developments which shaped the contours of ancient Palestine. None will prove hegemonic because of the multiplicity of discourses, political, religious, social, intellectual, and artistic. Hence this study encompasses two convenient, if not conclusive, periods of time, starting with Constantine in the early fourth century and ending with Abd al-Malik in the late seventh century. The first acknowledges new types of conflict which Constantine's conversion put in motion; the second marked the entry of Islam into the conflictual conversation in which triumphant religions engaged with biblical territories. Architecture lends visual testimonies to the ways in which these processes were conducted, first with the Constantinian Church of the Holy Sepulchre atop the Roman forum in Jerusalem, and then with the Dome of the Rock atop the Temple Mount, both structures defining and defying the recollections that had constituted the landscape.

2. SOURCES

The diversity of the land and of its inhabitants is well reflected in the range of the sources that relate to Palestine in late antiquity. These include, on the Jewish-Palestinian side, rabbinic exegetical works,

---

[7] See the reservations regarding the application to Palestine of the terms 'late Roman', 'late ancient', or 'Byzantine', G. W. Bowersock, 'The Greek Moses: Confusion of Ethnic and Cultural Components in Late Roman and Early Byzantine Palestine', in H. Lapin (ed.), *Religious and Ethnic Communities in Later Roman Palestine* (Bethesda 1998), 31–48, esp. 34–5. See also the counter-arguments of Lapin in his 'Introduction' to the collection, pp. 1–28, esp. 6–7. On periodization see also L. I. Levine, 'Between Rome and Byzantium in Jewish History: Documentation, Reality and the Issue of Periodization', in idem (ed.), *Continuity and Renewal: Jews and Judaism in Byzantine-Christian Palestine* (Jerusalem 2004), 7–48 (Heb.). With the exception of the Sinai this study is mostly confined to the Palestines within the present borders of the State of Israel.

synagogal poetry in Hebrew, popular poetry in Aramaic, as well as a body of material culture mostly derived from numerous archaeological digs and surveys. None lends itself too readily to a chronological organization or an analytical structure. Nor can this material be ignored. Never easy to decode, the Jewish sources which Palestine bred in late antiquity provide invaluable insights into the Zeitgeist and the ways in which the Jews of Palestine coped with changed realities.[8]

The Christians of Palestine, natives, residents, and visitors alike, produced vast literature in the shape of sermons, treatises, biblical exegesis, letters, poems, biographies, speeches, histories, diaries, and maps, in addition to visible remains in the shape of corpora of churches, monasteries, and countless artistic items unearthed in dozens of archaeological excavations on both sides of the Jordan. The Samaritans of late ancient Palestine boasted their own literature, prose and poetry alike, as well as a corpus of synagogues, artefacts, and even estates. Muted, the pagans of Palestine, by no means a homogeneous group, did not disappear, as strikingly seen in the continuity of the temples on the slopes of Mount Hermon. A body of inscriptions, in Greek, Hebrew, Aramaic, Latin, and 'Arabic' provides additional information regarding the dwellers of Palestine, as do papyri, especially the cache from Nessana. Coins, singly and collectively, inform the observer of the function of places, such as the hoard discovered in Ramat Hanadiv, a Herodian estate that became, inter alia, a place of pilgrimage in late antiquity.[9]

Some of the most illuminating and crucial evidence is derived from archaeological surveys and excavations. For example, two important monographs appeared recently on two types of settlement on Mount Carmel, one focusing on an estate owned, in all likelihood, by a wealthy Samaritan who scrupulously avoided the use of imported ceramic ware. The find points to the extent of the Samaritan orbit in

---

[8] Throughout the emphasis is on Palestine, Palestinian Jewry, and Palestinian sources. I do not deal with the Diaspora, or Diaspora literature or Diaspora Judaism and the relationship with Palestinian Jewry. These are important matters which deserve a separate treatment. Unless otherwise stated, the translations are my own. See also Appendix.

[9] Y. Hirschfeld (ed.), *Ramat Hanadiv Excavations* (Jerusalem 2000).

Palestine and to the wealth accumulated by individual Samaritans. The other excavation on Mount Carmel unearthed a mixed Jewish and non-Jewish settlement boasting a communal synagogue. The sanctuary was apparently destroyed in the early fifth century, bearing an astonishing testimony to a fanciful hagiographical narrative woven around the destructive trails which a Mesopotamian monk forged through Palestine at the very same time.

That historians have thus far shied away from integrating the archaeological data into their work is hardly surprising in view of sharp divisions among archaeologists over the interpretation of important monuments and of patterns of settlement. Two raging debates demonstrate the difficulties facing historians who are bold enough to tackle material culture. One concerns the dates of the numerous synagogues that have been identified in eastern Galilee and the Golan. Their dates have shifted recently from the second/third centuries (i.e. 'Roman') to the fifth/sixth centuries (i.e. 'Byzantine').[10] This is a move which raises a host of questions, such as the nature of rural economics (most of the synagogues were built in villages, including small ones); the sources of artistic inspiration; the relationships between legal theory and realities (imperial laws imposed severe restrictions already from as early as the fifth century on the construction of new synagogues); and the precise spread of Jewish settlement 'zones', if indeed there existed exclusively Jewish areas. The redating of synagogues has already resulted in new approaches to the religions of Palestine, such as Schwartz's hypothesis which assigns the birth of synagogal Judaism to late antiquity as an offshoot of late ancient Christianity.

The other debate, possibly even more crucial for fuller comprehension of period, places, and people, has addressed the Islamic 'conquest' of Palestine in the early seventh century. Recent reanalysis of the finds from sites ranging from Syria to the Negev shows clear signs of continuity beyond the seventh century and points to the

---

[10] Y. Tsafrir, 'The Synagogues at Capernaum and Meroth and the Dating of the Galilean Synagogue', in J. Humphrey (ed.), *The Roman and Byzantine Near East* (Ann Arbor 1995), 151–61; J. Magness, 'Synagogues in Ancient Palestine: Problems of Typology and Chronology', in Levine (ed.), *Continuity and Renewal*, 507–25 (Heb.) and the responses of Foerster and Strange in the same volume.

absence, in most places, of traces of violence and destruction.[11] This is indeed tantalizing but also problematic. Palestine has had its fair share of natural disasters, including earthquakes, droughts, and invasions of shifting sands, and it is often difficult, if not impossible without the aid of literary sources, to pinpoint a date at which places were abandoned. Even in settlements such as the urbanized zone of the northern Negev the nature of life beyond the seventh century is difficult to determine. No major new constructions, for example, can be identified anywhere. Moreover, the Negev had experienced continuous waves of migrations and of nomadic sedentarization, namely continuing cycles of settlement-abandonment-resettlement, and it is not easy to date the various phases of its development.[12] The impact of the Islamic conquest, therefore, has to be measured by several criteria, including its impact on the wine industry of Palestine, which clearly declined from the seventh century, and on the economic resources of each community that became an object of a new tax system. While the revised chronology of the Islamic conquest points indeed to life beyond 640, the quality of this life remains to be established. With all due caution, historians risk losing large chunks of the picture if they ignore the work accomplished by archaeologists. In this study I incorporate as much material culture as seems relevant in order to enliven and illuminate the literary sources.

3. CONFLICT

The hybrid nature and anomaly of the sources which the historian must use, from poetry of the synagogue to rabbinic lore, and from biographies of holy men and theological treatises to speeches

---

[11] J. Magness, *The Archaeology of the Early Islamic Settlement in Palestine* (Winona Lake 2003).

[12] Cf. the vicissitudes of the castellum at En Boqeq, a military outpost along the *limes Palestinae*, on the western coast of the Dead Sea, 13 km. south of Masada. In the course of its three centuries (mid-4th–early/mid-7th CE) the fort underwent several phases of construction, destruction, rebuilding, etc. M. Gichon, *En Boqeq: Ausgrabungen in einer Oase am Toten Meer*, 1st cent. (Mainz 1993). At the very same spot the Romans had an industrial centre, active with interruptions between the late 1st cent. BCE and the early 2nd cent. CE, for the production of perfumes and medicines from local plants. M. Fischer *et al.*, *En Boqeq, ii: The Officina: An Early Roman Building on the Dead Sea Shore* (Mainz 2000).

pleading for mimes, each in a different language, present a few shared *topoi*.[13] One, intra-communal conflicts, seems characterized by verbal and physical violence. The second, inner-communal conflicts, highlights the divisions which shaped the recorded history of each community. A third was formed by international politics, primarily by the conflict between Rome and Persia in which Palestine was never in the forefront. At any given time the complex density of Palestine's different levels of reality and imagination and its multiple discourses offered a wealth of reflections on identity, on citizenship, and on the place of individuals in the community.

To lend coherence to narratives which are distinct yet overlapping, a 'normative' outline along linear chronology risks obliterating the divisions which promoted distinctions and disputes as well as spheres of activities that often overlapped. Unlike conventional histories of specific regions or provinces, the present study explores one corner of the Roman Empire, Palestine, through a single theme, that of conflict. I emphasize 'theme', as opposed to a central 'hypothesis', because no one explanation can account for the extraordinary diversity and developments that Palestine experienced in late antiquity.

Approaches aimed at explaining the peculiarities of Palestine have resulted in histories based on ethnic or religious dichotomies, in themselves valuable but by their very nature also myopic. Thus an analysis focusing solely on Jews and Judaism, or on a central Jewish institution like the synagogue, creates an impression of ubiquitous Jewish presence at the expense, for example, of the not insubstantial Samaritan communities which are often difficult to tell apart.[14] A description of the expansion of Christianity and the creation of a Christian holy land perforce minimizes the role played by actual Jews, pagans, and Samaritans and their respective notions of sacred

[13] On the use of languages in distinct religious and ethnic contexts, F. Millar, 'Ethnic Identity in the Roman Near East 325–450: Language, Religion and Culture', *Mediterranean Archaeology* 11 (1998), 159–76; and S. H. Griffith, 'From Aramaic to Arabic: The Languages of the Monasteries of Palestine in the Byzantine and Early Islamic Period', *DOP* 51 (1997), 11–31.

[14] M. Avi Yonah, *The Jews of Palestine: A Political History from the Bar Kokhba War to the Arab Conquest* (New York 1976) (Eng. trans. of the 1946 Heb. original), S. Schwartz, *Imperialism and Jewish Society 200 BCE–640 CE* (Princeton 2001), L. I. Levine, *The Ancient Synagogue* (New Haven 2000).

places.[15] A presentation of the Samaritan revolts of the fifth and sixth centuries, central indeed to the formation of Samaritan identity in late antiquity, has little room for other forms of violence and for conflicts, no less fierce, that involved words and not only weapons.[16] Even a nuanced history of communal relationships in a single century misses a sense of continuity.[17] To the best of my knowledge the only attempt to take into account the huge array of evidence, literary as well as archaeological, has been produced, not surprisingly, by an archaeologist, and in French.[18] Besides this important contribution virtually all recent studies, even on Jerusalem, have been collective enterprises, many in Hebrew, and even these tend to focus on one community and to range from one discipline to another.[19]

Constant intertwining suggests therefore the impossibility of writing about Palestine solely from the point of view of a Christian 'majority' (or even a Jewish 'minority') not only because of absence of statistics but also because there was not one monolithic Christian community but rather many groups with Christian affinity or agenda of one type or another. The vicissitudes of the episcopal seat of Jerusalem and of the ascetic communities of the neighbouring Judaean desert provide one example of the rivalries and mutations within Palestinian Christianity.[20] Nor is it possible to measure with any precision which groups did rabbis and the writings associated

---

[15] R. Wilken, *The Land Called Holy: Palestine in Christian History and Thought* (New York 1992); A. Jacobs, *Remains of the Jews: The Holy Land and Christian Empire in Late Antiquity* (Stanford 2004).

[16] R. Pummer, *Early Christian Authors on Samaritans and Samaritanism* (Tübingen 2002).

[17] G. Stemberger, *Jews and Christians in the Holy Land: Palestine in the Fourth Century* (Edinburgh 2000) (Eng. trans. of the 1997 German edn.).

[18] C. Dauphin, *La Palestine byzantine* (Oxford 1998), 3 vols.

[19] Z. Baras *et al.* (eds.), *Eretz Israel from the Destruction of the Temple to the Muslim Conquest* (Jerusalem 1982) (Heb.); G. C. Bottini *et al.* (eds.), *One Land—Many Cultures: Archaeological Studies in Honor of Stanislau Loffreda* (Jerusalem 2003); idem *et al.* (eds.), *Christian Archaeology in the Holy Land. New Discoveries* (Jerusalem 1990); L. Levine (ed.), *Jerusalem: Its Sanctity and Centrality to Judaism, Christianity and Islam* (New York 1999); Y. Tsafrir and S. Safrai (eds.), *The History of Jerusalem: The Roman and Byzantine Periods (70–638 CE)* (Jerusalem 1999) (Heb.). E. Stern and H. Eshel (eds.), *The Samaritans* (Jerusalem 2002) (Heb.); Levine (ed.), *Continuity and Renewal* (Heb.); C. Hezser (ed.), *Rabbinic Law in its Roman and Near Eastern Context* (Tübingen 2003).

[20] See Ch. 5.

with the rabbinic class in Palestine represent. The differing orientation of synagogues throughout Palestine suggests that not all Jews
living within rabbinic orbits subscribe to rabbinic norms. Disagreements among the rabbis themselves over multiple issues, as well as
between rabbis and communal institutions such as the patriarchate,
should alert historians to the ambivalence of generalizations.

The theme of conflict has enabled me to weave together strands of
distinct histories, of peoples and of places, highlighting Palestine's
polyethnicity, and religious, cultural, topographical, and architectural diversity. That conflict is endemic in social relations and is,
in fact, a form of human association has been established long ago
by social scientists.[21] Its dynamics have been further illuminated as a
perpetual 'process of becoming', actions impacting structures and
vice versa across time and space.[22] Two social scientific approaches
facilitate the analytical horizons of the historian of late ancient
Palestine. One examines the make-up of communities in terms of
a struggle to establish cultural boundaries and group solidarity by
identifying 'deviant' internal groups as negative reference points.[23]
The other investigates how communities cope with outside
threats and how, in order to strengthen counter-arguments, these
are warded off through an adaptation of elements of the alien
culture.[24] Beyond basic physical contact the notion of conflict in
its widest cultural sense is broadly conceived to include direct
cultural competition, encounters between civilizations, syncretism
and borrowings resulting from such competition and encounters,

[21] G. Simmel, *Conflict and the Web of Group Affiliations*, trans. K. H. Wolff and
R Bendix (Glencoe, Ill., 1955); L. A. Coser, *The Functions of Social Conflicts* (New York
1956); L. Kriesberg, *The Sociology of Social Conflicts* (Englewood Cliffs, NJ, 1973). See
also the modifications of this functionalist framework as formulated by the so-called
structuration theorists, J. H. Turner, *The Structure of Sociological Theory* (Homewood,
Ill., 1974).

[22] A. Giddens, *Studies in Social and Political Theory* (London 1977); idem, *Central
Problems in Social Theory* (London 1979); P. Abrams, *Historical Sociology* (Ithaca, NY,
1982).

[23] K. T. Erikson, *Wayward Puritans: A Study in the Sociology of Deviance* (New York
1966).

[24] E. Durkheim, *The Rules of Sociological Methods*, trans. W. D. Halls (New York
1982); E. A. Nielsen, *Three Faces of God: Society and the Categories of Totality in the
Philosophy of Emile Durkheim* (New York 1999).

and intracivilizational struggles within distinct groups over central doctrines and organization.[25]

Key cultural categories provide an understanding not only of moments of conflict but also of the ideological operations that spawn multiple versions of the same contested texts. The attempt to neutralize the other works both ways. We get two opposing versions, one which assigned the main constructive role to one side and the destructive one to the other. The study of conflict examines different interpretations of the same myths and of the same events. An accurate attitude would be to assess up to what point each of the rival discourses—that of the motionless same and that of the moving other—laboured to preserve an autonomy, supporting, but at the same time threatened by the arguments of its neighbour, which aimed at erasing all alterity from a story. The temptation to convert the other back into the ranks of the same is powerful. Hence the history of conflict often becomes that of a circular argument. Conflict is the way of reversing the discourse of others to proclaim that, decidedly, one is not like them.

Moments of violence, verbal or physical, proclaim the unique character of each combatant. Moments of contest are self-referential. Antagonism plays a positive and integrative role internally as it sharpens boundaries and heightens awareness primarily vis-à-vis divergent elements. Conflict has a collectivizing effect vis-à-vis external factors. It increases internal cohesion and, in this sense, it has a double function, constructive and destructive. The question what identity or identities conflicts construct remains problematic largely because personal and communal identities comprise a multiplicity of factors.[26] In addressing these issues theories of social identity help in the understanding of the development of collective identities vis-à-vis the other and the self.[27]

In the case of Palestine the territory has been successively inhabited. Its dwellers have argued for a permanent image that rooted them in the land while assigning impermanence to the other. At

[25] B. Nelson, *On the Roads to Modernity*, ed. T. Hoff (Totowa, NJ, 1981).

[26] A. Blasi, 'Symbolic Interactionism as Theory', *Sociology and Social Research* 56 (1972), 453–65.

[27] H. Tajfel, *Human Groups and Social Categories* (Cambridge 1981).

many points in the historical narrative conflict, external and internal, has proved to have been a critical stimulant. Internal conflicts were a catalyst for the development of new views, or the forceful articulation of views which carried considerable weight. Thus, a sense of threat from 'heretics' within was part of the motivation to ensure the preservation and transmission of sound or 'orthodox' teaching. External conflicts, in the form of hostility, accusations, polemics, and violence focused attention on the aspects of identity which united groups and lent them distinction.

Because Constantine's adoption of Christianity entailed the deconstruction of 'Rome' as a secular entity and its reconstitution on a religious basis, 'becoming' and 'being' a Jew, a Christian, a pagan, or a Samaritan in late ancient Palestine assumed a cultural significance considerably beyond the perimeters of religion. With the de-secularization of imperial institutions, primarily of the emperor himself, the imperial 'supermarket of religions' changed profoundly.[28] Instead of competing systems, each offering different qualities of religious doctrines, experiences, insights, myths and stories, Constantine's conversion entailed the delegitimation of religious pluralism and tolerance, precisely and paradoxically the two traits which Christianity, as a *religio illicita*, had once strongly espoused.[29] The victory transformed the parameters of identity, radicalizing attitudes to the other and to the self. Polemical moments, texts, and attitudes and their interdependence highlight this radicalization while conflict theories help to unravel the fundamental kinship between faith and social identity.[30] Ideologues developed a boundary rhetoric which was based on principles of accentuation and assimilation and of creating insiders and outsiders. Written texts, oral confessions of faith, and rituals dramatized and embodied key dimensions of the faiths of each group. Rituals like baptism, for example, marked the transition from peripheral to core membership.

[28] J. North, 'The Development of Religious Pluralism', in J. Lieu, J. North, and T. Rajak (eds.), *The Jews among Pagans and Christians in the Roman Empire* (London 1992), 174–93; idem, 'Religious Toleration in Republican Rome', *Proceedings of the Cambridge Philosophical Society* 205 (1979), 85–103.

[29] R. Markus, *The End of Ancient Christianity* (Cambridge 1991).

[30] G. G. Stroumsa, 'From Anti-Judaism to Antisemitism in Early Christianity?', in O. Limor and G. G. Stroumsa, *Contra Iudaeos: Ancient and Medieval Polemics between Christians and Jews* (Tübingen 1996), 1–26, esp. 9–10.

Like conflict theories, sociology of religion provides a mechanism for understanding differences and rivalries.[31] The study of Jewish–Christian relations, for example, has enlisted conflict theory to explain the birth and development of Christian anti-Judaism as an extension of a competition between a new religion and an old yet still dynamic and combative one.[32] It has demonstrated how theological discourse, disenfranchising laws, and violent attacks conspired to destabilize if not to eliminate Judaism. More recently, scholars have emphasized how conflict catered more to intrinsic need of self-affirmation, dealing with 'debates' which cast the Jews as straw figures, complementary characters to heretics and pagans who were the other object of Christian polemical writings.[33]

In the last decade the concept of a 'clash of civilizations', as elaborated by Samuel Huntington, has become something of a vogue in describing contemporary conflicts and in predicting the shape of things to come.[34] At the heart of such gigantic conflicts stand cultures which coexist solely in conflict because they are in essence irreconcilable. Late ancient Palestine provides a forerunner of the ways in which citizenship coalesces around culture and religion. My investigation focuses on the shaping of patterns of cohesion and conflict as they revolved around alignments of identity. At a micro-level this study provides an analysis of forms of conflict in one multicultural society during a period in which the West, in this case the Roman empire, was in

[31] M. Weber, *From Max Weber: Essays in Sociology*, trans. H. H. Gerth and C. Wright Mills (New York 1946); L. Febvre, *A New Kind of History*, trans. K. Folca (New York 1973); V. Turner, *Dramas, Fields and Metaphors. Symbolic Action in Human Society* (Ithaca, NY, 1975); M. Halbwachs, *On Collective Memory*, trans. L. Coser (Chicago 1992).

[32] M. Simon, *Verus Israel*, Eng. trans. (Oxford 1986); J. Parkes, *The Conflict of the Church and the Synagogue: A Study in the Rise of Antisemitism* (London 1934). But see M. S. Taylor, *Anti-Judaism and Early Christian Identity: A Critique of the Scholarly Consensus* (Leiden 1994), *passim* for reservations regarding the applicability of conflict theory to Jewish–Christian polemics. Taylor contends that this model fails to take into account Christian internal dynamics which generated theological confrontations with a projected rather than with living Judaism,

[33] R. Ruether, *Faith and Fratricide: The Theological Roots of Anti-Semitism* (New York 1974); J. Cohen (ed.), *Essential Papers on Judaism and Christianity in Conflict* (New York 1991).

[34] S. P. Huntington, *The Clash of Civilizations and the Remaking of World Order* (New York 1996).

decline, as was the East, namely the Persian-Sassanid empire, while in the south a new power, that of the Arabs, was gathering momentum.

Ancient sources offer ready support for the paradigmatic polarization that came to characterize the sanctification of Palestine as a Christian Holy Land. They underline the intellectual and cultural interests that denounced yet gave weight to conflicting interpretations of the same events and same sacred texts. Hence the examination of exemplary cases confers concreteness on the contradictions of history. Moving from texts to religious and cultural contexts one is better equipped to go back and to see the inextricable intermingling of actual history and the temporalities of the clashes which strive to turn the now into an always.

Palestine in conflict and Palestine in concord. It remains to be seen whether these categories confine us to speaking the language of our sources or of our own times. It is vital to expose society to what it rejected ideologically yet lived in the time of the event. It is necessary to examine the forces of conflict that established the political stage as much as they destroyed it. And it is crucial to listen to the multiplicity of voices and to respect the multilayered instances of enunciation without isolating a particular discourse. To focus on turbulence means to widen and develop the examination of layers of order which society carefully constructs. Violence, wars, plagues, epidemic, insurrection, all ultimately wound and weaken the fabric of society which they target.

Consigned to a single smallish territory, Palestinian contests and confrontations provide symbols of the perennial nature of 'civilized' clashes. Local conflicts, limited as they were, nevertheless informed larger clashes, and vice versa. Within the centuries-old rivalry between Rome-Byzantium and Sassanid Persia the province of Palestine had a marginal role. But the Persian conquest of Jerusalem in CE 614, in itself only one indication of the shrewd strategy of Chosroes, elicited greater verbal vehemence than the entire campaign which brought the Persians to the gates of Constantinople.[35] For Jews, ready to identify Chosroes with Cyrus, his remote biblical ancestor, Persian control over Jerusalem suggested a possible revival of old hopes of

---

[35] H. Sivan, 'From Byzantine to Persian Jerusalem: Jewish Perspectives and Jewish-Christian Polemics', *GRBS* 41 (2000), 277–306.

renewing rituals on the Temple Mount. Christian characterization of the same experience, likewise rooted in the Hebrew Bible, cast the conquest as a repetition of the Babylonian seizure of the city with its attendant deprivation and exile. Neither proved right. The most crucial break with the past came in 692, with the erection of a golden mosque on the same site.

1

Prologue: From Constantine
to Abd al-Malik

Mogueime had already shown himself to be somewhat different from the common soldier when the debate took place about the conquest of Santarem and the rape and beheading of the Moorish women, and if it is true that at the time he betrayed a tendency to let his imagination run riot, then, ironically enough, it could be that for this very same reason, if truth is to prevail, we will find the difference in his nature stemming from doubt, from the subsequent reordering of a fact, from the oblique verification of his motives, from an ingenuous questioning of the influence each one of us has over the actions of others without knowing it, an influence deliberately denied by those who claim to be entirely responsible for their own actions.

José Saramago, *The History of the Siege of Lisbon*, trans.
Giovanni Pontiero, p. 202

This novel, whose title suggests a book on Portuguese history, permits the author to speculate about the difference between historiography, historical novels and 'stories inserted into history' which is the type of book Saramago himself prefers to write.

Giovanni Pontiero (ibid. 313)

1. CONSTANTINIAN LANDSCAPES

Some time around 300 a young Roman soldier encountered a young Palestinian, perhaps in a dream, perhaps through the suggestive words of a fiery itinerant preacher. The result was a personal choice that changed the outlook of an empire. When Constantine elected to adopt a Palestinian creed as his chosen faith he inherited a set of values that anchored the life of Jesus in the soil of a remote and once troublesome province.[1] Had he undertaken a journey to Jesus' home-land which his efforts had lifted from comfortable obscurity into universal limelight he would have found a land soaked in biblical memories and embellished with classically inspired pagan temples, circuses, and theatres. He never did.

Yet, imperial politics lent coherence and reality to the complex affairs of Palestine in late antiquity. History, in its basic sense of an orderly account of events leading from one emperor to another, was shaped in centres of power, far away from Palestine. Decisions taken in Constantinople prompted, as in the case of the Samaritans of Palestine, a series of revolts which punctured an ever fragile intra-communal balance.[2] Inner court intrigues reverberated all the way to Palestine, sending imperial women to visit and even to live in the province where their propinquity, piety, and wealth maximized the presence of the Church.[3] In the early seventh century the centuries-long conflict with Persia reached the gates of Jerusalem, bringing with it both the imperial army and the emperor. It was the first imperial 'visit' to Palestine since Maximinus celebrated his birthday at Caesarea in 306 with the sending to the beasts of women and men convicted of Christianity.[4] It proved to be the last.

If Constantine had embarked on a road to Jerusalem in 335, say to attend the dedicatory celebration of the church of the Holy Sepulchre which had been constructed with generous imperial funding, one ideal point of departure would have been the port of Phoenician Tyre. Already in 315 the town boasted an active bishop and a large

---

[1] The conversion of Constantine, a perennial topic of interest, has been the subject of several recent reassessments including E. Hartley *et al.* (eds.), *Constantine the Great: York's Roman Emperor. Catalogue of an exhibit* (York 2006).

[2] See Ch. 3 below. For the war of words which the court, through legislation, conducted against Judaism, Samaritanism, and other minorities, H. Sivan, 'Canonizing Law in Late Antiquity: Legal Constructs of Judaism in the Theodosian Code', in M. Finkelberg and G. G. Stroumsa (eds.), *Homer, the Bible and Beyond: Literary and Religious Canons in the Ancient World* (Leiden 2002), 213–25. See also M. A. Rabello, *Giustiniano, Ebrei e Samaritani alla luce delle fonti storico–litterarie, ecdesiastiche e giuridiche*, 2 vols. (Milan 1987–8).

[3] See Chs. 5 and 8.   [4] Eusebius, *Mart. Pal.* 6.3–7.

church. Both were objects of praise by Eusebius, bishop of Palestinian Caesarea, who would have acted as the emperor's trusted guide to the biblical antiquities of the area.[5] At Tyre the imperial visitor would have been greeted by Paulinus the bishop, his small yet enthusiastic congregation, as well as by representatives of other communities. Among the latter would have been members of Jewish priestly castes (*cohanim*), perhaps sons of the men who hastened to greet the emperor Diocletian during his passage through Tyre.[6] Their presence would have accentuated a process of distortion by which the Jewish and Christian communities in neighbouring Palestine defined themselves. Oblivious of provincial boundaries and imperial dictates, the rabbis incorporated the area of Phoenician Tyre in a 'Land of Israel'. The 'map' overtly recognized the presence of Jews in the region and their competence to abide by rules and rituals which obligated communities with a Jewish majority.[7] Based on the same difficult and ambiguous text, Eusebius' ingenuity translated the geography of the Hebrew Bible (= Old Testament) in terms of Christian scholarship to create a different kind of gazetteer of biblical localities (the *Onomasticon*). Such symmetrical scholarly acts laid the foundations of Christian reformulation of the same territory.[8]

In 335, the year of Constantine's *tricennalia*, the thirtieth anniversary of his accession to the imperial throne, Tyre was the scene of a major ecclesiastical council. The city provided easy access to the prelates from Egypt and Syria who had been summoned to address, and redress, divisive theological issues which had originated with Athanasius of Alexandria.[9] The imperial attempt to deal with such

---

[5] On the date of the Tyre encaenia, T. D. Barnes, *Constantine and Eusebius* (Cambridge, Mass., 1981), 162. On the dedicatory celebration in general, M. A. Fraser, 'The Feast of the Encaenia in the Fourth Century and in the Ancient Liturgical Sources of Jerusalem', (Ph.D. diss. University of Durham 1995; available through the internet). See also H. A. Drake, *Constantine and the Bishops: The Politics of Intolerance* (Baltimore 2000), *passim*.

[6] *PT Ber.* 3.1 on *cohanim* requiring specific rabbinic dispensation to cross a cemetery on the way to the imperial gathering at Tyre. See also F. Millar, *The Emperor in the Roman World* (Ithaca 1977), 31.

[7] See Ch. 6.

[8] J. Neusner, *Judaism and Christianity in the Age of Constantine* (Chicago 1987), *passim*.

[9] D. Arnold, *The Early Episcopal Career of Athanasius of Alexandria* (Notre Dame 1991), *passim*.

issues locally, through synods in Palestinian Caesarea and Phoenician Tyre, underlined a misclassification which deemed Alexandrian 'heresies' a local provincial matter.[10] The selection of Caesarea and of Tyre further highlighted the threads which linked Christianities throughout the region in moments of conflict and conciliation.

Neither synod was attended by Athanasius of Alexandria, who suspected, rightly, an adverse conclusion. He opted instead to escape to Constantinople, a manoeuvre which anticipated, by more than a century, the activities of Juvenal of Jerusalem in the aftermath of the 451 ecumenical council of Chalcedon.[11] The bishops assembled at Tyre were not allowed to disperse to their respective homes. Constantine ordered them to repair to Jerusalem, where they were to lend their august presence to the festivities accompanying the dedication of the church of the Holy Sepulchre. The absence of the emperor himself was not to impair the lavish scale of the solemnities which Marinus, the imperial *notarius*, orchestrated on the occasion and in honour of its summoned guests.[12] A crowd of all ages and both sexes surged in waves to meet the bishops, kissing their feet, plucking the fringes of their garments, and presenting their little ones to them.[13]

An imperial journey to Jerusalem, if undertaken in the 330s by an emperor intent on surveying the progress of Christianity in his realm, would have presented a few options. Even at Tyre, notwithstanding its imposing cathedral-church, it was rather the circus which drew the attention and admiration of casual visitors.[14] Directly east, along a road that traversed Phoenicia from Tyre to Damascus, was Caesarea Philippi (Paneas), a town at the foot of Mount Hermon. Even before Constantine, Paneas had been a popular pilgrimage spot both for admirers of Pan and devotees of Jesus. In the early fourth century a pious dignitary *en passant* would have had an opportunity to view

[10] The Caesarea synod was to take place in 334; P. Lond. 1913, Bell, 45 f.; Soz. *HE* 2.25; Theod. *HE* 1.28. Athanasius, *Festal Letters*, index, s. A. (Robertson 503). See Ch. 8.

[11] See Chs. 5 and 8.

[12] Eusebius, *VC* 4.41–6.

[13] Such is the unflattering description by Jerome of the solemn march of John of Jerusalem from the church of the Resurrection in his letter to Pammachius, 11; and n. 34, p. 25.

[14] *Expositio totius mundi et gentium* (ed. J. Rougé), 32.

there a bronze statue of Jesus in the act of performing a miracle.[15] Non-Christians would have argued, however, that this same artistic object represented the god Asclepius healing a sick woman.[16] This was the kind of disagreement in which each side, sharing practices, invoked its own history. The success of the (Christian) copy over the (pagan) model highlighted the process that privileged Christianity's relationship with Christ in a territory with pagan and Jewish roots. Matching gestures with biblical narratives, the Jesus-erstwhile-Asclepius derived divine dimensions from mimesis because the identifier could mould their words on a world which was known to everyone.

Unhappy faces of citizens would have reminded the emperor of the crushing burden of taxes which rendered the remote court, and an immediate ruler, unpopular in spite of organized *adventus* fanfare. The inhabitants of Paneas threatened, under Diocletian, to leave their town *en masse* to avoid paying taxes. The threat was met with a cynical remark: 'They will not go and even if they do, they will return'.[17] Not all the town councillors, members of the *boule*, would have been present during festivities honouring an emperor. The 'honour' of serving the council was burdensome. Even the wilderness of the Jordan appeared attractive by comparison with the imperial tax collector in civilized Paneas.[18]

From the height of Mount Hermon at whose foot spread the town of Paneas, an emperor could have caught glimpses of the milestones which designated the newly devised provincial boundaries between Phoenicia, Arabia, and Palestine. A sense of the artificiality of divisions drawn at the court would have been carried on whiffs of winds blowing simultaneously from the hilly plateau of the Golan, which officially belonged to Palestine, from the hilly Bashan, which was assigned to Arabia, and from watery Paneas, which belonged to Phoenicia. The successors of Diocletian and Constantine would continue to shift provincial boundaries, adding to Palestine, detracting from Arabia, and finally creating (in 409, *CTh.* 7.4.30), three Palestines (Palaestina prima, secunda, and tertia), each with its capital (Caesarea, Scythopolis, and Petra/Halusa respectively).

But for milestones which acted as witnesses of boundaries, be they of provinces, of estates, or of villages, the landscape of the Golan

---

[15] Eusebius, *HE* 7.18.   [16] Ibid. and below, Ch. 2.
[17] *PT Shev.* 9.2 (38d).   [18] *PT San.* 15.2 (26b).

(Jawlan) south of Paneas presented an image that conformed more with communal, even credal division, rather than with governmental dictates. At Paneas an emperor could feast on rice of exceptional quality cultivated by Jewish farmers who paid taxes in Phoenicia but who were, like those of Tyre, also held responsible for the tithe paid by residents of the rabbinic 'Land of Israel'.[19] From Paneas the *cursus publicus* (the Roman imperial post) southwards crossed the Golan. Authorized travellers could stop at staging posts (*mansiones*) which offered accommodation, repasts, and change of horses. One such *mansio*, at Naaran, was located on the crest of a basalt promontory.[20] It had started as a fortress, later acquired a chapel, and afterwards was augmented by a monastery and a hostel (*xenodochion*). The plan reflected distinct aspects of life in the periphery—the tenacious pursuit of livelihood, the ever-present threat of hostile incursions, the allure of relative isolation for the pursuit of monastic vocation, and the determination of pilgrims to cross uncharted territories on the way to desired destinations.

In the fourth century, settlements like Golanide Farj near Naaran would have engendered bewilderment. Their position on raised ground indicated danger yet the presence of a hostel suggested neutrality; their urban architecture evoked the design outline Jewish towns in rabbinic discourses yet the profusion of contrasting religious symbols and multiplicity of languages suggested the servicing of different groups, creeds, and cultural habits. The village of Farj consisted of clusters of fortifiable building units whose outer walls formed a continuous defence wall. It contained a structure identified as a synagogue as well as architectural elements bearing typical Jewish symbols. And it provided a model of what the rabbis defined as a Jewish townlet (*ayarah*).[21] Yet, inscriptions in Greek and early Arabic, in addition to those in Hebrew and Aramaic, and an ubiquitous presence of incised crosses, seem signs of rupture that suggest not homogeneity but heterogeneity.

[19] *M Dem.* 2.1.
[20] C. Dauphin and S. Gibson, 'Ancient Settlements in their Landscapes: The Results of Ten Years of Survey on the Golan Heights (1978–1988)', *Bulletin of the Anglo-Israel Archaeological Society* 12 (1992–3), 11, date unclear, perhaps fourth, perhaps third cent.
[21] *T Eruv.* 4.4–5; Dauphin and Gibson, 'Ancient Settlements', 19–22.

At Farj, a settlement not atypical of the northern Palestinian periphery, lived Jews, pagans, and Christians in configurations that defy facile generalizations. The proximity of the Golan to the eastern Galilee, bastion of Judaism in late antiquity, created a sphere of exchange and a strong bond.[22] The presence of Jewish-Christians, surmised from the juxtaposition of Jewish and Christian symbols within the same architectural and artistic context, proposes antithetical meanings with a specification that was derived rather than primal. The use of Arabic and of Christian symbols has been linked with the arrival (in the fifth century) of Monophysite Ghassanid whose Hawran *hirta*, Jabiya, was just to the east and whom the government invited to provide protection for a zone threatened by other Arab nomads who were allied with Persia.[23] At Farj, Jews, Monophysites, and polytheists engaged in complex relations that witnessed the efflorescence of Christian 'heresies', the partial sedentarization of Arabic nomads, and the tenacious preservation of Judaism.

Remote as the village appeared, its surviving stones show how closely fastened to the centre the periphery could have been. One lintel at Farj featured on the same surface a menorah, the quintessential Jewish symbol of antiquity, a fish, symbolic letters (omega, epsilon, and sigma), and a cross. The latter's dimensions, considerably larger than those of all the other symbols, would have been understood to imply a duplication of the cross which towered above the Jerusalemite Rock of Calvary.[24] If this indeed had been the intent, the competing language of symbols stressed the blocking of one creed by another, a process further underlined by the conversion of Farj's Jewish synagogue into a Christian centre of worship (mid-fifth century?).[25] There was no reverse procedure.

---

[22] On the Galilee see the articles assembled in L. I. Levine, *The Galilee in Late Antiquity* (New York 1992).

[23] On the Ghassanid see I. Šahid, *Byzantium and the Arabs in the Fifth Century* (Washington, DC, 1989), and idem, *Byzantium and the Arabs in the Sixth Century*, i (Washington 1995).

[24] J. E. Taylor, *Christians and the Holy Places: The Myth of Jewish-Christian Origins* (Oxford 1993), 39.

[25] C. Dauphin *et al.*, 'Païens, juifs, judéo-chrétiens, chrétiens et musulmans en Gaulanitide', *POC* 46 (1996), 334.

Constantine had set great store by efforts to plant Christian sanctuaries in areas where one creed had been dominant and where 'no one had dared to build churches'.[26] Lending unqualified support to individual enterprises, such as those initiated by converts from Judaism to Christianity, the emperor appreciated those who best knew the tactics of introducing credal heterogeneity. In the 330s an alliance between a Jewish convert (Joseph)—who had been an intimate of the family of the Jewish patriarchs—and Constantine, resulted in formal imperial endorsement of a wide-ranging plan to introduce Christianity into eastern Galilee where Jews had been a majority for centuries and Judaism was widely practised. Diocaesaea (Sepphoris) was singled out as was Tiberias. At Sepphoris the introduction of a church into the urban landscape would have posed a challenge to the tenor and rhythm of Jewish life and to the kind of Jewish–pagan symbiosis that had promoted Hellenistic aesthetics in the town, dictating the dimensions of a gentle communal interaction.[27]

To win ground in Tiberias, where a church was planned on the grounds of a public building (the Hadrianeum), perhaps originally a temple, Joseph and his former co-religionists engaged in a stratagem of sorcery. Tiberiade Jews who favoured maintaining the space as a bathhouse tried to prevent the erection of the church through magic; Joseph enlisted Jesus to cancel out Jewish spells. A crowd of interested spectators cheered the 'winners' as though it was a chariot race.[28] Joseph's reported 'triumph' in Tiberias, if historical, had multiple meanings. It provided a most trenchant statement of Constantine's equation between kingdom and creed. It affirmed the constitution of the new imperial creed with the substitution of Christ and Constantine for Hadrian and the Hadrianeum. And it demonstrated the superiority of Christian over Jewish 'magic' since the sign of the cross repeatedly achieved what other faith symbols failed to accomplish.

---

[26] The phrase comes from the narrative of the life of Joseph, a Jewish convert appointed *comes* by Constantine, Epiphanius, *Panarion.* 30 and 103–4, 114–15, 180–2.

[27] Constantine detached territory from Sepphoris in favour of Helenopolis near Nazareth and Naim, A. H. M. Jones, *The Later Roman Empire* (Norman, Okla., 1964), 46; Stemberger, *Jews and Christians in the Holy Land*, 9.

[28] *Pan.* 12, proclaiming that 'one is the god who helps Christians'. Cf. chariot races in Gaza where creed rather than sportive skills was judged the winner, see Ch. 8; on Joseph and his activities, see Ch. 4.

The competition over Palestinian landscapes as articulated by Joseph and espoused by Constantine set out to define both city and citizens as components of a country of Christianity. The location of Joseph's main recorded activity, Tiberias, was carefully calculated to enhance the exploit in the full flow of nascent Christian imperialism.[29] The city was the home of the Jewish patriarch, the most elevated position in the Jewish community empire-wide.[30] Tiberias boasted a decisive Jewish majority and its city council (*boule*) was, in all likelihood, entirely Jewish. Even the Hadrianeum-turned-bathhouse, designated to become a church, had been the arena of ceremonial conversion. The Palestinian Talmud reports that in order to purify the space and render it usable for Jewish bathing, a local rabbi orchestrated a statue bashing which a local gentile executed.[31] By the early fifth century Tiberias lost the patriarchs but not its Jewish aristocracy.[32] Two centuries later, when Heraclius stopped at Tiberias on his triumphant march to restore the True Cross to Jerusalem, he made a point of imposing his costly presence on Benjamin, the wealthiest Jew in the city.[33]

In Tiberias, as elsewhere in Palestine, architecture became a weapon in an arsenal of words and actions that mobilized violence. Joseph's endeavours in the lower Galilee were recorded by Epiphanius, a Palestinian from Eleutheropolis (Beth Govrin) who became a bishop of Salamis in Cyprus. Epiphanius gained fame as the compiler of an influential list of heresies into which he inserted the story of Joseph (*c.*370). The narrative dealt with open dissension between Jews and former-Jews in the Galilee. It also criticized the Tiberiade patriarchy, an institution at which Jewish sages and priests also

[29] E. Reiner, 'Joseph the Comes of Tiberias and the Jewish-Christian Dialogue' in Levine (ed.), *Continuity and Renewal*, 355–86.

[30] On the patriarchy, D. Goodblat, *The Monarchic Principle* (Tübingen 1994); M. Jacobs, *Die Institution des jüdischen Patriarchen* (Tübingen 1995); L. I. Levine, 'The Status of the Patriarch in the Third and Fourth Centuries', *JJS* 47 (1996), 1–32; Stemberger, *Jews and Christians*, 230–68.

[31] *PT AZ* 4.4 (43d). Cf. *GenR* 79.6 on the purification of the city from corpses by R. Shimon b. Yohai.

[32] According to CTh 16.8.29, by 429 the patriarchate was replaced by two sanhedrins in Palaestina I and II respectively. A. Linder, *The Jews in Roman Imperial Legislation* (Detroit 1987), no. 53.

[33] H. Sivan, 'Palestine between Byzantium and Persia (CE 614–619)', in *La Persia e Bisanzio. Atti dei Convegni Lincei* (Rome 2004), 77–92, and 47–50.

levelled criticism. What the anti-heretical tirades of Epiphanius failed to reveal, however, was the fact that the compiler himself, an apparent model of orthodoxy, was accused of heresy by the bishop of Jerusalem:

We were present when the bishop Epiphanius spoke against Origen in your (i.e. John of Jerusalem) church. He was the ostensible, you the real object of attack. You and your crew grinned like dogs, drew in your nostrils, scratched your heads, nodded to one another and talked of the 'silly old man'. Did you not, in front of the Lord's tomb, send your archdeacon to tell him to cease discussing such matters?[34]

So multiple breaks existed between ethnic groups, cultures, and creeds, and among themselves. The process that attempted to substitute one religion for another transcended its agents. Joseph's activities threatened the cohesion of Jewish society. Epiphanius' appearance in Jerusalem revealed principal cleavages in Palestinian Christianity.

Had Constantine passed through Tiberias, as Heraclius would do three centuries later, he would have arrogated the hospitality of the Jewish patriarch, the richest man in town and one of the wealthiest in the land. Against patriarchal wishes the welcoming party would have probably included a delegation of Jewish priests. Imperial policies vis-à-vis Jewish leadership contributed, in the fourth century, to the elevation of the patriarch to the rank of *spectabilis* and to the showering of privileges on this inherited position.[35] Paradoxically, the patriarch was to become an ally of the emperor in a territory where political practice stressed rather than soothed credal divergences. Allowing a certain measure of autonomy to this Jewish aristocrat confirmed the uniqueness of the patriarchy in the general economy of social relations.[36] Unlikely at first glance, the alliance between

---

[34] Jerome, To Pammachius against John of Jerusalem, 11; Eng. trans. NPNF.

[35] Stemberger, *Jews and Christians*, 228–45 on power and political influence.

[36] Note, however, that priests and not the patriarch were the men who allegedly met with the emperor Julian to discuss the imperial plan to rebuild the Temple in Jerusalem in 363 and priests were also the alleged recipients of a letter from the empress Eudocia regarding permission to re-enter Jerusalem around 440. Both instances, however, are recorded in hostile sources, the Syrian Julian romance and the biography of Barsauma, composed after the elimination of the patriarchy by Theodosius II (CTh. 16.8.29, CE 429). On the former, M. van Esbroeck, 'Le soi-disant Roman de Julien l'Apostat', *OCA* 229 (1987), 191–202; on Barsauma see Ch. 2.

Christian emperors and the descendants of the house of David accounted, in all likelihood, for the gentle pace of the Christianization of Palestine in the fourth century. The removal of the patriarchy at the start of the fifth century heralded a strategy of violence which contrasted strongly with the realism of the previous century.[37]

From Tiberias one could reach Jerusalem by heading directly south, not however without making an obligatory stop in lovely Scythopolis (Beth Shean). At Scythopolis, Constantine could have dined with Joseph, who elected to retire to the anonymity which a bustling city boasting a pagan majority and an Arian minority was well able to afford a converted Jew. Another invitee to such an exclusive dinner party would have been the city's bishop, successor of the prelate who had attended the ecumenical council of Nicaea in 325. Orthodoxy and Arianism, like Christianity and paganism, found fertile battlegrounds in fourth-century Scythopolis. Constantius II, Constantine's son and successor, attempted to silence a vociferous Italian bishop who had preached unmitigated orthodoxy, by exiling him to the Arian 'safety' of Palestinian Scythopolis.[38] Far from the main arenas of dogmatic debates, in a neighbourhood full of polytheists, a converted Jew, an Italian exile, and a Palestinian expert on heresy could converse amiably with a newly converted emperor over a table covered with plush local linen.

To proceed from Scythopolis directly to Jerusalem meant passing through the city of Neapolis and the region of Samaria. Curiosity might have impelled Constantine to climb Mount Gerizim, the sacred centre of Samaritanism near Neapolis. On the top stood a temple to Jupiter which, under the leadership of the legendary Samaritan reformer Baba Rabba, became the target of repeated

---

[37] It seems likely that it also ushered in a new Judaism, formulated in response to and under the influence of Christianity, as D. Boyarin, *Dying for God: Martyrdom and the Making of Christianity and Judaism* (Stanford 1999), *passim*, and S. Schwartz, *Imperialism and Jewish Society 200 BCE to 640 CE* (Princeton 2001), *passim*, have argued. The relations between the Jewish patriarchs and the representatives of the government in Palestine reflect, however, an uneasy political alliance. Libanius, *Ep.* 1251 (Stern, *Greek and Roman Authors*, 598) hints at patriarchal influence over the *consularis Palestinae* (in this case Priscianus, early 360s), but Libanius, *Ep.* 1105 and Jerome, *Ep.* 57.2 also refer to strained relations between the patriarch and the *consulares*, Hilarius (392/3) and Hesychius respectively. In the latter case the enmity led to the governor's execution under Theodosius I (*PLRE* 1, Hesychius 4).

[38] Eusebius of Vercellae apparently lived in Joseph's house, where Epiphanius met him. On Eusebius see F. dal Covolo *et al.* (eds.), *Eusebio di Vercelli e il suo tempo* (Rome 1997).

Samaritan assaults.[39] It was also possible to take the long route to Jerusalem by turning from Scythopolis westward in the direction of the Mediterranean. It would have been a worthwhile diversion. The city of Caesarea Maritima, constructed by Herod in honour of his Roman imperial patron Augustus, was an apt choice for the headquarters of the provincial administration of the Palestinian provinces.[40]

In Caesarea the presence of Samaritans was very much in evidence, especially in the ranks of the provincial administration.[41] Many Samaritans also served in the Roman army. Samaritan soldiers would have been put, from the late fifth century onward, in an awkward position. They would have been called upon to suppress the rebellions of their own co-religionists or to engage in combating Monophysite monks fighting for their faith. Was it their intimate familiarity with the 'secrets' of empire that made them appear formidable when, in response to growing governmental restrictions, they embarked on a series of insurgencies? Viewed from Constantinople the disruption caused by the Samaritans appeared to pose a grave threat to the fragile balance of creeds and cultures in Palestine.[42]

The metropolis of Caesarea was ethnically colourful. Besides Samaritans it boasted a sizeable Jewish community whose rabbis worried about the suitability of Samaritan wine for the performance of Jewish rites.[43] In the early fourth century, when Constantine would have graced the city with his presence, he would have been invited to attend a show in the theatre which overlooked the Mediterranean or to enjoy a chariot race in the renowned local hippodrome, a favourite pastime of urbanites.[44] Even in the sixth century residents were willing to pay taxes in order to maintain such shows, in spite of

[39] The chronology of Samaritan activities in the 4th cent. is unclear, see Ch. 3. It is not altogether unlikely that Baba Rabba was active during the reign of Constantine. On the removal of an idol by Poemenia (in the late 4th cent.?), *Life of Peter the Iberian*, with H.-G. Kippenberg, *Garizim und Synagoge* (Berlin 1971), 100.

[40] K. Holum, *King Herod's Dream* (New York 1988), *passim*.

[41] *PT AZ* 1.2 (39c).

[42] See Ch. 3.

[43] *PT AZ* 5.4; Stemberger, *Jews and Christians*, 217–29.

[44] J. Humphrey, 'Prolegomena to the Study of the Hippodrome at Caesarea Maritima', *BASOR* 213 (1974), 2–45. On Caesarea's annual festivity in which all were invited to participate, including the administration, citizens, strangers, and which, as late as the early 6th cent. provided forums for stage and rhetorical entertainment, Choricius, *Apol. Mim.* 95–6 and Ch. 8.

ecclesiastical and rabbinic objections.[45] An imperial *adventus* in a provincial capital would have been accompanied by lengthy panegyrics. Caesarea boasted a school of rhetoric whose professors were exceptionally well paid.[46] It would have been no idle school exercise to ponder on the selection of suitable themes for an imperial panegyric honouring a monotheistic emperor.[47]

A walk through the streets of Caesarea meant a passage paved with reminiscences of paganism. City centres, streets, squares, public buildings, and temples were all elements of urban landscapes with pagan distinction and patriotism. Decorated with numerous sculptures of gods, heroes, and emperors, these structures solemnly attested local pride and civic spirit.[48] Giant statues, carved with remarkable skill out of red porphyry imported from Egypt, forged complementary links between citizens, religion, and empire. Was it Constantine who ordered the removal of two heads which had topped two imposing statues, one of Jupiter, the other of Hadrian, and their relocation from their original (temple?) setting to a public square?[49]

Ceremonies intended to confirm civic identity had, at that point, nothing to do with Christianity. Yet, at the dawn of the fourth century Caesarea also boasted an ancient and well-organized episcopate, a spectacular theological library which Origen had left behind him, a small but affluent Christian congregation, spots soaked and sanctified with the blood of Christian martyrs and an erudite bishop whose familiarity with Constantine's own history was second to none. These proclaimed the continuous nature of the city itself in the very act of abandoning well-trodden paths. Behind the apparent permanence of civic structures a new spirit introduced tensions and changes.

---

[45] B. Lifshitz, 'Une inscription byzantine de Césarée en Israël', *REG* 70 (1957), 118–32 (Anastasius or later); idem, 'Césarée de Palestine, son histoire et ses institutions', *ANRW* ii.8 (Berlin 1977), 490–518. See also L. and J. Robert, 'Bulletin épigraphique', *REG* 71 (1958), 344.

[46] Libanius, *Or.* 31.42.

[47] C. E. V. Nixon and B. Saylor-Rodgers, *In Praise of Later Roman Emperors: The Panegyrici Latini* (Berkeley 1994), *passim* for samples.

[48] See Ch. 8.

[49] Y. Tsafrir, *Eretz Israel from the Destruction of the Second Temple to the Muslim Conquest*, ii: *Archaeology and Art* (Jerusalem 1984).

In the vicinity of the capital an advertisement of the emperor's new creed would have caused the revival of dormant communities. Just north of Caesarea was ancient Dor (Dora, Doar), which Eusebius' *Onomasticon* registered as a deserted spot and whose ruins were greatly admired by passing pilgrims.[50] Yet excavations revealed a local temple which had been set on fire to make room for a church. The date is unclear but the early half of the fourth century seems a likely context.[51] Dor's church harboured a chip of the rock of Golgotha (church of the Holy Sepulchre). The excessive importance early accorded to Jerusalemite relics, especially of the true cross, contributed to a share of a fantasy of the universality of Christianity even when the overwhelming majority of the citizens of the empire were still polytheists. By 333 a Gallic pilgrim recorded the affiliation of Dor with the province of Palestine.[52] Dor had belonged to Phoenicia. Its transfer from one province to another, possibly under Constantine, was a token of imperial acknowledgement of credal affinity with the imperial court.

Perhaps the most satisfying stop for a Constantine travelling along the Mediterranean coast in the early fourth century would have been at Maiumas-Constantia, Gaza's port town. The local wine industry was renowned throughout the empire. Maiumas' inhabitants had collectively opted to convert to Christianity (*c*.325?). The gesture, rare at so early a date, was amply rewarded. Constantine conferred on the harbour the status of a *polis*, detaching it from the jurisdiction of Gaza and renaming it Constantia.[53] By identifying the authority of the *polis* with that of Christ, the harbour community conformed to a widely attested practice of linking cities with tutelary deities. Associated with traditional civic values, the act of Maiumas enrolled Jesus among the great figures of national tradition. He was now competing with Marnas of Gaza in the pantheon of civic cults.

[50] *Onom.* 78.8–120; Jerome, *Ep.* 108.8. On the antiquarian nature of these comments, L. Di Segni, 'The Date of the Binyamina Inscription and the Question of Byzantine Dora', *Atiqot* 25 (1994), 183–6.

[51] C. Dauphin, *La Palestine byzantine*, 3 vols. (Oxford 1998), iii. 698.

[52] *IB* 19.10. M. Avi Yonah, *The Holy Land: A Historical Geography from the Persian to Arab Conquest* (rev. version Jerusalem 2002), 143, ascribes the transfer to Diocletian.

[53] Soz. *HE* 2.5, 5.3; Eus. *VC* 4.38.

Echoes of cheerful revellers might have reached the ears of an emperor hoping to be lulled to sleep by the undulation of the Mediterranean. The inhabitants of nearby Gaza were known for their fun-loving and public holidays which affirmed, somewhat nois-ily, the polytheistic character of their city.[54] To recuperate, someone might have taken Constantine to visit Hilarion, the area's first recorded and native-born ascetic, who settled at Thabata, south of Maiumas.[55] But even Hilarion, ultimately, would feel the urge to seek greater solitude than that offered by Gaza's hinterland. In 361 he left for Egypt never to return.[56]

Souvenirs of unqualified imperial support emboldened excessive assertions of Christian devotion along the southern coast of Pales-tine. Around 360, three monks from Maiumas set out to destroy pagan sanctuaries in Gaza. The timing proved miscalculated. On the throne was a polytheistic emperor who viewed with disfavour mis-sionary enterprises to convert temples. The brothers were lynched by a furious mob. The ringleaders were arrested by orders of the pro-vincial governor. Julian countered by ordering their release.[57] Defin-ing Christian civic values in terms of spontaneous laying down the law, individuals appropriated actions which dispensed with local governmental authority. Urbanism acquired a polemical character. Militancy constituted reality and was interpreted after the event as a stage in the educational process of urbanites. Substituting Christian-ity for the hegemonic city of polytheistic traditions, Gaza and Maiu-mas engaged in a discourse regarding the conversion of town and countryside. As cultural and spiritual centres their relationship with the central imperial power was no longer collective. Under Constan-tine, Maiumas brandished its faith as the very symbol of what it meant to be an urban congregation against perceived threats of a world dominated by polytheism.

---

[54] N. Belayche, 'Pagan Festivals in Fourth Century Gaza', in B. Biton-Ashkelony and A. Kofsky (eds.), *Christian Gaza in Late Antiquity* (Leiden 2004), 5–22.

[55] Jerome, *Vita Hilarionis*. For recent excavations at the site, R. Elter and A. Hassoune, 'Le Monastère de saint Hilarion: les vestiges archéologiques du site de Umm el-'Amr', in C. Saliou (ed.), *Gaza dans l'antiquité tardive* (Salerno 2005), 13–40.

[56] The excavations at Umm el-Amr revealed an inscription which confirmed that Hilarion's remains were transported back to his monastery in 372, one year after his death, Elter and Hassoune, ibid. 23–4.

[57] Soz. *HE* 5.9.

Turning inland the crowning glory of the entire journey would have been a visit to the churches which Constantine had commissioned in Jerusalem, Bethlehem, and Mamre. That the initial and most significant investment of the emperor should have been in localities associated with biblical events is hardly surprising.[58] The transformation of existing spaces into sanctuaries placed polemics at the heart of the process. Conflict was born from within, to be followed by a series of operations whose aim was to ensure the unequivocal victory of Christianity.

At Mamre an annual fair brought together sellers and buyers in the joys of commercial and cultural exchange regardless of religious affiliation.[59] It was the kind of inter-communal interaction resented by puritan rabbis as by pious princesses.[60] And it was the kind of censure which Jews, Christians, and pagans ignored, each group happily focusing on its object of veneration, Abraham, Jesus, and the angels respectively. Constantine's church at Mamre set out to purify the place primarily of its pagan associations. The process of purification entailed, like the one a rabbi had engineered at Tiberias (pp. 23–4), the smashing of idols and of altars. Constantine's activities at Mamre initiated a process of idealization in which the suppression of paganism became an integral part of political practices while the appropriation of Judaism mediated Christian autonomy. A church planted in Mamre, perhaps an odd choice amidst a host of biblically associated localities, served as a trophy in a new war directed also against Judaism. It was a bloodless war, for the most part, yet one which Constantine and Palestinian theologians were determined to win.

The site of the sacred oak that had served as the scene of a biblical annunciation (Gen. 18), Mamre, together with nearby Hebron, further marked the northern 'boundary' of an area called 'Daroma' (the south) which in late antiquity stretched from 'En Gedi on the Dead Sea to the territory of the city of Eleutheropolis (Beth Govrin).[61] The

---

[58] E. D. Hunt, *Holy Land Pilgrimage in the Later Roman Empire AD 312–460* (Oxford 1982); P. Maraval, *Lieux saints et pèlerinages d'Orient* (Paris 1985).

[59] Soz. *HE* 2.4.

[60] *PT AZ* 1.5 (39d); Eus. *VC* 3.52.

[61] Avi Yonah, *The Holy Land. A Historical Geography,* 161 with map on p. 160; J. Schwartz, *The Jewish Settlements in Judea after the Bar Kokhba War until the Arab Conquest* (Jerusalem 1986) (Heb.).

latter, situated half way between Gaza and Jerusalem, was an important urban centre which in the fourth century counted among the
'best cities' of Palestine.[62] The composition and fate of its population
can be gleaned from an excavated cemetery which contained burial
caves prepared for the dead of Eleutheopolis between *c.*200 and 750
CE.[63] These yielded hundreds of oil lamps which bore identifiable
religious symbols. The excavators assigned lamps with Jewish symbols to a period between the late second to the fourth centuries.
The earliest Christian symbols were apparently incised on lamps
dated to the fourth or fifth century. It appears that the cemetery
underwent a curious transformation, starting as Jewish and ending as
Christian, a process not unfamiliar from elsewhere in Palestine,
especially around Jerusalem.[64] Did the vicissitudes of the Eleutheropolis dead reflect those of the living? Already around 200 the rabbis
had exempted Jews there from the obligatory tithe, presumably in
order to alleviate their lot in an overwhelmingly non-Jewish and
competitive environment and to prevent their flight from their
land.[65]

Up to the second century and the Bar Kokhba revolt (CE 132–5)
the Daroma region had been the heart of the Jewish settlements in
Judaea. After 135 it was largely denuded of its Jewish population. In
the late 130s the market at Mamre was flooded with Jews captured by
the Romans in the course of the suppression of the revolt. The
overflow of slaves was directed to the market of Gaza.[66] Eusebius
named several large Jewish villages in Daroma of his time (*c.*300).
Their inhabitants were known mostly for their uncompromising
devotion to Hebrew. This was the language in which they paid their
respect to the dead. In Hebrew they further recorded their gratitude

---

[62] *Expositio* 30; Amm. Marc. 14.8.11.

[63] J. Magness and G. Avni, 'Jews and Christians in a Late Roman Cemetery at Beth
Guvrin', in H. Lapin (ed.), *Religious and Ethnic Communities in Later Roman Palestine*
(Bethesda 1998), 87–114.

[64] Magness and Avni, ibid. 110–13. G. Avni, 'Christian Secondary Use of Jewish
Burial Caves in Jerusalem in Light of New Excavations at the Aceldama Tombs', in
F. Manns and E. Alliata (eds.), *Early Christianity in Context: Monuments and
Documents* (Jerusalem 1993), 265–76.

[65] *PT Dem.* 2 (22c).

[66] Jerome, Comm. in Zach. 3.11.4; *Chron. Pasch.* 474 (Dindorf), with Hunt, *Holy
Land*, 136.

to generous donors to local synagogues, a custom that markedly contrasted with the 'epigraphical habits' of their Galilean brethren who preferred to resort to acknowledgements in Greek and Aramaic.[67] The proximity of Daroma to centres of Christian learning like Bethlehem and Jerusalem meant that Christians who desired to acquire mastery over the language required the services of these Hebrew speakers. Some, like Epiphanius' teacher at Eleutheropolis, were glad to have eager pupils regardless of their faith.[68] The purists among these Jews mocked such efforts:

The Jews boast of their knowledge of the Law when they remember several names which we generally pronounce in a corrupt way because they are barbaric and we do not know their etymology. And if we happen to make a mistake in the accent [the pronunciation of the word as affected by vowels] and in the length of the syllables, lengthening short ones and shortening long ones, they laugh at our ignorance, especially as shown in aspiration and in some letters pronounced with a rasping of the throat.[69]

Jerome's assessment of the value of the spoken language for the 'science' of biblical exegesis attributed specific knowledge to his Jewish teachers while undermining their claim to an authoritative interpretation of Scripture solely based on linguistic criteria. The Daroma dwellers were deemed fanatic linguists. They should be understood in conjunction with their synagogues. The ornamentation of these sanctuaries points to conscientious efforts to imitate Temple rituals, perhaps the result of the presence of descendants of Jerusalemite priestly families in this area.[70] Purity of language went hand in hand with the strength of forged associations with the heyday of Judaism when Temple worship was in full flow.

---

[67] *BT Eruv.* 53a–b; on the Daroma synagogues of En Gedi, Eshtemoa, and Susiya, L. I. Levine (ed.), *Ancient Synagogues Revealed* (Jerusalem 1982), 116–28; the inscriptions appear in Naveh. See also S. Safrai, 'The Synagogues south of Mt Judah', *Immanuel* 3 (1973–4), 44–50. On the influence of Greek even on liturgy, S. Safrai and M. Stern (eds.), *The Jewish People in the First Century*, i–ii (Assen 1974–6), *passim*. The expression is borrowed from R. MacMullen, 'The Epigraphical Habit in the Roman Empire', *American Journal of Philology* 103 (1982), 233–46.

[68] *Epiphanii Vita* 1–2, 4–5 (*PG* 41, cols. 24–5, 28–9).

[69] *Comm. ad Titum*, 3.9, trans. in the *Jewish Encyclopaedia* s.v. Jerome, 116.

[70] D. Amit, 'Priests and the Memory of the Temple in the Synagogues of Southern Judaea', in Levine (ed.), *Continuity and Renewal* (2004), 143–54 (Heb.).

The ground-breaking nature of the process by which Christianity claimed autochthony in Palestine was captured by Jerome, resident in Bethlehem from 386, in an epitaph commemorating a friend:

> Within this tomb a child of Scipio lies,
> A daughter of the far-famed Pauline house,
> A scion of the Gracchi, of the stock
> Of illustrious Agamemnon himself.
> Here rests the lady Paula, well beloved
> Of both her parents, with Eustochium
> For daughter, she the first of Roman noble women
> Who hardship chose and Bethlehem for Christ.
> You see here, hollowed in the rock, a grave.
> It is Paula's tomb whose soul high heaven now holds.
> She who Rome and friends, riches and home forsook
> Here in this lonely spot found her final rest.
> For here Christ's manger was, and here the kings
> To him, both God and man, their offerings made.[71]

A miniature masterpiece of classical rhetoric the epitaph elegantly breached discourses at once irreconcilable and complementary. The contradiction stemmed from a host of pagan ancestors, a vital factor in establishing Paula's outstanding lineage. But the genealogy that bonded the pious Paula with Homeric kings and Republican heroes also provided ideological justification for a new kind of imperialism. To redefine the terms of an *agon* that necessarily ended with Paula's symbolic victory Jerome expounded the principles of Christian renunciation of wealth and birth. No less heroic than Agamemnon and the Gracchi, Paula's asceticism contrasted ephemeral achievements with an eternal acquisition.

Epitaphs became camouflage for hegemonic speech, juxtaposing oppositions, stated or implied, and linkages. Paula's ultimate reward, burial in the natal city of the founder of her faith, advanced a polemical definition of history which juxtaposed a particular set of familial circumstances, material of traditional epitaphs, with a eulogy of the grave itself. Presenting the power of Christianity to reclaim the land of Christ Jerome's catalogue of Paula's exploits grafted the reality of death onto a declaration of credal solidarity. To distance herself from her origins did not result in condemnation of the self to

---

[71] Jerome, *Ep.* 108.34, trans. NPNF, slightly modified.

oblivion. Rather, the eulogy demonstrated how such a decision ensured that Paula remained on the horizon of history.

Inscribing Paula in a genealogy that specifically referred only to remote ancestors and to her own daughter implied a transfiguration that called into question the conventional relationship that moulded contemporary society.[72] The connections implied duplication: a mother and a daughter, the latter the recipient of the maternal eulogy, who formed a 'couple' perpetually engaged in pious pursuits that defied obligations and expectations of class. This was a non-traditional view of women that made ample room for a new kind of female virtue. Within a Palestinian context Jerome might have been startlingly original. Although contemporary Jewish women were inserted into multiple public and private contexts, the criteria of conventional behaviour still stigmatized 'rebellious' wives, namely wives who denied sex to their husbands, as well as women who were found to have sexual liaisons prior to marriage, bathed in public or did spinning in the market.[73] To advance, as Jerome did, an identity of merit that bonded generations of women in a crystallization of ascetic unity and sexual renunciation, would have been beyond the norms even within a gender topography that saw the intermingling of men and women in public.

Topoi of epitaphs implicitly revealed polemical relationship with the tradition of funerary inscriptions. The letter that contained the account of Paula's life depicted her initial visit to Palestine as a pilgrimage through a 'Holy Land', a rite of passage that conferred a concrete dimension on the Bible while allowing the practitioner to distance herself from a traditional background in which greatness belonged to victories in war. The description further fitted into a pattern that stressed the profound differences in inspiration between Christian, Jewish, and pagan perceptions of the land. Pilgrims, like Paula and the huge number of Christians who flocked to Palestine in late antiquity, engaged in a set of ceremonies that insisted on the uniqueness of the Christian experience, turning it into a focal point of Christian civilization. Through their eyes, as much as through didactic lectures and theological essays, it is possible to gain a sense of the fight undertaken for the sake of the salvation and the freedom that Christianity was believed to bestow.

---

[72] See Ch. 7.   [73] *T Ket.* 7.6. See Ch. 7.

Traces of collusion between history and eulogy also penetrated late ancient Jewish funerary inscriptions which produced a chronology that deliberately hinged on a trauma, namely the date of the destruction of the Temple (68/9 CE).[74] The dating defied traditional provincial and newly conceived calendars, declaring Judaism's autonomous entity and its privileged if perverse relationship with the Divine. In synagogues the generosity of individuals was commemorated as an example of communal solidarity. The synagogue, the heart of a Jewish community, also provided sombre reflections on collective experiences.[75] At 'En Gedi on the Dead Sea, a synagogue inscription combined praise and polemics:

May they be remembered for good: Yose and Ezron and Hizziqiyu, sons of Hilfi.

Anyone causing a controversy between a man and his mates,
Or anyone who slanders his mates in front of gentiles,
Or anyone who steals the property of a mate,
Or whoever reveals the secret (mystery?) of the town to gentiles—
He Whose Eyes roam over the whole earth,
He Who Sees hidden things,
He Will Set His Face on that man and on his seed and will uproot him from under the heavens.
And all the people say: Amen, Amen, Sela.[76]

In the village of 'En Gedi, as in that of Bethlehem, the contents of inscriptions bore the mark of an agonistic spirit, be it the implied superiority of Paula's asceticism vis-à-vis the feats of her illustrious ancestors or the competing activities that could usher civic strife within the congregation. Readers would not have missed the subtle interplay between difference and similarity, between right and wrong.

---

[74] See Ch. 6.

[75] On the role of synagogues in general, P. A. Harland, *Associations, Synagogues, and Congregations: Claiming a Place in Ancient Mediterranean Society* (Minneapolis 2003). For a valuable summary of the state of synagogue research, H. A. McKay, 'Ancient Synagogues: The Continuing Dialectic between Two Major Views', *Currents in Research: Biblical Studies* 6 (1998), 103–42. Useful bibliographical lists relating to the synagogues of Eretz Israel are also available via the Internet: www.daat.ac.il/daat/bibliogr/tavori, produced by J. Tavori.

[76] L. I. Levine, 'The Inscription in the 'En Gedi Synagogue', in idem (ed.), *Ancient Synagogues Revealed*, 140–5, text and trans. (trans. slightly modified). Naveh, no. 70. Sixth cent. (?).

In the community of 'En Gedi secrecy and solidarity, expressions of effective morality, constituted the test of identity. The threat of divine detection ranged God on the side of the congregation, balancing the sense of the temporal loss which permeated the funerary inscriptions that dated death within an era of destruction.

When confronting potential transgressors synagogue audiences contrasted past donations with future actions to confirm the needs of the present. During synagogue services poetic compositions enlivened prayers and enriched biblical readings and exegesis. Composed and performed in Hebrew, synagogal liturgical poetry (*piyyut*) has posed a continuous puzzle—how could communities maintain and support such complex literary creations which most could not even understand?[77] The popularity of this poetic genre to this very day suggests that comprehension of contents was less important than the ritual act of using a Holy Tongue. Put otherwise, Hebrew *piyyut* represented a liturgical idiom that constituted the most significant ongoing creative impulse in Jewish worship.[78]

Christian intellectuals who settled in Palestine, like Origen and Jerome, fully grasped the significance of acquiring Hebrew, as did the rabbis whose opinions were recorded in the Palestinian Talmud:

Whoever is situated in the land of Israel...and speaks the Holy Tongue, and recites the *shema* [prayer] in the morning and in the evening, is promised life in the world to come.[79]

Biblical interpretation went further. Commenting on Genesis 2: 23, a *midrash* stated that:

Just as the Torah was given in the Holy Language so was the world created with the Holy Language.[80]

It would have been difficult to miss the challenge that this dynamic structural interdependence of language, creation, and world order posed to contemporary Christianity. By transforming words and letters

---

[77] D. H. Aaron, 'Judaism's Holy Language', *Approaches to Ancient Judaism* 16 (1990), 92.

[78] Ibid.

[79] *PT Shab.* 1.3 (3c).

[80] *GenR* 31.8 quoted in Aaron, 96. On the derivation of rabbinic concepts of language from Platonic philosophy, Aaron, 98–9.

into cosmogonic forces the rabbis created an exegetical tool which rivalled Christian exegesis of the same sacred text. It also enabled the rabbis to maintain control over the development of Judaism itself. Rabbinic hermeneutics appropriated the power derived from knowing how to use Hebrew by imbuing it with holiness as God's language.[81]

Rituals and ceremonies harmonized the official/scholarly inter-pretation with practices that assigned time and place to the creed's self-celebration. The stakes were high because they touched the very possibility of reading Scripture. In synagogues Jews reaffirmed their identity. In churches Christians did the same. On holy days Chris-tians sought baptism, a rite of initiation performed by ecclesiastical officials in appointed sanctuaries. The ritualization of baptism be-came a central component in the self-definition of Christians. It also became a tool of inner polemics. When Jerome voiced his displeasure with the bishop of Jerusalem the censure revealed chasm and dis-unity:

A few months ago, about the day of Pentecost, when the sun was darkened and all the world dreaded the immediate coming of the Judge, forty candi-dates of different ages and sexes [came] to your presbyter for baptism. There were certainly [at least] five presbyters in the monastery [in Bethlehem] who had the right to administer baptism but they were unwilling to do anything to move you to anger for fear you might make this a pretext for reticence concerning the faith. Is it not you who ... commanded your presbyters at Bethlehem not to give baptism to our candidates at Easter so that we had to send them to Diospolis (Lod) to the confessor and bishop Dionysius for baptism? Who, then, is the cause of rending the church apart? We who outside our cells hold no position in the church or you who issue an order to your clergy that if any one says Paulinianus was consecrated presbyter by Epiphanius, he is to be forbidden to enter the church? ... Are we schismatic or is not he the schismatic who refuses a habitation to the living, a grave to the dead, and demands the exile of his brethren?[82]

Written on the eve of an imminent Hunnic incursion of Palestine (CE 395) Jerome's tone stigmatized what he viewed as the injustice, despot-ism, and impiety of the bishop of Jerusalem. The precise identity of the

---

[81] Aaron, 100.

[82] To Pammachius against John of Jerusalem, *PL* 23.393–4; Eng. trans. in NPNF, slightly modified.

candidates for baptism was not disclosed. For the purpose of the invective it was immaterial. They could have been pilgrims or locals who sought refuge in the church in times of panic.[83]

Since Jerome himself had been ordained presbyter *c.*380 the vituperation was indicative less of issues of conversion to Christianity and more of the precarious nature of the relationship between the Jerusalem bishopric and its monastic hinterland. Baptism was one murky zone; ideology another. Yet, ascetics and urban bishop did not necessarily pose a clear-cut antithesis. The well-regulated machinery of ritualistic Jerusalem could handle mass baptism as well as mass monkish demonstrations.[84] Egeria, in the 380s, showed how efficiently the clergy operated throughout Palestine (and beyond).

Paula's pilgrimage demonstrated how the entire world came to Palestine to glorify the land of the Bible as the only territory capable of creating true Christians. The important point is that they came not from Palestine but from elsewhere. The shapers and shakers of Palestinian Christianity, with few exceptions, had been outsiders for whom Palestine presented the sole terrain that could transpose the reality of the present into a mythical-biblical perspective. The view was not universally shared. It seemed just as easy to transport the 'Holy Land' into a different urban context. Around 500, in the reign of the emperor Anastasius, a noble woman of Paula's calibre, Anicia Juliana, commissioned a large church to be built in the heart of Constantinople along the lines of Jerusalem's Jewish Temple. Not, perhaps, the Solomonic structure but rather a sanctuary modelled on the visionary architecture according to the prophet Ezekiel.[85] Such investments ensured the position of the capital as a second Jerusalem, reiterating the Constantinian act of creating a second Rome. When Daniel the Stylite embarked on a pilgrimage to Jerusalem a man

---

[83] As suggested by Z. Rubin, 'The Spread of Christianity', in Z. Baras *et al.* (eds.), *Eretz Israel* (Jerusalem 1982), 240 (Heb.).

[84] Note also Jerome's criticism of this very same ritual machine which, he claimed, operated in a city that was like any other city, full of people, prostitutes, mimes, buffoons, etc., *Ep.* 54.

[85] As argued by C. Milner, 'The Image of the Rightful Ruler: Anicia Juliana's Constantine Mosaic in the Church of Hagios Poleuktos', in P. Magdalino (ed.), *New Constantines: The Rhythm of Imperial Renewal in Byzantium* (Aldershot 1994), 73–81, esp. 74–6. On ambivalent attitudes to Solomon's temple in the 6th cent., G. Dagron, *Constantinople imaginaire* (Paris 1984), 303–6.

whom he encountered on the road convinced him to go to Constantinople instead. The 'revelation' promised the ascetic that the Lord was everywhere he desired to seek Him.[86] The time for a typological sorting out also meant a time of separation from a theology that positioned a Palestinian 'Holy Land' at the heart of Christianity.

2. ANASTASIAN LANDSCAPES

Between Constantine and Anastasius (491–518), both objects of Palestinian panegyrists, a new polemical discourse organized ideologies of Christian orthodoxy in ways that affirmed local divisions yet defied facile schematization.[87] From the fourth century onward the arid hinterland lying between Jerusalem and the Dead Sea swarmed with humans, ascetics seeking solitude, pilgrims seeking ascetics, monks seeking salvation, none too reluctant to meddle in the religious politics that affected the Holy City.[88] Solitude, then, conferred scant solace or tranquillity. The conflicts which characterized the religious landscape of the empire throughout the fifth century spilt over to the Palestinian periphery, to cities as well as to monastic deserts.

Had Anastasius visited Jerusalem he would have no doubt headed to the imposing church which the empress Eudocia, who had resided in the city for two decades (*c.*440–60), had erected in honour of Saint Stephen. In 516 it was chosen as the only sanctuary sufficiently capacious to hold no less than 10,000 monks when the ascetics of the nearby Judaean desert monasteries descended on the city.[89] They had come in person to attend the first public appearance of a newly installed

---

[86] P. Brown, *The World of Late Antiquity* (London 1971), 141.

[87] A. Chauvot, trans. and comm., *Procope de Gaza, Priscien de Césarée. Panégyriques de l'empereur Anastase* (Bonn 1986). On the possible Palestinian, rather than Mauretanian provenance for Priscian, J. Geiger, 'Some Latin Authors from the Greek East', *CQ* 49 (1999), 606–17, esp. 606–12.

[88] On pilgrimage see Hunt, *Holy Land*; Maraval, *Lieux saints*; and J. Wilkinson, *Jerusalem Pilgrims before the Crusades*, rev. edn. (Warminster 2002). Anastasius' own contribution to the Christianization of this region consisted of a church built in the place where 'the Lord was baptized' and where the Epiphany was celebrated annually on 6 Jan. Wilkinson, *Jerusalem Pilgrims*, 321; F. M. Abel, 'L'Église du baptême du Christ', *RB* 41 (1932), 245–8.

[89] Cyril of Scythopolis, *Vita Sabae* (E. Schwartz, *Kyrillos von Skythopolis*, 2 vols. (Leipzig 1939), i. 148–52).

patriarch, John III (516–24), the man whom the emperor supported and who succeeded Elias, the man whom Anastasius had deposed. At stake was communion with bishops who represented what the monks considered heretical. Following the controversial council of Chalcedon (451) a struggle between Chalcedonians and Monophysites generated a dialectical quest for the right form of faith. It often bordered on violence. The assembly at St Stephen's was one episode in a chain of relationships of kinship and mutual tension that linked monks and patriarchs as well as setting them in opposition to one another.

Anastasius' intervention in Palestinian religious politics originated in initiatives of the Jerusalemite episcopate.[90] In 511 Sabas, head of a famed monastic community in the Judaean desert, was asked by Elias, the patriarch facing the likelihood of deposition, to intervene on his behalf at the court. In an accompanying letter Elias introduced Sabas as the 'colonizer and patron of our desert and the light of all Palestine'.[91] The monk, by then in his seventies, was also entrusted with a mission to request the cancellation of the extra levy which the emperor, in pursuit of financial and administrative reforms, had imposed.[92] The success of the delegation (Elias was not deposed and extra taxes were remitted) attested Sabas' powers of persuasion. It also indicated an imperial conviction of the marginality of Palestinian religious and economic affairs.

Yet, the 516 mass gathering in Jerusalem, even if not attended in person by the emperor, would have provided a convincing demonstration, if such were needed, of the web of intrigues which inextricably tied court and province, imperial religious policies and the politics of the patriarchate of Jerusalem. John had promised communion with Monophysites, the party on whose side the emperor tended to range himself. Under intense pressure from the Judaean desert monks John changed his mind. The emperor ordered his arrest. The *dux Palaestinae* released him from prison. The liberated patriarch summoned the monks to the city. The emperor's nephew was simultaneously expected in Jerusalem in fulfilment of an oath taken in time of captivity. Contrary to plans and expectations John

---

[90] On Anastasius' religious policy, F. K. Haarer, *Anastasius I. Politics and Empire in the Late Roman World* (Cambridge 2006), 115–62.

[91] *Vita Sabae* 50 (Schwartz 141) with J. Patrich, *Sabas, Leader of Palestinian Monasticism: A Comparative Study in Eastern Monasticism* (Dumbarton Oaks Studies 32; Washington, DC, 1994), 303.

[92] Ibid. 311–12.

publicly affirmed his commitment to the principles of Chalcedon. The *dux* had to flee to the safety of Caesarea, the provincial capital from which, if necessary, one could board a ship for Constantinople. The emperor's nephew had to swear allegiance to Chalcedon and to allocate an exceptionally generous donation to the church of the Holy Sepulchre and to the monks of the Holy Land.[93] Rarely rationalistic, what happened in Jerusalem did matter beyond Palestine.

To escape the pressure cooker which was Jerusalem at the turn of the sixth century a visiting Anastasius would have headed to the Mediterranean coast to be received there with gladness and gratitude. The city of Gaza offered exceptional amenities. In Anastasius' time the city presented a veritable microcosm of the best that the empire could boast. Goods and delicacies arrived there from remote Africa and Arabia and the nearby Negev, and thence often to the court. These included, in 496, a gift of two giraffes from the 'king of India' (to be precise, Axum/Ethiopia) to Anastasius via Gaza.[94] The gift inaugurated a mutually useful treaty between the Christianized kings of African Axum and the court at Constantinople which culminated in campaigns led by the Axumites against the Judaized king of Himyar (Yemen) who had converted to Judaism with the help of Tiberiade priests (*c.*520).[95]

Gaza's school of rhetoric was famous throughout the provinces as the best place to acquire a first-rate classical education. Palestinians with intellectual and court aspirations, like Procopius, came to Gaza from Caesarea to study with the finest teachers of the day.[96] For Anastasius, hardly an object of admiration in monastic and episcopal circles in Palestine, Gaza would have been refreshingly welcoming. Its able orators, no less piously Christian than the ascetics of the Judaean desert, felt equally at ease composing imperial panegyrics in the best

[93] *Vita Sabae* 50 (Schwartz 141) with J. Patrich, *Sabas, Leader of Palestinian Monasticism: A Comparative Study in Eastern Monasticism* (Dumbarton Oaks Studies 32; Washington, DC, 1994), 306–8.

[94] P.-L. Gatier, 'Les Girafes de Gaza', in C. Saliou (ed.), *Gaza dans l'Antiquité tardive* (Salerno 2005), 78; idem, 'Des girafes pour l'empereur', *Topoi* 6 (1996), 903–41.

[95] Z. Rubin, 'Byzantium and Southern Arabia—the policy of Anastasius', in D. H. French and C. S. Lightfoot (eds.), *The Eastern Frontier of the Roman Empire*, ii (Oxford 1989), 383–420; I. Šahîd, *The Martyrs of Najran: New Documents* (Subsidia Hagiographia 49; Brussels 1971), 11–117; J. Beaucamp *et al.*, 'La Persécution des chrétiens de Nagran et la chronologie himyarite', *Aram* 11–12 (1999–2000), 15–83.

[96] On arguments for and against the possibility, G. Greatrex, 'Stephanus, the Father of Procopius of Caesarea?', *Medieval Prosopography* 17 (1996), 133.

tradition of the genre, biblical exegesis, or learned discourses on the beauties of a mechanical clock. Had Anastasius reached Gaza by sea he would have been greeted with a poem honouring the disembarkation, delivered in pure Attic Greek by John, one of the city's notable masters of classical rhetoric.[97]

At Gaza no wild beast shows or mimes would have been prepared in honour of the emperor. Anastasius had abolished both in 499 and 502 respectively.[98] He would have attended services at the Eudoxiana, a church built with generous funding from the empress Eudoxia at the dawn of the fifth century, or at any of the other churches that had sprouted in the city since. In honour of the elderly and sombre Anastasius Gaza's council might have ventured, at the most, to stage the tragedy written by a local man, Timotheus, whose subject was the emperor's most popular financial measure, the abolition (in 498) of the hated *chrysargyron* tax (the *collatio lustralis*). Had Anastasius met the tragedian in person no doubt he would have been greatly impressed with the range of this Gazan erudite—Timotheus was a poet, philologist, and zoologist, the author of a treatise on exotic animals.[99] In fact, in the sixth century Gaza was 'the' place to discuss virtually any topic, from the Bible to classical poetry, and from traditional urban rituals to Christian theology.

At a distance deemed short by the standard of imperial journeys, the cities of Jerusalem and Gaza presented strikingly different façades at the dawn of the sixth century. One sported a seemingly unending procession of monks and pilgrims demonstrating an array of piety; the other espoused vastly different types of entertainment, including mimes that mocked Christian rituals. The least ambiguous difference between the two cities would have been the presence or rather the absence of non-Christian groups. None is attested at that date in Jerusalem. A hint of Jewish presence in Gaza, however, was gleaned from remains of what had been a local synagogue. An inscription dated to the reign of Anastasius (CE 507) commemorated a donation

---

[97] F. Ciccolella, *Cinque poeti bizantini. Anacreontee del Barberiniano Greco 310* (Alessandria 2000), anac. 1.

[98] Josh. Styl. 34, 46; Proc. Gazae, *Pan.* 15, 16, with A. H. M. Jones, *The Later Roman Empire*, 2 vols. (Norman 1964), 232 and n. 35. The most famous defender of mimes was another Gazan, Choricius, who composed a speech, *Apologia Mimorum*, in which this form of entertainment was vigorously extolled.

[99] R. Kruk, 'Timotheus of Gaza's On animals in the Arabic Tradition', *Le Muséon* 114 (2001), 355–87.

of a mosaic to the local synagogue by two Jewish wood merchants, Menahem and Yeshua, sons of Isses. The mosaic contained medallions enclosing wild animals (lioness, tigress, zebra, and giraffe), the very topic of Timotheus' treatise, as well as other inscriptions in Greek and an image of a man who, but for a lyre on his knee, looked like a seated emperor. An inscription in Hebrew letters identified this figure as David. The overall classicism of the mosaic presented close parallels with mosaics in synagogues and churches in the vicinity of Gaza, suggesting an artistic discourse that had less to do with specific religiosity and more with popular aesthetics.[100] It further reflected a ready adaptation by ordinarily opposing groups of an iconography flexible enough to fit contrasting credal messages.[101]

Among occasional revellers in the Gazan festivities soldiers could be seen. The sight of soldiers in Jerusalem ordinarily spelt trouble. At Gaza they would have been members of the *limetanei*, the soldiers who protected the southern Palestinian periphery.[102] One such, the *numerus Theodosiacus*, was stationed at Nessana in the Negev whence an astonishing find of some 250 papyri opened vistas hitherto unknown and unsuspected.[103] Operating mostly on camel back, Nessana's unit was typical of a local militia.[104] To judge by their names many of its members were of Arab or Nabataean extract. Their main task was to protect the cultivated areas against Bedouin excursions.

---

[100] See the detailed comparison of giraffes on mosaics in Palestinian synagogues, baptisteries, monasteries, and other structures in Gatier, 'Girafes de Gaza', *passim*, esp. 80. Gatier, 'Des girafes', 936, further proposes to see the imagery of Anastasius as a source for the Gazan David.

[101] The striking similarities between the mosaics of the Gaza synagogue, the Nirim (Maon) synagogue, and the Shellal, Bir Shama, and Hazor churches have been ascribed to the same workshop, M. Avi Yonah, *Art in Ancient Palestine* (Jerusalem 1981), 389–95; A. Ovadiah, 'The Mosaic Workshop of Gaza in Christian Antiquity', in D. Urman and P. V. M. Flesher (eds.), *Ancient Synagogues* (1995), ii. 367–72. On the relations between late ancient Jewish and Christian art in Palestine, R. Hachlili, 'Aspects of Similarity and Diversity in the Architecture and Art of Ancient Synagogues and Churches in the Land of Israel', *ZDPV* 113 (1977), 92–122; F. Vitto, 'The Interior Decoration of Palestinian Churches and Synagogues', *BF* 21 (1995), 283–300.

[102] B. Isaac, *The Near East under Roman Rule* (Leiden 1998) for collection of relevant articles.

[103] See Ch. 2.

[104] In general, B. D. Shaw, 'The Camel in Roman North Africa and the Sahara; History, Ideology and the Human Economy', *Bulletin de l'Institut fondamental d'afrique noire*, Dakar 4 (1979), 663–721, repr. in idem, *Environment and Society in Roman North Africa* (Aldershot 1995).

The precise relationship between these troops and the legion stationed in Aila on the Red Sea is unclear. Perhaps members of the Nessana unit had to assist in exceptional operations such as the campaigns led by Romanus, *dux Palaestinae, c.*500, to recover the island of Iotabe (south of Aila) which controlled much of the trade with the Indian Ocean.[105] The move would have accorded with a decree of Anastasius which allowed for the detachment of individual soldiers for special service.[106]

Heading back north the emperor might have crossed the Galilee. If his arrival coincided with a Jewish 'sabbatical year' he would have realized that the burden of being a Jew was no lighter than that of an imperial taxpayer and in many instances even heavier. The plight of taxpayers had been graphically described in Timotheus' drama; that of law-abiding Jews was depicted in a passage of biblical exegesis of the verses that prescribed a repose for the land:

Scripture speaks of those who observe the Sabbatical year (*shomrei sheviit*). It is common in the world for a man to perform a precept for a day, or a week, or a month. But for a whole year? And yet this man sees his field untilled, his vineyard untended, he gives up his living and still he says nothing! Is there a hero greater than this man?[107]

A trip through the Galilee would have introduced the emperor to a prosperous area about which his court might have known rather little. Its eastern part was dotted with Jewish settlements, many endowed with synagogues. In the western part the spread of churches

---

[105] Malchus, *Frg.* 1. The precise location of Iotabe has been a matter of controversy, P. Mayerson, 'A Note on Iotabe and Several Other Islands in the Red Sea', *BASOR* 298 (1995), 33–6; and idem, 'The Island of Iotabe in Byzantine Sources', *BASOR* 287 (1992), 1–4, repr. in idem, *Monks, Martyrs, Soldiers and Saracens* (Jerusalem 1994), 352–5. See also F. M. Abel, 'L'Île de Jotabe', *RB* 47 (1938), 510–38; B. Isaac, *The Limits of Empire* (Oxford 1990), 247–8; M. Sarte, *Trois études sur l'Arabie romaine et byzantine* (Brussels 1982), 154 f. On the Jewish community on the island, Y. Dan, 'Jews and Sea Trade in the Indian Ocean before the Islamic Period', *Studies in the History of the Jewish People and the Land of Israel* 5 (1980), 153–8.

[106] Isaac, *The Near East*, 452, 460. Nessana's camel corps had to send two camels to the churches in Characmoba, some 150 km. east, P. Colt 35 (C. J. Kraemer (ed.), *Excavations in Nessana*, iii: *The Non-Literary Papyri* (Princeton 1958)).

[107] *LevR* 1.1, redacted *c.*500. Passage quoted in D. Stern, 'Midrash and the Language of Exegesis: A Study of Vayikra Rabbah, Chapter 1', in G. H. Hartman and S. Budick (eds.), *Midrash and Literature* (New Haven 1986), 109.

attested the vigorous pace of the Christianization of Palestine.[108] The scale of the synagogues and their decoration reflected considerable means and a sense of security derived perhaps from the relative remoteness and insignificance of the region.[109] Imperial bans on erecting new synagogues had apparently little effect in this part of the empire. The floors of the Galilean synagogues appeared to project not defiance but nonchalance. They provided viewers with a mixture of Jewish and polytheistic symbols which recognized their aesthetic value while legitimizing their Jewish interpretation.

The likelihood of an emperor visiting a Jewish sanctuary in the Galilee was negligible but in Nazareth, at least according to an Italian pilgrim who visited the Holy Land c.570, the synagogue contained a book ascribed to Jesus' schooldays, as well as a school bench which Christian visitors could easily move but the Jews were unable to drag outside.[110] Connoisseurs of female beauty could (and did) marvel at the attractive Jewesses of Nazareth.[111] Nazareth presented a Galilean-type symbiosis punctured by sarcasm: a tongue-in-cheek weight-lifting match between Jews and Christians in the synagogue coupled with Mary's Jewish 'daughters' as a source of considerable attraction for discerning Christian pilgrims. The paradox appeared elsewhere in urban areas with mixed population: in Scythopolis Jews and non-Jews participated in mimetic feasts, regardless of communal affiliation, particularly when drinking and eating provided bonding elements; at Capernaum, urban planning, by accident or by design,

---

[108] Strikingly reflected in the number of churches revealed in archaeological surveys and excavations, A. Ovadiah, *Corpus of the Byzantine Churches in the Holy Land* (Bonn 1970) and the various supplements in *Levant* 1981 and 1982. On the changing landscape of the north see R. Frankel *et al.*, *Settlement Dynamics and Regional Diversity in Ancient Upper Galilee* (Archaeological Survey of Upper Galilee) (Jerusalem 2001), with useful maps.

[109] The date of the Galilean synagogues has been undergoing constant revisions. See Introduction, n. 10. A sort of consensus seems to emerge regarding the 5th, perhaps even the 6th cent., a date that would parallel the efflorescence of church building in the western-Christianized Galilee. An analysis of the proportions of several has pointed to a *terminus post quem* of the early 4th cent., D. Chen, 'The Design of the Ancient Synagogues in Galilee', *LA* 28 (1978), 193–202. The most comprehensive survey of synagogues to date is Levine, *The Ancient Synagogue* (2000).

[110] *Anonymus Placentini* (text in *Itineraria et alia geographica*, ed. P. Geyer, CCSL 175, 129–53). Eng. trans. in Wilkinson, *Jerusalem Pilgrims*, 129–51.

[111] Ibid. On the cave-cum-church in town, J. Taylor, *Christians and the Holy Places*, 221–67.

placed the church and the synagogue cheek by jowl, as though to suggest a convenient mutual attendance at services or to remind each other of constant rivalry.[112] It would appear that at least in the first half of the sixth century a general state of prosperity was pre-eminently responsible for moments of conciliation. Amidst several factors, pilgrimage assumed a conciliatory function.[113] The economic efflorescence set off by Holy Land pilgrimage in late antiquity had been noted by the pilgrims themselves. For a pious man from Italian Piacenza who meandered through Palestine c.570 the place was paradise.[114]

In 628 the emperor Heraclius swept through Palestine after defeating the Persians near Nineveh.[115] Strictly speaking the journey was not a necessity.[116] But Heraclius came to restore, in person, the True Cross, the most precious relic of Christendom, to its original setting in the church of the Holy Sepulchre. It had been removed by the Persians in CE 614 after a short but bitter siege of the city. Heraclius reached Jerusalem to enthusiastic reception.

When the blessed and pious Heraclius had received the Lord's Holy Cross... he set out with all the royal retinue, honouring the holy, wonderful and heavenly discovery which he brought with him to the holy city with all the vessels of the church which had been saved... There was no little joy on that day as they entered Jerusalem. Sounds of weeping and wailing were heard, tears were flowing all around... king, spectators and soldiers were choking with emotion... [117]

On the way to Jerusalem the emperor had stopped in Tiberias. The Christian community in the city had lost its bishop who had fled the

---

[112] See Ch. 4.
[113] As noted by Taylor, *Christians*, 290–1.
[114] *Anon. Plac.* 5. On the limited impact of pilgrimage and monasticism on the rural economy of late ancient Palestine, D. Bar, 'Settlement and Economy in Eretz-Israel during the Late Roman and Byzantine Periods (70–641 CE)', *Cathedra* 107 (2003), 24–46 (Heb.).
[115] W. Kaegi, *Heraclius: Emperor of Byzantium* (Cambridge 2003).
[116] A. Frolow, 'La Vrai Croix et les expéditions d'Héraclius en Perse', *REB* 11 (1953), 88–105 on the journey as an attempt to legitimize the emperor's incestuous marriage; C. Mango, 'Héraclius, Sahrvaraz et la vrai croix', *TM* 9 (1985), 105–17 on the Jerusalem episode as a political and religious gesture aimed at demonstrating the Christian unity of the empire.
[117] Sebeos, 41 (R. W. Thomson *et al.*, *The Armenian History attributed to Sebeos*; TTH, Liverpool 1999), slightly modified. Cf. Strategius (version A), 24.9.

advancing Persian army back in 614. In the absence of this dignitary Heraclius and his entourage were entertained by a wealthy Jew by the name of Benjamin.[118] Amidst festivities unnamed Christians accused Benjamin and his co-religionists of aiding the Persians and harming the Christians. Benjamin affirmed the accusation, adding that since the Christians were enemies of the Jewish faith they deserved their lot. Pardoning him, Heraclius issued a formal declaration protecting Jews and proceeded to convert Benjamin to Christianity. The ceremony of baptism was celebrated in Neapolis, formerly bastion of Samaritans and Samaritanism.

The imperial promise to protect the Jews of Palestine was rescinded under pressure from the Christian leadership in Jerusalem. Heraclius would later (in 634) order an empire-wide baptism—all Jews under Roman rule were to be baptized as proof of loyalty to emperor and empire. The Persian presence in Jerusalem, although brief (CE 614–28), had resharpened an ancient conflict over the Temple Mount, the single space left outside the vigorous building programme of Christian Jerusalem. During the Persian interlude Jews were allowed to settle in Jerusalem. The permit produced euphoria. After 500 years of having been banned from the city, amidst intense messianic speculations, an altar was erected to Yahweh on the Temple Mount and sacrifices renewed.[119] The Christian establishment in Jerusalem blamed the Jews for their woes during the Persian siege of the city.

Flushed with victory and piety Heraclius sealed his triumphant entry to Jerusalem with what would have been the most unthinkable of all. Challenging the words of Jesus who had prophesied the perpetual desolation of the Temple Mount, Heraclius apparently planted a church where the Temple of Solomon had once stood.[120]

---

[118] Events recounted in Theophanes, *Chron.* 328, s.a. 627/8; Cf. Eutychius 1089–90. See Sivan 'Palestine' (above, n. 33).

[119] For texts and the problems of dating J. Reeves, *Trajectories of Near Eastern Apocalyptic* (Leiden 2005). On these episodes see Sivan, 'From Byzantine to Persian Jerusalem (2000).

[120] The matter is not entirely clear. See F. E. Peters, 'Who built the Dome of the Rock?', *Graeco-Arabica* 1 (1983), 119–38; and C. Mango, 'The Temple Mount AD 614–638', in J. Johns and J. Raby (eds.), *Bayt al Maqdies: Abd al Malik's Jerusalem* (Oxford 1992), 1–16. The identification of Heraclius with King David, promoted by the emperor himself and reflected in the so-called David plates, may have facilitated such a dramatic departure from norms of centuries. On the plates, S. Spain Alexander, 'Heraclius, Byzantine Imperial Ideology and the David Plates', *Speculum* 52 (1977), 217–37. On the Davidic aspirations of Heraclius, W. Brandes, 'Heraclius between Restoration and

At that spot where the last testimony of Jerusalem's Jewish (and pagan) past existed, he implemented the final step in the Christianization of the Holy City. The conversion of the Temple which Yahweh had envisaged as a monument to peace into a talisman of victory in war, symbolized the defeat of Rome's greatest enemy and of Christianity's most enduring rival.

A few decades later, in 692, Abd al Malik dedicated the Dome of the Rock on the exact same spot. Positioned on mythical foundations, the church that Heraclius might have built and the Dome of the Rock that the caliph did build formed the supreme expression of annexation. The Dome brought about a powerful return of imaginary representations. Its shape, an octagonal, found rare yet striking echoes in two octagonal churches which had been dedicated to Mary, one atop Mount Gerizim, the holiest Samaritan space (*c.*480), and the other near Jerusalem, on the road to Bethlehem (the Kathisma) (*c.*430).[121] Opposing Mary with Mohammed, and Solomon with Abd al-Malik, the Dome of the Rock was meant to rival both Judaism and Christianity. It would divert pilgrimage from Mecca which Umayyad Jerusalem was poised to rival if not to surpass, and it would recapture the grandeur of Solomon's Temple while affording believers a reassuring gate to the Last Days.[122]

Few articulated the complex web of imageries and associations better than Bajila of Jerusalem:

In which direction are you going? To Jerusalem. When you enter, go into [the Dome of] the Rock from the northern gate. Then go forward towards the *qibla*. On your right there is a pillar and a column and to your left there is a pillar and a column. And between pillars and columns you see a black marble paving stone. This is the one over the gate of Paradise. Pray on it to Allah: May he be exalted and glorified for any request made there is granted.[123]

Early Islamic interpreters of Marian narratives in the Quran associated her pregnancy, departure, rest, and giving birth with the so-called

---

Reform. Some Remarks on Recent Research', in G. J. Reinink and B. H. Stolte (eds.), *The Reign of Heraclius. Crisis and Confrontation* (Leuven 2002), 17–40, esp. 19. On Heraclius' image as the *restaurator crucis*, J. W. Drijvers, 'Heraclius and the *restitutio crucis*. Notes on Symbolism and Ideology', ibid., 175–90, esp. 184–5 on the new age.

[121] See Ch. 6.
[122] A. Elad, *Medieval Jerusalem and Islamic Worship* (Leiden 1995), 158–63.
[123] Al Wasiti, quoted in Elad, *Medieval Jerusalem*, 79.

Mihrab Maryam which had been located on the Temple Mount, next to the Gate of Repentance and the so-called Cradle of Jesus.[124] The transfer of Christian traditions relating to Jerusalem, Bethlehem, and the Kathisma to the Temple Mount revealed an ever more imaginary installation of conflicting traditions intended to harmonize the history of the city in a timeless framework. Hence multiple readings of the Mount could ignore neither its historical development nor the relative stability of its sanctity that always reflected the same image of itself.[125] Entering Jerusalem meant entering eternity. But in 628 Heraclius could only inscribe his actions in a creative present. Although the restoration of the True Cross to its original 'cradle' testified to the recent threats that hung over the city, the emperor's presence in Jerusalem and in Palestine indicated an ultimate split between Rome and the Roman East.[126]

[124] P. A. Arce, Culte islamique au Tombeau de la Vierge', *Atti del congresso assunzionistico orientale* (Jerusalem 1951), 177–93; Elad, *Medieval Jerusalem*, 93–5.

[125] R. Gonen (ed.), *Contested Holiness: Jewish, Muslim and Christian Perspectives on the Temple Mount in Jerusalem* (Jersey City 2003).

[126] On the fate of the Christian communities of Palestine, R. Schick, *The Christian Communities of Palestine from Byzantine to Islamic Rule* (Princeton 1995); on the territory, M. Gil, *A History of Palestine 634–1099* (Cambridge 1992).

2

The Periphery of Dreams and Deserts

I travelled [through Palestine] with a sort of anticipation, as
though I was entering a covenant with the dead and with the
living...It was an instructive journey. I made my way among
murderers and historical sites, deserts and tanks, gods who had
been rejected and humans who had been exiled...I say, therefore, to everyone who heads to these bewitching landscapes: Do
not forget two important items in your luggage, a copy of
[Goethe's] Faust and ecstasy. A tropical hat is not a necessity.
Indispensable, however, are shivers through the spine and
transports of the soul...

> Shandor Marai, [Reflections on] *Diary of a Journey*, 1937,
> *Eretz Acheret* 18 (2003) (Heb.)

1. MINDSCAPES

Once upon a time, perhaps around 600, a solitary monk on Mount
Sinai abruptly left his cell, crossed the desert in an easterly direction,
joined a Jewish community near the Dead Sea, converted to Judaism,
got himself circumcised, married, preached against Christianity, and
died a painful death. Antiochus, the unsympathetic narrator of this
remarkable metamorphosis, claimed that it was the result of dreams
induced by the devil.[1] In repeated nightly visitations the demon

---

[1] Antiochus Monachus, Homily 84 (*De Insomniis; Peri Enhypnion*), PG 89, cols.
1688–91. A few passages are translated in P. Mayerson, 'Antiochus Monachus' on
Dreams: An Historical Note', *JJS* 35 (1984), 51–6. The division of dreams into

52   *The Periphery of Dreams and Deserts*

presented the ascetic dreamer with two strikingly contradictory images. One, drawn in dark and sombre hues, depicted Christian martyrs, apostles, and ordinary believers leading a life full of shame. The other, suffused with cheerful colours, showed Moses, the prophets, and ordinary Jews living a joyous life.[2]

The homily that contained this exemplum set out to demonstrate that 'dreams are nothing other than things of the imagination and hallucinations of a mind led astray, an illusion of evil demons bent on deceiving us'.[3] Antiochus' rhetoric delineated an intimacy between journeys of the mind and travels of the body. Dreams, in this case, dictated a new abode and a new life. But when sombrely and soberly contemplated, these visions occasioned distrust rather than reassurance. For Antiochus, who used the dream narrative to harangue his ascetic community, dreams presented a double grievance: self-initiated interpretation and unwarranted action. By accrediting visions the dreaming monk displayed faith in his own power of interpretation, thus disrupting a discourse which regulated ascetic life through a tight discipline over body and soul. By discounting such dreams, Antiochus could ignore the problems that visions evoked. The abandonment of ascetic life, of Christianity, and of the Sinaitic community represented a rebellion. To leave the desert in search of worldly pleasures meant leaving the faith. The attraction of Jewish life appeared incomprehensible, an inevitable result of devilish dreams.

creditable and discreditable, according to their senders, is discussed by Tertullian, *De Anima*, 45, 47. Demons naturally inspire false dreams, just as they induce false prophecies.

  [2] Cf. this vision with the strikingly similar one in the Babylonian Talmud *Pesahim* 50a: Rabbi Joseph the son of Rabbi Joshua ben Levi fell sick and [seemingly] gave up the ghost. When he recovered his father asked him: 'What did you see?' He said: 'I saw an inverted world—the exalted were low and the low were exalted'. Cf. also the Palestinian *midrash* of *Ruth Rabba* 3.1: Rabbi Meyasha the grandson of Rabbi Joshua ben Levi was made unconscious by his illness for three days. When he regained consciousness his father asked him: 'Where were you?' He replied: 'In a confused world . . . where I saw many people who were held in honour here and are in disgrace there', with S. Lieberman, 'The Martyrs of Caesarea', *Annuaire de l'Institut de Philologie et d'Histoire Orientales et Slaves* 7 (1939–44), 437–8. Cf. also the Protevangelium of James, 17 (2nd/3rd cent.) where Mary, about to give birth to Jesus, sees a vision of two peoples, one weeping and lamenting, the other rejoicing and exulting, the former representing the Jews, the latter the gentiles.
  [3] *PG* 89, col. 1688, trans. Mayerson, 'Antiochus Monachus'.

Mindscapes, like landscapes, had their rules and regulations. Dreams were acceptable, indeed necessary, in order to find some meaning and reassurance in a harsh life conducted in the middle of a desolate landscape like the Sinai. Nightly visions properly interpreted provided a guarantee of safe outcome for hazardous enterprises. A monk who planned to climb Mount Sinai had a vision on the eve of the expedition.[4] He saw himself standing in a palace and warmly greeted by its king. The next morning the dreamer consulted his superiors and upon receiving approbation he ascended the mountain in the company of a specially assigned priest. Reaching the top of Mount Sinai, a mass was said and the pious climbers presented God with requests which were then promptly fulfilled, just as the dream had predicted and subsequently interpreted. This orderly procedure of dream–interpretation–action was markedly contrasted with the initiative of the monk whose dream led him to abandon the life of contemplation in favour of the life of the flesh. In the words of Barsanuphius, the dreaming man was 'an enemy unto himself', a 'man without advice'.[5]

Conversion dreams, like the one told by Antiochus, may not have been a rarity nor so derisively recounted.[6] When they were reported

[4] Anastasius, A collection (Vat. Gr. 2592, fo. 138), F. Nau, 'Le Texte grec des récits du moine Anastase sur les saints pères du Sinaï', *OC* 2 (1902), A36, p. 81. Text and translation also in B. Flusin, 'Démons et Sarrasins. L'Auteur et le propos des *Diègè-mata stèriktika* d'Anastase le Sinaïte', *TM* 11 (1991), 398–9.

[5] *Ep.* 693, F. Neyt et al., (eds. and trans.), *Barsanuphe et Jean de Gaza: Correspon-dance* (SC 426, 427, 450, 451, 469; Paris 1998–2002). On this passage, L. Perrone, 'The Necessity of Advice: Spiritual Direction as a School of Christianity in the Correspondence of Barsanuphius and John of Gaza', in *Christian Gaza in Late Antiquity* (2004), 144. In general on order and discipline, P. Rousseau, *Ascetics, Authority and the Church in the Age of Jerome and Cassian* (Oxford 1978), *passim*.

[6] There is need to draw a typology of conversion scenes of individuals and of collectivities. While dreams lead individuals to assume a new type of life, mass conversion is often induced by a timely display of miracles by an individual confronting a potentially hostile audience. The narratives woven around the Palestinian excursions of the Christian monk Barsauma suggest this pattern vis-à-vis pagans, Jews, and Samaritans (see Ch. 1; Nau, *ROC*, 1913 and 1914, for the Syriac texts and partial translation, dating the events to the first half of the 5th cent.), as do the exploits of Hilarion which Jerome (*Vita Hilarionis*) unfolded, likewise within a Palestinian context. The story of the conversion of the Jews of Crete in the early 5th cent. (Soc. *HE* 7.38) provides a different model of conversion from Judaism to Christianity, induced not by an agent of the 'winning' or converting side but by a representative of the community about to be converted. See also the collection of

by the dreamers themselves they, too, entailed self-interpretation. As a result of a vision in which no less a personality than St Peter appeared to a nobleman of Iberia (Georgia) while he was a pampered hostage in Constantinople (*c.*430), the young man decided to abandon the splendours of the imperial court and whatever prospects he had back home in favour of a monastic vocation. In the vision, St Peter took the dreamer for a tour of heaven, pointing out the Father, the Son, and the Holy Spirit, all bathed in light, not unlike the prophets of the Hebrew Bible in the dream of the Sinaitic monk.[7] Peter also presented the dreamer with a lecture on the nature of the Trinity, clearly espousing Monophysite dogmas. Leaving the capital surreptitiously, the Iberian prince, accompanied solely by a single friend yet well equipped with relics of his favourite Persian martyrs as well as with a piece of the true cross, headed to Palestine. The vision determined both his career and his creed. Adopting the name of his saintly patron, Petrus (the Iberian), who had been born in a Christian family, ultimately became the Monophysite bishop of Maiumas, the port-city of Gaza. Luckily for the pious prince, his biography was recorded by a devout disciple.[8] Had the self-interpreted vision and the subsequent 'conversion' been introduced by an orthodox writer, Petrus the Iberian would have fared no better than Antiochus' introspective monk.

Travels of the mind, not unlike pilgrimages, contained realms that could not have been predicted, let alone protected against. Dreams provided an unmapped space and time, a freedom in which to nurture organic relations that developed in spite of, or perhaps only because of the vicissitudes of a world in which God did not easily reveal his meanings. In a dream, the command of God or of the devil becomes integrated over time into one's full creative life. The interpretation of dreams, like biblical exegesis in late antiquity, depicted hermeneutical situations in which theologians, clerics, rabbis, and other figures of authority exercised ingenuity.[9] Antiochus

articles in K. Milss and A. Grafton (eds.), *Conversion in Late Antiquity and the Early Middle Ages: Seeing and Believing* (Rochester 2003).

[7] John Rufus, *Plerophoriae* 37 (ed. and trans. F. Nau) (PO 8; Paris 1912).

[8] E. Schwartz, *Johannes Rufus, ein monophysitischer Schriftsteller* (Sitzungsbericht der Heidelberger Akad. D. Wiss., phil.-hist. Kl.; Heidelberg 1912), *passim*.

[9] On biblical interpretation see Ch. 6. On hermeneutic rules of the Haggadah and dream interpretation, S. Lieberman, *Hellenism in Jewish Palestine* (New York 1950),

did not reveal how the dream which he narrated would have been interpreted by the monk's immediate superior. But the dilemma of dreams, and specifically the question of who had the authority, and the key, to interpret spheres of sleep, confronted not only church theologians but also rabbis. When consulted by dreamers, the rabbis endeavoured to control the free interpretation of the symbolic and the uncoded nature of dream's images.[10] And just as Antiochus' scorn was fed by a model that called for the exclusion of all alterity, namely that of a Jew and that of dreams, the rabbis endorsed interpretations which were solely and solidly based on their own notion of correctness, excluding unauthorized interpreters.[11]

Preferring to dismiss or belittle dreams and their spectrum of interpretation, rabbis nevertheless realized that to inhabit the unconsciousness meant to get a grip over life in a situation arbitrarily controlled by nature, by tax collectors, and by serendipity.[12] A dream lent itself to purposefulness that overcame anxiety, and in dreams human experience became a vessel for godliness, challenging grave doubts about the possibility of the embodiment of the godly. Like classical dream masters, the rabbis elected to keep dream interpretation to its technical sense by smoothing over tensions between personal life and the imagination.[13] They discussed the relations between images and words, between what one 'sees' in a dream and what the dreamer articulates with words. The connection between dream and mouth, the essence of rabbinic dream interpretation, hinged on an invisible

68–82; on parallels between Artemidorus' *Oneirocriticon* and rabbinic dream intepretation, H. Lewy, 'Zu dem Traumbuche des Artemidorus', *Rheinisches Museum* 48 (1893), 398–419.

[10] R. Ulmer, 'The Semiotics of the Dream Sequence in Talmud Yerushalmi Ma'aser Sheni', *Henoch* 23 (2001), 305–23, esp. 318–19. In general, A. Kristianpoller, *Traum und Traumdeutung, Monumenta Talmudica* 2 (Vienna and Berlin 1923); B. Stemberger, 'Der Traum in der rabbinischen Literatur', *Kairos* 18 (1976), 1–42.

[11] The rabbinic discourse on dreams in *LamR* 1.18 casts Samaritan dream interpreters in the proverbial role of false 'prophets'.

[12] Rabbinic objections are neatly summarized in the dictum that 'dreams make no difference' (literally, 'matters learnt through dreams cannot elevate or diminish'), *T. Maaser Sheni* 5.9; *LamR* 1, 1.18; *BT San.* 30a. See also the rabbinic dictum that 'all dreams follow the mouth', *BT Ber.* 55b, or that 'dreams are fulfilled according to their interpretation, other than dreams induced by alcohol', *GenR* 89.8 (Theodor–Albeck).

[13] B. J. Koet, ' "Sag lieber, dass er diesen Traum positiv deuten soll": Über die Traumdeutung nach einem rabbinischen Traumbuch (Babylonischer Talmud Berachot 55–57)', *Kirche und Israel* 17 (2002), 133–49.

yet predictable path that linked human sphere of dreaming with the faculty of speech. The awareness that to perceive figures in a dream generates situational ambiguity or rather contrasting interpretations dominated rabbinic discourse of dreams:

Rabbi Johanan said: A dream follows its interpretation, except when it is of wine: some dream they are drinking it and it is a good omen, while others dream they are drinking it and it is a bad omen. Rabbi Abbahu said: Dreams are of no consequence either for good or for ill.[14]

Rabbinic theories of dream show that the recovery of reality proceeds ambiguously, counter to memory, and ridiculously predictable.[15] It seems that the rabbis were wary of all modalities of interpreting. Given the fact that dreams constituted oral testimony they were invalid because they were distorted either through informants' partiality or by memory. Hence information meant deformation and memory was in bad company:

R. Samuel said: A man is shown in a dream only what is suggested by his own thoughts... This is proven by the fact that he is never shown a date palm of gold nor an elephant going through the eye of a needle.[16]

Dreams became a parody of reality; the zeal to examine them was also parodic.[17]

Dreams and the seduction of hearing occupied a peculiar place in the rabbinic micro-cosmos, made all the more bizarre by the ubiquity of dreams and their crucial significance in the Hebrew Bible. The interpretation of dreams in the Talmud and Midrash was based on and laced with biblical verses which strip dreams of their individuality. It was as though

---

[14] *LamR* 1.18. Cf. *BT Ber.* 55b and 57a.

[15] The main guide is incorporated in *BT Ber.* 55a–57b. See P. S. Alexander, 'Bavli Berakhot 55a–57b: The Talmudic Dreambook in Context', *JJS* 46 (1995), 230–48. Cf. J. Z. Smith, 'Towards Interpreting Demonic Powers in Hellenistic and Roman Antiquity', in *ANRW* II, Principat 16.1 (Berlin 1978), 425–39; and P. Cox Miller, *Dreams in Late Antiquity* (Princeton 1994), 55–65 (on dreams and daemons). See also M. Niehoff, 'A Dream which is not Interpreted is like a Letter which is not Read', *JJS* 43 (1992), 58–84.

[16] *BT Ber.* 56a.

[17] R. Kalmin, 'Dreams and Dream Interpreters', in idem, *Sages, Stories, Authors and Editors in Rabbinic Babylonia* (Atlanta 1994), 61–80, esp. 65, draws distinctions between the hostile attitude of Babylonian amoraim to professional interpreters and Palestinian tannaim who are cast as such professionals.

dreams, like the Torah, were texts that require specific, authoritative exegesis but that, once more like the Torah, they could bear a variety of meanings which remain *in potentia* till unlocked and actualized by interpretation.[18] In the Hebrew Bible dreams anticipated major events in Israelite history.[19] Biblical dreams were literary metaphors verified through religious rituals. Their interpretation required that they be presented, like Joseph's famed dreams, as a demonstration of the superiority of divine justice over royal law.[20] Nor was a polemical aspect absent in the rabbinic trend to marginalize or rather to dismiss dreams as commonplace.[21] Such a tendency gains comprehension in view of the importance of dreams in the re-creation of Palestine as a Christian Holy Land.

The daily imagery of dreams, on the one hand, and dream ambiguities, on the other, highlight the use of dreams as a bridge between mindscapes and landscapes.[22] In the hands of skilful navigators dreams became, instead of a phenomenon embedded in a text, the text itself. Dream apparitions spurred discoveries of the true self and of long-forgotten burials. They engineered transfers of relics from past to new environments through rituals of reinstallation that moulded moments of communal bonding.

2. ENVISIONING THE LAND

Self-interpreted dreams prompted a sequel that guaranteed their meaning for the dreamer as against the rule of authoritative interpretation. The dreaming monk of the Sinai ensured his participation in the rosy

---

[18] Alexander, 237.

[19] *BerR* 68.12 on Jacob's dream at Beit El.

[20] *LevR* 3.5.

[21] Noteworthy is the marginalization of dreams as inspirers of prophecy, BT *Ber.* 57b, with E. E. Urbach, 'Homilies of the Rabbis on the Prophets of the Nations and the Balaam Stories', *Tarbiz* 25 (1956), 280 (Heb.).

[22] I am unaware of a study devoted to the cartography of visions in late antiquity. Yet, the periphery of dreams stretches along exceptionally wide horizons. For example, dreams were used to determine the value of church silver ornaments. *Life of Theodore of Sykeon* 42 (Festugière, *La Vie de Théodore de Sykéon* (Brussels 1970); Eng. trans. E. Dawes and N. H. Baynes, *Three Byzantine Saints* (London and Oxford 1948)); and John of Ephesus, *Lives of the Eastern Saints* 54–5 (E. W. Brooks, PO 19, 191–6). Hagiographical texts brim with visions which chart the course of their protagonist's life, John Rufus' *Life of Peter the Iberian* (Raabe, 1895), *passim*.

vision of his dream by uprooting himself from the holy mountain to the Dead Sea. According to Antiochus the ex-ascetic settled in Noara (Naaratha, Naaran), and/or Libyas (Livias), both locations on the banks of the Jordan river near Jericho, to become an active member of the local Jewish community. His 'translation' of a dream land into the northern region of the Dead Sea is instructive.[23] Since the devil might not have been conversant with the cultural geography of late ancient Palestine it seems that the monk selected his new abode either on the basis of information provided by pilgrims he met in the Sinai or by simply following a major pilgrim road out of the Sinai.[24] One of these roads led from Mount Sinai to Aila (Eilat) on the Red Sea and thence northward via Petra and the Via Nova Traiana, turning westward to Jerusalem via Livias and Jericho. Along this road the erstwhile monk would have encountered a landscape that had become thick with monastic establishments where ascetics practised the life that the monk willingly left behind.[25] The first Jewish settlements along this road were Livias and Naaran.

Jewish presence in Naaran had been attested at the start of the fourth century by Eusebius and confirmed, at the end of the same century, by Jerome.[26] The continuity of the Jewish habitat in Naaran was reflected in the presence of a synagogue constructed, it seems, as

[23] Virtual tours of contemporary landscapes seems a rare feature of dreamland in late antiquity. A notable example is the complete tour of Jerusalem, with its important Christian monuments, allegedly completed by Peter the Iberian (*Vita Petri* 98–100) in order to allay criticism raised about Peter's avoidance of the actual city while residing in the vicinity. See Ch. 5.

[24] The pilgrim of Piacenza (cf. Ch. 1, p. 46, n. 107), 40, refers to two routes for travelling from the Sinai back to Jerusalem in the late 6th cent., one via Egypt and the northern coast of the Sinai to Gaza, and the other via Aila and Petra. A third led through the central Sinai and the Negev. P. Mayerson, 'The Pilgrim Routes to Mount Sinai and the Armenians', *IEJ* 32 (1982), 44–57.

[25] J. L. Federlin, 'Recherches sur les laures et monastères de la plaine de Jordanie et du désert de Jerusalem', *La Terre Sainte* 20 (1903), 117–331; O. Sion, 'The Monasteries of the "Desert of the Jordan"', *LA* 46 (1996), 245–64, who surveyed between Jericho and the Dead Sea alone 19 cell-clusters, ranging in size from 6 to 44 cells and from 31 sq. m. in area to 248 sq. m. The majority of these monastic settlements were established between the middle of the 5th cent. and the middle of the 6th. See also Sion, 'Jordan Desert Asceticism', *Qadmoniot* 29 (1996), 25–32 (Heb.).

[26] *Onomasticon* 136. See now G. S. P. Freeman-Grenville *et al.*, *Palestine in the Fourth Century: The Onomasticon by Eusebius of Caesarea* (Jerusalem 2003), 76.

late as the sixth century.[27] Its mosaic bears a profusion of Jewish symbols, including two menorahs, the most popular Jewish symbol of late antiquity; the ark or a schematic temple; and the ubiquitous and oddly quintessential 'Jewish' symbol of late antiquity, namely the zodiac with the chariot of the sun in its midst.[28] One half of the mosaic pavement was covered with a tapestry of intricate geometrical patterns and punctuated by 'inhabited' medallions enclosing images derived from nature. Besides a taste for popular decorative elements, the Jews of Naaran, unlike many of their contemporary co-patriots, appeared fond of biblical scenes, as a rare depiction of Daniel in the fiery furnace suggests.[29] They were also forward in expressing allegiance to the congregation, as several Hebrew and Aramaic inscriptions clearly demonstrate, including one that specifically referred to past and future (!) donors to the community's 'holy place' (*makom*

---

[27] H.-L. Vincent, 'Le Sanctuaire juif d'Ayn Duq', *RB* 28 (1919), 532–63; idem and B. Carriere, 'La synagoga de Noaarah', *RB* 30 (1921), 579–601; idem and P. Benoit, 'Un sanctuaire dans la région de Jéricho: La synagogue de Naarah', *RB* 68 (1961), 163–77 with excellent b/w photos. See also *ESI* (*Excavations and Surveys in Israel*) 7–8 (1988/9), 93–5. Z. Ilan, *Ancient Synagogues in Israel* (Tel Aviv Ministry of Defense, 1991), 249–50 (Heb.), dates the Naaran synagogue to the 6th–8th cents. The building measures 15 × 19 metres.

[28] Avi Yonah, *Art in Ancient Palestine*, *passim*. The bibliography on Jewish synagogal symbols is considerable. See, among many, R. Hachlili, 'The Zodiac in Ancient Jewish Art: Representation and Significance', *BASOR* 228 (1977), 61–77; eadem, 'The Zodiac in Ancient Jewish Synagogal Art', *Jerusalem and Eretz Israel* 1 (2003), 87–122 (Heb.), interpreting the zodiac as a ritual calendar reflecting the prominence of the synagogue in communal life; L. A. Roussin, 'The Zodiac in Synagogue Decoration', in D. R. Edwards (ed.), *Archaeology and the Galilee. Texts and Contexts in the Graeco-Roman and Byzantine Periods* (Atlanta 1997), 83–96.

[29] On the rarity of Daniel in Jewish liturgy and synagogue iconography, M. Bar Ilan, 'Review of Sokoloff/Yahalom, *Jewish Aramaic Palestinian Poetry*', *Mahut* 23 (2001), 180 (Heb.), who brings the Dura Daniel as a sole parallel with Naaran. See, however, the fragmentary lion of the synagogue mosaic in Susiya which may have represented Daniel in the lions' den, Ilan, *Ancient Synagogues*, 315. On the translation of biblical scenes from texts into artistic depictions, Z. Weiss, 'Biblical Stories in Early Jewish Art: Jewish-Christian Polemic or Intracommunal Dialogue', in L. I. Levine (ed.), *Continuity and Renewal* (Jerusalem 2004), 245–69 (Heb.), who interprets the narrative art as polemics, as does Levine, ibid. 44, with regard to the menorah. See also R. Berliner (Landau), 'What are Daniel and the Lions doing on the Ark in Naaran's Ancient Synagogues', *Judea and Samaria Research Studies (Mehkarei Yehuda VeShomron)*, 3 (1993), 213–19 (Heb.; Eng. abstract on p. xxii), on the intertwining of the Temple motif with that of Daniel, and the zodiac, as signifiers of the divine creation and salvation, with Daniel's salvation assigned to the fifth day of creation, when the animals were created.

kadosh = synagogue).[30] The openness of this community to strangers appears as remarkable as its haphazard attitude to the precision of language—several grammatical errors have been spotted in the inscription.[31]

Jewish midrashic sources depicted the gentile (Christian?) community in neighbouring Jericho and the Jews of Naaran as bitter rivals, without specifying the type of enmity or rivalry between the two.[32] A sixth-century Life of Chariton, a key figure of fourth-century Judaean desert monasticism, referred to the establishment of a monastery between Jericho and Naaran in order to stem 'the insults borne (by Jericho's Christian community) at the hand of the Hebrews of Noeron'.[33] Antiochus alluded to polemical activities that the converted ex-monk undertook on behalf of his new creed. Perhaps the ex-ascetic also had a hand in the deliberate effacement of the figures that had graced the synagogue mosaic of Naaran itself. Indeed, he might have been a pioneering iconoclast among his newly adopted co-religionists.[34] Iconoclastic tendencies among the Jews

[30] J. Naveh, *On Mosaic and Stone* (Jerusalem 1978), nos. 58–67 (Heb.) and the much abbreviated summary of idem, 'Ancient Synagogue Inscriptions', in L. I. Levine (ed.), *Ancient Synagogues Revealed* (Jerusalem 1982), 133–9 with sketch of the Naaran mosaic on p. 136.

[31] On these errors, Naveh, esp. nos. 59 and 65.

[32] *LevR* 23.5: 'The Lord had commanded concerning Jacob that they who are around him become his adversaries (Lam. 1: 17), just as Hallamish [had become in the case of] Nawe, and Jericho [in the case of] Naaran' (trans. J. Slotki, London: Soncino, 1939) (slightly modified). Cf. *LamR* 1.17, 52.

[33] AASS 7, 578 (Sept. 28). See also G. Garitte, 'La Vie prémétaphrastique de Saint Chariton', *Bulletin de l'Institut historique belge de Rome* 21 (1941), 21; Eng. trans. by L. di Segni, in V. L. Wimbush (ed.), *Ascetic Behavior in Greco-Roman Antiquity* (Minneapolis 1990), 393–6. On the intra-Christian polemic aspects of the vita, J. Binns, *Ascetics and Ambassadors of Christ: The Monasteries of Palestine 341–631* (Oxford 1994), 46–7.

[34] Acts of iconoclasm/vandalism have been customarily assigned to the Islamic era, but the possibility of a Jewish iconoclastic movement already in the 6th cent. if not earlier cannot be dismissed. Cf. the damage inflicted on figures in churches, such as at Anab-el-Kebir in Har Hebron, Y. Magen *et al.*, 'The Church at 'Anab el-Kebir', *Qadmoniot* 36 (2003), 50 (Heb.); and in Kursi (on the Sea of Galilee), V. Tzaferis and D. Urman, 'Excavations at Kursi', *Qadmoniot* 6 (1973), 62–4 (Heb.). Apparently, the synagogue mosaics at Susiya and Sepphoris underwent remodelling aimed at concealing figures such as the sun-god, P. Figueras, 'Mythological Themes in Palestinian Mosaics from the Byzantine Period', *Aram* 15 (2003), 53. On Jewish iconoclasm, A. Ovadiah, 'Art of the Ancient Synagogues in Israel', in D. Urman and P. V. M. Flesher (eds.), *Ancient Synagogues* (1995), 316. At Susiya the Daniel mosaic was replaced with a geometrical pattern.

around Jericho might have been responsible for the erection of a new synagogue in the early seventh century between Jericho and Naaran, in close proximity to the latter. Unlike Naaran's non-committal ornamentation, the new synagogue displayed strictly non-figurative mosaic decoration, depicting the Torah ark, Jewish symbols (menorah, *shofar,* and *lulav*), and a Hebrew inscription announcing 'Peace on Israel'.[35] Did Jewish iconoclasts, beginning their anti-images campaign in Naaran, prefer to end it by building their own synagogue where they could carry their own brand of purist, perhaps even ascetic Judaism? Did such a movement, if indeed real, start in the Jewish settlements around the Dead Sea, so isolated amidst a growing Christian population likewise given to extreme forms of asceticism? Was the iconoclastic campaign an element in a communal effort to solidify its identity amidst increasing hostility from Christians?

In 'En Gedi on the Dead Sea a synagogue inscription, inscribed in Hebrew and Aramaic, conveyed the closing of communal ranks against non-conforming insiders and outsiders. It threatened with excommunication anyone who might disclose the 'secret' of the place to 'gentiles' (*amameia*). And it highlighted local pride of descent by listing communal 'ancestors' not only according to conventional patriarchal genealogy (Abraham, Isaac, Jacob, etc.) but also according to pre-deluge Genesis chronology, as though to guarantee its own longevity. Language displayed in public became an instrument of polemics. The mere use of words, no less than the employment of images or the meaning of text, indicated alliances. At 'En Gedi the contents targeted potential 'heresy' in the community itself while

---

[35] Ovadiah, ibid. On the date of the Jericho synagogue, *c.*620, Ilan, *Ancient Synagogues,* who links its erection with the expulsion of Jews from Jerusalem by the Sassanids. There are no details at all about the expulsion either in the direction of the Dead Sea or anywhere else for that matter other than a vague reference in a 10th-cent. Karaite source that specifies Tiberias, Gaza, and Zoara as Jewish centres of pilgrimage during a period when Jews were banned from Jerusalem, Sahl ben Masliah in A. Harkavy, 'Me'asef Nidahim', 13, *Ha'meliz* 15 (1879), 640 (Heb.). If the reference has any historical validity it points to the area south of the Dead Sea as a centre of Jewish activity. Yet, the presence of tombstones in Zoara which do not date beyond 601 suggests otherwise. On Zoara's funerary inscriptions, J. Naveh, 'The Zoar Tombstones', *Tarbiz* 64 (1995), 476–97 (Heb.) and see Ch. 6. On Jerusalem Jewry during the Sassanid occupation of the city, Sivan, 'From Byzantine to Persian Jerusalem' (2000) and eadem, 'Palestine between Byzantium and Persia' (2004).

proclaiming an unambiguous link with the greatest biblical antiquity. The builders of the new Naaran synagogue expressed their strict uniconic monotheism through a zodiac mosaic which, instead of containing images of the labours and the months widely popular in the Galilee primarily in synagogues, defiantly drew up a verbal list of them.[36]

Naaran, with its thriving Jewish community, seemed a sensible selection for a newly converted monk. That of Livias, if correctly reported by Antiochus, is puzzling. Livias, although strategically situated along the road linking the Via Nova Traiana with Jerusalem and the rest of Palestine, was famed for its hot water springs and was rich in biblical associations.[37] But the presence of Jews is not indicated in any contemporary source.[38] On the other hand, already as early as the fourth century the empty plains around Livias had attracted the attention of imaginative Christian guides and curious pilgrims.[39] In the 380s Egeria read a passage from Deuteronomy at a place, somewhere near Livias, where Moses had allegedly written that very book.

The region of Livias presented a congenial soil for the fulfilment of dreams. According to John Moschus, a writer who, like Antiochus, had close Sinaitic connections, a Jerusalemite monk named John set out from Jerusalem to the holy mountain of the Sinai.[40] Just after crossing the Jordan and reaching the periphery of Livias, John fell gravely ill. Finding refuge in a cave, the feverish monk was visited by an apparition that ordered him to desist from his efforts to reach the Sinai. Unimpressed, the monk refused to obey. The apparition reappeared and, identifying itself as John the Baptist, proceeded to assure

---

[36] On the 'En Gedi synagogue and its inscriptions, D. Barag *et al.*, in L. I. Levine, *Ancient Synagogues Revealed* (1981), 116–19 and 140–5 (6th or 7th cent.).

[37] M. Piccirillo, 'The Jerusalem–Esbous Road', *Studies in the History and Archaeology of Jordan* 3 (1987), 165–172; idem, 'La strada', *LA* 46 (1996), 285–300.

[38] Unless obliquely hinted at in an early 7th-cent. homily honouring the assumption of Mary and attributed to Theoteknos of Livias where he blames the Jews for not glorifying 'their sister Mary' and for rejecting her Son, accusations that are both general and ultimately undatable, A. Wegner, 'Aux origines de la croyance en l'Assomption: L'Homélie de Théoteknos de Livias en Palestine (fin du VI–début du VII siècle', in *De Primordiis Cultus Mariani*, vol. iv (Rome 1970), 327–39; Eng. trans. in B. E. Daley, *On the Dormition of Mary* (Crestwood, NY, 1998), 71–81.

[39] Jacobs, *Remains of the Jews*, 118.

[40] *Pratum Spirituale* 1 (*PG* 87.3, 2853). The narrative is placed in the time of bishop Elias of Jerusalem *c.*500.

the sick but persistent monk that the tiny cave where he was lying 'was greater than the Sinai' because Jesus himself had frequented it. To win the monk over the Baptist had to strike a deal: 'Promise me that here you will stay and I will restore your health instantly'. Cured, the monk established a *laura* in a locality which had been already hallowed by association with Elijah.[41]

In the engagement between two forms of piety, the monk's and the Baptist's, the search for an existing holy place (Mount Sinai) was contrasted with the 'discovery' of a new one. Galvanized into giving up his Sinaitic dream, the monk lived up to his promise. Indirectly, the establishment of a Jerusalemite laura east of the Jordan extended Jerusalem's sphere of influence beyond the Judaean desert. The dream-induced 'discovery' may have been further calculated to erase completely the faint souvenirs of biblical and Jewish associations which had roots in this territory. A monastery honouring Jesus' baptism had been located in a place called Qasr el-Yehud, the 'Castle of the Jews'.[42] It is difficult, however, to discern whether the name embeds an older (i.e. pre-Christian) or a more recent (i.e. late ancient) memory.[43]

Reconciling etymologies, dreams produced places but places also produced dreams. Stories of the rediscovery of localities long hidden from human eyes delighted travellers already conditioned to absorb the unnatural. Peter the Iberian, a man whose life had been punctuated by dream visions, journeyed from Livias to Nebo and Madaba (*c.*480), and was promptly introduced to dream-topography.[44] He began with bathing in Livias' hot springs, a therapeutic immersion

---

[41] Sapsas or Sapsaphas, the Place of the Willows, where it is identified with Ainon, M. Piccirillo, 'Aenon Sapsaphas and Bethabara', in *The Madaba Map Centenary 1897–1997* (Jerusalem 1999), 219–20; E. Alliata, 'The Pilgrimage Routes during the Byzantine Period in Transjordan', in ibid. 122.

[42] Y. Hirschfeld, *The Judean Desert Monasteries in the Byzantine Period* (New Haven 1992), 293–4; Sion, 'The Monasteries of the "Desert of Jordan"' (see n. 25, 58), 249–50.

[43] Perhaps the reference is to Iraq el Emir, the famed castle of the Tobiad family in the 2nd cent. BCE. It is curious that the name commemorating Jewish presence remained attached to the place rather than the association with John the Baptist and Jesus.

[44] *Vita* pp. 86–89 (Raabe). Eng. trans. in Saller, *Mt Nebo* (1941), 343–7, repr. in M. Piccirillo and E. Alliata, *Mount Nebo: New Archaeological Excavations 1967–1997* (Jerusalem 1998).

which failed to cater to his austere taste. He then headed to nearby
Mount Nebo, a locality which Christian tradition identified with
Moses' burial. There local monks made Peter privy to a local history
of holiness: led by a dream-vision, a local shepherd had found
himself in a large and luminous cave exuding sweet smells. In the
cave he suddenly saw a venerable old man reclining on a bed.
Without further ado the shepherd identified the elderly loner as
Moses. Rushing to tell the villagers about this vision, the shepherd
was able to lead them back to the mysterious cave which he had the
sense to mark with stones. Convinced of the link between Moses and
this cave, the villagers proceeded to construct a church honouring
the cave's biblical occupant. In no time at all 'those afflicted in soul
and affected with sufferings of the body' gathered at the sanctuary
and were healed.[45] To judge by the magnificent and costly array of
mosaics in the churches around Nebo, discoveries of this sort became
a source of substantial income for local communities suitably
rewarded for their biblical exegetical enterprises.[46] While in Madaba,
Peter the Iberian also performed a rain miracle, a feat that earned
him accolades as a second Elijah-cum-Moses.[47]

   Dreams displayed an interplay between an imaginary landscape and
geographical realities, transferring to Christians the initiative of con-
quering a holy land that the Hebrew Bible had allocated to the Israelites. The contribution of dreams to the history of sacred topography
functioned at several levels. They re-elaborated biblical geography;
they re-enacted the idea of visionary periphery by divorcing it from
ambiguity; and they forged a direct and unmediated link between
textual figures and collective needs. 'Reading' dreams contributed to

---

[45] *Vita Petri* p. 86 (Raabe); Hunt, *Holy Land Pilgrimage*, 59.
[46] The mosaics, some of the most beautiful ever discovered in these parts of the
empire, are surveyed by Piccirillo in idem and Alliata, *Mount Nebo, passim.*
[47] John Rufus, *Vita Petri* 90. B. Biton-Ashkelony, 'Imitatio Mosis and Pilgrimage
in the Life of Peter the Iberian', in eadem and A. Kofsky (eds.), *Christian Gaza in Late
Antiquity* (2004), 112–14. On presenting contemporary heroes as latter-day biblical
prophets, D. Satran, *Biblical Prophets in Byzantine Palestine: Reassessing the Lives of
the Prophets* (Leiden 1995), 97–105. Cf. the disappearance of Moses, the quintessential biblical hero, from the Passover Haggadah, the central text 'recalling' the biblical
desert experiences, which does not refer to the great leader in a single word. The
silence may be construed as polemics responding to the centrality of Moses in the
construction of a Christian holy land, as of images of an ideal Christian monarch. See
also Ch. 6.

establishing features of asceticism that escaped direct rulings. Edifying stories of the sort that led one monk to abandon a pilgrimage to Mount Sinai and another to abandon Sinaitic monasticism altogether were interwoven into the history of Palestinian Christianity in general and of monasticism in particular. In this interactive and creative topography, dreams directed a thread of history that shifted the model of Christian asceticism from dialectics towards action.

3. THE HOLY MOUNTAIN: MAKING THE IMPASSABLE PASSABLE

The essential plasticity of dreams reduced the vast complexity of Palestine's layered land into a single dimension of biblical references. They became exemplary fragments of a history that late ancient Christianity resumed as it built up a tradition that in itself was derivative. To interpret dreams *ad terram* meant to divest the mindscape of a singular freedom, the kind of liberty which is acknowledged in an *ad hominem* interpretation. The translation of visions into territorial realities constructed a historical universe in which centres and peripheries operated along lines dominated by impulses and necessities. Antiochus claimed that the devil visited the Sinai where he invaded the susceptible mind of a monk. The choice of location seemed deliberate. The emergence of deserts, like the Sinai and the neighbouring Negev, from obscurity or rather somnolence into unprecedented prosperity, illustrates how language effectively translates mindscapes into landscapes by transforming peripheries into horizons of centrality.

When Egeria visited the southern Sinai in the early 380s the mountains swarmed with monks who surrounded her as she visited and prayed in the central sanctuary of 'Mount Sinai', the very location of the Theophany. The transformation of this arid landscape into a central tourist zone in late antiquity had been achieved, nearly single-handedly, by groups of pioneering ascetics.[48] The fact that the

---

[48] Sivan, 'Pilgrimage, Monasticism, and the Emergence of Christian Palestine in the Fourth Century', in R. Ousterhout (ed.), *The Blessings of Pilgrimage* (Urbana 1990), 54–65.

Sinai featured on a universal map of pilgrimage shows how monastic determination and pilgrims' curiosity combined to create a zone of monastic and rural settlements that became self-sufficient and able to cope with harsh climatic conditions.

Its prominence was not, however, a foregone conclusion. In the late third century the Sinai had been taken to symbolize the 'old' obsolete Jewish covenant, in contrast with Mount Sion which symbolized the 'new' Christian covenant:

From the prophetic writing (Ps. 2: 6) it is clear that Sion is holy and spiritual, a mountain where the Son of God was appointed King by the Holy Spirit, proclaiming the will and kingdom of his father. But Sinai was made an earthly mountain in a dry land. It is in Syrian Palestine, where also the Judaean region is to be found in which lies the city that killed prophets and where Christ was crucified by the Jews.[49]

Sinai, in this biblical exegesis, became contiguous with Judaea and Jerusalem, a relic of a past that no longer mattered but that could be gazed upon dispassionately. Sion was tantamount to the Cross and hence a sacred precinct of immediacy and relevance.[50] These contrasting perspectives failed to check countless women and men for whom the Sinai retained the sanctity which the Exodus epiphany had bestowed on it since biblical antiquity.

The annexation of the bulk of the Sinai peninsula to the province of Palaestina III (*c.*400?) effectively created an inner desert (*interiorem heremum*) or a desert beyond the desert, a vast stretch of sand and solitude between Egypt and the Negev (southern Palestine) where pilgrims could experience, first hand, the formative stages of the biblical Exodus.[51] The connection between 'Mount Sinai' (Jebel

---

[49] *De Montibus Sinai et Sion* 3 (CSEL 3.3, 106), trans. in A. Hamilton, 'Jerusalem', in P. Allen *et al.* (eds.), *Prayer and Spirituality in the Early Church* (Everton Park, Qld. Australia, 1998), 295, who dates it to the second half of the 3rd cent.

[50] Hamilton, ibid.

[51] For the expression *interiorum heremum*, the Piacenza pilgrim, CCSL 175: 145–7. The date of the transfer of the southern Sinai and the Negev to Palestine has been a matter of debate. M. Avi Yonah, 'On the Date of the Limes Palestinae', *Eretz Israel* 5 (1959), 135–7 (Heb.), followed by Y. Tsafrir, 'Why were the Negev, the Southern Transjordan and the Sinai transferred from the Provincia Arabia to Provincia Palestina at the end of the Third Century?', *Cathedra* 30 (1983), 35–56 (Heb.), have opted for *c.*300, in conjunction with the erection of the Diocletianic *limes* and the transfer of the sole legion in Palestine from Jerusalem to Aila in reaction to perils posed by

Musa) and the site of the biblical Theophany had been forged by an enterprising Syrian ascetic, Julianus Saba, who established a small church on its peak, a token of victory of faith and resolution.[52]

To escape being honoured ... he (Saba) set out for Mount Sina (sic) with few of those closer to him, entering no city or village but *making passable the impassable desert*. They carried on their shoulders the necessary food, I mean bread and salt, and also a cup made from wood and a sponge tied to a piece of string, in order (if ever they found the water too deep) to draw it up with the sponge, squeeze it into the cup, and so drink it. Accordingly, after completing a journey of many days, they reached the mountain they longed for, and having worshipped their own Master passed much time there, thinking the deserted character of the place and tranquillity of soul supreme delight ... [53]

Echoes of this singular 'conquest' reverberated all the way back to Saba's home where (Pseudo) Ephrem celebrated the 'conquest' with three hymns (14, 19, 20) which compared Julianus Saba with Moses, favouring the former over the latter (Hymn 20).[54] Hymn 19 was cast as polemics with the Jews:

Saracens. P. Mayerson, 'Palaestina vs. Arabia in Byzantine Sources', *ZPE* 56 (1984), 223–30, repr. in idem, *Monks, Martyrs* (1994), 224–31, and idem, 'Justinian's Novel 103 and the Reorganization of Palestine', *BASOR* 209 (1988), 66, opted for *c.*390 as the date of the final transfer after a series of provincial mutations throughout the 4th cent. The archaeological evidence seems ambiguous. The military camp at Oboda (Avdat) had been abandoned, according to one interpretation, by the early 2nd cent. following the annexation of the Nabataean kingdom, T. Erickson-Gini, 'Nabatean or Roman? Reconsidering the Date of the Camp at Avdat in Light of Recent Excavations', in P. W. M. Freeman *et al.* (eds.), *Limes XVIII: Proceedings of the XVIIIth International Congress of Roman Frontier Studies held in Amman, Jordan* (Sept. 2000) (BAR Int. Ser.; Oxford 2002), 113–30; and according to another interpretation, in the early 4th cent., A. Negev, 'The Nabataeans and the Provincia Arabia', in *ANRW* ii.6 (1977), 622–4. The later date gains some corroboration in the light of events such as the construction of a large rectangular fort in Nessana in the early 5th cent., H. D. Colt (ed.), *Excavations at Nessana*, i (London 1962), 16, 32. Whether the two, namely the abandonment of one camp for another, are indeed chronologically interrelated, is still an open question.

[52] Theodoret, *Historia Religiosa* (ed. P. Canivet and A. Leroy-Molinghen, 2 vols. Paris 1977–9). Eng. trans. R. M. Price, *A History of the Monks of Syria by Theodoret of Cyrrhus* (Cistercian Studies 88; Kalamazoo 1985). On Julianus Saba see also Soz. *HE* 3.14. For a survey of Sinai 'explorers', visitors, and monastic establishments see Uzi Dahari, *Monastic Settlements in South Sinai* (Israel Antiquities Authority, Reports 9; Jerusalem 2000), *passim*.

[53] Price, trans. p. 29.   [54] CSCO 322–3 (1972).

The circumcised who boast of Mount Sinai
You (Julianus) humbled
Great is this news.
On the mountain of the Father stands a church for the Son ...
Of stone is the heart of a doubter made
That two are the mountains of sanctity
Here is the church on Mount Sinai
And on Mount Zion is the Golgotha ... [55]

Julianus Saba, according to his poetic co-patriot, united the Old and the New Testaments not only by defying Jewish traditions, but also by placing a church on the very spot where God and Moses conversed, and by linking Jerusalem with the Holy Mountain.[56]

While remoulding the mountainous landscape to fit the needs of contemporary Christian theology, Saba's pilgrimage to the Sinai re-semanticized the biblical meaning of the Sinai. A few decades later another venerable Syrian figure, Symeon the Elder, embarked on a Sinaitic journey that took him along a path paved with visions and studded with miracles, culminating in a week-long fasting and contemplation that ended with the mysterious depositing of three apples in his hand.[57] Notwithstanding the difficulties of facing hunger and thirst, these pilgrimages show how the desert between Egypt and the Holy Land, the alleged land of the Exodus, was integrated into Christian spirituality and the map of pilgrimage already by the mid-century.

For Jewish theologians the essence of the Sinai was made familiar not by embedding the divine message within a cartographic context, but rather in its sublimation into a vast chain of oral transmission. Tractate 'Avot' (Fathers) opens with a statement that reaffirmed a direct transmission of God's words from Moses straight to the rabbis. It enshrined the moment of Sinaitic revelation in the exegetical act of unveiling the text which in itself was both continuous and independent

[55] Trans. in Dahari, *Monasteries*.
[56] No Jewish tradition identifies Mount Sinai-Jebel Musa with the place of the biblical Theophany. According to Eusebius (*Onom.* sub Sin., Exod. 16: 1): Sin is 'the desert that stretches between the Red Sea and the Sinai desert. After Sin, they came to Rephidim, and after that to the desert of Sinai where beside Mount Sinai Moses received the revelation of the law. Scripture says that the desert of Sin is called the same as Kades by the Hebrews but not by the Septuagint' (trans. Freeman-Grenville). Jerome does not add to these basics.
[57] Theodoret, *HR* (Price, p. 67).

of the specificity of place and time.[58] By endlessly recreating God's lost voice, the ritual act of studying the Torah grounded the myth of the Sinai in the voices of the sages-teachers. Teaching and learning filled the space interjected by time with the motionless repetition of statements stripped of their geographical specificity.

To canonize the Sinai the rabbis projected a model of tradition vis-à-vis a model of revelation, replacing the mountain with scripture. By contrast, Christians sought to authenticate the Bible in the contemporary landscape, a quest that wrested a marginal territory out of centuries-long oblivion. Julianus Saba's identification of Mount Sinai amidst the mountains of the southern Sinaitic peninsula posed a new challenge to those who sought the desert in order to unite with God. The long trek to the mountain stood within a linear temporality that merged sacred topographies of the past and the present, succinctly yet poignantly pronounced in graffiti of anonymous pilgrims who 'have gone around Moses' and who 'saw Jerusalem' along the path up Mount Sinai.[59]

Already in the early 380s there were monastic establishments in the oases of Pharan, Raitho, and Jebel Musa (Mount Sinai), all visited by the indefatigable Egeria. When she climbed the 'mountain of Moses' she found there a cave,[60] not unlike the one 'discovered' near Livias by the fortunate shepherd (pp. 62–3). In late antiquity the wandering Israelite leader successfully served as a textual bridge between the Sinai and eastern Jordan. Moses' 'presence' in the Sinai rendered the inaccessible accessible, recasting the Sinai as a periphery within a periphery, yet an integral part of a Christian *patria*.

By the end of the sixth century the Sinaitic monastic community impressed a traveller with its global character:

Here we beheld a multitude of monks and hermits bearing crosses and singing psalms. They came to meet us and, falling to the ground, did reverence to us. We did the same, shedding tears. They then led us into the valley between

[58] M. Fishbane, 'Oral Tradition in Judaism', in *Scripture beyond the Written Word*, workshop (June 2002, Istanbul) (downloaded from the internet). See also S. Weingarten, '"And This Shall Be A Token To Thee" (Ex. 3: 12): *Lapis Sinaiticus* in Jewish and Christian Traditions', *JJS* 54 (2003), 1–20.

[59] M. Stone, *Armenian Inscriptions from Sinai: An Intermediate Report* (Sydney 1979), 3–5, 12.

[60] *Itinerarium Egeriae* (*IE*) 3.4, J. Wilkinson, *Egeria's Travels in the Holy Land* (Jerusalem 1981).

Horeb and Sinai. . . . The monastery (there) is surrounded by walls and in it there are three abbots learned in Latin, Greek, Syriac, Egyptian (Coptic) and Persian (Bessic), and many interpreters of each language.[61]

Yet, when pilgrims finally reached the summit of Mount Sinai their eyes first met neither Saba's church nor with pious monks but with the following sight:

On this mountain, on part of the hill, the Saracens had set up their own marble idol, white as snow. Their priest remained there as well, dressed in a Dalmatic and a linen cloak. At the new moon, when the time of their festival arrived, the marble started to change color. It became as black as pitch as soon as the moon appeared and they began to worship. When the time of the festival was over the idol regained its original color, a truly amazing sight.[62]

The Sinai sanctified soil served two vastly different communities, that of the monks of the mountain, on the one hand, and of the pagan Saracens, on the other. With its cells, sanctuary, and statue, the landscape provided stability in a game of mobility in which the same territory fulfilled different purposes.

Relations between monks and 'Saracen' marauders in this desert periphery were modulated by murders and miracles. The Saracens, only nominally Roman subjects, spread over the desert all the way from Egypt to east of the Jordan and beyond even to Syria.[63] Saracens assumed a variety of roles, from soldiers serving empire and emperor, to guides, labourers, guards, traders, robbers, and killers, thus contributing to a peculiar kind of symbiosis punctuated by conflict and compromise.[64] The 'wolves of Arabia' also provided converts.[65] Their dependence on settlers for survival was recorded by an Italian pilgrim who, in the sixth century, was struck by pitiful spectacles of entire

---

[61] *Anon. Plac.* 37 (Wilkinson; trans. A. Stewart in PPTS).

[62] Ibid. 38 (Wilkinson) trans. in Jacobs, *Remains*, 136–7 (slightly modified). The idol may have been placed on Mt. Horeb, fully facing the church on Mt. Sinai.

[63] Ps. Nilus, *Narrationes*, ed. F. Conca, *Nilus Ancyranus: Narratio* (Teubner 1983), 12, on their distribution (an older version appeared in *PG* 79). J. Retsö, *The Arabs in Antiquity* (London 2003).

[64] P. Mayerson, 'Saracens and Romans: Micro–Macro Relationships', *BASOR* 274 (1989), 71–9 and Mayerson's other contributions in his collected essays, *Monks, Martyrs, Soldiers and Saracens* (Jerusalem 1994). See also F. Millar, 'The Theodosian Dynasty and the Arabs: Saracens or Ishmaelites?' in E. Gruen (ed.), *Cultural Borrowings and Ethnic Appropriations in Antiquity* (Stuttgart, 2005), 297 f.

[65] For the expression, Cyril of Scythopolis, *Vita Euthymii*, 24 (Schwartz).

families dressed in rags and begging for bread from travellers.[66] Aggressive or submissive, Saracens spiced the lore of the Sinai by infusing the predictable tenor of the desert with serendipity. Tales of the monks of the Sinai relayed the heroism of the ascetics of the desert who formed objects of deadly amusement for Arab raiding parties.[67] There were stories such as that of the forty martyrs of the Sinai, and of the 700 monks slaughtered at Raitho by 'barbarians', and of monks and pilgrims abducted to be sold in the Negev slave markets.[68] These deaths formed the nucleus of a Sinaitic corpus of tales of martyrdom which commemorated a uniquely Palestinian ascetic mode without parallels either in contemporary Syria or in Egypt.

Monastic life in the southern Sinai centred around the settlements of Mount Sinai, of Wadi Pharan, and the town of Raitho, localities identified with various stations along the biblical Exodus, all clustering near water sources.[69] Around the springs of Raitho sprang both Saracen dwellings and ascetic settlements and cells. The town's

[66] *Anon. Plac.* (Geyer, 212–13).

[67] Nau, 'Le Texte grec'; and B. Flusin, *Saint Anastase le Perse et l'histoire de la Palestine au debut du VII S.*, 2 vols. (Paris 1992), *passim.* See also the account of Ps. Nilus, *Narrationes* (above, n. 63) with P. Mayerson, 'Observations on the "Nilus" Narrationes: Evidence for an Unknown Christian Sect?', *Journal of the American Research Center in Egypt* 12 (1975), 51–74, and idem, 'The Ammonius Narrative: Bedouin and Blemmye Attacks in Sinai', in *The Bible World: Essays in Honor of Cyrus H. Gordon* (New York 1980), 133–48. Mayerson correctly detects in this monastic lore traces of authentic traditions and topography in spite of the stringent criticism of Robert Devreesse, 'Le Christianisme dans la péninsule sinaïtique dès origines à l'arrivée des Musulmans', *RB* 49 (1940), 205–23, esp. 216–22. On monastic lore coupled with pilgrimage Sinaitic experiences, D. Caner, 'Sinai Pilgrimage and Ascetic Romance: Pseudo-Nilus *Narrationes* in Context', in L. Ellis and F. Kidner (eds.), *Travel, Communications, and Geography in Late Antiquity: Sacred and Profane.* Proceedings of the IV Shifting Frontiers in Late Antiquity Conference (San Francisco 2001) (Aldershot 2004), 135–47.

[68] Ammonius (story of the 40 martyrs); Epiphanius the martyr VII.4 (*PG* 120. 259–72) on the massacre, with H. Donner, 'Die Palästinabeschreibung des Epiphanius Monachus Hagiopolita', *ZDPV* 87 (1971), 42–92, p. 71.

[69] Dahari, *Monastic Settlements in South Sinai,* identified about 70 monastic units around wadi Pharan and Mount Sinai. Compare the spread of monasteries along the coast of the northern Sinai, P. Figueras, *From Gaza to Pelusium: Materials for the Historical Geography of North Sinai and South-West Palestine 332 BCE–640 CE* (*Beer Sheva* 14; Beer Sheva 2000), esp. pp. 130–53 on the Christianization of the northern Sinai, and pp. 157–258 for gazetteer.

church provided a centre of prayer and a shelter from the Bedouin.[70] The proximity of Egypt was instrumental. It provided inspiration for desert asceticism and a market where 'Saracens' traded dates grown by the monks in the Sinai for wheat cultivated in Egypt.[71] Pharan, a town of some 80 dunams (8 hectares), boasted a bishop and a monastery on top of its acropolis, besides a large church and numerous dwellings.[72] Believed to have been the biblical Rephidim (Exod. 17: 8–13), Pharan was the military, administrative, economic, and ecclesiastical centre of the southern Sinai. It owed its prosperity and sustainability, as well as susceptibility to raiding parties, to its strategic location between Egypt and the Sinai. The town's dwellers provided guards for the local monasteries although Pharan appeared as vulnerable to Saracen raids as were the isolated cells of the desert. According to one account of martyrdom, the heroism of the Pharanides equalled, if not surpassed, the bravery of the Sinaitic monks.[73]

The precarious balance between locals (or sedentarized Saracens), monks, nomads, and pilgrims rested on mutual need, with monks providing miracles and nomads providing protection from other nomads.[74] Monks worked miraculous cures and exorcized demons, activities that generated communal contacts and even conversion. When a monk named Moses cured a chieftain by the name of Zocom,

[70] Ammonius, Syriac version (7th cent.?); Eng. trans. in A. Smith Lewis, *The Forty Martyrs of the Sinai Desert* (Hora Semiticae 9; Cambridge 1912), 1–24. The church was called *castrum*, no doubt designating its double function, and perhaps identified with the citadel built by the emperor Anastasius *c.*500 in the wake of a 'barbarian' raid that killed several monks, John of Nikiu, *Chronicle* 125 (R. H. Charles, text and trans., 1916).

[71] Ammonius (*Relatio de sanctis patribus, barbarorum incursione in monte sina et Raithu peremptis*, ed. F. Combefis, *Illustrium Christi Martyrum lecti Triumphi* (Paris 1660), 88–122).

[72] Dahari, *Monastic Settlements*, 15–20; 135–6.

[73] Ps. Nilus, *Narrationes* (*PG* 79. 657B–661B). Passage translated in Mayerson, 'Observations on the "Nilus" Narrationes', 66. The passage contains a speech by a widow who lost her son in a Saracen raid. She tries to inspire the hero with bravery and piety.

[74] R. Solzbacher, *Mönche, Pilger und Sarazen: Studien zum Frühchristentum auf der südlichen Sinaihalbinsel von den Anfangen bis zum Beginn islamischer Herrschaft* (Altenberge 1989). See also the articles gathered in D. Valbelle and C. Bonnet (eds.), *Le Sinaï durant l'antiquité et le Moyen Âge: 4000 ans d'histoire* (Paris 1998). The possibility that much of the land around the southern Sinai was owned by monasteries and leased to laymen requires some consideration, in spite of lack of evidence. On the topic, M. Kaplan, *Les Propriétés de la couronne et de l'église dans l'empire byzantin (V-Ve S.)* (Byzantina Sorbonensia 2; Paris 1976), *passim*.

the latter converted to Christianity, acquired the name of Obedianus and in turn engineered the conversion of 'all the people living on the frontiers of the Ishmaelites who inhabited the region of Pharan'.[75] Moses' endeavour, if historical, generated an 'understanding', namely an oral contract between the inhabitants of Pharan and a succession of tribal chieftains, a kind of symbiosis based on gifts for the chieftains in exchange for protecting the locals from non-allied nomads.[76] One result was that during Saracen festivals pilgrims could travel in relative safety through the Sinai to the holy mountain but once the festivities were over perils returned.[77]

Remoteness notwithstanding, the monks of the Sinai were kept abreast of matters 'abroad' by constant travels between Egypt, the Sinai, the Judaean desert, and Jerusalem, not to mention the presence of pilgrims from afar.[78] The monks' contribution to theological debates ranged from hagiography that extolled the virtues of Sinaitic asceticism and monasticism to treatises defending monothelitic principles.[79] John Rufus, a staunch supporter of Palestinian Monophysites, narrated how Zosimus, a Monophysite monk, travelled from the Sinai to Jerusalem with the intention of retreating to Bethel.[80] He was deterred from completing his journey by a vision of the biblical patriarch Jacob who chided him for betraying his orthodoxy (i.e. Monophysite faith). Bethel was a community of 'renegades' (i.e. Chalcedonians) and therefore inappropriate. The monk complied.

[75] Ammonius, 99–101, quoted in Mayerson, 'Saracens and Romans: Micro–Macro Relationships', 74. The story of the conversion is discounted by Devreesse, 'Le Christianisme', 219, who regards it as a 'miracle with longevity' based on Sozomen, *HE* 6.38 (conversion of Mavia by Moses). The presumed date is around the middle of the 4th cent.

[76] Ps. Nilus (Conca, 38); Mayerson, 'The Saracens and the Limes', *BASOR* 262 (1986), 35–47, esp. p. 44.

[77] *Anon. Plac.* 34, 38 (Wilkinson). See also Mayerson, 'The Pilgrim Routes to Mount Sinai and the Armenians', 44–57, esp. 46–7.

[78] John Moschus, *Limonarion* 16, 116. On the links between Egypt and Palestine in general in late antiquity, Binns, *Ascetics and Ambassadors*, 157–9 and *passim*.

[79] Anastasius (Nau, p. 53, n. 4); Ammonius (above, n. 71). See also Theodore of Pharan, identified with the presbyter Theodore of Raitho the writer of *Praeparatio de Incarnatione*, E. Elert, 'Theodore von Pharan und Theodor von Raithu', *Theologische Literaturzeitung* 76 (1951), 67–76; H. G. Beck, *Kirche und theologische Literatur im byzantinischen Reich* (Munich 1959), 383 n. 154.

[80] *Plerophoriae*, 30. See also Lorenzo Perrone, 'Dissenso dottrinale e propaganda visionaria: Le Pleroforie di Giovanni di Maiuma', *Augustinianum* 29 (1989), 451–95.

A not atypical ascetic peregrination would take a man seeking monastic tutoring to monastic centres in Egypt, the Sinai, and Palestine, regardless of provincial boundaries and perils:

Silvanus, a native of Palestine, to whom, on account of his high virtue, an angel was once seen to minister, practised philosophy... (?) in Egypt [Scetis]. He then lived at Mount Sinai and afterwards founded at Gerar in the wadi [Gaza region] a very extensive and most noted coenobium for many good men.[81]

John of Climachus and Anastasius the Sinaitic, John the Sabaite and Antiochus made substantial contributions to the genre of edifying biographies of ascetics, following in the footsteps of Palladius' Lausiac History.[82] The Holy Mountain left an indelible imprint on all these, as did the 'Saracens', making the existence in so harsh and perilous an environment a leitmotif of the narratives of heroism that aspired to delineate a brutal opposition between Christians, beloved of God, and Saracens, allies of the Devil.[83]

Living in a desert seemed to define a type of citizenship that was peripheral to the institutional language of legality that defined domicile and residence in terms of towns and taxation. The relationship of individuals to the territory was controlled by nature, by past associations, by sentiments of piety, and by movements of 'Saracens'. To characterize the occupation of the Sinai in late antiquity means to grasp at a sense of colonization that is absent from the logic of migration and settlement, yet is also of the way that the empire had of occupying the soil.

Undergirded by piety, the sight of the mountain dispelled the difficulties of journeying through the desert. The natural splendour

---

[81] Sozomen, *HE* 6.32. On Silvanus, D. Chitty, *The Desert a City* (Oxford 1966), 71; M. Van Parys, 'Abba Silvain et ses disciples: Une famille monastique entre Scété et la Palestine à la fin du IVe et dans la première moitié du Ve siècles', *Irenikon* 61 (1988), 315–31. See also B. Biton-Ashkelony and A. Kofsky, 'Gazan Monasticism in the Byzantine Period', *Cathedra* 96 (2000), 79–81 (Heb.).

[82] Flusin, 'Démons et Sarrasins', 397–8. For the intellectuals of the Sinai and their activities especially in the second half of the 6th cent. and the beginning of the 7th, including Theodore of Raitho, John Climachus, Daniel of Raitho, and Anastasius, see V. Beneševic, 'Sur la date de la mosaïque de la Transfiguration au Mont Sinaï', *Byz.* 1 (1924), 145–72; and Flusin, *Saint Anastase.*

[83] Flusin, 'Démons et Sarrasins', 408. The contrast is a major theme of the 'Nilus' *Narrationes*, narration 3, Mayerson, 'Observations on the "Nilus" Narrationes' 51–74, esp. 52 and 60.

of the Sinai was considerably enhanced when Justinian endowed a monastery at the foot of the mountain. Skilful mosaicists decorated the apse of the monastery's church with the Transfiguration, medallion busts of apostles, prophets, and other biblical figures, including a David who looked very much like the imperial Justinian of San Vitale in Ravenna.[84] In complete reciprocity between seeing and being seen, pilgrims to the Sinai recognized a certain sense of displacement and different dynamics. Some, most notably Armenians, elected to share their impressions with posterity by leaving graffiti along the road to the mountain.[85] Iberian pilgrims in the Sinai, like the Armenians who translated their emotions into a few pithy phrases, asked God for mercy in the belief that such requests were directly communicated to God because they were uttered in precisely the same locations where Moses had conversed with the deity.[86] Westerners chose to commemorate their visit in terms of an agon between pious 'Romans' versus impious 'Syrians'.[87] Others, mindful of the public monuments seen along their route to the holy land, inscribed the words *Senatus P(opulus) Q(ue) R(omanus)*, as though the very repetition of this traditional formula in the heart of the Sinai endowed the Exodus desert with Roman identity.[88] Even Jews, stumbling into the Sinai either as soldiers or in some other guise, left graffiti on Sinaitic rocks, written 'to the One God' in the hope of invoking divine succour also through the magical use of the Alphabet.[89]

The emergence of the Sinai desert from peripheral obscurity to a central place in the ascetic and pilgrimage maps of late ancient Palestine

[84] G. K. Forsyth and K. Weitzman, *The Monastery of St Catherine at Mount Sinai: The Church and the Fortress of Justinian* (Ann Arbor 1973); J. Elsner, *Art and the Roman Viewer: The Transformation of Art from the Pagan World to Christianity* (Cambridge 1995), 99–123. Cf. David in the Gaza synagogue, Ch. 8, 346.

[85] M. E. Stone, *The Armenian Inscriptions of the Sinai* (Cambridge, Mass., 1982). See also Mayerson, 'The Pilgrim Routes to Mount Sinai and the Armenians', 44–57.

[86] M. van Esbroeck, 'The Georgian Inscriptions', in Stone, *The Armenian Inscriptions of the Sinai* 179.

[87] W. Adler, 'The Latin Inscriptions' = App. II in Stone, ibid. p. 183, no. 1: *cessent Syri ante Latinos Romanos*.

[88] Ibid. p. 185, no. 2: *factus Senatus PQ Romanus ex imp.*

[89] A. Negev, 'Inscriptions on Rock no. 5 in Wadi Haggag. Sinai', *Eretz Israel* 12 (1975), 134–6 (Heb.); L. Di Segni, '*Eis theos* in Palestinian Inscriptions', *SCI* 13 (1994), 106. One inscription is assigned to 299/300, the other to either the same date or later in the 4th cent.

is brought home in documents that demonstrated the intimate link between commerce in commodities and in piety. A papyrus from Nessana in the Negev gives a partial account of the income and expenditures of a caravan travelling from the Negev to the southern Sinai and back.[90] This group of merchants traded animals, especially camels, and conveyed food products and money from the Negev to the Sinai. The papyrus outlines the preparations for the journey, including the sale of camels, purchase of slaves, and the highlight—a visit to the Holy Mountain and other holy sites in the southern Sinai. The merchants hired a Bedouin guide for the not inconsiderable sum of three *solidi*.[91] Prepared thus for the necessities of the journey through the desert, the traders completed a number of transactions along their road, trading items such as pack animals, wool, oil, textiles, barley, and wine. The papyrus also alludes to the return journey, this time without the services of a guide, and the setbacks encountered, not the least the loss of a camel which was recovered by a member of the Bani al-Udayyid who held the animal for ransom.[92]

The mythical origins of the landscape, so firmly entrenched in the biblical narrative of the Exodus, established an order in which passivity and activity mingled to tell a story of the victory of 'civilization' over barbarism, human over nature, and of Christianity over the foreignness of the terrain. How integral the Sinai had become in the Palestinian Christian discourse of sanctity in late antiquity is seen

[90] C. J. Kraemer (ed.), *Excavations in Nessana*, iii: *The Non-Literary Papyri* (Princeton 1958), pap. 89, pp. 251–8 dated to the end 6th/beginning 7th cent.

[91] The guide or recipient of the money may have been a Saracen tribal chief who controlled the territory which the caravan intended to traverse, P. Mayerson, 'P. Ness. 58 and two Vaticinia ex Eventu in Hebrew', ZPE 77 (1989), 283–6. The payment was a reasonable expense in view of the uncertainty of travelling throughout Palestine. In Samaria, for example, road robbers attacked travellers, esp. Christian pilgrims on the way to Jerusalem, H. Delehaye, *Vita Danielis Stylitae* 10–11, AB 32 (1913), 130–3, referring to c.450. In the early 6th cent. journeys between cities, and especially around Caesarea, were so dangerous that they required consistent action on the part of the governor, Choricius, *Laudatio Aratii et Stephani*, 35–7 (ed. R. Foerester and E. Richtsteig) (Leipzig 1929), 58–9. The potential profit of these pursuits even overcame credal differences—a gang of Jews, Samaritans, and Christians was active around Emmaus in the middle of the 6th cent., John Moschus, *Pratum Spirituale*, 165 (PG 87. 3032).

[92] On the possible location of this tribe, perhaps in the south-west Negev Highlands, G. Avni, *Nomads, Farmers, and Town Dwellers: Pastoralist–Sedentist Interaction in the Negev Highlands, Sixth–Eighth Centuries CE* (Jerusalem: Israel Antiquities Authority, 1996), p. 79.

in an unfinished saga on the eve of the Islamic conquest. Sophronius, patriarch of Jerusalem, complying with the last will and testament of his friend John Moschus, carried John's remains all the way from Rome to Palestine (CE 619). He was unable, however, to bury John on top of the Holy Mountain because the area between Ashkelon (Ascalon) and the Sinai was blocked by Arab tribes.[93] Few missions illustrate with such poignancy the numerous functions and multiple levels of the social and religious experience of the Sinai desert. John Moschus wanted to be buried there because for him Mount Sinai embedded the soil of a 'fatherland' which conferred membership in a singular desert clan.

4. PERIPHERAL VISIONS: THE NEGEV

The road that Sophronius could not traverse had been frequented in late antiquity by steady streams of pilgrims, merchants, monks, marauders, Bedouin, and soldiers intent on reaching the Sinai and Egypt.[94] When the hero of a gruesome adventure story traced the footsteps of a lost son whom 'Saracens' had abducted in the Sinai, he ran him down, alive and content contrary to all expectation, in the household of a priest in the city of Elusa.[95] In late antiquity Elusa (Halusa) was the capital of the Negev, perhaps for a while even of the province of Palaestina III, and a major station along the road between Jerusalem and the Sinai.[96] The city boasted churches, including a 'cathedral', a theatre, schools, and public structures, as well as a

[93] *PL* 74. 862. A. A. Vasiliev, 'Notes on Some Episodes concerning the Relations between the Arabs and the Byzantine Empire from the Fourth to the Sixth Century', *DOP* 9–10 (1956), 306–16.

[94] Mayerson, 'The Pilgrim Routes', 44–57 on the roads via Egypt, the Negev, and Jordan.

[95] Ps. Nilus, *Narratio* 6 (*PG* 79. 676B–680A).

[96] Y. Dan, 'Palaestina Salutaris (Tertia) and its Capital', *IEJ* 32 (1982), 134–7 proposed Elusa as the provincial capital rather than Petra. The hypothesis is attractive if difficult to support. On the Negev with its microclimates and regions, G. Avni, *Nomads, Farmers, passim*, esp. 67–9. For another recent reassessment of the same area see J. Magness, *The Archaeology of the Early Islamic Settlements in Palestine* (Winona Lake, Ind. 2003), *passim*. See also R. Rubin, *The Negev as a Settled Land: Urbanization and Settlement in the Desert in the Byzantine Period* (Jerusalem 1990) (Heb.).

population that depended, regardless of rank and resources, on judicious and intense use of the scarce water resources of the region.

A 'gateway to the desert that extended to the Sinai', Elusa provided a test-case for the prowess of the primordial Palestinian hermit, Hilarion of Gaza.[97] Some time in the middle of the fourth century Hilarion appeared there, accompanied by a large crowd of monks. He proceeded to preach Christianity in the middle of a pagan festival that conveniently gathered the locals at the temple of the goddess of the Morning Star (Aphrodite).[98] Impressed by Hilarion's miraculous cures, the 'semi-barbarian' audience converted then and there, as Jerome asserted in his laudatory biography of the monk.[99] Archaeologists have identified three churches in Elusa, none, however, dating to the fourth century. The number appears impressive yet less startling when compared with the four identified churches in the neighbouring and much smaller town of Rehovot-in-the-Negev.[100]

[97] *Caput heremi qui vadit ad Sina, Anon. Plac.* (Geyer, CSEL, p. 181). On Elusa, J. D. Elliot, 'The Elusa Oikoumene' (Ph.D., Mississipi State University, 1981). Little of the recent excavations at Elusa has been published and the city is still largely covered with sand dunes.

[98] Jerome, *Vita Hilarionis*, 25.

[99] The welcome accorded to Hilarion included a cheerful greeting in Aramaic from welcoming crowds of 'pagans', a reception that stands in marked contrast with those accorded to the Mesopotamian monk Barsauma a few decades later who usually discovered the gates of cities closed and the locals unwelcoming, F. Nau, 'Résumé de monographies syriaques: Histoire de Bar Sauma de Nisibis', *ROC* 8 (1913), 270–6, 378–89, and *ROC* 9 (1914), 113–34, 278–89, 414–19, *passim*. On Hilarion in Elusa see also Millar, *The Roman Near East 31 BC–AD 337*, 399. On Jerome as hagiographer, A. A. R. Bastiaensen, 'Jérôme hagiograph', in G. Freyburger and L. Pernot (eds.), *Du héros païen au saint chrétien* (Collection REA 14; Paris 1997), 97–123. On the value of hagiography in general, R. Lane Fox, 'Life of Daniel', in M. J. Edwards and S. Swain (eds.), *Portraits: Biographical Representation in the Greek and Latin Literature of the Roman Empire* (Oxford, 1997), 175–225.

[100] A. Negev, 'The Churches in the Central Negev: An Archaeological Survey', *RB* 81 (1974), 400–22; and idem, 'The Cathedral of Elusa and the New Typology and Chronology of the Byzantine Churches in the Negev', *LA* 39 (1989), 129–42. On the churches of Rehovot, Y. Tsafrir *et al.*, *Excavations at Rehovot in the Negev*, i *The North Church*. Bagatti's suggestion that the appearance of so many churches in relatively small towns may be attributed to ritual and doctrinal differences, with each church serving a different community, cannot at present be borne out, B. Bagatti, *Antichi villaggi cristiani della Guidea e del Neghev* (Jerusalem 1983) (Eng. trans. 2002), with the comments in the review by L. Perrone in *Cristianesimo nella storia* 5 (1984), 602–7. The proliferation of churches in the region is a well-documented process—at Umm el Jimal no less than fifteen churches have been identified, serving a population of some 5,000 inhabitants, B. De Vries, *Umm el Jimal: A Frontier Town and its Landscape in Northern Jordan* (JRA Suppl. 26; Portsmouth, RI 1998), *passim*.

A bishop of Elusa attended the council of Ephesus in 431 but the appearance of this dignitary does not necessarily imply that Hilarion's mission was a complete success.[101] Around 375 Epiphanius reported the celebration of pagan festivals in Elusa which replicated the festivities celebrated in Petra and Eleutheropolis.[102] In the early fifth century, when the Syrian monk Barsauma crossed the Negev on his way from Jerusalem to the Sinai, his biographer claimed that pagans were the 'masters of the region and of the cities' along the (Negev) desert route which the monk traversed.[103] The theatre of Elusa, built in the second century, continued to function at least until the middle of the fifth century, as suggested by an inscription commemorating the repaving of its floor by the biblically named Abramios, son of Zenobius, in 454/5.[104] Contemporary ecclesiastical strictures notwithstanding, the theatre could be used not only for mimes but also for public declamations and for displays of the town's not inconsiderable pool of rhetorical talents.[105]

Life in Elusa in late antiquity, to judge by the meagre sources that referred to the capital of the Negev, was modulated by the ever-present threat of shifting sands.[106] In time of drought the water which Elusa's residents had to imbibe tasted like seawater and their

---

[101] The name of the bishop was either Theodolus or Ampela (Abdallah?). Other bishops include Arethas who attended Chalcedon in 451, Petrus who signed the synodical letter of Jerusalem in 518, and Zenobius who participated in the synod of Jerusalem in 536. The dignitary who employed the abducted youth of the Ps. Nilus *Narrationes* may have been a bishop or a priest.

[102] Epiph. *Pan.* 51.52; P. Mayerson, ' "Palaestina" versus "Arabia" in Byzantine Sources', 223–30, repr. in idem, *Monks, Martyrs* (1994), 224–31.

[103] F. Nau, 'Résumé', *ROC* 8 (1913), 378–89. The description applies to the area of the 'desert route' which is to be identified with a road crossing the Negev on which Barsauma embarked when he travelled from Jerusalem to the Sinai. See also Ch. 6.

[104] A. Negev, *The Greek Inscriptions from the Negev* (Jerusalem 1981), 92; L. Di Segni, 'Dated Greek Inscriptions from Palestine from the Roman and Byzantine Periods' (Ph.D., Hebrew University, 1997). The name suggests that Abramios was Christian. His father may have been a member of a family that numbered well-known rhetors, including a teacher of Libanius in the mid-4th cent., O. Seeck, *Die Briefe des Libanius* (Leipzig 1906; repr. Hildesheim 1966), 315–16.

[105] A. Segal, *The Theatres in Eretz Israel in Antiquity* (Jerusalem 2000) (Heb.).

[106] The sands won and Elusa was abandoned in the 8th cent. Cf. the impressions recorded by the pilgrim of Piacenza in the late 6th cent. and those of the Negev surveyors in the early 20th cent., C. L. Woolley and T. E. Lawrence, *The Wilderness of Zin* (London 1936), 23, 126–7.

bread contained more barley than wheat.¹⁰⁷ Some Elusans, not surprisingly, preferred to live in Egypt in luxury, rather than to linger
under Elusa's hazy skies.¹⁰⁸ Others, like Mary, a young woman who
lost her husband on their wedding night, left the city abruptly and
disappeared in the direction of the semi-desert around the Dead Sea,
like the dreaming monk of the Sinai.¹⁰⁹ Of those who stayed a few
retired to a *laura* near by, like Victor, or engaged in hagiography in a
celibate cell, like Paul.¹¹⁰ The fate of the academy to which Libanius
alluded is unknown.¹¹¹ If the school-texts found in Nessana, 'a village
in the district of Elusa', are an indication, literary Greek and Latin
were taught till, perhaps, the seventh century.¹¹²

The biography of the rhetor Eudaimon encapsulates the extraordinary role that Elusa played in the fourth century in the life of
southern Palestine and eastern Egypt.¹¹³ Born in Egyptian Pelusium
in the northern Sinai peninsula, Eudaimon taught rhetoric in Syrian
Antioch where his path crossed that of Libanius, the city's most
famous rhetorician in late antiquity. He moved back to Palestine,
to Elusa in 357/8 but, initially at least, did not fare well. In view of
Antioch's prominence and centrality Eudaimon's decision suggests
that he had multiple ties in Elusa—he had studied there, had relatives
there, and his parents resided in relatively nearby Pelusium. With
Libanius' help Eudaimon became Elusa's officially appointed teacher
of rhetoric, a position that made him independent of the whims of
private students and of their unreliable parents and enabled him to

¹⁰⁷ Procopius of Gaza, *Ep.* 2 (Garzya and Loenertz, *Procopii Gazae Epistolae et Declamationes* (Studia Patristica et Byzantina 9; Rome 1963)).
¹⁰⁸ Ibid.
¹⁰⁹ *Anon. Plac.* 34.
¹¹⁰ On Victor, John Moschus, *Pratum Spirituale* 164 (*PG* 87.3. 3032); Paul composed a Life of Theognius (bishop of Bitylion), *AB* 10 (1891), 73–113. No remains of
monasteries have been discovered to date, unless one of the churches unearthed
belonged to a monastery.
¹¹¹ *Ep.* 132.
¹¹² *P. Ness.* 16–18, 24, 27 (Kraemer).
¹¹³ The following is based on M. Schwabe, 'Eudaimon and the School of Rhetoric
at Elusa', *Zion* 2 (1937), 106–20 (Heb.). See also Kaster, R. A., *Guardians of Language: The Grammarian and Society in Late Antiquity* (Berkeley 1988) and Al. Cameron,
'Wandering Poets: A Literary Movement in Byzantine Egypt', *Historia* 14 (1965),
470–509. The relevant letters of Libanius are *Eps.* 255 (Foerster 258), 315, 108, 132,
164, 826, 1057, 632.

engage in poetic pursuits. This Egyptian-Palestinian 'friend of the Muses' became so well known that he was invited to hold chairs of rhetoric in Constantinople and in Alexandria.[114] He preferred the latter, at least to judge by his presence in Antioch, with Libanius, in the early 390s.

Talented individuals, like Eudaimon in Elusa, contributed to the disbursement of Hellenistic *paideia* throughout the southern Palestinian periphery. Persuasive eloquence played a decisive role in civic life: it instilled official values and it inserted Elusa into an unchanging temporality that lifted the city from the sands of the peripheral desert. The urban tone and regional importance of Elusa were reflected in references to offices of a regional land record and a regional court of justice.[115] Above all, Elusa's preeminence was evidenced in a Negev calendar which numbered years 'according to the era of Elusa'.[116]

Elusa's prosperity in late antiquity provides a hint of the spectacular renaissance which the southern periphery of Palestine, and especially the Nabataean caravansarais, experienced in that period.[117]

---

[114] On the expression, Libanius, *Ep.* 108: *tois Mousaon hetairos hoios.*

[115] *P. Ness.* 24, 29 (Kraemer).

[116] *P. Ness.* 56, 57 (Kraemer); Negev, *The Greek Inscriptions*, nos. 18, 19.

[117] On the Nabataean Negev prior to the Roman annexation, A. Negev, *Masters of the Desert: The Story of the Nabataeans* (Jerusalem 1983), and *Nabatean Archaeology Today* (New York 1986). On problems relating to Nabataean precise ethnicity, Retsö, *The Arabs*, 364–91. See also R. Rosenthal-Heginbottom (ed.), *The Nabataeans in the Negev* (Haifa, 2003). T. Erickson-Gini, 'Crisis and Renewal: Settlement in the Central Negev in the Third and Fourth Centuries, with an Emphasis on the Finds from Recent Excavations in Mampsis, Oboda and Mezad 'En Hazeva' (Ph.D., the Hebrew University of Jerusalem 2004) discusses the 2nd and 3rd centuries. I am grateful to Tali for providing me with a copy.

The reshaping of the Negev may be dated to *c.*300, with the transfer of the sole Palestinian Roman legion from Aelia (Jerusalem) to Aila (Eilat-Aqaba), and the stationing of a camp, and the dux Palaestina, in Beer Sheva. On the latter, P. Fabian, 'The Late Roman Military Camp at Beer Sheva: A New Discovery', in *The Roman and Byzantine Near East* (JRA Suppl. 14; Ann Arbor 1995), 235–40 who regards BS as the administrative headquarters of the *limes* as well.

Neither the pace nor the precise extent of the Negev's newly refurbished centres can be established. The earliest dated papyrus at Nessana belongs to the mid-5th cent. The earliest churches are usually dated to the late 4th/early 5th cent. but very few were excavated and the sequence of their pottery remains problematic. At Avdat (Oboda) the last dated Nabataean inscription belongs to CE 126 while the first Greek inscription dates to CE 241 (Negev, *The Greek Inscriptions from the Negev*; idem, 'Nabatean Inscriptions from Avdat', *IEJ* 13 (1963), 113–24. Curiously, the earliest specimen of

South of Elusa, the townlets and villages of Shivta, Mamshit, Rehovot, Avdat, Nessana, and Saadon punctured the uniformity of the
desert with large, not to say luxurious houses, public bathhouses and
squares, hostels, churches, monasteries, and industrial structures.[118]
The unfortunate narrator of the 'Nilus' narrationes (above) learnt
that his son had been taken by his abductors to the slave market in
the 'village of Sobeita' (Shivta) to be sold to the highest bidder.[119]
Pilgrims who strayed to Shivta from the main road could find in this
prosperous community spiritual sustenance in any one of the three
local churches, as well as room in the local monastery or hostel.
Hungry travellers could enjoy local delicacies laced with locally grown
olive oil, and the thirsty could quench their thirst with locally
produced wine or with a glass of water drawn from one of Shivta's
numerous cisterns. There, as in any other Negev townlet, the services
of 'Saracens' or Arab guides and the protection of imperial soldiers
facilitated communications with the southern Sinai and, above all,
with the Holy Mountain.

Similarly other urbanized centres in the northern Negev, Shivta
was surrounded by a huge expanse of agricultural terraces which
provided mute yet eloquent testimony to the endless engagement of
human diligence in a merciless battle with the elements.[120] In the

---

an Arabic inscription also belongs to Avdat (M. Sharon, *Corpus Inscriptionum Arabicarum Palaestinae*, i (Leiden 1997), 190–4, dated to *c.*150 CE). But there are no buildings
that can be dated earlier than the 2nd cent. CE in the northern Negev nor are there signs
of permanent occupation before the 4th or even the 5th cent., with the exception of
Mampsis (Mamshit; Kurnub) which apparently flourished from the late 1st cent. CE
onward, A. Negev, *The Architecture of Mampsis: Final Report* (Jerusalem 1988);
R. Rubin, 'Urbanization, Settlement and Agriculture in the Negev Desert: The Impact
of the Roman-Byzantine Empire on the Frontier', *ZDVP* 112 (1996), 49–60, esp. 51.

For a survey of the urbanized Negev, Y. Shereshevski, *Byzantine Urban Settlements in
the Negev Desert* (Beer Sheva 5; Beer Sheva 1991), esp. pp. 20–36 (Kurnub–Mamshit);
36–48 (Eboda–Avdat); 49–60 (Nessana); 61–82 (Subeita–Shivta); 83–90 (Elusa);
90–102 (Saadi) and *passim* on urban characteristics and aspects of urbanization.
See also K. C. Gutwein, *Third Palestine: A Regional Study in Byzantine Urbanism*
(Washington, DC, 1981).

[118] Cf. other marginal areas, such as the Syrian desert, which also enjoyed unparalleled prosperity in late antiquity, C. Foss, 'The Near Eastern Countryside in Late
Antiquity: A Review Article', in *The Roman and Byzantine Near East* (1995), 213–34.

[119] *PG* 79. 676A.

[120] Y. Hirschfeld, 'Man and Society in Byzantine Shivta', *Qadmoniot* 125 (2003),
2–17 (Heb.); idem, 'Social Aspects of the Late Antique Village of Shivta', *JRA* 16
(2003), 395–408.

village itself, cisterns, canals, pools, and public baths provide visible tokens of the victory of human ingenuity and determination.[121] Two-storied stone houses with courtyards and vaulted entries, markets, winepresses, pottery workshops, and camel sheds display a defiance which was continually nurtured by streams of pilgrims and monks and by generous donations.[122] At Shivta, the grid system which characterized a classically planned city disappeared in favour of an urban plan which preferred convenience to rigidity and order.[123] Perhaps this unruly sort of urban order reflected the nomadic origins of the inhabitants who clustered around clans and chieftains rather than around a municipal governing body.

In this type of settlement survival largely depended on the organization of water. Ostraca found in the area of the large pools in Shivta suggest that civic identity depended on judicious sharing of responsibilities for maintaining and repairing the cistern systems.[124] Ironically, the excavations of the early 1930s headed by Dunscombe Colt had to be abandoned because the excavators ran out of water.[125] A recent survey of the townlet counted 170 dwellings, arranged in clusters which were often surmounted by a tower.[126] A few abutted the church, an unusually close proximity that reflected the pride of ownership in both house and church. Several houses had wine cellars which housed the products of local wineries whose popularity extended all the way to Gaul.[127] The wealth of Shivta's inhabitants could be measured in the ubiquitous attention to architectural decoration. Of those left in situ, lintels chiselled with rosettes and crosses

---

[121] A. Segal, *The Byzantine City of Shivta, Negev Desert, Israel* (BAR IS 179; Oxford 1983).

[122] P. Mayerson, 'Urbanization in Palaestina Tertia: Pilgrims and Paradoxes', *Cathedra* 45 (1987), 19–40 (Heb.), repr. in Eng. in idem, *Monks, Martyrs* (Jerusalem 1994), 232–45.

[123] The observation holds true also for late ancient Scythopolis, as it does for the other urban centres in the Negev, Y. Tsafrir and G. Foerster, 'From Byzantine Scythopolis to Arab Baysan: Changing Urban Concepts', *Cathedra* 64 (1992), 3–30, esp. 21 (Heb.); idem, 'Urbanism at Scythopolis-Bet Shean in the Fourth to the Seventh Centuries', *DOP* 51 (1997), 85–146.

[124] H. C. Youtie, 'Ostraca from Sbeita', *American Journal of Archaeology* 40 (1936), 452–7.

[125] One report was published, C. Baly, 'Shivta', *PEFQS* 68 (1935), 171–81.

[126] Hirschfeld, 'Shivta', *Qadmoniot* (2003), *passim*.

[127] Gaza wines, a denomination which in all likelihood covered also the wine produced in the Negev, were well known throughout the empire.

reflect a taste for ornamental doorways and for aniconic motifs.[128] Barely three decades before the Muslim invasion, in 607, a new (mosaic?) floor was inlaid in the floor of Shivta's northern church.[129]

A walk through the streets and the central square of Shivta evinces a paradigm reflecting an experience of living which combined a contrast—an arid environment with the quality of urban living at its best. Two factors, however, signalled a difference in ambiance between the Negev periphery and the rest of Palestine. One was the constant presence of the military, a reminder of larger imperial concerns, as of the perennial rivalry between Rome and Sassanid Persia, and of the unpredictable presence of Bedouin inside and along the *limes*. The other was the overwhelming investment in water conservation, so much so that a recording of the transfer of ownership from one person to another listed, in addition to the basic elements of land and house, one quarter of a cistern and the right of ownership over points of entry and exit of the water flow.[130]

Our information about the inhabitants of the Negev urbanized zone and their concerns has been immensely enriched by a cache of papyri discovered in one of the churches by the Colt expedition during a season of excavation conducted in Nessana in the early 1930s.[131] The texts, mostly in Greek but also in Latin and Arabic, furnish precious insights into the lives of the soldiers, ecclesiastics, educators, and wealthy members of the Nessanan and other Negev communities between the mid-fifth and the late seventh centuries, thus bridging the crucial period of transfer as the region passed from Roman to Islamic hands.[132]

[128] A. Segal, *Architectural Decoration in Byzantine Shivta, Negev Desert, Israel* (Oxford 1988).

[129] Negev, *Greek Inscriptions*, nos. 66, 75.

[130] P. *Ness.* 32 (Kraemer). On these water cisterns, O. Moran and D. Palmach, *The Water Cisterns on Negev Mount* (Sde Boker 1985) (Heb.).

[131] L. Casson and E. L. Hettich (eds.), *Excavations at Nessana: Literary Papyri* (Princeton 1950). Kraemer (ed.), *Excavations at Nessana: Non-Literary Papyri*. See also H. M. Cotton *et al.*, 'The Papyrology of the Roman Near East: A Survey', *JRS* 85 (1995), 214–35.

[132] The find can now be compared with the recent discovery of papyri in Petra, J. Frösén, A. Arjava, M. Lehtinen (eds.), *The Petra Papyri*, i (ACORP 4; Amman 2002). The papyri disclose remarkably similar concerns but span only the 6th cent. On Petra and its vicinity see the still incomparable, Alois Musil, *Arabia Petraea*, 3 vols. (Vienna 1907–8).

A perusal of the Nessana papyri reveals a double preoccupation: one with mind/soul (education, literacy, theology); the other with the body (food, property, taxation, marriage, inheritance). The so-called literary papyri contain, inter alia, a full copy of the famed correspondence between Abgar of Edessa and Jesus of Nazareth, a copy of the acts of St George of Lydda, and a variety of theological texts, all confirming the picture of piety already drawn from the astonishing presence of no less than six churches in the 'village'.[133] It would be otiose, but perhaps not altogether unprofitable, to speculate about the identity of the person(s) who brought to Nessana or copied there the Abgar–Jesus exchange of letters since the text enjoyed immense popularity.[134] Its presence in Nessana suggests that a Nessanan resident made a pilgrimage to Edessa, where s/he got a copy, as did Egeria in the early 380s, or that the text migrated to Nessana among the precious movable possessions of a migrant Syrian family. Be that as it may, in the arid Negev the story of the water miracle which Jesus' letter performed in Edessa would have lent a poignant edge to the familiar narrative.[135]

The centrality of Christianity, Jesus, and Jerusalem in the lives of the Negev urbanized zone was further reflected in Nessana's spatial and visual perceptions. The architecture of Nessana's South Church combined elements borrowed from the Jerusalemite Anastasis with classical Vitruvian principles.[136] Nessana's church of Sergius and Bacchus, apparently served by a community of monks with close ties with the monastic establishments of Mount Sinai, drew worshippers from as far as Elusa and Beer Sheva.[137] Recent excavations have revealed another church of significant dimensions (45×36.5 metres

---

[133] The churches are listed in P. Figueras, 'Monks and Monasteries in the Negev Desert', *LA* 45 (1995), 401–50, esp. 425–30.

[134] *Itin. Eg.* 19.6; for the Letter of Abgar, Wilkinson, *Egeria*, 151–2. A. Mirkovic, *Prelude to Constantine. The Abgar Tradition in Early Christianity* (Frankfurt 2004).

[135] *Itin. Eg.* 19.12–13. On Edessa's water supply, Wilkinson, *Egeria* (above, n. 60), 284–7.

[136] D. Chen, 'Byzantine Architects at Work in Oboda, Nessana and Rehovot, Palaestina Tertia. A Study in Paleo-Christian Architectural Design', *LA* 35 (1985), 291–6 with pls. 40–2.

[137] *P. Ness.* 79 (Kraemer); Figueras, 'Monks and Monasteries, 425–7. *P. Ness.* 89.23 refers to a Father Martyrios of Mount Sinai who may have been a superior of Mount Sinai in 595, Kraemer, *Excavations in Nessana*, 254, 259 n. 23.

overall), bringing the total number of sanctuaries in this smallish settlement to four (or five).[138] The existence of an individualized local calendar wholly based on saintly figures points to an inordinate degree of pious devotion.[139] Although no biblical sites were identified around Nessana or the other Negev townlets, the presence of 'antiquities' proved attractive. At least one monastery was established on the ruins of an Israelite fortress. Another, Nestorian (?), was carefully placed near an ancient Israelite city on the banks of Nahal Beersheva.[140]

Among donors to Nessana's churches was a family from Syrian Emesa. It numbered Sergius, an ex-assessor and monk, Palut, his sister, and John, her son who was a deacon and formerly a member of Emesa's curia.[141] Perhaps the family settled in Nessana after the ex-assessor retired from active duties in the area.[142] Their membership in Nessana's monastic landscape reinforces the impression of accelerated 'Hellenization', seen also in the ubiquity of Greek and in the extraordinary role that Christianity played in the life of the Negev in late antiquity. The presence of fragments of books 2 to 4 of the *Aeneid* among the Nessana papyri, together with a long and detailed Latin-to-Greek glossary of the poem, all dating to the sixth century, opens intriguing vistas into the acquisition of Latin not only in the Greek

---

[138] D. Urman, 'Nessana Excavations 1987–1995', in idem (ed.), *Nessana. Excavations and Studies*, i (Beer Sheva 2004), 1*–118*.

[139] G. E. Kirk and C. B. Welles, 'The Inscriptions', in Colt (ed.), *Excavations at Nessana*, i (1962), 151–2 n. 38. The list includes saints like Mark, Bliphimus, Manicus, and Ambrose; 'fathers' like Cyril, Zenobius, and Chariton; and 'mothers' like Anna and Martha. On these, Y. E. Meimaris, *Sacred Names, Saints, Martyrs and Church Officials in the Greek Inscriptions and Papyri pertaining to the Christian Church of Palestine* (Athens 1986).

[140] On Tel Ira and its Israelite past, Figueras, 'Monks and Monasteries', 442 (not marked on the map provided on p. 402). On Tel Masos and its monastery, V. Fritz and A. Kempinski, *Ergebnisse der Ausgrabungen auf Hirbet al-Msas-Tel Masos 1972–1975*, 2 vols. (Wiesbaden 1983). The latter appears to have been a Nestorian monastery founded, it is claimed, under the Umayyad, a dating opposed by Figueras, 443.

[141] Kirk and Welles, 'Inscriptions'. The inscription is dated to the year 496 of the era of Halusa (Elusa), namely CE 609.

[142] Figueras, 'Monks and Monasteries', 429, believes that they founded a monastery in Nessana on the occasion of their visit to the town. Whether the sister/mother from Emesa came to join the women's monastery, the existence of which is assumed by Figueras, ibid., is unknown.

East but in the school(s) of so remote a spot as Nessana and at so late a date.[143]

Several clans left their imprint on Nessana's epigraphical scene. An inscription bearing the name of Stephanos, son of Patricius and member of a family which boasted two abbots and a nun in Nessana, boldly proclaimed: 'Christ wins. Christ reigns. Stephanos, son of Patricius made... may the envious burst!'[144] The family was prominent. The Nessana ecclesiastical archives recorded the deeds and properties of Patricius, son of Georgius, who led the local church and the monastery. His son, Georgius, was the recipient of letters, in Greek and Arabic, from the new Muslim masters of Palestine in the seventh century. Inscriptions, mostly in Greek, conformed to a familiar pattern of epigraphic material known from other parts of the land, although the names recorded were of mixed Semitic (Nabataean or Arabic), Greek, and biblical origins.[145] Onomastic diversity was overlaid by the unifying factor of a common creed, Christianity.

Whether, as the excavators believed, the bulk of Nessana's population was Arabic, in other words urbanized native Bedouin presided over by a Greek-speaking imported minority, is possible but difficult to prove.[146] If this had indeed been the case, it seems that Nessana ex-nomads proved uncommonly open to both Hellenization and Christianization, unlike their nomadic Negev 'brothers' who remained pagan throughout late antiquity, converting directly to Islam after the Islamic invasion. Whether local or 'imported', the elusive ethnicity of the urbanized Negev is linked with another contentious question—was the Negev 'renaissance' in late antiquity the result

---

[143] J. Geiger, 'The Latin Language in Roman Palestine', *Cathedra* 74 (1994), 3–21 (Heb.); and idem, 'How much Latin in Greek Palestine?' in Hannah Rosen (ed.), *Aspects of Latin: Papers from the Seventh International Colloquium on Latin Linguistics, Jerusalem 1993* (Innsbruck 1996), 39–57.

[144] Kirk and Welles, 'Inscriptions', nos. 305, 306, 318; Di Segni, 'Dated Greek Inscriptions from Palestine', no. 318, CE 577.

[145] A. Negev, *Personal Names in the Nabatean Realm* (Qedem monographs 32; Jerusalem 1991).

[146] Kirk and Welles, 'Inscriptions', 132. See also D. J. Wasserstein, 'Why did Arabic Succeed where Greek Failed? Language Change in the Near East after Muhammad', *SCI* 22 (2003), 257–72, esp. 259–60 on a process of change which involved religious acculturation, Christianization, and even broad ethnic changes. See also Robert Hoyland, 'Language and Identity: The Twin Histories of Arabic and Aramaic—Why did Aramaic Succeed where Greek Failed?', *SCI* 23 (2004), 183–99.

of massive government investment in the shape of planned sedentarization of Bedouin in order to bolster the *limes*, or the result of 'natural' and less guided developments, such as growing demand for land in the wake of changing demographics and climatic conditions?[147]

Nessana boasted a police force that regularly patrolled the roads which crossed the region in order to protect inhabitants, traders, and pilgrims.[148] Security concerns featured on inscriptions commemorating the generosity of eminent individuals towards defraying the significant costs involved in maintaining law and order.[149] The town's fort, comparable with those at Avdat and Kurnub, may have belonged to the reconstructed *limes* of Palaestina Tertia.[150] The soldiers at Nessana, a camel corps known as the loyal Theodosiani, left archives which show how well they blended with the civilians whom they had been appointed to guard. Upon dispersal in the mid-sixth century

---

[147] For the former, M. Haiman, 'Agriculture and Nomad–State Relations in the Negev Desert in the Byzantine and Early Islamic Periods', *BASOR* 297 (1995), 29–53; for the latter, Hirschfeld, 'Shivta', *passim*, esp. p. 4, referring to newly acquired internal security, increase in humidity, and the privatization of imperial land coupled with massive investment in peripheral areas. See also P. Smith, 'People of the Holy Land from Prehistory to the Recent Past', in T. Levy (ed.), *The Archaeology of Society in the Holy Land* (Leicester 1995), 58–74, and A. S. Issar and M. Zohar, *Climate Change: Environment and Civilization in the Middle East* (Berlin 2004).

[148] P. *Ness.* 35, 37 (Kraemer). On security concerns, Kraemer, *Nessana*, iii, no. 16 (*c.*560 CE) refers to Saracen attacks the Pharan area. See also B. Isaac, 'The Army in the Late Roman East', in idem, *The Near East under Roman Rule* (Leiden 1998), 437–69, esp. 452–60.

[149] Di Segni, 'Dated Inscriptions', no. 310: In the reign of the invincible Flavius Justinianus and of Flavia Theodora, Flavius Su... comes of the most loyal imperial guards [and?...] auditor, wishing to provide for the security of [Nessana?]. The reading is problematic. It is unclear if the subject is one person, *comes* and *discussor*, or two, one *comes*, the other an *auditor*. Di Segni prefers the latter and identifies the first as Summus, dux Palestina in 531–3 and 537/8, connecting his presence in the Negev with the expedition to recover the island of Iotaba, Choricius, *Laudatio Summi*; and *In Aratum et Stephanum*, 66–76. On the vicissitudes of this important imperial outpost, see among many, F.-M. Abel, 'L'Île de Jotabe', *RB* 47 (1938), 510–38.

[150] Colt, i. 6–26. The Tenth Legion was moved from Jerusalem to Aila (Eilat) *c.*300; Palaestina Tertia experienced a series of administrative and military mutations in the course of the 4th cent. till its 'limes' reached its largest scope by attaching to it a hefty section of the province of Arabia including the southern Sinai. On these much contested movements, Tsafrir, 'Why were the Negev?' (above, n. 51), and Mayerson, 'Justinian's Novel 103' (above, n. 51).

these soldiers had little trouble reintegrating into the community as civilians, taxpayers, landowners, and permanent residents.[151]

United by the perpetual struggle against land erosion, by concerted efforts to preserve water, and by Christian piety, soldiers, civilians, monks and clerics formed the backbone of the urbanized Negev society of late antiquity. The singularity of the Negev amidst its isolation stands out. Settled by nomads who sought stability, monks who sought inspiring desert surroundings, migrants who may have seen lucrative opportunities in commerce and pilgrimage, soldiers who had been acclimatized to its conditions, the prosperity of the wilderness periphery in late antiquity can be attributed to a dynamism that overcame the inherent difficulties of living in an arid territory. In the democracy of the desert Christianity became the unifier, a presence nearer and more potent than the provincial governor and even the emperor.

Surrounded by a closely-knit belt of terraced wadis and agricultural farms the urbanized settlements of the Negev lowlands thrived on the production of olive oil and wine.[152] The published farms show a replication of the luxury elements that characterized homes in the nearby townlet, suggesting mutual dependence in matters of taste as in economic interests.[153] Such intricate and intimate exchange is hardly surprising. More astonishing was the spread of farming well into the heart of the desert, namely the Negev Highlands south of the urbanized and rural zones of the lowlands, a parched terrain that can yield livelihood only with the greatest difficulty.[154] Extensive surveys of these remote areas have yielded a wide range of rural

---

[151] The dispersal is derived from the contents of the so-called Beer Sheva edict, a tax list of the annual urban toll, city by city, which reflects an imperial move, under Justinian, to transfer the burden of services ordinarily performed by *limetanei*, such as patrols, the escort of travellers, the manning of stations, and the protection of hostels, to civilians and to the local communities. Among the recent bibliography on this controversial document, Di Segni, 'Dated Greek Inscriptions' (1997), no. 262*, and eadem, 'The Beer Sheva Edict Reconsidered', *SCI* 23 (2004), 131–58.

[152] Y. Kedar, *The Ancient Agriculture in the Negev Mountains* (Jerusalem 1967) (Heb.); M. Evenari et al., *The Negev: The Challenge of a Desert* (Cambridge, Mass., 1971); P. Mayerson, *The Ancient Agriculture Regime of Nessana and the Central Negev* (London: British School of Archaeology in Jerusalem, 1960).

[153] Rubin, *The Negev as a Settled Land* (Heb.), 128–55 on farms in the area of Rehovot in the Negev.

[154] Avni, *Nomads, Farmers, passim*, esp. p. 3.

and nomadic activities, pointing to an exceptional extent and intensity of cultivation.[155] The uniformity of construction materials and plans throughout the area surveyed indicates, according to its surveyors, a relatively brief period of activity and occupation.[156] Altogether, of the nearly 650 sites recorded in two sections totalling about 200 square kilometres, about half were attributed to the so-called Byzantine–Early Islamic period (6th–8th cents). By one estimate there were no less than 300 farms in the Negev Highlands in late antiquity, scattered over a large area, and totalling some 800 families or 4,000 individuals, a considerable number by all accounts, and one which seems to lend support to the hypothesis of central, governmental initiatives behind so extensive an enterprise.[157]

The most striking and controversial feature of the ruralized nomadic Negev is the presence of installations interpreted as representations of religious cults. These are flat stone slabs, not much taller than one metre, which appear to have been deliberately placed next to each other, thus forming a short row of *stelae*.[158] Such 'monuments' often appeared in settlements which also boasted low-walled rectangular structures punctured by a niche in one wall and interpreted as open-air mosques, each with a *mihrab*.[159]

---

[155] Near Sde Boker in the central Negev, 233 sites were identified as 'Byzantine' (4th–early 7th cent. CE), and 12 as 'early Arab' or 'Islamic'. See Y. Lender, *Map of Har Nafha (196). Archaeological Survey of Israel* (Jerusalem 1990), *passim*. But the compilers also insist that it is difficult to draw clear distinctions between the 'Byzantine' and 'early Islamic' periods (pp. xxiii–xxv). Cf. M. Haiman, *Map of Har Hamran Southeast* (199) (Jerusalem: Israel Antiquities Authority, 1993), and idem, 'Agriculture and Nomad', 29–53, esp. 31, opposing Lender's conclusions and suggesting instead that most of the 233 sites belong to the 7th and 8th cents. and are the result of state (Umayyad) sponsorship of settling Bedouin. Cf. the cautionary note sounded by Avni, *Nomads*, 8–9 regarding the lack of dating criteria for precise chronological analysis.

[156] Cf. an adjacent surveyed sector where 143 sites were identified as 'Byzantine-Early Islamic' (6th–8th cents.), Avni, *Nomads*, 19.

[157] Haiman, 'Agriculture', 41. Note, however, the much smaller estimate of Avni, *Nomads* (Hebrew abstract), of 1,200–1,300 people.

[158] Avni, *Nomads*, 27, based on Yehuda Nevo, *Pagans and Herders: A Re-Examination of the Negev Runoff Cultivation Systems in the Byzantine and Early Arab Periods* (Sde Boqer 1991), *passim*, who maintains that even the agricultural system served cultic purposes. See the objections of Haiman, 'Agriculture', 49 n. 11; and of D. Whitcomb, Review of Avni, *Nomads*, and of Rosen and Avni, *The Oded Sites*, BASOR 311 (1998), 100–2, esp. 101. See also C. Foss, 'The Near Eastern Countryside in Late Antiquity: A Review Article' (above, ii. 118).

[159] Avni, *Nomads*, with references to other areas in the Negev Highlands.

Juxtaposed with Arabic rock inscriptions found in the Negev Highlands, these 'mosques' indicated precocious conversion of the Bedouin directly from paganism to Islam.[160] If correctly interpreted, the religious culture of the nomadic Negev in late antiquity stood in striking contrast with that of the urban and rural Negev. In the latter, the exceptional number of churches per town/village, the number of monasteries, and the extensive use of Greek in both inscriptions and papyri, reflected a wholesale adoption of Hellenized Christianity in faithful imitation of the culture of the Palestinian centre.[161]

To what extent the Islamization of the Negev also entailed the decline and ultimate abandonment of towns, villages, and farms, and at what date, has become the object of another lively debate. Inscriptions in Arabic, all postdating the Islamic conquest, attest the rapid spread of the language in the Negev but their location, on faces of rock shelters in relatively isolated spots, shows how Arabic began to supplant Greek but not what happened to the Greek-speaking citizens of the Negev.[162] Surveyors of the Negev Highlands have tended to date the floruit of many sites to the 6th–8th centuries, implying that the Islamic conquest of the early seventh century did not entail a clear break with the past.[163] According to one opinion, the shift from Byzantine to Islamic overlords might have even induced prosperity in areas which had been sparsely settled, if at all before.[164] Whether the efflorescence of the ruralized Negev Highlands in late antiquity was due to the decline of the urbanized lowlands, or whether both towns and villages flourished at the time, cannot be

---

[160] M. Halloun and M. Sharon, *Supplement to the Map of Har Nafha: Ancient Rock Inscriptions* (Jerusalem: Israel Antiquities Authority, 1990). The possibility that these are imported Arabs, already converted, needs to be examined. If this is the case it would support Haiman's contention of state-sponsored transplantation.

[161] Although no location in Palestine, with the exception of Jerusalem, boasted the staggering number of churches of the localities east of the Jordan, A. Michel, *Les Églises d'époque byzantine et umayyade de la Jordanie (Provinces d'Arabie et de Palestine), V–VIIIs: Typologie architecturale et aménagements liturgiques* (Turnhout 2001), counting 18 churches in Gerasa, and 14 in Umm al-Rasas.

[162] Y. Nevo, *Ancient Arabic Inscriptions of the Negev* (Jerusalem 1993); Wasserstein, 'Why did Arabic?', 261.

[163] Avni, *Nomads, passim*; Haiman, 'Agriculture', 37 (referring to coins dating to the end of the Umayyad period).

[164] Haiman, 'Agriculture', *passim*.

established at this point in time.[165] A recent reanalysis of the surveys and excavations conducted thus far in the urbanized zones of the Negev has likewise emphasized continuity, rather than abandonment or even decline, well beyond the early seventh century.[166] But even if most or all the townlets did continue to exist, the intensity, extent, and dynamics of the Negev urbanized zone remain a mystery which pottery assemblies alone cannot resolve. The continuous occupation of the site is, in itself, insufficient to indicate the nature and quality of life there.[167]

With such strikingly varied interpretations by archaeologists, the historian must conclude that the late ancient period in the history of southern Palestine (= Palaestina III) represented a symbiosis of town and country, or rather of townlets and deserts exploited by industrious farmers, traders, and monks with an intensity not surpassed since. Overcoming huge obstacles, the dwellers of the desert became inseparable constituents of the landscape that they reclaimed. Outside the towns, locals and strangers mingled in the territory of the desert, protected by its remoteness and aridity, as well as by forts and

[165] Avni, *Nomads*, for the former; Magness, *Islamic Settlements*, for the latter. In 1993–4, Peter Fabian excavated a domestic dwelling in Oboda (Avdat), which was destroyed by a devastating earthquake in the early 7th cent., the same natural disaster that evidently demolished the whole of the town ('Evidence of Earthquake Destruction in the Archaeological Record: The Case of Ancient Avdat', in *Big Cities World Conference on Natural Disaster Mitigation in Conjunction with the Tenth International Seminar on Earthquake Prognostics. Abstracts*. January 1996, Cairo, p. 25). I owe this reference to Tali Erickson-Gini. Seismological studies indicate that this final destruction was caused by a compressional seismic wave that originated 15 km. south/southwest of Oboda, A. M. Korjenkov and E. Mazor, 'Seismogenic Origin of Ancient Avdat Ruins, Negev Desert, Israel', *Natural Hazards* 18 (1999), 193–226. Similar problems faced Shivta, see Korjenkov and Mazor, 'Earthquake Characteristics Reconstructed from Archaeological Damage Patterns: Shivta, the Negev, Israel', *Israel Journal of Earth Sciences* 48 (1999), 265–82.

[166] Magness, Islamic Settlements, 177–94, has assembled the evidence for continuity, in some cases till the 10th cent., in Avdat, Rehovot, Nessana, and Shivta. The cases for Halusa, the only *polis*, is not so clear. To judge by the evidence of Procopius of Gaza at the start of the 6th cent., the end of Halusa was already then in sight as the sands began to move toward the city. P. Mayerson, 'The City of Elusa in the Literary Sources of the 4th–6th Centuries', *IEJ* 33 (1983), 247–53.

[167] Cf. the situation at Scythopolis where the excavators admit the impossibility of distinguishing between 'late Byzantine' and 'early Islamic' layers, while insisting on a general pattern of urban decline, or rather on the decline of classical urban traditions, Tsafrir and Foerster, 'Scythopolis', 27–9.

soldiers. The myths of the desert were woven into dialogues of piety and of profit that, like the place itself, were fixed and yet moving.

5. BEYOND DREAMS: THE PERIPHERY
OF THE NORTH (THE GOLAN)

According to an inflammatory biography of the famed theologian Maximus the Confessor (c.580–662), the saint was born to a Samaritan producer of textiles from the area of Shechem (Neapolis). On one of his sales expeditions the Samaritan fell in love with a beautiful Persian woman. She was then a slave in a Jewish household in the city of Tiberias where he used to trade his wares.[168] When she fell pregnant she demanded her lover ransom her; his family proposed her execution. The couple fled to Golanide Khisfin, a village near the 'border' between the provinces of Palestine and Arabia. There they found refuge in the house of Martyrius, a local priest who also baptized them in secret and allowed them to live on church property. Two sons were born to the converted couple. Upon the parents' early demise, Martyrius deposited the children in a monastery in the Judaean desert (Chariton's). One child died, the victim of a camel bite; the other grew up to become a noted theologian, albeit of

---

[168] S. Brock, 'An Early Syriac Life of Maximus the Confessor', 91 (1973), 299–346, esp. 302–15 for the Syriac text and 314–19 for an English translation. *Vita Maximi* 5 identifies the 'biographer' as George of Reshaina, one of Maximus' monothelite adversaries and a disciple of Sophronius of Jerusalem. Brock dates the MSS to the 8th cent. See also B. Z. Kedar, 'A Dangerous Baptism at Khisfin in the Late 6th Century', in D. Jacoby and Y. Tsafrir (eds.), *Jews, Samaritans and Christians in Byzantine Palestine* (Jerusalem 1988), 238–41 (Heb.), who ponders the (fragile) position of Christians in Khisfin vis-à-vis the relative strength of Samaritans (and Jews?) in the community at so late a date. Conventional biographies of Maximus place his birth in Constantinople, in a cradle of the nobility, see R. Devreesse, 'La Vie de S Maxime le Confesseur et ses recensions', *AB*. 46 (1928), 5–49, esp. 14 on birthplace and upbringing. On the Georgian versions of Maximus' life, which for the most part follow the Greek narratives, Lela Khoperia, 'Old Georgian Sources concerning Maximus the Confessor's Life', *Le Muséon* 116 (2003), 395–414, with ample bibliography. Cf. this Samaritan–Persian/free–slave union to the marriage of an Arab trader with a Jewish slave maid from Sepphoris, Al Bakhari, quoted in S. Klein, *Sefer HaYishuv* (Jerusalem 1977, repr. of 1939 edn.) (Heb.), 2, 53 (Sepphoris 1).

convictions severely condemned by the biographer and by other defenders of monothelitism.

The narrative clearly meant to discredit Maximus from birth by assigning to him mixed parentage, a bonded mother and a father who had sex with a slave belonging to his host and trade partner. The authenticity of Maximus' mixed parentage is doubtful but his alleged Palestinian origins deserve attention.[169] The topographical context of the tale embeds information that throws valuable light on the Golan in late antiquity.[170] The writer of the pseudo-biography depicted the population of Khisfin, a village or townlet between Nawa (in Arabia) and the Sea of Galilee (in Palestine), as a colourful mixture of creeds. Especially instructive is the image of the village as a location in a faraway region, a periphery that offered an ideal refuge for women and men who had to hide from familial wrath.[171] Recent surveys and some excavations provide both illumination and some rectification. No less than three churches have been identified in Khisfin, one belonging perhaps to a monastery.[172] With this relatively large number of sacred structures, it is curious that the baptism of Maximus' parents had to be conducted in secrecy.

Such a seemingly inexplicable circumstance made even Maximus' 'biographer' wonder. He accounted for the need for concealment as fear of Samaritan revenge, adding, however, that Martyrius was well connected, in fact a kinsman of the powerful 'governor of Tiberias and the surrounding area'. Whether or not the Samaritans on the

---

[169] Michael the Syrian, *Chronicle* (Chronique de Michel le syrien Patriarche Jacobite d'Antioche, ed. J. B. Chabot, Paris 1901), ii. 443–4 refers to Maximus as 'Maximus from Hisfin near Tiberias'. A Monophysite, Michael probably echoed an anti-Chalcedonian tradition as encapsulated in Maximus' 'biography'.

[170] I focus here mainly on the Golan within the borders of Israel.

[171] Cf. *PT Ket.* 11.1 (34b) which records the flight of a Galilean sage, who had to escape the wrath of the Tiberiad patriarch, to Naveh (Nawa) in the Bashan (Arabia), east of Khisfin. The episode is dated to the middle of the 4th cent. See B.-Z. Rosenfeld, 'The Crisis of the Jewish Patriarchate in the Fourth Century', *Zion* 53 (1988), 256 n. 61 (Heb.).

[172] Z. Maoz, 'Hispin', in *NEAEHL* 2. 586–8 (*The New Encyclopedia of Archaeological Excavations in the Holy Land*, ed. E. Stern, 4 vols. (New York and Jerusalem 1993)); D. Urman, 'Public Structures and Jewish Communities in the Golan Heights', in idem and P. V. M. Flesher (eds.), *Ancient Synagogues: Historical Analysis and Archaeological Discovery* (Leiden 1995), 373–617; V. Tzaferis and S. Bar Lev, 'A Byzantine Inscription from Khisfin', *Atiqot* 11 (1976), 114–15.

Golan, themselves in all likelihood refugees, had either the desire or the power to avenge the conversion and marriage of a single individual remains open to doubt.[173] One other explanation occurs. An inscription from Khisfin hints at intra-Christian polemics, rather than at Samaritan–Christian strife.[174] Originally inscribed on a lintel, probably from a church, the text commemorated a *katholike ecclesia*, a phrase designating either episcopal jurisdiction or, more likely, a distinction between two Christian factions, 'them' and 'us', orthodoxy and heterodoxy.[175] The precise nature of this 'catholicism' was not defined, nor has the date of this inscription been established. Whether Martyrius belonged to a Christian minority group in Khisfin that preferred privacy to open strife is another unsolved puzzle.

A singular omission of Maximus' 'biography' relates to the absence of Jews. With the exception of a reference to a Jewish household of Tiberias, no Jew made an appearance in the narrative. Yet, both archaeological data and written sources indicate the presence of a substantial Jewish community on the Golan. At Khisfin itself archaeological surveys have yielded a doorpost stone with a three-branched menorah and a lintel bearing symbols ordinarily associated with Jewish public structures (palm-tree or *lulav*, rosettes, a vine branch with a cluster of grapes, a garland with a Hercules' knot).[176] Khisfin was numbered among the 'forbidden' towns in the rabbinic 'territory' of Susita (Hippo).[177] Its inclusion within the rabbinic 'borders' of the 'Land of Israel' signified that, by rabbinic standards at least, Khisfin

---

[173] Malalas, *Chron.* p. 447 (Dindorf), on Samaritan flight to the Trachon following the failure of the revolt of CE 529. See also Ch. 3.

[174] R. C. Gregg and D. Urman, *Jews, Pagans and Christians in the Golan Heights: Greek and Other Inscriptions of the Roman and Byzantine Eras* (Atlanta 1996), nos. 71–3; 75–82; 84, 86–90.

[175] Gregg–Urman, no. 82*. Cf. floor mosaic inscription which refers to a renovation of the 'holy house' (*hagion oikon*) from CE 618 (Gregg–Urman, no. 83*).

[176] Urman, 'Public Structures', 559.

[177] *T. Shev.* 4.10 (66.4–6); *PT Dem.* 2.1 (22d), dating perhaps to the 3rd–4th cent. but perhaps earlier. The 'borders' are also delineated, with a few significant divergences, on an inscription from Rehob/Rehov near Scythopolis, usually dated to the 5th or 6th cents. Ilan, *Ancient Synagogues*, 186–9, includes the text of the inscription (p. 188); Y. Sussman, 'The Inscription in the Synagogue at Rehov', in L. I. Levine (ed.), *Ancient Synagogues Revealed* (Jerusalem 1981), 146–61, and 152–3 (trans.), and idem, 'A Halakhic Inscription from the Beth Shean Valley', *Tarbiz* 43 (1973–4), 88–158 (Heb.). See Ch. 6. On the relationship between legal theories and territorial

was a locality where Jews had to abide by rules pertaining to certain diets and to sabbatical (seventh-year) regulations. Perhaps by Maximus' time (late sixth–early seventh centuries), the Jewish community at Khisfin had dwindled, its inhabitants replaced by Samaritans and Christians. The Golan (Jawlan) lies between arable and arid zones, with the Syrian desert and the Hauran to the east and the Galilee to the west. It is scarce in permanent water sources and in consistently rich soil. Geographically and geologically the Golan's diversity ranges from fertile patches that can support cities (such as Panias-Caesarea Philippi and Hippos-Sussita) to intractable desolation.[178] Devoid of papyri and of pilgrims' accounts, the northeastern regions of late ancient Palestine, although densely populated, remain a periphery awaiting the intensity invested in the archaeology of the Negev. The rich epigraphical finds from the Golan are problematic since the majority of the inscriptions are either without a date or are undatable. Khisfin's dwellers, for example, had a preference for Greek, at least when recording deaths and donations in stone. Whether Greek was also used as the medium of daily communications rather than Syriac is likely but difficult to establish. Jews in the Golan often resorted to Aramaic and Hebrew to commemorate the dead and to honour local euergetism.

The history of 'border' towns, such as Khisfin, features moments of tension mingled with routine and repetition. The balance between the two was often impossible to establish. The excavations of another Golanide settlement, Farj (north of Khisfin and bordering on Arabia), provide an instructive example of the intricacies of the northeastern periphery of late ancient Palestine.[179] A preliminary publication of the village's Greek inscriptions reveals a mixture of Graeco-Roman

realities, Claudine Dauphin, 'Interdits alimentaires et territorialité en Palestine byzantine', in *Mélanges Gilbert Dagron, Travaux et Mémoires* 14 (2002), 147–66.

[178] D. Urman, *The Golan: A Profile of a Region during the Roman and Byzantine Periods* (BAR IS 269; Oxford 1985); Z. Maoz, *Jewish Settlements and Synagogues in the Golan* (Kazrin 1980) (Heb.); Ilan, *Ancient Synagogues in Israel* (Heb.), 61–113 (for the Golan's synagogues and their Hebrew or Aramaic inscriptions); L. Roth-Gerson, *The Greek Inscriptions from the Synagogues of Eretz Israel* (Jerusalem 1987) (Heb.) (for the Greek inscriptions) and Gregg–Urman, *passim*.

[179] Dauphin *et al.*, 'Païens'; eadem, 'Farj en Gaulanitide: Refuge judéo-chrétien?', *POC* 34 (1984), 233–45.

and Semitic names on a scale appreciably smaller than the one known from the Negev.[180] On one Greek inscription a sole surviving word, God (*theos*), flanked by two *menorot*, aspired to proclaim Jewish monotheistic identity, perhaps in deliberate contrast, if not overt polemics with other, non-Jewish forms of one-God worship.[181] Of the nine Farj inscriptions identified as Christian, one basalt lintel avowed the lordship of Jesus (*kyrie*) while another recalled a pious vow to him.[182] A third referred to the Fates, *Moir(ai)*, perhaps a Christian appropriation of pagan references to death.[183]

Farj's Aramaic and Hebrew inscriptions, inscribed on basalt fragments and decorated with Jewish symbols, pose problems of interpretation. One, bearing (in Aramaic) the Greek formula of *kurie eleison* (Lord, have mercy) has been variously interpreted as either Jewish or Christian.[184] Such confusion shows the constricting character of the remains of the Golan's material culture and the elusiveness of proliferated traditions when tempered with innovations. A triad of *menorot* on basalt lintels from the village appears to have balanced Jewish symbols with a quintessential Christian tenet.[185] Another inscription has been taken to designate the site of a 'Beit Midrash' or house of study, a stunning proposition, if true.[186] This centre of learning, apparently active between the second and the

---

[180] Urman, 'Public Structures', 414 with Gregg–Urman, nos. 132–7.

[181] Dauphin *et al.*, 'Païens', no. 5, pp. 312–14 and fig. 6–7.

[182] Gregg apud Dauphin, 'Païens', nos. 13–21, esp. nos. 14 and 16.

[183] Gregg apud Dauphin, no. 21; for the theme of Fate as death, R. Lattimore, *Themes in Greek and Roman Epitaphs* (Urbana 1962), 150–1.

[184] Sebastian Brock apud Dauphin *et al.*, 'Païens, juifs', pp. 308–10, no. 2. The difficulties of reading and deciphering inscriptions on basalt are fully acknowledged, p. 307. If the second reading is correct, it cannot antedate the 5th cent. since the phrase is not attested before the 380s, Brock, 309. Dauphin, ibid., 334, emphasizes the rarity of a transliteration of the formula *kyrie eleison* into Hebrew characters and suggests a Judaeo-Christian milieu linked with the taking over of the synagogue and the Christianization of the Jewish quarter in the 5th cent. The scenario is possible, if unsupported. Z. Maoz, 'Comments on Jewish and Christian Communities in Byzantine Palestine', *PEQ* 117 (1985), 63 objects to Jewish identification proposing instead a Christian sect composed of newly converted Jews who integrated a traditional Jewish symbol (such as menorot) into their iconography. This appears unlikely.

[185] For drawings of these triple menorot, C. M. Dauphin, 'Jewish and Christian Communities in the Roman and Byzantine Gaulinitis: A Study of Evidence from Archaeological Surveys', *PEQ* 11 (1982), figs. 10; eadem, 'Païens', figs. 1 and 5, p. 335.

[186] Brock apud Dauphin, no. 3 (pp. 310–11).

fourth centuries, would have been contemporaneous with another Golanide 'academy' located at Dabbura.[187]

The village of Farj began its life as an estate owned by a Jewish family. Later it expanded to become a village or townlet (*ayara*) with land parcelled out to individual owners.[188] Its mixed heritage in late antiquity points to unsolved ambiguity—did the Jewish, (Jewish-)Christian, and later Ghassanid seasonal gatherings at Farj coexist peacefully or uneasily?[189] Rabbinic sources alluded to strained relations between Jews and 'gentiles' on the Golan, singling out Jewish Nawa on the border between Palaestina and Arabia, a few kilometres east of Farj, and Nawa's neighbour 'Halamo' (Halamish or Alamusa, a townlet 12 km. east of Nawa).[190] Located along the road linking the Hauran with the Golan and Phoenicia, both towns were episcopal seats in the sixth century.[191] In that same century the halakhic inscription of the Rehov synagogue incorporated the region of Arabian Nawa in a dietary map of the 'Land of Israel'.[192]

Although the Golan has very few sites with identifiable biblical connotations (Kursi and Beit Saida being notable exceptions), its position along the roads leading from Damascus to the Mediterranean and thence to Egypt contributed to a strategic desirability that dictated the transfer and settlement there of Ghassanid Arabic-speaking tribes. These new migrants might have absorbed the descendants of the Golanide Itureans who, like the Negev Nabataeans, had once spread over the Golan. Around CE 100 the Itureans disappeared into a historiographical fog, leaving behind scores of stones which they

---

[187] D. Urman, 'Jewish Inscriptions from Dabbura in the Golan', *IEJ* 22 (1972), 21–3, no. 6 dated to the end 2nd/early 3rd cent. See also V. Elizur (Noam), 'A Glimpse into the World of a Golanide Tanna: Rabbi Eliezer the Qappar', *At Atar* 4–5 (1999), 59–66 (Heb.).

[188] Dauphin, 'Farj', 241–4; eadem, 'Païens', 319–24. Cf. the Hauran and other eastern regions, P.-L. Gatier, 'Villages du Proche-Orient protobyzantin (4ème–7ème siècle): Étude régionale', in G. R. D. King and Av. Cameron (eds.), *The Byzantine and Early Islamic Near East*, ii: *Land Use and Settlement Patterns* (Princeton 1994), 17–48.

[189] Dauphin, 'Païens', *passim*, for an optimistic view.

[190] *LevR* 23.5 (Margaliot), perhaps reflecting a 4th-cent. situation. On the identification of the two rival townlets, G. Reeg, *Die Ortsnamen Israels nach der rabbinischen Literatur* (Wiesbaden 1989), 253; M. Sartre, *L'Orient romain* (Paris 1991), 331 n. 3; and B.-Z. Rosenfeld, 'Nawa: Capital of the Bashan from Herod to the Muslim Conquest', *Al Atar* 4–5 (1999), 83–93, esp. p. 91 (Heb.).

[191] E. Habas, 'The Nawa-Der'a Road', *SCI* 14 (1995), 138–42.

[192] Sussmann, *Tarbiz* (1973), 124; see also Ch. 6.

venerated and stacks of 'Golan ware' misnamed Iturean pottery.[193] Iturean sanctuaries reached even the uninviting slopes of Mount Hermon, at the very north of the Golan. One of the temples built there to an unknown divinity continued to operate till the Islamic invasion, when it fell into natural decay.[194]

Ghassanid presence, the result of a decision of the imperial authorities to guarantee sensitive 'border' regions like the Golan, further reinforced a Monophysite form of Christianity in the periphery. The transfer of the Ghassanid to the Golan tipped credal and ethnic balance in favour of Christianity and of Arabs.[195] It further contributed to bringing the margins closer to major cult centres through annual pilgrimages—the Ghassanid frequented the sanctuary of John the Baptist in Golanide Er-Ramthaniyye and of Sergius in Rusafa along the Roman–Persian frontier.[196]

Modern interpreters of the Golan's material culture have drawn two distinct maps of its late ancient human habitat, one of separation, the other of intermingling. The first, largely based on the distribution of Golanide synagogues, depicts the south-central Golan as a distinctly Jewish area, indeed a periphery within a periphery.[197] The rest of the Golan, it has been further surmised, remained an area altogether devoid of Jews. The projection is undermined by the heterogeneous character of several sites beyond the Golanide Jewish 'pale'.[198] Even within the predominantly Jewish area

[193] On problems of the precise identification of the Itureans and their relations with those identified as 'Arabs', Retsö, 407–8. On the Hermon area and its Iturean dwellers, R. Mouterde, 'Antiquités de l'Hermon et de la Beqa', *Mélanges de l'Université Saint Joseph*, Beirut 29 (1951–2), 21–39; Shimon Dar, 'Sanctuaries of the Hermon', in A. Kasher *et al.* (eds.), *Greece and Rome in Eretz Israel* (Jerusalem 1989), 296–316 (Heb.); and idem, *The History of Hermon: Settlement and Temples of the Itureans* (Tel Aviv 1994) (Heb.) (Eng. abs. pp. 375–6); and M. Hartal: 'Khirbet Zemel: Northern Golan. An Iturean Settlement', in Z. Gal (ed.), *Eretz Zafon: Studies in Galilean Archaeology* (Jerusalem 2002), 75*–117*. See also A. H. M. Jones, 'The Urbanization of the Iturean Principality', *JRS* 21 (1931), 265–75.

[194] Dar, *The History of Hermon, passim.*

[195] Dauphin, 'Jewish and Christian Communities in the Roman and Byzantine Gaulanitis', 132; eadem, 'Farj' (below), 244–5.

[196] On the latter, E. Key Fowden, *The Barbarian Plain: Saint Sergius between Rome and Iran* (Berkeley 1999), *passim*, esp. 141–9.

[197] This is the image propounded by Zvi Maoz and criticized by Urman, 'Public Structures', *passim*, who also encloses a list of Maoz' relevant publications (ibid. 638).

[198] Dauphin, 'Païens, juifs', 305–40; eadem, *La Palestine byzantine* (1998), *passim.*

of the Golan Jews did not live in complete isolation. The ornamental art of numerous synagogues in the central Golan reveals a significant degree of artistic exchange with Christian and pagan art.[199]

A recent investigation of patterns of continuity of 45 Jewish settlements in the central Golan has elicited an instructive model of development.[200] Based on qualitative analysis of about 5,000 pottery shards which had been recorded in various surveys, the examination has yielded a threefold settlement typology. About one third (39%) of the Jewish habitations existed throughout the 'Roman' and 'early Byzantine' eras, namely between the first and the sixth centuries (type A); an equal number (35%) seem to have lasted from the first to the fourth centuries (type B); while about a quarter (24%) of the settlements recorded existed only between CE 400 and 600 (type C). In nearly all the settlements which disappeared by about 350 CE (type B) there were no traces of monumental synagogues, a fact which jars with the striking number of synagogues identified in settlements belonging to type A. At the height of its late ancient 'renaissance', between 350 and 450 CE, the economy of the Golan was characterized by an intense oil production. Remains of some 65 oil presses which could produce about 500 tons of olive oil bear witness to heightened demand and supply in the period.[201] A process of dramatic decline has been observed for the period around the middle of the sixth century.[202]

The exceptional density of Jewish sanctuaries in one zone of the Golan (centre–south) is difficult to interpret and raises several questions. Did Jews continue to live voluntarily on this relatively poor soil because of its proximity to the predominantly Jewish eastern Galilee,

[199] R. Hachlili, 'Late Antique Jewish Art from the Golan', in *The Roman and Byzantine Near East: Some Recent Archaeological Research* (JRA Suppl. 14; Ann Arbor 1995), 183–212.

[200] H. Ben David, 'The Lower Golan in the Late Second Temple, Mishnah and Talmud Periods' (Ph.D. Bar Ilan University, 2000) (Heb.).

[201] H. Ben David, 'Oil Presses and Oil Production in the Golan in the Mishnaic and Talmudic Periods', *Atiqot* 34 (1998), 1–61.

[202] Cf. the scholarly consensus regarding an economic downturn around the middle of the 6th cent. throughout the eastern provinces, C. Morrison and J.-P. Sodini, 'The Sixth Century Economy', in A. E. Laiou (ed.), *The Economic History of Byzantium* (Washington, DC, 2002), 171–220; M. G. Morony, Economic Boundaries? Late Antiquity and Early Islam', *Journal of the Economic and Social History of the Orient* 47 (2004), 166–94.

or were they confined by dictates of government and hostile neighbours, or both? Because research relating to the number and distribution of churches on the Golan is still in its infancy, and the dating
of synagogues is undergoing a radical re-evaluation, it is impossible
to provide even a tentative answer to the question of religious
distribution in late antiquity.[203] The identified synagogues on the
Golan vary in orientation and plan.[204] Their ornamentation displays
a curious mixture of conformity and contrast.[205] Above all, the
incised architectural fragments unearthed throughout the area display striking similarities with the art of the Galilean synagogues,
indirectly corroborating the redating of the latter to the fifth if
not the sixth century, the dates generally accepted for the majority
of the synagogues of the Golan.[206] Such a building 'boom' in both the
Golan and the Galilee indicates that Jews ignored imperial restrictions
on the construction of new synagogues.[207]

In the southern Golan rabbinic maps listed nine Jewish 'towns'
within 'the boundaries of Sussita' and eight in the eastern Golan
within the 'boundaries of Nawa'. In late antiquity the city of Sussita
was largely a Christian city, as was Arabian Nawa.[208] Established in
Hellenistic antiquity, Sussita's bishops attended ecclesiastical councils

---

[203] B. Isaac, 'Inscriptions and Religious Identity on the Golan', in *The Roman and
Byzantine Near East 2* (1999), 179–88.

[204] Urman, 'Public Structures', *passim*. At Deir Aziz, about 4 km. south of Gamla,
the platform of the ark was fixed into a southern wall, suggesting a prayer direction to
the south rather than the more prevalent west.

[205] Note the variation on the number of the menorah branches, five, nine, and the
'classical' seven, Hachlili, 'Late Antique Jewish Art from the Golan', catalogue nos. 7,
10 (nine branches); 5, 6, 11, 13, 17 (five branches).

[206] See for example the ongoing excavation at Um-el-Kanatir (*www.yeshuat.com*)
with Ilan, *Ancient Synagogues*, 63–4, who considers Um-el-Kanatir's synagogue one of
the most important synagogues of the Golan. On the history of modern exploration
till the early 1990s, Urman, 'Public Structures', 546–51. The site is, in all probability,
to be identified as the home of a donkey-carrier who made a living by transporting
pilgrims from the Golan to Jerusalem once a month, *PT Ber.* 9.13 with S. Klein, *Sefer
haYishuv* I.143; S. Safrai, 'Jerusalem Pilgrimage after the Destruction of the Second
Temple', in A. Oppenheimer *et al.* (eds.), *Jerusalem in the Second Temple Period:
Abraham Schalit Memorial Volume* (Jerusalem 1980), 383 and n. 39. On redating the
Galilean synagogues, J. Magness, 'When were the Galilean Synagogues Built?', *Cathedra* 101 (2002), 19–38 (Heb.); eadem, in Lee Levine (ed.), *Continuity and Renewal*
(2004), 507–25.

[207] Linder, *The Jews in Roman Imperial Legislation, passim*.

[208] On the Sussita district and its settlements, Urman, 'Public Structures', 555–605.

already in the fourth century.[209] The city boasted at least five
churches, including a monumental basilica and tri-apsidal baptistery,
the latter with a sunken cruciform font of a type common in the
Negev churches.[210] Like the Negev churches, those in Hippos-Sussita
contained cisterns or water reservoirs under the atrium in order to
collect rainwater from the roof and from the peristyle to serve the
needs of the church and rituals of purification.[211] At the western edge
of the central street of Sussita the remains of a structure identified as
a synagogue were surveyed.[212] Neither its date nor its extent have
been established but its marginal position suggests a community
pushed to the edge of town, a minority whose space, like that of
Sussita's once powerful polytheists, had been overtaken by the
expanding Christian community. The progress of Christianity was
matched by regression of the Jewish zones in the city.

Visual and verbal references indicate a symbiosis punctured by
polemics. In CE 377, a man by the name of Flavius Naaman consecrated a martyrium honouring John the Baptist in a locality now
known as Er-Ramthaniyye which, like Farj, was not far from the border
with Arabia.[213] In addition to relics of the Baptist, Er-Ramthaniyye
boasted a profusion of secular and ecclesiastical structures, including
facilities for storing water and for corralling animals.[214] The
martyrium itself was apparently placed within a complex which

[209] Epiph. *Pan.* 73.26; Soc. *HE* 3.25; B. Bagatti, *The Church from the Gentiles in
Palestine* (Jerusalem 1971), 56, 94.

[210] C. Epstein and V. Tzaferis, 'The Baptistery at Sussita-Hippos', *Atiqot* 20 (1991),
89–94, who compare the font with those in Shivta, Avdat, and Mamshit. See now
A. Segal *et al.*, *Hippos-Sussita: Fifth Season of Excavations (2004) and Summary of all
Five Seasons (2000–2004)* (Haifa 2005).

[211] Epstein–Tzaferis, p. 93 n. 3.

[212] Ilan, *Ancient Synagogues*, 99.

[213] Dauphin, 'Païens', no. 25, and pp. 335–6, regarding 'Naaman' as an Arabic
name. 'Flavius' in this context is clearly not a personal name (*pace* Dauphin) but a
status indicator, J. G. Keenan, 'The Names Flavius and Aurelius as Status Designations
in Late Roman Egypt', *ZPE* 11 (1973), 33–63; and ibid. 13 (1974), 283–4, esp. 301–3;
see also idem, 'An Afterthought on the Names Flavius and Aurelius', *ZPE* 53 (1983),
245–50, and Alan Cameron, 'Flavius: A Nicety of Protocol', *Latomus* 47 (1988), 26–33.
The name-as-designator appears both in the Nessana and the Petra papyri.

[214] The relics reached the Golan after the destruction of the Baptist shrine at
Sebaste during Julian's reign *c.*360 and the dispersal of his relics. J. W. Crowfoot *et al.*,
Samaria-Sebaste, i (London 1942). C. Dauphin and S. Gibson, 'Landscape Archaeology at er-Ramthaniyye in the Golan Heights', in J.-L. Fiches and S. van de Leeuw
(eds.), *Archéologie et espaces: Actes des Xe rencontres internationales d'archéologie et*

had contained a monastery and a baptistery, serving locals and nomads who would have gathered in the village to celebrate the annual feasts honouring the Baptist.[215] Flavius Naaman was *clarissimus* and *ordinarius* of an *arithmos*, a unit whose name is not preserved. His own name, a composite of Latin and Semitic elements, indicates his (military) status and his (Semitic) origins.[216] He attained a high rank in society and enough wealth to endow a structure in a prominent place in his chosen locality. Nor was Naaman shy of publicly proclaiming his religious affiliation, an affinity further reflected in the name given to his (only?) daughter, Thekla. His own name, Naaman, and the selection of the patron saint for his daughter suggest recent conversion and/or baptism. The coincidence of name with the Ammonite general who had been baptized by the prophet Elisha and cured, on that occasion, from leprosy (2 Kgs. 5: 1–19) might have appealed to the latter-day Naaman.

In the 370s, when Naaman commemorated his life-changing course, avowing loyalty to the arch-baptizer, Epiphanius of Salamis, originally from Palestinian Eleutheropolis (Beit Govrin), reported a scene of conversion from Judaism to Christianity which bore instructive parallels with Naaman's conversion. Epiphanius' protagonist was Joseph, a confidant of the Jewish patriarch (*nasi*) at Tiberias.[217] While on his deathbed, the patriarch summoned the city's bishop and allegedly received secret baptism at his hands. The sole witness, besides the two participants, was Joseph. Appointed guardian of the young patriarch, Joseph accompanied his volatile charge to the baths of Golanide Hammat Gader. When the young man fell in love with a chaste Christian woman who frequented the baths, Joseph resorted to magic in order to bewitch the young lady. The spell failed and Joseph himself fell gravely ill. Haunted by dreams which featured Jesus, the ailing aide was promised a cure in return for conversion from Judaism to Christianity. The transaction was duly accomplished and ultimately Joseph was rewarded with the rank of *comes* by the emperor

d'histoire, Antibes (Juan les Pins 1990), 435–65; and eidem, 'Pèlerinage ghassanide au sanctuaire byzantin de Saint Jean-Baptiste à er-Ramthaniyye en Gaulanitide', in *Akten des XII internationalen Kongresses für christliche Archäologie* (Münster 1995), 667–73.

215 Fowden, *Barbarian Plain*, 148–9.
216 Keenan and Cameron (above, n. 213).
217 Epiph. Pan. 30. See also Ch. 1 and Ch. 6.

Constantine himself. Epiphanius further recorded that the Christian-ized Joseph undertook missionary activities among Jews in the Galilee without apparently scoring significant success.

On the Golan, the *ordinarius* Naaman cast himself as a counterpart of the *comes* Joseph, both men undertaking building initiatives in or near areas which had large Jewish communities. Joseph was credited with the intention of erecting churches in Tiberias and Sepphoris, two bastions of Galilean Judaism; Naaman considered himself a pioneer of Christianity in regions which had yet to be 'conquered'. The transition from active military service to the service of Chris-tianity appeared smooth, suggesting that in the Golan, military men, rather than monks like Hilarion in Elusa, were pioneers of converting missions. By the sixth century, Naaman's church grew to encompass a monastery, chapel, and a funerary cave, and it required restoration, a task undertaken by one Balbionos, another *clarissimus*.[218] The inscription commemorating the latter's enterprise was incised around a palm tree with nine branches, a style unique to the Golan.[219] The motif was repeated on the walls of a structure iden-tified as a Ghassanid monastery in the same settlement.[220] The choice of this decorative element might have been calculated to link Gola-nide Er-Ramthaniyye with Palmyra-Tadmor which became a Ghas-sanid base and with other Ghassanid bases along the *limes Palaestina*.[221] But the nine-branched palm can also be 'read' as a deliberately inverted *menorah*, and specifically of the nine-branched

---

[218] Dauphin, 'Païens', 336–7. Gregg–Urman, no.155.

[219] Photograph of the inscription and the palm motif in Dauphin, 'Païens', pl. VIa. On its uniqueness, ibid., p. 337. Note, however, the variation on this motif in contemporary Zoora/Zoar on the Dead Sea, Y. E. Meimaris and K. F. Kritikakou-Nikolarupoulou, *Inscriptions from Palaestina Tertia*, ia: *The Greek Inscriptions from Ghor es Safi (Byzantine Zoora)* (Athens 2005), 1–13, where the editors count 31 tombstones, all Christian, depicting schematized palm trees and dating to between 372 and 481 CE. See also Ch. 6.

[220] Dauphin, 'Jewish and Christian Communities', 140 and fig. 12.

[221] Dauphin, ibid. See also Eusebius, *Onom.* 96, 100, 146 (Thaiman of the Palm Trees, Thamar, Thermoth, Palmetis, Theman), forms that reflect the confusion between Tadmor (Palmyra) and Tamar (an oasis in the Negev (Asasan Thamar, *Onom.* 8), see R. Chapman in Freeman-Grenville *et al.*, *The Onomasticon of Eusebius*, p. 159. The Golanide palm carving could also, then, represent the Negevite home of the persons who commissioned it. On the widespread use of palm trees on tombstones from Zoar, see n. 219, where, according to the editors, they symbolized triumph or victory.

variation which is known from several Golanide locations such as Yahudia, Ahmadia, and 'En Nashut.[222]

At the start of the fourth century a battle of faiths took place in the northern Golanide city of Paneas (Caesarea Philippi), inaugurating a new era in the history of this periphery. An ancient statue of Pan was replaced with two of Jesus, further disrupting an age-old ceremony of a water sacrifice.[223] It seems that a Christian man witnessing the miraculous disappearance of the sacrifice into the water prayed to Jesus to put an end to the popular delusion of demonic powers. The prayer was answered, or so it seems. The town became a popular site of Christian pilgrimage. In the early 360s Julian the emperor ordered the replacement of Jesus with a statue of himself which, after his death, was subject to decapitation.[224] The headless statue might have continued to grace a public square in Paneas, as did those of Zeus and Hadrian in Caesarea, a token of victory of faith at the expense of civic aesthetics.

Nearly two centuries later, at the end of sixth century, the relative remoteness of the Golan was fractured with the arrival of imperial emissaries intent on executing an anti-'heretic' and anti-Jewish agenda. A leading Ghassanid chieftain was arrested in 581 and soon afterwards the protection system that kept the settlements of the Golan within the boundaries of the eastern Roman empire collapsed. The region continued to be inhabited but its new inhabitants left faint imprints.[225] The heyday of the late ancient Golan, days of oil (and of wine), of synagogue construction boom, of verbal rivalries and artistic polemics, was over.

---

[222] Ilan, *Ancient Synagogues*, 65 (Ahmadia), 95 (Yahudia), 102 ('En Nashut).

[223] Eusebius, *HE* 7.17–18. Taylor, *Christians and Holy Places*, suggests that the bronze statues represented Asclepius healing a sick woman, later interpreted by Christians as Jesus healing the woman with the issue of blood (Mark 5: 25–34; Matt. 9: 20; Luke 8: 43–8). See Ch. 1.

[224] Sozomen, *HE* 5.21 (Julian's statue); Philostorgius, *HE* 7.3 (Pan's statue).

[225] Note, however, Al Iakoubi's epitaph for Paneas/Banias, 'capital of the Golan', trans. G. LeStrange, *Palestine under the Moslems: A Description of Syria and the Holy Land from AD 650–1500* (London 1890), p. 34. See also the brief survey and comments of V. Tzaferis and R. Avner, 'The Excavations at Banias', *Qadmoniot* 23 (1990), 110–14 (Heb.) of which the most fascinating aspect is the complete absence of archaeological data for the period between the third and twelve centuries, a gap that hints at abandonment during late antiquity and the early Islamic eras.

To reflect on the formation of landscapes in late antiquity it is useful at times to start, as this chapter has, with mindscapes, the terrain of dreams and of dialogues beyond the limits of time and space. Within a specific Christian context these mental visions generated topographical discourses that elevated designated localities out of their present and into a biblical past. Dreams gave a prefiguration and a legitimacy to all territorial expansion. The rise of the southern Sinai and of the summit of Jebel Musa to the rank of a holy mountain created a locus of sanctity with two categories of citizens, monks and pilgrims, and a third of non-citizens, the 'Saracens'. An intense religious life and a dynamic relationship with nature and nomads dominated a search for sanctity and a desire to experience the Bible in a manner unmediated by layers of more recent history. Slipping along uncharted paths, pious Christian travellers followed revived biblical tracks which had been conjured along a dream-map and translated into a new geographical reality.

So intense was the rush to the Sinai that it injected the entire southern periphery with new life. Located between Jerusalem and the Sinai, caravansarais along the Negev roads became prosperous towns, benefiting from the attraction of the holy mountain and from imperial needs. Monks, pilgrims, and soldiers brought a religious orthodoxy that penetrated the politics of Palestine's southern periphery, becoming a necessary mediation of social experiences. Away from major pilgrim routes, in the northern periphery, Jews, Samaritans, pagans, and Christians of the orthodox and heterodox varieties prospered without hindrance. If the Sinai provided opportunities for touristic as well as for scholarly tours of the past, a Golan itinerary passed through settlements where synagogues and temples provided a reminder of an unbroken continuity that Christianity punctured. Nowhere were there neutral spaces because it was impossible, even in the late ancient peripheries of Palestine, to take a walk without encountering the past. In the land where the Bible was part of the fabric of Jewish, Samaritan, and Christian historical consciousness, visions and memories spoke. And some also knew how to make them speak as each creed brandished its heroes and tenets in the faces of the others.

3

Recalcitrance, Riots, and Rebellion: The Samaritans and the Emergence of Intolerance

PRELUDE: SAMARITANS CELEBRATING SUKKOT

Desolation reigns outside,
Devastation is in the townships.
The Good One turned his face from us.
When the Compassionate One does not help
And does not remember his beloved,
Then fathers and sons
Perish by Wrath, for it is great...
Signs indicate
That in the generation in which we are living
There is no man who is not a companion of sinners:
Fathers and sons,
Mothers and children,
As they rebelled in concert,
So they are afflicted with punishments...
O people, look and be fearful
of the great desolation that is in the world;
Woe is to us that we were not prepared to learn.
Neither by the earthquake did we learn
Nor by the punishment of the locusts did we learn.
Let us fear the punishment of death
Before the fountain of abundance dries up...

A. S. Rodrigues Pereira, *Studies in Aramaic Poetry*,
437–8   (slightly modified)[1]

---

[1] A. S. Rodrigues Pereira, *Studies in Aramaic Poetry, c. 100 BCE–c. 600 CE: Selected Jewish, Christian and Samaritan Poems* (Assen 1997).

These are the verses of Marka (Marqah), the most famous Samaritan poet of late antiquity whose poems still form part of living Samaritan liturgy.[2] The sentiments expressed were fully justified. In the fifth and sixth centuries the Samaritans became the bearers of communal rebellion in Palestine. Their rural and urban communities were embroiled in bitter and bloody strife with their Christian and Jewish neighbours and with representatives of the Roman government. Samaritanism became a symbol of dissension. In late ancient political discourses of 'orthodoxy' and 'heresy', as of centre and periphery, the Samaritan case expressed subversion, a process of dissolution, and of the breaking apart of a community. Rejected as well as accepted by Jews, persecuted yet also tolerated by the Roman emperors, the Samaritans occupied a difficult position in Palestinian society of late antiquity.

Samaritan annals, all late compilations of uncertain historical value, provide a patchy coverage of the era of rebellion which dramatically reduced their number to a level from which they never recovered.[3] The writings are barely reconcilable with late ancient Christian sources which zoomed in on Samaritans as rebels against Roman order.[4] In Samaritan memory chronicles, like the *kitab* of Abu'l Fath (14th cent.), linked the dawn of late ancient Samaritanism with reform and rebellion, both led by a legendary figure, Baba Rabba, to whom the Samaritans ascribed a renaissance of law, liturgy,

---

[2] On Marka see A. D. Crown, R. Pummer, and A. Tal (eds.), *A Companion to Samaritan Studies* (Tübingen 1993), s.n. Marqa, pp. 152–3. On Marka's work, J. MacDonald, *Memar Marqah*, 2 vols. (Berlin 1963), esp. xviii–xx. Marka is usually dated to the 4th cent.

[3] J. A. Montgomery, *The Samaritans: The Earliest Jewish Sect, their History, Theology and Literature* (Philadelphia 1907; repr. 1968), 300–11, for a summary of Samaritan sources. See also P. Stenhouse, 'Samaritan Chronicles', in A. D. Crown (ed.), *The Samaritans* (Tübingen 1989), 218–65. On the difficulties of relating the information preserved in Samaritan chronicles to events recorded in late ancient sources on Samaritan history, A. D. Crown, 'The Samaritans in the Byzantine Orbit', *BJRL* 69 (1986–7), 107. For a comprehensive bibliographical guide, A. D. Crown and R. Pummer *A Bibliography of the Samaritans. Revised, Expanded and Annotated*, 3rd edn. (ATLA Bibliography Series 51; Lanham, Md., 2005). On patterns of 'native' revolts, see S. L. Dyson, 'Native Revolt Patterns in the Roman Empire', ANRW II.3 (1975), 138–75.

[4] Conveniently gathered in R. Pummer, *Early Christian Authors on Samaritans and Samaritanism* (Tübingen 2002).

and lore.[5] Baba Rabba's 'biographies' are difficult to decode. His life, placed by modern interpreters anywhere between the early third and the early fourth centuries, came to reflect the vicissitudes of Samaritan history itself.[6] Born during a period of Samaritan persecution when the Roman government forbade circumcision, the child nevertheless underwent this all-important ceremony which his father, a Samaritan high priest, administered with the help and connivance of a Christian cleric, Germanus, the bishop of Neapolis.[7] The gesture, a bodily mark that binds newly born males to their community, forged a temporary Samaritan–Christian bond based, it seems, on commonality of a persecuted minority.

In Samaritan memory the benevolent prelate of Neapolis became the subject of a blessing: 'May Germon [scil. Germanus] the Roman overseer be remembered for good forever'.[8] Christians, viewed with benevolence, as sanctified in the Gospels, only the 'good' Samaritans who followed Jesus; their late ancient descendants were viewed with indifference bordering on hostility.[9] Baba Rabba's surreptitious introduction into the world of Samaritanism harboured symbolism of what was to come. The story of his circumcision points to moments of Samaritan–Christian collaboration precisely over potentially divisive issues. Defying the Roman government while attempting to unify the Samaritans became the hallmark of Baba Rabba's

---

[5] A. Tal, 'The Hebrew and Aramaic Literature of the Samaritans', in E. Stern and H. Eshel (eds.), *The Samaritans* (Jerusalem 2002), 519–36 (Heb.).

[6] The dates of Baba Rabba are hotly contested. For brief summary, R. T. Anderson and Terry Giles, *The Keepers: An Introduction to the History and Culture of the Samaritans* (Peabody, Mass., 2002), 58–60. On possible conflation of Baba's reconstructed biography in Samaritan sources and the history of Arsenius, a famous 6th-cent. Samaritan, Pummer, *Authors*, 287. On Arsenius, Procopius, *Anec.* 27.3–19 and 26–31, and below.

[7] It is unclear whether the ban was ever lifted as far as Samaritans were concerned; it was lifted for Jews, A. M. Rabello. 'The Ban on Circumcision as a Cause of Bar Kokhba Rebellion', *Israel Law Review* 29 (1995), 176–214. Germanus' precise position is likewise unclear. He may have been a bishop or a Roman official sympathetic to Samaritan plight.

[8] J. Bowman, *Samaritan Documents relating to their History, Religion, and Life* (Pittsburgh 1977), p. 162; Cf. Chronicle Adler, 223–4 (E. N. Adler and M. Seligsohn, 'Une nouvelle chronique samaritaine', *REJ* 45 (1902)).

[9] The most famous encounter was between Jesus and the Samaritan woman, John 4. See also Acts 8. For Christian negative attitudes, Justin, *Apologia* 53; Epiphanius, *Pan.* 55, 78, 80.

vision and his acts. In his lifetime he achieved the possibility of communal harmony through institutional and religious reforms which reshaped the structure of Samaritan collective interaction.

The scope of Baba Rabba's architectural and artistic initiatives must be fully appreciated within a context of centuries of void— there are no traces of Samaritan synagogues between the first century BCE and the fourth century CE.[10] Accredited with far-reaching enterprises, Baba Rabba built eight synagogues in settlements with a Samaritan majority. Recent excavations suggest that the new leader spared no expense—the sanctuaries linked with his name were endowed with magnificent mosaics which easily rivalled those known from Palestinian Jewish synagogues, Christian churches, and private dwellings.[11] They consistently displayed a number of traits including aniconism based on a relatively small repertory of religious symbols, like the Torah ark, which served as a visual proclamation of the central tenets of Samaritanism.[12]

To spread the word of renewal and reinvigoration he appointed sages, laymen, and priests who were to manage communal affairs along the lines which he had delineated.[13] Above all, Baba Rabba engineered the renewal of worship on Mount Gerizim, the holiest of Samaritan lands. He developed its sacred area by building a well of

---

[10] Nor is it possible to identify any of the excavated Samaritan synagogues with those accredited to Baba Rabba in Samaritan sources, Magen, 'The Areas of Samaritan Settlement in the Roman-Byzantine Period', in Stern–Eshel, *The Samaritans* (2002), 267 (Heb.).

[11] Y. Magen, 'Samaritan Synagogues', *Judea and Samaria. Research Studies* 2 (1993), 229–64 (Heb.), with map of excavated synagogues on p. 264 (Eng. summary, xx–xxi). idem, 'Samaritan Synagogues', in F. Manns and E. Alliata (eds.), *Early Christianity in Context: Monuments and Documents* (Jerusalem 1993), 193–230; and idem, 'Samaritan Synagogues', in Stern-Eshel, *The Samaritans* (2002), 382–443 (Heb.).

[12] F. Dexinger, 'The Beliefs of the Samaritans in the Byzantine Period', in Stern–Eshel, *The Samaritans* (2002), 496–518 (Heb.).

[13] The inclusion of laymen among the newly appointed men who were to become the religious leaders of the community appears to reflect a decline in the status of priests, a process that stands in a curious contrast with the apparent rise in their status in contemporary Judaism, see Dexinger, 'Beliefs', 499–500; and O. Irshai, 'The Priesthood in Jewish Society of Late Antiquity', in Levine (ed.), *Continuity and Renewal* (Jerusalem 2004), 67–106 (Heb.). See also the reservations of Z. Weiss, 'Biblical Stories in Early Jewish Art: Jewish–Christian Polemic or Intracommunal Dialogue', in L. I. Levine (ed.), *Continuity and Renewal* (2004), 245–69, esp. 256–7.

purification and a 'house for prayer', perhaps even a synagogue.[14] This was the territory that stood at the heart of the controversy which marked and marred relations between Samaritans and Christians. Bloody clashes over this holy area occurred already in the days of Baba Rabba. His alleged victories over Roman troops became the occasion of a celebration which the Samaritans still maintain. The narrative of conflict and conflagration, as recorded in Samaritan sources, provided an aetiology for the (re)formation of cult and of childhood:

One night all the people were mustered and ascended Mount Gerizim and Baba Rabba was in the van of the troops. Levi [his nephew] then arose with the might and power of God and smote the guards of the king, the monks and the priests, crying out in a loud voice: 'The Lord is a man of war. The Lord is His name'. And when Baba Rabba heard the voice of Levi his nephew, they all raised their voices saying as he had said. They unsheathed their swords and killed many of the Romans, not ceasing until they had wiped out everyone who was on Mount Gerizim.

Then they kindled the fire on the top of the dome and all the Samaritans arose and killed all the overseers who had been put over them. Not one of them remained. And they continued throughout the whole night to burn the churches of the Romans, destroying them until they effaced the name from Mount Gerizim and round about.

From that day onward, at the beginning of the seventh month, children of the Samaritans gather wood together and set fire to the wood of their Succah-booths on the last night of the festival (of the Tabernacles), on the eighth day of the solemn assembly which concludes the festivals of the land.[15]

Yet, when summoned to the imperial court Baba Rabba complied with the order, believing, perhaps, in his ability to pave the way for

---

[14] Y. Magen, 'Mount Gerizim during the Roman and Byzantine Periods', *Qadmoniot* 120 (2000), 133–43 (Heb.).

[15] *The Kitab al-Tarikh of Abu'l Fath*, trans. P. Stenhouse (Sydney 1985), 156/199. The translation here is a composite of J. Bowman, *Samaritan Documents*, 154–5 and of J. M. Cohen, *A Samaritan Chronicle: A Source-Critical Analysis of the Life and Times of the Great Samaritan Reformer Baba Rabbah* (Leiden 1981), II.19.65, p. 206. This episode appears to be related twice by Abu'l Fath, once with Levi as a main protagonist, and once with Baba Rabba as the sole hero (Bowman, 147). It also demonstrates the confusion that reigns in Samaritan chronicles, which appear to believe that Baba Rabba's opponents were Christian, whereas the target of demolition on top of Mount Gerizim must have been the temple built in honour of Zeus.

reconciliation with the Roman authorities.[16] Samaritan sources, the only texts that preserved the story of Baba Rabba, engulfed his court appearance with a harmony that projected a symbiosis of two cultures, one of crosses, the other of camels, each with its own distinct image:

When he [Baba Rabba] drew nearer [Constantinople] King 'Philip' summoned the crowd to go out to meet him and all the people went out with crosses and images and in prayer. All the kings walked alongside the camel of Baba Rabba, who alone continued riding. And it was a great day for him when he entered Constantinople with great pomp. No other king had so entered . . . [17]

Underlying this idyllic merging of the 'desert' and the 'city' was a scenario of disagreement. The king's advisers proposed execution for Baba Rabba, as befitting a rebel; the 'king' opposed the idea, preferring to neutralize the Samaritan leader by removing him from Palestine and keeping him at the court. Although Baba Rabba wanted to return home he remained in the capital, for all intents and purposes as a hostage. Upon his deathbed he entrusted his son to a Jewish friend. Ironically, when he died, Baba Rabba was interred with pomp and ceremony in a beautiful tomb over which the Romans built a beautiful church.

Baba Rabba's activities suggest a process of Samaritan unification through opposition to a common enemy, namely Rome. He had to contend with centuries of internal dissension and external persecutions and his success seemed due to a renewed focus on rituals linked with Mount Gerizim. His victory over the Roman 'overseers', whether myth or reality, became an object of annual commemoration through fire rites performed by children 'at the beginning of the seventh month', the period designated for the celebration of the Feast

[16] Cf. the links between the imperial court and the Jewish patriarchs in the 4th cent., Stemberger, *Jews and Christians in the Holy Land: Palestine in the Fourth Century* (Edinburgh 2000), 230–1. Baba Rabba's history may preserve echoes of the status of the Jewish patriarch under the early Christian emperors, precisely when the Samaritans, too, had authoritative leadership.

[17] Bowman, 157. The claim of singularity is predictable yet untrue. Cf. the entry of Athanaric, the Gothic king, to the same city in 383, and his lavish funeral, see H. Sivan 'From Athanaric to Ataulf: The Shifting Horizons of "Gothicness" in Late Antiquity', in J.-M. Carrié and R. Lizzi Testa (eds.), *Humana Sapit: Études d'antiquité tardive offertes à Lellia Cracco Ruggini* (Bibliothèque de l'antiquité tardive 3; Turnhout and Paris 2002), 55–62.

of the Tabernacles (Succoth). The children's ritual of burning appears a unique manner of ending a festival originally designed to recall the Exodus from Egypt.[18]

1. THE SAMARITAN ROAD TO REBELLION

Like Baba Rabba's life, Samaritan history in late antiquity was full of contradictions.[19] It spoke of vigorous resistance to evolving imperial ideologies and of violent conflicts, of individual success and of collective failures. Everything was played out between pairs of opposites, Samaritans versus Christians, Samaritans versus governor and government, Samaritans versus Jews, peasants versus landowners. To settle differences the government invariably flexed its legal and military muscle, rendering conflict a central theme of its relations with the Samaritans. Unleashing a torrent of judicial rhetoric, the emperors employed legalities to marginalize Samaritans and Samaritanism. Repeated bloody clashes between the Roman government and the Samaritans in Palestine provided confirmation that the empowerment of orthodoxy entailed the suppression of conflictual groups.[20] Samaritan chronicles and Christian writers habitually resorted to vocabularies that strove to establish two antagonistic and irreconcilable poles. Within the infinite multiplicity of exchanges violence came to constitute the totality of the landscape. Both Samaritan and Christian writers generalized Samaritan–Roman conflicts in terms of 'rebellions'. The reality of this vocabulary is open to various interpretations.[21]

[18] See Ch. 4. Cf. the role of children in the rituals marking the end of a famine in the 8th cent., M. Levy-Rubin, *The Continuatio of the Samaritan Chronicle of Abu L-Fath Al-Samiri Al-Danafi. Text, Translated and Annotation* (Princeton 2002), 66.

[19] In general, Crown, 'The Samaritans in the Byzantine Orbit', *passim*.

[20] Modern estimates of the numbers of Samaritans in the 5th cent. vary from 90,000 to 200,000, Dauphin, *La Palestine byzantine*, i. 280–3, also on distribution of Samaritan settlements. On the Samaritan rebellions in late antiquity see the useful overview of Menahem Mor, *From Samaria to Shechem: The Samaritans in Antiquity* (Jerusalem 2003), ch. 12 (Heb.).

[21] L. Di Segni, 'The Samaritans in Roman-Byzantine Palestine', in H. Lapin (ed.), *Religious and Ethnic Communities* (Bethesda 1998), 51–66, prefers to classify the 484

The roots of the Samaritan–Christian/Roman conflict are to be sought within a double context of Palestinian Christianity, the relentless drive to enliven the Bible through the superimposition of a Christian Holy Land on existing maps, and the emergence of intra-Christian controversies, especially after the council of Chalcedon (CE 451). In the early fifth century Poemenia, an energetic and well-connected pilgrim, was instrumental in destroying a Samaritan 'idol' atop Mount Gerizim.[22] Hers must have been a peculiar interpretation of Samaritanism's strict monotheism. In the middle of the fifth century the imperial drive to bring the Bible to life was recorded in Samaritan sources as an example of the violation of the sanctity of Samaritan space:

In the days of the high priest Eleazar the Christians came and laid waste to the field of Joseph's tomb. They said that they wanted to take the remains of Joseph the patriarch away. They would excavate by day but during the night [the ground] would revert to its previous state. So they seized some Samaritans and made them go and dig. Sad and weeping, the [seized men] did not have their heart in their work. When Friday came, towards evening, they arrived at the entrance to the cave and kept on appealing to God for help, saying: 'This is the night time and we are no longer able to do any work until the Sabbath is over'. Afterwards, they would say 'There is no light left for work' and stopped the work as soon as the Sabbath commenced.[23]

A sign appeared in the sky, thunder with gusty winds and fire erupted from the mouth of the cave to heavens. There was fire on Mount Gerizim. A pillar of cloud returned to the mountain. This was what was written about in the Holy Torah. These [miracles] were a witness to the mighty desires of gentiles to own Joseph. Then the Christians came and put up a building over the grave which the Samaritans then demolished. They then took seven people from among them and executed them. So they then seized the high priest Eleazar and leaders of the Hukama and hanged them . . .

---

events as 'riots' rather than 'rebellion'. Di Segni, 'Mutual Relations between Samaritans, Jews and Christians in Byzantine Palestine', *New Samaritan Studies* (1995), 185–94; and 'Samaritan Revolts in Byzantine Palestine', in E. Stern and H. Eshel (eds.), *The Samaritans* (Jerusalem 2002) 454–80 (Heb.).

[22] John Rufus, *Vita Petri* (Raabe, p. 30). See also Palladius, *Historia Lausiaca* 35.14–15; with Hunt, *Holy Land Pilgrimage*, 159–67, and P. Devos, 'La Servante de Dieu Poemenia d'après Pallade, la tradition copte et Jean Rufus', *AB* 87 (1969), 189–212.

[23] Cf. alleged Jewish resistance to Helena's search for the true cross, A. Jacobs, *Remains of the Jews* (Stanford 2004), 176–82.

After this, during the reign of Marqitus [Marcian] war broke out between the Samaritans and the Christians over the tombs of the high priests Eleazar, Ithamar and Phineas—peace be upon them—for the Christians wanted to take them from the Samaritans. The ruler of Caesarea sided with the Samaritans, as did others. The Christians had an immense army. The ruler of Caesarea asked: 'Why should all the people perish? Let one champion stand out from among these and another champion from among those and we will be with whomever God gives the victory to, and will aid him'. The Christian champion took the field, a powerful and huge man. The Christians said to him: 'We are all relying upon you'. They also had a dog with them which was like a lion and could swallow two cats. Taking the field for the Samaritans was a man called Bustiya from Kfr 'Aqr. He was like a devouring whirlwind of fire. He knelt in the presence of the Almighty God, the Giant of Giants, and set out to do battle with a sincere heart and pure intent. The dog leapt at him; he dealt it a blow which broke its legs. God gave the victory to Bustiya who killed his opponent. The Christians then fled as did all those who were with them. After this contest no one returned to demand the tombs of Eleazar, Ithamar and Phineas.[24]

The Samaritan 'victory', it may be noted, was negotiated by the provincial governor who was, in all likelihood, Christian, yet considerably more sensitive to local varieties than the court at Constantinople.[25] Since many Samaritans served in the Roman army stationed in Palestine the downsizing of potentially full-scale conflict with an uncertain outcome, and its channelling into a sporting event, was the most sensible measure that the local administration could adopt. Increasingly rigid, however, the imperial court often stuck to an

---

[24] *Kitab* (above, n. 15), 236–9 (slightly modified). Cf. Chronicle Adler (above, n. 8), 234–5), which provides a condensed version of the same events. The events narrated may have taken place in the middle of the 5th cent. Pummer, *Early Christian Authors*, 112, suggests that Christians had taken possession of Joseph's tomb at the beginning of the 5th cent. See also J. Jeremias, *Heiligengraber in Jesu Umwelt* (Göttingen 1958), 33, and Dauphin, *La Palestine byzantine*, i. 285. The Samaritan sources appear to echo an imperial hunt for the bones of the patriarchs, esp. Joseph, which had been undertaken at the behest of Theodosius I (379–95) and Theodosius II (408–45). Such quests prompted numerous discoveries of burials in various parts of the province, raising Samaritan chagrin. J. Purvis, 'Joseph in the Samaritan Tradition', in *Studies on the Testament of Moses* (Missoula, Mont., 1975), 147–53.

[25] This may have been the occasion that prompted the unusual tribute of a golden statue to a Nonnus, the 'leader' who has been identified as Fl. Nonnus, Consul in 445. C. M. Lehmann and K. G. Holum, *The Greek and Latin Inscriptions of Caesarea Maritima: Joint Expedition to Caesarea Maritima Excavation Reports*, 5 (Boston 2000), no. 25.

openly hostile course of action which its local representatives found singularly ill suited to their management style and local balance.

Court and Samaritan ideologies, seemingly irreconcilable, united in action to stem the tide of 'heresy' among the Christian communities in Palestine. The irony is palpable—the persecutors of Samaritanism used Samaritans to persecute their own co-religionists. In the wake of the council of Chalcedon (CE 451), which condemned Monophysite doctrines associated with Eutyches, Palestinian supporters and opponents of Chalcedonian 'orthodoxy' became embroiled in bitter strife.[26] Champions of Chalcedon, backed by local army units, attacked monasteries deemed 'heretic', killing monks and destroying churches. In Neapolis, a thriving city in the heart of Samaria, a region densely dotted with Samaritan settlements, Roman and Samaritan soldiers, at the instigation of Juvenal of Jerusalem, decimated anti-Chalcedonian monks.

Christian sources bitterly recalled the ruthlessness of the Samaritans, as well as the miraculous healing of a blind Samaritan who applied the blood of a martyred monk to his eyes, and subsequently converted to Christianity.[27] The authorized involvement of Samaritans in intra-Christian conflicts drew protests from Palestinian monkish circles, who appealed to the court over the head of the governor. In 453, Pulcheria, by then empress and wife of Marcian, addressed these concerns:

His Serenity [Marcian] ordered an accurate search to be made about the looting of property which is said to have been done boldly by Samaritans. He has decreed that as many things as should have been shown to have been seized should be restored by them both to the most holy churches and to those who have lost these, and that the persons found guilty should undergo legal correction . . . [28]

Her words echoed Marcian's promise to investigate anti-Samaritan allegations:

You have accused the Samaritans of committing terrible and lawless deeds against the most holy churches and murders or some other unnatural sins.

---

[26] R. Price and M. Gaddis, *The Acts of the Council of Chalcedon*, 3 vols. (TTH; Liverpool 2005).

[27] Zacharias of Mytilene, *Hist.* 3.6, text and translation in Pummer, 237–40.

[28] Mansi, *Sacrorum conciliorum nova et amplissima collectio* 7. 511–12; text and translation in Pummer, 234 n. 12.

We have ordained that after an accurate inquiry is to be conducted studiously by Dorotheus, the admirable count, the stolen things must be restored to the most holy churches and to those who have lost these and that the persons found guilty of these things must undergo punishment according to the laws since vengeance in these matters cannot be a private matter... [29]

The tenor seemed calculated to effect a rapprochement between the monastic and ecclesiastical establishments in Palestine and to exonerate the court from employing non-Christians who invaded churches and monasteries and killed monks in the name of the law.

Attacks on Christian persons and property, sponsored by the Orthodox imperial court and carried out by Samaritan soldiers displayed the virtue of an impeccable logic which acted upon requests without full investigation. The army preserved the function of law and order but applied it to the enhancement of doctrinal standing. Concerned to impute destructiveness and bloodshed to Samaritan rather than to Roman soldiers, the complaining monks and the imperial court focused on imputations which were barely central to the heart of the matter, namely the ongoing struggle between Chalcedonian Juvenal and Monophysite Theodosius over the see of Jerusalem. The imperial investigation into Samaritan looting restricted the reading of these events from one among Christians to one between Samaritans and Christians. Monks became victims of Samaritan murderous harassment in an ironic inversion of the subsequent history of the Samaritan communities of Palestine. Christian suspects of lawlessness emerged victorious from the accusations brought against them because they in turn accused the military arm of the empire of perpetrating crimes which a Christian empire could not condone. It was a matter of time before government and local church would collaborate to collide with the Samaritans.

2. RECALCITRANCE

As an illustration of the growing rift between Palestinian Christian orthodoxy backed by Constantinople, and Samaritanism, the bloody clash between the emperor Zeno and the Samaritans in 484 seems

---

[29] Mansi, 7. 494, 496, text and trans. in Pummer, 233 n. 10, slightly modified.

instructive. It is documented in both Samaritan and Christian sources.[30] The narratives of Procopius, a Palestinian by origin, and of Malalas exemplify the varying perceptions of Samaritan violence.[31] Procopius emphasized the anti-Christian flavour of the events; Malalas focused on its anti-Roman hue. In an excursus on the architecture of Mount Gerizim, Procopius recorded that:

During the reign of Zeno the Samaritans suddenly banded together and fell upon the Christians in Neapolis in the church while they were celebrating the festival called Pentecost. They destroyed many of them, striking by sword Terebinthius, the man who was then the city's bishop whom they found standing at the holy table performing the mysteries. The Samaritans slashed at him, cutting off the fingers from his hand. They also railed at the mysteries, as is natural for Samaritans to do, while we honour them with silence (*De Aedif.* 5.7.5).

The 'suddenness' of the onslaught suggests that such a course of events had been foreign to Samaritans and unfamiliar to Romans.[32] It put the burden of assault on the shoulders of Samaritans alone, exonerating the local Christians and indirectly justifying the penalties which the emperor later imposed on the Samaritans. Procopius indicated that Samaritan unity was another unusual aspect of the revolt which, in his description, was specifically anti-clerical. The geography of the clash, namely the city of Neapolis, points to a Samaritan–Christian conflict over the urban space vacated by the

---

[30] Crown, 'Samaritans in Byzantine Orbit', 128, sees the events of 453 (alluding to the excavations of the bones of Eleazar etc. and the role of Samaritans in the Monophysite struggle) as foreshadowing the revolt under Zeno. Accusations against Samaritans as enemies of orthodoxy, and hence friends of Monophysites, were raised in a letter of Chalcedonian monks to the emperor Marcian to which he and Pulcheria replied by commissioning an investigation into these allegations, *ACO* II, 1, 3 (ed. E. Schwartz), pp. 127. 15–17; 129.12–16.

[31] Texts and translations are in Pummer. For detailed analysis, Di Segni, 'Samaritan Revolts in Byzantine Palestine', in Stern–Eshel, *The Samaritans* (2002), 454–80 (Heb.).

[32] The timing of the rebellion is puzzling. The Samaritans believed that Zeno's preoccupation with the usurper Illus might divert attention away from Palestine. Y. Dan, *The City in Eretz Israel during the Late Roman and Byzantine Periods* (Jerusalem 1984) (Heb.), 45, suggests that the revolt followed, rather than preceded, the Christian occupation of Mount Gerizim and the conversion of the Samaritan synagogue there to a church.

polytheists who had dominated the city till at least the early fifth century.[33]

Verbal mockery of Christian rituals coupled with physical attacks against bishop and parishioners created a distinct impression of an anti-governmental uprising. Both types of violence challenged Christianity by attacking it at its very root, namely the ecclesiastical hierarchy and liturgy. This Samaritan mode of operations attempted to modify drastically the imprint that Christianity was leaving on the cityscape. Far from being an exception, this model became the rule that expressed the resentment at the growing suppression of privileges and of increasingly circumscribed space. Confronted with Christianity in the heart of their habitat, the Samaritans asserted the veracity of their own brand of monotheism in violent actions and in pithy declarations. Samaritan inscriptions often consisted of key biblical phrases and of basic credal tenets, like the one found on Mount Gerizim that defiantly announced: 'He is the God of Gods, Lord of Lords, and there is no God besides Him.'[34]

In an attempt to normalize the practice of suppression, the imperial retaliation set out to limit the extent of Samaritanism by reducing its meaning. Zeno punished those responsible for the bishop's mutilation and banished all Samaritans from Mount Gerizim, the holiest of Samaritan sanctuaries. He ordered the erection of a church honouring Mary on top of the mountain. To stem Samaritan unity and violence Zeno also placed a garrison in Neapolis, a city with a substantial Samaritan population. These painful measures appeared to have been directed at a substitution of Samaritanism with Christianity by tipping the balance in favour of the territory's Christian communities. The extraction of the venerated mountain

---

[33] On the pagan character of the city and the continuity of the temple to Zeus, Magen, 'Areas of Samaritan Settlement' (below, n. 38), 262–3. The Madaba map (mid-6th cent.) still shows the theatre which had been built on the city's outskirts in the 2nd cent., Magen, 'The Roman Theater of Shechem', in E. Schiller (ed.), *Zeev Vilnay's Jubilee Volume* (Jerusalem 1984), i. 269–77 (Heb.), and idem, *Flavia Neapolis: Shechem in the Roman Period* (Jerusalem 2005) (Heb.), *passim*.

[34] Y. Magen, Mount Gerizim—A Temple-City', *Qadmoniot* 23 (1990), 82 (Heb.); for the inscriptions which are dated to the 4th cent. (p. 79), and perhaps linked with the Samaritan 'renaissance' of Baba Rabba, and to the 'Middle Ages' (p. 81), all found in the area of the church that Zeno built. See also Ch. 2 (Jewish inscription of Golanide Farj).

from the creed created a flagrant and deliberate gap bound to be felt. The Samaritans could not recreate Samaritanism without Gerizim as the rabbis did with Judaism without the Temple. In Procopius' brief narrative the revolt symbolized the opposition between right and wrong, with the Samaritans acting as the image of disunity that must be suppressed.

These same events of 484 were described by Malalas not in terms of a solitary attack on a single Christian church during a Christian festival but as a full-scale rebellion, equipped with a leader and leading to war. The scene of the insurgency was transferred from Neapolis to Caesarea, capital of Palestine, where the Samaritans apparently maintained their majority.[35] Malalas' narrative focused on the career of a man named Iustus who was crowned by Samaritan supporters in Caesarea. Once installed, Iustus' first act was to preside over chariot races in the city's famed hippodrome. Then he and his followers set fire to the local church (St Procopius?) and killed many Christians. In an inevitable clash with the soldiers of the *dux Palaestinae* the newly elevated Samaritan 'emperor' lost both the battle and his head. Zeno's punitive measures included the confiscation of the property of wealthy Samaritans and the banning of Samaritans from service in the Roman army.

Both Malalas and Procopius agreed about the most crucial outcome of the affair, namely the conversion of the Samaritan holiest sanctuary atop Mount Gerizim into a church honouring Mary. In this Zeno hardly set a precedent. Some 350 years earlier Hadrian had planted a statue of Jupiter atop the Temple Mount in Jerusalem to signify the end of a Jewish rebellion and the triumph of Roman religion over Judaism. The differences between the two versions of the 484 events are obvious and puzzling. For Procopius the actions of the Samaritans constituted a religious riot in the sense of a 'violent action, with words or weapons, undertaken against religious targets by people who were not acting officially or formally as agents of

---

[35] *PT Dem.* 2.1 (22c) asserts that in the 4th cent. the number of Samaritans in Caesarea equalled that of Jews and gentiles combined. By the late 5th cent. most of the peasant farmers of Caesarea's agricultural hinterland were Samaritans, Procopius *Anec.* 11.29. Dan, *The City*, 46 reconstructs the events from both sources, suggesting that the revolt broke out in Samaria and then spread to Caesarea.

political and ecclesiastical authority'.[36] He 'translated' what may have been a routine urban discourse consisting of mutual railing at the other's rites through words and gestures into a contentious episode that justified a major modification of the landscape.[37] For Malalas the essence of the Samaritan violence consisted of a 'classic' pattern of usurpation, taking place not in a remote provincial town but in the provincial capital itself.[38] Each narrator reflected a distinct strand of Samaritan contemporary ideology—resistance to the encroaching Christianization of their heartland, and a quest for a leader who, like Baba Rabba, could reunite them.

Samaritan chroniclers preserved an astonishingly coherent account of the traumatic clash between their ancestors and the imperial power, depicting the Samaritans as victims of imperial zealous piety and ascribing to Zeno a series of extraordinarily harsh measures, including an attempt to convert the Samaritans by force. Here, as elsewhere, the Christians emerged not as monotheists but as idol worshippers, just as they did in contemporary Jewish sources:

In the 13th year of Nathaniel's pontificate, Zaitun (Zeno), king of Byzantium, came to Nablus (Shechem, Neapolis) and oppressed the Samaritans and obliged them to embrace the religion of the Christians under pain of being burnt to death or pressed to death or tortured by fire. He began looking for the important men of the community and the *Hukhama* (body of sages) and the priests.

Zaitun said to them: 'If you will not kneel before this cross, then you will all be killed'. They said: 'We surrender our lives to death for the sake of our Lord to whom alone we will kneel'. So he killed them.

[36] N. Z. Davis, 'The Rites of Violence', in eadem, *Society and Culture in Early Modern France* (Stanford 1975), 152–88 (quotation at 153).

[37] Cf. the ritualized railing of Christian children at Samaritan synagogues in Scythopolis, Ch. 4 (Purim).

[38] Di Segni, 'Samaritan Revolts', 465 claims that the 484 events were not a fully-fledged rebellion, as Malalas aspired to show, but a pogrom within the context of circus faction rivalry. She is certainly correct in rejecting the automatic ascription by archaeologists of traces of destruction and of abandonment to either the late 5th or the early 6th cent., as do S. Dar, 'Samaritan Rebellions in the Byzantine Period: The Archaeological Evidence', in Stern–Eshel, *The Samaritans* (2002), 444–53 (Heb.); and Magen, 'The Areas of Samaritan Settlement in the Roman-Byzantine Period', 245–71 (Heb.) who also discerns a phase of 'resettlement' at the end of the 6th cent., after apparent abandonment.

He then took seventy *Hukhama* (sages) and tried to force them to kneel to idols. They refused. So he had them executed in the middle of the market place near the standing column. And the Samaritans used not to walk in front of these columns, only behind them.[39]

Then Zaitun, may God curse him, took the synagogue which Aqbun had built and put a throne in it, and made in front of it a place of sacrilege. He then went out and came to the synagogue of Baba Rabba and asked: 'To whom does this place belong?' They said: 'This place belongs to the Samaritans. They pray in it to God their Lord before this mountain'. He said: 'But it does not have an image on top of it'. They told him that they prayed to a being who was unseen and immaterial.

Zaitun had Nathaniel the great high priest brought and assembled the leaders of Israel and said to them: 'Sell me the mountain of your Qibla'. They answered: 'We and all that we possess are at the disposal of the king'. He did not stop until he had taken the temple and all around it, the water pool and the cistern of water, to the north. He added buildings to the temple and surroundings, and to the cistern of water. He built a church inside the temple and on the church he constructed a very high tower which he painted white and from which lamps were hung to glow in the night to let those in Constantinople and Rome see . . . A large number of houses were emptied and villages were ruined by the oppression of Zaitun, may God curse him . . . [40]

In Samaritan memory the clash occurred at a stage in which two systems of values were coexisting in conflict. The chronicles preserved a basic opposition between Christianity and Samaritanism, reducing it to a rhetorical antithesis which nevertheless reflected the real power relations between Christians, backed by the government, and Samaritans. Christianity was idolatry while the Roman ruler was behaving as an active missionary.[41] Echoes of classic scenes of martyrdom, as recorded in the books of the Maccabees where Judaism and Hellenism were cast as two antagonistic modes of faith with

[39] Cf. the role of columns in the mourning and protest over the execution of Christians in the days of persecution, Ch. 8.

[40] *The Kitab al-Tarikh of Abu'l Fath*, trans. P. Stenhouse, pp. 239–41. The reference to idols may echo Samaritan tradition of buried idols in the mountain, a tradition based on Gen. 34: 4 and 2 Kgs. 17, still discussed in Epiphanius' time, with Pummer, 140–1.

[41] Cf. the story about Heraclius in Palestine and the conversion of the Jew Benjamin, Theophanes, *Chron.* with Sivan, 'From Byzantine to Persian Jerusalem', *GRBS* 41 (2000), 277–306.

Greeks as persecutors and Jews as martyrs, seemed to permeate the encounter between Zeno and the Samaritan leaders.[42] The commonality of themes hints at a curious historical process which witnessed the transfer of martyrdom mentalities from Jews to Samaritans as each faced the threat of a new culture and a new creed vigorously advanced by the superpower of the day.

Zeno's decision to convert the Samaritan holy precinct on Mount Gerizim into a church was a step calculated to undermine the very essence of Samaritanism. It symbolized the violent uprooting of the creed from its sacred centre and of the people from a site which enshrined their history and their specific traditions of biblical exegesis. Procopius, a native of Palestinian Caesarea, was fully aware of the extent of this blow to Samaritan theology. This is why he set out to weave the 484 events into a history not of a deluded usurpation but of the mountain precinct. And this is why Zeno's church emerged as the fulfilment of Jesus' prophecy (John 4: 21–3) regarding the approaching end of Samaritanism.[43] To sustain the claims of Christianity to be an all-embracing universal theology, Procopius digressed from Constantinople to Palestine and from Justinian's church to the appropriation of the site by Zeno.

What neither the Samaritan chroniclers nor the Byzantine historians commented upon was the crucial fact that the octagonal church of the Theotokos was an exact replica of an earlier sanctuary also honouring Mary's maternity. In 1992 excavations along the road leading from Jerusalem to Bethlehem unearthed a large church of distinctive octagonal shape which ancient sources identify as the Kathisma (Mary's resting place).[44] The church's earliest phase has

---

[42] Macc. I and II with vast literature on each. In general, J. W. van Henten and F. Avemarie, *Martyrdom and Noble Death: Selected Texts from Graeco-Roman, Jewish and Christian Antiquity* (London 2002), *Passim*.

[43] The text itself suggests no such interpretation. On the church, Y. Magen, 'The Church of Mary Theotokos on Mount Gerizim', in G. C. Borrini, L. di Segni, and E. Alliata (eds.), *Christian Archaeology in the Holy Land: New Discoveries. Essay in Honor of Virgilio C. Corbo* (Jerusalem 1990), 333–42; idem, 'Mount Gerizim and the Samaritans', in F. Manns and E. Alliata (eds.), *Early Christianity in Context: Monuments and Documents* (Jerusalem 1993), 91–148.

[44] R. Avner, 'The Recovery of the Kathisma Church and its Influence on Octagonal Buildings', in *One Land—Many Cultures: Archaeological Studies in Honor of S. Loffreda* (Jerusalem 2003), 173–86. See also Ch. 6, 237–40.

been dated to the first half of the fifth century, thus preceding Zeno's church by some half a century. Why Zeno's architects used the same plan, with very minor modifications, to proclaim Christianity atop the most venerable Samaritan sanctuary remains a matter of speculation. The emperor might have intended the church to become a centre of Marian pilgrimage in close conjunction with Mary's cult in the Jerusalem orbit.[45] He might have envisaged streams of pilgrims converging on Samaritan territories on their way to Jerusalem and to Mary's Kathisma. According to the testimony of an Italian pilgrim a century later, this is precisely what had taken place.[46]

Samaritan reactions to this catastrophe, recorded solely by Procopius, are revealing because they point to intra-Samaritan dissension as well as to the role of Samaritan women as spearheads of resistance:

At a later time, when Anastasius (491–518 CE, Zeno's successor) was holding the imperial office, the following happened: Some of the Samaritans, incited by a woman's suggestion, unexpectedly climbed the steep face of the mountain (Gerizim), since the path which leads up from the city was carefully guarded and it was impossible for them to attempt to ascent by that route. Entering the church suddenly, they slew the guards there and with a mighty cry summoned the Samaritans in the city. The latter, however, through fear of the soldiers, were by no means willing to joint the attempt of the conspirators. And not long afterwards, the governor of the district arrested the authors of the outrage and put them to death.[47]

The allocation of a leadership role to an unnamed Samaritan(?) woman is intriguing. Women, collectively and individually, played a minor role in Samaritan annals. There is no reference in Samaritan chronicles, for example, to Baba Rabba's mother or wife, but there is a whole story about the fruitful collaboration of two women, a Samaritan and a Jewess, to save his life. No woman graced the accounts of the 484 events but a decade or two later the flag of resistance was raised by a woman. A woman also featured as one of

---

[45] Two other notable examples of an octagonal sanctuary are well known—the church in Capernaum and the Dome of the Rock in Jerusalem, the former dating to the 5th cent., the latter to 691/2. It is unclear to whom the Capernaum octagonal church was dedicated (Taylor, *Christians and the Holy Places*, 272–3). Could it have been Mary?

[46] *Anon. Plac.*, 129.   [47] *De Aedif.* 5.7.10–14, apud Pummer, 302–4.

the two main protagonists in a tale that pits Christian ascetic virtue against Samaritan female wiles.[48]

The plot hatched by the unnamed woman to retake Mount Gerizim hardly amounted to a fully-fledged rebellion. In Procopius' recording the narrative was calculated to discredit the pious enterprise from its very infancy, precisely by accrediting a woman as its initiator and by branding it as an impious and deluded scheme. The story bears the usual Procopian elements, including a surprise attack on unsuspecting Christians, the localized nature of the events, and the decisive and brutal nature of the suppression by the authorities. Procopius' logic, by definition expected to side with Church and court, defended the bloody outcome by attributing it to the unaccountable behaviour of Samaritans, limiting what might have been a widespread discontent to a tiny group of hotheaded men following the whim of a woman.

The Samaritan attempt to reoccupy the church that had occupied their holiest precinct appears symptomatic of a type of violent communication which mediated Samaritan–Christian relations in late antiquity. In the narration of the disorders brought about by the Samaritan revolts Christian writers depicted Samaritan violence against both government and Church in ways suggesting that the threat to Christians in Palestine menaced the empire itself. The tendency to glide between the particular and the general, Palestine and the empire, was especially apparent in the reports of the disturbances under Justin and Justinian in the sixth century (529, 555/6). These highlighted only moments of violent clash as though contacts between Samaritans and Christians invariably involved a 'rebellion'.

3. REBELLION

Procopius and Malalas, in rare agreement, claimed that the Samaritan 'revolt' of 529 started as an inter-communal conflict in Scythopolis, capital of Palaestina Secunda. It was an affair which the governor (*dux Palaestinae*) was expected to know how to handle,

---

[48] See Ch. 4.

presumably by squashing it in its inception. But matters got out of hand. Members of the Samaritan community, clashing with both Christians and Jews, set fire to many parts of the city. Apprised of these events, the imperial court acted promptly and drastically. Orders were issued to behead the governor, an act of official violence which failed to calm the feelings which were now running high in Scythopolis.

According to Malalas (second edition), the cause of the urban outburst of Samaritan violence was a ritual assault carried out by Christian children against Samaritan synagogues in the city.[49] But Malalas, who also asserted that this was a widespread custom on every Sabbath both in Palestine and outside it, failed to explain what, precisely, ignited the violence in the year 529 and why it occurred, of all places, in Scythopolis.[50] Perhaps the most curious aspect of this phase in the cataclysmic violence of the period was the singling out of the governor, rather than the governed, as the object of initial imperial wrath and retribution. According to Zacharias Rhetor the 529 revolt was in essence a repetition of the 484 one, as though only one pattern of unruly behaviour suited Samaritans. This time the 'tyrant' was named Julian and Samaritan actions included the burning of estates and of churches and the killing of many Christians around Neapolis and Caesarea.[51] It seems that Julian cast himself as a messianic king, reflecting an apocalyptic mood that accompanied the uprising and that the visions of the poet Marka (quoted above, p. 107) likewise reflected.[52] In hindsight, Samaritan chronicles echoed the misleading euphemism presenting the precise inversion of reality as a smokescreen to hide what had actually happened.

Municipal racing arenas appeared to provide an ideal context for incipient rebellions in late ancient Palestine. The Samaritan 'king' presided over chariot races in Neapolis and ordered the execution of the ultimate winner because the charioteer happened to profess

[49] See Ch. 4.

[50] *Excerp. Hist.*, trans. in Jeffreys, Jeffreys, and Scott, *The Chronicle of John Malalas*, 260, repr. in Pummer, 275–6.

[51] Malalas, *Chron.* 18.446. Dauphin, i, 288–90 on sites affected by the revolt. Zacharias Rhetor, *Hist.* 9.8, apud Pummer, 240–1, if indeed the entry relates to 529.

[52] John of Nikiu, *Chron.* 93.4–5, apud Pummer, 379–80 claims that the Samaritan leader declared that he was a king and that God had sent him to re-establish the Samaritan kingdom. On messianic expectations, Kippenberg, *Garizim*, 121.

Christianity.[53] Cyril, a native of Scythopolis, added that the Samaritans executed the bishop of Neapolis and his priests by roasting them together with remains of Christian martyrs.[54] And he further alluded to one serious and immediate outcome of the rebellion, namely the cessation of traffic as Christians, pilgrims and residents alike, were unable to travel along the roads of Palestine.[55] This was also the point at which the emperor intervened with orders to stem the rebellion with help from the troops stationed in Palaestina Tertia, a manoeuvre that occasioned alarm as far as Gaza—not, however, at the prospect of rebellious Samaritans but rather at the terror evidently borne by the imperial troops. Gaza's bishop, Marcianus, organized provisions for the passing soldiers to ensure the safety of his flock.[56] The repression of the revolt was swift and brutal. The extent of the damage inflicted on the Palestinian provinces was so great that the bishops of Ascalon and Pella asked for remission of taxes.[57] Numerous Samaritans were killed.

Some facts are revealing. At its inception, the Samaritan revolt of 529 was aimed at both Jews and Christians within a specific urban orbit. The governor's inaction hints at events which were, perhaps, a regular feature of urban history, bursting and fading within a rhythm all of their own. The imperial call to arms was issued not upon investigation but, one presumes, upon requests from locals. For

[53] Cf. the criticism of Choricius of Gaza regarding the madness and disorder that such shows introduced, *Apol. Mim.* 114 (369, 3–8); 116–18 (371, 3–18), and Ch. 8, 330 ff. Samaritan annals echo these events with references to a David–Goliath like encounter in the arena in Caesarea, between a Samaritan and a Christian champion which ended, not surprisingly, with Samaritan victory, and with another reference to a Roman governor who knew how to restrain communal violence by channelling it into sports, Abu'l Fath apud Stenhouse, 238–9. On the role of races, Al. Cameron, *Porphyrius the Charioteer* (Oxford 1973) and *Circus Factions* (Oxford 1976).

[54] Cyril of Scythopolis, *Vita Sabae* 70, Price.

[55] *Vita Sabae* 70. The plight was presumably general, and road banditry endemic but it suited Cyril to emphasize the problems of pilgrims. John Moschus refers to a bandit by the name of Cyriacus who headed a gang of Christians, Jews, and Samaritans in the region of Emmaus-Nicopolis (*Pratum Spirituale* 165, apud Pummer, 346–7), active, it seems, at the beginning of the 7th cent., in a collaboration for gain which transcended sectarian boundaries. John is careful, however, to emphasize Cyriacus' empathy with Christians versus the hostility displayed by his Samaritan and Jewish followers.

[56] Choricius, *Laud. Marc.* ii.24 (34, 10–20) (C. Glucker, *The City of Gaza in the Roman and Byzantine Periods* (BAR IS 325; Oxford 1987), 55).

[57] *Vita Sabae* 70.

Procopius the suppression of the revolt was not only brutal in nature but also ruined nature itself. The precise extent of the material damage which Palestine sustained as a result of the clashes between Samaritans, Christians, and government forces is difficult to gauge. Archaeological excavations have pointed to destruction and possible abandonment of rural settlements with no comparable traces in the cities.[58] There is a widespread tendency to assign visible ruins throughout Samaria to the aftermath of the 484 or 529 revolts although it is virtually impossible to date the debris with such precision.[59] When excavations at al-Boraq, some 20 kilometres south-west of Shechem (Neapolis) in the heart of a territory considered the Samaritan hub, revealed a church, the site was interpreted as a Christian rural settlement which had been damaged in one of the Samaritan revolts. Or, alternatively, as a Samaritan settlement whose dwellers destroyed the church which their Christian neighbours had planted in the middle of the village.[60]

On Mount Gerizim excavations have unearthed a layer of ashes that has been linked with the abortive attempt to 'conquer' the mountain in 572, or with fortifications that Justinian built in order to prevent further Samaritan attempts to seize the sanctuary.[61] Controversy also has surrounded the interpretation of the important site of Horbat Midgal (Zur Natan), strategically located on the slopes of Mount Shomron and midway between present-day Tul Karem and Kalkilia. The village boasted a Samaritan synagogue decorated with exceptionally beautiful and well-executed mosaics. It was later used as a church, perhaps as a result of the planting of Christian settlers on lands abandoned by Samaritans in the late fifth, or early sixth, centuries.[62] A structure in the village, which has been interpreted as a monastery, appears to lend credence to the hypothesis of an

---

[58] This is just one problem related to Samaritan 'archaeology'. Another relates to the identification of Samaritan synagogues, R. Pummer, 'How to Tell a Samaritan Synagogue from a Jewish Synagogue', *BAR* 24 (1998), 24–35.

[59] Magen, 'The Samaritans in the Roman-Byzantine Period', *passim*; idem, 'The Areas of Samaritan Settlement', *passim*; idem, 'Samaritan Synagogues', *passim*; S. Dar, 'Samaritan Rebellions in the Byzantine Period: The Archaeological Evidence', all four in Stern–Eshel, *The Samaritans* (2002), 213–44; 245–71; 382–443; 444–53 respectively.

[60] Magen, 225; Dar, 449.

[61] Magen, 225.

[62] E. Ayalon, 'Horbat Migdal (Tsur Natan): An Ancient Samaritan Village', in Stern–Eshel, *The Samaritans*, 272–88; Magen, 'Samaritan Synagogues', ibid. 429.

accelerated pace of Christianization which the Samaritan landscape experienced in the wake of the revolts. The fate of the Samaritans of Zur Natan is unclear. Around 570 a pilgrim from Piacenza encountered Samaritans throughout the region of Samaria. No numbers were given in the pilgrimage diary but the Samaritans plainly gave the impression of life structured around strict separation between Samaritans and gentiles. Material remains in Zur Natan point to Samaritan (re)occupation in the seventh and eighth centuries. Perhaps, then, after a gap of four decades (*c.*530–70) some Samaritans returned to their village and, in the wake of the Islamic conquest, many more followed suit.[63]

History proposes its own commentary and conclusion. In the late eighth century the donors of a colourful mosaic to a church in a military encampment east of the Jordan (Umm al-Rasas, Kastron Mefaa) recorded their vision of sacred geography with the help of medallions enclosing famed localities.[64] Jerusalem naturally featured as did several other cities frequented by pilgrims. Among these was the city of Flavia Neapolis, or Shechem, the see of the benevolent bishop Germanus who had helped to circumcise Baba Rabba, and a major Samaritan centre where several clashes between Samaritans and Christians had taken place. In the eighth century Neapolis was represented by neither a Samaritan synagogue nor a Christian church but by a famed pagan temple, indeed the sanctuary which centuries before had been dedicated to Zeus Hypsistos. Procopius of Gaza referred, in the early sixth century, to a temple of Zeus on Mount Gerizim. The assertion has been contested by archaeologists who have assigned the temple's *terminus ante quem* to the fourth or, at the latest, the fifth century.[65] Notwithstanding either the ancient or

[63] Magen, 'The Areas of Samaritan Settlement', *passim*, has been the most vigorous defender of the gap and resettlement hypothesis.

[64] For images of the Madaba map see the website of the Franciscan Cyberspot. On the identification of the structure featured in the icon of Neapolis, N. Duval, 'Essai sur la signification des vignettes topographiques', in M. Piccirillo and E. Alliata, *The Madaba Centenary*, available via the Internet under the Franciscan Cyberspot. On the date of the mosaics, M. Piccirillo, 'Le iscrizioni di Umm al-Rasas-Kastron Mefaa in Giordania I (1986–1987)', *LA* 32 (1987). On the fort see D. Kennedy, *The Roman Army in Jordan* (London 2004), 137–9.

[65] R. L. Hohlfelder, 'A Twilight of Paganism in the Holy Land: Numismatic Evidence from the Excavations at Tell Er Ras', in idem (ed.), *City, Town and Countryside in the Early Byzantine Era* (New York 1982), 77–9.

modern chronology of Zeus' Neapolitan temple or the bloody history of the Samaritans in this urban orbit, the mosaic of Kastron Mefaa reinstated Neapolis as a classical urban space unaffected by the passage of time.

4. SAMARITANS AND JEWS

Malalas characterized the 529 troubles in Scythopolis as 'ethnic riots' (*taraches ethnikes*). In his reading, Samaritans opposed Jews, as well as Christians, in a striking alignment or realignment.[66] In Scythopolis religious festivals like the Jewish Purim generated tension which rippled all the way to Constantinople.[67] The aggressive behaviour of Christian children in that volatile environment, an expression of ritualized hostility between Christians and Samaritans, was responsible, at least according to Malalas, for the Samaritan outburst in 529 and the brutality of its suppression. Yet, communal enmity was ordinarily channelled through the arena of spectacles and festivities. Difficulty resided in the ability, or incapacity, of the local authorities to judge an event as an expression of routine violence or as a disturbance which merited aggressive intervention.

Whom did Samaritans regard as enemies? The Christian establishment was an obvious cause of discontent and rebellion. Harsh imperial laws were responsible, according to Procopius, for the outbreak of the 529 uprising.[68] From the beginning of the fifth century imperial legislation inserted the Samaritans into a motley group designating the unacceptably non-orthodox.[69] Between 404

---

[66] *Chron.* 18.445.3 (Dindorf) ranges Samaritans versus Christians and Jews; Theophanes, *Chron.* and Cedrenus (Bekker), pp. 646–7, range Jews with Samaritans against Christians. Di Segni, 'Revolts', 476. See the reservations of Y. Dan, who regards Malalas' reference to Jews as a late addition and the late Byzantine sources as fanciful, 'Jewish–Samaritan Relations in Eretz Israel in the Late Byzantine Period (6–7th centuries)', *Zion* 46 (1981), 71–2 (Heb.).

[67] See Ch. 4.

[68] *Anec.* 9.14–30; 27.6–10.

[69] A. M. Rabello, 'The Samaritans in Roman Law', in Stern–Eshel (eds.), *The Samaritans* (2002), 481–95 (Heb.); idem, 'The Samaritans in Justinian's Code 1.5', in A. Tal and M. Florentin (eds.), *Proceedings of the First International Congress of the*

and 553 the government increasingly associated Samaritans, and Jews, with heretics, as though all non-orthodox groups, regardless of the intricacy of their own beliefs, marked the boundaries of religious dissidence.[70] Casting the 'other' as intrinsic to its vision of non-conformity, Constantinople advanced policies of Christian unity based on the rejection of all creeds but orthodoxy. Imperial constitutions accentuated vocabularies of intolerance and hatred which matched the language of physical violence adopted by the Samaritans and exerted by the Romans.

Imperial laws, many of which had to be repeated due to lack of enforcement, imposed restrictions on the capacity of heterodox groups, if persistent in their 'mistaken' ways, to function as integral components of the Christian-Roman commonwealth. The possession of Christian slaves, for example, became a major bone of contention, to judge by the number of laws that address this issue. Service in the imperial administration was severely curtailed, as well as basic rights of bequeathing one's property upon will. Marriage between a Christian and a Jew was likewise banned.[71]

It is difficult, however, to assess the level of application of these laws, and the extent of enforced and voluntary non-participation. There is no way of knowing how many governors responded to the call to enforce the regulations, nor how many 'heretics' (including Jews and Samaritans) were actually hauled to justice and punished. The procedure was not cheap. In the new Justinianic codex of 534 the

---

Société d'Études Samaritaines, Tel Aviv, 1988 (Tel Aviv 1991), 139–46; and 'The Samaritans in Justinian's Corpus Iuris Civilis', *Israel Law Review* 31 (1997), 724 f. (repr. in idem, *The Jews in the Roman Empire: Legal Problems from Herod to Justinian* (Aldershot 2000), no. xi. On Jews in late Roman imperial legislation, Sivan, in 'Canonizing Law' (2002).

[70] Linder, *The Jews in Roman Imperial Legislation*, no. 33 (CTh. 16.8.16, 404, issued by Honorius at Rome); no. 52 (CTh. 16.8.28, 426, issued by Valentinian III at Ravenna) no. 54 (Nov. Theod. 3, 438, issued by Theodosius II at Constantinople); no. 56 (CJ 1.5.12, 527, issued by Justin and Justinian at Constantinople); no. 58 (CJ 1.5.13, 527/8, issued by Justinian and repeating CTh. 16.8.28 of the previous century!); no. 59 (CJ 1.10.2, between 527 and 534, issued by Justinian in Constantinople); no. 60 (CJ 1.5.21, 531, issued by Justinian in Constantinople); no. 64 (Nov. 45, 537, issued by Justinian in Constantinople); no. 65 (Nov. 131, 545, issued by Justinian in Constantinople).

[71] See H. Sivan, 'Rabbinics and Roman Law: Jewish–Gentile (Christian) Marriage in Late Antiquity', *REJ* 156 (1997), 59–100.

emperor banned Samaritans and heretics from teaching (CJ 1.5.18), limited the right of Samaritans to bear testimony (CJ 1.5.21), and designated Samaritan synagogues for destruction (CJ 1.5.17) while exempting Jewish synagogues from the rules of *hospitalitas* (CJ 1.9.4).[72] Such distinctions, undoubtedly a source of the guarded attitude of Jews to the Samaritan revolts, underwent a dramatic change in the middle of the (sixth) century.

Aiming their frustration, in 529, at Christians and at Jews produced therefore an anomaly and a question—did Samaritan–Jewish relations in Christian Palestine imitate anti-Jewish and anti-Samaritan Christian-imperial discourses, or did they evolve their own distinct language? To what extent was interaction between minorities structured by government and by economic, political, judicial, and ideological conditions?

Active displays of violence between minority groups in late ancient Palestine appear rare. Verbal violence is another matter. Rabbinic references to Samaritans (Cutheans/*kuthim*) reflect a turning point around 300.[73] The cause of this estrangement appears to have been Diocletian's command to demonstrate loyalty to the emperor and empire by pouring a libation to the gods. Imperial discrimination kindled fears among rabbis about the acceptability of Samaritan wine since Samaritans, unlike Jews, were not exempt from the imperial law of libation.[74] Before the late third century only wine produced in Samaritan villages adjacent to pagan ones had been forbidden. From about 300 onward all 'Cuthean' wine was considered 'corrupt' and hence forbidden to Jews unless it came in sealed vessels with recognizable seals.[75] In Caesarea, Samaritan wine was banned from Jewish tables.[76] The Palestinian Talmud, in the name of Rabbi Abbahu of

[72] Di Segni, 'Revolts', 477 n. 107. On *hospitalitas* see H. Sivan, 'On *Foederati, Hospitalitas* and the Settlement of the Visigoths in AD 418', *American Journal of Philology* 108 (1987), 759–72.

[73] The history of Jewish–Samaritan relations in late antiquity has a complex ancient history of its own, beginning with the Hebrew Bible, S. Talmon, 'Biblical Traditions on Samaritan History', in Stern–Eshel, *The Samaritans* (2002), 7–27. Montgomery, *The Samaritans.*

[74] *PT AZ* 5.4 (44d).

[75] *PT AZ* 5 (44); *BT AZ* 31a.

[76] Caesarean rabbis would have had plenty of opportunities to observe Samaritans since it is said that they formed the decisive majority in Caesarea in that period, *PT Dem.* 22c, quoted in Stemberger, *Jews and Christians*, 41 n. 7.

Caesarea, stated that since 'the majority of the administration of Caesarea is Samaritan, they must be treated like pagans, in case of pagan festivals'.[77] Rabbinic fears of pollution provided a curious counterpart to the reported obsession of Samaritans with purity.[78] Whether correct or false, the rabbinic belief that Samaritans in the cities were willing to convert rather than to risk their lives was also nurtured by Christians, in spite of repeated violent demonstrations to the contrary.[79] According to the anonymous biographer of Barsauma, a Mesopotamian monk whose 'pilgrimages' in Palestine in the early fifth century were accompanied by clashes with locals and conversion of non-Christians by force, the zealous ascetic managed to convert Samaritans through benign methods of verbal and healing demonstrations. In the city of Sebaste, near Neapolis, he engaged a Samaritan sage in a public debate. When he won the battle of words Barsauma was asked by the locals to prove his healing prowess.[80] He proceeded to dispense an ointment which miraculously cured the wife of the Samaritan man who had lost the disputation. The woman promptly converted to Christianity. The necessity of a miracle suggests initial resistance. Nor did the narrator disclose whether her husband did the same. If need be, Barsauma did not hesitate to resort to threats of bodily violence accentuated by burning sanctuaries. Such pressures were reflected in Samaritan annals which repeatedly referred to moments of forced conversion.[81] In the sixth century, under growing governmental pressure to convert, many Samaritans who refused to convert to Christianity apparently preferred paganism and even Manichaeism.[82] The most famous Samaritan philosopher of late antiquity, Marinus, who taught at the Academy in Athens, 'fell in love with Hellenism'.[83]

[77] *PT AZ* 1.2 (39c), quoted in Stemberger, *Jews and Christians*, 221.

[78] *Anon. Plac.* 136.

[79] Procopius draws distinctions between rural and urban Samaritans, the former, readier to convert under pressure became, somewhat oddly, 'polytheists and Manichees'; the latter preferred to resort to arms *Anec.* 11.29. On these two terms which probably reflect the historian's disdain for Samaritan *conversos*, Di Segni, 'Revolts', 469 n. 71.

[80] Nau, 'Résumé', ROC 9 (1914), 114–15. Barsauma's Palestinian 'excursions' are traditionally dated to the first half of the 5th cent.

[81] Abu'l Fath (Stenhouse), *passim*.

[82] Procopius, *Anec.* 11.26.

[83] Damascius, apud Photius, quoted in M. Stern, *Greek and Latin Authors on Jews and Judaism* (Jerusalem 1980), 673–4.

One bone of doctrinal contention between Jews and Samaritans revolved around the Samaritan denial of the resurrection of the dead, a frequently noted aspect of Samaritanism:[84]

Rabbi Eliezer, son of Rabbi Jose, said: In this matter I refuted the books of the 'sectarians'[85] who maintained that resurrection is not deducible from the Torah. I said to them: 'You falsified the Torah [by omitting the words *to them* from the text],[86] yet it availed you nothing. For you maintain that resurrection is not a biblical doctrine, but it is written: *the soul shall be utterly destroyed, thus his iniquity shall be upon him* (Num. 15: 31). Now, [seeing that] he shall be utterly cut off in this world, when shall his iniquity be upon him? Surely in the world to come!'[87]

Samaritan emendations of the Bible, introduced to suit their strict Pentateuchal theology, were considered by the rabbis as tampering with the sacred text.[88] Yet, it was also possible for Samaritans to be (re)accepted into the Jewish fold providing they renounced three principles, namely their belief in the centrality of Mount Gerizim, their denial of resurrection, and their rejection of Jerusalem.[89] To what extent this call to recant such central issues was answered remains unknown.

Challenging Samaritanism, the rabbis, with the assistance of select biblical passages, threw doubt on the Samaritan association of Mt. Gerizim and Mt. Ebal with Shechem (Neapolis) and relocated the Samaritan sacred precincts to Jericho.[90] But the Samaritans themselves anchored their sacred geography in the Ten Commandments which they extended to include a tenet about Mount Gerizim as the holy of holies:

When the Lord your God has brought you into the land of the Canaanites...you shall set up large stones, coat them with plaster and inscribe

---

[84] Pummer, index, s.v. and below, 139 ff.

[85] 'Minim', an error for 'kuthim' or 'cuthaeans', namely the Samaritans. R. Herford, *Christianity in Talmud and Midrasch* (1903; repr. 1975), 231–4, on the basis of parallel passages in the *Sifre*.

[86] Deut. 11: 21; cf. Deut. 1:8.

[87] *BT San.* 90b, Soncino.

[88] Cf. Samaritan modifications of the Decalogue apud Bowman, *Samaritan Documents*, 9–25.

[89] *Kutim* 28.

[90] *Sifre Deut.* 56; *PT Sota* 29a–b, followed by Eusebius, Epiphanius, and Procopius of Gaza, with Stemberger, *Jews and Christians*, 86.

upon them all the words of this teaching. When you cross the Jordan you shall set up these stones ... on Mount Gerizim. There, too, you shall build an altar to the Lord your God ... that [is the] mountain on the other side of the Jordan ... near Gilgal ... near Shechem.[91]

The poet Marka endowed Mount Gerizim with thirteen names, all based on biblical passages, a few also found in rabbinic sources as names for Jerusalem.[92] In effect, the Pentateuch lent scriptural support to either interpretation regarding the 'chosen place' and Judges 9: 7 specifically placed Mount Gerizim near Shechem (Neapolis).

Another bone of contention between Judaism and Samaritanism was the Samaritan belief that the vessels of the Mosaic Tabernacle were hidden on Mount Gerizim.[93] The rabbis claimed that the Samaritans hid there not the Torah Tablets but idols.[94] The assertion was coloured with stories of travels and travail—once a rabbi who had resolved to embark on a pilgrimage to Jerusalem was harassed by a Samaritan who tried to make him abandon the journey with taunts about the 'mount of rubble' (or dung heap) (i.e. the Temple Mount) and worship instead at the 'mount of blessing' (i.e. Gerizim).[95] Perhaps the destruction of the Temple in 70 and its far-reaching implications for Judaism encouraged the confidence of the Samaritans in the veracity of their own choice of sacred territory.

[91] Passage quoted in Sara Japhet, 'From the King's Sanctuary to the Chosen City', in L. Levine (ed.), *Jerusalem* (New York 1999), 12.

[92] A. Ben-Hayyim, *Tevat Marka: A Collection of Samaritan Midrashim* (Jerusalem 1988), 150–1 (Heb.); MacDonald, *Memar Marqah: The Teaching of Marqah*.

[93] *PT AZ* 5 (44d); *GenR* 81; *DeutR* 3. Epiphanius repeats this assertion, Pummer, 141.

[94] Kippenberg, *Garizim*, 251. Jewish–Samaritan polemics have a long history and the legend of the treasure under Mt. Gerizim goes back at least to the 1st cent. BCE and to the Copper Scroll of Qumran which refers to this contentious point, H. Eshel, 'The Development of the Attribution of Sanctity to Mount Gerizim', in Stern–Eshel, *The Samaritans* (2002), 192–209, esp. 201. See also I. Kalimi and J. D. Purvis, 'The Hiding of the Temple Vessels in Jewish and Samaritan Literature', *CBQ* 56 (1994), 679–85.

[95] *GenR* 81 is the sole version that pits the Temple Mount against Mount Gerizim; the version in *PT AZ* 5 (44d) dispenses with Jerusalem and places the encounter in Neapolis (Shechem). See S. Safrai, 'Jerusalem Pilgrimage' (1980), 388–9 (Heb.).

Several rabbinic passages illustrate the radicalization of Jewish–Samaritan relations in late antiquity such as the harsh sentences pronounced in a midrash, citing Ezra Nehemiah.[96]

Anyone who eats Samaritan bread is as though he has eaten pork. Nor may one convert a Samaritan and further they have no portion in the bodily resurrection, as it is said: 'Not for you but for us' (Ezra 4: 3), not in this world, neither in the world to come. Nor shall they have any portion or inheritance in Jerusalem, as it is said: 'For you shall have neither portion nor justice nor memorial in Jerusalem' (Neh. 2: 20).[97]

Yet, Christian travellers through Samaritan lands emphasized the strict rules of purity which prevailed among Samaritans, who even burnt the footprints of the non-Samaritans who traversed their streets.[98] When negotiating with Christian shoppers, Samaritans did not allow a purchaser to touch the goods before buying them. A buyer, moreover, had to deposit the money in a pool of water before a Samaritan seller would accept it.[99]

In the history of recalcitrance and rebellion which had characterized both Jews and Samaritans under Roman rule, the two groups ordinarily stood alone in moments of violent clash with the authorities. The Samaritans did not lend support to the Jewish revolts either in 66 or in 132. With the possible exception of the 529 rebellion, Jews did not assist Samaritans in the fifth- or sixth-century insurgencies. Jewish reluctance to become involved in the dangerous enterprises undertaken by Samaritans against Christians in Palestine was reflected in the poetry of Yannai, a composer of liturgical poems who lived in the fifth or sixth century. Yannai repeatedly called upon his co-religionists to maintain calm and to suppress defiance.[100] Cautioning prudence, his verses nevertheless hinted at readiness

[96] The compilation is usually considered gaonic (9th cent.) but includes earlier material. Stemberger, *Introduction to the Talmud and Midrash*, 356–7. The late ancient provenance of this passage appears warranted by the assimilation of Samaritans and Christians, as by the objection to Samaritan principles which imperial Roman law also addressed (below).

[97] G. Friedlander (ed. and trans.), *Pirke de Rabbi Eliezer* 38 (London 1916; repr. New York 1981).

[98] *Anon. Plac.* 8.3, apud Pummer, 350–1.

[99] Ibid. 8.4–5.

[100] J. Yahalom, *Poetry and Society in Jewish Galilee of Late Antiquity* (Tel Aviv 1999), 76 (Heb.).

among some to join Samaritan insurrections. He counselled these men not to 'push the end' since Rome's demise would come one day but not at the hands of Samaritans:

> Beware of those around you
> Do not place faith in their plots
> Rather, regard your 'brothers' as your enemies
> Because time will bring an end to your common foe... [101]

Whether this advice was heeded because of its common sense or because of the bitter lessons of the past is difficult to ascertain. The last Jewish stand against Rome, the so-called Gallus revolt of the mid-fourth century, apparently entailed bloody clashes with pagans and with Samaritans.[102] In 529 the Samaritans tried to recruit Persia to their side by promising to provide Chosroes with both Samaritan and Jewish able-bodied men to conquer Palestine.[103] The timing was miscalculated. The results, for the Samaritans, were disastrous.

Driving relentlessly towards a vision of a Mediterranean Christian commonwealth, the emperor Justinian issued, in 553, a lengthy constitution that aspired to regulate synagogue services among Jews (Novella 146).[104] According to its preamble the law was issued in

[101] Ibid. with Piyutei Yanna, 2. p. 125.

[102] The 'Gallus revolt' of the early 350s, when Gallus controlled the eastern provinces, has become a subject of scholarly controversy. From the brief and extremely vague allusions in near-contemporary sources it appears that the anti-government activities extended from Jewish settlements in the Galilee all the way to Lydda. Roman revenge was harsh in the extreme and cities like Sepphoris were completely destroyed. On this elusive episode, Barbara Geller Nathanson, 'The Fourth Century Jewish "Revolt" during the Reign of Gallus', (Ph.D., Duke University 1981). On the absence of evidence attesting calculated destruction in Sepphoris see, Z. Weiss and E. Netzer, *Promise and Redemption: A Synagogue Mosaic from Sepphoris* (Jerusalem 1996), 8. The problem of identifying a layer of destruction is compounded by a well-attested earthquake which took place in 363 that, according to Weiss and Netzer, did destroy the city (ibid. 8–9). See also the reservations of Gabi Bichovsky regarding the value of monetary hordes as indicators of rebellion, 'Numismatic Finds from Synagogues as Evidence of the Gallus Revolt', a lecture given at the conference on *New Studies on the Ancient Synagogue and its World* (Bar Ilan University, 10 June 2004), abstract pp. 22–4. See Ch. 8.

[103] Malalas, *Chron.* 446 (Bonn) (no ref. to Jews); Theophanes, *Chron.* 178–9 (de Boer) (Samaritans and Jews). J. Starr, 'Byzantine Jewry on the Eve of the Arab Conquest (565–638)', *JPOS* 15 (1935), 282 also refers to Jewish–Samaritan collaboration in 555 (below) and 578.

[104] Text and translation in Linder, *Jews in Roman Imperial Legislation*, no. 66. P. T. R. Gray, 'Palestine and Justinian's Legislation on Non-Christian Religions', in

response to internal communal quarrels over the use of languages. The precise location of these linguistic quibbles was not disclosed but most scholars have placed it in Constantinople. The law marked a radical departure from the habits of the chancellery vis-à-vis Jews and, as I believe, Samaritans. One striking novelty was its terminology. Until 553 all laws dealing with Jews and Judaism, and with Samaritans and Samaritanism, had employed the terms *Iudaioi* or *Samaritanoi* respectively.[105] Novella 146 used only the term 'Hebrews'.[106] Scholars have interpreted the denomination as referring to Jews alone; the contents of the law itself suggest that it addressed both Jews and Samaritans.[107] The reversion to biblical terminology, as

B. Halpern and D. W. Hobson (eds.), *Law, Politics and Society in the Ancient Mediterranean World* (Sheffield 1993), 241–70; E. Klingenberg, 'Justinians Novellen zur Judengesetzgebung', *Aschkenas* 8 (1998), 7–27; idem, 'Roman Imperial Legislation Prohibiting Jews from Owning Gentile Slaves', *Jewish Law Association Studies* 4 (1990), 89–98. For a recent reassessment, L. Rutgers, 'Justinian's Novella 146 between Jews and Christians', in R. Kalmin and S. Schwartz, *Jewish Culture and Society* (Leuven 2003), 385–407, who classifies the law as a rhetorical example of intra-Christian polemics which had little or nothing to do with 'real' Jews. W. Horbury, *Jews and Christians in Contact and Controversy* (Edinburgh 1998), 242 links the novella with imperial banning of both the Shema and the Tefilah (the Amidah or Eighteen Benedictions).

[105] The exception was, perhaps, Nov. 139 (Linder no. 63) which deals with polygyny in two localities, one named Sindus komes (the village of Sindus), the other Tyre. The inhabitants of the latter are called 'Hebraii'; there is no ethnic or religious designation for the dwellers of the village. The law could have addressed the custom of both Jews and Samaritans.

[106] Cf. the terminological shift in Theophanes' *Chronography* when reporting the conversion of the Jewish synagogue of the Copper market to a church (AM 5942 (de Boor), p. 159 (*The Chronicle of Theophanes Confessor*, trans., introd., comm. C. Mango and R. Scott, Oxford 1997), and his reference to Justin's appropriation of the same synagogue, the synagogue of the Hebrews in the Chalkoprateia, in 576–7 in order to build a church there (AM 6069 (de Boor); p. 367 (Magno/Scott). A. Panayotov, 'The Synagogue in the Copper Market of Constantinople: A Note on the Christian Attitudes towards Jews in the Fifth Century', *OCP* 68 (2002), 319–34. Cf. the use of the terms 'Jews' and 'Hebrews' in Eusebius for whom 'Jews' proper, unlike the 'Hebrews', took their origin from Judah, 'from whose tribe the kingdom of the Jews was established long afterwards' (*PE* 7.6.2). The 'Hebrews' were then the pre-Mosaic friends of God who had adhered to purely ethical monotheism while the Jews were those who kept the Mosaic law, or Judaism (*DE* 4.17.5; *PE* 1.6.2, 6; 7.6–8; 7.7.1; cf. Josephus, *Ant.* 1.5), which was too localized (in Jerusalem) to suit a worldwide movement (*DE* 1.3) like Christianity whose principles were universal (*PE* 7.8.37).

[107] Modern observers have emphasized similarities between Jewish and Samaritan midrashic traditions, the dependence of Samaritan beliefs on Jewish institutions, and the difficulties of distinguishing between Jewish and Samaritan synagogues, Z. Safrai,

though to suppress living Jews and living Samaritans, recalled the criticism that contemporaries, like Procopius of Gaza, levelled at Justinian's Jewish policy, which included a ban on celebrating Passover if the feast happened to precede Easter in any given year.[108]

The novella attempted to build linguistic bridges between non-Christian believers and Scriptures. It charted a new territory in the sphere of governmental intervention, reflecting imperial determination to appropriate the text most holy to all three communities, Christian, Jewish, and Samaritan. Justinian extolled a direct and unmediated approach to the text which dispensed with erudite interpreters. The constitution claimed that 'it is commonly agreed that one raised up on the Holy Books is far readier to discern and to choose what is better... than he who does not understand a thing in them but clings only to the name of religion (*onoma threskeia*) as though held by holy anchors'.[109] The novella insisted on the reading of Scripture in Greek, if Greek was the preferred language of the congregation, so as to enable everyone to form her/his own interpretation. It further accused experts, *exegetai*, of maliciously falsifying the Scriptures, thus undermining the kind of expertise that ensured compliance with internal communal rules.

One item of the law addressed doctrinal principles, specifically castigating those who denied the resurrection, the Last Judgment, and the existence of angels, three fundamentals of Christianity. It would be difficult, not to say impossible, to associate the denial of these tenets with the Judaism(s) of late antiquity.[110] But these are precisely the principles, or rather their absence which, rightly or wrongly, both Jewish sages and Christian theologians associated

---

'Samaritan Synagogues in the Roman-Byzantine Period', *Cathedra* 4 (1977), 84–112 (Heb.).

[108] Procopius, *Anec.* 28.16–19. On this legislation, J. Juster *Les Juifs dans l'empire romain*, 2 vols. (Paris 1914), i. 282–3, 356–7 and the new interpretation of S. Stern, *Calendar and Community* (Oxford, 2001), 85–7, who regards it as primarily an anti-Novatian rather than anti-Jewish law.

[109] Linder, for text and translation.

[110] On Jewish worship of angels in late antiquity, Clement of Alexandria, *Stromata* 6.5.41; M. Simon, 'Remarques sur l'angélolatrie juive au début de l'ère chrétienne', *Comptes rendues de l'Académie des Incriptions et Belles Lettres* (1971), 120–34; M. Smith, 'Helios in Palestine', *Eretz Israel* 16 (1982), 199–214; Origen, *Contra Celsum* 1.26, 5.6. Roussin, 'The Zodiac in Synagogue Decoration', 90–2.

with Samaritanism.[111] Origen and Epiphanius, as well as the Babylonian Talmud, asserted that the Samaritans denied the resurrection
of the dead.[112] The truth of the matter is not so easily established. The
resurrection of the dead, as well as the last judgement and ultimate
revenge were components of Samaritan eschatology in late antiquity.
So was angelology although there is a debate whether references to
angels *in loco Dei* in the Samaritan Pentateuch indicated an actual
belief or a scrupulous avoidance of even a hint of polytheism.[113]

Barsauma's biography lends corroboration to the swift legal association of these doctrinal issues with Samaritans and not with Jews:

On a Sabbath Barsauma reached a Samaritan city where the inhabitants
denied the resurrection, and the Son of God, saying that there is neither
Holy Spirit nor angels... The Samaritans do not accept any book of the
Bible other than the Law of Moses... [114]

Justinian's novella imposed exile on those who denied resurrection,
the Last Judgment, or the existence of angels so as to 'completely
purify the nation of the Hebrews (*ethnos ton hebraion*) from the error
introduced into it'. It also authorized the application of corporal
penalties, confiscation of property, and banishment in cases of resistance to the 'liberty' which the law granted in linguistic matters
within the sacred realm of the synagogue.

These verbal attacks on Judaism and Samaritanism, both cast as
deluded 'Hebrews', provided Jews and Samaritans in Palestine with
a common cause which, for the first time in centuries, united them
in anti-governmental demonstrations. In 554/5 Jews and Samaritans in the city of Caesarea rose against Rome. Malalas, the main
source for these events, failed to furnish a specific reason, but the
proximity of the events he narrated to the issuance of Novella 146,
and the location of the events in the Palestinian capital suggest that
the spark was provided by an attempt to extend the law's sphere of

---

[111] Epiphanius, *Haer.* 13.1.1, apud Pummer, 153.

[112] Origen, Homily on Numbers 25: 1 (*PG* 12. 763), Epiphanius, *Pan.* 9.2.3 (*GCS*
25, 198). *BT San.* 90b. F. Dexinger, 'The Beliefs of the Samaritans in the Byzantine
Period' in Stern–Eshel, *The Samaritans* (2002), 516–17 (Heb.).

[113] Dexinger, 517–18. The Torah refers to God as Elohim, a plural noun, and the
Samaritan Pentateuch uses the word 'angels'.

[114] Nau, 'Résumé', *ROC* 9 (1914), 118, referring to the monk's third 'pilgrimage' to
Jerusalem in 435–8.

application to Palestine. So unusual was the Samaritan–Jewish partnership against Rome that Malalas described it as the ganging up of circus factions.[115] In reality, it may have been just that. Caesarea was renowned for its hippodrome. A race might have elicited a verbal clash which inspired the use of a vocabulary that transformed a protest into a violent demonstration of civil unrest and sedition.[116]

The characterization of the Caesarean episode as circus riots underscored a constellation of paradoxes inherent in a spectacle of Jews and Samaritans as Blues and Greens, as well as the inherent danger in such sporting assemblies.[117] True to pattern, the circus riots turned to attacks on Christians and on churches in Caesarea, this time the rioters killing not the bishop but the governor. In another version of the same events Malalas described the sanctuaries under attack as 'churches of the orthodox' as though careful distinction was drawn by the attackers in matters of internal Christian doctrinal strife. The emperor ordered an investigation into the killing of the governor. Those found guilty were hanged or beheaded, others had their hands cut off, and yet others suffered loss of property. A swift and brutal end obscured the true significance of the alleged Samaritan–Jewish collaboration in Caesarea in 555/6. While such a course of action tallied with the history of the Samaritans in late antiquity, Jewish reactions to the strictures of imperial laws remain unrecorded.[118] If Malalas' assertion was correct, the Jewish

[115] Pummer, 268. Y. Dan, 'The Circus and its Factions in Eretz Israel during the Byzantine Period', *Cathedra* 4 (1977), 142–6 (Heb.); Al. Cameron, *Circus Factions* for the larger picture.

[116] Caesarea's hippodrome, perhaps the initial scene of the 'revolt', was one of the best known arenas in the Near East (with those of Antioch, Laodicea, Berythus, and Tyre), *Expositio Totius Mundi* 32 (Rouge); and J. H. Humphrey, 'Prolegomena to the Study of the Hippodrome at Caesarea Maritima', *BASOR* 213 (1974), 31–45.

[117] An inscription from Jerusalem (5th/6th cent.) refers to the Blues, P. Thomsen, 'Die lateinischen und griechischen Inschriften der Stadt Jerusalem', *ZDPV* 44 (1921), 6–7, no. 10, and idem, *ZDPV* 64 (1941), 208, no. 10; *SEG* viii. 213; as does another, from Umm idj-Djimal in southern Hauran and from Taff in the Trachon, E. Littman, D. Magie, and D. R. Stuart, *Princeton University Archaeological Expedition to Syria*, III A (Princeton 1921), p. 149; Al. Cameron, *Porphyrius*, 74–8.

[118] The building of synagogues throughout the Galilee and the Golan may be considered a form of response, if indeed these date to the 6th cent., as has been recently maintained by Jodi Magness. See also Ch. 2.

participation in the Caesarean uprising of 555/6 was the first instance in two centuries of active resistance to imperial proscriptions.[119]

Novella 146 bonded Jews and Samaritans as enemies of the Christian faith. The actions of Jews and Samaritans in Caesarea in 555/6 displayed a desperate reciprocity of perception. When an intrepid pilgrim engaged in buying merchandise from Samaritans, they treated him as though Christianity and Christians were the polluting elements of the land.[120] The edict against the liturgical traditions of Jews and against Samaritan doctrines was meant to facilitate conversion to Christianity. It transformed axes of religious and political allegiance into opposing camps and was instrumental in the formation of a religious discourse increasingly intolerant of Jews and of Samaritans.

The discourse of recalcitrance and resistance that characterized Samaritans in late antiquity was caught between two reefs. On one side ranged a repetition of governmental legal statements that disadvantaged and condemned; on the other stood the uniqueness that Judaism assumed vis-à-vis Samaritanism. As though the land produced its own rhythm of rebellion, the Samaritans replaced the Jews as bearers of recalcitrance and revolt. The lessons which the failures of two Jewish revolts had generated were forgotten. Barely a decade after the troubles of 555/6 the government called upon Photius, Belisarius' stepson, who had been installed as the head of the Nea monastery in Jerusalem, to suppress an otherwise unrecorded Samaritan rebellion.[121] When not engaged in anti-Samaritan activities Photius fought Monophysites and financed his operations through extortion. The two hats of this imperial representative, monastic and military, reflected the complexity of the landscape of conflict in late ancient Palestine.

---

[119] A vague reference of Theod. Anag. recalls a Jewish riot in Caesarea, during the reign of Theodosius II (*c.*440) in the course of which several Christians were killed (*HE* 336, ed. G. C. Hansen).

[120] *Anon. Plac.* 8, and above, 129.

[121] John of Ephesus, *HE (pars tertia)*, 1.32; 2.29–39, 69–70 (ed. E. W. Brooks) (CSCO 106. Script. Syri 55; Louvain 1952). Di Segni, 'Samaritan Revolts', in Stern–Eshel (2002), 479–80.

4

Contesting the Sacred:
Forms of Ritualized Violence

1. POLITICS OF MEMORY AND OF FORGETFULNESS

The feast of Purim commemorates a biblical fantasy—a contest of wits between a beautiful and resourceful Jewish queen and a wily gentile court minister in Persia. At stake was the very survival of the Jews in the Persian empire.[1] He (Haman) plots to kill them all; she (Esther) counterplots to save them all. The power to judge is deposited in the hands of a pleasure-seeking monarch (Ahasuerus) who is also, not coincidentally, Esther's husband as well as Haman's patron. The fate of the Jews is decided in the course of a banquet which Esther hosts with Haman as its unlikely guest of honour. Virtue, in this case female and Jewish, wins; and evil, in the shape of a short-tempered and conceited gentile, loses. The scroll of Esther 7: 10 records the hanging of Haman (as does Esther 8: 7); and Esther 9: 14 refers to the hanging of his ten sons. The essence of the biblical celebration is neatly summed up as 'days in which the Jews gained respite from their enemies, when sorrow turned into gaiety and mourning into a holiday; days of feasting and fun, of exchanging edible gifts and of displaying charity towards the poor' (Esther 9: 22). Purim is the one day in the year when Jews are urged, indeed commanded, to get drunk. But Purim, in the scroll of Esther, is also accompanied by an extraordinary outburst of violence directed against those identified as 'enemies' and 'Jew-haters' (Esther 9: 16), a

---

[1] On the scroll of Esther, see my *Dinah's Daughters: Gender and Judaism from the Hebrew Bible to Late Antiquity* (Philadelphia 2002), Ch. 3.

textual aspect which has made Christian commentators distinctly uneasy.[2]

On 29 May 408 Purim became the object of an imperial law:

Emperors Honorius and Theodosius Augusti to Anthemius, Pretorian Prefect:
The governors of the provinces shall prohibit the Jews from setting fire to (H)aman in memory of his past punishment during a certain ceremony of their festival, and from burning with sacrilegious intent (*sacrilega mente*) a form cast in the shape of a holy cross (*species adsimulata sanctae crucis*) in contempt of the Christian faith (*christiana fides*), lest they mingle the sign of our faith (*fidei nostrae signum*) with their jests (*iocis*). They shall also restrain their rituals (*ritus*) from ridiculing Christian law (*christiana lex*) because if they do not abstain from matters which are forbidden they will promptly lose what had been thus far permitted to them.[3]

Where, precisely, these feasts were celebrated; who had been the government informants regarding their allegedly anti-Christian character; and why the emperor(s), with one (Theodosius II) barely a few days on the throne, chose this specific moment to censure the festivities, was not specified. The ruling indicates that by the beginning of the fifth century Purim was perceived as an occasion generating self-conscious religious tension rather than light-hearted gaiety. The language of the law encased imageries which presupposed Purim a Jewish act of violent sacrilege culminating in a mock re-enactment of the crucifixion.[4]

---

[2] Luther's hatred for the scroll was notorious, as that of earlier Christian theologians, C. A. Moore, *Esther* (The Anchor Bible Commentaries; Garden City 1971), pp. xxv–xxxi. Visual images relating to Purim are rare even within a Jewish context, the Dura Purim panel being an exception, H. Sivan, *Biblical Images: The Dura Europos Synagogue. Guide to the exhibit* (New Haven 1978).

[3] CTh. 16.8.18 (=CJ 1.9.11), in A. Linder, *The Jews in Roman Imperial Legislation*, 236–8 (transl. slightly modified): *Iudaeos quodam festivitatis suae sollemni Aman ad poenae quondam recordationem incendere et sanctae crucis adsimulatam speciem in contemptum Christianae fidei sacrilega mente exurere provinciarum rectores prohibeant, ne iocis (or: locis) suis fidei nostrae signum inmisceant, sed ritus suos citra contemptum Christianae legis retineant, amissuri sine dubio permissa hactenus nisi ab inlicitis temperaverint.*

[4] E. Horowitz, 'The Rite to be Reckless: On the Perpetration and Interpretation of Purim Violence', *Poetics Today* 15 (1994), 9–54 for a brief overview of Purim 'violence' throughout the ages. Also idem, *Reckless Rites: Purim as the Legacy of Jewish Violence* (Princeton 2006).

Singling out Purim, perhaps the least Jewish of all Jewish calendrical feasts, the imperial decree seemed emblematic of an atmosphere of growing imperial intolerance vis-à-vis Jewish practices in late antiquity. The law crystallized a moment of visual and verbal clash created by contrasting interpretations of the biblical text in different religious communities. One group, Jewish, used the holiday to recall the bitter-sweet fortunes of the past; the other, Christian, projected a different order of reality in which crucial events in biblical 'history' were seen to signify abuse rather than victory. CTh. 16.8.18 is unusual because it invoked credal differences in order to warrant intervention in what amounted to theatrical intracommunal polemics. According to a rabbinic midrash, gentiles in Palestine's capital Caesarea used precisely the same methods which Purim promoted to ridicule Jewish customs in public:

Rabbi Abbahu (of Caesarea, *c.*300) opened his discourse with the text '*They that sit in the gate talk of me*' (Psalm 69: 13). This, he said, refers to the nations of the world [i.e. gentiles] who sit in theaters and circuses … and as they eat, drink and become intoxicated, they scoff [at the Jews] … They take a camel into their theaters, they put their shirts upon it, and ask one another: 'Why is it mourning?', to which they reply, 'The Jews observe the law of the sabbatical year and have no vegetables, so they eat this camel's thorns, and that is why it is in mourning'. They [the gentiles] next bring a corpse with a shaven head into the theatre, asking one another: 'Why is his head shaven?' To which they reply: 'The Jews observe the Sabbath and whatever they earn during the week they eat on the Sabbath. Since they have no wood to cook with, they break their bedsteads and use them as fuel. As a result they sleep on the ground, covered with dust and then anoint themselves with oil [to prevent bad smell?]. Consequently oil has become expensive' [hence they shave their heads to spare oil consumption] … [5]

[5] *LamR Proem.* 17 (= 3.5) (ed. Vilnah and Buber). Eng. trans. A. Cohen, *Midrash Rabbah: Lamentation* (London 1939; repr. 1961), slightly modified. The possibility that these 'gentiles' were Christians and not pagans, as has generally been assumed, cannot be excluded in light of the enormous popularity of mimes as public entertainment in Caesarea in the 4th cent. (*Expositio Totius Mundi* 32) and in other places, such as Gaza, as late as the 6th cent. where a famed orator, Choricius of Gaza, rose to its defence (*Apologia Mimorum*). Some of these mimes ridiculed also Christian rites like baptism, see Ch. 8 below, and S. Elm, 'Marking the Self in Late Antiquity: Inscriptions, Baptism, and the Conversion of Mimes', in B. Vinken and B. Menken (eds.), *Stigmata* (Weimar 2003), 47–68, and R. Lim, 'Converting the Un-Christianizable: The Baptism of Stage Performers in Late Antiquity', in Mills and Grafton (eds.),

Jewish texts of late antiquity unfolded a remarkable competitive energy with regards to the Esther-Purim scroll which, despite its relative brevity, spawned one of the richest stores of talmudic, midrashic, and early rabbinic literature connected with any book of Scripture.[6] Already in the first century CE biblical exegesis associated Purim with Passover as twin poles of Jewish hopes for national redemption:

On the fourteenth and fifteenth of [Adar] are the days of Purim, on which mourning is prohibited. These are days on which miracles were performed for Israel through Mordechai and Esther who established them as festival days. Rabbi Yehoshua ben Qarha (2nd century) said: 'Since the days of Moses no prophet has endeavoured to establish a new ordinance except for the ordinance of Purim, even though the redemption from Egypt is commemorated for seven [days] and the redemption of Mordechai and Esther is commemorated in a single day'. Another exposition: 'If in the case of the redemption from Egypt a decree [of destruction] was issued only against males (Exod. 1: 22), and the result was that they established these as festival days [i.e. Passover], how much more [appropriate], in the case of the redemption of Mordechai and Esther, when a decree [of destruction] was issued for both males and females (Esther 3: 13), is the obligation to observe these as festival days every year!'[7]

Conversion, 84–126. Besides social relations, themes of mimes also included perennial 'burning' issues like adultery, R. W. Reynolds, 'The Adultery Mime', *CQ* 40 (1946), 77–84, and P. H. Kehoe, 'The Adultery Mine Reconsidered', in D. F. Bright and E. S. Ramage, *Classical Texts and their Traditions: Studies in Honor of C. R. Trahman* (Chico 1984), 89–106. The rabbinic quasi refrain from using the words Christ and Christian may be compared with a similar attitude on the part of Libanius who never uses these terms even when he obliquely alludes to Christianity. F. Millar, 'Libanius and the Near East', *Scripta Classica Israelitica* 26 (2007), 170.

    [6] In general, I. Davidson, *Parody in Jewish Literature* (New York 1907). For medieval exegesis see also B. D. Walfish, *Esther in Medieval Garb: Jewish Interpretation of the Book of Esther in the Middle Ages* (Albany 1993). L. Ginzberg, *The Legends of the Jews* (Philadelphia 1909–38), iv. 299–402 remains basic.
    [7] *Megillat Taanit*, 12 (adar), quoted in M. G. Wechsler, 'The Purim-Passover Connection: A Reflection of Jewish Exegetical Tradition in the Peshitta Book of Esther', *JBL* 117 (1998), 324 n. 12. On the contested date of this source, B.-Z. Lurie, *Megillath Taanith* (Jerusalem 1964) (Heb.). See now V. Noam-Elizup, *Megilat Taanit* (Jerusalem 2003) (Heb.). Rabbinic appreciation of the message of Purim is also reflected in *PT Meg.* 1.5: 'Rabbi Abbahu in the name of rabbi Eleazar: "The reference to 'each and every year' (Es. 9: 27) serves to draw an analogy from a year which is intercalated to one which is not intercalated, with the result that we come to the following conclusion: just as in a year which is not intercalated Adar is next to Nisan, so in a year which is intercalated Adar is next to Nisan." Said Rabbi Helbo: "It is so as to link up one redemption with another."' This attitude is especially instructive in view of the debate regarding the admission of the scroll of Esther into the canonized

The rabbis also 'updated' the events which the scroll had narrated to include ritual cursing of gentiles (later Christians).[8] Of these modifications, the most striking was the assimilation of Haman with Christ through a common mode of death by crucifixion. Esther referred to Haman's lot as hanging; in *Genesis Rabbah* the protagonists, Jews and gentiles alike, faced crucifixion.[9] The association might have been prompted by the Septuagint, which 'translated' the scroll's reference to hanging as crucifixion.[10]

Late ancient Palestinian poetry (*piyyut*) provides the most poignant articulation of Purim as a ritual containing both a recreation of biblical 'events' and a re-enactment of its message of salvation through a 'violent' climax.[11] Written in Hebrew and Aramaic these compositions attest the polemical nature of the passionate and continuing attachment of Palestinian Jews to their national festivals.[12]

Hebrew Bible (*BT Meg.* 7a), see Z. S. Leiman, *The Canonization of Hebrew Scriptures: The Talmudic and Midrashic Evidence* (Hamden, Conn. 1976), 120–6; J. Tabory, *Jewish Festivals in the Time of the Mishnah and Talmud* (Jerusalem 1995), 323–67 (Heb.).

[8] The cursing may have had long antecedents, A. Damascelli, 'Croce, maledizione e redenzioni: Un'eco di Purim in Galati 3.13', *Henoch* 23 (2001), 227–41. On Purim's cursing of Haman, T. C. G. Thornton, 'The Crucifixion of Haman and the Scandal of the Cross', *JTS* 37 (1986), 419–26 and idem, *JTS* 38 (1987), 419–31.

[9] *GenR* 30: 8: 'Mordechai was yesterday ready to be crucified; and now he crucifies his would-be crucifiers'. Cf. *LevR* 28: 6 'When Esther heard how matters stood she issued a proclamation throughout the province, saying: "Let no one open his shop in the market. Let all the people go out, for the head of the Jews is about to be crucified"' (Eng. trans. J. J. Slotki, *Midrash Rabbah: Leviticus* (London 1939; repr. 1961), modified. The date of the composition of these *midrashim* has been hotly debated. Most scholars believe that they date to the 5th cent., if not earlier, M. Margulies, *Midrash Vayyikra Rabbah* (Jerusalem 1960), part v, pp. xxxi–xxxiii.

[10] Thornton, 'Crucifixion', 419–26, traces Christian traditions which comment on the Jewish Purim custom of 'crucifying' Haman. None is earlier than Jerome (*c.*400) and all may depend on both the LXX and Jewish exegesis. For the medieval context see C. Roth, 'The Feast of Purim and the Origins of Blood Accusations', *Speculum* 8 (1933), 520–6; and also W. Wind, 'The Crucifixion of Haman', *Journal of the Warburg Institute* 1 (1937), 245–8. I do not deal with the affair at Imstar which took place outside Palestine and later than the law (Soz. *HE*).

[11] M. Sokoloff and J. Yahalom, *Jewish Palestinian Aramaic Poetry from Late Antiquity. Critical Edition with Introduction and Commentary* (Jerusalem 1999), 170–219 (Heb.).

[12] On the employment of Aramaic especially as a vehicle of public lament, Yahalom, *Poetry and Society in Jewish Galilee of Late Antiquity,* 50–9 (Heb.), and idem, 'Angels do not Understand Aramaic: On the Literary Use of Jewish Palestinian Aramaic in Late Antiquity', *JJS* 47 (1996), 33–44. On rabbinic opposition to the use of Aramaic in prayer, *BT Sotah* 33a with Yahalom, *Poetry and Society,* 53–4.

The Aramaic Purim poems reveal assumptions and tensions implicit in contemporary modes of religious intolerance and tolerance. They articulate the ambiguity of Jewish existence. Substantiating the continued viability of the Jews in their ancestral land and elsewhere through tenacious adherence to traditional festivities, the words of the *piyyutim* also project conditions for their collective destruction. A moment of impending tragedy looms large at the start of the biblical tale of Esther: 3: 6 records Haman's design to kill all the Jews of Persia because of the affront of a single man, Mordechai the Jew (Esther's 'cousin'). Taking a clue from this ominous beginning, one Purim poet of late antiquity marshalled the entire biblical past in search of gentiles who, like Haman, acted as tragic signifiers who came to grief. The poetic text, basically a burlesque, paraded biblical gentiles from Nimrod (Gen. 10: 9) through the Pharaoh of Egypt (Exod. 1) and Sanherib the Assyrian (2 Kgs. 18) to Nebuccadnezzar the Babylonian (2 Kgs. 25). To these gentile potentates the poem joined Shimshi the scribe (Ezra 4: 8), a man whom midrashic mutations amalgamated with one of Haman's sons, sending both to the cross.[13] The poem ended with an invocation which called on God (who had been conspicuously absent from the biblical scroll), to help Israel by bringing calamity to the Romans and (?) the Arabs:

Let the Lord of Heaven revive these miracles
Let God bring, now, in these days salvation to beloved children
Let the hour draw near when the nation is redeemed
And when gladness abides...
And just as once it was in Shushan (Susa) the capital,
Let the Lord look with mercy from heaven
And redeem the beloved nation from seventy [hostile] peoples.
Let the One who had settled accounts with these also annihilate the others;
Let the Lord inflict revenge on Romans and [Saracens]...[14]

[13] Poem 1 line 41 (Sokoloff–Yahalom, p. 173), and ibid. on Shimshi's midrashic interpretation.
[14] Sokoloff–Yahalom, *piyyut* 26, lines 42–9. Unless otherwise stated, the translations are mine. The reference to the Saracens (Arabs) may well be a reworking of an earlier and different denomination. The phenomenon of various transmissions is well documented for synagogal poetry, Sivan, *GRBS* 2000. The use of the term 'Saracens' is interesting. It is used in *GenR* (commentary on Gen. 18: 2) where Rabbi Lewi (*c.*300), commenting on the three 'angels that Abraham saw', classifies them as an Arab, Nabataean, and a Saracen. The reference may constitute the earliest reference to the Saracens, Jan Retsö, *The Arabs in Antiquity*, 529.

Dividing the world into a hostile, anti-Jewish half, and a defenceless Jewish half, the poet connected the two through divine justice. The adversaries of the past, represented by specific biblical individuals, became the general category of the present, namely 'Romans' or 'Arabs', abstractions of all the forces which chose the language of violence over words. With the crucifixion of the arch villain, Haman, poetic justice was achieved as the poem reached a violent resolution.[15]

Haman and Christ emerge as two sides of the same coin, a point which another Purim poem drives home through a comic competition among trees over the 'honour' of furnishing the wood for Haman's cross.[16] In the proem the poet positioned Haman as a man in search of Christ not for spiritual sustenance but as a sharer of his ultimate fate:

> Listen to me, O trees and all the plants
> Which had been sown since the beginning of the world:
> The son of Hamadan [sc. Haman] sought to go up
> To the Alexandria[17] of the son of Pantera... [18]

Why Alexandria? Rabbinic sources (*T Hul.* 2.24; *BT AZ* 16b–17a) identified the 'son of Pantera' with 'the son of the cross' (Ben Stara, *stauros*), namely Jesus, who went to Egypt, land of witchcraft and sorcery, in search of training in magical practices:[19]

Rabbi Eliezer said to the sages: He is Ben Stara who brought sorcery out of Egypt by tattooing [its secrets] on his body. They responded: He was a fool and one does not bring a proof [based on what] fools [do]. Who is the son of Stara? He is the son of Pantera' (*BT Shab.* 104b).

Perhaps Alexandria had a specific relevance to the locality where the recitation of the *piyyut* took place and where the Purim that prompted the imperial law took place. Since the city is not

---

[15] Cf mimic laughter at the crucifixion, Elm ('Marking the Self'), above, n. 9.

[16] Sokoloff–Yahalom, *piyyut* 29, pp. 183–7.

[17] Reading unclear; see Sokoloff–Yahalom, 183. On the possibility that 'Alexandria' is indeed the correct reading, 160 ff.

[18] Sokoloff–Yahalom, *piyyut* 29.1–4, p. 183.

[19] D. Rokeah, 'Ben Stara who is Ben Pantera: Towards the Clarification of a Philological Historical Problem', *Tarbiz* 39 (1970), 9–18 (Heb.). The Egyptian link is based on a single, late reference to the flight into Egypt (Matt. 2: 15–23). On Nilotic scenes which contain a stylized image of Alexandria, see pp. 160, 165.

mentioned in the biblical narrative of Purim (i.e. the scroll of Esther) its inclusion in the *piyyut* points to contemporary events and locations that appealed to the poet and to the poem's immediate audience in Palestine itself.

As the poem weaves a complex network of images borrowed from other associative sequences, primarily the Hebrew Bible, nature is appointed to 'unite' Haman and Jesus, the two enemies of Jews and Judaism. One by one the trees refused to part with their wood, each asserting a preferential function.[20] The vine excused itself because it has a vital role as provider of wine for libation; the fig tree preferred to produce fruit for celebrations and primordial clothing; the olive tree insisted on supplying only oil; the palm tree refused on ideological grounds; and the oak claimed that it had fulfilled its appointed 'historical' role by providing a lasting rest place for Rebecca's wetnurse and by ensnaring Absalom (Gen. 35: 8; 2 Sam. 18: 9). Only the thorn bush, devoid of any nutritional function, 'volunteered' to become the cross.[21] Themes of fertility and sterility are implicit in these evocations of nature's fecundity, its destructive aspects, and of human fertility (Gen. 35: 8). The biblical scroll ridicules nature's unwarranted bounty in Haman's case because his sons do not reach maturity just as his evil designs are aborted; the Purim poem mocks the futility of anti-Jewish enterprises and the sterility of Christianity.

Esther 1 opened with a royal display of abundance of food and drink, shared by all the dwellers of the Persian capital. The Purim

[20] Cf. the 'discussion' regarding an appropriate tree for a wooden idol, *DeutR* p. 56 (Lieberman) with the discussion in Lieberman, *Hellenism in Jewish Palestine*, 116. Cf. Targum Sheni in which the citron, one of the four Succoth species, asks that Haman will not be hung off its tree, M. Kasher, *Torah Shlema: Megilat Esther* (Jerusalem 1994), pp. 326–7, 362–3 (Heb.). Disputation-poems between personified objects, such as cedar and vine, and gold and wheat, are also known in late ancient Syriac, S. Brock, 'Syriac Dispute Poems: The Various Types', in G. J. Reinink and H. L. J. Vanstiphout (eds.), *Dispute Poems and Dialogues in the Ancient and Medieval Near East* (Leiden 1991), 109–19.

[21] The poem is fragmentary but the lacunae are easily combed through other versions of the same 'contest'. Note also that in a different context a (burning) bush is selected as a scene of divine revelation, a selection which the rabbis explain 'because the bush is clean and the gentiles do not make it an idol' (Mekhilta deRashbi, p. 2, Hoffmann), and specifically, as medieval rabbis and Theodoret argued, because it is impossible to carve from the bush a face of an image (Theodoret, *PG* 80. 229c), with Lieberman, *Hellenism*, 116 n. 11.

poem which dwelt on these verses emphasized not universal participation but rather the refusal of a single subject to share in the
common festivities:

> Once upon a time there was a Jew in Sushan (Susa), a veritable Jew,
> Mordechai, 'pure-myrrh'.[22]
> Many were the Jews in Shushan, the imperial capital.
> And all of them shared in the [royal] banquet.
> Therefore no longer were they considered Jews.
> Men and women, [members] of the beloved nation,
> How they mingled amongst gentiles!
> Only Mordechai did not eat; him therefore the One chose,
> And to him the One said: You alone can be called 'a Jew'.[23]

The harmony projected in the biblical scroll is thrown into conflict
and the cause of the disruption is not, as Esther 1 asserts, the refusal
of the king's wife to join the all-male banquet but the non-compli-
ance of a Jewish man.

Two antagonistic approaches emerge as the poem positions Jewish
ecumenism versus separatism. Because delicacies and intoxicating
drinks were crucial aspects of the Purim holiday, its rituals also
paved a road to communal conciliation, glossing over intra-Jewish
polemics and inviting wider communal participation. Purim's hilar-
ity bestowed a temporary freedom which ascribed a common tonal-
ity to the forbidden. There is a religious ceremony, namely the
reading of the scroll in synagogues, and a day of rejoicing unfit for
any other activities other than eating, drinking, and making merry.
This is a moment of liberation that frees the entire community,
Jewish and gentile, from strains of division. CTh. 16.8.18 implies
that the feast attracted non-Jews. The law betrays fear of Christians
sharing, unwittingly, in rituals which mocked Christianity, and,
paradoxically, of potential pollution through close contacts with
non-Christians during these public spectacles.[24]

---

[22] The poet plays on the meaning of the name Mor-dechai (myrrh and purity).
[23] Sokoloff–Yahalom, *piyyut* 30.1–8, p. 187.
[24] Cf. episcopal criticism of Christians participating in pagan religious festivities, such as the Lupercalia; Gelasius, *Lettre contre les Lupercales et dix-huit messes du sacramentaire léonien* (Paris 1959); Augustine, *Sermon* Dolbeau 26, in F. Dolbeau (ed.), *Vingt-Six Sermons aux peuples d'Afrique* (Paris 1996), 345–417, with B. Caseau, 'Sacred Landscapes', in G. W. Bowersock *et al.* (eds.), *Interpreting Late Antiquity* (Cambridge, Mass., 1999, 2001), 27.

Nor was the imperial court altogether erroneous. Religious festivals, whether Jewish celebrations of biblical miracles or Christian festivals honouring martyrs and saints, articulated pride in the *patria* where the occasion took place. The dynamism and dimension of such festivities is reflected in descriptions of the events surrounding the feast of St Stephen in late ancient Gaza. A festival honouring the proto-martyr consisted of processions through the market place and central streets of the town, of numerous visitors and inhabitants lining the streets to behold the sights and to hail the march, of markets and even of nocturnal spectacles consisting of mimes and theatrical performances.[25]

Purim is also a memory of vengeance, one that cannot be erased and is ever present. The last poem in the Purim cycle, a closure which reasserted the call for redemption, culminated in a verbal confrontation between Haman and Jesus. Once again Haman proclaimed his intimate affinity with other biblical figures who had plotted the annihilation of Israel. But in this poem Haman was firmly embedded in contemporary Palestinian context as 'the fool of Scythopolis (Beth Shean)', a phrase that contained a double allusion, one to Jesus whom the rabbis likened to a fool (*BT Shab.* 104b), the other to the capital of Palaestina Secunda. Haman was cast as an evil man of low origin who hoped to curry favour at court by maligning Jews.[26] In this Purim poem Haman becomes the object of a harangue by another 'deluded' Palestinian, Jesus (here called the 'anonymous'), who sets out to dispel Haman's delusion about the uniqueness of his execution:

Do you really believe that you alone were crucified?
I too shared your lot!
Fastened unto wood, my image in churches (?) is painted unto wood.
Nailed to a cross, my flesh slashed at hand-breadth length,

[25] Choricius Gazae, *Marc.* ii and iii, with F. K. Litsas, 'Choricius of Gaza and his Descriptions of Festivals at Gaza', *Jahrbuch des österreichischen Byzantinistik* 32 (1982), 427–36.

[26] Sokoloff–Yahalom, *piyyut* 33, vs. 28 (*Ha shatya dbayishan*) and *Tifsha dkfar karnus* (vs. 49). On the latter see also *LevR* 28: 6. To be precise, the poem places Haman in a village called Krenos which has been identified in the hinterland of Scythopolis, *PT Dem.* 2b, 22c; Cf. the inscription at nearby Rehov with Y. Sussman, *Tarbiz* 43 (1973–4), 115–17 (Heb.).

I am the son of one who carries wood (carpenter)!
Lashed by rods,[27] of woman born (?), they call me 'the savior' (*christos*).
Pierced with nails,
My limbs clamped into place,
A barley eater is better off than me.[28]
This is the end of the pierced one(?), disgraced in every town.
Thus said 'Jesus'.[29]

The lines provide an uncanny echo of the imperial decree which banned the mock crucifixion of Haman on Purim. Both law and lore attest the assimilation of Haman with Jesus and the ritual of festive mocking on Purim.[30]

Burning a human effigy on a cross might have become the highlight of the festival of Purim in late antiquity. In Christian art, by contrast, human depictions of the crucifixion were rare before the fifth century in the west and before the sixth in the east.[31] Could Purim have been partially responsible for this aversion to putting Christ on a cross? Constantinople's harsh reaction to the Purim bantering of the cross confirms the role of the crucifixion in the promotion of an imperial

---

[27] The term 'rods' or 'whip', *iskotis*, reflects the Greek word for a leather strip or a whip (*skutos*). On the use of Greek words in Aramaic poetry, Yahalom, 'Angels', 42–3.

[28] The editors of the poem were uncertain whether the reference to barley consumption refers to an ass or a gladiator, Sokoloff–Yahalom, 217. If the latter, they maintain that the poem could not have been written much later than the early part of the 5th cent., soon after the imperial decree which closed the schools of gladiators (T. Wiedemann, *Emperors and Gladiators* (London 1992), 156–9). The above-quoted law suggests that Purim in this form, with the crucifixion of Haman as the highlight, was celebrated at least until 408. On the consumption of barley bread as a hallmark of the poor in late antiquity, Libanius, *Ep.* 1.8; Procopius of Gaza, *Ep.* 2. Cf. rabbinic views on barley as food fit for animals, *T Sot.* 3.7; *PT Beitza* 1.11 (61a); *BT Moed Katan* 28a; *BT Kidd.* 62a.

[29] Sokoloff–Yahalom, *piyyut* 33, 85–90. Jesus called in the poem *ploni* (someone); cf. *EccR* 1: 8. Probably a late addition.

[30] Yahalom. 'Angels', 42–3 also sees this *piyyut* as reflecting Jewish–Christian polemics over the interpretation of Ps. 21, with K. Corrigan, *Visual Polemics in the Ninth Century Psalter* (Cambridge 1992), 48–9, 170. On this poem see O. Münz-Manor, 'Carnivalesque Ambivalence and the Christian *Other* in Aramaic Poems from Byzantine Palestine', in G. Stroumsa and R. Bonfil (eds.) *Jews in Byzantium* (forthcoming). I am grateful to Ophir for providing me with an advanced copy.

[31] V. Grossi, 'Cross', in *Encyclopedia of the Early Church*; G. Q. Reijners, *The Terminology of the Holy Cross in Early Christian Literature* (Nijmegen 1965). See also N. Baynes, 'The Icons before Iconoclasm', *HTR* 44 (1951), 93–106; and Av. Cameron, 'The Language of Images: The Rise of Icons and Christian Representations', *Studies in Church History* 28 (1992), 1–42.

vision of an exclusively Christian commonwealth.[32] Within a Palestinian context the centralization of the cross as the emblem par excellence of Christian orthodoxy is eloquently reflected in persistent exhortations of Cyril of Jerusalem to his flock:

We should not be afraid to acknowledge the Crucified. We should boldly trace the cross with our fingers as a seal on our forehead and over everything: over the bread we eat, the cups we drink, when we come in and when we go out, before we go to sleep, when we go to bed and when we get up, on journeys and at rest. It is a powerful protection; to suit the poor, it costs nothing; to suit the weak, it costs no labor since it comes as a gift from God. It is a sign for the faithful and a terror to demons.[33]

A rivalry of labels cast the cross as a contentious issue, reflected, for example, in contemporary ornamentation of oil flasks (*ampullae*). Christian flasks proclaimed the cross as a source of life; Jewish, and Samaritan inscriptions tersely insisted that 'God is One'.[34] In a Purim context Cyril's representation of the cross as an integral component of the daily life of a Christian became an anachronistic paradox.

---

[32] Cf. the centrality of the Menorah, the Jewish symbol par excellence, on the mosaic of the Beth Shean synagogue, a rarity in spite of the ubiquity of this symbol on coins, graffiti, lamps, glass vessels, sarcophagi, and chancel screens. Within a monumental context the Menorah appears only in Dura Europos and on Titus' arch. L. I. Levine, 'The History and Significance of the Menorah in Antiquity', in idem and Weiss, *From Dura to Sepphoris*, 131–53. A photo of the Beth Shean Menorah mosaic appears in the same volume on p. 98. It is worth noting, too, that in 409, the emperors banned 'paganized' spectacles, CTh. 2.8.25.

[33] *Catechesis* 13.36, trans. E. Yarnold, *Cyril of Jerusalem* (London 2000), 160–1. On Cyril and his role in Christianizing Jerusalem see Ch. 5 below.

[34] On the ampullae bearing a cross at the centre with an inscription about its significance, N. Feuchtwanger, 'Late Sixth Century Metal Ampoules', in D. Jacoby and Y. Tsafrir, *Jews, Samaritans and Christians in Byzantine Palestine* (Jerusalem 1988), 47–8 (Heb.). For the 'God is One' formula which accompanies a menorah, Lehmann and Holum, *The Greek and Latin Inscriptions of Caesarea Maritima*, no. 137. It is dated to 408–11 by L. Di Segni, 'A Jewish Greek Inscription from the Vicinity of Caesarea Maritima', *Atiqot* 22 (1993), 133–6 and eadem, 'The Date of the Binyamina Inscription and the Question of Byzantine Dora', *Atiqot* 25 (1994), 183–6, responding to D. Barag, 'The Dated Jewish Inscription from Binyamina Reconsidered', *Atiqot* 25 (1994), 179–81, who prefers 540 CE. For the Samaritan inscription, also from Caesarea, Lehmann–Holum, *Inscriptions*, nos. 138–40 with L. Di Segni, '*Eis theos* in Palestinian Inscriptions', *SCI* 13 (1994), 94–115. See also the reservations of W. Horbury, 'A Proselyte's heis theos Inscription near Caesarea', *PEQ* 129 (1997), 133–7 about the ascription of such formulas mostly to Samaritans rather than to Jews or to proselytes. The precise affiliation of the monotheistic formula 'eis theos' has been hotly contested. E. Peterson, *Eis Theos: Epigraphische, formgeschichte und religionsgeschichtliche Untersuchungen* (Göttingen 1926) opts for a Christian formula;

If for Cyril the cross was a reminder of Christ's sufferings, for Purim revellers it was a reminder of a victory won by remembering the wrong they had suffered. Purim ceased to be integrative when the cross became a means of identifying membership in the Christian community. Haman's 'crucifixion' and the association of the re-demptive values of Purim with the 'passion' of Passover, sharpened the historical and physical boundaries between Jews and Christians.[35] Purim scenes re-enacted the humiliation and ultimate victory of the Jews in a stylized fashion. Such 'shows' staged a ritualized vengeance of a 'pugilistic event' which emphasized communal boundaries while displacing violence from the Bible to a contained ritual.[36]

At the dawn of the fifth century, Jewish–Christian credal animosity had a character of ritualistic humour which also suggests mutual tolerance. In Pre-Constantinian Caesarea gentiles mocked Jewish habits in the theatre; in the early fifth century Jews mocked Christianity in the streets.[37] Such fragile balance, always susceptible to pressures from outside, was especially vulnerable in Palestine where local and imperial campaigns strove to promote the hybrid terrain as a Christian holy land. Christian manifestations of faith focused on parades honouring relics or living saints, thus complementing yet competing with Purim parades. Both provided public moments of bonding, as Cyril of Scythopolis emphasized in his description of a reception in honour of Sabas and John of Jerusalem which took place in Scythopolis:

F. Trombley, *Hellenic Religion and Christianization c. 370–529*, 2 vols. (Leiden 1993–5), app. V, p. 315 for Jewish origins and Christian adaptation; Di Segni, '*Eis theos*', for gnostic-pagan origins transmitted via Samaritanism to Christianity. See also Ch. 2.

[35] Cf. the words of Yose ben Yose, poet of the 5th cent. (?), who laments the fate of his people in words reminiscent of the Purim poems: 'How can we toss the blood (Mishna Yoma 1.2) when our blood is shed? . . . How can we be purified by wood (Ezekiel 41: 22) when we have stumbled under the wood (Lamentations 5: 13)?' Lines 8 and 32 of *eyn lanu kohen gadol* (we do not have a high priest), trans. in W. Horbury, 'Suffering and Messianism in Yose ben Yose', in idem and B. McNeal (eds.), *Suffering and Martyrdom in the New Testament* (Cambridge 1981), 154.

[36] For the expression, R. Girard, *Violence and the Sacred* (Baltimore 1977), 93.

[37] I refrain from delving into ritualistic cursing in synagogues during the obliga-tory prayer = The Benediction of the Minim. On this contentious topic see among many, R. Kimelman, '*Birkat Ha-Minim* and the Lack of Evidence for an Anti-Christian Jewish Prayer in Late Antiquity', in E. P. Sanders, A. I. Baumgarten, and A. Mendelson (eds.), *Jewish and Christian Self-Definition*, 3 vols. (Philadelphia 1981), ii. 226–44.

They [Sabas and John] went to Scythopolis, where all the citizens together with the most holy metropolitan Theodosius came out to meet them at the apostolic shrine of Saint Thomas. They made their entry with psalms, the liturgy was celebrated in the ancient church, the imperial letter [concerning the council of Chalcedon] was read out, and the four councils were inserted in the sacred diptychs.[38]

This scene was repeated in other Palestinian cities. In Jerusalem, the public reading of the imperial letter coincided with a local festival of 6 August, thus combining an event on the city's calendar of faith with an ad hoc presentation of a message celebrating the victory of imperial and local orthodoxy.[39]

Imperial rejection of Purim rituals points to a mode of decoding which considered the feast as an ordinary yet threatening form of Jewish communal conduct. What the law banned was a dissonance that proclaimed a Jewish living interpretation of the Bible. For Theodosius II, as for Constantine before him, to assert their creed was to establish an undisputed continuity between Christ and the Christian Roman empire as if neither Judaism, nor paganism for that matter, had been present in the intervening years.[40] But Judaism's staying power, so colourfully seen in the Purim festivities, symbolized a rotation of meanings signifying communal concord and opposition.[41] The tenacity of polytheism was a symbol of continuity not yet voided.[42] In the topography of time and of territory

---

[38] *Life of Sabas* 61 (163 Schwartz), trans. Price, *Lives of the Monks of Palestine by Cyril of Scythopolis*. The year is 518.

[39] *Life of Sabas* 60 (162 Schwartz), for Jerusalem; 61 (162 S) for Caesarea.

[40] A. Jacobs, *Remains of the Jews: The Holy Land and Christian Empire in Late Antiquity* (Stanford 2004), *passim*. S. Schwartz, *Imperialism and Jewish Society 200 BCE to 640 CE*, *passim*.

[41] Compare the covert polemics over the position of the Passover sacrifice. According to an early (pre-70?) custom (*PT Pes.* 7.1 (34a), the sacrificial animal was roasted with the body hanging and its head up, while the Mishnah (Pesahim 7.1) attests a change of orientation with the animal's head hanging down. The former resembled a crucified person, a semblance that may have induced the Mishnaic attempt to reduce the similarity between the Jewish ritual and the crucifixion which became the core of the Christian Easter, although a polemical intention (i.e. mocking the crucifixion) cannot be ruled out. See J. Tabory, *The Passover Ritual throughout the Generations* (Tel Aviv 1996), 96 (Heb.), and below, Ch. 6.

[42] In the 6th cent. Jacob of Serugh (Syria) complains that pagan sacrifices are still performed in the theatre, C. Moss, 'Jacob of Serugh's Homilies on the Spectacles', *Le Muséon* 48 (1935), 87–112, esp. 106, with Caseau, 'Sacred Landscapes', 28. On

which moments of credal conciliation mapped out, memory operated as a successful bridging of pasts and presents, but also as a locator of sites of conflict.

Underlying Purim, then, was a dimension of disorder which suggested two contrasting yet complementary poles. In an urban context with a hybrid population Purim prompted communal cooperation by temporarily eliminating group boundaries; but it also erected divisions by targeting another creed. For the court informants who had drawn attention to this Jewish feast Purim was perilous because it adumbrated choice and the existence of alternative models of social interaction. Gatherings of this sort had become a sensitive barometer of communal interaction. In the repetitive time of social practices in which rituals projected a state of being and thinking Purim was seen to assign to the 'other' and to the 'elsewhere' uneasy connotations. And because the festivities proclaimed the spatial and temporal proximity of the biblical 'other' and 'elsewhere', Purim celebration carried connotations far beyond its invocation of the past or immediate environment.

2. SEEN FROM SCYTHOPOLIS: PURIM IN AN URBAN CONTEXT

Twice in the longest Purim poem the poet placed Haman not in Susa, as the biblical scroll does, but in Palestinian Scythopolis (Beth Shean).[43] Neither law nor poem indicates where the Purim occasion which drew the attention and ire of the imperial legislator took place. Assuming that the reference to Scythopolis was not a fanciful poetic touch, the possibility that this city provided the catalyst scene that evoked the issuance of the imperial law merits careful consideration.[44] By 408, when the imperial decree was issued, Scythopolis was

paganism within the context of Palestinian periperies in late antiquity see Ch. 2 above.

[43] Sokoloff–Yahalom, *piyyut* 33, lines 28 (Beth Shean) and 49 (Kefar Karnus).

[44] The rules of rhythm suggest that this was not a mere coincidence but a careful choice dictated by both topography and meter. This is why the poet, where needed, uses 'Scythopolis' (Beth Shean) to rhyme with Susa (Shushan), and resorts to Karnus

the capital of a recently carved out Palestinian province, Palaestina Secunda, an area which included zones with a predominantly Jewish population (central and western Galilee).[45] Any attempt to suppress Purim's most visible ritual marks within this Palestinian urban context would have been more than a routine demonstration of imperial rhetoric. Aiming at a hybrid population of Christians, Samaritans, Jews, and pagans, a constitution banning the rituals of one group was tantamount to an attack on all non-conforming forms of religious expression. It was an invasion of the Palestinian cityscape in an attempt to redraw communal boundaries and perimeters.

Around 400 a Purim march through Scythopolis would have wound its way within the city walls with their six gates, along spacious paths and past public buildings, all spread at the foot of a towering acropolis once graced with a temple to Zeus.[46] Revellers would have advanced through colonnaded streets, treading over carefully laid mosaics donated by generous individuals such as Palladius and Sylvanus. At the city centre Purim participants could view fresh merchandise in the agora which succeeded a civic basilica, or

to rhyme with 'turnus'. M. Bar Ilan in his review of Sokoloff–Yahalom ('Aramaic Poems from Eretz Israel', *Mahut* 23 (2001), 167–88) (Heb.) assigns Scythopolis as the poet's home (p. 179). He prefers, however, to dismiss the possibility of the poet's familiarity with the rabbinic tradition that connected Mordechai and Haman with Kefar Karnos (*BT Meg.* 16a; *LevR* 28.5) in favour of linking the poem's geographical horizon with the inscription of Rehov near Scythopolis which conflates, like the poem, Scythopolis with Kefar Karnos (p. 179).

[45] CTh. 7.4.30, with Y. Tsafrir, 'The Provinces in Eretz-Israel: Names, Limits and Administrative Zones', in Z. Baras et al. (eds.), *Eretz Israel from the Destruction of the Second Temple to the Muslim Conquest* (Jerusalem 1982), i. 350–86, esp. 371–2, for CE 409 as the date of partition. Stemberger, *Jews and Christian in the Holy Land*, 7, opts for a date around 400. P. Mayerson, 'Libanius and the Administration of Palestine', *ZPE* 69 (1987), 251–60 prefers the year 390. See also G. Mazor and R. Bar Nathan, 'Scythopolis. Capital of Palestina Secunda', *Qadmoniot* 27 (1994), 117–37 (Heb.).

[46] According to Cyril of Scythopolis' Life of Sabas, the city's Christians preferred the 'ancient church' to the one on the summit (*Vita* 163.2, *Lives of the Monks of Palestine by Cyril of Scythopolis*, trans. Price, p. 172. Full reports of Beth Shean's recent excavations, headed by Y. Tsafrir, are soon to be published. Interim publications include Y. Tsafrir and G. Foerster, 'Urbanism at Scythopolis-Bet Shean in the Fourth to the Seventh Centuries', *DOP* 51 (1997), 85–146, and eidem, 'From Scythopolis to Baysan: Changing Concepts of Urbanism', in G. R. D. King and Av. Cameron (eds.), *The Byzantine and Early Islamic Near East*, ii (Princeton 1994), 95–115. See also J. T. Raynor, 'Social and Cultural Relationships in Scythopolis/Beth Shean in the Roman and Byzantine Periods' (Ph.D., Duke University 1982).

drink from one of the city's public fountains. At the crossroads of two of Scythopolis' main streets, the marching Purim bands could contemplate the imposing façade of what had been a temple dedicated to Dionysos, the city's legendary founder and erstwhile tutelary divinity. Abutting the sanctuary was an aqueduct which provided fresh water to newly installed latrines. Those who could read would have recited aloud the verses which commemorated the contributions of individuals to public projects that beautified Scythopolis.

Purim provided a link with the city's polytheistic traditions, not the least with Dionysos, god of wine and intemperance, and Scythopolis' very own patron.[47] Because of the holiday's irresistible mixture of fun and food, the feast's ecumenical and 'dionysiac' character would have generated appeal beyond the boundaries of creed and ethnicity:

The nations of the world when given a holiday, eat, drink, carouse and go into their theaters and circuses and thus anger You; but it is the way of Israel, too, that when You give them holidays, they likewise eat, drink, are merry and go to their synagogues and academies and pray.[48]

Near the theatre Purim participants might have chatted about performances at the theatre, a much beloved centre of entertainment to judge by its tenacious survival to the very end of antiquity. Whispers might have been exchanged about shows which had been mounted in the amphitheatre, about the increasing encroachment of commercial centres, and about visits to local brothels.[49] A Purim procession through the western part of the city would have passed a large private house of a wealthy Jewish family whose sons, Leontius

[47] None of the four hitherto excavated temples has been associated with the cult of Dionysos, Y. Tsafrir, 'The Fate of Pagan Cult Places in Palestine: The Archaeological Evidence with emphasis on Bet Shean', in H. Lapin (ed.), *Religious and Ethnic Communities in Later Roman Palestine* (Bethesda 1998), 197–218, p. 214. See also L. Di Segni, 'A Dated Inscription from Beth Shean and the Cult of Dionysos Ktistes in Roman Scythopolis', *SCI* 16 (1997), 139–61.

[48] *Pesiq. Rab.* Additions 84 (ed. Ish Shalom, p. 200), quoted (with a misprint) in Z. Weiss, 'Greco-Roman Influences on the Art and Architecture of the Jewish City in Roman Palestine', in H. Lapin (ed.), *Religious and Ethnic Communities* (1998), 241. On rabbinic objections to Jewish attendance of spectacles and games, ibid. 243. According to the Rehov inscription, Scythopolis was exempt from rabbinic diet-sabbatical rules, an exemption reflecting a Jewish minority in town. See Ch. 6.

[49] C. Dauphin, 'Brothels, Baths and Babes: Prostitution in the Byzantine Holy Land', *Classics Ireland* 3 (1996), 52–3.

and Jonathan, possibly Scythopolis' first recorded hotel magnates, recorded their passion for art and literature in mosaics. One floor featured scenes from the *Odyssey*; another depicted a Nilotic festival. A viewer conversant with rabbinic lore would have made a mental association between the Alexandria of this Nile mosaic and Purim poems which incorporated the city into the lives of Jesus and Haman.[50] The Nile festivities, an annual holiday celebrated by all regardless of creed, entailed the kind of playful mimes as did Purim.[51] Leontius' family might have originated in Alexandria. Their choice of a typical Egyptian scenery of Nilotic imageries would have expressed their affinity with their original provenance.[52] Along the Purim march the more pious among the revellers could have briefly prayed at Leontius' private synagogue or prayer room. Christian participants might have piously peered into the house adjacent to Leontius' inn. It was owned by a man who was an avid collector of *eulogiae*, souvenirs of pilgrimage, especially the kind that featured biblical images.

In the fourth century a Purim march would have passed (or bypassed) five temples dedicated to five different divinities.

---

[50] Above for verbal connection. On Nilotic scenes in Palestine, E. Dvorjetski and A. Segal, 'The "Nile Festival" Mosaic and its Relation to the Cultural Life in Eretz Israel in the Roman and Byzantine Periods', *Bamah Dramah Quarterly* 141–2 (1995), 100–5 (Heb.); Z. Weiss and R. Talgam, 'The Nile Festival Building and its Mosaics: Mythological Representations in Early Byzantine Sepphoris', in J. H. Humphrey (ed.), *The Roman and Byzantine Near East* (JRS Suppl. 49; Portsmouth, RI, 2002), 55–90, esp. 70–1. 'The personification of the Nile, a Nilometer, and a schematic depiction of Alexandria were found at Bet Shean in the House of Leontius, a complex belonging to a rich Jew. An adjoining panel represents the story of Odysseus and the Sirens, a third room served as a synagogue or prayer room' (Weiss–Talgam, 71, with N. Zori, 'The House of Kyrios Leontius at Beth Shean', *IEJ* 16 (1966), 123–34. The Sepphoris Nile mosaic belongs to a building constructed around 400 (Weiss–Talgam, 60). These mosaics appear in a secular or religious context, pagan, Jewish, and Christian (Weiss–Talgam, 72). The Christianization of the Nile festival is strikingly seen through a 6th-cent. papyrus from Antinoe in Egypt which is cast as a traditional hymn addressed to the Nile with an ending in the shape of an appeal to Christ, M. Mandrefi, 'Inno cristiano al Nilo', in P. J. Parsons and J. R. Rea (eds.), *Papyri Greek and Egyptian edited by Various Hands in Honor of Eric Gardner Turner* (London 1981), 56, with H. Maguire, 'The Good Life', in Bowersock *et al.* (eds.), *Interpreting Late Antiquity* (Cambridge, Mass., 1999, 2001), 250.

[51] *Song of Songs Rabbah* 1.1; *PT Sotah* 36b, quoted in Dvorjetski and Segal, 'The Nile Festival'.

[52] Ilan, *Ancient Synagogues in Israel*, 179 (pp. 176–9, on Beth Shean synagogues), on the Alexandrian origins.

In the fifth, four (or less), survived to witness the erection of two synagogues, one Jewish and one Samaritan, and a monastery. The monastic complex appeared remarkable on account of its latrines.[53] The Jewish synagogue was located on the other side of a large yard that separated it from the house of Leontius. Its inscriptions, in Greek and Aramaic, commemorated donations without, however, naming individuals, and recorded the collective efforts of a 'sacred group' that contributed to repairs in the synagogue.[54] Such studied anonymity strove to extol the congregation at the expense of individuals as though faith alone provided a bonding matter.

By 408 a Purim march would have passed a golden statue of the empress Eudoxia, wife of Arcadius, which Artemidorus, the provincial governor and presumably resident of Scythopolis, had erected.[55] According to its inscription, Eudoxia, who died in 404, was 'queen of all the earth, visible from afar'. The Homeric epithet underscored Scythopolis' Hellenistic character and the shared aesthetics of its citizens.[56] But the empress's shiny 'presence' in Scythopolis also reminded viewers of the links which tied province to court through the mediation of female members of the imperial family. In contested urban territories in Palestine, like Scythopolis and Gaza, the name of Eudoxia signalled decisive and divisive imperial intervention in local affairs. In 400 the empress lent weighty support to Porphyry, Gaza's belligerent bishop, in his campaign against Gazan paganism. With her indispensable assistance, Porphyry obtained an imperial decree which authorized the demolition of pagan temples in the city,

---

[53] C. Dauphin, 'Leprosy, Lust and Lice: Health and Hygiene in Byzantine Palestine', *Bulletin of the Anglo-Israel Archaeological Society* 15 (1996–7), 67, with N. Zori, 'An Archaeological Survey of the Beth Shean Valley', in *The Beth Shean Valley. The 17th Archaeological Convention* (Jerusalem 1962), 124–98 (Heb.), pp. 188–9, no. 143.

[54] The inscriptions are reproduced in Ilan, *Ancient Synagogues*, 176. See also Roth-Gerson, *The Greek Inscriptions*, 33–43.

[55] Tsafrir, 'Fate', 217, with K. G. Holum, *Theodosian Empresses: Women and Imperial Dominion in Late Antiquity* (Berkeley 1982), 48–78. The inscription reads: 'Artemidorus set up a golden [statue of] Eudoxia, queen of all earth, visible from every place in the country' (Tsafrir, 'Fate', 217).

[56] On Scythopolis' self-conscious presentation as a Greek city, as directed against the Aramaic-speaking countryside and against the Jews, J. Geiger, 'Language, Culture and Identity in Ancient Palestine', in E. N. Ostenfeld (ed.), *Greek Romans and Roman Greeks: Studies in Cultural Interaction* (Aarhus Studies in Mediterranean Antiquity III; Aarhus 2002), 233–46, esp. 240.

including the one dedicated to Marnas, Gaza's tutelary divinity.[57] The church, erected on top of the destroyed temple and inaugurated on Easter Sunday of 407, was duly named after the empress (the Eudoxiana). Henceforth the Gazan Christian congregation, which up to that point had more than sufficient space in a small church dedicated to 'Peace', could listen to sermons in surroundings which were far larger than its needs.

Since the nature of the locale was rarely fully understood by the central authorities in Constantinople, the Purim law of 408, with its emphasis on the cross as an object of Jewish violence, served to inflate Jewish–Christian animosity, just as imperial support of Porphyry's campaigns of demolition had done in Gaza. In both cases the voice of distant Constantinople would have enabled a Christian urban minority to gain a firm and irreversible foothold within the local power structure. Local struggles were given a decisive twist through the intervention of imperial resources and royal women, like Eudoxia and Pulcheria, the latter most likely the agent behind the Purim law which appeared when she was the undisputed power behind the throne.

When Porphyry set out to 'conquer' the Gazan landscape he inaugurated his episcopate with a series of 'miracles', providentially providing cure to the ailment of the land and of the city's inhabitants. One episcopal prayer put a stop to a devastating drought; another saved a young mother from death during delivery, and a third a ship from sinking. In Constantinople, Porphyry disentangled an

---

[57] The sole source of information for the Gazan events is Mark the Deacon, *Life of Porphyry*, 76 (H. Grégoire and M. A. Kugener (eds. and trans.), *Marc le Diacre: Vie de Porphyre évêque de Gaza* (Paris 1930) (also in C. Mango, *The Art of the Byzantine Empire 312–1453: Sources and Documents* (1972; repr. Toronto 1986), p. 31). See the doubts raised relating to its author, date, and authenticity by R. MacMullen,*Christianizing the Roman Empire AD 100–400* (New Haven 1984), 86–8, with P. Peeters, 'La Vie géorgienne de Saint Porphyre de Gaza', *AB* 59 (1941), 65–216. See also G. Fowden, 'Bishops and Temples in the Eastern Roman Empire', *JTS* 29 (1978), 53–78. The removal of pagan temples occurred in several stages, with a recorded failure in the case of the Marneion which was demolished by a miracle rather than by human hands (Mark, *VP* 71). On Gaza, Glucker, *The City of Gaza in Roman and Byzantine Periods*; Trombley, *Hellenic Religion and Christianization*, vol. i; R. Van dam, 'From Paganism to Christianity at Late Antique Gaza', *Viator* 16 (1985), 1–20. On the activities of the Gazan delegations in Constantinople, Stemberger, *Jews and Christians*, 70–1, 197. See also Ch. 8 below.

empress from the embarrassment of not producing a male heir.[58] As a stranger to the land (he was from Thessalonike but spent time in Jerusalem as keeper of the true cross), Porphyry entered the arena of municipal politics in Gaza as bearer of religious violence rather than of civic order.[59] Around 402 he publicly interrogated Julia, a 'pagan' philosopher who had reached Gaza from Antioch.[60] Porphyry had hoped to use this form of 'entertainment' as a forum enacting Christian victory. When the debate went badly for him he called on Jesus to strike Julia dumb. Julia's sudden death was followed by 'mass' conversion in the city. Notwithstanding Porphyry's endeavours, Christians were still a minority in Gaza in the late fifth century.[61] Nor did Gaza's powerful pagan elite remain idle. They staged a retaliation which prevented Porphyry from accomplishing the complete Christianization of his diocese.[62] Only occasions like chariot races elicited admissions of inferiority on the part of pagans, and then only when their favoured champion was losing to a charioteer assisted by the prayers of a Christian holy man.[63]

Although Scythopolis was not as rich a city as Gaza it boasted weaving workshops renowned throughout the empire.[64] Such excellence bred imperial concerns. Already in 339 an imperial law 'protected' female weavers from Jewish men who were, in all likelihood, the owners of rival weaving establishments.[65] Because of its position

---

[58] List in MacMullen, 87–8, based on the Georgian text.

[59] R. Lim, *Public Disputation, Power and Social Order in Late Antiquity* (Berkeley 1995), 82; Van Dam, 'From Paganism to Christianity', 1–20.

[60] On these events, Lim, 83–7 prefers to see Julia as a Manichee, according to the Greek version, versus her identification as a pagan philosopher in the Georgian version.

[61] By 1987 there were only three datable Gazan inscriptions identified as 'Christian', D. Barag, 'The Kingdom of Heaven in a Christian Epitaph of 474 CE from Gaza', *Eretz Israel* 19 (1987), 242–5 (Heb.). But see now C. Saliou, 'Gaza dans l'antiquité tardive: nouveaux documents épigraphiques', *RB* 107 (2000), 390–411 (see Ch. 8 below).

[62] *Vita* (Greek), 95–9.

[63] Jerome, *Life of Hilarion* 11.11: 'Marnas has been conquered by Christ'. See also Y. Ashkenazi, 'Paganism in Gaza in the Fifth and Sixth Centuries', *Cathedra* 60 (1991), 106–15 (Heb.).

[64] Dan, *City*, 196–7; Diocletian; CTh. ( ); A. H. M. Jones, 'The Cloth Industry under the Roman Empire', *Economic History Review* 2 (1960); see also *PT Ket.* 1.3; *Kidd.* 3.3.

[65] CTh. 16.8.6 (Linder, 148); see Sivan, *REJ* 1997. The law does not refer to Scythopolis but the reference to an imperial *gynaikeion*, of which Scythopolis was one, and to close proximity between Jews and Christians point to a Palestinian

midway between Antioch and Alexandria, Scythopolis was also selected as a venue for gruesome treason trials launched by Constantius II in 359.[66] The sight of accused women and men, hauled all the way from Syria and Egypt, was hardly calculated to inspire communal tranquillity.

In the sixth century the religious landscape of Scythopolis, by then altogether devoid of temples, gained another monastery and a church.[67] Statues of divinities which once had graced temples, public baths, and many public places were mutilated and thrown into pits when not reused in new constructions.[68] One of Scythopolis' temples provided building material for a church.[69] Similarly to other Palestinian cities, Scythopolis also experienced a dramatic increase of population. The demographic curve was reflected in a building boom, in the conversion of public monuments into housing projects and in the planting of houses and shops on the pavement of busy streets.[70] These modifications implied that urban dwellers of all persuasions lived in close proximity to each other in a degree of density which was conducive to a life-style of alternating tension and reconciliation, besides acting as a conduit of disease.[71]

The religious, social, and political metamorphosis of Scythopolis at the turn of the fifth century, when the imperial law on Purim was issued, seemed emblematic of competing issues in late ancient Palestine. In the same urban space, Jewish, Christian, and Samaritan

environment. On this and CTh. 10.20.8 (CE 374) which does refer to Scythopolis, see also Stemberger, *Jews and Christians*, 176–81.

[66] Amm. 19.12.1.

[67] Tsafrir, 'Fate of Pagan Cult Places', in Lapin (ed.), *Religious and Ethnic Communities* (1998), 212–17. On the synagogues, Ilan, *Ancient Synagogues*, 176–82, who objects to the identification of the synagogue north of Beth Shean with a Samaritan one, in spite of its (Greek) inscription in Samaritan letters (J. Naveh, 'A Greek Dedication in Samaritan Letters', *IEJ* 31 (1981), 220–2).

[68] Tsafrir and Foerster, 'Urbanism', *DOP* 51 (1997), 129–30, on the large number of decapitated divinities.

[69] Tsafrir, 'Fate'. The church, on the city's acropolis, was round—an unusual architectural form. Its construction was dated to the mid-fifth century, based on the similarity of its capitals to those of St Stephen's Church that the empress Eudocia had commissioned in Jerusalem in the 430s, G. M. Fitzgerald, *Beth-Shan Excavations 1921–1923. The Arab and Byzantine Levels* (Philadelphia 1931) 18–30.

[70] Dauphin, 'Leprosy', 73, with G. Foerster and Y. Tsafrir, 'City Center (North): Excavations of the Hebrew University Expedition', in *The Bet Shean Excavation Project (1989–1991), Excavations and Surveys in Israel* 11 (1992), 3–32, esp. 18–19.

[71] Dauphin, 'Leprosy', 74.

nabobs allocated room and money for the establishment of synagogues, churches, and monasteries, a collective show of competing generosity and piety. The survival of the theatre and presumably of its shows suggests civic tenacity which transcended religious censorship and imperial restrictions. To judge by the social dynamics that shaped theatrical performances, the stage both maintained and reinforced the cohesion of the community in a context of social rituals and spectacles in which the audience formed a 'political community'.[72]

Visual if not verbal syncretism underscored interaction. When Leontius endowed a synagogue (or prayer room) in his own vast home in Scythopolis in the fifth century he placed this sacred precinct next to rooms embellished with mosaics depicting scenes from the *Odyssey* and images of the Nile festival.[73] For him, as for those who prayed at the adjacent synagogue, the Egyptian festivities honouring the life-giving water were stripped of both a specific Egyptian context and pagan roots. What was left was an occasion celebrating rejuvenation and beauty in nature. In this symbiotic Scythopolis the feast which celebrated the achievements of a biblical beauty crystallized manners of communal contacts and conflicts, shaping an urban milieu where Purim rituals represented a violent paradigm for mutual toleration. Participation in the 'game' of Purim occurred within a hierarchy, urban, Roman, Christian, which it also threatened.

The 'judicial savagery' that marks the language of CTh. 16.8.18 provided a reminder of the violence which punctured the tenor of tranquillity that archaeological finds appear to project.[74] The question whether textual brutality, such as the one permeating the biography of Porphyry and the legal texts, went hand in hand with

---

[72] Cf. the Athenian theatre as a theatre of competing civic ideologies and of a dialogue between public and stage, O. Longo, 'The Theater of the Polis', in J. J. Winkler and F. Zeitlin (eds.), *Nothing to do with Dionysos?* (Princeton 1990), 12–19; the quote is taken from ibid. 'Introduction', 6.

[73] See above p. 160. Weiss–Talgam, 71, 82. On Jewish familiarity with 'Hellenism', S. Lieberman, *Hellenism in Jewish Palestine*, 100–14; G. Foerster, 'Allegorical and Symbolic Motifs with Christian Significance from Mosaic Pavements of Sixth-Century Palestinian Synagogues', in G. C. Bottini *et al.* (eds.), *Christian Archaeology in the Holy Land: New Discoveries* (Jerusalem 1990), 545–52. See also Dauphin, *La Palestine*, iii. 780–2 for a summary.

[74] For the expression, R. MacMullen, 'Judicial Savagery in the Roman Empire', *Chiron* 16 (1986), 147–66; repr. in idem, *Changes in the Roman Empire: Essays in the Ordinary* (Princeton 1990), 67–77.

physical violence is difficult to determine. The ferocity of the texts of
the Purim poems and of the Purim law may serve as an index of the
escalating hostility of Christian leadership towards Judaism, and as
literary counterparts of intra-communal strife.[75]

Violence was multifarious. The Purim poems vented Jewish anger
on an effigy of the mythic-biblical Haman by nailing him to a
contemporary cross. During Julian's reign pagans desecrated the
bones of Patrophilus, the 'Arian' bishop of Scythopolis, in a post-
mortem ritual which included digging out the bishop's grave, scatter-
ing his bones and 'insolently hanging up his skull, affixing it as
though it were in the form of a lamp'.[76] The identification of the
perpetrators as 'pagans', if correct, suggests an act of violence against
a creed (Christianity) which came to be embodied in the corpse of
the deceased bishop.[77] It is especially curious because Patrophilus
gained notoriety, at least among theologians with orthodox leanings,
not for any anti-pagan activities but rather for his outspoken support
of the doctrine of Arius of Alexandria. Christian counter-anger was
vented on statues of divinities which used to embellish the city's
public spaces.[78] An exceptionally large number of mutilated, primarily decapitated statues hints at one shape of violence in the city.

What made CTh. 16.8.18, if indeed it had been prompted by the
situation in Scythopolis, of special significance is the testimony
which it bore of a new type of militant orthodox Christianity that
aimed at buildings, cult objects, and rituals. It charts the road that
transformed Scythopolis, among other cities, from a city of contesting minorities to one dominated by orthodox Christianity. And it
reflected a heightening of textual acerbity around 400 of which
Jerome stood as a spokesman. From his cell in Bethlehem he visual-
ized a Christian Palestine devoid of 'Jewish serpents, the incredible
stupidity of Samaritans, and the most blatant impiety of pagans', all
with ears closed to the 'truth', and all dangerous vis-à-vis a tender

---

[75] A. Wharton, 'Erasure: Eliminating the Space of Late Ancient Judaism', in
L. I. Levine and Z. Weiss (eds.)., *From Dura to Sepphoris* (JRA Suppl. 40; Portsmouth,
RI, 2000), 200.

[76] *Chron. Pasch.* 362, trans. M. and M. Whitby, TTH.

[77] Cf. the 'battle of the statues' in Golanide Paneas (Caesarea Philippi in Phoenicia),
Eus. *HE* 7.17; Soz. *HE* 5.21 and above, pp. 19–21. Cf. also Ambrose, *Ep.* 40 on Jews
burning Christian basilicas in Gaza and Ascalon (Ashkelon). But *Chron. Pasch.* (TTH,
p. 37) ascribed the Gazan and Ashkelon rampage to pagans.

[78] Tsafrir and Foerster, 'Urbanism', 129–30.

Christian 'flock'.[79] The vision found a counterpart in wry rabbinic comments on Christian efforts to seduce Jews by words:

Said the emperor to Rabbi Tanhum: 'Come and let us all be one people'. 'Very well', the rabbi answered, 'but we who are circumcised cannot possibly become like you. Rather you become circumcised and be like us'.[80]

The Purim poems provided yet another response to the growing monopoly of Christianity by voicing a ritual of lamentation over the present which, like the past, placed Jews in the hands of gentiles. The biblical text was manipulated to project a future day of deliverance from the yoke of Haman/Christianity/Rome. Purim's popularity and persistence meant that its annual re-enactment destabilized the coherence which the Christian emperors of the eastern empire sought to lend their 'commonwealth'. The attempt to suppress Purim's most visible ritual marked a textual turning point in the religious policies of Constantinople with regards to non-Christian groups in Palestine. Barely four years before the Purim constitution (in 404) Arcadius confirmed the privileges granted to Jewish patriarchs throughout his domains (CTh. 16.8.15). In 415, however, Theodosius II demoted the Tiberian patriarch Gamaliel and restricted his authority. The emperor further banned the construction of new synagogues and ordained the demolition of abandoned ones (CTh. 16.8.22). In addition, the law forbade circumcision of non-Jews and ordered the patriarch to hand over any slave who converted to Christianity.

3. SAMARITANS IN SCYTHOPOLIS

In late ancient Scythopolis, Purim festivities left a mixed legacy. By the sixth century the pattern of communal animosities shifted from Jewish–Christian to Samaritan–Christian. A crucial stage in the

---

[79] Jer. *Ep*. 93: *atque utinam sanctorum orationibus, non nos inquietarent Iudaici serpentes, et Samaritanorum incredibilis stultitia, atque gentilium apertissimae inpietates, quorum turba quamplurima et ad veritatem praedicationis omnino auribus obturantes, in similitudinem luporum gregem Christi circuientes, non parvas nobis excubias et laborem incutiunt, dum volumus oves Domini custodire ne ab his dilacerentur!*

[80] *BT San*. 39a; Herford, 283, thinks the emperor was Julian.

deteriorating relations between the Samaritans and the imperial government started with an incident characterized by ritual violence:

There was once a custom in Palestine and the entire East. Every Sabbath, after reading the Gospels, Christian children used to proceed from the church in the direction of Samaritan synagogues, jokingly stoning their homes, since the Samaritans were accustomed to isolate themselves at their homes on that day. Once the Samaritans could no longer tolerate yielding to Christians, and when the children left the church after the reading of the Gospel and walked to the synagogues of the Samaritans, starting to pelt them with stones, the Samaritans went out against the children with ready swords and killed many. Some of the children escaped to the holy altar of the church of holy Basil, whence they were pursued by some Samaritans who killed them under the very altar.[81]

The march of the Christian children which ended on so bloody a note occurred in Scythopolis in 529.[82] The events are striking because the reaction to ritualized violence far exceeded the norm. The juvenile festivities, aimed at a vulnerable minority, extended the customary damage inflicted on buildings to blood-shedding. Yet, until 529, the ritual of children hurling stones and insults at Samaritans and their homes had not incited broader riots. That year, the Samaritans revolted.

Stoning in Scythopolis had been a game, and specifically a children's game and the children appeared to have been the only participants in anti-Samaritan violence. Perhaps it was felt 'safe' because the actions were protected by the ritual context in which they took place and because the children's liberties were temporally circumscribed. But why children? Legal immunities may have played a role as did the belief that a child's voice could speak pure truth because it

---

[81] Malalas, *Excerpta* 44 (de Boer).

[82] On the identification of the locality as Scythopolis, based on Malalas' reference to a church dedicated to Basil, L. Di Segni, 'Scythopolis (Bet Shean) during the Samaritan Rebellion of 529 CE', in D. Jacoby and Y. Tsafrir (eds.), *Jews, Samaritans and Christians in Byzantine Palestine* (Jerusalem 1988), 223 (217–27) (Heb.); eadem, in Stern–Eshel, *The Samaritans* (Jerusalem 2002), 454–80 (Heb.). See also above, Ch. 3. Cf. the role of children in pagan–Christian relations in Gaza where a 7-year-old accused the pagans of offering human sacrifices in the Marneion, an allegation that contributed to the success of the campaign carried by Porphyry against the temple, Mark the Deacon, *VP* (Grégoire–Kugener, p. 127). The initiative could have hardly been that of the child. See also Ch. 8 below.

was thought to speak from outside the networks of social relations which dictated adult behaviour.[83] Moreover, children articulate most frankly a society's 'persecutory mythopoesis' because they mimetically reproduce the persecutory fantasies and realities of their environment and thus confirm them.[84] Clever strategists sought to expand the boundaries between communities through manipulating children's rituals. Reading the gospels in church and then marching to Samaritan synagogues constituted 'educational' activities in that they were intended to instil in children a sense of the divisions that constituted their world. Participation in violence was a step to full membership in the community. It was an age-specific way for children to show their religious zeal within a hierarchy of roles.

After the massacre of the children the Christians in Scythopolis proceeded to a gruesome murder of Silvanus, the most eminent Samaritan in Scythopolis. A group of Christians seized and burnt him in the middle of the city.[85] According to Cyril of Scythopolis, hardly an unbiased reporter, Silvanus had been 'plotting against the Christians', thus engaging in 'a war against God'.[86] Cyril did not disclose the precise nature of Silvanus' anti-Christian activities. Recently revealed inscriptions rather suggest that Silvanus had been actively involved in acts of patronage which included building projects throughout Scythopolis.[87] His style of execution shows that by the beginning of the sixth century, over a century after the issuance of the Purim decree, the public burning of the enemies of one's faith became a demonstration of the power of revenge. Because Silvanus' son, Arsenius, was living in Constantinople, he was able to exert influence over Justinian and Theodora to act against 'the Christians of Palestine'.[88] Only the combined efforts of a specially assembled

---

[83] Cf. N. Z. Davis, 'The Reasons of Misrule', in eadem, *Society and Culture in Early Modern France* (Stanford 1975), 97–123, at 108; and R. Trexler, 'From the Mouths of Babes: Christianization by Children in Sixteenth Century New Spain', in *Church and Community, 1200–1600* (Rome 1987), 549–73.

[84] R. Girard, *Des choses cachées depuis la fondation du Monde* (Paris 1978), 171.

[85] *Life of Sabas*, 70.

[86] Ibid. 61.

[87] Di Segni, 'Samaritan Revolts in Byzantine Palestine', in Stern–Eshel, *The Samaritans*, 454–80 (Heb.).

[88] *Life of Sabas*, 70.

Palestinian delegation, which included the famed ascetic Sabas, de-
flected the imperial wrath which Arsenius had kindled.

Nor did Cyril provide a precise day for the burning of Silvanus.[89] It
might have fallen on a Purim. If it did, the lynching would have been
a sinister re-enactment of the burning of Haman on a cross. Poetic
accounts of Purim in late antiquity presented biblical events as a
sequence with a repetitive rhythm of threatened annihilation and of
vengeance. The feast of Purim culminated with the burning of
Haman. Christian vengeance in the sixth century reached a climax
with the execution by fire of a live Samaritan. From a theatre of the
ridicule which integrated various groups, the ideology of Purim was
appropriated by Christians to make brutally clear the sharp boundaries, historical and physical, that separated Christians from Samaritans. More than the deliberate demolition of pagan temples or of
Samaritan and Jewish synagogues, this mode of applying violent
rituals to reality encapsulated the tipping of the balance in favour
of Christianity.

The type of attack on Silvanus had a history. During Succoth
(Feast of Tabernacles = Feast of Booths), Samaritan boys engaged
in a ritual which bore a striking resemblance to the Purim banned by
Roman law:

Thereby originated the Samaritan custom [celebrated] until now—boys of
the cities and villages burn [effigies of] the notorious ones (i.e. Romans) as a
memorial of that night on which their ancestors burnt the overseers who
prevented Israel from serving God.[90]

Acts and words of children on such occasions, especially small-scale
infantile violence that mirrored large-scale adult violence, neatly
summed up the relationship between the local and the general. The
guided violence of Samaritan children, as that of Christian children,
projected a macrocosm in which communications among adults

---

[89] Di Segni, 'Scythopolis', 226 dates the murder to June 529, the same month as the
killing of the children and after the outbreak of the revolt in Samaria (April–May
529). This chronology requires a revision.

[90] Abu'l Fath, *Chronicle*, trans. J. Bowman, *Samaritan Documents* (Pittsburgh, Pa.,
1977), 147, slightly modified = P. Stenhouse, *The Kitab al-Tarikh of Abu'l Fath*
(Sydney 1985), 186. See also Ch. 3 above. This may appear to be a doublet of the
information provided by Abu'l Fath in conjunction with the Roman occupation of
Mt. Gerizim (Bowman, 155).

were channelled through such periodic manifestations.[91] Violence
had become an efficacious means of communicating a range of
sentiments that guided relations between communities.

In Samaritan annals this annual scene of setting fire to effigies of
enemies commemorated the actual burning of the Roman 'overseers'
who opposed Baba Rabba, the great Samaritan reformer.[92] The
precise historical circumstances are as hazy as those related in the
scroll of Esther. The killing by incineration occurred on 'the evening
of the first of the seventh month'.[93] The involvement of children,
which invoked the ritual attacks of Christian children on Samaritan
synagogues and houses, suggests an early inculcation of communal
consciousness among both the Christian and Samaritan communities in Palestine. The Samaritan ceremony of the burning effigies, so
similar to the ritual burning of Haman on a cross, served several
functions: it provided a peaceful outlet for expressing hatred of Rome
while inspiring hopes of future vengeance based on past precedent; it
bonded children with adults in a ritual which allocated a specific
place for boys; and it underlined the frontiers of faith through
children's 'crusades'.

Roman reactions to this form of Samaritan resistance were not
recorded. The Samaritan manner of celebrating Succoth was not
banned. But in 438 the government of Theodosius II issued a law
which grouped together, for the first time in the legal history of the
eastern empire, Samaritans and Jews in collective prohibitions.[94] The
preamble to this constitution cast the emperor as the guardian of the
only 'true religion' and all those who did not share the empire's
'ceremonies of holiness' were branded demented and blind.[95] The
rhetoric clearly aimed at promoting orthodoxy by vitiating all other

[91] Malalas 40.
[92] Bowman, 147. The identity of these 'overseers' is unclear—they may have been
representatives of the Roman provincial governor or bishops, Bowman, 199 n. 192.
Chronicle Adler, pp. 93–4 (Adler and Seligsohn, 'Une nouvelle chronique samaritaine', *REJ* 45 (1902), 70–98), which appears to refer to the same events, does not link
the custom of burning effigies on the first of the seventh month with the burning of
the overseers. See above, Ch. 3.
[93] Bowman, 147.
[94] Western laws had done so in 404 (CTh. 16.8.16); in the east, CTh. 13.5.18 of CE
390 alleviated the burden of liturgies which had been imposed on Jewish and
Samaritan communities in Egypt.
[95] Nov. Theod. 3 (CE 438), text and translation in Linder, 326–32.

forms of religious worship. Jews and Samaritans were excluded from the ranks of municipal and imperial office-holders.

By the late sixth century, after a series of bloody clashes that inflicted enormous damage on lives and property, Samaritan resistance to the constant encroachment of Christianity acquired a distinctly ritualized hue. A hagiographical narrative dating to *c*.570 traced this sublimation of violence. One story, clearly conceived to exemplify the protagonist's virtue and exceptional stamina, related how a Samaritan (?) woman, a perfect antithesis of Jesus' Samaritan woman, attempted to tempt him. The episode took place in Porphyreon, a village at the foot of Mount Carmel (near Haifa). In a cave near the village lived a saintly man named Jacob. His presence and reputation as a healer drew visits from admiring fans, including Samaritans who subsequently converted to Christianity.[96] The saint's success prompted the local Samaritans, evidently worried about losing membership to their Christian neighbours, to engage in tactics aimed at undermining Jacob's ascetic fame:

They [the Samaritans] summoned a shameless and indecent woman, gave her twenty gold coins, and promised to give her the same again if she tripped the servant of God, Jacob, so that, seizing the opportunity, they would be able to drive him from their regions. The woman yielded to these promises...

It was late in the evening as she knocked at Jacob's door [*sic!*]...He tarried...She continued shamelessly to knock, imploring him to let her in. When he opened [the door] and saw her he first believed she was an apparition. Making the sign of the cross, he shut the door, and facing east he prayed fervently to God...But she did not stop knocking, loudly calling: 'Have mercy on me, servant of God, and open for me so that I do not become food for the beasts before your cell...' Unwillingly he let her in...[97]

In response to the monk's question, the woman identified herself as a nun stranded for the night who came to Jacob's cell because of her fear of wild beasts. The two subsequently shared Jacob's space, she in the outer cell and he in the upper cell. Later in the night the woman burst into a prolonged crying, asking the saint to comfort her

---

[96] *Vita Jacobi*, text and trans. in Pummer, 326–31. The date is some time in the 6th cent., probably the 570s, Pummer, 326.
[97] *Vita* 3–5, with Pummer, 329–30.

with the sign of the cross so as to alleviate her chest pain. The monk obliged but to avoid the ever-looming temptation he kept burning his hand in the fire which he had lit to keep the woman warm. Realizing that the plot had failed, the woman 'confessed' her share in the Samaritan strategy. She was then made to confess again, this time in public, at the local church and under the supervision of the local bishop. The bishop then mounted an expedition against the Samaritans, chasing them away from the village and from the districts where they had been living.

What started as a form of entertainment aimed at deflowering a male virgin of both virtue and reputation became, upon the individual's 'victory', an organized communal action against all the Samaritans of the region. Using weapons of force to combat Samaritan wit, the two parties fought with unequal might. The Samaritans groomed the woman because they had felt threatened by the attraction which the saintly Jacob exerted over their members; the Christians retaliated by getting rid of all the Samaritans because they felt menaced by the continued demonstration of Samaritan staying power in face of so much pressure from both the local and imperial establishments. The Samaritans cast Jacob as a Samson and hoped that he would meet the same fate at the hands of a contemporary Delilah. By employing sexual armoury the Samaritan strategy appeared fully cognizant of the role that sex, temptation, and tempting women played in the ideology of Christian sanctity.

What makes the Samaritans especially interesting was the adoption of a new discourse that espoused ritualized iconolasm to express their continuing defiance even after their staggering losses:

They [the Samaritans] perpetrated exceedingly outrageous and blasphemous atrocities against the Divine Word who became incarnate for us; against the immaculate glorious Mother of God, against the venerable and precious cross and against the saints... with shamelessness and impiety hitherto unheard of...[98]

[98] *Ep. ad Justinum Juniorem*, text and trans. in Pummer, 323–5, based on J. Mendham, *The Seventh General Council, the Second of Nicea, in which the Worship of Images was Established* (London 1849), 259–63. The date of the events narrated is 572. See, however, the reservations of P. van den Ven, 'Les Écrits de S. Syméon Stylite le Jeune avec trois sermons inédits', *Le Muséon* 70 (1957), 2–4, who prefers the reign of Justinian and a date before 565.

The author, the famed stylite Symeon the Younger, never set foot in Palestine. Consequently, he was exceedingly vague about the nature of the Samaritan 'blasphemy'. The Samaritans he accused were 'atheistic, impure and abominable', their activities requiring prompt imperial intervention. His letter considered the Samaritan entry into Christian sanctuaries as a violation both of the boundaries of a specific Christian area and of welfare of the empire itself.[99]

Unlike the burning of effigies on Purim and Succoth, the Samaritan iconoclasm seemed to be played out not in the streets but indoors, and specifically within a Christian sacred precinct. The complaint was initiated by the local bishop, passed to the 'patriarch of the orient', thence to Symeon and to the court.[100] Symeon's idiosyncratic reading of the events projected a Samaritan form of ritual violence meant to challenge Christian domination. The clash underlined Samaritan competitive energy as a source of intra-communal conflict that generated so much anxiety as to send the local bishop in search of outside help. Lifted out of its local context, the Samaritan war against images called for more anti-Samaritan laws so that,

The rest of them may spend all the days of their accursed and schismatic existence in fear... and the spirit of Jesus... shall accurse to the lowest depth of the abyss to destroy them with a never ending destruction...

Symeon's insistence that icons could not defend themselves meant that it was the duty of the emperor, as the supreme defender of the faith, to avenge this form of impiety. In May 572, perhaps in response to Symeon's letter, Justin II issued a decree (Novella 144) which rescinded all rights left to Samaritans by law, with the exception of the right to bequeath rural property. It even penalized, with exile and confiscation of property, Samaritan *conversos*, if detected celebrating the Sabbath or some other Samaritan holy day. Samaritans became belligerent 'heretics'. The vision of Samaritan iconoclasm and abysmal impiety, powerful enough to move the court in the sixth century,

---

[99] Assuming that the church was in neighbouring Porphyreon and not in the Castra Samaritanorum itself, Pummer, 319.

[100] Porphyreon remains unidentified, Pummer, 320–1, although both localities were on Mt. Carmel. For an attempt to identify these, A. Zigelman, 'Castra or Porphyrion?', *Michmanim* 15 (2001), 32–6 (Heb.). See also TIR. J-P, 204.

enjoyed a curious afterlife. At the second council of Nicea in 787 Christian iconoclasts were labelled 'Samaritans'.[101]

In 'battles' between Samaritans and Christians, the winners were virtually preordained. The specific ways in which minorities designed their strategies of survival and counter-offensive, be it through Purim rituals or Samaritan iconoclasm, were invariably interpreted as expressions of defiance which transcended the local. Because relations between Christians and minorities in late ancient Palestine came to be increasingly structured around Christian institutions and their supportive ideologies, the need to function within this framework forced non-Christians to participate in their logic. Rituals, processions, symbols, and icons, so important in the promotion of Christianity, were adopted into a Jewish–Christian and Samaritan–Christian discourse to promote barriers and to articulate challenges. Mock crucifixion and iconoclasm, attempts to violate the sexual integrity of Christian holy men, and attacks on churches became the practical expressions of an imbalance in power that characterized the landscape of Palestine in late antiquity.

4. FIRE AND WATER: RITUALIZING THE CONVERSION OF THE LAND

On the slopes of Mount Carmel, some 11 kilometres from the Mediterranean coast, lies the site of Sumaqa, an ancient village comprising about 20 dwelling complexes, industrial installations (oil and wine presses, as well as workshops), water cisterns, a Jewish synagogue, burial caves, and agricultural terraces.[102] Its origins went back to the Persian period (c.500–300 BCE) but the heyday of this rural settlement belonged to the Roman era, and specifically to the

---

[101] This was the conclusion voiced by John, legate of the east, after Symeon's letter was read at the second council of Nicaea, Mansi, 13. 164 with Pummer, 320.

[102] S. Dar, *Sumaqa: A Jewish Village on the Carmel* (Tel Aviv 1998) (Heb.). Note the relationship between the inhabited area (about 30 dunams) and the adjacent agricultural terrain which the villages tilled (about 5,400 dunams), the latter mostly covered with grapevines. Dar estimates c.800–900 inhabitants during Sumaqa's period of prosperity.

second and third centuries, when Sumaqa enjoyed prosperity and tranquillity.[103] Development projects at that time, including the construction of a well-built synagogue in the centre of the village, reflected the considerable means at the disposal of these rural Carmelites. Around CE 400 signs of deliberately inflicted damage have been detected. The synagogue and several private houses were heavily damaged. Some repairs were applied but the village contracted, entering a period of irreversible decay that lasted till the end of the sixth century when it was abandoned.

It is impossible to establish with complete certainty the identity of the agents of destruction of Sumaqa's Jewish sanctuary and property. It is possible, however, to link the early fifth-century layer of demolition with the *modus operandi* of Barsauma, a Mesopotamian monk whose meandering through the region invariably involved attacks on sacred precincts of non-Christians.[104] Although not specifically cited as a milestone along Barsauma's 'pilgrimages', Mount Carmel presented manifold attractions for zealots of his sort. Carmel had been the scene of a famous and ferocious clash between Elijah, defender of Yahwist monotheism, and the prophets of Baal, Yahweh's main rival (1 Kgs. 18). Moreover, with its mountainous landscape and relatively isolated rural settlements, the territory of Carmel provided impunity to actors of vandalism.[105]

---

[103] This continuity stands in a marked contrast to the abandonment of the Herodian villa of Ramat Hanadiv on the southern edge of the Carmel range, between the early 2nd and the early 5th cent., Y. Hirschfeld and R. Birger-Calderon, 'Early Roman and Byzantine Estates near Caesarea', IEJ 41 (1991), 86 and at greater length in Y. Hirschfeld (ed.), *Ramat Hanadiv Excavations* (Jerusalem 2000), *passim*.

[104] The suggestion has been made by Dar, *Sumaqa*, who also considered the damage a possible result of neighbouring wars. For Barsauma's biography, Nau, 'Résumé', ROC 8 (1913), 270–6; 379–89 and ROC 9 (1914), 113–34; 278–89. See also idem, 'Deux épisodes de l'histoire juive sous Théodose II d'après la vie de Barsauma le Syrien', REJ 83 (1927), 184–206; and E. Honigmann, *Le Couvent de Barsum et le Patriarchat Jacobit d'Antioche et de la Syrie* (Louvain 1954). On the genre of hagiography and its caveats, Lane Fox, 'The Life of Daniel', in Edwards and Swain (eds.), *Portraits*, 175–225.

[105] The number of settlements that can be ascribed to the 4th–7th cents. is impossible to ascertain. A survey of Carmel detected 259 (out of total of 357) sites dated to a 'Hellenistic–Byzantine' range, namely those that can be assigned to the millennium between c.300 BCE and 640 CE, H.-P. Kuhnen, *Studien zur Chronologie und Siedlungsarchäologie des Carmel (Israel) zwischen Hellenismus and Spätantike* (Wiesbaden 1989). On the use (and abuse) of archaeological surveys, G. Barker and D. Mattingly (eds.), *The Archaeology of Mediterranean Landscapes* (Oxford 2000), *passim*.

Whether Barsauma was selective or haphazard in his choice of locations remains unclear. Sumaqa did not have protecting walls and was vulnerable to hostile outsiders. Its grim fate contrasts sharply with the nearby Carmelite estate of Marinus.[106] Owned by an affluent Samaritan and boasting a Samaritan synagogue, this large estate of *c.*2,500 dunam (250 hectares or *c.*830 acres) was abandoned, apparently voluntarily, around the middle of the fifth century, to be resettled some 75 years later (*c.*625).[107] The reasons for the abandonment, or the resettlement for that matter, are unclear. Perhaps both were the outcome of natural and man-made disasters. Barsauma might not have been able to identify privately owned Samaritan synagogues or to derive glory from attacking a single family. If indeed Sumaqa's Jewish synagogue and homes fell victim to Barsauma's fanaticism, the detected destruction provides a sample of his methods vis-à-vis Jews, pagans, and Samaritans. When arriving, for example, at a pagan settlement, such as (the Negebite?) Reqm dgaia, Barsauma would have threatened to wage war and bring the place down unless the citizens opened the city gates to him.[108] Admission was invariably granted. He would then apply a miraculous remedy to a desperate collective need, such as lack of water. The miracle would bring about a general conversion. Opposition would be met with demonic affliction.

Through confrontation with local leaders Barsauma set out to demonstrate Christian superiority via a match of responsibility. He performed miracles calculated to challenge the ability of local priests to respond to communal needs. The demonstrations proved that his divinity, unlike the divinities venerated in the locality, controlled the elements as well as the devil. Conspicuously absent from such narratives were representatives of local and provincial order.[109] Although Barsauma's biographer insisted on his hero's impartiality when it came to conducting campaigns against non-Christians, the

---

[106] S. Dar *et al.*, *Raqit: Marinus' Estate on the Carmel, Israel* (Jerusalem 2003), *passim*, esp. 147–50.

[107] It is not entirely clear whether the 75 missing years represent abandonment or a gap in the evidence.

[108] Nau, *ROC* 8 (1913), 383. The precise location of Reqm dgaia is unclear. It is to be sought in the Negev, and may be identical with one of the townlets, such as Avdat or Mamshit. See Ch. 6 below.

[109] The exception was Jerusalem, see Ch. 5.

scale of the confrontation was markedly different. When encountering Jewish settlements Barsauma targeted the synagogue rather than the leaders. Towns singled out by him had spectacular synagogues, like the golden one which graced Rabat Moab (Areopolis), east of the Jordan:

> Nowhere was there a synagogue equal to this one, other than the temple that Solomon himself built in Jerusalem. It was built with large and carefully-hewn stones, encrusted with gold and silver, and lit with golden chandeliers . . . [110]

At Rabat Moab, the Jews, numbering no less than 15,000, had been prepared. Barsauma's reputation as a destroyer of sanctuaries must have preceded him. He and his few followers apparently managed to breach the walls. The defenders retreated to the synagogue, perhaps deluded into believing that Barsauma would respect the sanctuary's right of asylum. Doors were shut and stones were thrown. One stone hit the head of one of Barsauma's 'brothers' but miraculously split without injuring the man. The closed doors suddenly opened. Barsauma was confronted with the stunning beauty and riches of the synagogue. He ordered his men to desist from looting. The synagogue and everything in it had to be set afire. Nothing was left— wood, stones, gold, silver, and precious stones burnt to cinder.[111] It is unclear whether conversion to Christianity also occurred. The omission of all references to such a consequence is as suggestive as the biographer's reticence regarding the fate of the pagan temples whose priests Barsauma had outwitted and converted.

An outsider to Palestinian tenors, Barsauma, carrying radical foreignness and condemnation, challenged what was immutably entrenched in the soil. In the spaces that he sought to alter to fit his own notions of a land fit for Christian pilgrims he isolated his perceived obstacles through rivalry, dispute, and destruction. An invader, his destructive pilgrimages embedded a claim based on an appropriation of the biblical wars which the Israelites carried in the name of Yahweh against non-Yahwists. By attacking synagogues Barsauma attempted to wipe out Jewish and Samaritan specificity,

[110] Nau, *ROC* 8 (1913), 383.
[111] Although one follower got away with gold, to be chased away by Barsauma, ibid. 385.

and to dissolve it, as well as polytheism, in the generality of non-conformity. Jews, pagans, Samaritans, were no longer Roman citizens of various religious and ethnic affiliation but rather neutralized elements. The biases of both monk and narrator are strikingly obvious, casting the former as the sole spokesperson for the true God, precisely like an Elijah. It was natural that such zeal would eventually be aimed even at Barsauma's co-religionists. Bent on purifying Christianity itself, Barsauma found himself accused of using magic and of subverting the imperial establishment. In response to these accusation he simply stated, like would-be martyrs of the pre-Constantinian era of persecution: 'I am Barsauma the Christian'.[112]

The phenomenon of missionary monks was not new.[113] Jerome's hero, the Gazan monk Hilarion, emerged from the self-imposed isolation of meditation and basket-weaving to go to Halusa (Elusa) in the Negev to convert the 'Saracen' pagans.[114] His arrival (*c*.350 CE), 'accompanied by a great procession of monks' coincided with a major festival celebrated at the temple of Venus.[115] After healing an ailing chieftain Hilarion was rewarded with the conversion of both leader and tribesmen. Whether conversion was accompanied by the destruction of the temple was not stated. What made Barsauma's trail unique was the plan and scale of 'baptism': the use of water miracles to convert pagans and the application of fire to undermine Judaism. The dissemination of Christianity, as perceived by Barsauma, proceeded as a rectification of the landscape, taking care to lend it uniformity by erasing creeds, castes, and communal sanctuaries. The elimination of the distinct ritual and religious past was meant to engage in a solemn affirmation of the glory of Christianity.

Carefully structured and peppered with miracles, the narratives that glorified Barsauma suggest that the whole plot had been well organized, the converting individuals few, and the initial expectations

---

[112] Nau, *ROC* 9 (1914), 280.

[113] Cf. Z. Rubin, 'Christianity in Byzantine Palestine: Missionary Activity and Religious Coercion', *Jerusalem Cathedra* 3 (1983), 97–113.

[114] I know of no specific study that outlines a typology of conversion and of mission. Palestinian 'methods' of conversion, especially of Jews, can be compared with the most detailed account of forced communal conversion, that of the Jews of Minorca, prompted through the arrival of the Palestinian relics of St Stephen. S. Bradbury, *Severus of Minorca: Letter on the Conversion of the Jews* (Oxford 1996).

[115] Jerome, *Vita Hilarionis*. See also Ch. 2 above.

of success minimal. The efflorescence of synagogues, recently redated to the fifth, if not the sixth century CE, underlines the futile savagery of both imperial laws and Barsauma's activities.[116] Yet, these early fifth-century vignettes also highlight the manner in which non-Christian rituals were devalued. Barsauma's attempts to make the foreign local and the local foreign, and the agonistic nature of the legal rhetoric employed vis-à-vis non-Christians (and heretics) associated the naturalization of Christianity with dissension and destruction.

To judge by Barsauma's Palestinian trails, few converted willingly in the early half of the fifth century. Yet, around 360 Epiphanius, the Palestinian-born bishop of Salamis (Cyprus), met at Scythopolis a converted Jew by the name of Joseph.[117] According to Joseph's own testimony he had been a member of the close circle of the *nasi*, the Jewish patriarch in Tiberias, and a sole witness, through peeping, of the deathbed baptism of this dignitary administered, in solitude and secret, by the local bishop.[118] Appointed guardian of the heir to the patriarchate, Joseph busied himself with extricating the young man from various acts of mischief while himself experiencing visions that encouraged conversion. During a mission to Asia Minor Joseph discovered the Gospels. He underwent baptism, was rewarded with a meeting with the emperor Constantine, and was awarded the rank of a *comes*. He ultimately settled in Scythopolis, a city where he and another secret convert from Judaism to Christianity formed the nucleus of Christian orthodoxy.

Joseph's road to self-conversion and his subsequent missionary activities placed him in open conflict with his former co-religionists. When he had been caught reading the Gospels in Cilicia the local Jews lashed him in the synagogue until the bishop of the town

---

[116] See the comments in Ch. 2, 101–2.

[117] *Pan.* 30 (*GCS* 25, 338–48). Eng. trans. F. Williams, *The Panarion of Epiphanius of Salamis* (Leiden 1987), i. 122–9.

[118] On Joseph and his history see the recent analyses of E. Reiner, 'Joseph the Comes of Tiberias and the Jewish–Christian Dialogue in Fourth Century Galilee', in Levine (ed.), *Continuity and Renewal* (Jerusalem 2004), 355–86 (article title in Hebrew: 'The Seal of Christ and the Potion that Failed'); and of S. C. Goranson, 'Joseph of Tiberias Revisited: Orthodoxies and Heresies in Fourth Century Galilee', in E. M. Meyers (ed.), *Galilee through the Centuries: Confluence of Cultures* (Winona Lake 1999), 335–43.

extricated him. When he set out to convert a conspicuous public monument in Tiberias, the confrontation between Joseph and the Jewish community bore distinct resemblance to biblical scenes which pitted Elijah against the prophets of Baal.[119] Joseph became an Elijah paradoxically converted to Christianity while the Tiberiade Jewish opponents bore the role of the defenders of idolatry. The lime kilns of Tiberias provided the battlefield. The weapons were water and fire, precisely those which Barsauma would later wield. In the first round the temple which Joseph coveted was converted into a ritual bathhouse to serve the needs of Tiberias' Jews. The conjunction of place and time were pertinent. The temple was a locus of ambivalence, a relic of an imperial pagan past appropriated to serve the specific needs of Tiberias' Jewish community, two associations which Joseph's church set out to challenge.

When the walls of the watering establishment, built with stones that had once graced the temple, reached a certain height Joseph needed lime to accomplish his mission. He had kilns built outside the city but at that point 'those natural born Jews wasted their time on magic and jugglery to put a spell on the fire' (*Pan.* 30.12). Apparently the fire smouldered, failing the spells. Joseph arrived at the scene.

He ordered water to be fetched in a vessel, took it in the sight of all—a crowd of Jews had gathered to watch, eager to see how it would turn out and what Joseph would try to do. Tracing the sign of the cross on the vessel with his own finger, he cried out: 'In the name of Jesus of Nazareth, whom my father and all those here present crucified, may there be power in this water to annul all sorcery and enchantment these men have wrought, and to work a miracle on the fire so that the Lord's house may be finished'. With that he wet his hand and sprinkled the water on each furnace. The spells were broken, and in the presence of all the fire blazed. The crowds then cried: 'One is the God who helps the Christians', and withdrew.[120]

What started as a routine building operation turned into a public match of wit and faith in which Joseph engaged in a power demonstration.

---

[119] Reiner, 'Joseph', 385 and *passim*. idem, 381–2, claims that Epiphanius modelled the narrative on Eusebius' description of the church of the Holy Sepulchre (*Vita Constantini* 3.25–40). For Jacobs, *Remains of the Jews*, 50 n. 125, the story of the church in Tiberias, and specifically its Jewish 'aspects', formed a counterpart to that of Julian's attempt to build the temple.

[120] *Pan.* 30.12 (Williams's translation, slightly modified).

Its elements included the sign of the cross over the water-jug, blessings that aimed at countering Jewish imprecations, and ceremonious
pouring of water over smoke. The purpose of the show was to free the
space that inhibited the encroachment of Christianity into urban
sanctuaries.

Joseph's biography represented a stage at which the transformation
of Palestine was perceived in terms of a mission of construction.
A few decades later the mission changed dramatically to become a
message of destruction, as Barsauma's biography shows. The
churches that Joseph built staked a claim to the land, serving as a
focus of Christian identity for those who were to follow its call. If an
eminent Jew like Joseph could see the 'light', there was no reason why
others would not follow. In fact, at Tiberias, as Epiphanius himself
admitted, the admiring spectators of the magic show of water and fire
went home without converting.[121]

In Joseph's narrative the dynamics of interaction suggest mutual
contacts that privileged ritualized shows of endless configurations.
Some spectacles had the potential of developing into a violent confrontation. When the players were placed within a local context, like
the protagonists of Joseph's tale, violence was contained and rituals
prevailed. When the protagonist was a stranger, the locale was interpreted in terms that required manipulative and hostile overtaking.
Barsauma's rationale dictated the violation of the landscape because
his patriotism, purely Christian, could not be contained in the
Roman notion of citizenship. Similarly, when Palestinian protagonists went abroad, their appearance spelt dissension. The bones of
St Stephen, unearthed in CE 415 not far from Jerusalem, reached
the island of Minorca to upset a territory which, until then, had been
a model of communal harmony:

In the end, even the obligation of greeting one another was suddenly broken
off, and not only was our old habit of easy acquaintance disrupted, but the
sinful appearance of our long-standing affection was transformed into

---

[121] There are no archaeological traces of churches in the eastern Galilee before the
5th cent. At Sepphoris, another place where Joseph allegedly built a church, even the
synagogue does not appear to antedate the 5th cent., and at least one of its donors was
a Gelasius, *scholasticus and comes*, and son of Aetius the *comes*. Ilan, *Ancient Synagogues*, 220–1; Roth-Gershon, *The Greek Inscriptions*. On its date, Weiss–Netzer,
Promise and Redemption. A Synagogue Mosaic from Sepphoris.

temporary hatred, through love of eternal salvation. In every public place battles were waged against the Jews over the law, in every house struggles over the faith.[122]

In this remote outpost of the western empire, the deposition of the relics engineered a campaign, led by the local bishop, to forcibly convert the Jews of the island by targeting the leaders of the community and its sanctuary.

Because of the centrality of the concept of Palestine as a Christian holy land, the tenor of social interaction was susceptible to external pressures.[123] Constantine set out to reordain Palestinian sacred geography in Jerusalem and its vicinity. Following a report of Eutropia his mother-in-law, who had been outraged by the colourful trade fair at Mamre (near Hebron), Constantine entrusted the *comes* Acacius with the task of 'purifying' the spot from its pagan associations.[124] According to Constantine,

One benefit, and that of no ordinary importance, has been conferred on us by my truly pious mother-in-law, in that she has made known to us by letter that abandoned folly of impious men which has hitherto escaped detection by you. The criminal conduct thus overlooked must now through our own means obtain fitting correction and remedy... for surely it is a grave impiety indeed that holy places should be defiled by the stain of unhallowed impurities... She assures me that the place which takes its name from the oak of Mambre, where we find that Abraham dwelt, is defiled by certain of the slaves of superstition in every possible way... Since it is evident that these [pagan] practices are inconsistent with the character of our times and unworthy of the sanctity of the place itself, I desire your reverence to be informed that the illustrious count Acacius has received instructions to the effect that every idol which shall be found [in Mamre] shall immediately be consigned to the flames; that the altar be utterly demolished; and that if any one, after this decree, shall be guilty of impiety of any kind in this place, he shall be visited with penalty... (NPNF, *VC* 3.52–3).

[122] *Epistula Severi* 5, trans. Bradbury, *Severus of Minorca*, 84–5.

[123] Wilken, *The Land Called Holy*, passim. Jacobs, *Remains of the Jews*, passim.

[124] On the Mamre-Terebinthus fair and its 'international' character, W. Bacher, 'Die Jahrmarkt an der Terebinte bei Hebron', *ZAW* 29 (1909), 294–311; S. Krauss, 'Der Jahrmarkt von Batnan', *ZAW* 29 (1909), 148–52. Z. Safrai, 'The Fairs in Eretz Israel during the Period of Mishna and Talmud', *Zion* 49 (1984), 139–58. On the site and its excavations, E. Mader, *Mambre* (Freiburg 1957).

The government's heavy-handed manner lent conflictual colour to celebrations which transcended communal boundaries. Imperial authorization of the use of physical force was directed primarily against pagan divinities and their altars, both consigned to fire and destruction. Less than a century later Barsauma would apply similar strategies without imperial approval.

Jewish rabbis shared with Constantine a dislike for the Mamre (Botna) fair, precisely because of the opportunities it afforded for mixing company (Jewish–gentile) and for extra-communal trade.[125] Festive proximity to gentiles made the rabbis as uneasy as Eutropia appears to have been outside her own circle of Christian piety. She constructed the merriment of Mamre as an affront to her concept of Christian sanctity; the rabbis feared intimacy with gentiles and inadvertent participation in pagan rites. The appropriation of the site by Christianity paradoxically ensured the continuous success of the fair, as Sozomen attested in the fifth century. Few could resist an astute and appealing combination of shopping opportunities with satisfying a personal search for piety:

This feast is diligently frequented by all nations: the Jews because they boast their descent from Abraham [who is buried in Mamre], the pagans because angels appear there to men, and by Christians because Christ was born there of a virgin ... Here some prayed to the God of all, some called upon the angels, poured out wine, burnt incense, or offered an ox, goat, sheep or a cock.[126]

The imperial attempt to transform Mamre into a site worthy of its biblical connotations, like the one launched to purge Purim of its blasphemous associations (both doomed to Failure), was advertised as a vindication of a 'divine law'.[127] This was a law based on the claim of Christianity to the Bible and the claim of Constantine to rule a

---

[125] Jews were strictly forbidden from attending the fair at Mambre-Botna, as well as those in Gaza and Acre, *PT AZ* 1.4; *Sifre Deut.* 30.6; Cf. Jerome, *Comm. in Jerem.* 31.39.

[126] Soz. *HE* 2.4. with Hunt, *Holy Land Pilgrimage*; A. Kofsky, 'Mamre: A Case of a Regional Cult?', in idem and G. G. Stroumsa (eds.), *Sharing the Sacred* (Jerusalem 1998), 19–30. For Jews the site also conjured up painful memory of the sale of thousands into slavery during the revolt against Hadrian in 135. Cf. Jerome, *Comm. in Zach* 4.11.4.

[127] Eus. *VC* 3.53.3 apud Hunt, *Holy Land Pilgrimage*, 102.

Christian empire. For Christians, Mamre was to become what Purim had become for Jews, a locus tying the past to the present where celebrants became spectators of their own history.[128] The transformation of Mamre, like that of Gaza *c.*400, was a process initiated at a local level and carried out by imperial decrees and soldiers. It provides an example of the decisive effect of imperial intervention and of the application of law to reality. Yet, such cases may have been an exception rather than the rule. The desacralization of pagan sites and their Christian sacralization was rarely an orderly affair, with a royal reporter, an imperial order, and prompt execution. Nor was the depaganization of urban space complete till at least the sixth century.

Presided over by Pan, god of the inexplicable and master of the echo, the public space at the city of Golanide Paneas (Caesarea Philippi) articulated the discourse of ritualized violence that marked the transformation of Palestine in late antiquity. From its foundation, annual celebrations honouring Pan in the city bearing his name, included a ritual whose highlight was the miraculous disappearance of a sacrifice in the waters of the local stream, believed to be the sources of the Jordan river. This was the ceremony that Astyrius, an early convert to Christianity described as a member of the Roman Senate and as a confidant of emperors, decided to disrupt during a visit to Paneas.[129] Taking pity on what he construed as the locals' deluded faith in the power of demons, Astyrius prayed to Jesus to put a stop to this delusion. As soon as the words left his mouth, the sacrifice surfaced. One miracle countered another with the more recent divinity banishing the divine trickster, Pan himself. Eusebius' words hint that Astyrius' demonstration banished Pan and paganism from Paneas.[130] The matter remains open to doubt.

Within the context of the *polis*, the introduction of Jesus into the world of Pan, and into the world of Judaism, necessitated the simultaneous holding of two apparently contradicting propositions. One relied on miracles, and hence on the unpredictable, in order to procure victory. The other recruited rituals which proceeded from

[128] To paraphrase Asterius of Amasean Hom. 9.2 apud Hunt, *Holy Land Pilgrimage*, 103,

[129] Eusebius, *HE* 7.17.

[130] Cf. rabbinic linking of the coming of the Messiah with the end of paganism at Paneas, *BT San.* 98a.

ritualized confrontation to open violence. For those who had to reinvent themselves, ritualized violence was an affirmation of difference and therefore an effective operator. To displace Pan it was imperative to undermine the foundations which bound such divinities to the soil. To replace Judaism, Christianity had to reinvent itself.

5

Jerusalem: The Contrasting Eyes of Beholders

A harsh town, Jerusalem is. History has imposed a heavy burden on her ever-bending back. Even now conflagrations of conflicts which had raged long ago continue to ravage her flesh, to feed her heavenly lineage, and to kindle the passions of her fanatics.

Go live your daily life in a city like this! Every time you leave home you embark on a winding path of history. On the way to your hairdresser in the centre of town you meet the prophet Isaiah, and king Agrippa and his majesty George V. Your daily walks are tantamount to encounters which cross the frontiers of time. Walking home you meet with two great sages, ben Zakai and ben Maimon, with far-seeing Hertzl, with the great conqueror Salah a Din, and with the towering literary figure of Agnon. Here as you stroll you can conjure Jesus marching along a narrow alley. In the background you ears are attuned to the din of the Roman army as it besieged the city as they are to riders of Islamic onslaught and to crusaders unsheathing bloody swords...

On one hill of the city is the house of parliament of the sovereign state of Israel; down below are the scars of the latest suicide bombing...

Go live in a city like this where sanity is scarce, where every stone may momentarily turn into a contested space.

If I were allowed to recreate Jerusalem from its foundations I would begin exactly as children do when they paint a picture. I would draw a house, with a roof and a window and a chimney, and a soft lawn in the front. Then another house, then another. In these houses ordinary people would dwell and not self-appointed missionaries. The denizens of this new Jerusalem would live in the city and not exist through her.

Yaakov Maor, 'Jerusalem Journal', in *Yediot Aharonot*, Succoth Eve, 10 Oct. 2003, p. 19, Heb. (slightly modified)

Nicolai Gogol never published the second half of *Dead Souls*. The Hebrew translator of the work accounted for the incompleteness by explaining that Gogol burnt the manuscript of part II after visiting Jerusalem where he had gone slightly mad. There are other and possibly more adequate explanations but none so apt. Those who live or who have lived in Jerusalem share in this madness and its antagonistic consciousness, subtle and brutal, encountering time and memory at points exceeding the frame of the temporal and the visible.

1. PROLOGUE: THE NAVEL OF THE UNIVERSE?

The day is the 8th of Av, the 5764th year since the creation of the world (in common parlance, 26 July 2004). The streets of Jerusalem around the Old City come to life. Thousands stream through the Jaffa gate, hundreds through the gate of Sion, all heading to the Wailing Wall to participate in the ancient ceremony that marks the eve of the Day of Mourning, a memorial of the destruction of the Temple in Jerusalem, first by the Babylonians, and a second time by the Romans. Animated conversations, occasional laughter, an astonishing Babel of languages, heavily attired ultra-orthodox and lightly clad seculars.

The immediate vision is neither of sadness nor of longing, although both sentiments become mourning. The crowds that fill the narrow alleys of the Old City create a revisionary narrative that sustains yet confounds tradition. The moment they capture represents the historical transformation of Jerusalem, and an ironic repetition. In 2004 it is possible to walk all the way to the Wailing Wall, the last vestige of the Temple Mount, but it is still impossible, for Jews only, to walk on the Temple Mount itself. Overhead hover helicopters, a token of modernity, and of the perpetual cloud of tension that envelops Jerusalem. Threats have been made by extremists.

I join a group that prefers to encircle the walls. The guide leads in a wheelchair, the way pointed out by a tiny torch fastened to his brow, and his voice, amplified by a microphone, blends an artful technology with stories of old. A gentle breeze alleviates the heat of the passing day. The huge monasteries that nestle against the walls are bathed in silence and darkness. This is, after all, the day of the Jews. I ruminate on what Saint Jerome once presented as a traumatic scenario, a proof of God disavowing the Jews. I witness a paradox— on the one hand, an image of a temple in ruins and of remembering that is not, in itself, original, and on the other hand, a new articulation as repetition with a difference.

The presence of many histories is always ambivalent, and in Jerusalem it produces a fissure between appearance and reality. There is the Jerusalem which is the invention of historicity, and there is the Jerusalem of fantasy, not merely a heavenly city but also a subject of cosmology, cosmogony, cartography, and of textuality. Each one of these Jerusalems projects a mode of authority with its own discriminatory discourse. In the interests of visibility and recognition, Jerusalem appears as a space that is permanently positioned as a golden mean, a borderland between perpetuation and recollection, between the past and the present.

In the early years of the fifth century Jerusalem obtained a permanent foothold at the heart of the great city of Rome.[1] A visitor to the Roman church of Santa Pudenziana could behold an artful depiction of the Palestinian city. At the centre of the Roman mosaic three elements, a mound, a human figure, and a symbol, simultaneously projected a terrestrial and a celestial Jerusalem. The first represented Golgotha; the second was Jesus seated in majesty on its top; and the third was a huge cross stretching from hill to heaven.[2]

---

[1] On the complex relationship between Jerusalem and Rome, V. Twomey, *Apostolikos Thronos: The Primacy of Rome as reflected in the Church History of Eusebius and the Historico-Apologetic Writings of Saint Athanasius* (Münsterische Beiträge zur Theologie; Münster 1982), 41–90. On Rome and the logistics of its Christian topography, J. Curran, *Pagan City and Christian Capital: Rome in the Fourth Century* (Oxford 2000), and E. D. Hunt, 'Imperial Building at Rome: The Role of Constantine', in K. Lomas and T. Cornell (eds.), *Bread and Circuses: Euergetism and Municipal Patronage in Roman Italy* (London 2003), 105–24.

[2] W. Pullan, 'Jerusalem from Alpha to Omega in the Santa Pudenziana Mosaic', *Jewish Art* 23/24 (1997–8), 405–17. See also B. Kühnel, 'Jerusalem in Christian Art

Few artistic images illustrate with greater conviction the complexity of Jerusalem's transformation in late antiquity. The Santa Pudenziana's vision of the Hill of the Crucifixion in Jerusalem highlights the politics of dislocation that shaped the transfer of the sacred from the Temple Mount, home of successive Jewish temples, to Golgotha (Calvary) at the heart of the Roman forum of Jerusalem.[3]

The Roman mosaic also marked a discontinuity, a disturbance of the authoritative representation of Rome's polytheistic past and an uncanny victory of Palestinian religiosity. Pudenziana's Jerusalem encapsulated the mixed and split imaginations that generated displacements and strategies of subversion which turned an urban space from side to side, like a coin with endless faces. Within the Roman context, of city and of empire, late ancient Jerusalem required a language of description that mediated between visual experience and the object of writing. An understanding of Jerusalem in the critical phase between Christianity and Islam necessitates the bridging of words that were culturally transparent and of images that disavowed visibility.

The Christian appropriation of Jerusalem in late antiquity is a well-documented process.[4] Unlike most historical developments it had a well-defined start with an enterprising emperor (Constantine) endowing a spectacular church (the Holy Sepulchre, CE 335) and a well-articulated end marked by the erection of a golden mosque endowed by a caliph (Abd al-Malik, CE 692) and placed on the Temple Mount. In between, accounts of pilgrims, monumental maps, sermons, and numerous references in a host of sources, not

from the Fourth to the Seventh Centuries', in S. Safrai and Y. Tsafrir (eds.), *The History of Jerusalem: The Roman-Byzantine Period 70–638* (Jerusalem 1999), 441–75 (Heb.). The mosaic is heavily and not too subtly restored.

[3] Y. Z. Eliav, 'Temple Mount as a Cult Place and as a Political Center in Judaism and Christianity: A Re-Appraisal', in Y. Reiter (ed.), *Sovereignty of God and Man: Sanctity and Political Centrality on Temple Mount* (Jerusalem 2001), 25–56, esp. 50 (Heb.).

[4] The bibliography on the history of late ancient or Byzantine Jerusalem is vast. A useful point of departure is Y. Tsafrir, 'Jerusalem', *Reallexicon zur byzantinisch en Kunst* 3 (1975), 525–615 and numerous publications by the same author. For a basic list with critical bibliography, K. Bieberstein and H. Bloedhorn, *Jerusalem: Grundzüge der Baugeschichte vom Chalkolithikum bis zur Frühzeit der osmanischen Herrschaft* (Wiesbaden 1994), 3 vols. The best collection of sources in translation remains F. E. Peters, *Jerusalem* (Princeton 1985).

to mention countless modern digs and probes, provide milestones or punctuation of an ideology which repositioned Jewish Jerusalem and Roman Aelia Capitolina at the heart of virtual and visual Christianities, and later of Islam.[5]

For Christians who never set foot in the city Jerusalem became a literary fiction or an 'iconic image', a heavenly city which, more than any other locality in Christendom, represented the essence of what it meant to be a Christian.[6] For Jews, all but barred from Jerusalem, the alienated space underwent a similar sublimation. Jewish prayers, biblical exegesis, and liturgical poems placed the city firmly in the centre of a religion that could no longer revolve around Jerusalem and its central sanctuary. Jerusalem in late antiquity subsequently emerged as a city of striking contrasts: a dynamic reality for numerous Christians, residents and visitors alike, but also a reconfigured space which determined Jewish law and lore. For Christians and for Jews, recasting Jerusalem meant that the very concept of sanctity and holiness underwent a concomitant revolution.[7] Late ancient Jerusalem became larger than life. It still is.

The centrality of Jerusalem in Jewish history and thought is poignantly reflected in the continuing belief that the city was the navel of the earth.[8]

As the navel is in the middle of a human being, the Land of Israel (*Eretz Israel*) is the navel of the world, as it is written: *dwellers of the navel of the*

---

[5] Wilken, *The Land Called Holy*; P. Walker, *Holy City, Holy Places? Christian Attitudes to Jerusalem and the Holy Land in the Fourth Century* (Oxford 1990). See also A. Wharton, *Refiguring the Post Classical City: Dura Europos, Jerash, Jerusalem and Ravenna* (Cambridge 1995) and eadem in *From Dura to Sepphoris*. One introduction to excavations within the last two decades is provided in H. Geva (ed.), *Ancient Jerusalem Revealed* (Jerusalem 2000). See also E. Mazar *The Temple Mount Excavations in Jerusalem 1968–78*, ii: *The Byzantine and Early Islamic Period* (Jerusalem 2003).

[6] On opposition to pilgrimage based on fear of competing cults, B. Biton-Ashkelony, *Encountering the Sacred: The Debate on Christian Pilgrimage in Late Antiquity* (Berkeley 2005).

[7] Cf. the comments of R. Markus, 'How on Earth could Places Become Holy? Origins of the Christian Idea of Holy Places', *JECS* 2/3 (1994), 257–71.

[8] P. S. Alexander, 'Jerusalem and the Omphalos of the World: On the History of a Geographical Concept', in L. I. Levine (ed.), *Jerusalem: Its Sanctity and Centrality to Judaism, Christianity, and Islam* (New York 1999), 104–19. On Jewish, or rather rabbinic attitudes to Jerusalem, I. M. Gafni, 'Jerusalem in Rabbinic Literature', in Y. Tsafrir and S. Safrai (eds.), *The History of Jerusalem: The Roman and Byzantine Periods (70–638 CE)* (Jerusalem 1999), 35–60. Below, on specific concepts of the Temple Mount.

earth (Ezekiel 38: 12). Just as *Eretz Israel* is located in the centre of the world so is Jerusalem in the centre of *Eretz Israel*, the temple in the centre of Jerusalem, the holy of holies in the centre of the temple, the ark at the centre of the holy of holies, and right in front is the foundation-stone of the whole of the universe.[9]

In this creative geography rabbinic imagination placed the foundation of the cosmos at the heart of the (defunct) Jerusalem temple. This was a fanciful amalgam of vertical and horizontal plans which formed a concentric sphere that radiated divine energy. It also stood for an imaginary boundary between the world above and the one below, between chaos and creation.[10] Such sentiments received an odd and contentious corollary in Origen's claim that Jerusalem was an entity beyond earthly grasp:

If Israel belongs to the sphere of souls and the city of Jerusalem is in heaven, it follows that the metropolis of the cities of Israel is Jerusalem in the heavens, and likewise the whole of Judaea. If we listen to Paul's divinely inspired wisdom, whatever has been prophesied and spoken of Jerusalem is of the heavenly city and it is of the place that contains the cities of the Holy Land that we must understand what Scripture announces.[11]

Rabbinic promotion of a literary Jerusalem posed a twofold challenge, one to Jewish biblical and post-biblical traditions, the other to Rome's domination.[12] Tacitus, like Titus, had been confident that Judaism would die with the loss of the Temple, its ritual core.[13] Both misunderstood the nature of Jewish commitment to city and to Temple. The birth of Aelia Capitolina as a garrison town in the second century was a traumatic event in the history of Jewish Jerusalem. It

[9] *Tanhuma to Leviticus*, Qedoshim 10, ed. Buber, 78, quoted in Alexander, 'Jerusalem', p. 114, modified.

[10] Ginzberg, *The Legends of the Jews*, v. 14–16, and *passim* with Z. Vilnay, *Legends of Jerusalem* (Philadelphia 1987), 5–36, 128–32, 269–79.

[11] *De Principiis* 4.3.8, trans. in Hamilton, 'Jerusalem', in Allen *et al.* (eds.), *Prayer and Spirituality in the Early Church*, 292, slightly modified.

[12] W. Müller, *Die Heilige Stadt: Roma quadrata, himmlisches Jerusalem und die Mythe vom Weltnabel* (Stuttgart 1961). Perhaps the elevation of Jerusalem and Eretz Israel served a double purpose in both an internal Jewish polemics (i.e. Palestinian versus Babylonian sages) and an external one (i.e. Jewish versus Roman). On the former, I. Gafni (ed.), *Land, Center and Diaspora: Jewish Constructs in Late Antiquity* (Sheffield 1997), 71–8.

[13] Tacitus, *Hist.* 5.13: *radice sublata, stirpem facile perituram.* Cf. Sulp. Sev. *Chron.* 2.30; Josephus, *War* 6.339.

further entailed an imperial ban that forbade Jewish life in Jerusalem. Generating a series of irreconcilable cityscapes, Jerusalem without Jews produced a meta-conflict between the submerged city of Jewish memory and its Roman and later Christian counterparts.

When Constantine legalized Christianity in the early fourth century the process of transformation continued as eloquently as the rabbinic remoulding of Jerusalem into a literary space had been.[14] Controversy over the identity of the city, between pagan Aelia and Christian Jerusalem, and between Jewish and Christian Jerusalems, resulted in stunning distortions of cartography. The rabbis located the navel of the world in the Land of Israel, in Jerusalem and in its Temple. The Madaba mosaic (6th century), a visual guide to the Christian Holy Land, depicted the city as a huge oval dominating the Palestinian landscape, hardly a reflection of Jerusalem's actual plan or size but a clear message of its position in the heart of every Christian.[15]

The reconfiguration of Jerusalem in Christian cartographic terms generated a paradox as striking as the verbal continuation of temple worship in rabbinic texts. In Christian Jerusalem there was a large yet a real void. Although Jerusalem itself dwarfed every other city in the area,[16] nowhere in the Madaba map did the imposing Temple Mount, once the heart and glory of Jewish Jerusalem, feature. To compound paradoxes, representations of the Temple, schematic yet unmistakable, began to multiply on floors and walls of synagogues throughout late antiquity, posing a direct challenge to Christian ideology which reasserted Judaism's demise by basing it on Temple and city alone.[17]

[14] E. D. Hunt, 'Constantine and Jerusalem', *JEH* 48 (1997), 405–24.

[15] See the comments of Y. Tsafrir, 'Byzantine Jerusalem: The Configuration of a Christian City', in Levine (ed.), *Jerusalem* (1999), 143–4. Also, A. Piganiol, 'L'Hémispherion et l'omphalos des lieux saints', *Cahiers archéologiques* 1 (1945), 7–14, especially on the highest point of the church of the Holy Sepulchre which, according to Eusebius (*VC* 3.38), Constantine 'presented to his God as a superb offering' (trans. Cameron–Hall, *Eusebius' Life of Constantine*). Cf. the roundness of Jerusalem in the Madaba map with literary perceptions of the city as a round one, Eucherius, 3 (CCSL 175: 237).

[16] This has been duly noted by practically all scholars of late ancient Jerusalem. For a recent survey of scholarship and ancient ideology, Eliav, 'Temple Mount as a Cult Place', 25–56 (Heb.). idem, *God's Mountain: The Temple Mount in Time, Place and Memory* (Baltimore 2005), esp. chs. 4–6.

[17] J. Magness, 'Helios and the Zodiac Cycle in Ancient Palestinian Synagogues', in W. G. Dever and S. G. Gitin (eds.), *Symbiosis, Symbolism and the Power of the Past* (Winona Lake, Ind. 2003), 363–89.

2. FROM AELIA BACK TO JERUSALEM

By the early 380s, barely half a century since the erection of the church of the Holy Sepulchre on the site of the crucifixion, a pious Christian pilgrim could spend months on end in Jerusalem, treading the cobbled streets, peering at localities hallowed by biblical souvenirs, visiting churches and monasteries, and participating in an unending feast of liturgical celebrations.[18] By the beginning of the seventh century, Jerusalem's patriarch could address the city from which he had been exiled by the Persians in verses that aspired to rival the Psalmist's poignant lament, as though Jerusalem had always been a Christian city.[19] Between Egeria in the late fourth century, and Zacharias, the banished bishop of the early seventh century, stood a process that denuded Jerusalem of its Jewish and pagan pasts and a landscape that had become a bone of endless contention.

Already the first Constantinian building in Jerusalem, the church of the Holy Sepulchre (CE 335), ushered in a rhetoric that aspired to highlight the futility of Judaism, a religion that had lost its sacred centre.[20] Contrasting the 'old' or Jewish Jerusalem with the 'new' or the Christian city, Eusebius, bishop of the Palestinian capital Caesarea, depicted the imperial endeavour as an affirmation of the city's new identity. The Jerusalem which Eusebius envisaged

[18] *Egeria's Travels*, trans. J. Wilkinson (1981). See also J. F. Baldovin, *The Urban Character of Christian Worship: The Origins, Development and Meaning of Stational Liturgy* (Rome 1987), esp. 45–104.

[19] Psalm 137: 1 (by the rivers of Babylon), reworked in Zacharia Hierosolymitani Patriarcha, *Epistola* (*PG* 86. 2, col. 3228). Cf. John the Almsgiver's word on the same events in 614, 'wailing and groaning bitterly, striving to outdo Jeremiah who had lamented the capture of the very same city, Jerusalem', Leontius of Neapolis, *Life of John the Almsgiver* 9 (H. Delehaye, 'Une vie inédite de Saint Jean l'Aumonier', *AB* 45 (1972), 23, trans. in R. L. Wilken, 'Loving the Jerusalem Below: The Monks of Palestine', in L. I. Levine (ed.), *Jerusalem: Its sanctity and Centrality to Judaism, Christianity and Islam* (New York 1999), 240 (slightly modified).

[20] The literature on the church of the Holy Sepulchre is vast. Among recent works, M. Biddle, *The Tomb of Christ* (Stroud 1999) and J. Patrich, 'The Church of the Holy Sepulchre: History and Architecture', in Tsafrir and Safrai (eds.), *The History of Jerusalem* (1999), 353–81. The centrality of the church is strikingly reflected in the Madaba map, see Piccirillo and Alliata (eds.), *The Madaba Map Centenary*.

immortalized the victory of Jesus over death and of Christianity over Judaism.[21]

The monument of salvation itself was the new Jerusalem built over against the one so famous of old which, after the pollution caused by the murder of the Lord, experienced the last extremity of desolation and paid the penalty of its wicked inhabitants. Opposite this the emperor reared with rich and lavish expenditure the trophy of the Savior's victory over death. This was the strange and new Jerusalem, proclaimed in the oracles of the prophets... [22]

The re-entry of Christianity to Jerusalem through the implantation of a church in the forum further pitted the Christian God against the gods once honoured there. Unfolding the 'history' that had preceded the erection of the Constantinian church, Eusebius recorded the discovery of Christ's tomb underneath a pagan temple.[23] The sanctuary was dismantled to make room for the church and the incident was elevated to the status of a divine revelation which confirmed the triumph of Christianity over paganism (*VC* 3.26–8). Eusebius offered a verbal purification of the site. The act echoed Jewish acts of purifying urban territory that had been 'polluted' by pagan use.[24]

Destruction and construction, two symmetrical acts thus accompanied the unearthing of the holiest burial in Christianity, symbolizing the interment of paganism. Jupiter and Aphrodite had to bow to Christ. Yet, the memory of Jupiter's victory over Yahweh was allowed to stay. Atop Temple Mount two statues, one of a divinity (Jupiter?),

[21] A. Linder, 'Jerusalem as a Focal Point in the Conflict between Judaism and Christianity', in B. Z. Kedar and Z. Baras (eds.), *Jerusalem in the Middle Ages: Selected Papers* (Jerusalem 1979), 5–26 (Heb.). On Eusebius' attitudes to Jerusalem, Z. Rubin, 'The Church of the Holy Sepulchre and the Conflict between the Sees of Caesarea and Jerusalem', *Jerusalem Cathedra* 2 (1982), 79–105, restated in 'The Cult of the Holy Places and Christian Politics in Byzantine Jerusalem', in Levine (ed.), *Jerusalem* (1999), 151–62, and largely followed by Walker, *Holy City, Holy Places? passim*; but see also the reservations of Cameron–Hall, *Eusebius' Life of Constantine*, 274 ff., esp. 280–4. On Eusebius' accuracy and his use of sources, B. Isaac, 'Eusebius and the Geography of the Roman Provinces', in D. L. Kennedy (ed.), *The Roman Army in the East* (JRA Suppl. 19; Ann Arbor 1996); repr. in Isaac, *The Near East under Roman Rule*, 284–309.

[22] Eusebius, *VC*, 3.33, trans. in PPTS.

[23] *VC* 3.26–8, dedicated to Aphrodite or to Jupiter, according to Eliav, *God's Mountain*, Ch. 3.

[24] Cf. the purification of Tiberias because it had been built on a pagan burial ground, Josephus, *Ant.* 18.38; *Pesiqta de Rab Kahana* 11.16. P. van der Horst, *Japheth in the Tents of Shem: Studies on Jewish Hellenism in Antiquity* (Leuven 2002), 127.

the other of an emperor (Hadrian?), memorialized both Jesus' prophecy regarding the area's perpetual desolation and the victory of pagan Rome over its rebellious Jewish subjects.[25] To insert Jerusalem into a system that lived by imagining its exclusion Eusebius introduced the contemporary town as a creation of Constantine, an old city with a new myth of origins that dispensed with sequential history. A vision of a selected past recreated Jerusalem's Christian identity along contesting terms. The texts and architecture that accompanied the birth and the primordial period of the nascent Christian city highlighted the moments when Aelia gave birth to a Jerusalem which had already been in existence from time immemorial.

Jerusalem's biblical roots supplied a mythic starting point for a history of the city that was not very historical. When Eusebius described the church of the Holy Sepulchre he compressed generations into a timeless present, merging what came before and after around the church:

In the province of Palestine, in the city which was once the seat of Hebrew sovereignty, on the very site of the Lord's sepulchre, he [Constantine] raised a church of noble dimensions and adorned a temple sacred to the salutary Cross with rich and lavish magnificence, honouring that everlasting monument, and the trophies of the Savior's victory over the power of death with a splendor which no language can describe (*Tric. Oration*, 9.16, NPNF trans.).

Appropriating all representational space, the language which Eusebius employed cast the city in terms of a spectacle, a space given over to public monuments and to specific moments. In the course of such an appropriation, when visuals took over the spoken word, the space of religion and religiosity was recreated.

An annual re-enactment of the dedication ceremony (*encaenia*) of the church of the Holy Sepulchre enshrined the new Jerusalem in the heart of Christians.[26] It was designed to invoke the biblical ceremony

---

[25] Dio Cassius 69.14, with the discussion in Tsafrir, 'The Topography and Archaeology of Aelia Capitolina', in idem and Safrai (eds.), *The History of Jerusalem* (1999), 157–8 (Heb.).

[26] *Itin. Eg.* 48.2; Soz. *HE* 2.26; Wilkinson, *Egeria's Travels*, 79–80; J. Schwartz, 'The Encaenia of the Church of the Holy Sepulchre, the Temple of Solomon and the Jews', *TZ* 43 (1987), 265–81 versus O. Irshai, 'Constantine and the Jews: The Prohibition against Entering Jerusalem—History and Hagiography', *Zion* 60 (1995), 170–3 (Heb.). On Jewish reactions to the Christian appropriation of Temple symbols in the context of Jerusalem, Schwartz, ibid.

of the dedication of Solomon's Temple and it bore uncanny echoes of Hanukkah or the Feast of Lights which marked the rededication of the Temple under the Maccabees in the second century BCE.[27] Egeria specifically referred to the joyous observation of this feast not only because of its deliberate coincidence with the day when the cross had been found, but also because its character was meant to revive the pomp and ceremony which had accompanied the biblical solemnities under Solomon.[28] Hanukkah was well suited to match the religious climate of a city that delighted in the charms of public displays. It represented an articulation of identity that coalesced around a Temple and a vision of its repurification. Each of its eight days encoded the experience of traditional practices and of Judaism's relation to its historic past. Both the Encaenia and Hanukkah occupied the same space of a totalizing discourse that reinscribed a biblical past on a more recent one. And both shaped a liminal form of religious identification that was peculiarly relevant to the Jerusalem landscape.

In the Jerusalem of early pilgrims, like the anonymous Bordelais who visited Palestine in 333, the ruins of the Temple with pagan statues on top provided a perfect counterpoise to the magnificent church of the Holy Sepulchre, observed in progress of erection.[29] It was as though the previous identity of the city acted as a mnemonic which reminded this new breed of tourists of a tense sequence of history which had led inexorably from the destruction of the Jewish temple in CE 70 to the defeat of Bar Kokhba in CE 135 and from Hadrian to Constantine.[30] The progression demonstrated the veracity

[27] M. Black, 'The Festival of Encaenia Ecclesiae in the Ancient Church with special Reference to Palestine and Syria', *JEH* 5 (1954), 84. Cf. the Armenian Lectionary 67 (ed. Renoux, PO 35.3) which reads John 10: 22–42 that likewise refers to Hanukkah precisely during the Encaenia.

[28] *Itin. Eg.* 48; 2 Chron. 5–6.

[29] J. Wilkinson, 'Christian Pilgrims in Jerusalem during the Byzantine Period', *PEQ* 108 (1976), 75–101; idem apud *Egeria's Travels* (1981); for the text, CCSL.

[30] G. Bowman, '"Mapping History's Redemption": Eschatology and Topography in the *Itinerarium Burdigalense*' (*IB*), in Levine (ed.), *Jerusalem* (1999), 179. Both Jews and Christians assumed that Hadrian established a pagan centre in Aelia in order to subvert their own past, O. Irshai, 'The Jerusalem Bishopric and the Jews in the Fourth Century: History and Eschatology', in Levine (ed.), *Jerusalem* (1999), 209.

of Christ's prophecies (Matt. 24: 1–2; Mark 13: 1–2; Luke 21: 6) even before the events had taken place.

Contemporary Jewish practices contributed a visible proof of this representation. Once a year pilgrims saw a pitiful crowd of Jews praying on the site of the destroyed Temple.[31] The spectacle, in fact a performance of an ancient duty and a testimony of the continuing practice of Jewish pilgrimage to Jerusalem, was also registered by Jerome, who viewed it as a living proof of the vagaries of the city's history.[32] The sight of Temple mourning evoked both Jesus' verdict of perpetual punishment and, at an unregistered and unconscious level, Tacitus' dictum of devitalized Judaism:

You can see with your own eyes a piteous crowd gathering on the day that Jerusalem was captured and destroyed by the Romans (the 9th of Av). Woebegone women stand with old men who appear weighed down with years. Bodies and clothes demonstrate the wrath of God. This mob of wretches congregates and groans over the ruins of their temple while the manger of the Lord sparkles, the church of his resurrection glows and the banner of his cross shines forth from the Mount of Olives.[33]

Jerome's satirizing of the Jewish custom of lamentation over the grim fate of city and Temple is instructive. According to a Talmudic behest, a Jew gazing at Jerusalem and the Temple in ruins must assume mourning gestures including the tearing of one's garments and the recitation of an appropriate verse.[34] For Jerome the Temple platform and the church of the Holy Sepulchre were two symbolic locations each encapsulating religious celebrations, ceremonies and rites which

---

[31] See Ch. 6 below. *IB*, alluding to a 'perforated stone' which the Jews anointed while lamenting and rending garments. On its placement, E. W. Cohn, 'Second Thoughts about the Perforated Stone on the Haram of Jerusalem', *PEQ* 114 (1982), 143–6.

[32] H. I. Newman, 'Jerome and the Jews' (Ph.D., Hebrew University 1997) (Heb.). On Jewish pilgrimage to Jerusalem in late antiquity, S. Safrai, 'Jerusalem Pilgrimage after the Destruction of the Second Temple', 376–93 (Heb.). But see the reservations of C. Hezser, 'The In(Significance) of Jerusalem in the Talmud Yerushalmi', in eadem and P. Schäfer (eds.), *The Talmud Yerushalmi and Greco Roman Culture*, ii (Tübingen 2000), 11–49.

[33] Jerome, *In Sophoniam* (On Zephania) 1.15–16 (CCSL 76A, 1970, 673–4), trans. in Peters, *Jerusalem*, 144. See also Ch. 6 below.

[34] *BT Moed Katan* 26a; D. Golinkin, 'Jerusalem in Jewish Law and Custom: A Preliminary Typology', in Levine (ed.), *Jerusalem* (1999), 416.

wove complementary yet oppositional bonds across Jerusalem's space.[35]

The imagery of a stark contrast between vibrant and triumphant Christianity on the one hand and deflated Judaism on the other was echoed, uncannily and bitterly, in synagogal poetry. Thus Yannai, an outstanding Jewish poet of late antiquity, confirmed Jerome's victorious words:

> The lights of Edom (Rome) grew strong and multiplied,
> The Lights of Zion were muffled and destroyed.
> The lights of Edom gained in power and glowed
> The lights of Zion faded and were extinguished... [36]

The verses reflected the bright lights that shimmered in churches and the slender candles that carried the burden of Judaism. But in Yannai's world the pitiful condition of the Jews was not so much an admission of the power of Christianity as a state which required divine attention, assistance, and compassion:

> Pray thee, God,
> Who will not weep?...
> Who will not lament?...
> Who will not wear sackcloth and mourn?...
> Until when will You not spare us and console us?
> Come back and be reconciled;
> Allow me to be consoled,
> Say,
> Holy... [37]

Synagogal liturgy, commemorating and perpetuating Jewish longings for the Temple and the holy city, provided a verbal rebuttal to

[35] On pagan Jerusalem and its environs, Taylor *Christians and the Holy Places*, 88–142. Rabbinic traditions ascribed to Hadrian the ploughing of the Temple Mount (*DeutR*, Eqev, 13; *BT Taanit* 29a), a fiction in view of the excavations of the last two decades, M. Ben Dov, *The Dig at Temple Mount* (Jerusalem 1982) (Heb.). It is unclear whether Hadrian built a temple on Temple Mount itself as Cassius Dio 69.12.1 asserts, an assertion repeated in a late source, B. Flusin, 'L'Esplanade du Temple à l'arrivée des Arabes d'après deux recits byzantins', in J. Raby and J. Johns (eds.), *Bayt Al-Makdis: Abd al-Malik's Jerusalem* (Oxford 1992), 17–31, esp. 27–8.

[36] *Piyyutei Yanai* ii. 37. Yannai's dates are uncertain. Y. Baer, 'The Pesher of Habakkuk and its Date', *Zion* 34 (1959), 37 interprets the reference to lights to candles burning in the church of the Holy Sepulchre. Yahalom, *Poetry and Society*, 77, dates Yannai to the 6th cent.

[37] *Piyyutei Yannai* 313, in Yahalom, *Poetry and Society*, 194.

the growing Christian pressure to contradict and appropriate the Jewishness of Jerusalem.[38]

Imperial ideology, continuing to espouse forced separation between Jews and Jerusalem echoed Eusebius' insistence on distinguishing between the sanctity of the Jewish temple and the secularity of Jerusalem.[39] Divorcing sanctuary from city, Eusebius called for an ecumenical Christianity which, unlike Judaism, did not depend on a single monument.[40] His research and writings endeavoured to translate Hebrew-Jewish Jerusalem into an environment which projected, at one and the same time, a heavenly sphere and an urban actuality. Navigating between a heavenly Jerusalem, a city in which all Christians could claim citizenship, and a Constantinian Jerusalem, an earthly entity with specific identity, Eusebius' reproduction of Jerusalem became twofold: a city of biblical descent and hence the common patrimony of all Christians and at the same time a territory which harboured a potential threat by its very roots in Judaism and in paganism.

3. CYRIL'S JERUSALEM

Polarity remained at the heart of the Christian discourse about Jerusalem. Between Eusebius and Jerusalem's monuments, present and absent, endless possibilities of new languages emerged to rehearse, interpret, and venerate the same story. In the middle of the fourth century, Cyril, bishop of Jerusalem, born and bred in the city, infused colour and meaning into the sporadic imperial imprints left by Constantine's endeavours.[41] Mediating a discourse of signifiers,

---

[38] Irhsai, 'The Jerusalem Bishopric and the Jews in the Fourth Century', 206; idem, 'The Christianization of Palestine (Review of Walker)', *Cathedra* 74 (1994), 39–47 (Heb.).

[39] On the debate surrounding bans and restrictions on Jewish presence in Jerusalem, O. Irshai, 'Constantine and the Jews', 129–78 (Heb.), essentially claiming that the history of the issue is anchored not in imperial but in local episcopal politics.

[40] Walker, *Holy City, Holy Places?* 347–401, esp. 383–96.

[41] J. W. Drijvers, 'Promoting Jerusalem: Cyril and the True Cross', in idem and J. W. Watt (eds.), *Portraits of Spiritual Authority: Religious Power in Early Christianity, Byzantium and the Christian Orient* (Leiden 1999), 79–95; idem, *Cyril of Jerusalem: Bishop and City* (Leiden 2004).

Cyril depicted Jerusalem as a genealogy of the cross and not of Constantine. His lectures projected a biblical Jerusalem that had been sublimated into a series of slow-moving spectacles and festivals which in turn marked the space of the city. There was no heavenly Jerusalem. Heaven was encapsulated in the potential of specific apparitions which ensured, and were ensured by, the sanctity of its space.

In Cyril's vision of his own see, Jerusalem emerged as a series of concentric circles of ever-increasing symbolic value. At the centre was the prelate's own church where he regularly addressed crowds of believers. Divine revelations, peculiar to the Jerusalemite environment, confirmed the value of both sanctuary and city. When in early May 351,[42] a traditional time of the *hamsin*, the hot desert wind that sweeps over Palestine in late spring, an enormous cross was painted over the skyscape of Jerusalem, the prelate, confident in the significance of the sign, hastened to report it to the emperor.[43]

In these holy days of the Easter season, on 7 May at about the third hour, a huge cross made of light appeared in the sky above holy Golgotha, extending as far as the holy Mount of Olives. It was not revealed to one or two people alone but it appeared unmistakably to everyone in the city. It was not as if one might conclude that one had suffered a momentary optical illusion; it was visible to the human eye above the earth for several hours. The flashes it emitted outshone the rays of the sun ... It prompted the whole populace at once to run together into the holy church, overcome both with fear and joy at the divine vision. Young and old, men and women of every age, even young girls confined to their rooms at home, natives and foreigners, Christians and pagans visiting from abroad, all together as if with a single voice raised a hymn of praise to God's only begotten son the wonder worker. They had the evidence of their own senses that the holy faith of Christians is not based on the persuasive arguments of philosophy but on the revelation of the spirit and power. It is not proclaimed by mere human beings but testified from heaven by God himself.[44]

---

[42] On the date, E. Bihain 'L'Épître de Cyrille de Jérusalem à Constance sur la vision de la croix (BHG3 413)', *Byzantion* 43 (1973), 264–96, esp. 266–7; H. Chantraine, 'Die Kreuzesvision von 351: Fakten und Probleme', *BZ* 86/7 (1993/4), 430–41.

[43] Philostorgius, *HE* 3.26; Sozomen, *HE* 4.5.1–5. On the contribution of Constantius II to the architecture of Jerusalem (the Anastasis), Cyril, *Cat.* 14.14 with W. E. Kleinbauer, 'Antioch, Jerusalem, and Rome: The Patronage of Emperor Constantius II and Architectural Invention', *Gesta* 45 (2006), 125–45, esp. 128–31.

[44] *Letter to Constantius*, trans. in Yarnold, *Cyril of Jerusalem*, 68–70, quote on p. 69.

This was the type of mass euphoria that ordinarily accompanied the miracles performed by holy figures and their funerals. The presence of powerful and ambitious bishops in Jerusalem precluded the domestication of live saints.

Cyril never criticized the Jews for regarding Jerusalem as a holy city.[45] Rather, he borrowed the ideology of the centrality of Jerusalem and refitted it with an envelope of Christian universalism. And, most carefully, he distinguished between city and Temple, the former convertible, the latter not.[46] Even if this Temple were to stand again it would have been a monument devoid of sanctity because Cyril's Jerusalem rested on the church of the Holy Sepulchre and not on the Temple, built or destroyed. Nor did Cyril refer to the Hadrianic temple which preceded the church of the Holy Sepulchre or even to the dramatic discovery of the 'true cross' under it.[47] His Jerusalem was never Aelia Capitolina, the official designation of the city since 135, but Jerusalem.[48]

The city over whose Christians Cyril aspired to preside represented the centre or navel of the earth, made homogeneous through the dispersion of fragments of the Cross throughout the empire.[49] Like no other location, however, Jerusalem offered the initiates an apprenticeship expressed in assemblies and ceremonies that instilled the value of joining the community. With persuasive eloquence Cyril could use the landscape of the city in which Jesus was crucified, buried, and resurrected to play the role of a history that linked the present to its past and future.

We did not really die nor were really buried or really crucified. Nor did we really rise again. This was figurative and symbolic. Yet our salvation was real. Christ's crucifixion was real. His burial was real and his resurrection was real.

[45] Walker, *Holy City, Holy Places?* 317.

[46] *Cat.* 10.11, with Walker, 318.

[47] Walker, 246. It is unclear what, exactly, had been under the foundations of the vast Constantinian complex besides a stone quarry. Patrich, 'Holy Sepulchre', for a list of archaeological remains which, as yet, cannot be linked to suggest a specific building. *Cat.* 15.15 prophesies the rebuilding of the Temple by the Antichrist.

[48] Walker, 319; and idem, 'Cyril of Jerusalem: The Apparition of the Cross and the Jews', in O. Limor and G. G. Stroumsa (eds.), *Contra Iudaeos* (Tübingen 1996), 85–104.

[49] *Cat.* 4.10; 13.28.

And all these He has freely made ours, that by sharing his sufferings in a symbolic enactment we may really and truly gain salvation.[50]

Texts like Cyril's catechumenal lectures (*c*.350) and Egeria's experiences in Jerusalem (*c*.380) followed liturgical pomp as it wound its way through the streets and from one church to another. Lived in or visited, the city activated two competing yet complementary representations of itself with antagonistic creeds brought together in one indivisible unity. What Cyril and Egeria chose to remember was a collective cohesiveness. Their Jerusalem was an amalgam of solemn processions of ecclesiastics, monks, and pilgrims that united its diversity.

Such idealization matched yet vied with rabbinic traditions that depicted the city as a huge urban sprawl and as the most beautiful city in the world.[51] In rabbinic writings Jerusalem was primarily depicted as a hub of piety intimately associated with learning, a city which had boasted no less than 480 synagogues, each with its own school![52] The statistics, whether correct or exaggerated, recreated Jerusalem as a vast space of scholarship with intellectual horizons that surpassed even those of Athens.[53] The city of the Temple, once marked with a civic and religious imprint, became a pure field of the mind with a form dictated by the demands of education and not of ritual.

As a counterpart to the city which Rome wrested from Judaism the rabbis postulated a future or 'heavenly' Jerusalem, a city destined to become a light to all the world, a sort of universal capital, regardless of creed and ethnicity.[54] This was a city with unlimited potential of

---

[50] *Myst. Cat.* 2.5, trans. in *The Fathers of the Church* 61. The authorship of the mystagogical lectures has been a subject of intense scholarly controversy. For their attribution to Cyril, A. J. Douval, *Cyril of Jerusalem, Mystagogue: The Authorship of the 'Mystagogal Catecheses'* (Washington, DC, 2001).

[51] *BT Kidd.* 49b (on Jerusalem's beauty); *LamR* 1.2 (on Jerusalem's enormous size, comprising 24 major roads with numerous minor roads, markets, houses, and untold number of inhabitants). On the heavenly Jerusalem as a reaction to ecclesiastical perceptions of the earthly Jerusalem and especially to Jesus' words on the demolition of the city (Matt. 24: 2), G. Stroumsa, 'Whose Jerusalem'? *Cathedra* 11 (1989), 119–24.

[52] *PT Meg.* 3 (63.4), with comments of Gafni, 'Jerusalem in Rabbinic Literature', 41.

[53] *LamR* 1.4.

[54] *Pesiqta de Rab Kahana*, Kumi Ori (Mendlbaum, 322); *Tanhuma* (Buber, Add. to Deut., pp. 4–5); *Avot de Rabbi Nathan* A, 35 (Schechter, p. 106), all three quoted in Gafni, 'Jerusalem', 45–6.

expansion, even all the way to Damascus, because it represented simultaneously a universal centre of inspiration and religiosity and a gathering place for all Jews.[55] Beyond the language of law, contemporary poetry of Jewish mysticism redirected prayer and liturgy away from the non-existent Temple into a heavenly shrine where priests and levites continued to exercise their ritual duties unhampered by mundane historical considerations.[56] In the so-called *hekhalot* literature the translation of traditions of Temple worship into heavenly spheres, mixed with elements of synagogal liturgy, provided a unique if controversial corridor which bridged the vicissitudes of the recent past and the institutions of the remote biblical past. As bearers of meaning, heavenly shrines, divine chariots, and angels unfolded history beyond the frontiers of conventional wisdom, thus broadening the horizons of the holy to a heavenly Temple well beyond the grasp of earthly powers.

In Christian eyes the process of endowing Jerusalem with a specifically Christian character signalled a double victory, that of Christian Jerusalem over Aelia Capitolina, its pagan precursor, and that of Christianity over Judaism, a creed that would not depart. By the early 360s the process of depaganizing Jerusalem seemed irreversible. In 362, when Julian, the polytheist emperor, contemplated Jerusalem from afar, a revival of the city's Hellenic-Roman heritage appeared a remote possibility. To pose a perfect counterpart to Constantine's Jerusalem, Julianic Jerusalem had to resume its Jewish character.

4. JULIAN'S JERUSALEM

The fragility of the Christian space so elaborately constructed by Constantine, Eusebius, and Cyril is evident in the violent reactions to Julian's designs to alter the Jerusalemite landscape by reviving its

[55] *Sifri Deut.* 1; *BT BB* 65b; *Tanhuma* (Psalms) 55.11, all quoted in Gafni, 46–7.

[56] R. Elior, 'From Earthly Temple to Heavenly Shrines: Prayer and Sacred Liturgy in the Hekhalot Literature and its Relation to Temple Traditions', *Tarbiz* 64 (1995), 341–80 (Heb.); eadem, 'Hekhalot and Merkavah Literature: Its Relation to Temple, the Heavenly Temple, and the Diminished Temple', in Levine (ed.), *Continuity and Renewal* (2004), 107–42 (Heb.).

Jewish roots.[57] Three decades after the Bordelais pilgrim meandered throughout the streets of Jerusalem, celebrating the succession of the worldly kingdom of the Jews by the spiritual empire of their Christian successors,[58] the emperor Julian, nephew of Constantine, conceived the idea of reviving the Jewish temple as an 'international' centre of sacrifices for Jews throughout the Empire.[59] The imperial campaign to reinvigorate both polytheism and Temple Judaism positioned Julian, somewhat ironically, as heir to the legacy of Solomon and Herod, controversial builders of the holiest Jewish sanctuary.

Such an all-embracing imperial pantheon was, in itself, hardly a novelty. In the early third century the emperor Elagabalus reputedly venerated in his palace a colourful mixture of figures, divine and heroic, drawn from classical polytheism, Judaism, Samaritanism, and Christianity (*HA Hel.* 3.5). His successor, Alexander Severus, kept in the sanctuary of his *lares* images of emperors, celebrities, Christ, and Abraham (*HA Alex. Sev.* 29.2). Julian, however, attempted to expand the horizons of polytheism by reversing history in the middle of the fourth century and fifty years after the legalization of Christianity.[60]

---

[57] Greg. Naz. *Orat.* 5.3.14–20; Ephraem Syrus, *Hymn against Julian* 4.18.23 (*The Emperor Julian: Panegyric and Polemic*, ed. S. N. C. Lieu (Liverpool, 2nd edn. 1989), p. 125); Rufinus, *HE* 10.38–40; Socrates, *HE* 3.20; Sozomen, *HE* 5.22; Philostorgius, *HE* 7.9; Theodoret, *HE* 5.22; Chrys. *Iud. et Gent.* 16.9–10 and *HcJul.* 4.20. Among many modern studies, M. Adler, 'The Emperor Julian and the Jews', *JQR* 5 (1893), 591–651; F. Blanchetière, 'Julien. Philhellène, philosémite, antichrétien: L'Affaire du temple de Jerusalem', *JJS* 31 (1980), 61–81; D. Levenson, 'Julian's Attempt to Rebuild the Temple: An Inventory of Ancient and Medieval Sources', in H. W. Attridge *et al.* (eds.), *On Scribes and Scrolls: Studies on the Hebrew Bible, Intertestamental Judaism, and Christian Origins Presented to John Strugnell* (Lanham 1990), 261–79; Y. Lewy, 'Julian the Apostate and the Building of the Temple', *The Jerusalem Cathedra* 3 (1983), 70–96; S. P. Brock, 'The Rebuilding of the Temple', *PEQ* 108 (1976), 103–7; idem, 'A Letter Attributed to Cyril of Jerusalem', *BSOAS* 40 (1977), 266–86; J. W. Drijvers, 'Ammianus Marcellinus 23.1.2.3: The Rebuilding of the Temple in Jerusalem', in J. den Boeft, and H. C. Teitler (eds.), *Cognitio Gestorum: The Historiographic Art of Ammianus* (Amsterdam 1992), 19–26; B. Mazar, *The Mountain of the Lord* (New York 1975); G. Stemberger, *Jews and Christians in the Holy Land: Palestine in the Fourth Century*, trans. R. Tuschling (Edinburgh 2000), 185–216.

[58] Bowman, ' "Mapping History's Redemption": Eschatology and Topography in the *Itinerarium Burdigalense*', 178.

[59] As explained by Julian himself in his letter to the Jews, a controversial document considered authentic by Stern, *Greek and Latin Authors* 2. 559–68, but rejected as an early fifth century forgery by P. Van Nuffelen, 'Deux fausses lettres de Julien l'Apostat', *VC* 55 (2001), 132–6. I find the latter unconvincing.

[60] On Julian's universal polytheism, G. Fowden, *Empire to Commonwealth: Consequences of Monotheism in Late Antiquity* (Princeton 1993), 52; and R. B. E. Smith,

Julian's vision, at least as projected in his letter to the Jewish communities of his realm, suggests mixed motivation, religious, political, positive (i.e. pro-Judaism) and negative (i.e. anti-Christianity):

When I have successfully concluded the war with Persia, I may rebuild by my own efforts the sacred city of Jerusalem, which for so many years you have longed to see inhabited, and may bring settlers there, and together with you, may glorify the Most High God therein.[61]

The letter, an uncanny echo of the biblical decree of Cyrus the Great (Ezra 1), remote ancestor of the Persian monarch whom Julian desired to depose, outlined an imperial ideology that sought to incorporate the grandiose Persian past into the Roman present. In the process of assimilating this strand of Near Eastern history Julian cast himself as the agent of repeated history that incorporated all marginalized edges. Yet, the articulation of the future in the letter also revealed the limitation of the plan and its dependence on an uncertainty.

According to contemporary Christian sources the project was launched only to reach an unexpected end through a divinely sent fire which consumed whatever had been constructed on the site. According to a less partisan view (Amm. 23.1.2–3), balls of fire caused by an earthquake halted the project's progress. The earthquake inflicted considerable damage not just in Jerusalem but also in other cities west and east of the Jordan, including Eleutheropolis, Scythopolis, Sebaste, Ascalon (Ashkelon), Caesarea, Paneas, and Petra.[62] In May 363, exactly a dozen years after Cyril had reported to Constantius II, Julian's uncle, the news regarding the apparition of a cross over Jerusalem, an order was given to halt work on the Temple Mount. The chronological coincidence contributed to the articulation of a discourse that elevated religious polarities to produce cross-referential justification of Christian presence in Jerusalem, as though

---

Julian's Gods: Religion and Philosophy in the Thought and Action of Julian the Apostate (London 1996), *passim*. Cf. the Palestinian inscription which describes Julian as *restaurator templorum*, W. Eck, 'Zur Neulesung der Julian-Inschrift von Ma'ayan Barukh', *Chiron* 30 (2000), 857–9.

[61] *Ad Communitatem Iudaeorum*, text and trans. apud Stern, *Greek and Latin Authors*, 559–61.

[62] K. W. Russell, 'The Earthquake of May 19, AD 363', *BASOR* 238 (1980), 51; P. C. Hammond, 'New Evidence for the Fourth Century Destruction of Petra', *BASOR* 238 (1980), 65–7.

the permutations of nature were staged to reinforce gross distinctions between 'defunct' and 'developing' creeds.

The precise scope of Julian's endeavour in Jerusalem remains a matter of scholarly debate.[63] Orosius claimed that after his return from the war against Persia, Julian intended to construct an amphitheatre in Jerusalem where bishops, monks, and the Christians of the city would have served as fodder for animals.[64] The extravagant claim construed a vision of Julian's Jerusalem as a peculiar mixture of pagan and Jewish elements. The vitality of paganism may have been doubted.

Christian contemporaries and near contemporaries were aware that a renewed centre of Jewish worship in Jerusalem would have reasserted the viability of Judaism in a way that 'would call into question the claims of Christianity'.[65] Theologians like Gregory of Nazianzus, poets like Ephrem, and ecclesiastical historians like Theodoret (*HE* 3.20) and Socrates (*HE* 3.20), vilified Julian while asserting that Diaspora Jews eagerly responded to Julian's call to revive the sacrificial cult of the Temple.[66] Their vehemence suggests that the possibility of resurrecting the holiest monument of Judaism on the holiest site to Jews was seen to undermine the bind of power that informed the Christian discourse of Jerusalem.[67] By threatening a return to a pre-Christian, indeed pre-Hadrianic urban plan, Julian's undertaking split the intercourse between identity and origin that the Christianization of Jerusalem engendered.[68]

In the negotiation of religious politics Julian staged the Jewish right to their ancestral traditions not just through verbal acknowledgement but also by questioning the right of Christian emperors to produce the sole authoritative interpretation of religiosity. Jerusalem

[63] Stern, *Greek and Latin Authors*, ii. 502 ff., esp. 506–11.

[64] *Hist adv. Paganos* 7, 30.5.

[65] R. L. Wilken, *Chrysostom on the Jews: Rhetoric and Reality in the Late Fourth Century* (Berkeley 1985), 139.

[66] J. Vogt, *Kaiser Julian und das Judentum* (Leipzig 1939); M. Parmentier, ' "No Stone Upon Another?" Reactions of Church Fathers against the Emperor Julian's Attempt to Rebuild the Temple', in M. Poorthuis and C. Safrai (eds.), *The Centrality of Jerusalem: Historical Perspectives* (Kampen 1996), 143–59. On Julian's controversial figure, Lieu, *The Emperor Julian*.

[67] L. Perrone, ' "The Mystery of Judaea" (Jerome Ep. 46): The Holy City of Jerusalem between History and Symbol in Early Christian Thought', in Levine (ed.), Jerusalem (1999), 225.

[68] Eliav, 'Temple Mount as a Cult Place'.

provided a form of identity that symbolized conflictual positions. The alleged alliance between an emperor (Julian) and a minority (Jews), diametrically opposed to the one previously linking emperors to Christianity, demonstrated the coincidental nature of the particular historical conjuncture that motivated Constantine's espousal of Christianity. Julian's plan vis-à-vis temple and Judaism represented an aggressiveness that had become the reserve of Christianity. Because the history of Jerusalem, as adopted by Constantine and articulated by Palestinian theologians, began with the Hebrew Bible, Julian's ideological plurality went beyond the binaries of power of Constantine–Jerusalem or even of Yahweh–Israel to reorganize a new sense of the process of identification.

In the ecclesiastical see of Jerusalem Cyril maintained a discreet silence.[69] The proposed shifting of the epicentre of worship away from the church of the Holy Sepulchre back to the Jewish Temple threatened to break his monopoly over ritualistic Jerusalem. But the plan to revive a Jerusalem-focused Judaism also implied a tacit acknowledgement of the city's significance for both Judaism and Christianity. Cyril, who had been restored to his seat with the accession of Julian, had to tread warily.[70] So did Palestinian rabbis. The spectre of a Jewish temple restored to its past splendour under the auspices of a polytheistic emperor might have appeared unpalatable. Rabbinic sources offered neither praise nor vituperation.[71] For the rabbis, Julian's Jerusalem presented a twofold problem. One was that the rebuilding of the holiest precinct of Judaism was to be launched by a gentile monarch who, unlike Cyrus, did not enjoy the endorsement of Yahweh's prophets. Another was the potential dislodging of the literary Jerusalem that generations of

[69] A letter, in Syriac, attributed to Cyril, deals with Julian and the Temple. The authenticity of this document has been contested, Brock, 'A Letter Attributed to Cyril of Jerusalem on the Rebuilding of the Temple'; P. Wainwright, 'The Authenticity of the Recently Discovered Letter Attributed to Cyril of Jerusalem', *VC* 40 (1986), 286–93. For Irshai, 'The Jerusalem Bishopric', 213–14, Cyril's *Cat.* 15 is a reworking of an earlier one in which Cyril responds to Julian's aborted vision of the Temple long after the emperor's death.

[70] Ibid. 204–20.

[71] But see M. Stern, *Greek and Latin Authors*, ii. 211, on an isolated Talmudic comment which appear to betray awareness of Julian's Jewish plans; and J. Schwartz, 'Gallus, Julian and Anti-Christian Polemic in Pesikta Rabbati', *TZ* 46 (1990), 1–19, on a possible midrashic exception to rabbinic reticence.

rabbis had lodged in Jewish memory as a mnemonic rather than a reality.

By rabbinic and apocalyptic criteria the Jerusalem Temple had to be built by God not only because God had ordained its destruction but also because the event had to have a profound significance for Judaism, transforming the 9th of Av from a day of general mourning to one of universal rejoicing.[72] A world-view which asserted that 'ever since the day when the Temple was destroyed, God will know no mirth till He builds Jerusalem and will return Israel to it' had no room for an enterprising polytheist.[73] A structure made by mere human hands, at the instigation of a non-Jewish emperor, was unlikely to last forever.[74] Yet, an inscription discovered in the area of the Temple hints at a different reception of Julian's plans.[75] There were Jews who greeted his vision with a jubilation that harked back to Isaiah's magnificent vision of a new Jerusalem (66: 14; Heb.). Beyond the biblical quote etched in stone it was possible to glean how an imminent divine justice was about to recapture a redoubtable biblical prophecy.[76]

Heightening polarities, imperial interventions in Jerusalem throughout the fourth century rendered the city an experience that transcended reality. Imbued with daunting religious power the topography of Jerusalem transformed the mundane world of late ancient urban spaces into a landscape that melded together the past and the present.[77] Although Julian's attempt to modify Jerusalem was of short duration it reinforced rabbinic displacement of the Temple with a written entity. The failure of the intended transformation of space further matched the existing Christian disposition of uprooting the Temple Mount from the cityscape of Christianized Jerusalem.[78] After

[72] *BT Ber.* 40a, based on Ps. 147: 2.

[73] *Lamentation Zuta*, Buber ed., p. 55, quoted in Gafni, 'Jerusalem in Rabbinic Literature', 44.

[74] *Fragmentum Epistulae* 295c–d, apud Stern, *Greek and Latin Authors*, 555–6.

[75] Mazar, *IEJ* (1975), 94.

[76] Cf. contemporary synagogal art interpreted as a gesture of alliance between the Jewish patriarch and Julian, especially in recognition of Julian's alleviation of taxes, L. I. Levine, 'Contextualizing Jewish Art: The Synagogues at Hammat Tiberias and Sepphoris', in R. Kalmin and S. Schwartz (eds.), *Jewish Culture and Society under the Christian Roman Empire* (Leuven 2003), 91–131, esp. 115.

[77] Wilken, *A Land Called Holy, passim.*

[78] Tsafrir, 'Byzantine Jerusalem', 144.

Julian, the Temple Mount disappeared from the purview of Christian Jerusalem. In the early 380s a diligent pilgrim like Egeria appeared wholly oblivious to its presence.

5. IMPERIAL IMPRINTS: EUDOCIA IN JERUSALEM

Neither Constantine nor Julian visited the city in which they invested or intended to invest substantial resources. Constantine delegated to his ageing mother, Helena, the task of 'inspecting with imperial concerns the eastern provinces with their communities and peoples'.[79] Her passage through Palestine resulted in the erection of three churches in close proximity in Jerusalem, Bethlehem, and Mamre.[80] Souvenirs of Helena's visit prompted influential narratives woven around her 'discovery' of the true cross.[81] The mode of mixing pious tourism with reclaiming biblical sites opened a new arena where imitative endeavours emerged as the necessary culmination of a fine life, a hypertrophy of values proper to late antiquity and to Christian female piety.[82]

The history of the euergetism of aristocratic and imperial women in the Holy Land in general, and Jerusalem in particular, went hand in hand with the permanence of traditional values of patronage and beneficence. Constantine acknowledged the agency of Eutropia, his mother-in-law, not only in undertaking a visit to holy places but also in taking it upon herself to compose a report on their current state of either repair or neglect.[83] In their investments in Palestine in the

---

[79] Eusebius, *VC* 3.42.

[80] Hunt, *Holy Land Pilgrimage*, 33–6; J. W. Drijvers, 'Helena Augusta: Exemplary Christian Empress', *SP* 24 (1993), 85–90.

[81] S. Borgehammar, *How the Holy Cross was Found: From Event to Medieval Legend* (Stockholm 1991); J. W. Drijvers, *Helena Augusta: The Mother of Constantine the Great and the Legend of her Finding of the True Cross* (Leiden 1992); idem and H. J. W. Drijvers, *The Finding of the True Cross: The Judas Kyriakos Legend in Syriac* (Louvain 1997).

[82] L. Brubacker, 'Memories of Helena: Patterns in Female Imperial Matronage in the Fourth and Fifth Centuries', in L. James (ed.), *Women, Men and Eunuchs: Gender in Byzantium* (London 1997), 52–75.

[83] Eusebius, *VC* 3.52–3. In general, N. Lenski, 'Empresses in the Holy Land: The Creation of a Christian Utopia in Late Antique Palestine', in L. Ellis and F. Kindner (eds.), *Travel, Communications and Geography in Late Antiquity* (Aldershot 2004), 113–24.

shape of churches, monasteries, and pilgrim hostels, and in their acts of patronage in Jerusalem, women like Helena, Eutropia, Poemenia, the Melanias, and Eudoxia and Eudocia (wives of Arcadius and Theodosius II respectively) created a collective portrait made up of an accumulation of religious and social virtues. Theirs was a valour inspired by zeal and piety.

In Jerusalem, female enterprises became an index of the involvement of laity in the evolving Christianization of the urban space and in its conflicts and principles. Their presence in Jerusalem created exceptional situations, sharpening and mitigating confrontations. By displacing yet dispensing traditional forms of patronage, these women highlighted what was really at stake in the Christianization of Jerusalem. Their share in the transformation of the city and its environs indicated that although the fundamental purpose was the same, namely to expand notions of aristocratic patronage, their specific activities framed and were framed within the context of cultural substitution of one religious system for another.

Eudocia's sponsorship of the cult of St Stephen provided one model for the association of politics and piety in a city where relics constituted its soul.[84] Stephen's late ancient career comprised a drama and a rhetoric that sharpened communal contrasts and culminated in outbursts of violence.[85] In the middle of an ecclesiastical synod which had convened in 415 in Palestinian Diospolis (Lod/Lydda) in order to deal with Pelagius, participants were apprised of a dream of a priest named Lucianus in which a Jewish dignitary, Gamaliel, urged the cleric to free Stephen's bones from his

[84] J. Burman, 'The Christian Empress Eudocia', in J. W. Perreault (ed.), *Les Femmes et le monachisme byzantine* (Athens 1991), 51–9; on Eudocia in Jerusalem, Jacobs, *Remains*, 153–8; J. Herrin, 'Public and Private Forms of Religious Commitment among Byzantine Women', in L. Archer *et al.* (eds.), *Women in Ancient Societies: An Illusion of Night* (Basingstoke 1994), 181–203. For foundations of other aristocratic women, Patrich, *Sabas*, 4–5 and S. Verhelst, 'Les Lieux de station du lectionnaire de Jérusalem', *POC* 54 (2004), 13–70. These included, around the middle of the 5th cent., a church-cum-monastery established by Bessa intra muros, a monastery at Gethsemane established by Flavia, and a monastic church on the road between Jerusalem and Bethlehem founded by Ikelia.

[85] E. Clark, 'Claims on the Bones of St Stephen: The Partisans of Melania and Eudocia', *Church History* 51 (1982), 141–56. The best known episode took place in Minorca, where the arrival of the bones prompted a campaign to baptize the Jews of the island, Bradbury, *Severus of Minorca: Letter on the Conversion of the Jews*.

grave.[86] The remains of the proto-martyr were duly 'liberated'.[87] John of Jerusalem, until then a controversial figure in the arena of doctrinal wars, hastened to identify Stephen as the 'first to wage the Lord's wars against the Jews' and proceeded to arrange for the transfer of the bones to Jerusalem.[88] On 26 December the relics were solemnly brought to the city and deposited in the church of Holy Sion (Sancta Sion).[89]

No less than four localities in Jerusalem vied over the honour of housing the relics.[90] Some three decades after their arrival, with the active agency of Eudocia, then a resident of the city, Stephen's relics were reinterred in a location outside the walls believed to have been the scene of his stoning. The ceremony took place on 15 June 460, the year of Eudocia's death.[91] With this enterprise the empress inserted into the landscape a monumental compound which represented the city's earliest registered record of Christianity. Hesychius, a presbyter in Jerusalem, seized the moment to proclaim the unique character of Jerusalemite Christianity whose tradition had originated with Stephen.[92] Local traditions transformed discoveries into legendary accounts and the distribution of relics into exploits embedding a new civic culture.

[86] Lucianus' letter about these events survived in several versions, two in Latin (*PL* 41. 805–8); Greek (originally published in St Petersburg in 1898 by A. Papadopulos); and Syriac. On problems relating to these versions, F. Nau, 'Sur les mots *politikos* et *politeumenos* et sur plusiers textes grecs rélatifs à saint Étienne', *ROC* 11 (1906), 199–219; P. Peeters, 'Le Sanctuaire de la lapidation de saint Étienne, à propos d'une controverse', *AB* 27 (1906), 359–68; and M. J. Lagrange, 'Le Sanctuaire de la lapidation de saint Étienne à Jérusalem', *ROC* 12 (1907), 412–28. On the identification of the scene with the present Bet Gemal, now a beautiful monastery near Bet Shemesh, some 25 km. west of Jerusalem, A. Strus, *Khirbet Fattir-Bet Gemal: Two Ancient Jewish and Christian Sites in Israel* (Rome 2003).
[87] Cf. the discovery of the bones of St James in Jerusalem in 351, with Rubin, 'The Cult of the Holy Places', in Levine (ed.), *Jerusalem* (1999), 154–5.
[88] M. van Esbroeck, 'Jean II de Jérusalem et les cultes de S Étienne, de la Sainte Sion et de la Croix', *AB* 102 (1984), 99–134.
[89] Bradbury, *Severus*, 19.
[90] S. Vailhé, 'Les Monastères et les églises St Étienne à Jérusalem', *Echos d'Orient* 8 (1905), 78–86.
[91] Rubin, 'Jerusalem in the Byzantine Period', in Tsafrir and Safrai (eds.), *The History of Jerusalem* (1999), 225. On Eudocia's church, C. Schick, 'Die Stephankirche der Kaiserin Eudokia bei Jerusalem', *ZDPV* 11 (1888), 249–57.
[92] M. Aubineau, *Les Homélies Festales d'Hésychius de Jérusalem* (Subsidia Hagiographica 59; Brussels, 1978), i. 244, quoted in R. Wilken, 'Loving the Jerusalem Below', in Levine (ed.), *Jerusalem*, 241.

The erection of a new basilica under Eudocia's patronage signalled an expansion of the Christian city beyond the limits of Jerusalem's northern walls. The area became dotted with monasteries, cemeteries, and residential buildings, demonstrating how a common faith could obliterate the boundaries between the living and the dead.[93] A peculiar combination of patronage and piety, already the twin pillars of the Constantinian narrative in Jerusalem, generated a paradigm that reshaped Jerusalem and its vicinity. Through a fierce competition over space and topography the distinction between Jerusalem's pagan and Jewish pasts, and Christian history, was blurred. During Eudocia's first visit to Jerusalem, in 438/9, her guest of honour, Cyril of Alexandria, presided over the interment of the relics of Persian and Armenian martyrs, a gesture symbolizing the internationalization of Jerusalem and its centrality in a new map of Christian religiosity. The martyrs bestowed additional sanctity on a geography already hallowed by souvenirs of Christianity's Martyr. They were housed by Melania the Younger, another aristocratic figure of Jerusalem, who allocated them a space adjacent to her monastery.

The architecture of relics expressed modalities of a pious takeover of Jerusalem's geography. Its language couched the redistribution of land, a violent process at heart, with a mantle of Christian concord. For Eudocia, politics was the practice of remembering a specifically Christian Jerusalem, an ideological construct inherited from her imperial predecessors. Her presence, first as a pilgrim and then as a resident, activated the transformation of both the city and of imperial properties around it into enclaves of imperial patronage.[94]

It would be difficult to overestimate the extraordinary juncture generated by continuous imperial presence coupled with an incessant stream of visitors, discoveries, and building projects. The history of Stephen after the discovery of his burial affected not only its immediate Palestinian environment but also the exigencies of the Church

[93] G. Avni, 'The Necropoleis of Jerusalem and Beth Govrin in the Fourth to the Seventh Centuries: An Example of Urban Cemeteries in Palestine in the Roman and Byzantine Periods' (Ph.D., the Hebrew University, 1997).

[94] John Rufus, *Pleroph.* 20, records how the priest of the village of Gantha, some 15 miles north of Jerusalem, which Eudocia owned, was asked by Juvenal of Jerusalem, on the verge of his departure for Chalcedon, to pray for him; E. Honigmann, 'Juvenal of Jerusalem', *DOP* 5 (1950), 264.

throughout the empire. When Petronius, bishop of Bologna and a contemporary of Eudocia, returned from a pilgrimage armed with a relic of Stephen, the presence of the Palestinian martyr generated an Italian replica of the Holy Sepulchre.[95] No other architectural form was deemed suitable to house so precious a relic. It projected a new sense of Christian unity affected by sharing in the sanctity of Jerusalem.

Stephen's translation from Mount Zion, heart of the early Christian community of Jerusalem, to the other side of the city completed a series of constructions which the empress had undertaken in and around Jerusalem. She was responsible for the erection of a wall which extended the southern limits to include Mount Zion. Beyond Jerusalem the empress commissioned the erection of a tower, a church, and a pool to augment the monastery of Euthymius in the Judaean desert.[96] The gesture was more than a mere display of pious euergetism, as Euthymius, who refused to see the empress in person, must have gauged. It provided a precedent for an intertwining of imperial politics and monasticism in the war that raged in the second half of the fifth century in the aftermath of the council of Chalcedon (CE 451) over the soul of the Holy Land. Honouring Euthymius, a monk renowned for his support of Chalcedonian orthodoxy, could be interpreted as taking sides.

In post-Chalcedonian Jerusalem, Eudocia stood between two opposing camps. One side was headed by Juvenal, bishop of Jerusalem, whose episcopal residence she had donated but whose volte-face at Chalcedon had provoked her displeasure.[97] On the other side were ranged Monophysite monks and believers, among them Eudocia's own protégé, Peter the Iberian. In 452 Juvenal was forced to flee Palestine for Constantinople. Amidst feverish correspondence between rebellious abbots and monks, and the new ruling couple in

[95] R. G. Ousterhout, 'The Church of Santo Stefano: A "Jerusalem" in Bologna', *Gesta* 20 (1981), 311–21. On the Holy Sepulchre complex as a 'theme park' in Italy, G. Stroumsa, 'Mystical Jerusalems', in Levine (ed.), *Jerusalem* (1999), 356.

[96] Cyril of Scythopolis, *Vita Euthymii* 30, with Y. Hirschfeld, 'A Church and Water Reservoir Built by Empress Eudocia', *LA* 40 (1990), 339–71.

[97] Honigmann, 'Juvenal', *passim*. Nicephorus Callistus, *HE* 14.50 on the bishop's residence. In general, R. V. Sellers, *The Council of Chalcedon: A Historical and Doctrinal Survey* (London 1953); A. Grillmeier, *Christ in Christian Tradition*, i: *From the Apostolic Age to the Council of Chalcedon*, trans. J. Bowden (Atlanta 1975); and idem and H. Bacht (eds.), *Das Konzil von Chalkedon. Geschichte und Gegenwart* 2 (4th edn.; Würzburg 1973). See also Ch. 6.

Constantinople, Marcian and Pulcheria, the situation in Jerusalem was deemed sufficiently turbulent to warrant military intervention.[98] The court requested Eudocia to induce her son-in-law, the western emperor Valentinian III, to join the efforts to bring to an end the Palestinian sectarian turmoil.[99] From Rome pope Leo urged her to wield influence in Jerusalem on behalf of Chalcedonian orthodoxy.[100] The empress, like the monks, proved recalcitrant. Only in 456, five years after the council of Chalcedon and a year after the traumatic events which included the assassination of her son-in-law, the Vandal sack of Rome and the abduction of her daughter by the Vandal king, did Eudocia consent to support Juvenal. A general amnesty followed.[101] But the strife was far from over.

A vocal supporter of St Stephen, Eudocia espoused the cause of a saint whose promotion often entailed violent anti-Jewish manifestations.[102] In 438 her presence in Jerusalem placed her at the centre of Jewish–Christian polemics over the Temple Mount. The sole source regarding the fluctuating relations between the empress, then a pilgrim to the Holy Land, and the parties to a plot which rapidly moved between monks on pilgrimage, the Jerusalemite Christian community, and the Jews, is a panegyrical biography dedicated to the life and miracles of the monk Barsauma of Nisibis and written at least a century after the death of its protagonist.[103] Approached by 'Jews of the Galilee' the empress apparently rescinded the imperial ban on the presence of Jews in Jerusalem, allowing them to pray at the ruins of the Temple. The permit was followed by a message sent

---

[98] Honigmann, 'Juvenal', 251–3.

[99] Leo, *Ep.* 117.

[100] Ibid. 123; Honigmann, 'Juvenal', 255, 258.

[101] Honigmann, 'Juvenal', 259.

[102] Hunt, *Holy Land Pilgrimage*, *passim*. In Edessa Rabbula converted the local synagogue into a church honouring Stephen and took the opportunity to forcibly convert thousands of Jews, *Chronicon Edessenum*, ed. Guidi (1903), 6, with J. W. Drijvers, 'The Syriac Julian Romance: Aspects of the Jewish–Christian Controversy in Late Antiquity', in H. L. J. Vanstiphout *et al.* (eds.), *All Those Nations— Cultural Encounters within and with the Near East: Studies presented to H. Drijvers* (Groningen 1999), 31–42, esp. 38.

[103] Nau, 'Résumé de monographies syriaques', *ROC* 9 (1914), 119–25; idem, 'Deux épisodes de l'histoire juive sous Theodose II', 184–206, esp. 193 ff. The biography is dated by Irshai, *Zion* (1995), 163 to the 6th or 7th cent.

from the Galilee to all the Jews of Persia (*sic!*) as well as to Jews in urban centres throughout the Roman empire:

To the great and powerful people of the Jews from the priests and the leaders of Galilee greetings. Know that the time of dispersion of our people has ended and the day of the reunion of our tribes is at hand. For the kings of the Romans have ordered that our city of Jerusalem be returned to us. Hasten and come to Jerusalem for the Feast of the Tabernacle, for our kingdom will be reestablished in Jerusalem.[104]

What followed, according to Barsauma's biographer, was a stunning encounter between no less than 100,000 Jews in black and in tears who had gathered on the Temple Mount, and a handful of monks on pilgrimage who allegedly happened to be there in order to view the place's pinnacle. Suddenly hail descended. The monks had already prudently left the scene. Many Jews were killed. The Jews accused the monks of murder. Public empathy in the city ranged on their side as the grim story unfolded:

The Roman (soldiers?), clerics and the Jews assembled. Breaking off olive branches they surrounded the palace of Eudocia who at that point was in Bethlehem ... saying: Numerous brigands arrived from Mesopotamia, dressed in the respectable habit of monks, but waging a deadly war in the city they devastated it ... [105]

Facing a trial for murder and Eudocia's wrath the monks professed themselves disciples of Barsauma. Simultaneously, crowds of Christians and monks were hastily summoned to come to the city to express their support for the monks and their leader. The provincial governor was called in from Caesarea. During an interview between the governor and one of the murderous monks an earthquake took place. When it transpired that no damage occurred Barsauma quickly declared that 'the cross had triumphed', a cry which was then repeated throughout the city. He then marched through the streets followed by a huge number of monks brandishing perfumes and incense. The events were duly reported to the emperor. Eudocia apparently feared for her life. Barsauma left triumphant.

---

[104] Nau, 'Résumé' (1914), 120; Eng. trans. in Peters, *Jerusalem*, 159.
[105] Ibid., 121.

Operations of this sort pitted monks against civil dignitaries and discreetly erased the distinction between imperial and monastic authority. To enhance one and to belittle the other Barsauma's panegyrist enlisted God as the avenging agent. If Eudocia, it was implied, grievously erred in allowing Jews access to the precincts of their destroyed Temple, God and Barsauma were there to ensure that justice would be done. The story contained elements that echoed Christian narratives of Julian's attempt to rebuild the Temple. In both cases a misguided ruler was blatantly criticized for distancing him/ herself from the cause of Christianity; in both, Jews and Judaism were cast as the proverbial other, the embodiment of contrasting values. Above all, a timely intervention from above, enunciated as an earth-quake and hail, addressed the breach.

What impelled Eudocia to display magnanimity which ran counter to imperial and ecclesiastical attitudes vis-à-vis Jews was left unex-plained. Perhaps she had been swayed by vast amounts of money which she received from Jews.[106] Although had this been the case it is surprising that Barsauma's biographer omitted such damaging evi-dence against the pro-Jewish empress. More likely, in a society where neutrality was impossible Eudocia tried to keep the two camps, Christian and Jewish, at bay by defying the pattern of taking sides which had evolved as the only way to recreate a totality out of a divided society. Her failure was not a foregone conclusion. The story suggests that Barsauma's presence and the pressure which the mon-astic establishment exerted prevented a regular resumption of Jewish pilgrimage to the Temple Mount.

Etched with a host of faces, the contentious landscape of Jerusalem could also assume the façade of a harmonious composition, a place of sharing rather than of discord. The city that met the uncritical eyes of pilgrims, like the Iberian prince Nabarnugius (better known as Peter), projected a striking vision, nearly a metaphor of sanctity:

---

[106] This is argued by Z. Rubin, 'Jerusalem', in Tsafrir and Safrai (eds.), *The History of Jerusalem*, 227–8, on the basis of several factors including the explicit reference of Jerome, *Inter. Zepph.* 1.15–16 to Jews bribing the city guard to enter Jerusalem in spite of permission to pray, once a year at least, at the ruins of the Temple. Interestingly, Theodoret, *Inter. Ezek.* 42 (*PG* 81. 1224) recorded the existence of a Jewish settlement in northern Jerusalem, perhaps on one of Eudocia's properties and as a result of her permission. A century later, Cyril of Scythopolis, *Vita Sabae* 54, 57, also referred to Jews in Jerusalem.

Jerusalem: Contrasting Eyes of Beholders

When [Peter and his companion] were near Jerusalem, the holy city which they desired, and saw from a height opposite it at a distance of five stadia, like the fleshing of the sunrise, the lofty roofs of the holy churches, of the saving and worshipful cross of the holy Anastasis, and of the worshipful Ascension on the mountain opposite, they cried out aloud, fulfilling the prophetic words, 'Look on Sion, the city of our salvation, your eyes shall see Jerusalem' (Isa. 33: 20, LXX) ... Casting themselves down on their faces they ceased not to worship from that height and, creeping on their knees, continually with their lips and their eyes greeting this Holy Land, they proclaimed the love that was burning inside them ... [107]

Around the middle of the fifth century a privileged pilgrim like Peter visited both shrines and people. When Peter arrived in Jerusalem he embarked on an aristocratic/ascetic round which included a visit to the Mount of Olives to the monastery of Melania the Younger, an erstwhile patroness from his court days in Constantinople.[108] His subsequent career, however, belied the initial spell of irenic concord that the city had seemed to radiate. Peter settled in Palestine, became a monk, and acquired fame for his staunch defence of Monophysite doctrines. For him Jerusalem became the seat of the hated Juvenal and of Chalcedonian orthodoxy. When he desired to pay homage to the city's saints, like Stephen, Peter could only do so by returning to Jerusalem not in the body but in a dream:

He entered first the Martyrium of St Stephen whom he had met before. He then went down to the cave and there worshipped at his sarcophagus. Coming out of there he hastened to the holy Golgotha and the holy Sepulchre. From there he went down to the church named after Pilate, then to that of the Paralytic, and then to Gethsemane ... After that he went to the holy Ascension, from there to the house of Lazarus, then embarked on the road to holy Bethlehem. After praying there he turned to the tomb of Rachel ... then descended to Siloam and thence ascended to Holy Sion.[109]

In the context of the ideological battle over the landscape of Jerusalem between supporters and opponents of Chalcedon, when all the

[107] *Vita Petri* 26–7, Eng. trans. in Biton-Ashkelony, 'Imitatio Mosis ... Life of Peter', in *Christian Gaza in Late Antiquity*, 115.
[108] A. Kofsky, 'Peter the Iberian: Pilgrimage, Monasticism and Ecclesiastical Politics in Byzantine Palestine', *LA* 47 (1997), 211–12.
[109] *Vita Petri* 98–100, Biton-Ashkelony, 'Life of Peter', 126–7. Kofsky, 'Peter the Iberian', 220–1.

sanctuaries were firmly in Chalcedonian hands, Peter's vision unfolded a new type of homage to the holy city—a spiritual pilgrimage that enabled believers to avoid bodily contamination while fulfilling a holy duty.[110]

6. JUSTINIAN'S JERUSALEM

Into this dense and evocative landscape the emperor Justinian, an enterprising builder, added a church honouring Mary (the Nea), a vast complex which included a hospital and a library(?), all squeezed onto the slopes of the Temple Mount and borne by a huge terrace.[111] In spite of its imposing dimensions and the detailed descriptions of contemporary eyewitnesses the church eluded modern discovery until the 1970s when, in the course of restoration, the Jewish Quarter of the Old City was excavated.[112] The church had apparently collapsed in an earthquake, perhaps in the middle of the eighth century, and vanished from sight.[113]

In his description of the Nea, Procopius emphasized Justinian's determination to construct a church worthy of his status and of Mary's, and the sheer difficulties involved in accomplishing it. For example, to find fitting columns the emperor required divine revelation which directed him to a local quarry and saved the imperial treasury the enormous costs of importing the necessary material. By one modern view the vision served to justify, if not to conceal, the source which Justinian's builders used to support the enormous

[110] Kofsky, 221. See, however, Biton-Ashkelony, 127, on barring Monophysites from visiting Jerusalem's sanctuaries. D. J. Chitty, 'Jerusalem after Chalcedon, AD 451–519', *The Christian East* 2 (1952–3), 22–32.

[111] The two contemporary descriptions are by Cyril of Scythopolis, *Vita Sabae*, 73; and Procopius, *De Aedif.* 5.6. For a modern description and discussion, Tsafrir, 'Jerusalem', in idem and Safrai (eds.), *The History of Jerusalem* (1999), 231. On the emergence of a stational Marian liturgy in Jerusalem, with services held at designated shrines in or near the city on designated days, S. Shoemaker, *Ancient Traditions of the Virgin Mary's Dormition and Assumption* (Oxford 2002), 132–41. See below, Ch. 6.

[112] Ben Dov, *The Dig at Temple Mount* (Heb.), 233–41; N. Avigad, *Discovering Jerusalem* (Jerusalem 1980), 229–46.

[113] Or was destroyed during the few years of Jewish domination in Jerusalem (614–17) (?) according to Ben Dov, 241.

church, namely pillars which had been removed from the ruins of the Temple Mount.[114] If correct, the use of Temple material would have blended perfectly with Justinian's gesture of endowing the Nea with treasures which had once belonged to the Jewish Temple.[115] The hypothesis further accounts for the belief, based on the later elusiveness of the Nea, that the church had been constructed and subsequently concealed below the Mosque of Al Aqsa on the Temple Mount itself.

An inscription discovered in the course of the excavations attested the close collaboration between the imperial patron and the local church in the city:

This is the project executed through the good will of our most pious emperor, Flavius Justinianus, and under the supervision and attention (*spoude*) of the most holy Constantine, presbyter and *hegoumenon*, in the thirteenth indiction.[116]

The central position and size of the church required the repaving of the southern part of the city's *cardo*, a costly enterprise resulting in the upgrading of the street.[117]

The history of Jerusalem, as Justinian's investments demonstrated, was a tissue of decisions, each accompanied by specific circumstances and all expressing a vision that carried the day. The city dominated the political manipulation of language and was in turn dominated by an assembly of factors that conditioned its development. The language to which Justinian subscribed had been the outcome of a rhetoric that collared images to words, and vice versa, to generate a seductive map of an earthly Jerusalem, a self-contained Christian universe, with its own churches, monasteries, hospitals, old age homes, hostels, cemeteries, and living and hospitality quarters. In

---

[114] Thus Ben Dov, 239–40.

[115] Proc. *BV* 4.9.5–9 on the disbursement of the treasure in the various churches in Jerusalem.

[116] B. Isaac, 'Epigraphic Remains from the Byzantine Period', in Tsafrir and Safrai (eds.), *The History of Jerusalem* (1999), 384–5.

[117] H.-L. Vincent and F. M. Abel, *Jerusalem nouvelle*, ii.2 (Paris 1925), 40 f.; K. Bieberstein, 'Die Porta Neapolitana, die Nea Maria und die Nea Sophia in der Neapolis von Jerusalem', *ZDPV* 105 (1989), 110–22; D. Chen, 'Dating the Cardo Maximus in Jerusalem', *PEQ* 114 (1982), 43–5; Tsafrir, 'Byzantine Jerusalem', in Levine (ed.), *Jerusalem* (1999), 142.

other words, a landscape which, with its conspicuous biblical affiliation, presented no ready alternative and hence was a prime target of
imperial investment.

The catalogue of constructions, a basic guide to the transformation
of Aelia Capitolina into a Christian Jerusalem, concealed endless
variations.[118] One was the rationalization of the elevation of Jerusalem
to the rank of the fifth imperial patriarchate, in the august company of
Rome, Alexandria, Constantinople, and Antioch, at the expense of the
provincial metropolitan and capital, Caesarea.[119] Another was the
role that the orthodox Palestinian monks bore in the theological
controversies which threatened and ultimately did split the eastern
church into orthodox and Monophysite camps.[120] An analysis of the
ethnic composition of Jerusalem's population in late antiquity
provides a fascinating insight into the attraction that this small
urban conglomerate exerted, and continues to exert, over believers.[121]

A mantle of unity, imposed through architecture, texts, rituals,
ceremonies, and propaganda, promoted a presentation of one consistent theme, that of a baptized urban space which promised its
citizens a direct passage from earthly to celestial domains. Yet, in the
process of forming the ideal of a purely Christian Jerusalem actual
theo-political divisions could not be ignored because the struggle
over Christian identity caused considerable dissension in the fifth
and sixth centuries. At the heart of such stasis stood the ascetic
dwellers of the 'desert of the Holy City' which extended from the
city through its suburbs and into the nearby Judaean desert.[122]

---

[118] Verhelst, 'Les Lieux de station', 13–70 for a list of foundations in and around
the city.

[119] Rubin, 'Jerusalem in the Byzantine Period', in Tsafrir and Safrai (eds.), *The
History of Jerusalem* (1999), 199–237; idem, 'The Church of the Holy Sepulchre and
the Conflict between the Sees of Caesarea and Jerusalem', 79–105.

[120] See esp. the role borne by Sabas: J. Patrich, *Sabas.*

[121] L. Di Segni and Y. Tsafrir, 'Ethnic Compositions of the Population of Jerusalem
in the Byzantine Period', in Tsafrir and Safrai (eds.), *The History of Jerusalem* (1999),
261–80, counting some 10,000 at the start of the 4th cent. and about 50,000 around
600, among whom were Latin-speaking westerners, Greek-speaking dwellers from
Constantinople and Asia Minor, Cappadocians, Armenians, Georgians, and Syrians.
It is also possible that Jews and Samaritans lived in the city in very small numbers.

[122] The denomination appears in late antiquity, Wilken, *A Land Called Holy*, 158;
Y. Hirschfeld, *The Desert of the Holy City: The Judaean Desert Monasteries in the Byzantine
Period* (Jerusalem 2002) (Heb.) (an earlier version appeared in English in 1992).

The centrality of Jerusalem in theological disputes sprang from a long and intimate history of interaction between the city and the hilly hinterland which lies between Jerusalem and Jericho. The bishops of the city needed the monks of the desert to bolster their position no less than the monks needed an external authority to act as arbiter of monastic disputes.[123] Among the monks many had been pilgrims who originally came to Jerusalem and decided there and then to settle in its 'desert'. Some became legendary. Euthymius, who had decided to live in the Pharan desert near Jerusalem after visiting the city in 405, was greatly admired by the empress Eudocia.[124] The literary talent of Cyril of Scythopolis ensured his lasting fame as it did the history of many monks of the Judaean desert in late antiquity.[125]

Fewer episodes illustrate the interdependence of the Jerusalem Church and desert asceticism more strikingly than the so-called monastic mutinies against Sabas, leader of the Great Laura monastery (=Mar Sabas).[126] Two 'uprisings' were recorded, each involving a faction of monks in Sabas' own monastery, and each ultimately arbitrated not in the desert but in the city itself. In 486 objections were raised to Sabas' leadership. One was his refusal to ordain priests; the other his rusticity, and both were considered fatal flaws.[127] Sallustius, patriarch of Jerusalem, was asked to arbitrate between Sabas and the 'aristocratic' monkish faction. He decided to reject the accusations.

Mediation from Jerusalem, then, played a conciliatory role in desert politics, although the formulas did not end conflicts. A second 'uprising' took place in CE 503 and lasted three years. Sabas had to retire to self-imposed exile, first far away from his laura and then in Jerusalem. In his absence the anti-Sabaitic monks declared their abbot dead. When they asked the patriarch of Jerusalem (Elias) to appoint another abbot he prevaricated. During the feast of the Encaenia (the dedication of the Holy Sepulchre) Elias miraculously

---

[123] Binns, *Ascetics and Ambassadors, passim.*

[124] L. Perrone, 'Monasticism as a Factor of Religious Interaction in the Holy Land during the Byzantine Period', in A. Kofsky and G. Stroumsa (eds.), *Sharing the Sacred: Religious Contacts and Conflicts in the Holy Land* (Jerusalem 1998), 67–98.

[125] See the important introduction to the edition of his work by E. Schwartz, *Kyrillos von Skythopolis* (Leipzig 1939). See also B. Flusin, *Miracle et histoire dans l'œuvre de Cyrille de Scythopolis* (Paris 1983).

[126] Much of the following is based on Patrich, *Sabas.*

[127] *Vita Sabae* 19, 35; with Patrich, *Sabas,* 197–202.

identified Sabas in the midst of a huge crowd of pious worshippers, thus paving the way for his return. The restoration prompted dissension rather than reconciliation. Scores of monks elected to leave the laura after demolishing Sabas' dwellings.

Reinstated, the fortunes of Sabas became even more intimately linked with those of Jerusalem in the early sixth century. Conflicts assumed a predictable pattern, as can only be expected in an urban space where the threat of conflict always loomed and where factions were eager to start a fight. In 513 Sabas organized a mass demonstration in support of the city's Chalcedonian bishop at a critical moment at which the latter's refusal to accept tenets of anti-Chalcedonian dogma put him at risk of losing both imperial favour and his see. There followed a scene of confrontation between government officials and monks in which, just as had happened nearly a century before when Barsauma launched his protest against imperial support of Jewish claims, ascetic authority won, mocking the idea of Jerusalem as a place of peace:

Sabas went up to the holy city with the other superiors of the desert. They drove those who came with Severus' (of Antioch) synodical letters from the holy city and, collecting a mass of monks from all directions in front of the holy church of Calvary, shouted out together with those of Jerusalem: 'Anathema to Severus and those in communion with him'. The *agentes in rebus*, magistrates and soldiers sent by the emperor (Anastasius) stood by and listened.[128]

Jerusalem's church squares provided a battlefield in which assemblies of noisy monks compelled the representatives of the authorities in charge of law and order to subscribe to their ideas of harmony. Constantinople had its say, however, when the emperor sent imperial troops to depose the patriarch, as he did again in 518 when John, Elias' seemingly more pliant successor, preferred to follow ascetic persuasion rather than imperial decrees.

Protesting against John's imminent imprisonment Sabas and no less than 10,000 monks gathered in St Stephens church, the only space large enough to fit such a large crowd. Inside the church, John, with Sabas at his side, anathematized all opponents of Chalcedon.

---

[128] Cyril of Scythopolis, *Vita Sabae* 148 (Schwartz); 158 (Price).

Outside the church, imperial troops and even Hypatius, the emperor's nephew, proved powerless.

After this outcome, the *dux* in fear of the multitude of monks fled to Caesarea. Hypatius assured the fathers with oaths: 'I come here not in communion with Severus (of Antioch) but out of desire for the honour of your communion'. He made an offering of a hundred pounds of gold coins to each of the holy churches of the Resurrection, Calvary and the venerable Cross.[129]

The brotherhood of the monks became an institution simultaneously reflecting endemic conflict in the city and a search for spiritual peace. United by a very strong bond this brotherhood in itself was a contradictory notion because it was completely artificial, brothers being brothers only by virtue of an individual decision.

Under Justinian, Sabas' staunch orthodoxy found ready allies at court. He prevailed upon the emperor to enlarge the plans for the Nea Church in Jerusalem and to add a hospital in the city to tend to the needs of sick foreigners. And he successfully obtained a temporary remission of taxes for the province after the quelling of a Samaritan revolt. Yet, the alliance between court and Palestinian ascetic leaders did not put a stop to dogmatic fermentation. A renewed controversy over dogmas attributed to Origen prompted violent demonstrations among the monks of the Judaean desert. A decision was made to expel the Origenist monks from the New Laura, the monastery that Sabas' opponents had established in 506. The place of the banished monks was promptly taken by orthodox ascetics, all carefully chosen by the bishop of Jerusalem.[130]

Through the eyes of the monks of the 'desert of the city', Jerusalem appeared at once a reality and an ideal. By adopting a theological position the monks designated a choice of policy that might legitimately depend on religious considerations, as well as on political interests, but that also assigned a quality of timelessness to its objectives. Monastic authors, when highlighting or suppressing the official institutions of the city's ecclesiastical establishment, set up the city as a stereotyped image, unfavourably compared with the desert

[129] Cyril of Scythopolis, *Vita Sabae* 152 (Schwartz); 161 (Price).
[130] Ibid. 331–41; Binns, *Ascetics and Ambassadors*, 207–19. On the controversy in general, E. Clark, *The Origenist Controversy: The Cultural Construction of an Early Christian Debate* (Princeton 1992).

realm of asceticism. Imagining a Jerusalem, the monks saw a city attuned to their needs, an arbiter of inner monastic dissension. A mutual friendship governed both Jerusalem's bishop and the monks of the desert, dividing yet uniting because without dissension, and its concomitant resolution, the monks could not be victorious. Their manner of life, as seen from the city, transformed the monks into edifying paradigms endowed with honourary status. Isolated in their monasteries, the monks were nevertheless integrated into the cityscape, their solitude succumbing to theological wars.

7. FROM PERSIAN TO MUSLIM JERUSALEM: POETIC AND EPISCOPAL POLEMICS

The collective glory of Jerusalem came to be poignantly reflected in the literature which emerged in the wake of far-reaching political mutations at the dawn of the seventh century.[131] In 614 the Persians conquered the city; several years later Heraclius re-entered the city in triumph; in 638 the city passed under Muslim rule and in 692 the Dome of the Rock was complete. Laments over the fate of Jerusalemite Christianity and over vanquished hopes to rekindle Jerusalemite Judaism, composed by erudite monks on the one hand and by skilful liturgical poets on the other, addressed timeless topics. A monk of Mar Sabas described the departure of the city's patriarch in terms clearly meant to recall biblical scenes of exile, as though a direct line led from the Babylonian Nebuchadnezzar to the Persian Chosroes and from the last Judaean king to the last patriarch.

They raised their eyes and beheld Jerusalem ablaze with flames and began to lament with tears. Some struck their faces, others threw ashes over their heads, others yet threw dirt in their faces, and more lifted their hands to heaven crying... O Lord, look how your enemies are rejoicing in the destruction of your city... [132]

---

[131] What follows is largely based on Sivan, 'From Byzantine to Persian Jerusalem', 277–306; and eadem, 'Palestine between Byzantium and Persia', 77–92.

[132] Strategius apud G. Garitte (ed.), *Expugnatio Hierosolymae* AD 614 (Arabic versions and Latin translation) (CSCO 340; Louvain 1973), 13. 14–20, Eng. trans. in Wilken, 'Loving the Jerusalem Below', in Levine (ed.), *Jerusalem* (1999), 247.

He (Zachariah the patriarch)...wept...saying...O Zion, what hope do I have, how many years before I will see you again. What use is there for me, an old man, to hope?...I beseech you to remember me when Christ comes to you...For if I forget you, O Jerusalem, let my right hand wither. Let my tongue cleave to the roof of my mouth if I do not remember you. Peace on you, O Zion, you who were my city and now I am made a stranger to you.[133]

Another monk, Sophronius, destined to become the last Roman-Byzantine patriarch of Jerusalem, composed a poem on the same events of 614, in which the Persian conquest was dramatized into confrontation between biblical Medes and Edom:

Deceitfully the Mede came from terrible Persia
Pillaging cities and villages, waging war against the ruler of Edom (Rome).
Advancing on the Holy Land, the malevolent one came
To destroy the city of God, Jerusalem... [134]

Harking back to the Hebrew Bible, the vocabulary employed in these farewells echoed liturgical poetry used in Palestinian synagogues. Thus, the biblical Edom, which had become hostile Rome in Jewish poetry, was transformed into a helpless Christian empire.

A sense of helplessness intermingled with hopes for divine succour and revenge characterized Christian literary reactions to the fall of Jerusalem, as it did synagogal liturgical poetry. Sophronius called upon Jesus to set Persia on fire in exchange for the conflagration of the holy places inflicted by the Persians.[135] Before him, Yannai the *paytan*, had called upon God to wreak vengeance not on Persia but on Rome-Edom:

> He loves blood and hence his name is Edom
> He is Esau. He is Edom.
> Remember, O God, the sons of Edom
> The sword made by a daughter of Edom.
> Bring slaughter to the land of Edom,
> Let fire light the fields of Edom... [136]

---

[133] Strategius, 14.12–16, Eng. trans. Wilken, 247. See also Wilken, *Land Called Holy*, 223.
[134] *Anacreonticon* 14.19–20 (Garitte, *Expugnatio*), Eng. trans. Wilken, 'Loving', 249.
[135] *Anac.* 14.73–4.
[136] J. Schirmann, 'Yannai the Paytan, his Poetry and his Worldview', in idem, *Studies in the History of Hebrew Poetry and Drama* (Jerusalem 1979), 41–65, at 54.

The sense of loss, so prominent in the works that commemorated the passage of Jerusalem from Roman-Byzantine to Persian hands, had permeated Hebrew liturgical poetry since the destruction of the Temple in 70 CE and the closure of the city to Jews in the second century:

> [We have] no burnt offering, nor trespass-offering
> no staves, nor mingled meal offerings
> no lot nor burning coals
> no oracle, nor fine beaten incense...
> no Jerusalem... [137]

Using archaic language, Christians and Jews exalted Jerusalem as each tried to come to terms with changing circumstances. In order to defend their claim to the city, the Christian establishment maintained the thesis that Christianity lent a mantle of sanctity to both a terrestrial and celestial Jerusalem. Evoking the long-established link between Jews and Jerusalem synagogal poetry declared unequivocally that divine law was behind the vicissitudes experienced by both city and people, the same rationale that promised future redemption and restoration.

Sophronius, whose poetry captured the poignancy of exile and loss, returned to Jerusalem as its patriarch with the Byzantine reconquest in 628, to die a decade later, shortly after handing over the city's keys to its Islamic conquerors.[138] For the next 63 years Jerusalem's Christian congregation fared without an official head.[139] The break had little to do with the new rulers of Palestine. The absence of a patriarch represented a dogmatic dilemma and a rekindling of the controversy over the tenets of Chalcedon.[140] The camp of Chalcedonian orthodoxy was, as before, represented by the monks of

---

[137] J. Yahalom, 'The Temple and the City in Liturgical Hebrew Poetry', in J. Prawer and H. Ben-Shammai (eds.), *The History of Jerusalem* (Jerusalem and New York 1999), 273.

[138] C. von Schonborn, *Sophrone de Jérusalem: Vie monastique et confession dogmatique* (Paris 1972).

[139] In the records of the council at Trullo appears an Anastasius as the bishop of Jerusalem (Mansi) but there are also conflicting testimonies which suggest that the gap may have been shorter. On this and what follows, M. Levin, 'The Struggle of Orthodoxy over the Control of the Jerusalemite Patriarchate in the Seventh Century', *Cathedra* 64 (1992), 31–58 (Heb.).

[140] See Ch. 6.

the Judaean desert; that of its rivals by Monothelites, heirs to the Monophysites. The very resumption of an ideological struggle over orthodoxy a century after the ostensible victory of Chalcedonianism, and when city and province were no longer under Christian sovereignty, endowed Jerusalem with a peculiar sense of autonomy.

Among the literary productions which accompanied the seventh-century phase of the war over the nature of Christ was a 'biography' of one of orthodoxy's most staunch defenders, Maximus (the Confessor).[141] The story planted Maximus in Palestine, and not in Constantinople, endowing him with a Samaritan father and a Persian mother, rather than with a noble home in the imperial capital. Its composer, Gregory, identified himself as a disciple of Sophronius of Jerusalem, Maximus' closest ally. The odd affiliation reflected a climate that made room for a Monothelite to become an assistant of the orthodox patriarch yet also an enemy of the patriarch's orthodoxy and its supporters.

Throughout the seventh century the wildly fluctuating tenor of the Jerusalem Church compelled popes in Rome to intervene repeatedly and often without success in Jerusalemite ecclesiastical affairs. The fact that one pope, Theodore (642–9), was Palestinian by origin, highlighted both Rome's keen interest in regulating so prestigious a see as Jerusalem and Rome's helplessness and inability to set up a patriarch acceptable to all factions.[142] The stakes were high indeed. In Constantinople, Antioch, and Alexandria the Monothelites gained the upper hand, leaving only Jerusalem as a battlefield where orthodoxy still had a chance to win.

For decades (c.630–c.683/90) the monothelite and the dyothelite (orthodox or dyophysite) factions waged war over the selection of a patriarch for the holy city, the former garnering support among the local Syriac-speaking population; the latter enjoying the backing of the monastic communities near the city, populated mostly by Greek-speaking ascetics who had originally hailed from non-Palestinian provinces. Because power relations in the arena of theology and dogma in Jerusalem had been invariably reduced to variations on

---

[141] See Ch. 2 above.

[142] L. Duchesne, *Liber Pontificalis*, i (Paris 1955), 331; J. Herrin, *The Formation of Christendom* (Oxford 1987), 252; Theodore's father was a bishop in Jerusalem and his family later migrated to Rome.

the monks-versus-authorities pattern, the rivalry over the credal affiliation of the city's patriarch was settled neither by pope nor by other patriarchs but by the strategically placed monks of the Judaean desert. Orthodoxy won.

Declaring differences, even against the background of resemblance, had been a fundamental characteristic of the agonistic structure of communal relations and ideologies in Jerusalem of late antiquity. The struggle over orthodoxy which pitted the ecclesiastical and civic establishments against and with the ascetic desert dwellers, highlighted how several systems could coexist in mutual suspicion yet also unite in mistrusting the outside world. Sets of oppositions proved instrumental in shaping the physical and human landscapes of the late ancient city. The landscape between paganism and Christianity, initially crucial to Constantine's plans in the early fourth century, began to lose its meaning a century later to become no more than a rhetorical antithesis and anachronism. But the Christianized space was never freed of the struggle against Jerusalem's Jewish past. The Jewish–Christian antithesis endowed the combat with criteria that opposed the ostensibly otiose claims of Judaism to the city with the vibrant presence of Christianity. Both creeds set out to glorify the same city, the city of the Bible, the city of the Temple and the city of Jesus' death. Within the borders of praise the indomitable space defined Jerusalem as the land of sanctity, larger than all other cities, a chief advocate of the very claim of Christianity to the Holy Land.

6

Contesting Scripture and Soil: Liturgical Dates and Seasonal Dieting

1. MATTERS OF MEMORY: THE THEOTOKOS AND THE TEMPLE

13th of August: Synax from Bethlehem for the holy Theotokos
Come today, O believers, and with this chant
Let us together embark along a corridor of the spirit
On this feast of the Theotokos.
Let us sing of the immaculate: rejoice, you who ascend from
the earth
To the sky under the guidance of your son
With the celestial bodies in an unending joy.
Open, O king, our lips so that we can sing
Of the virgin, bearer of salvation,
Who rises today from Bethlehem to Jerusalem
So as to rise thence to the heavenly Jerusalem
And to join in the living light of
Her eternal spouse, her son who is God of the universe.
Before her departure came a redoubtable apparition
Witnessed by all the inhabitants of Bethlehem:
From the sky a voice was heard like the herald
Who announces the arrival of your son,
And the apostles arrive on the halo of the light.

M. van Esbroeck, 'Un canon liturgique géorgien pour
Assomption de la Vierge'[1]

---

[1] Repr. in van Esbroeck *Aux origines de la Dormition de la Vierge* (Variorum 1995), XIV. 8.

Flocks of Christians chanted these words as they commemorated the death and assumption of the Mother of God. The Marian feast of 13 August was born, in all likelihood, in the middle of the sixth century.[2] It had been preceded by an earlier Marian feast, the 'Memory of Mary the Theotokos', which brought believers from Jerusalem to Bethlehem in remembrance of the fateful journey that had taken the pregnant Mary along the same road. Eulogies of Mary's imminent maternity survived only in fragments. According to the Armenian lectionary of Jerusalem, in the fifth century, if not before, the day of the Theotokos was celebrated on 15 August, and not the 13th, at the third mile from Jerusalem, where it was believed that Mary had once rested.[3] No less than two 'Kathisma' (resting) churches in close proximity furnished ample room for believers to follow the appropriate Scriptural readings which included the famed verses of Isaiah (7: 10–15) anticipating virginal pregnancy, as well as relevant passages from the New Testament.[4]

[2] D. B. Capelle, 'La Fête de la Vierge à Jérusalem', *Le Muséon* 56 (1943), 1–33 surveys the evidence of the Georgian and the Armenian calendar as well as the sermon of Chrysippus of Jerusalem. For recent comprehensive analysis, S. C. Mimouni, *Dormition et assomption de Marie: Histoire des traditions anciennes* (Théologie Historique 98; Paris, 1995); Shoemaker, *Ancient Traditions of the Virgin Mary's Dormition and Assumption*. What follows is largely based on Sivan, 'Contesting Calendars: The 9th of Av and the Feast of the Theotokos', in B. Caseau *et al.* (eds.), *Pèlerinages et lieux saints dans l'antiquité et le Moyen Âge* (Paris 2006), 443–56.

[3] F. C. Conybeare, *Rituale Armenorum* (Oxford 1905), 526. The Armenian lectionary, dated by Renoux to 419 (death of John of Jerusalem) and to 438–9 is a copy of an earlier Greek one, A. Renoux, *Le Codex Arménien Jérusalem 121* (PO 36; Turnhout 1971), 354–7. See also C. Renoux, 'Hierosolymitana: Aperçu bibliographique de publications depuis 1960', *Archiv für Liturgiewissenschaft* 23 (1981), 1–29 and 149–75; Wilkinson, *Egeria's Travels to the Holy Land*, provides an accessible overview and English translation of the old Armenian lectionary reading: 'Com. Mary Theotokos at second mile [*sic*] from Bethlehem, 15 August' (p. 274). Mimouni, *Dormition*, 383 for comparative tables.

[4] Archaeologists have argued whether the Kathisma which Ikelia had constructed in the episcopate of Juvenal of Jerusalem (422–58) was the first (i.e. the Old Kathisma) one or the 'new Kathisma'. Of the two excavated churches one, at Ramat Rahel, was attached to a monastery, both dating to the 5th cent., *TIR-IP* 212 (Ramat Rahel); the other, and larger (near Mar Elias) was an octagonal church just north of Ramat Rahel. For a survey of ancient sources and modern identifications, R. Avner, 'The Recovery of the Kathisma Church and its Influence on Octagonal Buildings', in *One Land-Many Cultures: Archaeological Studies in Honor of Stanislau Loffreda* (Jerusalem 2003), 173–86. See also the detailed discussion of S. J. Shoemaker, 'The (Re?)Discovery of the Kathisma Church and the Cult of the Virgin in Late Antique Palestine', *Maria: A Journal of Marian Studies* 2 (2001), 21–72.

Scripture provides no authority for the specific calendrical choice of 15 August.[5] In fact, the Virgin's earliest feast appears an anomaly since, unlike saints' days, it commemorated not her earthly death and heavenly birth but her divine maternity and the events of the Nativity.[6] Nor does Scripture authenticate the later (mid-sixth-century) transformation and extension of the feast from one celebrating Mary's maternity to one commemorating her death (dormition) and assumption.[7] Yet, the 15 August date of the first ever recorded memorialization of the Theotokos in Jerusalem was situated precisely at the moment when the Jewish community marked the darkest day in its history, the destruction of the Temple on the 9th of Av.[8] The

[5] The earliest is the Protevangelion of James, usually dated to the 2nd cent. J. E. Taylor, *Christians and the Holy Places: The Myth of Jewish-Christian Origins* (Oxford 1993), 101–3, dates the Kathisma-resting tradition to, at the latest, the 4th cent.

[6] Shoemaker, *Ancient Traditions*, 115–32, on the origins, shape, and development of Marian cult in late antique Jerusalem, esp. 122 on its anomaly. According to Ray (W. D. Ray, 'August 15 and the Development of the Jerusalem Calendar', unpub. Ph.D. diss., University of Notre Dame 2000), as summarized in S. J. Shoemaker, 'Christmas in the Qur'an: The Qu'ranic Account of Jesus' Nativity and Palestinian Local Tradition', *Jerusalem Studies in Arabic and Islam* 28 (2003), 24–7, the original 15 Aug. feast had been a second Nativity (and not Marian) feast, adopted in the 4th cent. from western Roman Nativity tradition, and celebrated in addition to the 6 Jan. Epiphany feast. The argument largely rests on a comparison of readings which includes Psalm 109 that appears irrelevant to a celebration of Mary. The fact remains, however, that the 15 Aug. in conjunction with Mary's maternity remains a Jerusalemite celebration which grew on Palestinian and not western soil.

[7] Capelle, 'La Fête' surveys the evidence of the Georgian and the Armenian calendar as well as the sermons of Hesychius and Chrysippus. For recent comprehensive analysis, Mimouni, *Dormition*, 378–433, and Shoemaker, *Ancient Traditions*, 115–41. Note the change of the date of the Memory feast from 15 August to 13 August according to the Georgian lectionary, which recorded liturgical developments from c.450 to 750, H. Leeb, *Die Gesänge im Gemeingottesdienst von Jerusalem (vom 5 bis 8 J.)* (Vienna 1970), 23–33. On the exaltation of Mary's death and assumption as a result of deep anxiety which Christians began to feel in the face of death at the end of the 4th cent., combined with a new emphasis on death as a struggle between 'good' (angels) and 'bad' (demons), and with 5th–6th-cent. theological attempts to connect death with salvation, see B. E. Daley, ' "At the Hour of our Death": Mary's Dormition and Christian Dying in Late Patristic and Early Byzantine Literature', *DOP* 55 (2001), 71–89.

[8] It should be mentioned that neither Jewish nor Christian calendars were as yet fixed. S. Stern, *Calendar and Community* (Oxford 2001), *passim*, esp. 172, on the Jewish calendar, noting that although the rabbis did, at least, partially, fix the calendar by the late 4th cent. local variations, as the one attested at Zoar, abounded. Divergences within the Christian calendar likewise multiplied, as the Easter–Passover controversy demonstrates.

overlapping of dates between the Christian and Jewish liturgical calendars could have hardly been a coincidence.[9] Mary's movable feast had been chosen as a peculiar reanimation of the Jewish national day of mourning, illuminating a type of exchange that completed the Christianization of the Jewish calendar in late antiquity.

That the earliest Marian feast of August was linked with the Virgin's maternity rather than her demise is not in doubt. Besides the Armenian Lectionary, the work of Hesychius highlighted the primacy of the natal function of the feast of Mary's memory.[10] Around 430 Hesychius, a priest and theologian of the Jerusalem diocese, delivered two homilies (nos. 5 and 6), both celebrating the Virgin's role in the Nativity.[11] What chiefly connected these with the Theotokos celebration of 15 August were the biblical readings (Isa. 7: 14; Ps. 109: 3 and 131: 8; Luke 2: 7) chosen by Hesychius to extol Mary, and by the Armenian lectionary, as the appropriate readings for the Feast of the Memory of Mary.[12] It is unclear where Hesychius

---

[9] The connection, and the origins of the feast, appear to have eluded the sharp eyes of Mary's feasts' recent biographers including Mimouni, *Dormition*, esp. 381, van Esbroeck, *Aux origines de la Dormition de la Vierge*, and Shoemaker, *Ancient Traditions*. It has been noted by S. Verhelst, 'Le 15 Août, le 9 Av et le Kathisme', *Questions Liturgiques* 82 (2001), 172–4, who, however, links the Memory of Mary day with a Jewish-Christian milieu. On the conjectural nature of the very existence of such a milieu in late antiquity, Taylor, *Christians and the Holy Places, passim*. Taylor (p. 108) did see the connection between the Marian Kathisma geography and rabbinic midrash (*PT Ber.* 5a and *LamR*).

[10] The fundamental study is K. Jüssen, *Die dogmatischen Anschauungen des Hesychius von Jerusalem*, 2 vols. (Münster 1931–4).

[11] The texts are edited in M. Aubineau, *Les Homiliés festales d'Hésychius de Jérusalem*, 2 vols. (Subsidia Hagiographica 59; Brussels 1978–80), i. 118–69 (Homily 5); 170–205 (Homily 6). Aubineau, pp. 184–6 opts for 15 August as the date of delivery for Hom. 5 and the Epiphany for Hom. 6, the latter conclusion is rightly contested by Mimouni, *Dormition*, 394–5 who restores its date to 15 August. The possibility that both homilies were delivered before, rather than after 431, must be carefully considered not only because the texts of Hesychius lack any firm reference to the official elevation of Mary but also because the Armenian lectionary and its readings for 15 Aug. reflect earlier (late 4th-/early 5th-cent.) liturgical practices. If this indeed was the case, the Jerusalem Church may be considered a prime pusher behind the move to enshrine Mary's maternal status empire-wide, and a prime beneficiary as well.

[12] Aubineau, 135. Striking similarities with the Marian homily delivered by Chrysippus of Jerusalem around the middle of the 5th cent. have been noted (Mimouni, 396 with bibliography), attesting the effort of the Jerusalemite Church to reinforce its unusual calendrical selection.

delivered these Marian homilies. A Kathisma church, or rather a spot between Jerusalem and Bethlehem, appears a likely candidate.[13] It may not be wise, however, to exclude a locality in Jerusalem itself where celebrants would have assembled prior to the departure for Bethlehem. Hesychius' reference to Mary as 'another Temple larger than heaven' (5.1), would have been designed to capture two allusions, one to a location whence the Temple Mount would have been visible, the other to Mary's pregnancy with a child destined to prophesy the destruction of that very Temple.

Hesychius' second Theotokos homily (no. 6) was marked by a distinct anti-Jewish hue, presupposing a Jewish–Christian controversy over the meaning of the feast that the Jerusalem Church had appropriated on Mary's behalf. At the core of this homily stood the theme of Mary's miraculous maternity, unfolded in a manner geared to meet Jewish doubts regarding the virginal parturition.[14] Hesychius contended (6.7) that 'the Jews' deliberately misinterpreted the words of the prophets regarding the birthplace of the messiah. Citing Micah 5: 1 (*and you, Bethlehem Ephrata, though you are little among the thousands of Judah, yet out of you shall come forth to me the one to be ruler in Israel...*), he claimed that Jewish exegesis vainly insisted on the unrevealed identity of this 'ruler-messiah'. To refute this messianic anonymity Hesychius marshalled a battery of quotations from the Hebrew Bible, as though by citing the Jews' own sacred Scripture he could effectively undermine the opponents' premises.

Christian–Jewish controversy over the matter of Mary's virginity had been raging since, at least, the second century.[15] With the ruined

[13] Since the church subsidized by Ikelia was built only in the middle of the 5th cent., some two decades after the delivery of the homilies, Aubineau, 137, 145–9 locates the rituals in the vicinity of the (future) Kathisma.

[14] On Hesychius' polemics with Judaism in exegetical context, S. Tampellini, 'Aspetti di polemica anti giudaica nell'opera di Esichio', *Annali di Storia dell'Esegesi* 16 (1999), 353–8.

[15] C. E. B. Cranfield, 'Some Reflections on the Subject of the Virgin Birth', *Scottish Journal of Theology* 41 (1988), 177–89 on the middle of the 1st cent. as a terminus ad quem for the origin of the Gospel accounts of virgin birth, suggesting that the rabbinic claim regarding a union between Mary and a Roman soldier named Panthera (from parthenos? from panther?) was developed as a response to Christian claims of Jesus' virginal conception, J. Klausner, *Jesus, his Life, Times and Teaching*, trans. H. Danby (New York 1979), 23–4, 48–51; C. Quarles, 'Jesus as Mamzer. Review Essay', *Bulletin for Biblical Research* 14 (2004), 243–55, esp. 251 and n. 22. See also

Temple Mount in the background, Hesychius' homilies actualized the debate in terms of calendrical opposition—the celebration of Mary's maternity on the one hand, and its implied Jewish commemoration of death and destruction on the other.[16] Such verbal skirmishes, in which the opponent was never identified beyond 'the Jews', ranged along biblical battlefields where Christian theologians and rabbinic interpreters relied on the Hebrew Bible and where each side borrowed key concepts from the other. The effectiveness of the argument, on the Christian side, resided in the very use of the Hebrew sacred scripture as in the constant appeal to visual aides derived from the biblical landscape of their own time. Eschewing the Jewish model, Palestinian Christianity sought to 'correct' and reconcile its reading of biblical and post-biblical history through a confrontation over the calendar. Between the bearing of Jesus and the destruction of the central sanctuary of Judaism, both 'fixed' for the same day, stood two fatalities that the Jerusalem Christian calendar sought to intertwine. The reckoning highlighted a crucial stage in an ongoing manipulation of the calendar as a result of Christian–Jewish contending calculations of the past.

Jewish biblical interpretation used similar weapons, including the appropriation of Christian themes and symbols, to embellish its reading of Scripture. A commentary on the Scroll of Lamentations, the obligatory synagogal reading for the 9th of Av, contains clues that account for the selection of this date for the oldest Marian feast.[17]

B. L. Visotzky, 'Anti-Christian Polemic in Leviticus Rabbah', *PAAJR* 56 (1990), 83–100. On Marian feasts as a stage for anti-Jewish demonstrations, S. J. Shoemaker, ' "Let Us Go and Burn Her Body": The Image of the Jews in Early Dormition Traditions', *JECS* 68 (1999), 775–823. See also M. Simon, 'Anti-Jewish Polemic: The Arguments Employed' in idem, *Verus Israel*, trans H. McKeating (Oxford 1986), 156–78. The composition known as *Toldot Yeshu* appears to belong to this milieu as well.

[16] What, exactly, was on the Temple Mount after the destruction of the Temple remains a matter of controversy, see the summary in Y. Z. Eliav, 'Hadrian's Actions in the Jerusalem Temple Mount according to Cassius Dio and Xiphilini Manus', *Jewish Studies Quarterly* 4 (1997), 125–44, concluding that the location of the pagan shrines implanted by Hadrian remains elusive.

[17] Ray and Shoemaker (above n. 6) delve into the calendar of Jubilees in order to account for the selection of 15 Aug. in the first place, suggesting that the original Jerusalemite Nativity feast commemorated Jesus' conception (with an emphasis on the Nativity and not on Mary) and that it was patterned after Jubilees' model of the visitation of Sarah/conception of Isaac which occurred 'in the middle of the sixth month' (i.e. mid-August). I intend to deal with this hypothesis elsewhere. Suffice it to

Discussing Lamentations 1: 16, the rabbis pondered the biblical phrases regarding 'the one who brings consolation' (*ha-Menachem*) and 'the one who revives the soul' (*meshiv nefesh*). One interpreter provided an exegetical narrative which bore distinct echoes of nativity narratives:[18]

> *Because the comforter is far from me, even He that should refresh my soul* (Lam. 1: 16). What is the name of the king Messiah? . . . Rabbi Judan said in the name of Rabbi Aibu: His name is 'Comforter' as it is said: The Comforter is far from me . . .
>
> The following story supports what R. Judan said. It happened that a man was ploughing when one of his oxen lowed. A passing Arab asked him: Who are you? The man answered: I am a Jew. The Arab said: Detach your ox and untie your plough. Why? asked the Jew. Because the Temple of the Jews is (to be) destroyed. How do you know this? Because of the lowing of your ox. While he was saying this the ox lowed again. The Arab then said: Harness your ox and tie up your plough because the deliverer (*go'el*) of the Jews is born. What is his name? Menahem (=the comforter of his people). What is his father's name? Hezekiah.[19] And where do you find them? At Birat Ha-Ar(a)ba, which is in Bethlehem in Judaea.
>
> The man sold his oxen and his plough and became a peddlar of baby garments. He went from one village to another and from one city to another till he arrived there (i.e. Bethlehem). [At Birat Ha-Arba] the women gathered. All but one, a mother of a baby, bought something. He asked her: Why do you not buy baby garments? She said: Because I fear that a harsh fate is in store for my baby. Why? Because on account of his birth the Temple is to be destroyed. He said: We trust in the Lord of the Universe—just as close on his birth it is to be destroyed so close on that day it will be rebuilt. Take then these linens for your child. She said: I cannot pay. He said: No matter. Come and buy these and within a few days I will come to your house to collect payment. She took some and departed.

say that there is no need to reach for a 2nd-cent. BCE esoteric calendar for an explanation readily available in contemporary, late ancient sources.

[18] The story appears twice in Palestinian sources, once in the Palestinian Talmud (*Ber.* 4.2, 5a, in Aramaic) within rabbinic discussions concerning the Amidah (=Eighteen Benedictions, the obligatory daily prayer); and once in Hebrew, in the exegesis of Lamentations 1.16 within the context of tales about mothers and sons. The relationship between the two versions is unclear. Although the PT was redacted c.400 and *LamR* probably later, the story itself may have circulated in at least two distinct versions long before both compilations were sealed. The employment of Hebrew, however, suggests a later date for the *LamR* version.

[19] On the messianic name of Menahem son of Hezekiah see also *BT San.* 98b.

Later he said: I will go and see how this baby is getting on. Arriving at her home he asked: How is that child? She answered: Did I not tell you that a harsh fate is in store for him? Misfortune has dogged him and a whirlwind swept him off.

Rabbi Abun said: Why should I learn this from an Arab when there is an explicit text which states: *And Lebanon* (i.e. the Temple) *shall fall by a mighty hand* (Isa. 10: 34) and *there shall come forth a shoot out of the stock of Jesse and a twig shall grow forth out of his roots* (Isa. 11: 1)?[20]

Of the anonymous protagonists the most elusive was the baby who disappeared in a single whiff of the storm. What happened to the other three also remains a mystery. Nevertheless, it must have been fairly simple to recognize in the tale a quintessential Christian dogma that centred on the relations between mother and child-messiah, here perversely depicted as a doomed baby and a fatalistic parent.[21] *LamR* incorporated Christian traditions unattested before the second century, including one that located Jesus' birth near and not in Bethlehem, and another that identified the Magi as Arabs.[22] Above all, the midrashic story imparted the ultimate counter-proof necessary to sustain the hope of rebuilding the Temple by depriving Jesus' prophecy of its perpetual relevance.

To endow the exegetical excursus with form and meaning the narrator placed his unnamed characters in a specific location in Bethlehem, at *Birat Arba*, a pointer that could hardly fail to evoke both the narrative of the Nativity as well as Jewish traditions of a Davidic messiah. Using a numerical pun (*arba/arabi/araba* can read as 'four', 'an Arab', or 'a willow'), the story further invalidated contemporary Christian interpretation of New Testament topography by moving a central stage of the 15 August Nativity from the third mile (Kathisma), with its distinct Marian connotations, to the

---

[20] *LamR* 1.16, parasha I, pp. 89–90 (Buber), Eng. trans. in *The Midrash Rabbah* (London 1977), 135–7 (slightly modified).

[21] R. E. Brown, *The Birth of the Messiah: A Commentary on the Infancy Narratives in Matthew and Luke* (Garden City 1977), 513–16 and *passim*. In the Palestinian Talmud's version the narrator attributes cannibalistic instincts to the mother who is ready to kill her own child in order to prevent the destruction of the Temple. The PT also calls the child 'the consoler' as though it was a personal name and describes Bethlehem as 'the royal capital'.

[22] Justin, *Dial.* 77.

fourth, with its implied link with Rachel who had been buried at Ephratha which Genesis 35: 19 identified as Bethlehem.[23] Above all, the connection forged between the birth and the deathly disappearance of the baby on the one hand and the destruction *and* rebuilding of the Temple on the other, strove to undermine the Christian dogma that had invested the proof of Jesus' power of prophecy with a perpetual state of desolation on the Temple Mount.

Lamentations Rabbah, the rabbinic discourse on the intent and scope of the biblical Lamentations of the 9th of Av, built an exegetical bridge between the Jewish national day of mourning and the Christian date of memorializing the mother of the messiah. The passage indicated rabbinic awareness of traditions relating to the Nativity narratives, and of the appropriation of 9th of Av as a Marian festivity. Concluding the debate with a reference to Isa. 11: 1 to prove that the 'consoler' will be a scion of David in an *unspecific future*, Rabbi Abun targeted Christian interpretation of the same verse as a prooftext of direct affinity between David and Jesus. This was the very verse, deliberately juxtaposed with Lamentations 1: 16, that provided an equation between Temple and Messiah that was as fundamental to Judaism as that between Jesus' second coming and the Temple was to Christianity.

To grasp why the 9th of Av would seem especially attractive to mark Mary's maternity and the Nativity within a Jerusalemite liturgical context it is useful to recall how the city's Christian community annually witnessed the perennially resuscitated sentiments that accompanied the mourning over the destruction of the Temple. In late antiquity the 9th of Av was the only day of the Jewish calendar when Jews were visible in Jerusalem:

[23] Taylor, *Christians and the Holy Places*, 103; on 107–9 she analyses, on the basis of *PT Ber.* 5a, this multifaceted pun as an allusion either to an 'Arab residence/fort' or to a 'willow residence', the latter signifying the grove of Adonis-Tammuz in Bethlehem and implying rabbinic cognizance of the Christian appropriation of pagan cults; Verhelst, 'Le 15 août', 171–2 reads Birat Arba as the 'fourth well'. On the development of the Kathisma as Nativity shrine, Shoemaker, *Ancient Traditions*, 80 ff. In the 4th cent. or later, the *Story of Joseph the Carpenter* located Jesus' birth beside the tomb of Rachel, which is about 1 km. from Bethlehem's grotto of the Nativity, Taylor, 102. *Itin. Burd.* 598 refers to Rachel's tomb at the distance of four miles from Jerusalem on the right of the way to Bethlehem and not in Bethlehem itself. In this the traveller apparently followed a Jewish tradition recorded in *T Sot.* 11.11 and apparently in Justin, *Dial.* 78.19, Wilkinson, *Egeria's Travels*, 162 n. 1 and Taylor, 100–1.

You can see with your own eyes a piteous crowd gathering on the day that Jerusalem was captured and destroyed by the Romans (the 9th of Av). Woebegone women stand with old men who appear weighed down with years. Bodies and clothes demonstrate the wrath of God. That mob of wretches congregates and groans over the ruins of their temple while the manger of the Lord sparkles, the church of his resurrection glows and the banner of his cross shines forth from the Mount of Olives.[24]

These gloomy images, recorded with venomous glee by Jerome, were echoed in a Jewish description which compared the happy heyday of pilgrimage to the city prior to the destruction of the Temple with the mournful post-70 situation:

In the past I used to go up to Jerusalem along well kept roads, but now through thorny hedges... In the past I used to go up and the trees formed a covering above my head, but now I am exposed to the sun... In the past I used to go up in the shade of the Holy One, blessed be He, but now in the shadow of [oppressive] governments... In the past I used to go up with baskets of first fruits on my head. Early in the morning they used to exclaim: '*Arise and let us go up to Zion* (Jer. 31: 6); while on the road they used to exclaim: *Our feet are standing within thy gates, O Jerusalem* (Ps. 122: 2), and when they were on Temple Mount they used to say: *Hallelujah, praise God in His Sanctuary* (Ps. 150: 1)... But now I go up with weeping and come down with weeping... In the past I used to go up in crowds of holiday makers... but now I go up in silence and come down in silence.[25]

Jews reaching Jerusalem in the fifth century from the south (the Daroma region), along the Bethlehem–Jerusalem road would have hardly missed the conspicuous presence of two churches aspiring to commemorate the Kathisma. The 9th of Av mourners would have coincided with the crowds that left Jerusalem for Bethlehem on the same day to celebrate Mary's maternity. Such encounters challenged Jewish perception of the 9th of Av as a day of universal lamentation

[24] Jerome, *In Sophoniam* (On Zephania) 1.15–16 (CCSL 76A, 1970, 673–4), trans. in Peters, *Jerusalem*, 144. On the ban on Jewish settlements in Jerusalem, Irshai, *Zion* 60 (1995). On the existence of a synagogue on Mount Zion, officially outside the territory of 'Jerusalem', *Itin. Burd*, with M. Ehrlich and D. Bar, 'Jerusalem according to the Description of the Bordeaux Pilgrim: Geography and Theological Aspects', *Cathedra* 113 (2004), 35–52 (Heb.). See also Ch. 5 above.

[25] *LamR* 1.17 (Soncino trans.).

in which the personified figure of Zion (Sion), mourning her fate and the loss of her children, had come to figure prominently in the dirges (*qinot*) recited on that day.[26] The *qinot* were usually inserted into the fourteenth benediction ('God of David, the builder of Jerusalem') which enshrined Jerusalem in Jewish daily prayers.[27] The encounter seemed also responsible for the transfer of the scene of the nativity from the Kathisma to Bethlehem.[28]

As the rabbis upturned the joy of Mary's memorialization back into reviving the memory of the melancholy of the day in the Jewish calendar, *Lamentations Rabbah* plough through a field of conflict dominated by powerful biblical bonds. In transferring the feast (in the sixth century) from one celebrating Mary as the mother of God to one commemorating her death, Christian reading of the life of Mary realigned itself with the sentiment that had permeated the Jewish day of mourning while insisting on the joyful aspect of Mary's ascension to heaven.[29] Reflecting a view that regarded as anachronistic the Jewish bonding of messianic hopes with the reconstruction of the Temple, the establishment of concomitant calendrical feasts underlined the real consequences of the academic pursuit of biblical interpretation in late antiquity.[30]

At the start of the Jewish–Christian 'dialogue' regarding Mary, an annual ceremony honouring her dissociated the 9th of Av from

---

[26] See the *piyyut* printed in I. Davidson, *Genizah Studies in Memory of Solomon Schechter* (New York 1928), iii. 148–50, beginning with: 'Do not call me Zion, rather call me deserted.'

[27] Yahalom, *Poetry and Society*, 251.

[28] Taylor, *Christians and the Holy Places*, 104 on traditions and transfer.

[29] It is impossible to date such convoluted processes. *Lamentations Rabbah*'s story seems to follow rather than to precede the introduction of the Memory of Mary's feast, and may lend indirect support to a date *c.*400, rather than later in that century. The substitution of the feast with Mary's ascension may have been an attempt to avoid the kind of rabbinic irony that permeates the interpretation of the 9th of Av as a day heralding the birth of a messiah. See the discussion of Shoemaker, *Ancient Traditions*, 78–80, 132 ff., and *passim*. Cf. the mutations of Mount Zion across Jerusalem as the name with its weighty connotations was transferred from the north-eastern hill to the south-western hill. See the debate between B. Pixner, 'Nazoreans on Mount Zion', in S. Mimouni and F. Stanley Jones (eds.), *Le Judéo-Christianisme dans tous ses états. Actes du Colloque de Jérusalem 1998* (Paris 2001), 289–316; and Taylor, *Christians and the Holy Places*, 207–20.

[30] On the acerbity of the clash over Mary's virginity and concomitant maternity, Shoemaker, '"Let Us Go and Burn her Body"' (above n. 15), 775–823.

15 August and the kathisma from Jesus' birth.[31] By the beginning of the seventh century, a culminating point in the history of the cult of Mary,[32] Jewish apocalyptic visions (*Sefer Zerubbabel*) which circulated in Palestine in the wake of the Persian conquest of Jerusalem in

[31] One more displacement-transference deserves attention. In late 4th-cent. Jerusalem, as presented in Egeria's travelogue, Lent consisted of eight rather than the usual seven weeks, and readings from the Hebrew Bible were taken from chapters 40–66 in Isaiah (S. Verhelst, 'Le 15 août', 174; idem, 'Une homélie de Jean de Bolnisi et la durée du carême en Syrie-Palestine', *Questions Liturgiques* 78 (1997), 216, but see also idem, 'Trois remarques sur la *Pesiqta de-rav Kahana* et le christianisme', in Mimouni and Stanley Jones (eds.), *Le Judéo-Christianisme dans tous ses états* (Paris 2001), 367–80, esp. 376–9). Egeria described Lent as a time when the 'clergy and lay people underwent an intensification of their regular round of worship' (Wilkinson, *Egeria's Travels*, 71, 263, 278–80), culminating in Easter, the holiest period of the Christian calendar, with week-long liturgical celebrations that formed an essential feature of city life in late ancient Jerusalem. Egeria's emphasis on collectivity, on marching, praying, singing, listening, mourning, and weeping (37.7, 9), suggests that in Jerusalem the identity of a Christian was defined not in terms of rich or poor but of participation in the practice of the liturgies. It was a time of dissolution of the present into the past, of integrated readings of select passages from the biblical Prophets who had foreseen precisely what Jesus was to undergo at Passover (*Itin. Eg.* 37.6). Lent typically also led to baptism, namely to admission and full membership in the community of believers. It meant personal renewal, even rebirth, time to hear of past deeds, and time to turn to the salvation that Jesus' death had promised. A similarly cohesive period in the Jewish liturgical calendar of late antiquity followed the 9th of Av, culminating in Rosh Hashanah, the first day of the Jewish year. During the seven Sabbaths following the 9th of Av, a period meant to bridge lamentation with hopes for future redemption, the *haftarot* (readings from the prophets) are based on Isa. 40–66, just like biblical readings during Lent, and are collectively known as the *haftarot* of consolation (L. M. Barth, 'The "Three Rebukes" and the "Seven of Consolation"': Sermons in the *Pesikta de Rav Kahana*', *JJS* 33 (1982), 503–15; E. Stern, 'Transforming Comfort: Hermeneutics and Theology: The Haftarot of Consolation', *Prooftexts* 23 (2003), 150–81). See also N. G. Cohen, 'Earliest Evidence of the Haftarah Cycle for the Sabbaths between 17 Be-Tamuz and Sukkot in Philo', *JJS* 48 (1997), 225–49 on their origins. It seems hardly a coincidence that Pentateuchal readings (*parasha*) on Rosh Hashanah include the narrative of the annunciation to Sarah (Gen. 21) while the accompanying *haftara* reads Sam. 1: 1, the birth narrative of the prophet Samuel. It would appear that the relocation of the Jewish cycle of consolation to Lent was deliberate.

[32] On Mary's imperial cult, Av. Cameron, 'The Virgin's Robe: An Episode in the History of Early Seventh Century Constantinople', *Byz.* 49 (1979), 42–59; V. Limberis, *Divine Heiress: The Virgin Mary and the Creation of Christian Constantinople* (New York 1994); Fowden, *Empire to Commonwealth*. On the 'finding' of Mary's robe in the Galilee in the time of Leo I, in the house of a pious Jewish virgin, N. H. Baynes, 'The Finding of the Virgin's Robe', *Annuaire de l'Institut de philologie et d'histoire orientales et slaves* 9 (1949), 87–97.

614 generated a Jewish messiah with a Jewish mother, a veritable counterpart to Mary.[33] In her most intriguing guise, this mother (Hephziba, 'the desired') featured in a verse version of the apocalypse embedded in a *piyyut* of lamentation written for the 9th of Av.[34] At the same time, a vision attributed to 'a priest of the Jews' in Tiberias predicted the imminent coming of the messiah, king of Israel, son of a virgin.[35] The metamorphosis suggests that calendrical ceremonies activated rather than concealed contacts. When Mary was repatriated after her phenomenal success in sixth-century Constantinople, the power of her maternity mobilized new Jewish perceptions of the messiah.[36] The same strategy led to tragedy. By orders of the Persian governor the Jewish messiah was executed. The second Persian empire, although initially garnering the success that the Achaemenids had once gained, failed to provide a Cyrus or a successful Zerubbabel.

Between two contemporary competing models which obeyed the same concept of time the language of biblical exegesis came to win a certain autonomy in relation to reality. At stake was the authenticity of the textual reading within a discourse that aspired to infuse

[33] On Palestinian, Jewish and Christian, reactions to the Persian invasion of Palestine in 614, Sivan, 'From Byzantine to Persian Jerusalem' (2000), and 'Palestine between Byzantium and Persia' (2004). The most famous apocalyptic work, the Book of Zerubbabel, has both prose and verse versions and enjoyed countless 'updating' in various contexts of messianic expectations. The prose was edited by I. Lévi, 'L'Apocalypse de Zorobabel et le roi de Perse Siroès', *REJ* 68 (1914) and 69 (1919), 108–15; Eng. trans. by M. Himmelfarb, 'Sefer Zerubbabel', in D. Stern and M. J. Mirsky (eds.), *Rabbinic Fantasies* (Philadelphia 1990), 67–90, who sees in Hephziba the Jewish counterpart of Mary (p. 69); and eadem, 'The Messiah in the Talmud Yerushalmi and Sefer Zerubbabel', in P. Schäfer (ed.), *The Talmud Yerushalmi and Graeco-Roman Culture*, iii (Tübingen 2002), 369–89. See also Shoemaker, ' "Let Us Go" '; 811–20. See now J. C. Reeves, *Trajectories in Near Eastern Apocalyptic: A Postrabbinic Jewish Apocalypse Reader* (Leiden 2005).

[34] Possibly also the earliest version of this highly popular composition. For the text, J. Yahalom, 'On the Validity of Literary Composition as a Historical Source', *Cathedra* 11 (1979), 125–33 (Heb.), and idem, *Poetry and Society in Jewish Galilee of Late Antiquity*, 90–2 (Heb.); E. Fleischer, 'On Solving the Date and the Provenance of R. Eleazar Birabbi Kilir', *Tarbiz* 54 (1985), 383–427 (Heb.) (linking two distinct *piyyutim*). See also Sivan, 'From Byzantine to Persian Jerusalem'.

[35] *Doctrina Iacobi* V.6 (G. Dagron and V. Déroche, *TM* 11 (1991), 193.

[36] By then, the location of the nativity cave in Bethlehem, and not on the road to town, had been firmly established, Taylor, *Christians and the Holy Places*, 112, completing the displacement of date and location for the memorialization of the *theotokos*.

the liturgy with geographical concreteness. Ironies followed. Rabbinic comments were considerably closer to the Gospels than to the biblical text (Lam. 1: 16) which they aspired to interpret. The tale of the peasant turned peddlar, the Arab, and the unnamed woman of Bethlehem animated the fluctuating fortunes of liturgical developments in late ancient Palestine. The feast of the 'Memory of Mary' highlighted a process of appropriation governed by complex strategies which reconstructed sacred time in which everything was organized in terms of the present whose reality embraced the Hebrew Bible while effacing Jewish derivation from this common past.

2. ARTICULATING THE LAND: DATING AND DIETING

Zoar (Zoora) is a village just south of the Dead Sea.[37] Genesis 19 records the flight of Lot and his family from Sodom to Zoar, an episode which in late antiquity elevated Lot into the ranks of Christian saints. A church dedicated to Hagios Lot with a cave in its midst generated a local cult promoted by monks and admired by pilgrims.[38] The most significant archaeological finds from Zoar are some 300 funerary *stelae* ranging from the fourth to the sixth centuries CE of which the majority are Christian.[39] Some 10 per cent of the inscriptions are Jewish, inscribed in Aramaic rather than Greek, the language of the Christian epitaphs, and often accompanied by a menorah. The most conspicuous aspect of Zoar's Jewish commemorative customs was the universal adoption of purely Hebrew chronology which dated death according to several converging criteria: the

[37] *TIR.J-P* (Zoora/Ghor es Safi). The area was incorporated in Palaestina Salutaris *c.*370 and in Palaestina Tertia *c.*400.

[38] C. Politis, 'The Sanctuary of Agios Lot, the City of Zoara and the Zared River', in *The Madaba Map Centenary* (Jerusalem 1999), 225–7, also available via internet on Franciscan Cyberspot. See also idem, 'Ancient Arabs, Jews and Greeks on the Shores of the Dead Sea', *Studies in the History and Archaeology of Jordan* 8 (2004), 361–70.

[39] Meimaris and Kritikakou-Nikolaropoulou, *Inscriptions from Palaestina Teria*, ia: *The Greek Inscriptions from Ghor es Safi (Byzantine Zoora)* (Athens 2005).

year of 'The Destruction of the Temple', the Hebrew day and month, and the sabbatical cycle (*shemitah*):[40]

This is the *nefesh*[41] of Mehirsha daughter of the *haver* (a sage? a pious man? a sorcerer?) Marsa, who died on the fifth day, 17 days into the month of Elul, the fourth year of *shemitah*, 362 years after the destruction of the Temple. Let her rest in peace (Isa. 57: 2). Shalom. Shalom. Shalom. Shalom (drawing of a menorah).[42]

This is the soul *nefesh* of... son of Migalus, who died on the day of the Sabbath (*shabbat*), on the twenty-fifth day of the month of *Tevet*, first year of the sabbatical cycle (*shemitah*), 386 after the destruction of the Temple (*hurban beit ha-mikdash*). Peace. Peace be on Israel.[43]

Here rests the *nefesh* of Yose son of Ufi who died in the city of Tefar in the land of the Himyarites and left for the Land of Israel and was buried on the sixth day, on the 29th of the month of Tamuz, the first year of the *shemitah* which is also the 400(?)th year from the destruction of the Temple. Shalom. Shalom on you as you lie here.[44]

All calendrical calculations in the Jewish section of the Zoar cemetery positioned the year of the destruction of the Temple (68/69 CE by their standard) as 'year zero', as though fitting a lasting trauma into a system that aspired to merge biblical and historical ways of counting time.[45] A similar calendar appeared simultaneously among Jewish communities in late ancient Palestine and later in the Jewish diaspora where it designated life-cycle events such as birth and marriage.[46]

[40] The Zoar dated inscriptions begin with 282 of the era of destruction (=CE 350), and end with 435 (or CE 503). In addition, many are further synchronically dated according to the sabbatical cycle. See Naveh, 'The Zoar Tombstones', *Tarbiz* 64 (1995), 476–97 (Heb.), and idem, 'Seven New Tombstones from Zoar', *Tarbiz* 69 (2000), 619–35. further bibliography in Stern, *Calendar and Community*, 88–9.

[41] Literally 'soul' here in the sense of a commemorative-funerary structure, H. Misgav, 'Development of Jewish Memorial Customs in the Roman-Byzantine Period', *Judea and Samaria Research Studies* 11 (2002), 123–36 (Heb.), at 131.

[42] Naveh, *Tarbiz* (1995), 491 tombstone 10 (CE 430).

[43] Joseph Naveh, *On Sherd and Papyrus* (Jerusalem 1992), 203–4 (Heb.) (inscriptions of Zoar), the conventional date is CE 454. The tombstone also bears an engraving of a menorah and incense shovel, two symbols ordinarily associated with Jewishness.

[44] Naveh, 'Seven New Tombstones', 624, tombstone 24 (CE 468).

[45] It may be worth noting that already the sages recorded in the Mishnah (redacted c.200) refer to a variety of dates to validate divorce writs including one counted from the 'Erection of the Temple' or the 'Destruction of the Temple' (*M Git.* 8.5).

[46] Stern, *Calendar and Community*, 88 n. 123 for ref. to locations and publications.

The all-pervasiveness of a calendar dominated by loss, specifically by that of Jerusalem's Temple, continued to animate the reflective domain of Jews. Whether mourning death or celebrating marriage, the spectre of the Temple, as of the living land, continued to hold sway in Jewish memory.[47] An intriguing question remains—on what day did the year start when counting the 'Era of Destruction'? On Rosh Hashanah (=1st of Tishrei) as did the ordinary Jewish year or on the 9th of Av, the traditional date of the Temple's destruction?[48] The former would have conformed to rabbinic calendrical standards; the latter would have presented an anomaly.

At Zoar the dating references occupied most of the writing. Their length surpassed both the indications of identity and the circumstances of death.[49] This spatial incongruity might have been adopted in tandem and as a collective challenge to the Christian system of dating within the same cemetery. Zoar's Christian tombstones regularly referred to the weekday (planetary/pagan or numerical), month day (Macedonian), year numeral (era of the province Arabia, starting with CE 106) and, from 438, the indication cycle.[50] An obsession with dating death with minute chronology appears to reign in Zoar's domain of the dead.[51] And monotheism:

> One (is) the God
> The Lord
> Of all.
> Monument of Petros (son) of
> Antys, who died
> Having a good name
> And a good conscience

[47] M. A. Friedman, *Jewish Marriage in Palestine. A Cairo Geniza Study*, 2 vols. (Tel Aviv and New York 1981), *passim*, for dating marriage according to various systems including the sabbatical cycle, the destruction of the Temple, the exile of king Jehoiachin, and even the Seleucid era.

[48] Naveh opts for the 9th of Av rather than 1st of Tishri or Rosh Hashanah, a suggestion opposed by Stern, *Calendar and Community*, 89. The Zoar calendar also diverges from the rabbinic calendar, Stern, 151–2.

[49] Misgav, 'Development of Jewish Memorial Customs', 130 (Heb.).

[50] Meimaris, *Inscriptions*, 46–54. Of the 321 tombstones, 293 bear a detailed chronological formula; Misgav, 'Development', 130–1.

[51] H. Cotton and J. Price, 'A Bi-Lingual Epitaph from Zoar in the Hecht Museum: The Greek Inscription', *Michmanim* 15 (2001), 10–12, ascribe dating system to the language used.

(at the age) of 33 years
in the year 334 on (the) 22nd
(day) of the month Dios, in the
4th day of (the) Lord
Be of good cheer
No one (is) immortal
In (this) world.[52]

Monument of the blessed
Ouales (Valens) (son) of
Eusebios, who died having
A good name and good faith
(at the age) of 48 years,
in (the) year... on (the) 14th
day (of the month)...
on the... day of the [Lord]
[be of good cheer]
no one is immortal.[53]

Epitaphs like Zoar's Jewish and Christian inscriptions celebrated a specific local identity in terms of time and traditional formulas.[54] The consequence of this amalgam was to enable the living to identify with the dead and to remember what it meant to be a Jew, or a Christian. In a community which consisted mostly of Semites with names derived from Nabataean, Arabic, and Aramaic, the cemetery provided a programme which extended arrangements and histories of the living. It reflected a precocious conversion of indigenous locals to Christianity. It confirmed an early (fourth-century) establishment of an ecclesiastical hierarchy, even with four deaconesses (attested between 444 and 454). Tombstones of soldiers reminded visitors of daily hazards of living in the region. The Jewish section of the cemetery indicated how minorities adjusted to a fast-changing environment.[55] The references to *shabbat* and *shemitah*, the Jewish holy day of the week and the sabbatical cycle respectively, further underlined a unity engendered through strict adherence to these unique

---

[52] Meimaris, *Inscriptions*, no. 162 (CE 439).

[53] Ibid., no. 282 (late 4th/early 5th cent.).

[54] About half of the buried Christians at Zoar bore theophoric names of which the most common were variations based on 'Allah', Meimaris, *Inscriptions*, 29.

[55] Note, however, the inscription commemorating an *archisynagogos* (Meimaris, *Inscriptions*, no. 7, pp. 99–101) which uses Christian dating formula. Perhaps the buried was a gentile donor to the local synagogue.

ways of resting—on the seventh day of the week, as the fifth commandment enjoined, Jewish households took a break from all labour;
on each seventh year the soil was to lie fallow, enjoying a rest.

The obligation of *shemitah*, as of tithe (*maaser*), both prescribed
by the Bible, raised in late antiquity questions relating to diet and to
borders. Observant Jews living in predominantly non-Jewish territory had to know what one was allowed to eat; which areas were
exempt from observing dietary requirements and which were obligated by them. To determine the geographical zones of biblical
commandments and hence the diet of their contemporaries, the
rabbis delineated a map of the 'Land of Israel' (*Eretz Israel*) which
consisted of locations and edibles deemed either 'permitted' or
'forbidden'.[56] Due to changing agricultural and dietary considerations the 'Land of Israel' became an elastic concept whose boundaries and bans fluctuated on the basis of several factors including
natural demography (the expansion and redaction in Jewish settlements), external pressure (Roman imperial restrictions and taxation), and general economic conditions.[57] Rabbinic discussions
regarding the territories subjected to, or exonerated from biblical
agricultural rules showed the rabbis establishing an internal map of
Judaism which reinforced Jewish perceptions of the sanctity of *Eretz
Israel* and of Jewish claims over it.

The rabbinic borders of the Land of Israel bore faint resemblance
to contemporary provincial boundaries. The main frame of reference

[56] *Sifre Deut.* 51; *T Shev.* 4.10; *PT Shev.* 6.1, redacted roughly between 250 and 400
CE but incorporating earlier documents. Y. Sussman, 'The Boundaries of Eretz Israel',
Tarbiz 45 (1976), 213–57 (Heb.) and, much more succinctly in idem, 'The Inscription
in the Synagogue at Rehov', in Levine (ed.), *Ancient Synagogues Revealed* (1982), 146–
51. Modern consensus, or rather lack of it, has assigned the oldest chronological layer
of this *baraita* to either the late 2nd cent. BCE (Hasmonaean) or to the late 1st cent.
BCE (Herodian), and the more recent to the 3rd, perhaps even the 4th cent. CE,
H. Hildesheimer and S. Klein, *Studies in the Geography of Eretz Israel*, trans. from the
German by H. Bar Darom (Jerusalem 1965) (Heb.); R. Frankel and I. Finkelstein,
'The Northeastern Corner of Eretz Israel in the Baraita "Boundaries of Eretz Israel"',
Cathedra 27 (1983), 39–46 (Heb.); C. Primus, 'The Borders of Judaism: The Land of
Israel in Early Rabbinic Judaism', in L. A. Hoffman (ed.), *The Land of Israel: Jewish
Perspectives* (Notre Dame 1986), 97–108.

[57] For estimates of the size of the Jewish population in late antiquity see
R. Yankelevitch, 'The Proportion between the Size of the Jewish and Gentile
Population in Eretz Israel in the Era of the Mishnah and the Talmud', *Cathedra* 61
(1991), 156–75 (Heb.).

was reconstructed biblical maps, one based on 'the land held by those who had migrated from Egypt' and coterminous with the Genesis-Exodus promised land, the other and much smaller territory was based on the territory occupied by those who returned from Babylonian exile under Ezra and Nehemiah (i.e. the Persian province of Yehud). The sum total of rabbinic concepts of what were deemed 'forbidden' (namely subject to restrictions) localities within exempt areas and 'exempt' locations (not subject) within 'forbidden' areas contributed to an oddly shaped 'Land of Israel' whose boundaries embraced the northern Palestinian periphery (Galilee, the Golan, and Bashan), a narrow strip along both banks of the Jordan, 'Daroma' (the Judaean hills south of Jerusalem and north of Beer Sheva), and a narrow strip along the Mediterranean coast between Ascalon (Ashkelon) and Tyre.[58] Strictly speaking, the map corresponded neither to the Exodus' promised land nor to Yehud but rather reflected the extent of contiguous Jewish settlements in late antiquity.

In times of hardship the rabbis altered the perimeters of the permitted in order to alleviate the lot of observant Jews.[59] The Palestinian Talmud recorded a series of concessions which exempted settlements with Jewish minorities (Caesarea, Scythopolis-Beth Shean, Eleutheropolis-Beth Govrin, Kefar Zemah) where it must have been cumbersome if not unrealistic to abide by the strict sabbatical and tithing rules.[60] Such dilemmas became apparent even in the eyes of non-Jews. Dietary difficulties which Jews experienced in predominantly gentile settings served as butts of ironic mimicry.[61] When exempt, the question remained whether an area was still considered part of the 'Land of Israel' or not and in which manner. The city of Ashkelon (Ascalon) was a case in point. The earliest recorded rabbinic boundaries placed Ashkelon outside the Land of Israel although the 'frontier' passed near by, perhaps even in an Ashkelonian suburb.[62]

---

[58] For a map see Dauphin, 'Interdits alimentaires et territorialité en Palestine byzantine', *TM* 14 (2002), 154.

[59] *PT Shev.* 9 with S. Safrai, 'The Practical Implementation of the Sabbatical Year after the Destruction of the Second Temple', *Tarbiz* 36 (1967), 12–21 (Heb.).

[60] *PT Dem.* 2.1 (22c). A. Büchler, 'The Patriarch R. Judah I and the Graeco-Roman Cities of Palestine', *Studies in Jewish History* (London 1954), 179–244.

[61] *LamR* Proem. 17 quoted in Ch. 4, above, p. 145.

[62] *PT Shev.* 6, 36c; *PT Yeb.* 7. 8a; *T Ahel* 18.18 with E. Fradkin, 'Jewish Ascalon in the Mishnaic Period', *Cathedra* 19 (1981), 3–10 (Heb.).

To substantiate the decision the rabbis relied on the Bible, which never included this Philistine city within the territory settled by the Twelve Tribes. A paradox emerged: while in matters pertaining to divorce Ashkelon was considered 'abroad', in matters of diet Jews living in Ashkelon had to abide by the rules binding their brethren in the Land of Israel since the city's air had been purged of 'gentile impurities'.[63]

Considerations of the purity or impurity of the land were the crux around which rabbinic maps revolved:

Whoever heads from Akko (Acre) to Achziv, to his east on his right, the road is pure, its produce subject to tithe and the [the rules of] the sabbatical year on account of [the laws pertaining to] the land of the peoples unless you are informed otherwise. But on the left towards the west, the road is impure on account [of the laws pertaining] to the land of the peoples and therefore exempt from tithes and sabbatical rules till you learn that it is under obligation.[64]

Whether Acre itself belonged to the 'Land of Israel' was a contentious subject which ended in stalemate, the decision being that it was both 'pure' and 'impure'.

Rabbinic exegetical geography sanctified the land through the observance of commandments. It created insiders and outsiders by the simple device of singling out settlements where Jews were obliged by, or exempt from, certain biblical rules. Such lists also reminded Jews that there was a certain homology among them which, like Oral Law, singled them out. The 'borders of the Land of Israel' integrated the biblical past into shifting presents. Through the rhetoric of biblical exegesis, on the one hand, and the realities of binding geography on the other, the projection of a 'Land of Israel' along biblical lines forged a direct bridge between the Jewish inhabitants of late ancient Palestine and their biblical ancestors. The territory which Jews in late antiquity occupied, although under foreign domination and largely peopled by non-Jews, was one in which they were entrenched and to which they had divine right.

The permanence of the Bible, on the one hand, and changing conditions, on the other, exerted constant rabbinic ingenuity. The

---

[63] *M Git.* 1.2. One rabbi even went so far as to include Ashkelon in the halakhic 'Land of Israel', an opinion which remained a minority consensus, *T Ahel.* 18.4.
[64] *PT Shev.* 6.1, 36b.

multiple character of the celebration of Scripture was reflected in the coexistence of Jewish and Christian biblical exegesis which focused on identifying and updating biblical localities. At the dawn of the fourth century, Eusebius of Caesarea, an indefatigable collector of biblical traditions, inaugurated a series of scholarly promenades through biblical alleys of which the so-called *Onomasticon* is the sole survivor.[65] A verbal map of Palestine, the *Onomasticon* relied on biblical toponymy and particularly on place-names from the books of Numbers, Deuteronomy, Joshua, and Judges, in other words the narratives that had established the hold of the Israelites over the land promised by Yahweh to their ancestors. Basically a scholarly venture, the *Onomasticon*'s Palestine was a recreation of the biblical promised land occasionally brought up to date. But since Palestine was not merely an exhibit of the past, the space which the *Onomasticon* conjured up was hardly neutral because none was less neutral than Palestine where the Bible was omnipresent.

Systematizing the Bible on the basis of place-names engendered an alphabetical arrangement of localities according to biblical books in the Christian canon. For many places, Eusebius merely restated the information given in the Bible, such as the four entries under the letter T(au) from the book of Joshua (Tina, Telem, and Tesan in the tribe of Judah and Tyrus in the tribe of Naphtali). But for other places Eusebius provided an updating which included references to distances and to the ethnic composition of the settlement.[66] He specified, for example, which settlements in Daroma were either

[65] The *Onomasticon* is one of a series of promised titles which Eusebius outlines in his preface and that have not survived. These included a map (?) of the allotments of the twelve tribes, and a plan of Jerusalem and its Temple. Its date has been a subject of scholarly controversy. For a summary of modern views, J. E. Taylor, 'Introduction' in eadem *et al.*, *Palestine in the Fourth Century: The Onomasticon of Eusebius of Caesarea* (Jerusalem 2003), 2–4. The basic study remains E. Z. Melamed, 'The *Onomasticon* of Eusebius', *Tarbiz* 3 (1932), 314–27, 393–409; 4 (1933), 78–96, 249–84 (Heb.). Melamed has opted for continuous revisions between 312 and 325, concluding that the *Onomasticon* is basically a Jewish work of several unidentifiable hands which underwent redaction at the hand of Eusebius, via Origen and his school, who 'Christianized' the text, a conclusion adopted by C. U. Wolf, 'Eusebius of Caesarea and the *Onomasticon*', *BA* 27 (1964), 66–96 (now available on the internet). See also idem, *The Onomasticon of Eusebius Pamphili compared with the Version of Jerome and annotated*, now available via www.tertullian.org/fathers.

[66] For a detailed analysis, P. Thomsen, 'Palästina nach dem Onomasticon des Eusebius', *ZPDV* 26 (1903), 97–198.

Jewish or Christian.[67] Entries for localities like Ashkelon and Achziv were composites harking back to the Bible with touches of contemporaneity. The entry for Ascalon (Ashkelon) specified that 'it is a most celebrated city in Palestine. In ancient times it was one of the 5 satrapies [of the Philistines] and allocated to Judah who did not rule it because he did not kill the foreigners in it.'[68] An underlying assumption was that its location was too well known to merit specific directives. For Achziv (Achzeiph) Eusebius provided orientation: 'the town fell to the lot of Asher from which it did not expel the foreigner. It is the same as Ekdippa, nine milestones from Ptolemais (Akko-Acre) on the way to Tyre'. These were the nine miles that the rabbis regarded as a boundary between the purity and impurity of the land (above, p. 249).

In several instances Eusebius provided information which linked the Hebrew Bible and the New Testament:

Bethsour (Josh. 15: 58)
Of the tribe of Judah or Benjamin. It is now the village of Bethsoro, 20 milestones from Aelia (Jerusalem) on the way to Chebron (Hebron). A spring is also shown there beside the mountain where, it is said, the eunuch of Kandake had been baptized by Philip (Acts 8: 38). There is also another Bethsour in the tribe of Judah, one milestone from Eleutheropolis.[69]

The entry led from the biblical past through a specifically Christian event to a present in which Christians were perceived as direct successors of the Israelite settlers.[70] It reflected a literary map unfolded like a story whose peaks corresponded to fluctuations of Christian history from the time of the patriarchs to late antiquity.

Aspects of biblical topography lent themselves to a redrawing of the very structure of the 'promised land' whose designation, genealogy, and individuality underwent profound transformation in late antiquity.[71] Through the *Onomasticon* biblical geography became part of the fabric of Christian consciousness. The Bible's 'ancient

---

[67] Freeman-Grenville *et al.*, *The Onomasticon*, 7.
[68] Ibid. 21.
[69] *Onom.* 52, Freeman-Grenville trans. in idem *et al.*, *The Onomasticon*, 35.
[70] D. Groh, 'The *Onomasticon* of Eusebius and the Rise of Christian Palestine', *SP* 18 (1983), 23–31; Jacobs, *Remains of the Jews*, 35.
[71] Wilken, *The Land called Holy*, on the emergence of a Christian Palestine; on monastic contribution to the process, Sivan, 'Pilgrimage, Monasticism', in Ousterhout, in *Blessings of Pilgrimage*.

history' was a history that was reworked to be used. It informed the actions of the present, brandishing its own version of the conquest, and it highlighted the geographical restrictiveness of the Jewish-Mosaic law which Eusebius located in Jerusalem alone.[72] Each locality in the *Onomasticon* denoted a tale, and the story gave prefiguration and legitimacy to Christianity's territorial claims.

By the time Jerome translated the *Onomasticon* into Greek (late 380s), imperial investment, pilgrims, and monks had set in motion a process which culminated in the transformation of the very same regions into a Christian holy land.[73] The change was reflected in key entries like Bethlehem. For Eusebius, Bethlehem, also called Ephratha, was a town affiliated with the tribe of Judah and located six milestones from Jerusalem. On the basis of Jewish traditions, he also situated in Bethlehem the tombs of Jesse and David. No reference was made to a Christian tradition, already mentioned by Origen, which placed the cave of the nativity in Bethlehem. Elsewhere Eusebius appeared fully cognizant of the tradition which identified the Bethlehem cave with that of the Nativity.[74] Jerome's updating consisted of the following:

About a thousand paces away is the tower of Ader which means the tower of the flock, meaning where in prophecy the shepherds became aware of the nativity of the Lord. Near the same Bethlehem is shown the tomb of [Herod] Archelaus, the former king of Judaea, which is at the beginning of the fork from the public highway to our cells. Bethlehem is also called the son of Efratha, that is of Mary, as is stated fully in the Book of Chronicles. Read history diligently![75]

Whatever Jerome had meant in his *Onomasticon* a few years later he described a cave in Bethlehem where 'the lover of Venus' [Adonis] had been lamented and where 'the infant Christ cried'.[76] Bethlehem, in Jerome's time, 'belonged to us'. In the implicit battle between

---

[72] *Commentary on Isaiah*, 322.37–323.3; Hollerich, *Eusebius' Isaiah*, 42.

[73] Wilken, *The Land Called Holy*; Hunt, *Holy Land*; P. Maraval, 'The Earliest Phase of Christian Pilgrimage in the Near East', *DOP* 56 (2002), 63–74; and idem, *Lieux saints*.

[74] Origen, *C. Celsum* 1.51 quoted in Taylor, *Christians*, 103; Eus. *Demon. Evan.* 3.2.47; 7.2.14.

[75] Freeman-Grenville, 31 for translation.

[76] Jerome, *Ep.* 58.3, dated to CE 395, quote in Taylor, *Christians and the Holy Places*, 96.

Jesus and Adonis, and between Rachel and Mary, Jesus and Mary won.

To appropriate authority over a work whose denotation had shifted from the Hebrew Bible to the Christian Scripture, categories of interpretation privileged meanings to the detriment of the 'other'. Multiplicity of interpretations did not put an end to difficulties or to doubts.[77] While the *Onomasticon* was designed as a scholarly aid to help Christians recover the ancient part of their polity, the commentaries on biblical books served as guides to literary remains. Relying on a tradition of anti-Jewish apologetics, to which other Palestinians like Justin Martyr had made substantial contributions, Eusebius' biblical exegesis focused on major texts of the Hebrew Bible that prefigured events narrated in the New Testament.[78] The use of the perennially popular Isaiah text(s) exemplified the mode in which a theologically charged geography established Christianity's continuity without conceding to Jewish opponents the rich historical terrain charted in this text.[79]

Commenting on Isa. 42: 11 (*Let the wilderness and its cities lift up their voice, the hamlets that Kedar inhabits. Let the dwellers of [the] Rock* (sela) *rejoice, let them shout from the top of the mountains*) Eusebius described Kedar as a location 'beyond Arabia at the edge of the desert, which they say is held by the Saracen people' and the Rock (Petra) as

A city of Palestine composed of superstitious men and saturated with demonic error... the course of events has confirmed the truth of [Isaiah's] words since in our day the churches of Christ are established even in that

---

[77] In general, see the various articles in C. Brekelmans and M. Haran (eds.), *Hebrew Bible/Old Testament: The History of its Interpretation*, i (Göttingen 1996). See also E. Z. Melamed, *Bible Commentators*, 2nd edn. (Jerusalem 1978), i, on biblical interpretation of the sages, in the Targums (esp. Onkelos, Jonathan, and to the Latter Prophets (Heb.). For Christian exegesis, R. P. C. Hanson, 'Biblical Exegesis in the Early Church', in P. R. Ackroyd and C. F. Evans (eds.), *The Cambridge History of the Bible* (Cambridge 1970), i. 412–53, and other articles in same collection. See also R. M. Grant, *A Short History of Biblical Interpretation* (New York 1948). W. Horbury, 'Jews and Christians on the Bible', Demarcation and Convergence (325–451)', in idem, *Jews and Christians in Contact and Controversy* (Edinburgh 1998), 200–25.

[78] On anti-Jewish apologetics, Simon, *Verus Israel*, 87–123, 165–213. On Justin, W. A. Shotwell, *The Biblical Exegesis of Justin Martyr* (London 1965).

[79] Hollerich, 133.

very city of the Petrans, and throughout its countryside, and in the desert places of the Saracens...[80]

Allowing for rhetorical exaggeration, the description of pagan Petra stressed a process of conversion which, at least according to recent archaeological excavations, remained more an aspiration than a reality in Eusebius' own time.[81] In the *Onomasticon* Petra was identified with Rekem (Reqm), a city in Arabia.[82] In this Eusebius followed Josephus (*Ant* 4.7, 1.161; 4.4 and 7.82), who had identified Rekem with Petra.[83] The *Onomasticon* further linked the desert of Rekem/Petra, which Eusebius called Kadesh Barnea, with a biblical miracle, the rock from which Moses teased water, and with Miriam, Moses' sister, who was buried there and whose grave was to be seen even in his own time (Num. 20: 1).[84] Late ancient Jewish biblical translations (*targumim*) contradicted this identification, suggesting instead a clear distinction between the 'Desert of Rekem', identified with the desert of Zin and with contemporary Petra, on the one hand, and Rekem Gaia or Kades Barnea, identified with a location between the Negev and the Sinai.[85]

The *Onomasticon* provided a basis for anyone interested in the application of biblical geography to contemporary realities. Because Eusebius modified a model that the rabbis used to define Jews and

---

[80] Eusebius, *CI* 272.34–273.18, trans. in Hollerich, *Eusebius' Isaiah*, 74. Recent excavations at Petra do not point to ecclesiastical structures prior to the 5th cent.

[81] Z. T. Fiema, 'Late Antique Petra and its Hinterland: Recent Research and New Interpretations', in J. H. Humphrey (ed.), *The Roman and Byzantine Near East*, 3 (JRA Suppl. 49; Portsmouth 2002), 191–252. The earliest church does not appear to antedate the 5th cent. See also the surveys in J. Frösén *et al.* (eds.), *The Petra Papyri*, i (ACORP 4; Amman 2002), and the lavishly illustrated book by Z. T. Fiema and J. Frösén, *Petra: A City Forgotten and Rediscovered* (Helsinki 2002). Note, however, the redating of the foundation of one of Petra's churches to the late 4th cent. following the 363 earthquake, P. Bikai, 'North Ridge Project', *ACOR Newsletter* (Summer 2002), 1.

[82] *Onom.* s.v. Rekem and Sela.

[83] On the various forms of the name, M. Weippert, 'Archäologischer Jahresbericht', *ZDPV* 82 (1966), 274–330, esp. 296–9.

[84] *Onom.* sub Kades Barnea.

[85] M. L. Klein, *The Fragments of Targums of the Pentateuch* (Rome 1980), i. 208. For Byzantine remains at the Sinaitic locality, identified as Ain Alkudirat, see *NEAEHL* s.v. Kades. In general, D. Ben Gad HaCohen, 'Kadesh and Rekem, Kadesh Barnea and Rekem Geah', *Judea and Samaria Research Studies* 11 (2002), 25–40 (Heb.).

Judaism, the *Onomasticon*'s paradigmatic polemics were striking as points of anchorage for the definition of a Christian Palestine. Compared with rabbinic ideology regarding the territoriality of biblical lands Eusebian perceptions of the contemporaneity of the same lands shows how he combined the literalness of Jewish biblical exegesis with criticism of this form of biblical interpretation in order to form a bridge between the Israelite past and the Christian polity of the present.[86]

3. THE MADABA MAP AND THE REHOV INSCRIPTION

Similarly to the contours of Eusebius' 'maps', rabbinic verbal 'maps' were list-texts that echoed and amplified contemporary claims to the promised land.[87] These became the indispensable foundations for religious consensus that bridged the space between scholarly inter-pretations of biblical topography and an audience of believers who were expected to comply with credal precepts. In the sixth century these lists were translated into monumental images which were placed in public places. The two outstanding examples were the (fragmentary) mosaic map in the church of Madaba, north-east of the Dead Sea, and the mosaic inscription in the synagogue at Rehov, south of Scythopolis. Neither is comprehensible without taking into account learned exegesis and the derivation that stripped it of abstracts.

Already in the 380s, when Jerome undertook a revised translation of the *Onomasticon* from Greek into Latin, the experiences of pilgrims and monks began to transform spaces into functioning

---

[86] Eus. *Comm. Isa.* 36.32–3. On Eusebius' use of Jewish sources, Hollerich, 109, 147–8. On the use of subsidiary sciences of etymology, chronology, ethnography, mythology, and geography and of existing lists of biblical Hebrew and Aramaic place- and personal names, such as *The Interpretation of Hebrew Names*, preserved in Jerome's Latin translation, Hollerich, 71. F. Wutz, *Onomastica Sacra: Untersuchungen zum Liber Interpretationis Hebraicorum Nominum des Hl Hieronymus* (TU 41; Leipzig 1914), variously attributed to Philo and to Origen.

[87] Dauphin, 'Interdits', emphasizes the rabbinic territorial ideology and its demographic dynamics.

practices made up of imaginary and real relationships with the biblical text. In the same 380s Egeria travelled throughout Palestine, then scantily clad with Christian structures, as though the land had been baptized.[88] By the mid-sixth century the multiple identity of the land was likewise suppressed in the Madaba mosaic map. The Madaba map carefully marked localities by referring to major public structures, which included walls, theatres, and baths. But the ubiquity of churches throughout demonstrated the hold that Christianity had taken on biblical lands. Settlements once associated by word only with the Bible boasted at least one church. Many had several. Equally eloquent were the spaces left out of the map. Neither Jewish nor Samaritans settlements or structures marred the uniform mantle with which Christian piety enveloped the mosaic.

The Madaba mosaic map seemed disposed to take the landscape literally.[89] It provided a visually updated illustration of Eusebius' *Onomasticon*. The map endowed all the cities with walls, a schematic representation that did not always correspond with their actual shape. In Gaza, about half of which is left on the map, it is possible to discern a theatre (or a *nymphaeum*), streets with colonnaded porticoes, and churches. The existence of a synagogue in sixth-century Gaza would not have even been suspected.[90] At Neapolis, once a city bustling with Samaritans, public structures were depicted with an exactitude which remains without parallel.[91] None hints at the presence of Samaritans in this part of Palestine. In its present shape, two entities dominate the map, the Dead Sea and Jerusalem. The Dead Sea emerged as an impressive topographical anchor wildly out of tune with its role in biblical history. Unlike the *Onomasticon*, the Madaba map positioned Jerusalem in its centre. It was a Jerusalem that barely corresponded with a geographical reality. But its shape, an oval, was strikingly reminiscent of the rabbinic *omphalos* which

[88] On the experiences of Egeria among many, Wilkinson, *Egeria's Travels, passim*; Hunt, *Holy Land Pilgrimage, passim*; Maraval, *Lieux saints, passim*; Sivan, 'Holy Land Pilgrimage' and 'Who was Egeria?'

[89] See the articles in *The Madaba Map Centenary* (1997), also available, with presentation of each locality, on the internet via Franciscan cyberspot.

[90] A. Ovadiah, 'The Synagogue at Gaza', in Levine (ed.), *ASR*, 129–32 (5th–6th cent.).

[91] Magen, *Flavia Neapolis* (2005).

designated the centrality of the city in the universe. Madaba's Jerusalem loomed larger than all other localities, and with more details than those selected for any other urban centre.[92] Its *cardo* and *decumanus* are easily discernible as are several of Jerusalem's main churches.

Faithful to itineraries of late ancient pilgrimage the mosaic included Egypt and the Sinai, two *sine qua non* areas that pilgrims assiduously frequented.[93] The Madaba map was comprehensive in its inclusion of villages and small settlements, as well as natural features. There were, as one could expect, distortions bred by the constraints of contemporary cartography which in turn led to imaginative improvisation. All images catered to the sensibilities of a public whose creed had been nurtured by the living land around it and by their own familiarity with the places on the map. Seen through the eyes of pious contemporaries the Madaba map presented a world of faith in which one took truth for symbols and symbols for the truth.

Proclaiming the identity of a Christian, the mosaic aspired to illustrate the history of God's salvation in a map. It formed a central complement to late ancient exegetical endeavours and to the territory that pilgrimage constructed.[94] The pictorial heirs of Eusebius' *Onomasticon* staked their claim to a holy land on its Christianization as well as on the immortalization of this process as a triumph of cartographic ideology. The erection of a monumental map of biblical lands signified the appropriation of both biblical and imperial history: the Bible because it provided the toponomy and the foundation of faith; the Empire because it provided the means, the techniques, and the ideology. As it celebrated Christian brotherhood, the Madaba map integrated the sanctified biblical territories into the social body of believers and their practices.

---

[92] With the possible exception of the (non-surviving) town of Madaba which was considerably smaller yet the proud possessor of this unique artefact. N. Duval, 'Essai sur la signification des vignettes topographiques', in *Madaba Map Centenary* via Franciscan cyberspot, also pointing to comparisons with the city depictions of the Umm al-Rasas mosaic.

[93] Hunt, *Holy Land Pilgrimage*; G. Frank, *The Memory of the Eyes: Pilgrims to Living Saints in Christian Late Antiquity* (Berkeley 2000).

[94] H. Donner, 'The Uniqueness of the Madaba Map and its Restoration in 1965', in *Madaba Map Centenary* (Franciscan Cyberspace).

Contrasting perceptions of the same 'promised land' by Jews and by Christians are vividly illuminated in a synagogue mosaic found at Rehov (Rehob), a small settlement just south of Scythopolis (Beth Shean).[95] Roughly contemporaneous with the Madaba map the Rehov synagogue mosaic contains only words. It is the longest inscription ever found in Israel. Heavily indebted to rabbinic texts, the mosaic listed localities whose fruits were forbidden on the seventh year and were tithed on the other sabbatical cycle years:

Shalom. These fruits are forbidden at Beth Shean in the Seventh Year, and in the other sabbatical cycle they are tithed (as) *demai*: marrows, melons, cucumbers, parsnips, mint, Egyptian beans..., leeks, seeds, dried figs, sesame, mustard, rice, cumin, dry lupine, large peas..., garlic, onions...pressed dates, wine and oil...

These are the places which are permitted around Beth Shean: from the south...gate till the 'white field'; from the west...gate till the end of the pavement; from the north...gate till Kefar Qarnos...; from the east... gate till the tomb of...Before the gate it is allowed; beyond it, it is forbidden.

The forbidden towns in the territory of Sussita are...

The towns which are doubtful within the territory of Naveh (Nawa) are...

The forbidden towns in the territory of Tyre are...and everything that Jews have purchased

The territory of the Land of Israel (namely) the places (settled) by the returnee from Babylon (are): The Ascalon junction, the wall of Strato's Tower, Dor, the wall of Akko (Acre)...upper Tarnegola of Caesarea (Paneas), Rekem Trachon, Zimra of the limits of Bostra, Jabbok, Heshbon, the brook Zered...fort of Raziza, Rekem Gaia, the garden of Ascalon and the great road leading to the desert.

These fruits are forbidden in Paneas on the Seventh Year...

These fruits are tithed at Caesarea (Maritima)...And where is the region of Caesarea? (It is) till Soran and the inn of Tibetah and the column...and if there is a place which was purchased by Jews our rabbis are suspicious of it. Shalom.

The towns permitted within the territory of Sebaste are...[96]

[95] Sussman, 'A Halakhic Inscription from the Beth Shean Valley', 88–158 for text and commentary. Levine (ed.), *Ancient Synagogues Revealed*, 152–3, and A. Demsky, in A. Houtman *et al.* (eds.), *Sanctity of Time and Space in Tradition and Modernity* (Leiden 1998), 361–3, for Engl. trans.

[96] 'The Rehov Inscription: A Translation', in Levine (ed.), *Ancient Synagogues Revealed*, 152–3 (modified).

The text holds several novelties. It lifted rabbinic debates out of their school context, removing ascription of specific opinions to specific rabbis, and inscribing in stone and in public an updated version of the rules regarding the duties incumbent on observant Jews along the borders of the 'Land of Israel'. Unlike its rabbinic models, the mosaic included the city of Sebaste and its environs. Once the heart of the Northern Israelite kingdom, in late antiquity this area was predominantly Samaritan. Following rebellions it was settled by Christians.[97] Nor did the Rehov lists merely reiterate biblical and post-biblical injunctions. The mosaic added a fine touch of urban planning absent from rabbinic discussions. The proximity of Beth Shean-Scythopolis to the Rehov community required finely tuned pointers such as the precise names of the city gates, and an exact orientation beyond walls and gates regarding the 'permitted' and the 'forbidden'. The verbal description of Scythopolis formed the closest parallel to the concept of urban depictions as conceived by the makers of the Madaba map. In both instances an emphasis was placed on the contours of urban spaces through careful delineation of walls, gates, and towers.

Because the Bible was the basis of all these efforts, the desire to elucidate the biblical truth was the power behind the choice to delineate sacred land in terms of history and actuality. These labours projected a citizenry whose structure was circumscribed by the exegetes' selectivity. In its largest circumference *Eretz Israel* of the rabbis, like the land promised to Abraham, extended from the eastern banks of the Jordan to the Sinai, and from Armenia to the Red Sea. Most of the sites listed in the Rehov inscription fell within the provincial boundaries of Palaestina I and II, extending solely from the Dead Sea to the Mediterranean and from the northern Negev to Hermon. Practical considerations outweighed the temptations of imaginary interpretation. Dietary lists had to qualify in actuality what Jews could, and could not, eat on the sabbatical year. Maps of a Christian Holy Land had to serve as guides for real travellers.

The adoption of the sabbatical principle in conjunction with the shifting frontiers of Jewish settlements served as a reminder of the main sources of communal diet and livelihood. At Rehov the

[97] A. Demsky, 'The Permitted Villages of Sebaste in the Rehov Mosaic', *IEJ* 29 (1979), 182–93; Z. Safrai, 'Marginal Notes on the Rehov Inscription', *Zion* 42 (1987), 1–23.

reminder was verbal. In other synagogues, representations of the zodiac, with its seasons and monthly labours, acted as visual confirmation of the rural character and calendrical concerns of Palestinian Jewry. The appearance of the zodiac as a centre piece of synagogal mosaics from the fourth century onwards has been linked with calendrical mutations and the need to advertise the fixing of festivals and the new moons.[98] Iconographical varieties, from a zodiac with Helios and his chariot in the centre (Beth Alpha) to a verbal list of months devoid of images altogether ('En Gedi), reflected local vocabularies and partialities as well as the centrality of the Hebrew communal calendar.

Rehov was situated near Scythopolis, the provincial capital of Palaestina Secunda, where Jews decorated their prayer halls with colourful mosaics laden with figural representations that owed much to polytheistic artistic sensibilities.[99] The community at Rehov inclined to aniconism. In this it sported an astonishing uniformity with the tastes of the 'En Gedi settlers, a Jewish village on the Dead Sea at a fair distance from Rehov. In the *Onomasticon* Eusebius qualified 'En Gedi as 'a large village of Jews'. Its sixth-century (?) synagogue mosaic contained a zodiac which had been stripped of its imagery to become a verbal list of months and labours, all in Hebrew.[100] The emphasis on abstracts, in shape of letters, rather than on images, represented a response to Hellenistic trends in Judaism itself as well as to Christianity's increasing use of pictorial imagery.[101]

The enumeration of localities and agricultural produce in biblical exegesis and in synagogues marked the soil as Jewish while devaluing the fact that the land itself was under the control of non-Jews. Pagans, Samaritans, and later Christians were neighbours whose presence, however, was a perpetual reminder of why certain items were forbidden to Jews. Constant and continuous interpretation of the

---

[98] A. G. Sternberg, *The Zodiac of Tiberias* (Tiberias 1972) (Heb.) on the link between the emergence and centrality of the zodiac and the patriarchal fixing of the calendar; R. Talgam, 'Similarities and Differences', in Levine and Weiss (eds.), *From Dura to Sepphoris*, 101. See also Ch. 8 on urban stories.

[99] See Ch. 8 on urban stories.

[100] D. Barag *et al.*, 'The Synagogue at 'En-Gedi', and L. I. Levine, 'The Inscription in the 'En-Gedi Synagogue', both in Levine (ed.), *Ancient Synagogues Revealed*, 116–19, and 140–5.

[101] Were the former responsible for erasing the images on the Naaran zodiac?

biblical texts immobilized what the Bible enshrined while integrating communities into the sacred precincts of the land and of biblical origins. Through lists, be they of localities, of biblical ancestors, or of priestly courses, it was possible to establish Jews in their own land as though a direct line led from the Bible to late antiquity via the Temple, and from Egypt through Babylon to the Holy Land.[102]

Rabbinic and Christian biblical interpretation reflected one way in which Jews and Christians argued their rightful place in a space concerned with origins. Within late ancient Palestine, Jews and Christians superimposed their notions of biblical geography, not without due attention to the realities of the land. The rabbis did not expect all Jews in localities where Jews formed a minority to abide by strict biblical rules.[103] Eusebius acknowledged the existence of Jewish settlement which the Madaba map, however, later ignored. In neither were the extrapolated scriptural boundaries sharply defined. The proximity of Jews, pagans, Christians, and Samaritans resulted in flexible definitions of spaces.[104]

The extent of intellectual activities fomented through Bible study throughout Jewish Palestine is further gleaned from the poetry of the synagogue (*piyyut*), an exegetical realm in which Hebrew retained a dominant role. Besides the extraordinary range and number of poems written for practically every occasion linked with ritual and service, composers of *piyyutim* also wielded their exceptional mastery over the language to record and comment on contemporary events. Poems commemorating the destruction of the Temple on the 9th of Av served to lament the fate of contemporary Jewry. In the wake of Heraclius' presence in Palestine in 628 a *piyyut* listed the localities most affected by the emperor's bloody trail.[105] These included several

[102] Cf. the inscriptions relating the 24 priestly guards in Palestine and as far as Yemen (Naveh 'Ancient Synagogue Inscriptions', in Levine, *ASR*, 133–9, and Levine, *The Ancient Synagogue*). Cf. poetic rendering of the same topic in the *piyyutim* of the Killir (*paytan*) written for the 9th of Av (6th cent.?) where he inserts references to the courses and their localities, Yahalom, *Poetry and Society*, 115; on biblical lists of patriarchs in the 'En Gedi synagogue, ibid.

[103] M. Bar Ilan, 'Why did the Tannaim discuss the border of Eretz Israel', *Teudah* 7 (1991), 95–110.

[104] D. R. Edwards, *Religion and Power: Pagans, Jews, and Christians in the Greek East* (New York, 1996), 103, relying on *M AZ* 3.4.

[105] E. Fleischer, 'Lament on the Killing of Jews in the Land of Israel during Heraclius' Time', *Shalem* 5 (1977), 209–27, esp. 224 (Heb.).

Torah study centres where specialists resided and where money was allocated to support the pursuit of such studies. The lament over their demise, skilfully intertwined with traditional elegy over the destroyed Temple, reflected a sense of threatened order.

Synagogal liturgical poetry, like synagogal art, hymnology, and church mosaics, reinforced the ingenuity and the deft linguistic touches that became weapons in Jewish–Christian encounters over Scripture. In Gaza, a city whose history was borne on the shoulders of fanatical bishops, erudite monks, learned grammarians, and devout ascetics, the mosaic of the synagogue, dated to CE 507, depicted a stylized Orpheus image dubbed 'David' in Hebrew characters. This 'David' wore the regalia of Byzantine emperors while playing the lyre for a group of ferocious animals of the kind that Romans viewed in theatrical *venationes*. Such events, on which both rabbis and Christian theologians frowned, became, in the hands of versatile practitioners of *piyyutim* like the famed HaKilir, a model for a gory staging of a mythic battle between Leviathan and Behemoth.[106] The poetic battle between the two monsters made synagogue audiences privy to acts of bestial cruelty to which only divine intervention put an end. The poem's inevitable conclusion, the triumph of God, reminded listeners that the fate of all, including the ultimate release of Israel from its present bondage, was in the hands of God alone:

> They (i.e. Behemoth and Leviathan) will be reconciled only
> To be slaughtered, butchered and defaced
> To become food for the pious
> Who will then realize that [Israel] is not forsaken (Jer. 51: 5)
> Then they will say 'Bless be He who is faithful' (Deut. 7: 9)
> Because every single thing did He ordain
> And brought about in its time[107]

When both monsters eventually died, their flesh served as meals for the righteous whose earthly descendants, it must be remembered, passed that hot August day of the 9th of Av in fasting

---

[106] J. Schirmann, 'The Battle between Behemoth and Leviathan according to an Ancient Hebrew *Piyyut*', *Proceedings of the Israel Academy of Sciences and Humanities* 4.13 (1970), 1–43; Yahalom, *Poetry and Society*, 250–8, esp. 257 naming the genre 'literary *kynegeion*'. The poem fits well into what Michael Roberts termed 'the jeweled style' of late ancient poetry (idem, *The Jeweled Style: Poetry and Poetics in Late Antiquity* (Ithaca 1989)). It was composed for the 9th of Av services.

[107] Schirmann, 'Battle', 32, lines 140–6; Yahalom, *Poetry and Society*, 255.

in remembrance of the destruction of the Temple. The poetic re-creation of the old opposition between land and sea through Behemoth and Leviathan within the very walls of the synagogue was a subtle way of making the values of Judaism triumph and of blurring the boundaries between the biblical past and its present adherents. The interpretation of the 9th of Av, when the *piyyut* was recited, in the context of war tempered the tumult of the destruction of the Temple, making it unnecessary to recount it. By insisting on the collective convictions of his listeners the poet exalted the perpetual kinship between God and Israel, then and in his own time.

To orchestrate the calendar around biblical injunctions and events involved a process of reconstruction and negotiation in changing contexts. The permanence of traditional signifiers, not the least the Bible itself, should not obscure the subtle transference and transformation that shaped scriptural interpretation. Because the celebration of Scripture was a paradigm of living, of beginning, and of renewal, the re-enacting of Scripture was measured in terms of ceremonies that reminded everyone that they were worthy descendants of biblical ancestors. Interpretative versatility became fundamental in establishing hegemony. While Palestinian Christian theologians advocated new types of patriotism that positioned celebrations at the outposts of the creed, Jews listened to exegetical narratives and liturgical poetry, twin texts that nurtured Jewish identity in the synagogue. To maintain a delicate balance between daily demands and a system of government that increasingly favoured one population group over another, a Jewish system had to retain and elaborate elements of a ritual calendar that guaranteed endurance.

4. PASSOVER AND EASTER: READING REDEMPTION AND REVENGE

Every year the reading of the Haggadah constitutes the heart of the Jewish Passover celebration which commemorates the story of Israel's deliverance from Egyptian bondage.[108] Every year the recitation of

[108] The oldest surviving version comes from the Cairo Genizah reproduced in E. D. Goldschmidt, *The Passover Haggadah: Its Sources and History* (Jerusalem 1960), 73–84 (Heb.).

the last days of Jesus and the anticipation of his second coming (the *parousia*) animates the Christian Easter ceremonies.[109] The message, for Jews and for Christians, is of salvation. The Exodus account, from its Egyptian inception to its Sinaitic epiphany, had been fundamental in the creation of Jewish identity.[110] Its influence on the shaping of crucial Jesus narratives, not the least of a miraculous birth amidst threats of death, is likewise evident.

After the destruction of the Temple in CE 70 Passover, the earliest celebratory injunction in the Hebrew Bible, came to signify for Jews a dramatic prefiguration of the divine promise of redemption; for Christians Easter marked the salvation that had already been effected. Such strikingly different interpretations point to a process of abstraction by which the same tradition endowed each group with an autonomous existence, dependent on, yet also independent of, each other. The very moments of biblical liberation and Roman destruction generated a fragile equilibrium between believers, God, and the environment forever associated with the celebration of the creed.[111] To inspire hopes of future delivery readings in the synagogue over the week of Passover drove home the gigantic dimensions of the Exodus. On the seventh day of Passover, when the narrative of the cleaving of the Red Sea was read in public, Aramaic 'translations' (*targumim*) of

---

[109] See the articles in P. F. Bradshaw and L. A. Hoffman (eds.), *Passover and Easter: Origin and History to Modern Times* and eidem (eds.), *Passover and Easter: The Symbolic Structuring of Sacred Seasons* (Notre Dame 1999). On the development of the Easter liturgy, K. W. Stevenson, 'The Ceremonies of Light: Their Shape and Function in the Paschal Vigil Liturgy', *Ephemerides Liturgicae* 99 (1985), 175 ff.; S. G. Hall, 'The Origins of Easter', *SP* 15 (1984), 554–67; on Passover rituals see B. M. Bokser, *The Origins of the Seder: The Passover Rite and Early Rabbinic Judaism* (Berkeley 1984) and idem, 'Ritualizing the Seder', *Journal of the American Academy of Religion* 56 (1988), 443–71.

[110] See my *Between Woman, Man and God: A New Interpretation of the Ten Commandments* (New York 2004), *passim*.

[111] On mutual influences emphasizing the Haggadah as a reflection of Christian–Jewish polemics see I. J. Yuval, 'Easter and Passover as Early Jewish–Christian Dialogue', in Bradshaw and Hoffman, *Passover and Easter: Origin* (1999), 98–124; idem, 'Those who skip: The Passover Haggadah and Christian Easter', *Tarbiz* 65 (1995), 5–28 (Heb.). Yuval theorizes that major elements of the Passover Haggadah were formulated or reformulated in response to Christian appropriation and interpretation of Passover's texts and rituals. Idem, 'Two Nations in Your Womb': Perceptions of Jews and Christians (Tel Aviv 2000) (Heb.), *passim*.

the Torah staged a dramatic battle between Moses and the Sea, reminiscent of the fierce encounter between Behemoth and Leviathan (above, pp. 262–3). In the course of an exchange the Sea contested Moses' right to change its shape and only conceded after Moses prayed to God for help. 'Hearing the voice of the Holy Spirit that talked to Moses from the fire, the sea held back its waves and the People of Israel passed through.'[112]

To codify origins Jews gather around the Passover table and listen to the Passover Haggadah. In evoking the Exodus the Haggadah recast the biblical event as pure allegory, an unwinding that on Easter came to be cited as a proof of Jesus' epiphany. Easter dismissed Passover in order to make things take place in a manner that recovered separation from Jewish origins. For Jews, Passover is a powerful reminder that Israel exists because there were 'first Israelites' or Hebrews, the women and men whom Moses led out of Egypt. The difficulty that Christianity faced was to give this biblical crowd a specifically Christian posterity.

In every generation, as Passover is reborn, Haggadic components challenge Christian readings of the same moments in the biblical common past. The Haggadah reads life and future redemption in the death of the persecuting Egyptians; Easter uses the death of Jesus to tell of the irremediable separation from Judaism that it generated. Generalizing the Passover/Easter in this way, the stories that they narrate describe the primordial creation of Judaism and the re-creation of a post-Temple Judaism on the one hand, and the creation and re-creation of Christianity on the other. In a distinct and disparate fashion both Easter and Passover form a bridge between the realism of Scripture and the abstraction of the auditory evocation. Between these two contemporary competing models existed all the distance that separated the two creeds. In late antiquity, Passover and Easter replicated each other, both reflecting the living diversity of religion in the Palestinian landscape.

---

[112] J. Heinemann, 'Remnants of Ancient *Piyyutim* in the Palestinian *Targum* Tradition', *Hasifrut* 4 (1973), 362–3 (Heb.). The popularity of this piyyut is attested by surviving multiple versions including a Samaritan one in which the Sea is ready to obey God and Moses without demur only insisting on not providing watery graves for the pursuing Egyptians, J. MacDonald (ed.), *Memar Marqah: The Teaching of Marqah* (Berlin 1963), i. 35; Heinemann, 'Remnants', 370–1.

Exodus 12: 14 ordained remembrance of 'the day of the deliverance from Egypt all your life'. The Passover Haggadah illustrates the meaning of this deceptively simple injunction with a tale about four sages who spent the whole of Passover night 'reminiscing' the Exodus.[113] When finally interrupted one confessed that only then he finally grasped the true significance of Exod. 12: 14. While this excursion has little to do with Passover itself it emphasized an understanding that the Exodus, and not any other event in history, was the moment that the Bible intended to remember forever as a law that could not be rescinded. Hence, the conclusion of this Haggadic excursus: 'and the sages reassert: all your life on earth; all your life till the coming of the Messiah'.

On Easter, Christians 'remember' the passion of Jesus, a custom that originated with Jesus himself as gleaned from narratives that echoed the Haggadic insistence on the nocturnal nature of rabbinic reflections on the Exodus during the first night of Passover.[114] Jewish and Christian competing narratives, each modelled on similar events, produced their own social practices based on exegetical fields that were inextricably intertwined. The appearance in the Passover Haggadah of the narrative about the four sages underlies rabbinic emphasis on the continuing applicability of the Haggadah since the Messiah had not arrived and the biblical injunctions regarding the need to remember, to narrate and to repeat, remained in force.[115]

Understanding the function of the biblical injunction to 'remember' and to 'tell' as collective sharing in the recitation, the Passover

---

[113] Passover Haggadah (Goldschmidt), 19–21, noting that the duty to allude to the Exodus is a component of the regular daily prayer (the Shema) 'borrowed' by the Haggadah compilers; Cf. *M Ber.* 1.10, *T Pes.* 10:12. Yuval, 'Those who skip', 7–8; idem, 'Easter and Passover', 99–102 suggests that the custom to 'tell' the Exodus originated after the destruction of the Temple in CE 70 in parallel fashion with the development of Easter as remembrance narrative of Jesus' passion, and that it marked a transition from a public ritual to one emphasizing the father's obligation to transmit the story to his son.

[114] *Epistula Apostolorum* 15, apud J. K. Elliott, *The Apocryphal New Testament* (Oxford 1993), p. 565, dated to the second half of the 2nd cent. Yuval, 'Those who skip', 8–9, draws comparisons between Herod and the Egyptian Pharaoh, Peter and enslaved Israel, and other elements common, according to him, to both Bible and Midrash, on the one hand, and Christian apocrypha on the other.

[115] Yuval, 'Those who skip', 10, comparing it with rabbinic insistence on the eternity of the commandments issued in the Sinai. See also S. T. Lachs, 'A Polemical Element in Mishnah Berakot', *JQR* 56 (1965), 81–4.

Haggadah celebrated the actions that the Hebrew Bible recorded. Over Easter the 'recollection' of the last moments of Jesus served to bind the community through the reassuring words of Jesus himself. In late ancient Palestine celebrating Easter in Jerusalem created a liturgical sphere that kept the community close to the events at the very stage of their enactment. The reading of the Haggadah in Jewish homes introduced Egypt into the immediacy of a Passover celebrated on the very soil of the promised land.

Read at home the Haggadah allowed broad participation in its ceremonies. In its most concrete form the Passover table united dissimilar elements, men and women, young and old, citizens and slaves, to provide a definition of who was a 'Jew'. During Passover this term meant not so much the suppression of social, ethnic, and gender barriers as the broadest participation in a religious task of recitation and recollection. The Haggadic use of Hebrew, probably understood by few, stood as an odd projection challenging the linguistic dominance of Greek and Aramaic in late antiquity. It continued to challenge linguistic dominance of other languages when Arabic became dominant in the aftermath of the Islamic conquest of the early seventh century.[116] The towering stature of the Hebrew Bible ensured the fundamental role of its language as a basis of religious and ethnic distinctiveness.

The Haggadah's didactic purpose is especially apparent in the recitation role which it assigned to the host's young son. Right after the opening benediction and the invitation to all and sundry to join the table, the child asks: 'Why is this night different from all others?'[117] In

[116] Wasserstein, 'Why did Arabic Succeed where Greek Failed?', 257–72, esp. 262–3. On the persistence of an Aramaic-speaking population in spite of Arabic penetration and the ensuing Arabization see R. Zadok, 'The Ethno-Linguistic Character of the Semitic-Speaking Population (excluding Jews and Samaritans) of Lebanon, Palestine and Adjacent Regions during the Hellenistic, Roman and Byzantine Periods: A Preliminary Survey of the Onomastic Evidence', *Michmanim* 12 (1998), 5*–36*, who uses 450 names, mainly from inscriptions, over a period of a thousand years. Perhaps the most interesting conclusion of Zadok's survey is the predominance of Arabic names over Aramaic names in 'peripheral areas' namely the Golan/Hermon and the Negev already from the Achaemenid period (p. 22*). See also Ch. 2. On Arabic-speaking groups and 'Arabs' in late antiquity, Retsö, *The Arabs in Antiquity*.

[117] Goldschmidt, *Haggadah*, 77 (Genizah's Haggadah). Cf. BT 117a: if his son is clever, he is the one who asks; if not, his wife does; if she is not, he himself asks, or even two disciples who already know the answer ask each other.

the most ancient Palestinian version, the one that the Cairo Genizah preserved, the question of 'difference' was answered through references to feasting customs.[118] One such related the consumption of roast meat. The paschal lamb that Jewish households roasted for the Passover meal nourished participants and kindled fantasies. The Palestinian Talmud instructed believers to roast the animal with its body hanging down and head up, a manner which bore a faint resemblance to images of the crucified Jesus.[119] The Mishnah ordained the opposite, namely the hanging of the animal's body with its head down.[120] The latter fitted the structure of Passover roasting ovens and represented an attempt to reduce the resemblance between the Passover sacrifice and the all-important Christian imagery of crucifixion.[121]

Because Passover is endlessly renewed, the words recited and the rituals performed have become a haven for the imagination. Passover offered possibilities of both rebuttal and of hope. Elements of the perennially appealing and perennially repeated story invited comparison. Following the book of the Exodus, rabbinic exegesis enshrined Egypt as an archetype of the 'enemy', often absorbed by 'Esau' to become a symbol of the 'kingdom' preceding national

---

[118] There is no consensus regarding the date of the final version of the Passover Haggadah whose earliest witness, at least as far as its reading in Jewish homes on the holiday's eve is concerned, is Melito of Sardis (2nd cent.), *On Pascha and Fragments*, ed. S. G. Hall (Oxford 1979). J. Lieu, 'Melito of Sardis: The *Peri Pascha*', in eadem, *Image and Reality: The Jews in the World of the Christians in the Second Century* (Edinburgh 1996), 199–240. The very word, *pessach*, which in Hebrew means 'to skip' has been taken to indicate Jesus' sufferings, on the basis of its meaning in Greek. See also Origen, *Treatise on the Passover*, trans. and annotated by R. J. Dally (New York 1992). As it now stands, the Haggadah is a pastiche of texts, nearly none originally composed for Passover and each dating to a different period, the whole redacted not earlier than the 8th–9th cent. in Babylon: Goldschmidt, *The Passover Haggadah*, 69–72; see also the criticism of Hoffman regarding Goldschmidt's chronological analysis, in *Beyond the Text: A Holistic Approach to Liturgy* (Bloomington 1987), 90–1.

[119] *PT Pes.* 7.1, the date is unclear but the custom appears to have preceded the one recorded in the Mishnah below. Cf. Justin, *Tryph.* 40 comments on the resemblance to images of crucifixion.

[120] *M Pes.* 7.1.

[121] Tabory, *The Passover Ritual throughout the Generations*, 92–105 (Heb.), who suggests that the Mishnaic modification may have been an attempt to mock the crucifixion, as was the crucifixion of Haman in Purim. See Ch. 4 above.

redemption.[122] Under Rome, 'Egypt' became 'Edom', an entity hostile to Jews and to Judaism, first identified with pagan and later with Christian Rome.[123] Like Egypt, Edom, too, was destined to experience divine wrath.[124] Numerical calculations helped to 'fix' the date of redemption to fit biblical chronology.[125] The month of anticipated salvation had to be Nisan, precisely the period of Passover.[126]

To articulate the modalities of Passover the rabbis omitted or harnessed biblical figures and moments that had migrated to Christian settings. In response to the growing importance of Moses in Christian theology the Haggadah omitted Moses altogether.[127] Simultaneously, a mythic Moses, precursor of the Messiah, appeared in Jewish translations of the Bible and in synagogal liturgy:

'Night of solemn observance' (Exod. 12: 42) is the night reserved for redemption, the night of the delivery from Egypt. Four nights are written in the book of memory: the first night is the one when God's plan to create the world was revealed; the second is that of the covenant with Abraham … ; the third is the revealing of God's revenge upon Egypt … and the fourth is when the world has completed the period prior to redemption, when evil will cease and oppression will be broken, when Moses will rise out of the desert and the king messiah from Rome, both leading the people according to the word of the Lord … This is the night of Passover … [128]

Because the delivery from Egyptian bondage figured in Samaritan eschatology that viewed Moses as the future deliverer, as well as in

[122] G. D. Cohen, 'Esau as Symbol in Early Medieval Thought', in A. Altmann (ed.), *Jewish Medieval and Renaissance Studies* (Cambridge, Mass. 1967, 19–48.

[123] *The Poetry of Yannai*, ed. M. Zulai (Berlin 1938), i. 298; Yahalom, *Poetry and Society*, 64–106.

[124] On Rome as Edom, Yuval, *Two Nations*, 25–34.

[125] Jerome, *Exegesis on Joel* (CCSL 76,I, 208) records that the Jews believed that Rome would be destroyed after 430 years. The point of departure for such calculations was usually the destruction of the Temple, dated to 68 CE. See D. Berger, 'Three Typological Themes in Early Jewish Messianism', *AJS Review* 10 (1985), 141–64; R. L. Wilken, 'The Restoration of Israel in Biblical Prophecy: Christian and Jewish Responses in the Early Byzantine Period', in J. Neusner and S. Frerichs (eds.), *To See Ourselves as Others See Us* (Chico, Calif. 1985), 443–72.

[126] *PT Rosh Hashanah* 11; *BT Rosh Hashanah* 11a–b; *BT Meg.* 6a.

[127] J. Petuchowski, ' "Do This in Remembrance of Me" (I Cor 11:24)', *JBL* 76 (1957), 293–8; Yuval, 'Those who skip', 17–20.

[128] M. L. Klein, *Genizah Manuscripts of Palestinian Targum to the Pentateuch I–II* (Cincinnati 1986), 221; R. Le Déaut, *La Nuit pascale: Essai sur la signification de la Pâque juive à partir du Targum d'Exode* (Rome 1963), *passim*.

Christianity which positioned Moses as a prototype for Jesus, rabbinic 'theology' preferred to de-emphasize Moses' redemptive role.[129]

By contrast, the sacrifice of Isaac (the *Aqedah* or *Akedah*) was elevated to a level of national redemption. According to one Jewish exegesis of the book of Exodus the month of Nisan marked, in addition to freedom from Egyptian bondage, the birth and the sacrifice of Isaac.[130] Christian versions of the same event regarded Abraham's readiness to sacrifice his beloved heir as a perfect prefiguration of the crucifixion.[131] The Jewish assimilation of Passover with the sacrifice of Isaac represented a tradition made from elements that Christianity appropriated to emphasize its distinctiveness. Sermons signalling rites of initiation in fourth-century Jerusalem provided an eloquent demonstration of the links which theologians had forged between the Exodus and the life of Christ:

> Turn now from past to present, from type to reality. Formerly Moses was sent into Egypt by God but now Christ is sent into the world by the Father. At that time Moses led a persecuted people out of Egypt, here Christ rescues all people from the tyranny of sin. There, the blood of the lamb was a charm against the destroyer; here the blood of the blameless lamb, Jesus Christ, is a sanctuary against demons ... [132]

Genesis 22 showed Abraham conducting the first sacrifice in compliance with God's expressed desire. This was the kind of love that could not be repeated, as far as Jews were concerned. Genesis 22: 8 qualified the binding as the equivalent of *a lamb for the burnt offering.* Synagogal poetry emphasized the readiness for sacrifice on the part of both father and son:

---

[129] *DeutR* 3.17 (Lieberman, *Hellenism in Jewish Palestine*, p. 91); A. Shnan, *One Bible and Multiple Translations: Torah Tales in Light of Aramaic Targumim* (Tel Aviv 1993), 119; S. H. Levey, *The Messiah: An Aramaic Interpretation—The Messianic Exegesis of the Targum* (Cincinnati 1974).

[130] *ExR* 15.11. On the various interpretations of the Aqedah, L. Kundert, *Die Opferung/Bindung Isaaks*, 2 vols. (Neukirchen-Vluyn 1998).

[131] P. R. Davies, 'Martyrdom and Redemption. On the Development of Isaac Typology in the Early Church', *SP* 17 (1982), 652–8; J. D. Levenson, *The Death and Resurrection of the Beloved Son: The Transformation of Child Sacrifice in Judaism and Christianity* (New Haven 1993).

[132] *Mystagogic Catechesis* 1.3, transl. in Douval, *Cyril of Jerusalem, Mystagogue,* 163, who also ascribed them to Cyril rather than to John of Jerusalem.

The father rejoiced to bind and the son to be bound...
Thou appointed for his atonement (or: absolution) a ram
and it was reckoned to him righteousness;
On this day we [also] will hear: I have found atonement.[133]

An early (fourth-century or earlier?) *piyyut* on the same subject presented Isaac as encouraging his father to apply the knife, to sprinkle the altar with his blood and to thank the Lord that he had been chosen as a sacrifice: 'Happy am I that the Lord (*Kyrios*) has chosen me from the entire world (*kosmos*)'.[134] The *piyyut*'s Palestinian Aramaic was sprinkled with Greek words which entered synagogal readings through the spoken language. The absence of the appellation '*kyrios*' for God in rabbinic literature of the same period suggests covert polemics with Christianity, which had adopted the Jewish Septuagint translation where *Kyrios* is the usual way of naming God.[135]

In Judaism, the sacrifice of Isaac provided a prefiguration of the Temple service on Mount Moriah (= Temple Mount) and of the atonement and future redemption that the service betokened.[136] The sacrificial cult of the Temple, once so central to Jewish life and society, had become an institutionalized memory after the disappearance of the sanctuary intended to reinforce these promises.[137] Recalling the sacrifice of Isaac meant reminding God of the promise given to Abraham as a reward (Gen. 22: 17–18).[138] Because the Temple itself was proof of Israel's commitment to be the chosen people its schematic representation in numerous synagogues

[133] Horbury, 'Suffering and Messianism in Yose ben Yose', 170.

[134] Heinemann, 'Remnants', 366–7, with Horbury, 'Yose', 170. Cf. *Liber Antiquitatum Biblicarum* 18.5; 32.2–3; 40.2; Josephus, *Ant.* 1.232; and *Targum Pseudo Jonathan* ad Gen. 22: 7–11, all quoted in P. W. van der Horst and M. F. G. Parmentier, 'A New Early Christian Poem on the Sacrifice of Isaac', in *Le Codex de Vision* (2002), 159–61.

[135] Heinemann, 'Remnants', 368. On the use of Greek terminology of this type in Hellenistic-Jewish literature including the Septuagint, E. E. Urbach, *The Sages: Their Concepts and Beliefs*, trans. I. Abrahams (Jerusalem 1979; repr. 1987). 106 f.; 400 f. (Heb. version).

[136] Horbury, 'Yose', 171; P. R. Davies, 'Passover and the Dating of the Aqedah', *JJS* 30 (1979), 59–67.

[137] Yalqut Shimoni, Vayyera, 99.

[138] On the various interpretations of the Aqedah narrative, E. Kessler, *Bound by the Bible: Jews, Christians and the Sacrifice of Isaac* (Cambridge 2004).

warranted a modification of behaviour while accounting for future hopes.[139]

Perhaps the most striking visual expression of the links that late ancient Jewish literature forged between Temple rites, the sacrifice of Isaac, and synagogal liturgy was reflected in a small mosaic (*c.*4.5 × 13.5 m.) which embellished the nave of a recently excavated synagogue in Galilean Sepphoris.[140] Its panels enclosed a profusion of scenes, symbols, and inscriptions in Greek, Aramaic, and Hebrew. The scenes included the consecration of Aaron and the Tabernacle-Temple's daily offering (Exod. 29); the angels' visit to Sarah and Abraham (Gen. 18); and the Binding of Isaac (Gen. 22). Symbols included a wreath flanked by lions; menorahs, incense shovel, an architectural façade, the Shewbread Table (Exod. 37) and basket of first-fruits. Dominating this mixture was a zodiac featuring a chariot of the sun in its midst with the twelve months encircling it.

The juxtaposition of the Binding of Isaac with other central symbols like the Zodiac and implements of Temple worship appeared also in the sixth-century synagogue mosaic from Beth Alpha near Scythopolis-Beth Shean.[141] At Sepphoris, unlike the conventional depiction of the Aqedah from Beth Alpha, it is possible to recognize two pairs of shoes left at the corner. Nothing in the biblical narrative accounts for the gesture. Only Moses (Exod. 3: 5) and Joshua (Josh. 5: 15) were required to take off their shoes in the presence of God or a divine emissary. The turning of the Aqeda into a prototype of Temple sacrifice transformed its scene of action, Mount Moriah, into a sacred territory which required those present to be barefoot in the presence of the divine.[142] Whether the Sepphoris mosaic's lone shoes heralded a new fashion in synagogue prayer or embossed an existing one in stone remains unclear. The latter seems implied in Origen's interpretation of Genesis patriarchal narratives where he insisted that the patriarchs were so pure as to render gestures like shedding shoes

---

[139] *Tanhuma* (Buber), Tetzave 10, describing past prosperity and alluding to a reinstatement of the blessings; R. Hachlili, *Ancient Jewish Art and Archaeology in the Land of Israel* (Leiden 1988), for art of the synagogues.

[140] Weiss and Netzer, *Promise and Redemption*.

[141] As well as in the Dura Europos synagogue.

[142] *ExR* 2.6: 'where the Shekhina (God's presence) is, one must not go about with shoes on'.

wholly superfluous.[143] The habit of praying barefoot in synagogues, implied by the Babylonian Talmud and attested in Palestinian traditions from the Cairo Genizah as well as in early Islamic references to Jewish prayer customs, demonstrates how biblical exegesis was applied, possibly in polemical context, to synagogal rituals.[144]

Even more unusual was the juxtaposition at Sepphoris of two biblical scenes, the one heralding the birth of Isaac (Gen. 18), the other his binding (Gen. 22). In a heavily damaged panel it is possible to discern the figure of Sarah listening in the tent to the message relating her imminent pregnancy. Sarah never appears in existing synagogue mosaics. The annunciation of Genesis 18 was selected by Christian exegesis as an archetype of the one to Mary and translated into church mosaics.[145] The exaltation of the memory of Mary and the increasing importance of her role in the Nativity distinguished the emphasis of Christian from Jewish representations of Genesis in which myth was fulfilled in 'history' and history in 'myth'. Between the fleeting appearance of Sarah and the careful arrangement of shed shoes at Sepphoris the collective imagery of the Jews who used the synagogue highlighted the fact that there was no innocent influence. Even synagogal imagery was not deaf to the charged language of biblical exegesis. Yielding to the prestige of the Bible, Jews and Christians harked back to a past as they injected archaic modes of celebrations with their specific histories and hopes.

As it mobilized biblical origins, Jewish exegesis had the potential of destabilizing Christian systematic use of biblical derivatives. Heightened cultural and ethnic awareness made such lessons a multipurpose text whose authoritative character intended to reassure Jews of their role as God's chosen people while aiming at Christian accreditation of the same sacred words. Exegetical competitions across credal boundaries and within them demonstrated how rivalries arranged themselves in the form of imitation, and how theological and liturgical vocabularies strove to transpose the power that the Bible exerted into the agonistic terrain of hegemony. Early Christianity resonated

---

[143] *Hom. ad Gen.* 8.7.

[144] Yahalom, *Poetry and Society*, 108–10.

[145] L. Thunberg, 'Early Christian Interpretations of the Three Angels in Gen 18', *SP* 8 (1966), 560–70; H. M. von Erffa, *Ikonologie der Genesis* (Munich 1995), ii. 91–103.

with various Easter debates that first focused on calendrical relations between Easter and Passover (the question of the 'Quartodeciman') and later on the more fundamental question of the Jewish reckoning of Passover as a determinant of Easter Sunday.[146]

While Passover celebrated a unique event, the Exodus, the annual practice of the celebration generated a process of repetition which secured a measure of equality with the original episode. Similarly, while the Binding of Isaac happened once only, the cyclical nature of history, as dictated by God and interpreted by rabbis, turned the uniqueness of the biblical representation into a milestone in a progression which was to end as it had started, namely with God's mercy and Israel's redemption:

God will show [the lamb to be sacrificed] (Gen. 22: 8). Remembering the sacrifice of Isaac God will take pity on his descendants. What is written afterwards? *And Abraham lifted up his eyes and looked and behold behind him (ahar) was a ram caught in a thicket* (Gen. 22: 13). What is the meaning of 'behind' (*ahar*)? Rabbi Judah son of Rabbi Simon said: After (= behind) all the generations, your children are going to be caught up in sins and entrapped in troubles. But in the end they will be redeemed by the horns of this ram... For that entire day Abraham observed how the ram repetitively got caught in one tree then freed itself, caught in a thicket and freed itself etc. The Holy One, blessed be he: Abraham, this is how your descendants will be caught by their sins and trapped by the kingdoms, from Babylon to Madai (the Medes), from Madai to Greece and from Greece to Edom [Rome]. Is that how it will be forever? In the end they will be redeemed by the horns of this ram.[147]

For attentive listeners the widening gap between Jewish and Christian practices posed the difficulty of establishing the truth.

---

[146] Eusebius, *HE* 5.23–5; C. H. Hefele and Henri Leclercq, *Histoire des conciles* (Paris 1907–52), I. i. 450–88. W. Peterson, 'Eusebius and the Paschal Controversy', in H. Attridge and G. Hata (eds.), *Eusebius, Christianity and Judaism* (Detroit 1992), 311–29. Stern, *Calendar and Community*, 124–3, for detailed discussion.

[147] *PT Taanit* 2.4, 65d.

7

Flesh and Blood? Women in Palestinian Societies

Taking a virgin bride used to be taboo in Maqaio.
'Striking red', as it was called, on the nuptial night
was seen as something highly inauspicious. Contrarily,
the husband's family would be very content with a female
pregnant before marriage, whose stomach struck out a long way...
There was nothing odd about this: in areas and periods of low
Production rate, people were the most important productive force
And giving birth was the most important task for women,
Much more important than maintaining moral chastity...

Han Shaogong, *A Dictionary of Maqiao*, trans. Julia Lovell
(Columbia UP, 1996), pp. 44–5

1. PRELUDE: HAIR AND HOME

It was told of Shimon son of Kimkhit that on the eve of Yom Kippur (Day of Atonement) he went to meet the king who accidentally splattered saliva on his clothing, rendering him impure. His brother Judah then assumed his position and served as the High Priest. Their mother thus saw two of her sons becoming the High Priests on one and the same day. Seven sons Kimkhit bore and all became High Priests. The sages asked her: What good deeds [of yours merited so distinct an honour]? She replied: I will be dead if the beams of my home ever saw a hair of my head.[1]

---

[1] The anecdote is transmitted in multiple versions in Palestinian sources, including *PT Yoma* 38d; *PT Horayot* 47d; *PT Meg.* 72aa; *LevR* 20.11; *NumR* 2.26; *ARNA* 35; as well as in the *BT Yoma* 47a; *Pesiqta de Rabv Kahana* 26; Midrash Tanhuma on

Kimkhit's response did not pass an aesthetic judgement on females' hair. Rather, it highlighted excessive piety by stretching *ad absurdum* rabbinic dictates regarding the appropriate appearance of women outdoors. Kimkhit, whose name harked back to 'flour' (*kemakh*), and hence to a basic necessity of life, showed how ill founded was the identification of a gender discourse made up of *topoi* such as hair and headgear. In her statement she implied that the genre of 'how to dress in public' proved to have been objectless.

Kimkhit's declaration provided an uneasy reconciliation of rabbinic rules explicitly designed to create 'women' with the models generated by the objects themselves. Her audacious statement, boldly appropriating credit while excluding any tribute to paternal impact, showed her worthy of her descendants. The humility which she exhibited vis-à-vis the beams of her own home determined the progress not of her relationship with her husband but rather of her motherhood. Between the roof and the mother, then, stood head-cover as a model worthy of imitation.

By exalting the chaste appearance maintained within the utmost privacy of her own home Kimkhit advanced the notions and maxims that contributed to a mass of elements meant to shape the lives of women within and outside the house. Her story framed the sphere of domesticity. It advanced a view which the rabbis used as a theoretical justification for a disadvantageous divorce:

These women are to be divorced without regaining their marriage settlement. One who transgresses the law of Moses, and of the Jewess (*dat yehudit*). What is the law of Moses? When she serves food which has not been tithed, have sex while menstruating, does not set aside 'hallah' and undertakes a vow but fails to keep it. What is then the 'law of the Jewess' (or Jewish law)? When she goes out with her hair bare,[2] spins in the market, and talks with everybody.[3]

parasha 'After the Death' 7 (Buber 9). On this story see Cynthia M. Baker, *Rebuilding the House of Israel: Architectures of Gender in Jewish Antiquity* (Stanford 2002), 64–70 with references to previous work.

[2] Uncovered or bare hair has been the usual understanding of the phrase 'sear paruah', but the possibility of messy rather than uncovered hair needs to be considered. Cf. Chrysostom, *On Virginity* 7, where a typical virgin is described as one who had messy hair, downcast eyes, and a dark cloak, with G. Clark, *Women in Late Antiquity* (Oxford 1993), 116.

[3] *M Ket.* 7.6.

Of the areas of potential transgression the rabbis were especially concerned with defining the 'ins' and 'outs', in other words the specific areas where a woman should cover her hair and where she might leave it uncovered. The 'out' began at the threshold, a 'frontier' of marital fidelity.[4] But in Kimkhit's 'universe' there was no distinction between the 'out' and the 'in'—the same sense applied to both, stressing the uselessness of words to describe the frontiers of domesticity.

Each of the rules regarding women in a state of marriage seemed to weigh on the respective value of what could be seen or heard. The visible had primacy over the reported or at least the latter was more difficult to assess. Discussions regarding tithed or non-tithed meals, and sex with menstruates, remained a matter of words, rumours, and complaints, in other words a negative uncertainty. Leaving one's hair uncovered outdoors, an act compounded by the image of public spinning and chatting, declared defiance. The emphasis on avoidance of participation in public activities was put in place to mobilize an image of conformity that set out to dominate rather than to transcend time and space. Marriage was a dynamic locus of communication which depended on what was not to be found.

If Kimkhit surprised her interlocutors with undertaking what was not expected of her, the ideology that bringing up model children required a paragon parent, each mirroring the virtues of the other, was freely preached by Jerome from Palestinian Bethlehem for the benefit of upper-class chastity:

A mother's nod should be to [a daughter] as much a command as a spoken injunction; [a daughter] should love her mother as her parent, obey her as her mistress, and revere her as her teacher... Entrust a daughter to a ... governess who is not given to much wine or is, in the apostle's words, idle and a tattler but sober, grave, industrious in spinning wool and one whose words will form a childish mind to the practice of virtue. For as water follows

---

[4] Baker, 128–30; 138–40. See also S. Stern, *Jewish Identity in Early Rabbinic Writings* (Leiden 1994), 244 for a discussion of the 'law of a Jewess', *dat yehudit*, as a code which denoted religious identity versus Baker on denoting marital status. On the female figure as a 'mediator' between 'them' and 'us', or Jews and gentiles, Baker, *passim*; J. Levinson, 'Mother of Nations: Literary Identities in a Changing World', in Levine (ed.), *Continuity and Change*, 465–85 (Heb.).

a canal drawn through the sand so one soft and tender in years is pliable for good or evil.[5]

Of course, if the home or rather the environment were found unsuitable for the upbringing of young women vowed to virginity, like Rome around the turn of the fifth century, a monastery in Palestine, especially one run by the girl's own grandmother and aunt, was deemed an excellent choice to achieve the desired combination of familial, educational, and vocational training.

> When you have weaned Paula as Isaac was weaned...send her to her grandmother and aunt. Give up this most precious of gems to be placed in Mary's chamber and to rest in the cradle where the infant Jesus cried. Let her be brought up in a monastery, let her be one amid a company of virgins, let her learn to avoid swearing, to regard lying as sacrilege, to be ignorant of the world, to live the angelic life, while in the flesh let her be without the flesh, assuming that all human beings are like herself...Let her become a companion in holiness...of one whose language and gait and dress are an education in virtue.[6]

While it was universally acknowledged that 'the good conduct of the children is to be traced back to the parent' and that 'the cause of virtuous children is often their parents who train them for the best things through education and upbringing', such axioms masked an ideal that was ultimately nothing more than the obverse of reality.[7] The core of the discourse remained a paradigm that construed an example from which reflection may rise to the model and vice versa. In certain conditions, however, the process became controversial:

> Rabbi Abbahu [of Caesarea, c.300] said in the name of Rabbi Yohanan. It is permitted for any man to teach Greek to his daughter because it would profit her. Simeon bar Ba heard this and said: It is only because Rabbi Abbahu wants to teach his own daughter Greek that he has attributed this teaching to Rabbi Yohanan. Rabbi Abbahu heard this and said: May [I be] cursed if I did not indeed hear this from Rabbi Yohanan.[8]

---

[5] *Ep.* 128.3, addressed to Gaudentius on the subject of bringing up his infant daughter Pacatula.

[6] Jerome, *Ep.* 107.13 (NPNF trans.).

[7] Quotes are from Choricius' eulogy of Maria, see below (with n. 48).

[8] *PT Shab.* 7d.

There is little doubt that this was a polemical reference. It pitted a sage living in a predominantly urban and gentile environment, not unlike the Rome that Jerome found unpalatable for prospective consecrated virgins, against a collective experience rooted in the silent immobility of daughters. The pairing of daughters and Greek seemed at first to be definitely rejected on the grounds of erroneous attribution. But the real criteria of rejection were both moral and intellectual. The proposed immersion of daughters in a 'foreign culture' as a component of paternally imparted (or approved) learning meant that other men could not mould their daughters on a world that was practically unknown to them.

Moved by a desire to create an exemplary woman, Christian theologians, as their Jewish rabbinic counterparts, celebrated a well-governed environment by delineating ill-fated divergences. Rabbinic discussions regarding the social repercussions of flawed virginity and of matronly recalcitrance stressed the dangerously slippery character of unmonitored behaviour. To give life to theoretical models of misconduct the rabbis projected a home that acquired its full significance upon confrontation between ideals and their denial. In a polemical and ambiguous way domestic conflicts acquired both meaning and effect far beyond the narrow perimeters of the home.

2. REVELATIONS OF THE FIRST NIGHT

The Mishnaic tractate on marriage settlements or endowments (*ketubbot*) begins with an image of a bridegroom hastening to bring a suit against his one-night-old bride on the morning after the wedding:

A virgin is to be married on Wednesday and a widow on Thursday because the courts sit in the villages twice a week, on Mondays and on Thursdays, and if he [the husband] has a charge [against his wife's] virginity he can quickly proceed to the court (*M Ket.* 1.1).

Bound by Deuteronomic dicta, and specifically by the so-called case of the slandered bride (Deut. 22: 13–21), the rabbis had to contend with biblical texts as well as with situations which, they reckoned, threatened the dissolution of marriage at the dawn of marital cohabitation. Deut. 22: 13–21 featured a suspicious husband accusing his wife of premarital sex.[9] The husband had to state in public his suspicion regarding the state of her hymen (*betulim*) upon the wedding night.[10] The affair involved not only the community's elders as arbitrators, but also the parents of the bride who were naturally eager to exonerate themselves of having transferred tarnished 'goods'.

Legally speaking, an accusation of premarital sex implied an unacceptable mode of female behaviour under paternal authority (Deut. 22: 21b: 'prostituting her father's house'). At stake, too, was the issue of property as an extension of wifely chastity, as well as a code of conduct between males. The woman whose life was at stake was not allowed to speak. She could not be a witness because there was no elaborate inquiry into the complexities of the case. The public trial took place between her parents, or rather father, and her husband. Parental defence 'rested' its case on a public display of the woman's 'tokens of virginity' (Deut. 22: 15, 17). These provided proof of the woman's eligibility at time of betrothal, as well as of complete paternal control over the daughter's body prior to marriage. Only males engaged in a judicial rhetoric which could turn deadly for the daughter/wife.

If the elders believed the father, the husband was heavily fined and had to stay married to the woman till the end of her life, forfeiting a basic husbandly right to divorce one's wife at will and unilaterally (Deut. 24: 1). The gravity of this penalty is reflected in the dictum that husbands' unjustifiable slander tarnished not only their own wives' reputation but also that of 'all the virgins in Israel' (Deut. 22: 19). If the elders believed the husband, the woman was to be stoned to death, like a blasphemer (Lev. 24: 23). The execution took place at the entry to her father's house, a grim lesson for all women who would 'prostitute' not only their body but also, and most crucially,

---

[9] For what follows see my *Between Woman, Man and God: A New Interpretation of the Ten Commandments, passim.*

[10] The precise meaning of the term *betulim* (Deut. 22: 14, 15, 17, 20) has been much contested. G. T. Wenham, 'Betulah: A Girl of Marriageable Age', *Vetus Testamentum* 22 (1972), 326–48. For a summary of scholarly views on this pericope, C. Pressler, *The View of Women found in the Deuteronomic Family Laws* (Berlin 1993), 25–8.

the reputation of their fathers as honest dealers in their daughters' virginity and marriageability. The disparity in sentencing is obvious. The woman had to pay with her life for a crime committed with her body. For sins of speaking, the man, if his allegation proved groundless, had to 'atone' with money and, perhaps, with social infamy, having undermined the reputation of an innocent family. But he lived, in either case, while the woman's sin, if she was found guilty, had to be eradicated through the obliteration of her body.[11]

Why would a husband even consider this mode of slander rather then, say, initiating divorce?[12] Num. 5: 14 stipulated a mysterious 'spirit of jealousy' as the moving force behind a sudden accusation of adultery.[13] Deut. 22: 13, and Deut. 22: 16 suggested that 'hatred' bred slander, and the term used also denoted a legal cause for a divorce.[14] The two biblical instances of husbands doubting their wives' sexual integrity (Num. 5 and Deut. 22) might not have been far apart since in both the issue hinged not on the ability of the husband to provide proof of wifely infidelity (either before or after the marriage), but on a judicial process or an ordeal that aimed at uncovering the concealed and that enabled the husband to get rid of his wife without forfeiting the marriage settlement.[15]

---

[11] Cf. Deut. 22: 28–9, which prescribes a similar punishment for raping an unbetrothed woman, versus Exod. 22: 15–16, that leaves the father room for refusing to marry his daughter to her seducer. T. Frymer-Kensky, 'Philosophy and the Case of Sex in the Bible', *Semeia* 45 (1989), 93, believes that death was merely a verbal threat intended to emphasize expectations of the virginal body of brides. Cf. similar expectations in Neo-Babylonian marriage contracts, M. T. Roth, ' "She Will Die by the Iron Dagger": Adultery and Neo-Babylonian Marriage', *Journal of the Economic and Social History of the Orient* 31 (1988), 186–206.

[12] Wenham, 'Betulah', believes that the woman was pregnant at her nuptials; Pressler, *View*, opts for fractured hymen.

[13] For full discussion Zlotnick, *Dinah's Daughters*, Ch. 4.

[14] Cf. marriage contracts from the Jewish community of 5th-cent. BCE Elephantine (Egypt) which contain a divorce clause allowing both wife and husband to initiate divorce on the basis of 'hate'. A. Cowley, *Aramaic Papyri of the Fifth Century BC* (Oxford 1923), 44 f.; B. Porten, in collaboration with J. C. Greenfield, *Jews of Elephantine and Aramaeans of Syene* (Jerusalem 1974), 20–3. On similar clauses in Palestinian marriage contracts from the Cairo Genizah, Friedman, *Jewish Marriage in Palestine*, 312 f.

[15] L. Stulman, 'Sex and Familial Crimes in the D Code: A Witness to Mores in Transition', *Journal for the Study of the Old Testament* 53 (1992), 57; and C. M. Carmichael, *The Laws of Deuteronomy* (Ithaca 1974), 168 suggest that the procedures were intended to protect hated wives by providing a public stage of potential vindication.

Strikingly, marital contracts from the fifth century BCE till the Middle Ages included a 'hate-clause' which granted women, and not just men, the legal ability to sue for divorce.[16] *PT Ket.* 5.10 recorded that:

Rabbi Yossi said: 'Those who put in writing [in the marriage contract] a "hate clause" [if she hates him or he her], the monetary conditions [attendant on subsequent divorce] are valid and the condition binding.'

But this allowance, which required written specification, remained a unique Palestinian provision, rejected by the Babylonian Talmud and subsequently by Jewish normative 'law'.[17]

Deut. 22 and Num. 5 highlighted how illusion and reality engaged in paradoxical crossing, itself a reflection of the ontological status of the feminine. At stake were not one but two perceptions of women: an ideal image of a chaste bride, in this case perhaps an illusion; and an adulterous wife who may turn out to be a phantom. Such a double spectre of femininity determined the proceedings and, at the same time, served as an objective referent through which men had to question their previous perceptions of the world and of women. The essential strategy for ensuring the 'success' of the agonistic operation in Deut. 22 required that the woman be sacrificed. When the father accused the husband of hating the daughter and of bringing 'shameful or defaming charges' (*alilat devarim*, Deut. 22: 16–17), both accusations were, at that point, irrefutable. Wrangling about the justice of respective claims, litigants quarrelled about a past without questioning the woman herself. The trial became a masculine agon whose 'winner' was hailed by a tribunal of local 'elders'. The hideous spectre of execution of an allegedly guilty woman lent the proceedings a concrete sense of a 'trial' which was, in fact, a spectacle calculated to instil fear in women and to promote the social status of the 'elders'.

Images of flawed virginity under the canopy continued to occupy normative visions of the female Jew. Wedding rituals in late antiquity

[16] Above, n. 14 (on Elephantine). M. L. Satlow, *Jewish Marriage in Antiquity* (Princeton 2001), 214, on the transition from bilateral to unilateral divorce which he further links with the emergence of rabbinic *ketubba* payment as a compensation and protection for the wife's loss of the right to initiate divorce.
[17] Friedman, *Jewish Marriage in Palestine*, 320 ff., esp. 322–5.

included a 'blessing of virginity' (*birkat betulim*), namely a brief benediction that a groom pronounced over a blood-stained cloth which he
would publicly display upon first emerging from the bridal chamber.[18]
The blessing, interspersed with biblical allusions to Num. 5, linked the
selection of Israel as a 'holy seed' with the sanctified purity of the
'daughters of Israel'.[19] It forged a crimson link between a textile reflection of bridal integrity and subsequent fertility of the marriage. Curiously, there is no record of this blessing in rabbinic sources of late
antiquity in spite of the emphasis on bridal virginity.[20] Instead, rabbis
offered a verbal tribute to virginity and attached monetary value to it:

A virgin's *ketubba* is two hundred; a widow's one hundred (*M Ket.* 1.2).

Stated otherwise, a woman might attract a larger settlement upon
her first marriage and a smaller one upon her second. Here one may
note that Mishnaic definitions of virginity embraced women who
had never been married as well as 'widows and divorcees' whose
marriage was believed to have remained unconsummated. Technically, 'virgins' were also female proselytes, captives, and slaves who
were converted, ransomed, or manumitted before the age of three
years and one day (*M Ket.* 1.2)! A 'widow', once more technically, was
all of the above categories but possessing a hymen the integrity of
which was no longer assumed. Different premiums for different
women depended, in this rabbinic reading, on the state of one's
hymen. To drive the point home the rabbis supplied males with an
opportunity to engage in litigation which exposed the intimacies of
the wedding night to the public.[21]

---

[18] R. Langer, 'The Birkat Betulim: A Study of the Jewish Celebration of Bridal
Virginity', *Proceedings of the American Academy for Jewish Research* 61 (1995), 59–94,
noting also (p. 71) that this ceremony obliterated any necessity to invoke adultery
procedures against a *sotah* (= suspected adulteress).

[19] For the text and its variants, Langer, 86–7; on biblical ideology of 'holy seed' and
marriage, see my 'The Silent Women of Yehud', *JJS* (2000); on post-biblical applica-
tions, *Dinah's Daughters*, Ch. 2.

[20] Langer, 66–71. Cf. the talmudic 'benediction of the groom' which is said in the
presence of 10 persons and is repeated for seven days (*BT Ket.* 8b).

[21] The precise scope and authority of rabbinic 'courts' remains unclear. The pre-
sentation of rabbis as judges promoted rabbinic authority in legal terms, H. Lapin,
'Rabbis and Cities: Some Aspects of the Rabbinic Movement in its Graeco-Roman
Environment', in P. Schäfer and C. Hezser (eds.), *The Talmud Yerushalmi and Graeco-
Roman Culture* (Tübingen 2000), 51–80, esp. 64–5.

Accused of premarital or rather pre-betrothal sex, a woman was, technically at least, not an adulteress because the alleged intercourse had taken place prior to betrothal. Her status as a defendant was unique. Although accusations for 'adultery' formed a familiar feature of family law in antiquity, this type of pre-betrothal 'adultery' and its peculiar timing was, to the best of my knowledge, intrinsic only to rabbinic rules. While Roman law, for example, allowed a betrothed man to sue his fiancée for 'adultery' during their engagement, he could only do so by virtue of *ius extranei* and not by that of *ius mariti*.[22] Roman jurists did not discuss suspicions or accusations of infidelity which the first marital intercourse might generate. Nor did Roman law assign specific dates for weddings of either virgins or widows, or aspire to impose precise figures of the (theoretical) value of virgins in the marital market.

Additional Mishnaic (Tosefta) speculations about the connection between bridal virginity, weddings on Wednesdays, and husbandly suspicions provided other perspectives, not without a tinge of humour:

If he [the husband] had a claim against [her] virginity, he could rush to court [thus the Mishnah]. If so, let her be married after the Sabbath [i.e. on a Sunday since the court also sat on a Monday]. Rather, because [wedding] preparations took all the days of the week, they [Mishanic authorities] established that a man should marry [a virgin] on Wednesday. From the era of danger (i.e. Jewish revolts and subsequent need to reorganize society) onward it became the custom [also] to marry on Tuesdays and the sages did not object. [But] if a man wanted to marry on Monday, they did not allow it unless it was a case of constraint (*onnes*, rape?), when it was permitted (*T Ket.* 1.1).[23]

[22] S. Treggiari, *Roman Marriage: Iusti Coniugi from the Time of Cicero to the Time of Ulpian* (Oxford 1991), 262 f.; cf. late Roman mutations, J. Evans Grubbs, *Law and Family in Late Antiquity: The Emperor Constantine's Marriage Legislation* (Oxford 1995), 205 f.; and A. Arjava, *Women and Roman Law in Late Antiquity* (Oxford 1996), *passim*. Cf. Sivan, 'Revealing the Concealed: Rabbinic and Roman Legal Perspectives on the Crime of Adultery', *ZSS.RA* 116 (1999), 112–46; and eadem, 'The Body of a Sinner. The Price of Piety: The Politics of Adultery in Late Antiquity', *Annales* 53 (1998), 231–53.

[23] On 'constraint' as rape, in a Palestinian context, M. Satlow, *Jewish Marriage*, 169 n. 39. On cases involving virginity in rabbinic sources, S. Valler, *Women and Womanhood in the Stories of the Babylonian Talmud* (Tel Aviv 1993), 39–55 (Heb.); and T. Ilan, *Mine and Yours are Hers: Revealing Women's History from Rabbinic Literature* (Leiden 1997), 191–9.

At the heart of this curious chronology lie accountancy and account-ability. If indeed the woman had initiated the 'crime' attributed to her she faced, theoretically, death. But if she had been a victim of a rape, both the Bible (Exod. 22: 15–16; Deut. 22: 27–9) and the Mishnah (*M Ket.* 3) proposed ways to deal with rapists/seducers, including marriage or ample compensation for her family. When, however, the bride's alleged lack of virginity had remained concealed up to the moment of the wedding, a battle of wits followed. The Bible (Deut. 22: 13–22) pitted fathers against bridegrooms as the parties most concerned with this issue; the Mishnah, however, confronted bridegrooms with brides:

When a man marries a woman but does not find in her virginity, she may say: 'After you betrothed me I was raped; your field had been flooded'. He says, however: 'This is not the case, rather, [this happened] before I betrothed you and hence the [marital] transaction had been contracted in error. Rabbis Gamaliel and Eliezer say: 'She is to be trusted'. Rabbi Joshua says: 'Not by her mouth do we live. She is considered to have lost her virginity prior to her betrothal, thus misleading him, unless she can bring proof of her assertion (*M Ket.* 1.6).

The 'case' of flawed virginity weighed arguments on both sides without proposing a definite solution. Notable in their absence were both the biblical (and post-talmudic) 'tokens of virginity' and the bride's parents. Nor was there an investigation into the causes of the accusation, the assumption being that since such a charge entailed a ban on subsequent sex within marriage no man in his right mind would launch it unless he really believed in it.[24] Specific references to penalties are likewise omitted, although it seems clear that divorce and wifely forfeiture of the *ketubba* were a likely outcome. The battle over lost virginity in the Mishnah became a verbal contest which hinged on the credibility (and, implicitly, the social status) of the litigants and, ultimately, on striking disagreements among the rabbis themselves (*M Ket.* 1.6–7).

The uniqueness of rabbinic perceptions regarding the problems that could plague marriage appeared striking by comparison with

---

[24] *BT Ket.* 9a: 'He who says "I have found an open opening" is trusted to make his wife forbidden to him…'. Here, too, there are disagreements regarding the circumstances and chronology of conjugal sex after the disclosure.

Roman perceptions of *stuprum,* namely extramarital intercourse with
unmarried women (virgins, widows, and divorcees).[25] While lovers
were never mentioned in rabbinic debates over bridal virginity,
Roman jurists considered both participants in the act culpable,
making the lover a sharer of infamy and penalty. But Roman juris-
prudence also drew a rather thin dividing line between *adulterium*
and *stuprum,* creating thus a legal limbo which left considerable
space for adultery suits and hardly any for *stuprum* litigation.[26] The
state of the bridal hymen on the wedding night was never, in itself,
a legal issue in Roman law. Not surprisingly, Roman definitions of
a matron or *materfamilias,* namely of a woman who bore legitimate
children, focused not on virginity at wedding but on her behaviour
during the marriage (*mores*).[27]

The complexity of the rabbinic picture of a troubled marriage in
its very inception is further illustrated in Mishnaic discussions of
the validity of marriage in which other crucial factors relating to
the woman's spiritual and physical integrity remained concealed.
Referring to vows and physical defects, *M Ket.* 7.7–8 stipulated
that deformities of women, if detected prior to marriage, could
invalidate pre-betrothal vows and the betrothal; if detected after the
wedding, they invalidated the marriage itself. At stake, however, was
the question of patent and concealed physical blemishes of brides:

All blemishes (*mumim*) that disqualify priests also disqualify women. If she
had blemishes when she had been living in her father's house [and her
betrothed wants to divorce her but her father demands her share of the
marriage settlement], the father must bring proof that these blemishes
developed after betrothal, hence his [the groom's] field has been swept
[but the betrothal remains valid]. If she entered the husband's power, he
[the husband] must bring a proof to the effect that she had blemishes prior
to the betrothal, hence he had been 'duped'. All this is according to Rabbi
Meir. Other sages elaborate: What is this all about? About blemishes which
remain concealed; as far as visible blemishes are concerned he [the groom]
has no [legal] leg to stand on. Moreover, if there is a bathhouse in that town,

---

[25] Treggiari, *Roman Marriage,* 199–202, 263–4; Evans Grubbs, *Law and Family,*
passim, esp. 215 on prosecution of unmarried women as well as of a *sponsa* by her
fiancé; Arjava, *Women,* 280–4.

[26] J. F. Gardner, *Women in Roman Law and Society* (London 1986), 121–5.

[27] *Digest* 50.16.46.1 (Ulpian).

the groom has no legal claim [against the father] even regarding concealed blemishes because these should have been verified by his female relatives (*M Ket.* 7.7–8).[28]

For sake of symmetry the Mishnah added that 'a man in whom defects arise [after marriage] is not compelled to divorce his wife' (*M Ket.* 7.9), but here, too, a disagreement emerged regarding the size and repulsiveness of these defects and whether they indeed warranted divorce. It was agreed, though, that concealed 'deficiencies' of the bride, including a fractured hymen, had the potential of undermining the carefully wrought agreements which accompanied betrothal and marriage. In either instance, deformity or flawed virginity, chronology was crucial because it reflected on the integrity of male-to-male dealings. Somewhat inexplicably, female relatives of the groom were not called upon to verify the virginity of the bride prior to the wedding.[29]

To make matters more complex the rabbis also allowed divorce, indeed (theoretically at least) even forced it if husbands had or developed blemishes (*mumim*). The category of repulsive husbands included men smitten with boils, men who boasted a smelly nose growth, dog-dung collectors, coppersmiths, and tanners (*M Ket.* 7.9–10). Crucial for the potential dissolution of the marriage were the nature and size of the defects (minor or major) as well as their chronology (pre- or post-marriage). The most lenient rule, proposed by Rabbi Meir (*M Ket.* 7.10), propounded that a woman who had believed that she could live with a man owning to a defect at betrothal, only to find out that she could not tolerate this deformity, was entitled to a divorce. But this enlightened view remained a one-person opinion, rejected by the majority, which agreed that only major and permanent blemishes developed during the marriage (?), justified divorce.

In late antiquity, rabbinic debates over the consequences of the detection of a fractured hymen revealed ambiguity. The Palestinian

---

[28] On this passage, see J. R. Wegner, *Chattel or Person? The Status of Women in the Mishnah* (New York 1988), 85 and Satlow, *Jewish Marriage*, 309 n. 56, with reference to *T Ket.* 7.10 on the nature of premarital vows and blemishes which include bad mouth odour; strong sweat; and moles.

[29] Especially odd in view of the apparent Palestinian custom of finger defloration, Langer, 67–8.

Talmud 'classified' a bride with flawed virginity as a 'sort of adulteress' (*safek sotah*, *PT Ket.* 1.1), reflecting perhaps Roman legal confusion over *adulterium* and *stuprum* (above, p. 286). In Palestinian parlance, finding an 'open door' or not finding blood on the wedding night constituted grounds for husbandly accusations. Strikingly, however, and contrary to *tannaitic* (Mishnah) divided opinions over the trustworthiness of the wife, the Palestinian Talmud exhibited an astonishing uniformity. Practically all the *amoraim* (rabbis) who reputedly acted as arbiters of female chastity ranged on the side of the accused bride.

Bridal pleas varied. A woman could assert that a premarital accident, such as falling off a ladder in her parents' home, had induced a loss of virginity; or that her own husband had been engaged in pre-wedding defloration; or that famine caused an apparent lack of hymenal blood (*PT Ket.* 1.1). Rabbinic arbitrators invariably voiced their agreement with such justifications, even adding experiment to vindication:

A certain man came before Rabban Gamaliel bar Rabbi. He said to him: 'Rabbi, I penetrated but found no blood'. She said to him: 'Rabbi, I am still a virgin'. The rabbi said: 'Fetch me two female slaves, one a virgin, the other not. These were fetched. He seated them over an open wine barrel. A scent of wine came through the mouth of the woman who was not a virgin but none emanated from the virgin's mouth. The rabbi then seated the accused wife in the same manner. No scent came through. He said to the husband: go and enjoy your purchase (*BT Ket.* 10a).

This show of support ran counter not only to the voices recorded in the Mishnah but also to folk beliefs about the fatal consequences of flawed virginity as reflected in a proverb which stated that 'a woman whose [virginal] blood is scarce, her children are few' (*PT Ket.* 1.1).

Rabbinic reflections on virginity cast husbands, temporarily, as enemies of their own wives and of women in general.[30] For the rabbis a viable solution to husbandly charges was a public reminder that the best synonym for 'virginity' was husbandly trust. When the wife ventured to re-establish her virginity by words she was believed

---

[30] For a different interpretation, N. Margalit, '"Not by Her Mouth Do We Live": A Literary/Anthropological Reading of Gender in Mishnah Ketubbot Chapter 1', *Prooftext* (2000), 61–86.

because the opposite prospect was considerably more threatening to rabbinic visions of social order. Talmudic dismissals of husbandly accusations reconstructed the encounter as one in which accusers faced not a wayward wife but rather a good one bent on his well-being. In the eyes of the *amora* (talmudic sage), wifely excuses exonerated the entire female sex from membership in the group of the untrustworthy. The stories recorded in *PT Ket.* 1.1 show that the outcome was a triumph neither for wife nor for husband but for the verbal and financial obligations which were undertaken upon matrimony.

Husbands and wives provoked each other, matching myth for myth in a contest which determined responsibility for the schism. Contrary to the biblical text, the rabbinic wife did not remain mute, a mere invisible witness of a process of which she was the centrepiece. By dismissing virginity as an index of husbandly moral authority, the rabbis made up for a perceived weakness of a system which privileged female chastity as an indispensable endowment for producing legitimate heirs and fully fledged Jews. Projecting Jewish males as men who maintain discreet silence about the body of their wives, the Palestinian Talmud deliberately undervalued the cultural icon of female virginity. Making the unfamiliar familiar, it insisted on prior commitment to communal religious ideology over personal dynamics of gender and sexual morality.

3. THE *MOREDET*: A JEWISH LYSISTRATA?

Tannaitic (Mishnah/Tosefta) and Amoraic (Talmuds) discussions of virginity indicate that, ideally and realistically, the marital endowment (*ketubba*) of virgins entailed an intact hymen. Weathering, then, the wedding night without unpredictable 'discoveries' a couple still needed, at least according to rabbinic visions of domestic order, a clear distribution of 'labour'. The Mishnah outlined seven wifely duties:

These are the tasks which a wife must perform for her husband: Grinding grain, baking and laundering, cooking, nursing her child, preparing his [husband's] bed, and spinning. If she brings [as dowry] one maid, she need not grind or bake or do the laundry; if she brings two [maids], she need not cook, or nurse her child; if three, she need not do his bed nor spin; if four, she may lounge [and do nothing]. Rabbi Eliezer, however, says: 'Even if she brings a hundred maids she is compelled to spin because idleness leads to lechery'. Rabban Shimon ben Gamaliel says: 'A man who has vowed that his wife shall not do work must divorce her and give her the *Ketubba* share because idleness breeds boredom [or: dull-wittedness] (*M Ket.* 5.5).[31]

Husbands, on the other hand, had a single routine marital obligation, namely conjugal sex (*M Ket.* 5.6).[32] The rabbis went so far as to specify the frequency with which this husbandly 'duty' must be discharged. Thus Torah students and camel-drivers need not engage in marital sex more often than once a month, and sailors only once every six months. Wifely compliance with this schedule might be taken for granted. What happened, however, when a wife refused to collaborate? The Mishnah transmits images of 'rebellion' within the marriage, appending penalties to these subversive activities:

She who rebels (*moredet*) against her husband loses seven dinars from her marriage settlement (*ketubba*) every week. Rabbi Judah says: [she loses] seven tarpikin (i.e. half a dinar). For how long can a husband deduct these amounts [from his wife's marriage endowment]? Till he exhausts it (or: as long as it lasts). Rabbi Yosi says: [he may deduct] 'Continuously, even from an inheritance which accrues to the wife' [during the marriage]. Similarly, a man who rebels against his wife must add to her *ketubba* three dinars weekly; Rabbi Judah says: 'Three tarpikin, rather' (i.e. half the amount) (*M Ket.* 5.7).

Neither the cause nor the nature of marital 'rebellions' was discussed. Nor did the Mishnah attempt to 'fix' an inception date for either deductions or additions. The juxtaposition of seven wifely obligations with a single husbandly one suggests that 'rebellion' was

[31] On the economic aspects of these duties, Wegner, *Chattel or Person?* 77 and Satlow, *Jewish Marriage*, 220. The number, seven, is of course a cliché. Cf. rabbinic calculations of biblical barrenness, with seven barren 'wives' including Zion, *Pesiqta de Rab Kahana* 20.1 and the discussion in J. R. Baskin, *Midrashic Women: Formations of the Feminine in Rabbinic Literature* (Hanover 2002), 136–8.

[32] *M Ket.* 4.7–12 enumerates other, non-daily duties, such as a husband's obligation to ransom his wife and to finance her healing in case of sickness.

linked with either a sex strike or with a wife's refusal to fulfil one of the seven duties.[33] More specific were the monetary fines to which rabbis subjected the *ketubba* of a rebellious wife. Here, however, something in the nature of an absurdity emerged. A weekly game of deductions is finite and can be of relatively short duration, depending on the size of a *ketubba*. A rebellious husband, by contrast, could, in theory at least, increase his wife's *ketubba* indefinitely, dragging an unhappy marriage for as long as his resources allowed. If both wife and husband were deemed 'rebellious', the exercise of alternate additions and subtractions could last for a while until the *ketubba* was exhausted. Besides contributing to a development of arithmetical skills, it might be asked what legalities the rabbis envisaged in cases which warranted outside intervention in marital intimacy.

The Tosefta provided a precise procedure to deal with rebellious wives (but not with rebellious husbands!). Once a wife was denounced as 'rebellious', a court of law (*bet din*) was to issue bi-weekly warnings for a maximum of four or five weeks (*T Ket.* 5.7). If she proved recalcitrant she stood to lose her entire *ketubba*.[34] This was a considerably shorter period than the one stipulated in the Mishnah for the 're-induction' of rebellious wives into domestic bliss. The Tosefta further extended the classification of a *moredet* to women who were betrothed, widowed (but awaiting levirate marriage), menstruating, and even sick (*T Ket.* 5.7). No woman, it seems, who was associated or about to be associated with a male could avoid either service or sex.

There is no agreement in either the Mishnah or the Tosefta regarding the precise nature and scope of wifely recalcitrance—was she a woman who only denies sex to her husband and/or one who commenced a labour strike? Most rabbis evidently did not relish the idea of a Jewish Lysistrata. Even so, there is no clear indication of

---

[33] Wegner, *Chattel or Person?* 79, opts for sex. For expanded discussion of this issue see S. Riskin, *Women and Jewish Divorce: The Rebellious Wife, the Agunah and the Right of Women to Initiate Divorce in Jewish Law. A Halakhic Solution* (Hoboken, NJ, 1989), 3 f.

[34] Cf. *BT Ket.* 64a which makes a *moredet* wait a year for a divorce while depriving her of food from her husband. *PT Kidd.* 1.2 (59a) refers to writs recording woman's rebellion: 'They write for him [for the husband] a writ of rebellion as a charge against her marriage contract.' On this and other rabbinic 'documents' relating to marital matters, C. Hezser, *Jewish Literacy in Roman Palestine* (Tübingen 2001), 297 f. and *passim*.

what constituted sexual rebellion—in other words, how often must a wife avoid sex in order to earn the label of *moredet*, consequently becoming an object of public remonstrance and risking the loss of her *ketubba*? The Palestinian Talmud shunned the issue of labour in favour of sex, contemplating the effect of economic and premarital conditions on the definition of a 'rebellious wife', as well as weighing the pain or pleasure of sex:

[Why seven and why three, as financial penalties decreed in the Mishnah] Rabbi Yossi ben Haninah said: 'Because she owes him seven (duties) he deducts seven [dinars, from the marriage settlement]; and because he owes her three (according to Exod. 21: 10, namely clothing, sustenance and sex) he adds three [dinars, to the marriage settlement]'. 'Think, however, about a situation in which a wife brings slaves. She then owes him nothing'. 'Contemplate, moreover, a situation in which the husband had married her on condition that he owes her neither clothing, nor sustenance or conjugal sex. He then owes her nothing.'

Why then [a wife is a subjected to a double penalty]? 'Because', according to Rabbi Yochanan, a man suffers more than a woman [from withdrawal of sex], as said [in Judg. 16: 16]: *she kept pestering him with words day after day and urged him...* 'How *urged him*?' Rabbi Isaac ben Lazar says: 'She suspended intercourse at a moment of ejaculation'. 'And what then is the meaning [of the rest of Judg. 16: 16] *and his soul was vexed to death*?' 'He and not she wanted to die'. Some say that she [Delilah] had other lovers. But Rabbi Nachman says in the name of Rabbi Nachman: 'She certainly wanted [sex from Samson]. Such is this organ: when starved, it is satiated; satiated, starved; satiated starved' [i.e. the greater the sex the greater the appetite] (*PT Ket.* 5.10).

Both the Tosefta and the Palestinian Talmud allocated to rebellious wives an uncommonly brief period of mind-changing, exhibiting harshness which had been absent from the Mishnah. Pondering the chronology of 'rebellion', the Palestinian Talmud weighed Torah regulations on menstruation versus rabbinic instructions.[35]

Rabbi Hiya taught: 'A letter recording a rebellion against the husband is issued to [the following categories of women]: betrothed, sick, menstruating and widow awaiting levirate marriage'. 'Does this mean that if her moment of rebellion coincided with her period [i.e. when she is ritually impure

---

[35] C. E. Fonrobert, *Menstrual Purity: Rabbinic and Christian Reconstructions of Biblical Gender* (Stanford 2000); R. K. Wasserfall (ed.), *Women and Water: Menstruation in Jewish Life and Law* (Hanover 1999).

according to the Torah], she is in fact obeying the Torah?' [i.e. the Torah and not her own will is her cause of rebellion]. 'We hold that if she rebelled prior to menstruating, her rebellion "dates" from that moment, even though she is not considered rebellious [by law, during menstruation], and consequently she is subject to punitive deductions throughout' (*PT Ket.* 5.10).

Such dicta brought to bear the collective pressure of husbands (i.e. family) and rabbis (i.e. public opinion) on subversive females and on forms of marital dissension caused by wives. The association of wifely rebelliousness with threats of marital dissolution cast rabbinic marriage as an institution which fostered morality and stability. By banning sex strikes the rabbis condemned a voluntary return of married women to a state of virginal purity within marriage because this state of being was opposed to the rabbinic definition of womanhood, which valued chastity within marriage but not in the marital bed itself. By conjuring spectacles which insinuated the power of rebellious wives to reduce not only their *ketubba* but also the marriage itself to nothing, the rabbis aspired to erase a fantasy of marital and social disorder which has women as the chief mischief-makers.

An explicit assimilation of 'bad' wives to rebellious ones reinforced rabbinic disapproval of recalcitrant wives:

Said Rabbi Hannina in the name of Rabbi Ishmael: 'A woman who is divorced on account of wicked reputation does not regain her dowry garments; a rebellious wife does'. Rabbi Simon in the name of Rabbi Joshua son of Levi, however, said: 'A rebellious wife, as well as a wife divorced for bad repute, receives neither alimony nor their dowry garments' (*PT Ket.* 5.10).

The image of a rebellious wife leaving home practically naked was both entertaining and ominous. By a rhetorical flourish the rabbis linked two categories of 'subversive' wives to insinuate disaster. The precise meaning of 'bad reputation' is as elusive as that of a *moredet. BT Ket.* 46b, for example, suggested that a husband could cause his wife to acquire an unsavoury reputation if he forbade her to lend or to borrow household items from her female neighbours.[36] The public standing of

---

[36] Cf. women's informal groups in biblical Israel as an expression of the intimate intertwining of 'public' (male) and 'private' (female) domains, C. Meyers, '"Women of the Neighborhood" (Ruth 4.17): Informal Female Networks in Ancient Israel', in A. Brenner (ed.), *Feminist Companion to the Bible: Ruth and Esther*, 2nd ser. (Sheffield 1999), 110 ff., esp. 111–16 (theoretical considerations).

a married woman, then, depended on her relationships with other women in the neighbourhood. Public exposure of rebellious wives damaged her husband's reputation in the neighbourhood.

One intriguing aspect of rabbinic projections of marital discord based on withdrawal of sex was an implication of the theoretical availability of sexual renunciation within marriage to both wives and husbands. Yet, this ostensible equality also singled out this practice as potentially disruptive. A chaste wife was perceived as a guarantor of social concord as long as her behaviour conformed with the ideals produced by men to guarantee a society based on gender differentiation. If she diverged from this gender stereotype, she challenged a social system which was carefully wrought around reciprocity among males. While marital 'asceticism' of Torah learners was expressed in terms of elevated moral existence, that of married women was tantamount to rebellion.

Vagaries of chance, profession, and choices favoured the position of men within marriage. The same system condemned marital stasis caused by recalcitrant wives because it tacitly recognized that this type of marital 'asceticism' could also serve women as a social matrix by which they could dissociate themselves from the equation of femininity with sexuality. By representing the interests of women in marriage through a pastiche promoting normative behaviour, the rabbis, even when censuring husbands for neglecting conjugal duties, reinforced submission to patriarchal authority.

4. BETWEEN DEFILEMENT AND DEFIANCE

Underlying rabbinic debates over virginal chastity and matronly obedience was the question whether the rabbis attempted to preserve an uncomfortable marriage at all cost or to facilitate divorce. Were the rules intended to prevent or to forestall wifely disobedience, to enable women to express their unhappiness in a marriage and to get a divorce, not, however, without considerable cost? Common to all discussions was the concern over precise ascription of paternity which unmonitored female behaviour, either before or during marriage, endangered.

Virgins and married women were two distinct categories in the rabbinic world-view, but the social reality behind this linguistic fact was that the subordination of all women ensured the ideal order of society. The ambiguity inherent in the situations which the Mishnah and the Talmud described, highlights the difficulty of integrating women into the envisioned stages that govern their lives. What the tales about women defending themselves against virginity charges demonstrate is how women turned weakness into strength by playing with their status as women, and how they tacitly united to oppose accusations that endangered their idealized progression from virginity into matrimony.

Rabbis and brides conspired to preserve the token image of fresh husbands as warriors, as men who penetrated and who elicited blood. Both endeavoured to embrace the tradition of the virtuous virgin, the fantasy to which husbands and fathers subscribed. Rabbis and husbands linked a presumed 'adultery' with the moment of betrothal which sealed a transaction between two males, the bride's father and her intended husband. At stake was neither august days for a virgin's nuptials nor prospects of husbandly accusations but rather an attempt to curtail the potential of women to challenge basic male assumptions regarding the physical property of women on the eve of their first marriage. By lending a comic tinge to the deadly seriousness of the biblical discussion of slandered brides, the rabbis attempted to preserve the dignity of the institution of marriage by forestalling this kind of marital discord.

Traditional female virtues, neatly summed up in the wifely seven duties, could enhance the status of a woman only within her own group since these were designed to stabilize and not to disrupt the social order. By labelling female independence within marriage as a 'rebellion' against male authority, rabbinic Judaism disallowed sexual renunciation, thus limiting women to social networks which could not exceed family and immediate environment. Chastity within marriage, a novel aspect of Christian domesticity in late antiquity, was censured because it could render female resistance to peer pressure respectable.[37] Rabbinic disapproval of conjugal continence ensured that this form of female independence became an expression of institutional disrespect.

---

[37] K. Cooper, *The Virgin and the Bride: Idealized Womanhood in Late Antiquity* (Cambridge, Mass., 1996), 87.

A wedding lacking a virginal bride and a wifely negation of marital obligations formed two poles of rabbinic discourses of sexuality. Presented as emblems of female merit, the possession of intact hymen and of submissive spirit delineated an explicit denial of rabbinic, as well as of Roman and early Christian, models which, in theory at least, espoused the mutuality of the conjugal debt. Although both Judaism and Christianity viewed women as supreme guardians of the household and as arbiters of male morality, brides were not invariably synonymous with virgins, nor matrons with submissive femininity. If the figure of the bride was extolled as an emblem of male concord, that of the 'virgin', if virginity was suspect, became a symbol of disruption. If wives were vital for procreation and male completion, sexual renunciation within marriage proved problematic.

Because marriage itself was a convention establishing the limits of female identity, the moment at which marriage was contracted held enormous practical and imaginative importance. It enshrined a change in personal status within the family and within the larger social system. What the discussions of virginity convey is a hint of the social trauma of renegotiating familial boundaries and relationships through marriage. What the images of wifely rebellion transmit is the fragility of realities and the tenuity of the bond.

It would be difficult to find a more candid observer of the world of women than Jerome:

Add to the other humiliations of nature the womb for nine months growing larger, the sickness, the delivery, the blood, the swaddling clothes. Picture to yourself the infant in the enveloping membranes. Introduce into your picture the hard manger, the wailing of the infant, the circumcision on the eighth day, the time of purification...[38]

And if pregnancy and delivery were not enough, the daily grinds of housekeeping demonstrated how thin was the line between reality and stereotypes when it came to domesticity:

The prattling of infants, the noisy household, children watching for her word and waiting for her kiss, the reckoning up of expenses, the preparation to meet the outlay... meanwhile a message is delivered that the husband and

---

[38] *Against Helvidius* 20 (Eng. trans. NPNF).

his friends have arrived. The wife, like a swallow, flies all over the house. She has to see to everything. Is the sofa smooth? Is the pavement swept? Are the flowers in the cup? Is dinner ready? Where amidst all this is there room for thinking of God?[39]

Perhaps these were precisely the images that drove women to embark on the unusual pursuit of pilgrimage to holy places. In the early 380s Egeria, a woman from Gaul, travelled for, at least, three years through countless 'sacred' locations in the Near East.[40] Her diary projected a mobile environment in which not even a faint echo of Jerome's chores is to be detected. Instead, Egeria's life on the road was crowded with sanctuaries, cells, priests, monks, and remarkably devoid of other women. To be fully integrated into the universe of pilgrimage Egeria might have had to shed her femininity as ascetic women did in late antiquity. She wrote for an audience composed of 'dear sisters' yet met only men along her years of meandering through Syria, Egypt, and Palestine.[41]

To define pilgrimage as an arena of public activity in which women had a role to play appears legitimate. Yet, the space so liberally projected for piety, regardless of gender, reduced the enterprise to a privileged sphere in which participation guaranteed the honours. In order to function in a Christian holy land, a territory which had been shaped by collective imagination, it was necessary to acquire an awareness of dramatically different yet time-consuming duties, such as participation in the daily liturgy of Jerusalem. These were the activities that infused coherence regardless of provenance and language.[42]

To exhaust the meaning of the experience of pilgrimage or asceticism as practised in late ancient Palestine meant the forgetfulness of an obvious and strange fact, namely that female ascetics and female pilgrims imitated male ascetics and male pilgrims.[43] If marriage and

[39] Ibid. 22. G. Clark, *Women in Late Antiquity*, 98–101.
[40] On Egeria's Gallic, rather than Spanish, provenance, see my 'Who was Egeria? Pilgrimage and Piety in the Age of Gratian', *HTR* 81 (1988), 59–71, Her diary has been translated with ample annotation by J. Wilkinson, *Egeria's Travels* (1981).
[41] H. Sivan, 'Holy Land Pilgrimage and Western Audience: Egeria and her Circle', *CQ* 38 (1988), 528–35.
[42] Jerome, *Ep.* 46.10.
[43] At least in the first phase when women like Melania the Elder and Paula left home, Rome, and family in 372 to embark on a journey that would end at the Mount of Olives. F. X. Murphy, 'Melania the Elder: A Biographical Note', *Traditio* 5 (1947), 59–77. In general, Hunt, *Holy Land Pilgrimage, passim.*

motherhood were as necessary and natural to women as they were led to believe, a woman could not become an ascetic or a pilgrim without profoundly disturbing the order of things. Jerome knew it and this is why he had to project an entirely new world order to justify his call to follow a 'primordial' virginal vocation and to uproot the self from 'normative' evolution. The women who followed Jerome's call to the Palestinian ascetic 'desert' were few and select. They had to possess the self-possession which enabled them to defy the consent of the social body which they sought to deprive of an anticipated future. Or at least they tried to mobilize a new life-style that, ironically, gave it its most complete form.[44]

To detach themselves from social conventions women like Eustochium and Melania the Younger, the second generation of aristocratic ascetics, used the same strategy that official eulogy of women employed to oblige women to remain in a specifically appointed cycle of perpetual activities. For Melania's biographer the tension between his heroine's innate nature and the demands of class reached its height with the birth and immediate death of a son and heir.[45] The apparent failure to protect child, rank, and inheritance animated a new relationship between wife and husband and a change of roles which led to a spiritual marriage coupled with massive disinvestment of their enormous properties. This was the first major step along a search for the self which culminated in a move to Palestine and to a life dedicated to scholarship and to a full ascetic vocation.[46]

For women like Melania the immersion in biblical scholarship meant the acquisition of cultural identity that only Palestine or rather the Holy Land could confer. What was especially remarkable

[44] See my 'On Hymen and Holiness in Late Antiquity: Opposition to Aristocratic Female Asceticism at Rome', *Jahrbuch für Antike und Christentum* 36 (1993), 81–93; and 'Anician Women, The Cento of Proba, and Aristocratic Conversion in the Fourth Century', *VC* 47 (1993), 140–57.

[45] *Vita Melaniae* 5–6 (ed. Gorce).

[46] A. Giardina, 'Melania the Saint', in A. Fraschetti (ed.), *Roman Women*, trans. L. Lappin (Chicago 2001), 190–207. E. A. Clark, *The Life of Melania the Younger* (New York 1984). In general on the phenomenon, A. Rousselle, *Porneia: On Desire and the Body in Antiquity*, trans. F. Pheasant (New York 1996); E. A. Clark, *Jerome, Chrysostom and Friends* (New York 1979); eadem, *Ascetic Piety and Women's Faith* (Lewiston, NY, 1986), *passim*; eadem, 'Ideology, History and the Construction of "Woman" in Late Antique Christianity', *JECS* 2 (1994), 155–84; P. Brown, *The Body and Society* (New York 1988).

about her was that the transformation was wholly self-achieved as though all it needed was not a human guiding hand, like that of the expert Jerome, but the inspiration solely derived from the land. The same Palestine which imposed constraints on Jewish women liberated Christian women, not all, of course, but the privileged who had come from the outside to spend time or to settle there. In interpreting the meaning of life in terms so different from the conventions that ordinarily dictated the female life-cycle, the meeting with unmediated holiness in biblical localities gave these outsiders the opportunity of affirming their individual valour.

Paula's epitaph, discussed in Chapter 1, pitted her mythical ancestors with the real adversaries whom she had to confront when leaving Rome for the Holy Land. Yet her biography also revealed the profound significance that her family's history had assumed precisely because she chose a dramatically different course. In recounting the lives of these women their biographers appeared to have allowed certain episodes to acquire mythical proportions as a foundation and justification for the behaviour of their protagonists. When Melania the Younger set out for Constantinople (436), apparently on a mission of conversion, her road from Jerusalem to the court resembled a triumphal march paved with receptions in every city.[47] During her stay in the capital she became a consultant on matters relating to 'heresy' (Nestorianism) and 'orthodoxy' and an intimate of the imperial family of Theodosius II, Eudocia, and their daughters. Following Melania, Eudocia embarked on her first pilgrimage to Palestine (438).

The scene of Melania's death, elaborately and minutely described by Gerontius, contained all the elements that presented those present with a signal distinction of what it meant to be in the company of a saint. The community paid Melania the honours ordinarily paid to its most valorous men, and in doing so expressed its cohesion and her greatness. In Melania's Jerusalemite monastery, homage to those about to die reflected a spirit that found its reflection in the cell where she was dying. Her greatness matched that of the living city whose citizens came to learn a lesson in piety while listening to her last words. Of the funeral honours accorded to Melania Gerontius found her attire

---

[47] *Vit. Mel.* 50–6 (Gorce).

worthy of recording. It was composed of remnants of cloths and of relics which had belonged to a gallery of saintly personalities (*VM* 69). No obituary was read. Melania's life constituted its own obituary. In death as in life, the Holy Land did not confer egalitarianism. When Maria, mother of two Palestinian bishops, died in Gaza in the first half of the sixth century, her funeral oration, pronounced by Choricius, the city's outstanding rhetor, hailed the dead as a model of domesticity.[48] Having been inculcated from infancy with the principles of the appropriate female virtues Maria's life inexorably led to a fine death at a great old age:

It is said that when still a girl and inexperienced with men, she lived virtuously, talking moderately and with a gentle voice and with her eyes lowered, blushing before she spoke. She knew the advice of Sophocles, not through studying [his drama] but from her own nature, namely that silence becomes all women, especially girls.[49]

Chorisius' allusion to Sophocles, used to point to Maria's befitting ignorance of the classics and to the appropriate demeanour of women in general, stands in striking contrast to the continuing employment of myth in the very school which produced the eloquence here practised. In Maria's and Choricius' Gaza, Greek myth and drama nurtured theatrical, rhetorical, and artistic presentations. Thus the story of Phaedra, whose unfortunate infatuation with Hippolytus, her step son, fascinated both Sophocles and Euripides, provided a popular theme for mimes, paintings and rhetorical exercises in Maria's Gaza. Choricius' teacher, Procopius, described in loving detail a representation of the myth that Maria could have viewed, and an anonymous poet composed anacreontics that depicted a Phaedra inflamed with moral and unlawful passion.[50] In the Gazan versions of the myth

---

[48] Choricius, *Or.* 7, Funeral Oration to Maria mother of Marcian, bishop of Gaza, and of Anastasius, bishop of Eleutheropolis (Eng. trans. F. Litsas, 'Choricius' (Ph.D., Univ. of Chicago 1980) (available via the internet), 204 ff.).

[49] Ibid.

[50] P. Friedlander, *Spätantiker Gemäldezyklus in Gaza* (Studi e Testi 89) (Città del Vaticano 1939), 5–19 for the text of Procopius' ekphrasis; R. Talgam, 'The Ekphrasis Eikonos of Procopius of Gaza: The Depiction of Mythological Themes in Palestine and Arabia during the Fifth and the Sixth Centuries', in B. Bitton-Ashkelony and A. Kofsky (eds), *Christian Gaza in Late Antiquity* (Leiden 2004), 209–34. For the verses of the anonymous called George of Gaza see F. Ciccolella, 'Phaedra's Shining Roses: Reading Euripides in Sixth-Century Gaza', *Scripta Classica Israelica* 26 (2007), 181–204.

Phaedra emerged not as a woman heroically battling an unwanted and unhappy love but as a lecherous character, unseemly and indecent, the very opposite of Maria.

At Maria's death-bed stood her children and listened to her last words: 'I have received the things I had longed for. It is a most welcome blessing for any woman to pass away while she is still in sound mind. For a mother should not bewail the fact that she is no longer a child, but a child should behold his mother as she dies.'[51] Maria's epitaph was a banal précis of women's maternal function:

> Do not shed tears beholding this tomb.
> Here lies an old woman
> Who is no cause worthy of tears.
> She lived a virtuous life and has left children of children,
> And offspring of the grandchildren too.[52]

Choricius was well aware of the inadequacy of current terminology to provide affirmation of the *topos* of Christianized motherhood. To die at an old age, serene, happy, a witness of the success of her children and grandchildren, hardly amounted to an account of noble deeds of the sort used to extol exceptional female piety. In using commonplaces, then, Choricius suggested that in the land of Christian epitaphs the vocabulary of an already existing rhetorical pattern should suffice. In a Palestinian city like Gaza in the sixth century, in the course of a funeral honouring a local woman, it was then possible to speak in *topoi* and to hint at something new at the same time. The absence of specific Christian references and the presence of classical allusions showed the speech to have been an exercise in imitation and adaptation. Maria, like rabbinic women, was generic. It would be impossible to reconstruct an authentic woman from her epitaph.

---

[51] Litsas, 25.   [52] Ibid. 35.

8

Urban Stories: Caesarea, Sepphoris, Gaza

1. THE CAPITAL: CAESAREA ON THE SEA

> Near the city gates was seen a spectacle beyond all description
> and tragic recital: everywhere human flesh was devoured and
> scattered. Limbs, flesh and entrails were to be seen even within
> the gates. After many days of such things a wondrous event
> happened. Suddenly, on a day when the air was clear and bright
> and the sky serene, throughout the city the pillars that sup-
> ported the public porticoes let fall drops, like tears. And though
> there was no mist in the air the market places and streets were
> moistened with sprinkled water. It was then immediately
> reported that the earth, the senseless stones and lifeless wood,
> unable to endure this foul and cruel deed, shed tears...
>
> Eusebius, *Mart. Pal.* 9.12 (Gr.)

The date is 309.[1] The location one of the gates of Caesarea Maritima,
capital of Palestine and its largest metropolis. The occasion the
aftermath of the trial of Christian men and women condemned to
torture and execution. The narrator is Eusebius, the city's foremost
theologian. By focusing on the weeping pillars, Eusebius presented
prominent features of an urban landscape that glorified the dead of
their own accord. First the gate that ordinarily linked urbanites with
their hinterland and the province, and then the urban interior with its
porticoes, pillars, streets, and stones. The signal honour accorded to
the last victims of the persecution endowed Caesarea's architectural

---

[1] On this passage and its date, Saul Lieberman, 'The Martyrs of Caesarea',
Annuaire de l'Institut de Philologie et d'Histoire Orientales et Slaves 7 (1939–44),
395–446, esp. 400 on the date.

elements with a religious dimension that amounted to a peculiar form of urban strife, a communal yet silent protest against governmental nefarious actions.[2] This civic act of the lamenting pillars reflected the emergence of a new type of patriotism that was to rest on the veneration of the Christian dead.

Eusebius' sympathy for the victims focused on the fact that they were deprived of decent burial and hence of a place in the 'domain of the dead'. By Roman standards of the time the executed Christian members of Palestinian urban communities, such as Scythopolis, Eleutheropolis, Gaza, and Caesarea, failed the test of citizenship. Yet, this apparent lack of solidarity was counterbalanced by an unofficial act that manifestly symbolized the city. When Eusebius insisted that pillars, streets, and the earth joined an imaginary funerary procession, his use of architectural formulae highlighted the urban distortion that the governor's action had introduced. The city, Eusebius' city, knew how to honour valour and piety. The description of mourning articulated a new concept of urbanism in which martyrs received a signal distinction that disregarded differences of status, sex, or age. A new sense of cohesion emerged, based on a common creed, Christianity, and on shared admiration for the individuals who died for the faith.

Although hardly original, the personification of grief through tearful pillars was striking.[3] It anticipated the kind of urban mass reaction triggered by the death of a 'holy' figure. Along a shared Mediterranean coast, in 491, when news about the demise of Peter the Iberian reached Maiumas, Gaza's port city and Peter's erstwhile see, throngs of men and women, young and old, rushed to his monastery to share in the burial ceremonies, to kiss his corpse and to embrace the holy remains.[4] Ready to snatch souvenirs in the shape of Peter's bodily parts his ardent admirers were prevented from pursuing their desire by Peter's ascetic colleagues, who had prudently placed the corpse in a sealed sarcophagus. The very nature of both demonstrations, that of the weeping pillars and that of the wailing

---

[2] On the urban landscape as reflected in Eusebius' martyr narratives, J. Patrich, 'The Martyrs of Caesarea: The Urban Context', *LA* 52 (2002), 321–46.

[3] Cf. Lysias, *Epitaphios* 21–3, which depicts a personified Greece cutting off her hair to show her grief for the citizens of Athens who had died in combat.

[4] *Vita Petri Iberi* (ed. Raabe), 142–3.

Gazans, implied a recognition of the role of exceptional individuals in infusing urban commonalities with a new meaning.

In Christian terms the story of the silent lament of inanimate public objects in Caesarea was cast in terms of an urban antithesis which invited contrasting interpretations. The phenomenon which Eusebius regarded as a common protest against governmental cruelty became, at the very same time and in the same urban context, an expression of grief for the passing of a great Jewish sage. 'When Rabbi Abbahu died, the pillars of Caesarea wept.'[5] Put otherwise, in Jewish memory the eloquent gesture of the stones of Caesarea did not mark the passing of Christian martyrs but rather the death of the city's greatest rabbi.[6]

Impervious to ethnic and religious background, the architecture of the city invited itself to take part in the end of an era. Stones were collared to serve rival propaganda aims. In exalting Rabbi Abbahu the Palestinian Talmud accounted for an otherwise unaccountable natural phenomenon. The grieving pillars, although subject of fundamental polemics, signified a deeper reality that witnessed the death of remarkable individuals. The Jewish interpretation of the sorrowful stones countered a Christian attempt to colonize the urban landscape by collaring the city's architecture. And since in his lifetime Rabbi Abbahu often engaged in polemics with members of other communities within the city, it was fitting that a dead Abbahu would become an equal claimant to the singular honour of a general act of mourning.

Yet a third interpretation of precisely the same phenomenon discounted both Jewish and Christian appropriation. The Samaritans of Caesarea calmly asserted that the pillars were not miraculously crying but merely perspiring.[7] There was no element of fantasy nor a spontaneous outburst of emotions but merely an impression in memory. For Christians, as for Jews, the pillars became monuments of a tangible reality of loss. For Samaritans, the proverbial 'other' in late ancient Palestine, such an assertion, admittedly preserved in a hostile source, intended to disprove the scope of Judaism (and of

---

[5] *PT AZ* 3.1 (42c) with Lieberman, 'Martyrs', 401.

[6] L. I. Levine, 'R. Abbahu of Caesarea', in J. Neusner (ed.), *Christianity, Judaism and Other Graeco-Roman Cults: Studies for Morton Smith at Sixty* (Leiden 1975), 56–76.

[7] *PT AZ* 3.1 where the Samaritans, as usual, are called 'kutim' and where the comment is cast as a direct reaction to the Jewish interpretation of the tearful pillars.

Christianity) rather than to describe the state of the pillars.[8] Conflictual interpretations cast the mantle of architecture as a thin veneer of communal differences.

Caesarea's gates, the scene of unburied and mutilated corpses of Christians at the dawn of the fourth century, formed an integral part of the urban layout. They embodied on the one hand the unity of the Caesarean community, and provided, on the other hand, a political and military symbol. Connecting the city with the province, the monumental arches that designated points of entry and of exit preceded the semicircular walls that Caesarea acquired only in the fifth century.[9] Already at a distance anyone heading to the city would have had an early taste of what was to come as the eyes fell on a magnificent *tetrapylon*, singled out for its beauty and uniqueness by a fourth-century précis of noted locations throughout the empire.[10] The decision to expose the bodies of the executed Christians at the gate reflected the view of government regarding the correct functioning of a public space where the unruly were to be persecuted even after death.

Moulded upon its object, Eusebius' story of the weeping promenade, porticoes, and markets shed light on the interconnectedness of the city which had been designed as a showcase of the orthogonal city plan. Organized social practices crystallized in close proximity around the governor's palace and the adjacent theatre and stadium. Both the *cardo* and the *decumanus*, the two main thoroughfares, guided the movement of humans and merchandise in a predictable pattern of traffic which the inhuman treatment of Christians, mourned by the colonnades, rendered grotesque. Eusebius' description highlighted the monumentality that united the city in a visual manifestation of its grandeur. But it also emphasized the divisions in the heart of Caesarea between Christians and pagans, rulers and ruled.

[8] K. Holum, 'Identity and the Late Antique City: The Case of Caesarea', in H. Lapin (ed.), *Religious and Ethnic Communities in Later Roman Palestine* (Bethesda, Md., 1998), 160–1 calls attention to the special voice of each community and how the appropriation of the pillars reinforced specific aspects of its history.

[9] For the date, Partrich, 'Martyrs', 325. See also J. H. Humphrey, 'Summary of the 1974 Excavations in the Caesarea Hippodrome', *BASOR* 218 (1975), 9, suggesting that the city was built no later than the 4th or the early 5th cent.

[10] *Expositio totius mundi* 26 (Rougé): *tetrapylon . . . quod unum et novum aliquod spectaculum.*

Once apprehended, a Christian or a criminal would have been taken to the court of the provincial governor which occupied a section of the *praetorium*, the living–working quarters of the highest Roman official of the land.[11] The complex commanded a magnificent position along a promontory which extended 100 metres into the Mediterranean. Under the inviting open courtyard of the governor's palace a vast system of water cisterns housed the prison where the would-be martyrs were held. A Greek inscription smeared in mud on the walls of the prison, 'Oh Lord, Procopia calls upon you to help her', may constitute the sole testimony of an otherwise unknown martyr of Caesarea.[12] She may have died in the oval stadium attached to the palace where, in late 306, an Agapius found his death as part of the public spectacles honouring the emperor's birthday.[13]

Caesarea's contested landscape appeared symptomatic of the ways in which the city was transformed in late antiquity. Verbal affirmation of identity was anchored in a conflict in which all sides resorted to the authority of venerable figures to whom the city owed its new vigour. Confrontational dialectics preceded actions. At the heart of the city, raised on a platform that afforded a magnificent view all around, the temple of Rome and Augustus which had been built at considerable expense by Herod in the first century BCE, continued to function throughout the fourth century.[14] Its affiliation with the two symbols of the empire, the ancient capital and the emperors, as well as its monumentality and beauty, would have ensured the continuing attachment of Caesarea's citizens no less than the presence of the provincial governor.[15] The strength of Caesarean Roman patriotism coupled with pride in its Hellenic tradition were likewise evident in the city's investment in education. Caesareans were willing to offer an Antiochene teacher a substantial salary in order to lure him from Antioch to their city Libanius *Or.* 31.42.

[11] A much-excavated spot, the promontory's praetorium has been the subject of numerous publications, Patrich, 'Martyrs', 330 n. 34 for basic bibliography.

[12] Patrich, 'Martyrs', 332.

[13] Eus. *Mart. Pal.* 3.1–3.

[14] The information on this temple is based on a summary, in typescript, by Ken Holum, generously provided by him. I also had the good fortune to participate in two seasons of excavations in Caesarea, in 1999 and 2000.

[15] Josephus, *BJ* 1.414. On the presence of pagans in 6th-cent. Caesarea, Procopius, *Anec.* 11.31–2.

Between the abandonment of the temple, *c*.400, and the erection of the church a century later, the elevated site was briefly occupied by a structure with an orientation that differed from that of both temple and church.[16] Perhaps the placing of this building represented a belated attempt to rectify the orientation of the temple, which had diverged dramatically from the city's axial regularity.[17] The excavators believe that this intermediate phase housed a secular building that ushered in a temporary 'desacralization' of the site. If this had indeed been the case it suggests a symmetry of urban anomaly—the transformation of secular space into sacred usage and vice versa.[18]

In the late fifth/early sixth century an octagonal church was built directly on top of the temple to Rome and Augustus. Originally the sanctuary was apparently a martyrium commemorating one of the city's martyrs in whose honour the city's pillars had shed tears long before, maybe Pamphilius, Procopius, or Paul. There were two Caesareans by the name of Paul, one martyred on 16 July 308 together with two virgins, Valentina and Ennatha; the other martyred on 6 February 309 or 310, a death also commemorated in the Jerusalem calendar.[19] The fame of the Caesarean Pauls ranged beyond Caesarea. Relics of one travelled beyond the river Jordan, to Kastron Mefaa (Umm al-Rasas), where a roof tile of the sixth-century church bore the inscription 'Hail, Saints Paul and Germanus'.[20]

The temple-turned-church, in its first phase (*c*.500), lacked an apse, or raised bema, to celebrate the Eucharist, an omission promptly

[16] For an updated chronology, with the temple destroyed in the second quarter of the 5th cent., the intermediary structure erected a decade later and destroyed in fire in the late 5th cent., J. A. Stabler, 'Caesarea Maritima: 2002 Land Excavations', available via *www.bibleinterp.com*.

[17] P. Richardson, 'Archaeological Evidence' for Religion and Urbanism in Caesarea, Maritima, in T. L. Donaldson (ed.), *Religious Rivalries and the Struggle for Success in Caesarea Maritima* (Waterloo, Ont., 2000), 11–34.

[18] See, however, below pp. 308–9, for a suggestion that links the journey of John of Caesarea and Porphyry of Gaza to Constantinople in 402 with the conversion of the temple into a structure in the service of the church.

[19] Eus. *Mart. Pal.* 8.5–12; 9.1–28. G. Garitte, *Le Calendrier Palestino-Géorgien de Sinaiticus 34* (Subsidia Hagiographica 30; Brussels 1958), 152. See also L. Di Segni, 'A Chapel of St Paul at Caesarea Maritima? The Inscriptions', *LA* 50 (2000), 398–9.

[20] M. Piccirillo, 'La chiesa di San Paolo a Umm al-Rasas', *LA* 47 (1997), 389–90, whose identification of the dedicatee, Saint Paul, is challenged, correctly to my mind, by Di Segni, 'Chapel' 399 n. 22, who prefers Paul of Caesarea, martyred with Germanus in the city (Eus. *Mart. Pal.* 9.4–8).

corrected with the creation of congregational space equipped with all the appurtenances to carry out communal rituals.[21] The walls of the church owed their magnificence to the stones that had once graced the temple and its immediate successor on the platform. Among the reused items were imported marble Corinthian capitals which boasted, in addition to lavish foliage, a conspicuous cross moulding at the centre below the boss.[22] If, as has been suggested, these columns had supported the unidentified building that preceded the church, the structure might not have been, after all, a 'desacralized' monument but perhaps an earlier church. Conversely, the pillars could have undergone 'baptism', as was rather common elsewhere when reusing architectural elements within the Christianized city space of late antiquity.[23]

Perhaps the most intriguing aspect of the Christianization of Caesarea's central temple was the relatively late date of construction, which marked an apparently benign transformation a whole century after the central sanctuary of Gaza's Marnas underwent violent conversion.[24] In Gaza the temple was set on fire and its fragments were used as slabs to pave a road which believers and animals were to trample in flagrant contempt for their previous function. The imperial order which sealed the fate of Marnas' temple was obtained as a result of a Palestinian episcopal delegation of a single pair, Porphyry and John, bishops of Gaza and Caesarea respectively, to the imperial court at Constantinople (400/401).[25] In the capital Porphyry managed to garner conspicuous success, with the repeated intercession of the empress Eudoxia. The result was the erection of a church atop the foundations of Marnas'

[21] Cf. the absence of an apsis, a focus of rituals, in the recently excavated Sepphoris synagogue, Z. Weiss and E. Netzer, 'The Excavations of the Hebrew University Expedition in Sepphoris 1992–1996', *Qadmoniot* 30 (1997), 16 (Heb.). Omission apparently not corrected.

[22] L. Roussin, 'A Group of Early Christian Capitals from the Temple Platform', in R. L. Vann (ed.), *Caesarea Papers* (JRA Suppl. Ser. 5; Ann Arbor 1992), 173–7.

[23] C. A. Marinescu, 'Transformations: Classical Objects and their Re-Use during Late Antiquity', in R. W. Mathisen and H. S. Sivan (eds.), *Shifting Frontiers in Late Antiquity* (Aldershot 1996), 285–98.

[24] But it compares well with the implantation of a church in late 5th/early 6th cent. atop a temple that had been in ruins since the 1st cent. BCE in Sussita, A. Segal and M. Eisenberg, 'Hippos-Sussita of the Decapolis: First Five Years of Excavation', *Qadmoniot* 38 (2005), 24–5 (Heb.). On Gaza see below pp. 328–47.

[25] The historicity of John has been doubted, Honigmann, 'Juvenal', 216, yet the existence of a Caesarean bishop cannot be doubted.

temple. What John achieved was an imperial gift of a large amount of money and a number of unspecified privileges.[26] Had he undertaken the journey merely to lend his august companionship to a bishop under his jurisdiction? Or was his purpose to secure the closure of the temple to Rome and Augustus?[27]

For a city of the size of Caesarea and its crucial role in the history of early Christianity, the number of edifices associated with religion, be it polytheism, Judaism, Christianity, or Samaritanism, seems strangely low. Of the city's sanctuaries, one temple, one Jewish and one Samaritan synagogue have been identified, as well as one church and possibly a chapel. By comparison with the sixteen churches of Gerasa, the octagonal Caesarean church, although strategically located and conspicuously elevated, was a reminder not so much of the Christianization of the Palestinian capital as of its self-celebration. The church's erection in a position of imperial dominance assigned Christian time to a space that had been allocated to the eulogy of the city, Rome, and the emperor.

Far from undermining the character of the city this apparent paucity of religious spaces reinforced the secular outlines of the Caesarean landscape. The omnipresence of the central government enabled Caesarea to retain an autonomous entity that had not lost all reference to the imperial framework that had moulded it. In the sixth century the city's lovely esplanade sported decapitated statues, one representing the emperor Hadrian, perhaps once at the Hadrianeum, the other another emperor or a divinity (Zeus?).[28] Besides the temple to Rome and Augustus, the existence of two civic structures, perhaps temples or basilicas, the Tiberieum and the Hadrianeum, has been conjectured solely through inscriptions.[29] The fate of the former after

[26] Mark the Deacon, *Vita Porphyry* 53.

[27] By one modern reading, the bishops of Caesarea were ceaselessly engaged in battling rival claims of the Jerusalemite episcopate, Z. Rubin, 'The See of Caesarea in Conflict with Jerusalem from Nicaea to Chalcedon', in A. Raban and K. G. Holum (eds.), *Caesarea Maritima: Retrospective after Two Millennia* (Leiden 1996), 562–7.

[28] R. Gersht, 'Roman Statuary used in Byzantine Caesarea', in K. G. Holum *et al.* (eds.), *Caesarea Papers* 2 (Portsmouth 1999), 389–98.

[29] Levine, *Roman Caesarea*, 18–22. The 6th-cent. inscription records the completion of building projects encompassing a basilica, its marble paving and mosaic, as well as steps (or stairway) of the Hadrianeum, W. Moulton, 'Gleanings in Archaeology and Epigraphy: A Caesarean Inscription', *Annual of the American School of Oriental Research in Jerusalem* 1 (1919–20), 86–90; Lehmann and Holum, *Inscriptions*, no. 43 (the Tiberieum); no. 58 (the Hadrianeum).

the first century is unknown. The second became the subject of a sixth-century inscription, which commemorated its restoration under the auspices of the provincial governor (*comes*) and a local dignitary (*pater civitatis*). By then, even if the Hadrianeum originated as a temple honouring Hadrian it came to denote a new type of alliance between the emperor and the city, both sharing the same creed.

Such investments in the cityscape and in its past reflected the continuing interest in maintaining and perhaps even expanding Caesarea's public space. Characteristics of urban identity, theatre, amphitheatre, stadium, hippodrome, government complexes, warehouses, remained in the landscape, their presence suggesting a contrast between figures of speech and figurative representations.[30] To Christians, Jews, and Samaritans the city gave a language in which they spoke of their Caesarea. Hence, in Eusebian terms, as in those of the Palestinian Talmud, the city was given a unity that expressed an underlying dissension.

Among the peculiarities of the history of the Palestinian capital in late antiquity was a discourse concerned with fierce allegiance to Christianity mingled with a deep sense of insecurity. Although the fourth century proved on the whole uneventful in that part of the empire, a citizen of Caesarea nevertheless felt compelled to hoard a collection of 99 gold *solidi* which methodically spanned the reigns of the Christian emperors of the century, from Constantius II to Honorius, with the notable exception of Julian.[31] Whether terrified by rumours regarding an imminent Hunnic invasion (CE 395) or merely concerned to preserve his precious gold for safer times, the unknown owner of the treasure took the trouble to place the coins in a cavity carefully cut into a large millstone whence they were unearthed, in the late twentieth century, in the course of a probe beneath a mosaic floor in one of the more affluent residential suburbs of the city.

---

[30] The latest building enterprise known is recorded on an inscription dated between 546 and 606 which refers to the construction of an enclosure wall, stairway, and monumental entrance of an unspecified building, a project organized by Flavius Strategius and financed by public funds, Lehmann and Holum, *Inscriptions*, no. 60.

[31] Peter Lampinen, 'The Gold Hoard of 47-c. Solidi found in 1993', in K. Holum, A. Raban, and J. Patrick (eds.), *Caesarea Papers* 2 (JRA Suppl. Ser. 35; Portsmouth 1999), 368–88.

Compulsion, however, might not have originated with a threat of Hunnic violence but rather with that of hunger and thirst, twin threats of life in late antiquity. Caesarea's water supply depended on two aqueducts, a low-level one constructed between 345 and 380, and a two-channelled high-level aqueduct, repaired in the mid 380s by the proconsul Flavius Florentius.[32] Water came at a premium, as did food in times of drought, and prudence was rewarded with a conscientious saving.[33] Scarcity of basic commodities was a cyclical affair in urban centres.[34] In the sixth century, for example, Jerusalem was hit by a drought for five years, beginning with the year 516 which coincided, not accidentally according to Cyril of Scythopolis, with the deposition of Elias, the city's Chalcedonian bishop.[35] After Jerusalem the famine hit Caesarea between 530 and 536. There the governor did much to alleviate the pressure.[36] If a story in the Palestinian Talmud can serve as a guide, astute farmers, more familiar than their urban counterparts with the vagaries of nature, built water reservoirs on their property and sold water for hefty prices in times of scarcity.[37]

Such episodes produced a paradox. Although Caesarea was the most important urban centre of Palestine in late antiquity its reconstructed history amounts to a series of accidents. In addition, only about 15 per cent of the area inside the late ancient walls has been thus far excavated. Nor is it easy to reconcile literary snippets with material data. The city's harbour (Sebastos) is a case in point. A main source of Caesarea's livelihood and wealth during the early Roman

[32] Diane Everman, 'Survey of the Coastal Area North of Caesrea and of the Aqueducts: Preliminary Report', in Vann (ed.), *Caesarea Papers*, 181–93; Y. Porath, 'Pipelines of the Caesarea Water Supply System', *Atiqot* 10 (1990), 100–10 (Heb.).

[33] On water as merchandise in times of famine, Dauphin, *La Palestine byzantine*, 508–9. In general, E. Patlagean, *Pauvreté économique et pauvreté sociale à Byzance* (Paris 1977).

[34] Eusebius (ref. in Lieberman, 'Martyrs', 434–5) states that peole used to eat 'hay', a statement corroborated by the contemporary (?) midrash of *Genesis Rabbah* 20.10, 194: 'Rabbi Isaac (late 3rd/early 4th cent.) said: [the verse] "You shall eat the grass of the field (Gen 3:18)" refers to the present day generations when a man plucks from his field and eats it while it is still herbage'.

[35] *Vita Sabae* 159.7–10.

[36] P. Mayerson, 'Choricius of Gaza on the Water Supply System of Caesarea', *IEJ* 36 (1986), 269–72.

[37] *PT AZ* 5.11.

era and, according to Josephus, spectacular by any standard, the harbour appears to have experienced a sharp decline in late antiquity, the culmination of a long process of silting, sinking, and ultimate disappearance. Around 500 the harbour became the subject of a rhetorical lament pronounced by an eloquent speaker from Gaza, Caesarea's rival port. Seeking to extol the virtues of the emperor Anastasius (491–518), Procopius of Gaza provided a single snapshot of Caesarea's harbour in late antiquity:

Since the port of the city named after Caesar had fallen into bad condition in the course of time and was open to every threat of the sea, no longer deserving in fact to be classed as a port but retaining from its former fortune merely the name, you (Anastasius) did not overlook the city's need and her constant laments over the ships which frequently, escaping the sea, were wrecked in the harbor. Those who awaited the cargoes suffered pitifully as they witnessed the destruction of what they most needed without being able to help. Thanks, however, to your good will, the city is rejuvenated and receives ships with good courage and is full of the necessities.[38]

Whether Procopius' praise of Anastasius' endeavour on Caesarea's behalf further indicated that the harbour entrance's had already been blocked and the channel sealed by around 500 remains controversial.[39] What Procopius' words suggest is that by the early sixth century, if not long before, Caesarea's harbour had lost its stature and possibly some of its use. Excavations of warehouses and granaries in the city point to the continuous prosperity of the Caesarean trading community. Around 300, for example, it was necessary to convert a Mithraeum into *horrea* and to construct other storage facilities along the inner harbour. A century later the volume of commercial operations required the addition of storage space on

---

[38] *Procopius Gazaeus Panegyricus in Imperatorem Anastasium* (*PG* 87c. 2817, 19), Engl. trans. in Levine, *Roman Caesarea*, 18.
[39] R. L. Hohlfelder, 'Caesarea's Master Harbor Builders: Lessons Learned, Lessons Applied?' in Raban and Holum (eds.), *Caesarea Maritima. Retrospective*, 88 n. 24. A. Raban, 'The History of Caesarea's Harbors', *Qadmoniot* 37 (2004), 20–1 (Heb.) points to evidence supporting Procopius' testimony but only in the north part of the inner harbour, an enterprise which he further connects with the construction of the octagonal church. By the mid-6th cent., the fate of the main harbour was sealed due to natural causes and operations were removed to an alternative harbour built along the naturally protected bit of the coast in the south portion of the city.

the north side of the *decumanus*.[40] North-west of the inner harbour an area of warehouses was reconstructed around 400 to serve the needs of the imperial *annona* for another two centuries, till the very eve of the Muslim invasion.[41] It appears, then, at least on the basis of archaeological finds, that the harbour witnessed renewed activity in the fourth century after a period of decline in the second and third centuries, and that it resumed, in part, the international scale which it had assumed in the first century.[42]

These dynamics appeared to belie the gloomy image that Procopius drew of the maritime traffic along the port. Yet, the planting of what might have been a chapel honouring Saint Paul in the heart of a commercial zone corroborates the rhetoric.[43] Perhaps a pious official wanted to surround himself with tokens of piety while hard at work. More likely this was a space converted from secular to sacred usage. Such 'conversions' from storage to sanctuary would not have been the first in the history of the Caesarean warehouses. Some time in the first century a Herodian warehouse had been transformed into a Mithraeum, reverting to its original usage around 300.[44]

Urban vagaries lent a veneer of comfort and conformity to diversity and disagreements. Caesarea's Jewish community, a vibrant minority in the provincial capital, boasted synagogues, schools, and at some point perhaps even a talmudic academy.[45] None has been

[40] J. Patrich, 'Warehouses and Granaries in Caesarea Maritima', in Raban and Holum (eds.), *Caesarea Maritima: Retrospective*, 146–73.

[41] K. G. Holum, 'The Excavations of the Combined Caesarea Expedition: The Warehouse near the Harbor and Temple Mount', *Qadmoniot* 128 (2004), 104 (Heb.). My gratitude to Ken Holum for sending me a copy of his article.

[42] J. P. Oleson, 'Artifactual Evidence for the History of the Harbors of Caesarea', in Raban and Holum (eds.), *Caesarea Maritima: Retrospective*, 376.

[43] The existence of which has been conjectured on the basis of fragments of ecclesiastical furniture as well as of painted Christian inscriptions, and of a bread stamp decorated with a cross and bearing the inscription: 'blessing of the Lord upon us and of Saint Paul'. See J. Patrich, 'A Chapel of St Paul at Caesarea Maritima?' *LA* 50 (2000), 363–82, without, however, venturing to date the structure. Di Segni, 'A Chapel of St Paul at Caesarea Maritima? 383–400, esp. 397–9 on the bread stamp, once again without dates.

[44] J. A. Blakely, *The Joint Expedition to Caesarea Maritima Excavation Reports*, vol. 4: *The Pottery and the Dating of Vault I. Horeum, Mithraeum, and Later Uses* (Lewiston, NY, 1987), 101–4.

[45] E. Habas, 'The Halachic Status of Caesarea as Reflected in Talmudic Literature', in Raban and Holum (eds.), *Caesarea Maritima: Retrospective*, 454–68.

identified thus far in the course of decades of excavations. Fragments of scholarship, like those of the great library of Origen in the city, have eluded modern probing. The sole Caesarean synagogue thus far unearthed was discreetly located at the edge of the city in a north-western corner.[46] It was a smallish structure (18 × 9 m.), its vicissitudes reflecting those of its parishioners. Constructed in the fourth century, it was destroyed soon after, rebuilt after a hiatus of a century, and then altered in the sixth or seventh century.[47] Among finds from the excavated site were two remarkable items, a plaque containing a list of the twenty-four priestly courses, and a community chest with thousands of coins.[48] The former demonstrated the continuing attachment of priests to their traditional divisions and duties long after the destruction of the Temple in Jerusalem; the latter hinted at the extent of communal resources. Wealthy Jews, and Christians, in Caesarea as elsewhere, like the local *archisynagogus* Beryllos son of Justus, contributed to various enterprises mostly by donating architectural elements such as mosaic floors.[49] Inscriptions commemorating such donations highlighted the universality of the relationship of power, wealth, and public benefaction while underscoring religious and ethnic rivalry.

Concrete evidence of the cultural alignment of local investments in sacred edifices invites reflection on patterns of communal exchange in the city. The historian Theodore Anagnostes recorded how, at the start of the fifth century, Caesarean Jews rioted and killed some Christians but managed to escape punishment through allegedly bribing the provincial governors, who were later dismissed by the

---

[46] Beyond the perimeters of the city in the Caesarean hinterland Jews were able to participate in services in local synagogues, such as the one in Shuni-Maioumas where an inscription bearing a menorah also proclaimed the unity of the divine, asking for assistance on behalf of Judah the Elder, L. Di Segni, 'A Jewish Greek Inscription from the Vicinity of Caesarea Maritima', *Atiqot* 22 (1993), 133–6, dating it to CE 408/9 and eadem, 'The Date of the Binyamina Inscription and the Question of Byzantine Dora', *Atiqot* 25 (1994), 193–6. Lehmann and Holum, *Inscriptions*, no. 137.

[47] Levine, *Roman Caesarea*, 41.

[48] Ibid. 44–5.

[49] Levine, 'Synagogue Officials: The Evidence from Caesarea and its Implications for Palestine and the Diaspora', in Raban and Holum (eds.), *Caesarea Maritima: Retrospective*, 392–400. Lehmann and Holum, *Inscriptions*, nos. 78–84 (the synagogue).

empress Pulcheria.[50] No reason was divulged for this action. The increasing religiosity of the imperial court contributed to the reshaping of the contours of an uneasy rather than irenic coexistence in Palestine.[51] A century later (CE 555) Jews and Samaritans burnt churches in the city, this time killing the provincial governor and destroying his property.[52] Whether these events were a sign of a deeper durable reality marking a fundamental confrontational streak in the urban fabric of late ancient Caesarea is likely, although difficult, to ascertain. While narratives left in men's memories etched moments of confrontation, buildings betrayed a tangible realization of civic life of uneventful continuity.

By rabbinic reckoning the largest ethnic community in Caesarea around the middle of the fourth century was that of the Samaritans.[53] Many Samaritans served on the staff of the provincial governor and must have wielded considerable influence in the city.[54] It is inconceivable that they did not have at least one synagogue yet, thus far, Samaritan sacred spaces have not been identified on the ground. One possible exception is an apsidal structure, orientated eastward towards Mount Gerizim, and unearthed in the Roman *praetorium* (government complex).[55] Whether or not this building was a Samaritan synagogue remains conjectural. A Greek inscription devoid of specific religious symbols was found in situ, calling for the salvation of one Silvanus and one Nonna, perhaps an eminent Samaritan couple.

Around Caesarea Samaritan villages proved the mainstay of the all-important rural hinterland. Samaritans were producers of wine which the rabbis did not allow Jews to drink unless it came in a sealed vessel, although the Samaritans' pious devotion to Scripture and to

---

[50] *HE* 336 (ed. G. C. Hansen), dated to c.439, Eng. trans. in Holum, 'Identity and the Late Antique City' (above, n. 8), 168. The action of the rebellious Jews, whose numbers may have been swollen by Samaritans, probably introduced disruption along the *cursus publicus*, if the inscription honouring Nonnus with a golden statue followed the restoration of order. Lehmann and Holum, *Greek and Latin Inscriptions*, no. 25; F. Millar, *A Greek Roman Empire* (Berkeley 2006), 143. See also above, Ch. 3.

[51] On imperial laws on Jews and Judaism, Linder, *Roman Imperial Legislation*, and Sivan, 'Canonizing Law' (2002), 213–25.

[52] Malalas, *Chron.* 15; Theophanes, *Chron.* a. 6048, see also Ch. 3, 140–1.

[53] *PT Dem.* 2.1 (22c).

[54] *PT AZ* 1.2 (39b) (c.300). [55] Patrich, 'Chapel of Saint Paul', 370.

monotheism was repeatedly attested, not least on a late ancient bronze ring, bearing biblical verses, from a village in the region of Caesarea.[56] In the course of repeated periods of unrest between CE 484 and 572, the livelihood and lives of numerous Samaritan farmers were forfeited, thus severing the co-dependency between city and countryside. The fact that in 555 Samaritans and Jews collaborated against the Christian establishment in Caesarea implies a pattern of shifting alliances and the growing vulnerability, if not despair of minorities, especially in the Palestinian capital. Christian sources recording these events as riots and rebellions depicted an urban space in which cycles of attack, punishment, and revenge modulated communal relations, a rhetoric calculated to de-neutralize social complexity into terms of Christian victory and non-Christian defeat.

Life in sixth-century Caesarea, when not threatened by ethnic riots, was punctuated by the twin problems generally besetting cities, namely fire and hunger, which could easily kindle widespread panic and sedition. In a panegyric honouring Stephanus, the provincial governor, the panegyrist referred to the case of a major fire that broke out one evening when the agora was full of people.[57] Commotion ensued. Stephanus promptly quelled both conflagrations, natural and man-made. He was fully aware that these could easily result in a *tarache*, or major urban disturbance, as had happened not infrequently in such situations. The city bred demagogues who were ready to incite crowds to acts of violence on such occasions.[58]

In so volatile an atmosphere pressure to conform to imperial ideology was increasing. Procopius of Caesarea registered the presence of crypto-Christians, converted under duress, perhaps from paganism, perhaps from Judaism or Samaritanism:

Those indeed who lived in my own Caesarea, and in other cities, deciding it silly to suffer harsh treatment over a ridiculous trifle of dogma, took the

---

[56] *PT AZ* 5.44; *BT AZ* 31a listing Samaritan settlements in close proximity to 'pagan' settlements. On these and the ring inscriptions in Samaritan script, Adam Zertal, 'The Samaritans in the District of Caesarea', *Ariel* 48 (1979), 110–16.

[57] Choricius Gazae III.39–43. L. Di Segni, 'The Involvement of Local, Municipal, and Provincial Authorities in Urban Building in Late Antiquity', in J. Humphrey (ed.), *The Roman and Byzantine Near East* (Ann Arbor 1995), 312–32.

[58] Al. Cameron, *Circus Factions, passim.*

name of Christians in exchange for the one they had borne before, by which precaution they were able to avoid the perils of the new law.[59]

The analysis is open to other interpretations. Late ancient urbanites acquired a reputation for facile conversion, yet once converted they were genuine enough Christians.[60] The imperial court, a cynosure of piety in the mid-sixth century, sought to unite the divided empire under the flag of Christianity at the expense of cultural, communal, and religious diversity. Procopius' words, recorded in a work not meant for wide circulation, could have expressed either approval or censure of the outcome of imperial decrees against non-Christians in general and Caesarean converts in particular.

2. SEPPHORIS IN THE GALILEE

At the dawn of the fourth century Caesarea's columns demonstrated a visceral disaffection with the treatment of Christian citizens. But masonic shows of solidarity were hardly the preserve of Mediterranean coastal orbits. When the Jewish sage Yose ben Halafta died, it was reported that the gutters in the Galilean town of Sepphoris flowed with blood.[61] A gesture of empathy with communal grief was expressed by pouring red into the streets, the result not of violent bloodshed but of the end of a natural life-cycle. In either case the city took its place as the author of an act of civic ceremony. At Sepphoris, as in Caesarea, the mute gesture of pillars and gutters joined in a social activity that paid tribute to humans with exceptional merit. Like the urbanites themselves, essential elements of the city's architecture mourned the passing of a notable wit or celebrity martyrs. Such exceptional collaboration further highlighted divergence from the norm. In the Christian version of events the mourning pillars

---

[59] *Anec.* 11.32, trans. R. Atwater, available via Paul Halsall website.

[60] G. Bonner, 'The Extinction of Paganism and the Church Historian', *JEH* 35 (1984), 339–57 on categories of converts in urban and rural settings.

[61] *BT San.* 109a; Cf. *BT Moed Kat.* 25b and *PT AZ* 3.42c; Lieberman, 'Martyrs', 401 n. 33. R. Yose ben Halafta lived around the middle of the 2nd cent. and taught at Sepphoris, Stemberger, *Introduction to the Talmud and Midrash*, 85 (the third generation of Tannaites).

emphasized the negation of final rites in honour of the dead. In the Jewish version, the gushing gutters added hue to the crowds that must have followed the last journey of the famed sage.

In the lower Galilee life in urbanized centres such as Sepphoris (Diocaesarea), a town roughly located between Tiberias and Caesarea, hinted at a tenor modulated by the dominant presence of one religion, Judaism. Towards the end of the fourth century Epiphanius of Salamis, formerly of Palestinian Eleutheropolis, described Sepphoris as predominantly Jewish, an impression to which narratives focusing on the town's sages and synagogues in the Palestinian and the Babylonian Talmuds, as well as in late ancient midrashic literature, lent unqualified support.[62] Recent excavations have unearthed an urban grid based on a unique intermingling of public and private edifices without, it seems, due regard to distinctions of wealth and class, an arrangement that suggests, perhaps, an archetype of a Galilean Jewish town.[63] Of the numerous synagogues that had once dotted the town, at least according to the Palestinian Talmud (*Kilayim* 9.32), there is, however, hardly a trace. Two are known to date and a single one, at the very outskirts of town, has been fully excavated (below).

By one estimate the territory of Sepphoris extended over 60 hectares, exactly half the size attributed to Caesarea.[64] It does not appear to fit the rabbinic category of a 'metropolis' (*kerach*), generally regarded as a walled space inhabited largely by non-Jews and consequently requiring the act of prayer twice, once upon entry and once upon exiting the city.[65] Since Sepphoris appears to have been predominantly Jewish even through late antiquity, it may be

---

[62] *Pan.* 30.11 (written in the 370s) depicts Sepphoris, together with Tiberias, Nazareth, and Capernaum as localities where, allegedly in the 330s, it was impossible to plant churches since their inhabitants were exclusively Jewish. Cf. Eusebius, *Mart. Pal.* 29. S. Miller, *Studies in the History and Traditions of Sepphoris* (Leiden 1984).

[63] Weiss and Netzer, 'Sepphoris during the Byzantine Period', 81–8; eidem, 'Architectural Development', 117–30. Here one ought to mention the reservations of J. Neusner regarding the very essence of urbanism in rabbinic *Weltanschauung* or rather what he terms the lack of engagement between rabbis and cities, 'The City as Useless Symbol in Late Antique Judaism', in *Major Trends in Formative Judaism*, i: *Society and Symbol in Political Crisis* (Chico, Calif., 1983), 29–40.

[64] M. Broshi, 'The Population of Western Palestine in the Roman-Byzantine Period', *BASOR* 236 (1980), 5.

[65] *PT Ber.* 9.5 (14b).i

accurately characterized as a middling town.[66] By rabbinic standards, towns of this sort evolved as a result of specific circumstances:

It must be built only in a locality with water and already populated. If there is no source of fresh water it must be brought from elsewhere. If the population decreases, settlers must be brought from elsewhere. Should the number dwindle, priests, levites and Israel must be added.[67]

The Palestinian Talmud further forbade Jews to live in a town which did not have a medical doctor (*rofé*), public bathhouse, a municipal kitchen garden (*ginunita shel yerek*),[68] not to mention a synagogue, a study hall, aqueduct, and wells. Whether such an ideal proved compatible with Sepphoris' actual development in late antiquity is difficult to ascertain. Life tended to steer a middle course between the requirements of Jewish law and the dictates of local circumstances.

Modern excavators of Sepphoris have associated significant structural changes with two events, a devastating earthquake in 363 mentioned in a spurious letter of Cyril of Jerusalem, and a Jewish revolt suppressed by Gallus which had taken place a dozen years before.[69] In spite of insinuations in Christian sources regarding the complete destruction of Sepphoris in the wake of the latter, the remains in situ do not disclose a deliberately violent hand.[70] The impression gained is that a catastrophe, man-made or, more likely, naturally occurring, hastened a building and expansion boom in one part of the city and ushered decline in another part where poorly planned buildings included installations interpreted as *miqvaot* or

[66] Z. Yeivin, 'On the Medium Size City', *Eretz Israel* 19 (1987), 59–71 (Heb.). See also S. Krauss, 'The Metropolis (*kerach*), City (*ir*) and Village (*kefar*) in the Talmud', *He-Atid* 3 (1923), 50–61 (Heb.).

[67] *T. Makkot* 3.8.

[68] *PT Kidd.* 4:12; cf. *BT Ned.* 49b.

[69] Brock, 'A Letter Attributed to Cyril', *BSOAS* 40 (1977), 267–86; Weiss and Netzer, 'Architectural Development of Sepphoris', 117–30. For a new evaluation of the revolt, M. Warner and Z. Safrai, 'Hoards and Revolts: The Chronological Distribution of Coin Hoards in Eretz Israel during the Roman and Byzantine Periods', *Cathedra* 101 (2001), 71–90. Fourth-cent. layers of destruction in the Galilee are regularly associated with the Gallus revolt, Y. and Y. Tepper, *Beit Shearim. The Village and Nearby Burials* (Tel Aviv 2004) (Heb.), *passim*.

[70] Weiss and Netzer, 'Sepphoris during the Byzantine Period', 81–9 and for what follows.

ritual baths, a sure sign of Jewish presence.[71] In late antiquity Sepphoris, like Caesarea, boasted a theatre, in use till the end of the
fourth/early fifth century; colonnades; public baths, and public
buildings graced with colourful mosaics celebrating events such as
the Nile festival, a theme that ran through the Palestinian urban
fabric from the Mediterranean to the Galilee.[72]

The assumption of Christian writers that in the middle of the fourth
century Sepphoris spearheaded an anti-imperial revolt draws an image
of a collectivity ready to stake its chances on a remote possibility of life
without Rome. Conformism and confrontation may appear as two
sides of the Sepphorean Jewish community. Material evidence conjures
up the city, at the dawn of late antiquity, as a space with a Jewish
identity that allowed for acceptance of other discourses. What nurtured
a sense of citizenship in this region of Palestine was a shared appreciation of aesthetics, intellectual and artistic, that espoused an astonishing breadth of Judaism in the Galilee of late antiquity. Public spaces
such as a civic basilica and a synagogue reinforced the impression of a
collectivity poised between textual strictures and civic culture.[73]

Sepphorean Jews were well documented in rabbinic literature, at
least till the closure of the Palestinian Talmud *c*.400.[74] During the
residency of the Jewish patriarch in the city two local clans vied over
the order of salutation of this dignitary. In this war of words one well-
connected group labelled its rivals *pagani*, an appellation intended
to underline the others' rusticity and ignorance.[75] The rabbis who

---

[71] See the note of scepticism of H. Eshel, 'A Note on "Miqvaot" at Sepphoris', in
Archaeology and the Galilee, 131–3.

[72] Cf. Choricius of Gaza on the Nile in one of the churches dedicated by bishop
Marcianus in the 6th cent., R. W. Hamilton, 'Two Churches at Gaza as Described by
Choricius of Gaza', *PEQ* (1930), 190.

[73] Z. Weiss, *The Sepphoris Synagogue: Deciphering an Ancient Message through its
Archaeological and Socio-Historical Contexts* (Jerusalem 2005).

[74] A. Büchler, *The Political and Social Leaders of the Jewish Community of Sepphoris
in the Second and Third Centuries* (London 1909); and F. Manns, 'Un centre Judéo-
chrétien important: Sepphoris', in idem, *Essais sur le Judéo-Christianisme* (Studium
Biblicum Franciscanum 12; Jerusalem 1977), 165–93. On the value of the Talmud as a
source of social history, J. Neusner, *Judaism in Society: The Evidence of the Yerushalmi*
(Chicago 1983).

[75] *PT Hor.* 3.7 (48c). On this passage see S. S. Miller, 'Those Cantankerous
Sepphoreans Revisited', in R. Chazan *et al.* (eds.), *Ki Baruch Hu: Ancient Near Eastern,
Biblical and Judaic Studies in Honor of Baruch A. Levine* (Winona Lake 1999), 550–1.
My thanks to Stuart for sending me copies of his Sepphoris articles.

recorded this episode designated the accused rather than the accusers as the learned group, thus emphasizing that social merit was to be judged by standards of devotion to learning rather than to proto-cols.[76] Public encounters between sages and 'minim' ('heretics'? 'apostates'? 'deviants'? pagans? Jewish-Christians?) became a source of empowerment for winners of such shows.[77] Stepping beyond the boundaries of intellectual exchange, the arena of public disputations provided a stage for talent shows that could not have taken place in conventional spaces of learning, praying, or teaching.[78] They threw into relief antitheses that existed in the urban landscape, especially rabbinic 'orthodoxy' and its opposition. To win in public, sages were not averse even to the use of magic.[79] In Sepphoris, as elsewhere in Palestine, these verbal encounters highlighted multiple systems of values that emerged in modes of both coexistence and conflict.[80]

Encounters between sages and the community at large reflected both the close connection and the distance between the learned and the untutored in town. In a public sermon Hanina, a famed sage (3rd century), interpreted the sin of the generation of the flood (Gen. 6) as theft. He elaborated his hypothesis, on the basis of Job 24: 16 (*in the dark they break into houses; by day they shut themselves in. They do not know the light*), by providing an extensive description of thieving

[76] Although the rabbis were fully aware of the power wielded by well-connected individuals and officials. See the warnings issued to the effect that only a fool would insult a curial in the market place since revenge could be swift and harsh, *Sifre Deut.* 309 (in Miller, 'Cantankerous Sepphoreans Revisited', 557).

[77] S. Miller, 'The Minim of Sepphoris Reconsidered', *HTR* 86 (1993), 377–402; idem, 'Further Thoughts on the Minim of Sepphoris', in *Proceedings of the Eleventh World Congress of Jewish Studies*, B1 (Jerusalem 1994), 1–8. Idem, 'New Perspectives on the History of Sepphoris', in E. M. Meyers (ed.), *Galilee through the Centuries: Confluence of Cultures* (Winona Lake 1999), 151, rejects the identification of Minim with a Jewish-Christian sect while emphasizing the lack of evidence for a Christian presence in Sepphoris prior to the late 4th/early 5th cens. On rabbinic indifference to nomenclature of precise categories of non-rabbinic circles, A. Segal, *Two Powers in Heaven* (Leiden 1977), *passim*.

[78] Lim, *Public Disputation, passim*.

[79] *PT San.* 7, 25d, attributes a list of magical skills, such as the ability to transform a melon into a deer, to famed rabbis who used these in public in order to demonstrate their superiority to local 'minim'.

[80] Cf. the famed clash between Porphyry of Gaza and Julia, his Manichaean opponent, M. Scopello, 'Julie, manichéenne d'Antioche', *Antiquité tardive* 5 (1997).

techniques. Thus the esteemed rabbi informed his listeners that in order to find desired objects by night a thief would smear them with balsam by day so as to sniff the odour as a guide after dark. Soon after the sermon no less than 300 burglaries took place.[81] The wrathful congregation confronted the sage with the effect of his words: 'You have shown the thieves the way'. His response was: 'How could I have known that you are thieves?'[82]

Nor did rabbis lose an opportunity to castigate uneducated priests, repeatedly asserting that tithes should have been allocated not to Torah-ignorant priests but rather to their learned rabbinic counterparts. Because Sepphoris attracted at least one of the priestly *mishmarot* (courses) that had officiated in the Jerusalem Temple before CE 70, the souvenirs of the great revolt of 66–70, and of Sepphoris' pro-Roman stand, lingered on, as did priestly claims of communal status.[83] Their presence might have stimulated a competition over the respective standing of sages and of priests in the community, an aspect of internal tensions known from elsewhere in Palestine.[84] Among the rabbis themselves innumerable disagreements created the impression of an implicit, as well as explicit, acerbic discourse, studded with dissension.

To recognize a Jewish Sepphoris beyond the narratives of the Palestinian Talmud largely depends on literary projections and on considerations of material culture, above all on interpretations of the much-publicized excavated synagogue. The latter is a smallish building in the north of town, seemingly far from the hustle and bustle of the centre. Its mosaics featured a profusion of biblically related themes including an aniconic Helios composed of a chariot drawn

[81] *PT Maas. Sheni* 5.55d;

[82] *BT San.* 109a links the Sepphoris sermon not with Hanina but with Yose ben Halafta. Miller, 'Those Cantankerous Sepphoreans Revisited', 565. In general, S. S. Miller, 'R. Hanina bar Hama at Sepphoris', in *Galilee in Late Antiquity*, 175–200.

[83] *PT Taan.* 4.68d. It seems, however, that the move only occurred in or after the 3rd cent., D. Trifon, 'Did the Priestly Courses Move from Judah to Galilee after the Bar Kokhba Revolt?', *Tarbiz* 59 (1990), 77–93 (Heb.).

[84] L. I. Levine, *The Rabbinic Class in Roman Palestine in Late Antiquity* (Jerusalem 1989), *passim*, and C. Hezser, *The Social Structure of the Rabbinic Movement in Roman Palestine* (Tübingen 1997), *passim*, for an analysis of the intricacies of intra-rabbinic relations. See also M. Swartz, 'Sage, Priest, and Poet: Typologies of Religious Leadership in the Ancient Synagogue', in S. Fine (ed.), *Jews, Christians, and Polytheists in the Ancient Synagogue* (London 1999), 101–17.

by four horses and surrounded by twelve months each inscribed in Hebrew letters; scenes from Genesis (the angels' visit to Sarah and Abraham and the 'sacrifice' of Isaac); and panels enclosing implements of Temple worship (Exodus 25) and depicting the dedication of the Tabernacle and the consecration of Aaron as high priest (Exod. 29).[85] Whether or not all these images would have accorded with rabbinic notions of Jewish monotheism or of the decoration appropriate to a place of worship, and the modern debate is far from settled, the synagogue's imagery was timeless and by then 'depaganized'.[86] If indeed pictures expressed polemics, the small synagogue appeared a contested institution, one of several set up to serve a diversity of interests.

Sepphoris' synagogal zodiac-cum-Helios, an imagery that gained considerable popularity in synagogues in late antiquity, hinted at an orchestration of ornamentation that promoted 'ecumenism' rather than particularism. In the predominantly Christian context of Gaza a Sol-Helios, twelve eagles, and the twelve labours of Hercules, formed the centrepiece of a public clock in the city's market place. The inauguration of this remarkable urban feature for measuring time was celebrated in a eulogy delivered on the occasion by a local rhetor (Procopius) (*c*.500) whose Christian piety, in spite of a lavish use of pagan imagery and metaphors, was not to be doubted.[87]

Devout Jews who wanted to worship in the Zodiac-Helios synagogue had to walk a fair way from the city centre. Along the route they would have passed a basilica where water festivities were held. Its colourful mosaics featured Amazons, hunters, a centaur, and Nilotic landscapes which included a procession heading to Alexandria to

[85] S. S. Miller, ' "Epigraphical" Rabbis, Helios, and Psalm 19', *JQR* 91 (2004), 27–76. My thanks to Stuart for sending me a copy.

[86] For a summary of interpretations, Miller, ' "Epigraphical Rabbis" ', 71–2. M.-D. Herr, 'Hellenistic Influences within the Jewish City in Eretz Israel from the Fourth to the Sixth Centuries', *Cathedra* 8 (1978), 90–4 (Heb.), concluded that the apex of Hellenization within the Jewish urban context was on the eve of the Muslim conquest.

[87] F. M. Abel, 'Gaza au VI siècle', *RB* 40 (1931), 10. For a reconstructed image of the clock H. Diels, 'Über die von Prokop beschreibene Kunstuhr von Gaza', *Abhandlungen der königlich preussischen Akademie der Wissenschaft, Philosophisch-Historische Klasse* 7 (1917), 1–39; D. Rehaut, 'Le Récitation d'ekphraseis: une réalité vivante à Gaza au VIe siècle', in C. Saliou (ed.), *Gaza dans l'Antiquité Tardive*, 197–220. See also R. Talgam 'Measuring Time in Sixth-Century Gaza: The Clock Ekphrasis of Procopius', in J. Patrich, L. Di Segni and R. Talgam (eds.), *Festschrift in Honor of Yoram Tsafrir* (forthcoming).

celebrate the Nile festival. Both synagogue and basilica belonged to the same era (early 5th century).[88] The likely participation of Jews in water feasts in this largely Jewish town suggests coexistence of images drawn from a pluralistic culture within a single dominant community. Whoever donated the mosaics had the satisfaction of seeing their names inserted into inscriptions that added texts to images. An Aramaic inscription in one synagogue commemorated the contribution of one Rabbi Yudan son of Tanhum, a member of a family that left its trace elsewhere in town.[89] A Greek inscription honoured the artists who designed and executed the Nile mosaics. While Aramaic seems to have been the preferred linguistic medium of engraving contributions to synagogues, the Sepphorean experience of heterogeneity was reflected in bilingual, Aramaic–Greek funerary inscriptions, such as the one that had once graced the tombstone of the brothers Yaakov and Nahum, sons of Rabbi Hosochi.[90]

The synagogue in northern Sepphoris was orientated towards the north-west and not towards Jerusalem. The orientation, seemingly in ignorance of the centrality of Jerusalem, appears to defy the dominance of normative rabbinic Judaism in Jewish spaces.[91] So did amulets which promoted the well-being of their wearers when appeals to rabbinic 'holy men' failed to halt a pestilence or to produce rain to alleviate a drought.[92] Women further embellished costly golden

---

[88] But see G. W. Bowersock, 'Inscriptions in the Nile Festival Building at Sepphoris: The House of the Daughter of the Governor (AD 517–18?) and her Husband Asbolius Patricius', *JRA* 17 (2004), 764–6.

[89] R. M. Nagy et al. (eds.), *Sepphoris in Galilee: Crosscurrents of Culture* (Raleigh 1996), p. 177 no. 25 (late 4th/early 5th cent.); Weiss and Netzer, *Promise and Redemption*; Naveh, *On Stone and Mosaic* (Tel Aviv 1978), 51–2, no. 29 (Heb.); F. Huttenmeister and G. Reeg, *Die antike Synagogen in Israel*, i (Wiesbaden 1977), 402–3.

[90] *Sepphoris in Galilee*, p. 186, no. 33, no date given.

[91] Z. Weiss, 'The Sepphoris Synagogue Mosaic and the Role of Talmudic Literature in its Iconographical Study', in L. I. Levine and Z. Weiss (eds.), *From Dura to Sepphoris* (JRA Suppl. 20; 2000), 28.

[92] Nagy, *Sepphoris in Galilee*, pp. 191–2, no. 39; C. T. McCollough and B. Glazier-McDonald, 'Magic and Medicine in Byzantine Galilee: A Bronze Amulet from Sepphoris', in D. R. Edwards and C. T. McCollough (eds.), *Archaeology and the Galilee* (Atlanta 1997), 143–9 (late 4th/early 5th); eidem, 'An Aramaic Bronze Amulet', *Atiqot* 28 (1996), 161–5. PT *Taan.* 3.66c on the people confronting the sage Hanina with an accusation of indifference to their plight, and with ineffectual prayers.

jewellery with universal symbols of fertility like cornucopia which served to invoke divine succour in cases of sterility.[93]

At an unknown date, perhaps around 500, two churches, each twice the size of the northern synagogue, were added to the landscape, both strategically placed along the intersection of the *cardo* and the *decumanus*. Greek inscriptions in situ commemorated an enterprising bishop named Eutropius who dominated the public scene by virtue of his elevated ecclesiastical position and because he engineered a restoration of one of the city's main thoroughfares.[94] To him one may ascribe a venture of scriptural exegesis—the association of the town with Anna and Joachim, the parents of Mary, for which there is no trace in the New Testament.[95] Eutropius and the two centrally located churches provided eloquent testimony of changed communal balance.[96] The building 'fever' which seized Sepphoris' Christian establishment extended to the city's fathers who erected a basilica in 517/518 and restored the city's gate which they further embellished with imperial portraits.[97]

Because synagogues and churches were active social centres where morality was preached and Scripture expounded they formed important landmarks in any given locality. Their administrators were visibly aspiring to positions of prominence.[98] When the inhabitants of a village near Sepphoris sought a community leader they looked for a man who could preach, judge, administer the synagogue, and teach the Bible and Oral Law.[99] A sage was duly recommended by the patriarch. At Sepphoris, the texts that commemorated the

---

[93] Nagy, *Sepphoris in Galilee*, p. 233 no. 140 showing a gold headpiece with a portrait of a 'tyche' on the central medallion, flanked by cornucopia and a branch of a plant, and bearing the inscription 'charis', grace or mercy, property perhaps of a Christian woman.

[94] E. Netzer and Z. Weiss, 'New Evidence for Late Roman and Byzantine Sepphoris', in J. Humphrey (ed.), *The Roman and Byzantine Near East: Some Recent Archaeological Research* (JRA Suppl. 14; Ann Arbor 1995), 170–3.

[95] *Anon. Plac.* 4 (Wilkinson, *Jerusalem Pilgrims*, 131).

[96] Weiss and Netzer, 'Sepphoris during the Byzantine Period', 84.

[97] M. Avi Yonah, 'A Sixth Century Inscription from Sepphoris', *IEJ* 11 (1961), 184–7; Di Segni, 'The Involvement' (1995), 318.

[98] S. Fine, *This Holy Place: On the Sanctity of the Synagogue during the Greco-Roman Period* (Notre Dame 1997); M. L. White, *Building God's House in the Roman World* (Baltimore 1990); L. I. Levine, *The Ancient Synagogue* (New Haven 2000).

[99] *PT Yevamot* 12.7, 13a quoted in L. I. Levine, 'The Sages and the Synagogue in Late Antiquity', in idem (ed.), *The Galilee in Late Antiquity* (New York 1992), 211 (*c*.200 CE).

achievements of Eutropius suggest a similar array of functions and responsibilities. The Palestinian Talmud characterized these sages in one apt phrase as 'guardians of the city', anticipating, it seems, the birth of the urban office of the *defensor civitatis*.[100] By the sixth century it was readily assumed that bishops shared the management of a city with civil administrators.[101] Herein lies the true parting of urban ways in patterns of relationships between rabbis and their towns, on the one hand, and bishops and theirs on the other. The rise of local ecclesiastical establishments, the unabashed support lent by the imperial court to Christian institutions, and the imperial legislation against minorities weakened the Jewish fabric of towns like Sepphoris.

Thus far the sole excavated synagogue in Sepphoris has been dated to the fifth century. Sepphoris' churches apparently belonged to the sixth. Were these the sole samples of evolving urban architecture? A recent and still ongoing debate regarding the dates of Galilean synagogues has reassigned the 'classically' inspired type, like Capernaum's synagogue, to the sixth century rather than the fourth.[102] Another view espouses a modified chronology with an early (2nd–3rd century) 'original' dismantled, moved, and reconstructed in a different Galilean location in late antiquity.[103] A third has advanced a similar process of remodelling but in the same location.[104] Without delving into the fine points of stratigraphy, pottery styles and dates,

---

[100] *PT Hagigah* 1.7, 76c, quoted in Levine, 'The Sages', 211; on *defensores*, CTh. 1.29 (368 CE) with Seeck, PW I. 8 (1901), 2365–71; Jones, *Later Roman Empire*, *passim*; and idem, *The Greek City from Alexander to Justinian* (Oxford 1940), *passim*; Dan, *The City*, 103–8 (Heb.).

[101] Dan, *The City*, 90–102 for an excellent summary of the duties/responsibilities/ privileges of the urban episcopate.

[102] Magness, 'Synagogues in Ancient Palestine', in Levine (ed.), *Continuity and Renewal*, 507–25; and the reservations of J. Strange, 'Some Remarks on the Synagogues of Capernaum and Khirbet Shema', in Levine (ed.), *Continuity and Renewal*, 530–43, who reassigns Capernaum to the 5th cent. The best basic survey of synagogues, churches, and architecture in general in late ancient Palestine remains Y. Tsafrir, *Eretz Israel from the Destruction of the Second Temple to the Muslim Conquest: Archaeology and Art* (Jerusalem 1984) (Heb.).

[103] Z. Maoz, 'The Synagogue at Capernaum: A Radical Solution', in J. Humphrey (ed.), *The Roman and Byzantine Near East*, ii (1999), 137–48, supported by M. Aviam, 'The Ancient Synagogue at Bar'am', in Levine (ed.), *Continuity and Renewal*, 552.

[104] G. Foerster, 'Has there indeed been a Revolution in the Dating of Galilean Synagogues?', in Levine, *Continuity and Renewal*, 526–9; and idem, 'The Ancient Synagogues of the Galilee', in Levine (ed.), *The Galilee in Late Antiquity* (1992), 289–319.

coins and their locations, and a host of other evidence marshalled in favour of one analysis or another, it is possible to observe a change of taste with regard to relations between believers and sanctuaries. In late antiquity much of the investment in synagogues was put into embellishing their floors with mosaics, rather than decorating their exteriors. At Sepphoris, Beth Alpha, Rehob, Naaran, and even along the east bank of the Jordan at Hammath Gader, the change was palpable.[105] Whether the new emphasis on interiors was conceived under the influence of Christian sacred architecture, or as a creative solution to imperial strictures that limited the extent and magnificence of non-Christian sanctuaries is difficult to ascertain. Perhaps the very use of a medium that had become intimately associated with churches reflected a defiant adoption of Christian ecclesiastical aesthetics.[106]

To exalt the martyrs of Caesarea and the sages of Sepphoris Christian and Jewish rhetoric borrowed an urban, basically pagan, vocabulary that seemed entirely appropriate. Such a strategy altered the usual meaning of words in relation to acts as did the use of paradigmatic elements like the Zodiac and Helios within a synagogal context or of the Nile within a basilica meant to serve the general public in Palestinian cities. What emerges from a quick perusal of the material culture of the hilly Galilean town of Sepphoris, as of the metropolis of Caesarea Maritima, is a realm where a series of constraints, imperial and communal, external and internal, ruled relations between groups and among them.

Conventional virtues urged the wealthy to register their affluence in terms of advertised donations to public causes. Simultaneously, an antithesis between communal regulations, be they Samaritan, Jewish, pagan, or Christian, and a tradition dictated by historical circumstances, associated law with compulsion. An appreciation of the function of visual representations in sacred, private, and civic structures suggests ecumenism as well as competition that required the mobilization of all one's energies against the other's hegemony

---

[105] For a typology, Foerster apud Levine, *Galilee*, 289–319.

[106] Nearly every dig of a church unearths a mosaic. See Ovadiah, *Corpus of the Byzantine Churches in the Holy Land*; and Y. Tsafrir, *Ancient Churches Revealed* (Jerusalem 1993).

precisely by harnessing opposing forces to a different locution. In the final analysis neither city proved startlingly original or even innovative. Tensions and factions might have been more ordinary than the spade reveals. After all, what was a city if not an amalgam of contradictions held together by ideals that expressed what the city wanted to be in its own eyes? And even then, could a visitor tell the difference between one city and another?

3. GAZA: A MEDITERRANEAN EMPORIUM

Responding to these questions Barsanuphius advanced a somewhat pessimistic view of urban subtleties:

Many there are who listen constantly to descriptions of some city, but when they happen to enter it, they do not know that it is the city in question.[107]

From his monastery near the thriving city of Gaza this ascetic 'great old man' recast relations between humans and urban landscapes as a mirror of the 'remembrance' of God by the believer. His sombre reflections on urbanism stood in striking contrast with the optimistic depiction of his sixth-century contemporary, Choricius of Gaza, whose panegyric of Marcianus, the city's bishop, suggested a distinction conferred by ecclesiastical structures:

Follow me toward the east gate of the city. If you descend from here and turn to the left you will no longer need to be shown the way since the church is plainly visible and is sufficient guide itself.[108]

Indeed, the central church of the city, the Eudoxiana, established on the ruins of Gaza's most famous temple, the Marneion, would have been hard to miss. It boasted thirty-two columns of brilliant green Carystus marble, the gift of the empress Eudoxia to Gaza's bishop.[109] These would have been inscribed with Eudoxia's name, a practice

---

[107] V 328 (ed. S. N. Schoinas, Volos 1960), trans. in F. Neyt, 'A Form of Charismatic Authority', *Eastern Churches Review* 6 (1974), 60.
[108] *Laudatio Marc.*, trans. in Hamilton, 'Two Churches at Gaza as Described by Choricius of Gaza', 187.
[109] Marc. Deac. *VP* 84.

familiar from Gaza's Jewish orbit.[110] And although the Gazan church pillars did not shed tears over the blood of martyrs they did radiate light like diamonds, symbolizing not only the immediacy of the remote imperial court but also the powerful presence of the Christian god amidst the city's near-extinct divinities.

The history of the city of Gaza in late antiquity invokes the fatality of an irreversible evolution. There it is possible to trace with remarkable exactitude the internal struggles that provided the basis for ultimate Christian hegemony. In Gaza the notion of Christianity was constituted on the basis of growth, be it that of a religious community or of a category. Around 400 the main tasks of the bishop of the city's fledgeling congregation were to orchestrate concerted attacks against the city's temples while concomitantly marshalling resources to invest in magnificent ecclesiastical structures. In the sixth century citizenship came to mean an awareness of a heritage that combined classical lineage with Christian legitimacy.

Gaza provides the modern historian of Palestinian cities in late antiquity with the ability to focus on two formative moments in its history, the appearance of Christianity in the city (mid–late fourth century) and the parallel prosperity of monasticism and rhetoric in the late fifth and early sixth century. To study these two periods one needs to examine the *topoi* of secular celebrations and of monastic advice, religious and civic stimulants, and the 'reality' behind the words of hagiographers and of skills teachers. It is, therefore, necessary to discern beyond expressions of day-to-day functioning of the city both the positive manifestations of brotherly amity as well as the shaping of polemics and the role of contestants in society.

On the Madaba map which guided pilgrims in the sixth century through a Christianized Palestine, Gaza, only partially preserved, was marked by colonnaded streets, white pillars, and red roofs.[111]

---

[110] C. A. M. Glucker, *The City of Gaza in the Roman and Byzantine Periods* (BAR IS 325; Oxford 1987), 144 no. 37. The inscription, in Aramaic and Greek, was enclosed in a tabula and embellished with Jewish symbols (menorah, shofar, lulav, and etrog), Naveh, *On Mosaic and Stone*, 90–1, no. 54*.

[111] See the Franciscan cyberspot on Gaza in the Madaba map as well as the verbal images projected in Choricius' contemporary orations, C. Saliou, 'L'Orateur et la ville: réflexions sur l'apport de Chorikios à la connaissance de l'histoire de l'espace de Gaza', in eadem (ed.), *Gaza dans l'Antiquité Tardive* (Salerno 2005), 171–95 with useful summarizing diagrams on pp. 193–4. Cf. Gaza in the Umm al-Rasas (Kastron

A careful scrutiny of the Madaba mosaic would yield the schematic delineation of the city's forum, the theatre, and a cruciform church, perhaps the Eudoxiana. Missing were the city's three public bathhouses and circus. The most striking illustration of Gaza's standing, situation, wealth, and culture in late antiquity was confirmed in a recent discovery of an ecclesiastical complex of imposing dimensions (c.400 square metres). Unearthed in Jabaliyah near Gaza, the church contained an array of colourful mosaics and a series of embedded inscriptions.[112] Decorative themes included bucolic and hunting scenes, the latter featuring exotic African animals. The Greek inscriptions, seventeen in number, both dedicatory and funerary, were dated according to the era of Gaza, conventionally between CE 496 and 732.[113] Taken together, script, images, and architecture projected an equilibrium that had been achieved through combat.[114] The mosaics, as well as numerous literary testimonies of Gaza's own intelligentsia, underlie a process of Christian appropriation of both the city space and of the city's history. By identifying themselves with traditions of euergetism, Christian donors reconstituted the civic along the lines that had been shaped by opposition.

Recent analyses of the changing faces of urbanism around the Mediterranean have traced the lineaments of erasure and violence as gleaned from physical remains, imperial laws, and occasional references in literary sources.[115] Gaza provides the observer with the one complete, albeit controversial narrative that presented the

Mefaa) St George's mosaic, better preserved but less distinct. On the stoas as shelter from rain, Choricius, II. 32.

[112] M.-M. Sadek, 'Gaza', *Les Dossiers d'archéologie* (Jan.–Feb. 1999), 46–67, esp. 62–4 and 66–7.

[113] C. Saliou, 'Gaza dans l'antiquité tardive: nouveaux documents épigraphiques', *RB* 107 (2000), 390–411. Gaza's inscriptions were collected by Glucker, *The City of Gaza*, 115–63.

[114] In a way, the combat never ceased as is clear from contrasting interpretations of a mosaic found in 1965 and featuring an Orpheus-like figure, a Hebrew inscription, and a Greek one commemorating the wood merchants Menahem and Yeshua, sons of Isses (CE 508/9). As recently as 1999 it was claimed that the archaeological context was 'très certainement d'une église' (Sadek, 61). See, however, A. Ovadiah, 'The Synagogue at Gaza', in *ASR*, 129–32.

[115] B. Caseau, '*Polemein Lithois*: La Désacralisation des espaces et des objets religieux païens durant l'Antiquité tardive', in M. Kaplan (ed.), *Le Sacré et son inscription dans l'espace à Byzance et en Occident*, 61–123 with ample bibliography. See also H. Saradi, 'The Dissolution of the Urban Space in the Early Byzantine Centuries: The Evidence of the Imperial Legislation', *Symmeikta* 9 (1994), 295–308.

deeds and the debates, the ideology and the rhetoric that launched
the trail of deletion. The story is a biography of Porphyry, Gaza's
bishop from 395 to 420, containing a record of 'his righteous deeds',
'wars', and of how he 'stood up against leaders and champions of the
madness of idols', (*VP* 1–2).[116] The themes appeared conventional
although in setting up Porphyry as an embodiment of the warriors of
antiquity, Mark, his disciple and biographer, diverged from the
models of a 'monk-bishop' as set up by theologians like Basil of
Caesarea. Mark's protagonist was not just a man of holiness and
miracles but one directly responsible for a profound change of urban
planning.[117] Following Porphyry and Mark, Gazans formed their
views of what constituted a successful episcopate on the basis of
their contribution to urban planning.[118]

Mark focused on Gaza as a seat of urban strife not only between
Christians and pagans, the main theme of the biography, but
also among Christians. Already the choice of Porphyry had been
mired in controversy, with the few Christians in the city unable
to decide among themselves on the right person for the job and
consequently empowering a delegation to appeal to the metropolitan
in Caesarea (*VP* 11).[119] What they primarily wanted was a man

[116] On the numerous problems facing the users of Porphyry's biography, Grégoire
and Kugener, *Marc le Diacre, Vie de Porphyre*. See the important review by F. Nau in
ROC 27 (1929–30), 422–41, esp. on the importance of P(arisinus), 431–2. Peeters, 'La
Vie géorgienne de Porphyre de Gaza', 65–216 detected a Syriac source for both the
Greek and Georgian version, a conclusion supported by Z. Rubin, 'Porphyrius of
Gaza and the Conflict between Christianity and Paganism in Southern Palestine', in
G. Stroumsa and A. Kofsky (eds.), *Sharing the Sacred*, 31–66 but opposed by
Trombley, *Hellenic Religion and Christianization*, 246–82. The debate regarding the
value of Mark's information continues. Recently, P. Chuvin, 'Christianisation et
résistance des cultes traditionnels', in *Hellénisme et christianisme* (Villeneuve d'Ascq
2004), 17–27 espouses its authenticity. For the quote see the English translation of
G. F. Hill, conveniently available via www.fordham.edu/halsall.
[117] Basil of Caesarea, *Ep.* 161; E. J. Fedwick, *The Church and the Charisma of
Leadership in Basil of Caesarea* (Toronto 1979); P. Brown, *Poverty and Leadership in
the Later Roman Empire* (Hanover, NH, 2002).
[118] Choricius, *Laud. Marc.* i and ii and below. Choricius further refers to a church
as 'naos', a term often used to apply to pagan temples or Jewish synagogues, rather
than the common 'ecclesia'. Y. Ashkenazi, 'Sophists and Priests in Late Antique Gaza
according to Choricius the Rhetor', in B. Biton-Ashkeloni and A. Kofsky (eds.),
Christian Gaza in Late Antiquity (Leiden 2004), 195–208, esp. 203 n. 39.
[119] The appointment, from Caesarea and not from Jerusalem, suggests the
predominance of the former, at least at this point, Honigmann, 'Juvenal', 216.

who would lead a fight against 'the idolaters' in the city (*VP* 12). What they got was a bishop who got to know his enemies even before setting eyes on his seat. Porphyry's initial advent to Gaza was paved, literally, with thorns, prickles, stench, and smoke (*VP* 17), all of which eloquently expressed the disenchantment of pagan dwellers of the villages around Gaza with the initiatives taken by their Christian neighbours.

Porphyry's first actions were to pit his newly gained authority against the city's well-entrenched divinities. When Gaza was stricken with one of the periodic droughts that Palestine habitually experienced, rain suddenly started on the day of the Nativity. On the eleventh day of the downpour, which coincided with the Epiphany (6 January), Porphyry conducted a celebration with much fanfare (*VP* 21) as though the rain was due solely to him and to his god. When a misunderstanding regarding funeral practices (*VP* 22–5) occurred, Porphyry caused the man who had been considered dead to rise in order to engage in a public debate regarding the appropriate urban place for burial. Emboldened by these successes Porphyry asked for an imperial writ authorizing the demolition of Gaza's temples (*VP* 26). Although it fell within the scope of imperial legislation regarding pagan sanctuaries the request was premature.[120] The rest of Porphyry's biography was consequently devoted to the elaboration of a single theme, the closure and destruction of Gaza's temples. The crowning glory in this protracted war was the demolition of the Marneion, Gaza's most venerable temple and the symbol of its adherence to the 'old ways' (i.e. polytheism).

Porphyry's belligerence delineated how, at the dawn of the fifth century, an individual cleric could position himself as a projection of what a citizen ought to be in an urban space undergoing transformation. The case of Gaza was brought to Constantinople. It was initially presented at the imperial court as civil strife in which pagans prevented Christians from paying taxes and from holding

[120] CTh. 16, with Y. Janvier, *La Législation du Bas-Empire romain sur les édifices publics* (Aix-en-Provence 1969). Caseau, '*Polemein Lithois*', 70, notes the confusing and confused character of the imperial legislation which simultaneously ordained the cessation of sacrifices and the closure of temples while protecting some temples as important features of urbanism.

office (*VP* 40).[121] When this failed to convince the emperor to condone the erasure of major monuments, Porphyry enlisted a vision in which the construction of a church rather than the demolition of temples was presented as a solution (*VP* 45). On paper he provided a list of requests which included : permission to overturn the city's idols, privileges for the holy church and for the Christians, and permanent revenue to support the city's ecclesiastical establishment (*VP* 46). The empress Eudoxia, Porphyry's staunch ally at the court, managed to elicit a decree that called for 'the overturning of all the temples unto their foundations and their burning with fire' (*VP* 51). She also donated a substantial amount of money to build a church in the middle of Gaza (*VP* 53).

Upon returning to Gaza Porphyry directed his destructive energy at a marble statue of a naked Aphrodite. The sculpture had graced a major intersection where it drew the homage of many women who kindled lamps and burnt incense to the goddess in the hope of securing harmonious marital relations (*VP* 59).[122] Among those who sought support from the goddess of love were also Gazan men whose marriage had fallen apart. Mark claimed that when their prayers went unanswered they blamed a demonic Aphrodite for the failure of their marriage and promptly converted to Christianity. Others, likewise feeling deceived by this deity for endorsing what turned into a disastrous marriage, bore the goddess a grudge (*VP* 60). There was, therefore, general jubilation when the statue suddenly fell just as Porphyry, armed with the imperial writ, marched through the centre of the city. Aphrodite, the maker and breaker of marriage, broke into many pieces, killing two bystanders who were mocking the Christian procession (*VP* 61). The episode was promptly interpreted as a match in which one divinity (Jesus) had vanquished another (Aphrodite).

---

[121] Hence the well-known response of Arcadius (*VP* 41: 'the city is idolatrous but well disposed in the matter of tax payment') which addresses precisely the issue raised by Porphyry. Curiously, Mark and subsequent editors of the text make no reference to civic insubordination in the city to which Soz. *HE* 7.15 and Theodoret, *HE* 5.21 allude in conjunction with Theodosius' laws on the closure of temples.

[122] Cf. the so-called Fountain of the Lamps at Corinth where over 4,000 votive lamps were recovered, mostly dating from the mid-5th to the 6th cents., and offered by pagans, Christians, and probably Jews too, R. Rothaus, 'Christianization and De-Paganization: The Late Antique Creation of a Conceptual Frontier', in Mathisen and Sivan (eds.), *Shifting Frontiers in Late Antiquity* (Aldershot 1996), 299–308, esp. 302–3.

Because the stakes were so high supporters of the new order converted public resentment at decisions resulting from dreams allegedly
sent by the gods into a paradigm of new politics. The establishment
of Aphrodite at a crossroads symbolized both the possibility of domestication yet also the threatening presence of familial discord.
The demonic had been chased out at the sight of the cross, as though
the two, Aphrodite and Jesus, had engaged in a war. The intersection
once presided over by Aphrodite's statue no longer constituted a
threat in connection with her cult. Instead, the space remained
empty, a reminder of a victory that ultimately remained hollow.
But the goddess continued to exert fascination over Gazans, her
beauty providing inspiration for a learned excursus on the intimate
links between poetry and painting. Its author, Procopius, a Gazan
rhetor of some note in the late fifth/early sixth century, incorporated
the goddess's praise in an oration celebrating the city's ancient
Rose Festival, possibly relying on a painting in one of the city's
public baths.[123]

After the fall of Aphrodite the imperial army arrived. A massive
departure of pagans followed, their empty homes promptly appropriated to billet soldiers (*VP* 63). In charge of the entire operation
was a man bearing the auspicious name of Cynegius, perhaps a
relative of the Praetorian Prefect who in the late 380s demonstrated
his Christian zeal by destroying temples throughout the provinces
under his authority.[124] The imperial letter given to Porphyry was read
in public, causing a loud protest throughout the ranks of pagans and
cheers through the Christian crowd (*VP* 63). The noise must have
been considerable, especially with the added din of the club-beating
which the soldiers administered to protesters. Following the recital
the troops, accompanied by laymen looking for loot, applied themselves to the demolition of temples and of statues, including the

[123] Procopius Gazae, *Epistulae et Declamationes*, ed. A. Garzya and R.-J. Loenertz
(Rome 1963), Dec. III, p. 89; G. Downey, 'The Christian Schools of Palestine:
A Chapter of Literary History', *Harvard Library Bulletin* 12 (1958), 310–11.
G. A. Kennedy, *Greek Rhetoric under the Christian Emperors* (Princeton 1983),
171–4, who further suspects Procopius of paganism and of late conversion, a suspicion that appears without foundation. Choricius, in his funeral oration, elaborates on
his teacher's (Monophysite?) Christianity and on his piety of long standing.
[124] *PLRE*; J. Matthews, *Western Aristocracies and Imperial Court* (Oxford 1975);
Fowden, 'Bishops and Temples', *JTS* (1978).

sanctuary of Aphrodite which may have been located not far from the already fragmented statue of the goddess (*VP* 64).[125]

Since the priests at the famed Marneion had the foresight to bar the temple and to hide its treasures, those engaged in the anti-pagan campaign had to stop in order to debate the 'best' way to deal with this beautiful structure—should it be dug out, burnt, or purified and reconsecrated a church? (*VP* 66). An unexpected mediation of a child reconciled the discordant voices. The infant called for the burning of a temple where human sacrifices allegedly had taken place. The strategy to ensure the success of the enterprise was pronounced, still by the child, in both Aramaic and Greek, the latter a language of which he had been entirely innocent (*VP* 66, 68). The intervention exorcised the incipient conflict by invoking Jesus as an omnipresence in situations which threatened to divide the congregation. And although the child's denunciation of the rituals at the Marneion countered the information provided in the *Vita* itself, his words decried the temple as a violation of urban space and of humanity.

The burning of the Marneion echoed the conflictual tone that Porphyry had adopted from the dawn of his episcopate, as did, apparently, nature itself. A tribune who had attempted to curbed the soldiers' desire to destroy the sanctuary was himself struck by a beam. His death in the course of duty replicated the episode that had hastened the demise of Gazan pagans through the falling Aphrodite (*VP* 70). Porphyry, aspiring to create a new order out of the erasure of the old, ensured the complete annihilation of his victims, consigning books and statues to fire and to latrine (*VP* 71). He further ordered that marble from the Marneion be incorporated in a pavement to be trodden under the foot of men, women, dogs, swine, and beasts (*VP* 76). More than other acts of war this marble metamorphosis acted as a reminder of the incompatibility of the pagan and the Christian city. For decades after the disappearance of the temple women and men did not walk upon the marbles (*VP* 76). The pavement, once a subject of a religious constraint, sealed the commitment of Gazan pagans to Marnas.

---

[125] It is, in fact, unclear what precisely had befallen the temples. Zacharias of Mytilene, a native of Gaza, claims that during the revolts against Zeno in 484–8, pagans in Gaza hoped to reopen their closed temples. W. E. Kaegi, *Byzantium and the Decline of Rome* (Princeton 1968), 67.

To complete the dismemberment of the temples and to inaugurate a Christian urban order, Porphyry devoted his energy to the construction of a church on the very location where the Marneion had stood. The decision ignited controversy among Christians regarding the shape of the church, a dispute that only the arrival of an imperial letter finally settled (*VP* 75). The distant yet decisive voice of the empress herself (Eudoxia) determined the architecture of the nascent sanctuary. In situating the Eudoxiana atop the Marneion Porphyry re-enacted a milestone in the history of Christianity in Palestine. Under Constantine the temple to Aphrodite in Jerusalem had been razed to make room for the church of the Holy Sepulchre.

As the congregation eagerly lent its collective energy to the construction of the church a miracle enlivened the proceedings, highlighting the paradigmatic role of the future Eudoxiana. Three little boys who had fallen into a well were found unharmed, each bearing the sign of the cross on their bodies (*VP* 80–3). The incident, according to Mark, exacerbated the tension between pagans and Christians (*VP* 83). It ensured that no reconciliation, at least under Porphyry, was to be effected. The arrival of the pillars, the gift of the empress, ushered in another mob scene with Christians rushing to the coast to bring the columns to the site of the burnt temple (*VP* 84).

In the *Life of Porphyry*, Mark constructed the story of the new church as a constitutive element in the history of both Porphyry and the entire Christian community at Gaza. Laced with miracles, the five years it took to erect the structure delimited the identity of Gazan Christianity, defining its position and status as central within the existing urban space. Once complete, the church continued to engender disagreement. Porphyry's own flock accused him of building a structure that by far exceeded the needs of the congregation (*VP* 93). A land dispute further reignited enmities between pagans and Christians, forcing Porphyry and Mark to leave Gaza hastily (*VP* 96). The situation necessitated the intervention of the provincial governor and the army (*VP* 98).

None of Porphyry's actions was calculated to contain hostilities. The efficacy of his methods, as exemplified in the burning of the Marneion, paved the way for the eradication of Gaza's pagan past. Its uniqueness must be emphasized. Although Porphyry became adept at court intrigues, the sole piece of imperial legislation of which the

Vita made mention were Eudoxia's orders which, strictly speaking, were not laws. Mark avoided all reference to imperial constitutions, such as CTh. 16.10.15 of 399 that ordained the preservation of ornaments of public works.

At the turn of the fifth century the episcopal road to power in Gaza's urban setting was paved with clashes composed of physical violence and public debates won through the sudden demise of opponents.[126] In the course of his episcopate Porphyry set in motion a process of Christianization that had, in fact, been in full swing in the region decades before he came to Gaza. Already under Constantine the citizens of Maioumas, Gaza's harbour town, converted to the imperial creed.[127] The town, or rather its bishop, Peter the Iberian, became prominent in the second half of the fifth century when the war between supporters and opponents of Chalcedon threatened to split the Palestinian Church. There had been little room for heresy in the narration of Porphyry's exploits.[128] But Peter aligned himself with the Monophysite camp in a campaign in which the monks of Gaza had the centre stage.

A culture that nurtured learning, asceticism, and doctrinal debates flourished in the monastic hinterland of Gaza from the middle of the fourth century through to the sixth.[129] Intimately intertwined

[126] The debate with Julia, a Manichee or pagan philosopher is the best-known example, *VP* 85–91.

[127] On Maioumas' conversion and the detachment from Gaza's jurisdiction, Soz. *HE* 2.5; Eus. *VC* 4.38. Subsequently the port-polis lost its status but maintained its independent episcopate. Ironically, when Gaza's bishop claimed jurisdiction over Maioumas-Constantia (early 5th cent.) in order to reincorporate it into its see, Constantia's citizens objected on the grounds that it was unseemly for a Christian bishop to revert to an arrangement introduced by a pagan emperor (Julian), Soz. *HE* 5.3. In the 5th cent. Maioumas disappears from the ecclesiastical lists, perhaps due to being amalgamated with the see of nearby Anthedon (F. M. Abel, *Géographie de la Palestine* (repr. Paris 1967), 203). Constantine or Constantius II, also carved out of Gaza's hinterland the Saltus Constantinianus, an action likewise aimed at undermining the pagan authorities of Gaza and at strengthening its fledgeling Christian community, L. Di Segni, 'The Territory of Gaza: Notes of Historical Geography', in Biton-Ashkelony and Kofsky, *Christian Gaza*, 52–3.

[128] Another notable omission is a reference to pagan attacks on the monks Zeno and Aiax, the former the head of the church at Maioumas, the latter of the one in Bithulion, Soz. *HE* 7.28.

[129] On Gazan monasticism, Biton-Ashkelony and Kofsky (eds.), *Christian Gaza in Late Antiquity* (2004) and eidem, 'Gazan Monasticism in the Byzantine Period', *Cathedra* 96 (2000), 69–110 (Heb.).

with Egyptian monasticism, the ideology of the desert was imported
to Palestine through Hilarion, a native of Thabatha and a disciple
of Anthony.[130] After his Egyptian initiation Hilarion settled in the
'neighbouring wilderness' of Gaza.[131] Hostility to cities, hubs of polytheism, guided his decision to avoid Gaza and city scenes altogether
(*VH* 33).[132] Yet, to gain adherents he had to leave his cell on choice
dates of the urban calendar. In the course of a horse race Hilarion
appeared on the Gazan racing stage as a sorcerer who de-demonized
a charioteer in exchange for conversion (*VH* 16), and as the inspir-
ational source for another who subsequently claimed that his victory
in the races amounted to a demonstration of Jesus' superiority over
'the people of Gaza who were enemies of God' (*VH* 20).

Tension ran high between monastery and city. In this climate
power relations between the monk and the urban community produced an uneasy balance made even more fragile with the growth of
the monastic community in the rocky 'desert' fringe of the city (*VH*
29, 31). Supporters of the charioteer who had lost the race to
Hilarion's protégé sought to kill the ascetic (*VH* 20). The vision of
Hilarion walking along the beach and humming psalms (*VH* 22) did
not endear him to Gazans, who preferred to present a benevolent and
cheerful face to visitors rather than that of dishevelled old men
strolling in solitude while talking to themselves. During Julian's
reign, citizens of Gaza presented a petition to the emperor asking
him to endorse Hilarion's execution (*VH* 33). The monk managed to
flee Palestine but his monastery was burnt.

When Hilarion died in Cyprus (CE 371) his body was brought to
Maioumas, whence it was carried in a stately procession, attended by
crowds of monks and towns folk, to be buried in his old monastery in
the Gazan hinterland (*VH* 46). A similar scene of general lamentation and grief was enacted 120 years later when the body of Peter the
Iberian, once bishop of Maioumas and before that a denizen of
another monastery near Gaza, was carried back to his brothers
(CE 491, *VPetri* 142–3).

Peter had once believed that the Gazan hinterland with its monastic establishments would offer him the peace he had craved when

---

[130] According to Jerome's *Vita Hilarionis*. Sozomen, *HE* 3.14; 5.10 also provides
some biographical details.
[131] *VH* 14.   [132] Ibid.

he fled Jerusalem and an intended ordination which Juvenal, Jerusalem's bishop, sought to confer. Peter chose to enter a life of asceticism and contemplation at a monastery between Gaza and Maioumas.[133] Juvenal's nephew, then bishop of Maioumas, managed to ordain Peter thus adding a reluctant priest to the ecclesiastical ranks in his town (CE 445, *VPetri* 51). Neither the nearby Mediterranean nor the city nor even the monastery provided Peter with the desired tranquillity. Gaza's monastic hinterland, led by formidable figures like Silvanus, Zeno, and Isaiah (450–90), became a target of monastic pilgrimage (*Pleroph.* 8) and a strategic centre in the war which the monks of Palestine waged on behalf of the Palestinian Monophysite camp against Chalcedonian dogmas and Juvenal of Jerusalem.[134]

Little in the monastic course of these ascetics appears to account for the passions which inflamed monasteries throughout Palestine during the so-called Monophysite controversy in the half-century following Chalcedon (CE 451). The outlines of this monastic 'insurrection' are well known.[135] Palestinian bishops and abbots who had attended the ecumenical council presented Juvenal, upon return, as a 'Nestorian' traitor. The Jerusalemite bishop changed camps during Chalcedon to rejoin imperial and Chalcedonian 'orthodoxy'. The reception planned for him at Caesarea promised to be anything but welcoming. Throngs of monks converged on the city, intent on confronting Juvenal. The governor decided to bar them from entering the city, convincing the monks instead to celebrate the Eucharist in the church of the Apostles which was outside the city walls (*Pleroph.* 10). Counselled by prudence, Juvenal escaped Caesarea

[133] *VPetri* 49.
[134] *Vita Isaiae Monachi*, ed. W. W. Brooks (CSCO Scriptores Syri, ser. 3, 25; Louvain 1907), 3–16. D. Chitty, 'Abba Isaiah', *JTS* 22 (1971), 47–72.
[135] For the term and a brief overview, Honigmann, 'Juvenal', 247–57; L. Perrone, *La chiesa di Palestina e le controversie cristologiche* (Brescia 1980), 89–103. On monastic violence in general, M. Gaddis, *There is no Crime for those who have Christ: Religious Violence in the Christian Roman Empire* (Berkeley 2005); K. M. Hay, 'Evolution of Resistance: Peter the Iberian, Itinerant Bishop', in Allen *et al.* (eds.), *Prayer and Spirituality in the Early Church*, 159–68; J.-E. Steppa, *John Rufus and the World Vision of Anti-Chalcedonian Culture* (Piscataway, NY, 2002) and the review by C. B. Horn, in *Hugoye: Journal of Syriac Studies* 6 (2003), downloaded from *www.syrcom.cua.edu/Hugoye*.

all the way back to Constantinople. A colleague, Severianus of Scythopolis, was killed, apparently by hired assassins. The rebellious monks turned to Jerusalem where they burnt houses, killing many including a deacon, and opened prisons allowing, it was claimed, criminals to escape.[136] Amidst the riots, the monks found time to elevate the Monophysite Theodosius to the see of Jerusalem.

A democratization of episcopal elections was introduced. The new Jerusalemite bishop appointed, or rather confirmed, candidates who had been proposed by popular vote (*VPetri* 54). Among these was Peter the Iberian, priest and now elected bishop of Maioumas.[137] The Monophysite euphoria lasted less than two years. Juvenal returned with an army and was reinstated with much bloodshed. 'Order' was restored in the holy city and elsewhere in Palestine, bolstered by an imperial decree of 453 which ordered the expulsion of all the bishops appointed by Theodosius during his brief tenure. The deposed Jerusalemite patriarch fled to the Sinai. Peter the Iberian, although the only one allowed to stay, preferred to leave for Egypt. Hostility to Juvenal fanned the flames of the Monophysite movement even in the absence of its leaders.[138] To placate the populace that continued to espouse the Monophysite cause the emperor later granted amnesty to all exiled 'saints' or monks, hoping to restore unity in Palestine.

Calculated to effect reconciliation these measures did not extinguish the conflict. More than half a century after Juvenal's death he was still portrayed as a devil in disguise, a traitor to orthodoxy and defiler of the holy city.[139] While vilifying Juvenal, John Rufus, the author of a biography of Peter the Iberian, presented his protagonist as a perfect foil to the ambitious prelate of Jerusalem.[140] In these two

---

[136] Marcian, *Letter to the archimandrites and monks of Aelia*, in *ACO* II.1, pars III, p. 125.2, with Honigmann, 249. The monks alleged that they had been innocent of violence which citizens of Jerusalem and strangers had committed.

[137] Only the laura of Euthymius in the Judaean desert remained loyal to Chalcedonian orthodoxy (Cyril of Scythopolis, *Vita Euthym.* 27).

[138] Honigmann, 'Juvenal', 262–6 and *passim*.

[139] *Plerophoriae*, with Honigmann, 'Juvenal'.

[140] J.-E. Steppa, 'Heresy and Orthodoxy: The Anti-Chalcedonian Hagiography of John Rufus', in Biton-Ashkelony and Kofsky, *Christian Gaza*, 92–3, with H. Bacht, 'Die Rolle des orientalischen Mönchtums in den kirchenpolitischen Auseinandersetzungen um Chalkedon (431–519)', in A. Grillmeier and H. Bacht (eds.), *Das Konzil von Chalkedon* (Würzburg 1953), ii. 193–314, esp. 292.

characters, the Monophysite monk of Gaza's 'desert', and the Chalcedonian patriarch of Jerusalem, it is possible to perceive the embodiment of the monastic rift that tore Palestine. One anecdote illustrates this contradiction. While Juvenal proved unscrupulous in his dealings with Palestinian opponents, not stopping at using soldiers to shed their blood, Peter had originally preferred not to join the monks who rushed to Caesarea to persuade the returning Juvenal to return to orthodoxy.[141] Only a heavenly vision which authorized the campaign as divinely ordained drew Peter from his cell to Caesarea. His arrival was timely. The commander of a military detachment was about to launch his well-armed men against the agitated Monophysite monks when Peter drew back his hood, revealed his face, and threatened the officer with divine fire. Surprised, the man prostrated himself and asked Peter's pardon. The surprise was occasioned through recognition. The commander had known Peter back in the days when the Iberian prince was a favourite at the imperial court.

Because religious wars had been congenial in Gaza the adoption of this form, conflictual and common, by opponents of Chalcedon, suggests that this was a customary manner of settling credal differences. Gaza's hinterland became the last stronghold of Palestinian Monophysites.[142] In the monastic establishments that dotted the region the fight for 'orthodoxy' continued largely through a vast propaganda programme transmitted and diffused by literati like Zacharias (Rhetor) and Severus (of Antioch).[143] Gaza's active role as a centre of anti-Chalcedonian activities led by Peter the Iberian and Abba Isaiah of Egypt ensured that the history of the city and its environs became the stories of great men.

In the annals of early Gazan Christianity the city became a target of reform, an unrepentant site of gods who no longer had a rightful space in the landscape.[144] Yet, in the sixth century the people of Gaza still

---

[141] *Pleroph.* 56.

[142] A. Kofsky, 'What Happened to the Monophysite Monasticism of Gaza', in *Christian Gaza in Late Antiquity*, 183–94 and for what follows.

[143] Y. Hirschfeld, 'The Monasteries of Gaza: An Archaeological Review', in Biton-Ashkelony and Kofsky, *Christian Gaza in Late Antiquity*, 61–88, for a list of monasteries.

[144] Van Dam, 'From Paganism to Christianity at Late Antique Gaza', 1–20.

celebrated the winter solstice festival which had originally honoured Dionysos/Bromios, god(s) of seeds and wine.[145] Like the Helios clock, the Brumalia marked a step in an immutable agrarian calendar. As late as 692 a church council named the 'infamous Dionysos' as the one not to be mentioned during the season of trampling grapes in the press. The antiquity of the celebration could not be ignored. The Bromalia probably involved chariot races as did the Consualia which, in Gaza, had marked the first appearance of Hilarion on the urban scene as a champion of Christian charioteers.[146]

Chalcedon's bitter adversaries would have been stunned at the evolution of Gaza in the sixth century. Funeral orations, panegyrics honouring military men, epithalamia, speeches celebrating festivals, orations defending mimes, as well as speeches commemorating the dedication of a church could have been produced by one and the same man whose Christian piety was lauded centuries later by no less a personality than the bishop of Constantinople.[147] Behind the irenic and prosperous façade which the city presented in its late ancient heyday lurked the unifying power of money. Like elsewhere in Palestine in the late fifth and early sixth centuries Gaza and its hinterland enjoyed an extraordinary level of prosperity, stemming primarily from the city's reputation as a producer and exporter of top-quality wine.[148] One contributing factor to Gaza's outstanding viticulture was monastic demographics. In ever-increasing numbers the monks of the Gazan region combined fierce missionary zeal with agricultural pursuits.[149]

---

[145] Choricius, *Oratio in Iustiniani Brumalia* 1–2 (ed. Foerster and Richsteig, 185), trans. in Litsas, 'Choricius' (Ph.D. 1980). The *Brumalia* had become the 'feast of the initial', which last twenty-four days for each of the letters of the Greek alphabet, F. Trombley, 'Brumalia', *Oxford Dictionary of Byzantium* 1 (New York 1991), 327–8. On the Gaza celebration, Ciccolella, 'Phaedra's Shining Roses', *passim*.

[146] *Vita Hilarionis* 11.3–5; N. Belayche, 'Pagan Festivals in Fourth Century Gaza', in Biton-Ashkelony and Kofsky, *Christian Gaza in Late Antiquity*, 11–12.

[147] Photius, 1. C. B 32 (Choricius). On Choricius see the various articles in C. Saliou (ed.), *Gaza dans l'Antiquité tardive* (Salerno 2005).

[148] M. Avi-Yonah, 'The Economics of Byzantine Palestine', *IEJ* 8 (1958), 35–51; Dauphin, *La Palestine byzantine*, *passim*. On the global character of Gazan exports, D. Pieri, *Le Commerce du vin oriental à l'époque Byzantine (V–VII s.). Le Temoignage des amphores en Gaule* (Beirut 2005), esp. 109–14; and P. Reynolds, 'Levantine Amphorae from Cilicia to Gaza: A Typology and Analysis of Regional Production Trends from the 2nd to the 6th Cent.', in J. M. Gurt, J. Buxed, and M. A. Cau (eds.), *Late Roman Coarse Wares*, i: *Cooking Ware and Amphorae* (BAR IS 1340; Oxford 2005), 563–611.

[149] On the distribution of monastic settlements in the region, Hirschfeld, 'The Monasteries of Gaza', 61–88, and figs. 1 and 6.

Already in the middle of the fourth century the calendar of monastic visits kept by Hilarion largely revolved around the dates of the vintage.[150] A century later Peter the Iberian was asked to pray over the vineyards of the villages surrounding Gaza. In local memory the vintage of the year blessed by Peter remained unmatched.[151] Beyond the Gazan hinterland, the wine industry spread as far south as the Negev townlets.[152] Wine produced in the Negev was shipped in Gazan ware all the way to Gaul, Italy, and Spain, to appreciative palates such as those of Sidonius Apollinaris in Clermont, Gregory in Tours, Cassiodorus in Ravenna, and Isidore in Seville.[153] The inter-dependence of the western Negev and Gaza was reflected not only in the distribution of the wine industry but also in the widespread adoption of the Gazan calendar.[154] In Beer sheva, Shivta, and Nessana, all localities outside the territory of Gaza (and outside Palaestina Prima), documents employed the era of Gaza to mark the passage of time (61 BCE).[155] In Gaza itself inscriptions habitually referred to the era of Gaza, including a Jewish inscription from the local synagogue and a Christian (orthodox) one from Horvat Gerarit, some 10 kilometres south-east of the city.[156]

The interaction between ascetics and agricultural practices was one aspect of Gaza's life in late antiquity. It opened wide vistas of wealth, well attested in the array of richly coloured mosaics from the area.

[150] Jerome, *VH* 42, P. Mayerson, 'The Wine and Vineyards of Gaza in the Byzantine Period', *BASOR* 257 (1985), 75–80.

[151] *V Petri* 95–6 (Raabe), with Mayerson, 'Wine and Vineyards', 76.

[152] *P. Ness.* 85, 3, 4, 7 (Kraemer, *Excavations at Nessana*, iii: *The Non-Literary Papyri*, 246–7) referring to 'Gazition', an all-purpose jar. See Ch. 2.

[153] Sid. *C.* 17.15–16; Greg. Tour, *HF* 7.29; Cass. *Var.* 12.12; Isid. *Etym.* 20.3, 7, cited in Glucker, *Gaza*, 93–4. On amphorae-producing kilns in the region of Gaza and Ashkelon, Y. Israel, 'Survey of Pottery Workshops, Nahal Lakish-Nahal Besor', *Excavations and Surveys in Israel* 13 (1993 [1995]), 106–7.

[154] Di Segni, 'Territory of Gaza', 43 and *passim* on the extent of the territory.

[155] Ibid. 41–2.

[156] B. Lifshitz, *Donateurs et fondateurs dans les synagogues juives* (Paris 1967), 57–9 n. 73a, on the Gazan synagogue mosaic dating to CE 569; Di Segni, 'Territory of Gaza', 56–8, on the one from the church at Horvat Gerarit, dating to 598/9. Di Segni advances the interesting hypothesis that this inscription commemorated the erection of a church outside the rather small settlement which may have already boasted a Monophysite centre of worship. The phenomenon of two sacred edifices, serving essentially the same small community, is paralleled at Naaran (see Ch. 2). Recent inscriptions from Gaza have been published by C. Saliou, *RB* 2000.

Some 12 kilometres south of Gaza the church of Kissufim, probably erected on the estate of a local nabob, yielded an intricate mosaic tapestry, while that of Shellal, some 24 kilometres south of Gaza, provided a comparable dazzling array.[157] Strikingly, the mosaic of the church at Shellal, of the synagogue at Maon (Menois), and of the Gaza synagogue (CE 508–9) are so similar as to suggest the same artistic hands.[158] The discovery of these mosaics poignantly illustrates how large the gaps are which pierce our knowledge of Gaza's material culture. Only a few surveys and excavations have been conducted.[159] Not a trace of the fifth-century Eudoxiana or of the building enterprises of bishop Marcianus in the sixth century has survived. What we can see of late ancient Gaza stands in striking if not pathetic contrast to the stature of the city's literary culture, unique in Justinianic Palestine, and exceptional even in the east.

In the first half of the sixth century one monastery amidst many stood out, that of Seridos, which housed Barsanuphius, John Dorotheus, and Dositheus, whose correspondence reflected a pattern of daily life suffused by the austere demands of the ascetic faith. Among hundreds of surviving letters, the responses addressed to parishioners provide a precious glimpse into the mundane as well as into the arbitration role of erudite and socially conscious monks.[160] There were queries regarding sales of land, the handling of slaves, the acceptability of incantations in order to save a sick animal, prices of commodities, dining with Jews and with pagans at their invitation, and buying from pagan merchants.[161] Among the brothers themselves monastic wisdom circulated in collections of pithy tales which enjoyed tremendous popularity in Palestine and beyond.[162] A few,

---

[157] R. Cohen, 'The Marvelous Mosaics of Kissufim', *Biblical Archaeology Review* 6 (1980), 16–23 (end 6th cent.); A. D. Trendall, *The Shellal Mosaic* (Canberra 1957).

[158] Levine, 'Between Rome and Byzantium', in idem (ed.), *Continuity and Renewal*, 39; A. Ivadiah, 'The Mosaic Workshop of Gaza in Christian Antiquity', in D. Urman and P. V. M. Flesher (eds.), *Ancient Synagogues* (Leiden 1995), 367–72.

[159] Saliou (ed.), *Gaza dans l'Antiquité tardive*, for a collection of brief overviews of the history of the city and its archaeology. See also 'L'Archéologie palestinienne', *Dossiers d'archéologie* 240 (Jan.–Feb. 1999), 46–67.

[160] In general, J. Hevelone-Harper, *Letters to the Great old Man: Monks, Laity and Spiritual Authority in Sixth Century Gaza* (Baltimore 2005).

[161] *Eps.* 648, 693–4, 753–4, 756, 775, 777.

[162] On the Gazan provenance of the Apophthegmata, L. Regnault, 'Les Apophtegmes en Palestine aux Ve–VIe siècles', *Irénikon* 54 (1981), 320–30.

however, remained edgy. When a layman asked the monks whether it was beneficial to tell many stories from the Bible and the lives of the ascetics, the answer was that silence was the greatest virtue. If one had to talk, the only appropriate subject were the sayings of the fathers.[163] When not dealing with admirers the learned monks of Gaza engaged in doctrinal conflicts, most notably in the so-called second Origenist controversy which they handled with a delicacy that reflected confidence in the uprightness of their own (Chalcedonian) orthodoxy.[164]

Gaza's ultimate Christianization along Chalcedonian lines entailed a literary renaissance. Besides feverish correspondence among monks and between the religious and lay orbits, the schools of Gaza produced a dazzling progression of intellectuals.[165] The writings of the illustrious scions of the schools of Gaza who rose to universal fame in the late fifth/early sixth century shed light on an environment that reached peace with its own past. Procopius (of Gaza), Choricius, Aeneas, and their colleagues and disciples (which included Procopius of Caesarea) employed their eloquence to commemorate exploits which enshrined contemporary modes of bridging urban modules.[166] Imperial panegyrics, praises of individuals, be they the city's bishop or the provincial governor, passionate pleas to allow educators to attend games, descriptions of marvels of human creativity, and a host of speeches on practically every public occasion, as well as works of erudite biblical exegesis showed how a city focusing on its economic and intellectual resources nurtured a new kind of egalitarianism in which religious factions and factionalism were phased out. The most valiant combatants were no longer monks or bishops with a missionary

[163] Barsanuphius, *Questions and Answers* 469.

[164] D. Hombergen, *The Second Origenist Controversy: A New Perspective on Cyril of Scythopolis; Monastic Biographies as Historical Sources for Sixth Century Origenism* (Rome 2001), in general, and idem, 'Barsanuphius and John of Gaza and the Origenist Controversy', in *Christian Gaza in Late Antiquity*, 173–81, on Gazan perspectives.

[165] G. Downey, *Gaza in the Early Sixth Century* (Norman 1963), who explains the Gaza phenomenon as a result of Justinianic anti-pagan or anti-Athenian legislation, and idem, 'The Christian Schools of Palestine', 297–319.

[166] R. A. Kaster, *Guardians of Language. The Grammarian and Society in Late Antiquity* (Berkeley 1988), *passim*.

zeal, as had been the case in the late fourth and early fifth century, but the preservers of the city's heritage, men who distinguished themselves as benefactors in battles fought on behalf of the whole community.

Choricius, possibly the outstanding rhetor of the day, composed a speech (*apologia mimorum*) defending a stunningly popular form of entertainment, the mime, which imperial bans failed to wipe out.[167] And although the pious Photius later chastised the Christian Choricius for undertaking this unseemly mission on behalf of those who 'mixed fables and pagan narratives' (*mythous kai istorias hellenikas*) when 'treating sacred subjects', the trenchant bishop of the imperial capital did not doubt for a moment Choricius' genuine attachment to Christianity.[168] Nor could one doubt the affection that continued to bond Gazans to the civic traditions that invited citizens to take part in celebrating their metropolis.

Sixth-century Gaza stood as a unique symbol of the harmonization of the city with itself and with its diverse hinterland. Its cosmopolitan character in an age which became more and more homogenized,[169] emerged even in its sixth-century synagogue mosaic where David, clearly identified through a Hebrew inscription, was manifestly copying a universal Orpheus, lyre and wild beasts included. Its donors were Jewish lumber merchants. A cycle of paintings which had graced a bathhouse and were eternalized in the words of the rhetor John of Gaza traced a *tabula mundi* which captured the wealth of the earth and the blessings of the city.[170] Whether these polytheistic images were created in the sixth century

---

[167] Jones, *LRE* 232, 977 elicits a ban of Anastasius in 502 from Joshua Stylite 46. V. Malineau, 'L'Apport de l'*Apologie de mimes* de Chorikios de Gaza à la connaissance du théâtre du VIe siècle', in C. Saliou (ed.), *Gaza*, 149–69 with ample bibliography. Note Choricius' avoidance of religious themes including parodies of Christian rituals like baptism (Malineau, 157). On the latter, C. Panayotakis, 'Baptism and Crucifixion on the Mimic Stage', *Mnemosyne* 50 (1997), 302–19.

[168] Photius, *Bibliotheca*, 160, 102b, 34–6 for quotes.

[169] Levine, 'Between Rome and Byzantium', in idem (ed.), *Continuity*, 32.

[170] G. Downey, 'John of Gaza and the Mosaic of Ge and Karpoi', in R. Stielwell (ed.), *Antioch on the Orontes*, ii (Princeton 1938), 205–12; H. Maguire, 'Truth and Convention in Byzantine Descriptions of Works of Art', *DOP* 28 (1974), 111–40.

or much earlier, their preservation suggests a *modus vivendi* which afforded the enjoyment of art *qua* art.[171] The education which the city's outstanding educators offered the community bridged the pagan past with the tranquillity of classical pursuits and Christian piety.

[171] As does the possession of Gazan lands by absentee landlords based in Petra, Frösén et al., *The Petra Papyri* I, no. 2 (written in Gaza and using the Macedonian calendar of the city). Cf rabbinic attitudes to images of Aphrodite in bathhouses, *M AZ* 3.4, with I. Stern, 'The Art of the Image in the Halakha during the Mishna and Talmud Periods', *Zion* 61 (1996), 397–419, esp. 404 (Heb.).

9

Epilogue

Three battles will take place in the land of Israel. One will be
waged by Hepheibah with Seroy the king of Persia. One will be
fought by the Lord God of Israel and Menahem son of Amiel
with Armilos, the ten kings who are with him, and God and
Magog. The third will be at Sela ha-Elef (the thousandth rock),
where Nehemiah son of Hushiel and Zerubbabel will see action.
The third battle will take place in the month of Av. After all this
Menahem will come accompanied by Nehemiah and all Israel.
All the dead will resurrect. Elijah the prophet will come
with them. They will come up to Jerusalem. In the month of
Av, during which they formerly mourned for Nehemiah and
for the destruction of the Temple, Israel will hold a great
celebration...

Sefer Zerubbabel, trans. J. C. Reeves[1]

In the pains preceding the birth and appearance of the messiah, the
month of Av reminded Jews of past misfortunes and of everlasting
hopes of salvation. On the 9th of Av the destruction of the Temple in
Jerusalem was commemorated in synagogues throughout Palestine
and the Jewish Diaspora. In the month of Av, on each 15 August,
Christians in Palestine celebrated a feast memorializing Mary's
maternity and the imminent birth of a messiah. Amidst an apocalyptic
web of wars hailing the resurrection of the dead and the transformation of the 9th of Av from a day of national mourning to one of
jubilation, the Islamic conquerors of Palestine conducted a series

---

[1] *Trajectories in Near Eastern Apocalyptic: A Postrabbinic Jewish Apocalypse Reader*
(Leiden 2005) (translation available via the internet).

of quick and decisive campaigns (CE 634–40).[2] Islamic historio-graphy cast Umar's victories in prophetic terms, as an expression of God's will and as a reward for accepting Islam.[3] Rome's defeat was due to its compromising God's oneness. Such terminology indicated how the stage was rearranged by using familiar principles to accom-modate the perceptions of the new rulers of the land.

Among the clauses of the so-called Treaty of Umar, the document(s) issued to regulate communal relations in newly conquered Palestine, Muslims and Christians were to share churches.[4] To facilitate the enforced proximity Christians were expected to conduct prayers in hushed voices and to curtail the exuberance of their ceremonies. The invasion of mosques into ecclesiastical spaces entailed architectural modifications. In the Kathisma, an octagonal church constructed in the early fifth century on the road between Jerusalem and Bethlehem, Mary and Mohammed were apparently worshipped side by side. In the first half of the eighth century a mosque with a prayer niche was placed in the south part of the church.[5] Throughout the partially converted sanctuary new mosaic floors were installed on top of the late Roman layer. Ornate and intricate, the mosaics reconfirmed the close affinities between the Kathisma and Jerusalem. They bore a striking resemblance to the mosaic tapestries of the newly completed Dome of the Rock, a mosque whose octagonal shape imitated the unique architectural layout of the Kathisma.

The history of the Kathisma showed in a nutshell how projections of creeds, or of civilizations, to use Huntington's language, operated both to punctuate historical events and to provide a context in which to comment on contemporary conflicts. On the 9th of Av Jews used to gather on the Temple Mount in Jerusalem to mourn the destruction

---

[2] P. Mayerson, 'The First Muslim Attacks on Southern Palestine', *Transactions and Proceedings of the American Philological Association* 95 (1964), 155–99, repr. in idem, *Monks, Martyrs*, 53–98. W. E. Kaegi, *Byzantium and the Early Islamic Conquest* (Cambridge 1992), *passim*.

[3] R. G. Hoyland, 'History, Fiction and Authorship in the First Centuries of Islam', in J. Bray (ed.), *Writing and Representation in Medieval Islam* (London 2006), 16–46, esp. 33.

[4] Available on the internet via Paul Halsall's website.

[5] R. Avner, 'The Kathisma Church on the Road from Jerusalem to Bethlehem', *Qadmoniot* 130 (2005), 117–21 (Heb.).

of the Temple. The moment, a single annual event, was captured through the critical eyes of an early Christian pilgrim in CE 333:

> Not far from the two statues of Hadrian [and where the Temple had once stood] there is a pierced stone which the Jews come and anoint every year. They mourn and rend their garments and then depart.[6]

The close association of the majesty of Rome, the demolished Temple once also majestic, and the string of Jewish mourners sharply edged in the memory of a voyager through Jerusalem, engendered Jewish polemical narratives which aspired to account for the very existence of Rome atop a territory sanctified to Yahweh. Embedded in a chronology which effortlessly glided between the present, the past, and biblical antiquity, rabbinic tales woven around the Book of Lamentations, the obligatory reading on the 9th of Av, told of profound misunderstanding that existed between Rome and Jerusalem, of vengeful empresses, bloodthirsty emperors, and of Jewish sufferings. In late antiquity this form of biblical exegesis acquired an anti-Christian hue, especially pronounced in narratives relating to mothers and infants.[7]

---

[6] *Itinerarium Burdigalense* 591, Eng. trans. Wilkinson, *Egeria's Travels*, 157. The scholarly debate on the existence and extent of Jewish pilgrimage to Jerusalem in late antiquity continues. Among recent contribution, C. Hezser, 'The (In)Significance of Jerusalem in the Talmud Yerushalmi', in P. Schäfer and C. Hezser (eds.), *The Talmud Yerushalmi and Greco-Roman Culture*, ii (2000), 11–49.

[7] *LamR* 1.16, sec. 45 = *LamR* 4.22. The story tells of the birth of an heir to the imperial throne on the 9th of Av, a day of sorrow for the Jews, and of his death on Hanukkah, a day of jubilation on the Jewish calendar. Both ceremonies, of lamentation and of joy, were misinterpreted at the court as expressions of deliberate provocation. The empress incited her husband to avenge the injured imperial majesty. The result was a bloody campaign which left many Jewish dead. This exegetical narrative appears three times in Palestinian rabbinic sources, once in the Palestinian Talmud (*Sukka* 5.1, 55b), and twice in *Lamentations Rabbah*. In the former it is inserted into a discussion regarding the main features of the feast of Tabernacles (*Sukkot*), and specifically on the profusion of lights during the holiday. The motif of light leads to 'reminiscences' regarding the blazing lights that used to illuminate the great synagogue in Alexandria which, together with the city's great Jewish community, had succumbed to a tragic fate under Trajan. In *Lamentations Rabbah* the Alexandrinian-Egyptian context disappears altogether. Instead, the story acquires a national-Palestinian dimension that highlights the uneasy relationships between Roman imperial power and Jewry in general and between Jewish feasts and their non-Jewish interpreters in particular. All manuscripts read Trajan as the name of the emperor but a better reading provides Hadrian. Cf. the confusion between Hadrian

As a reflection on the Christian 'conversion' of Jewish feasts, once the process is constructed, rabbinic folkloristic exegesis gains sense along the borderline between myth and history. The interpretation of Lam. 1: 16 (*LamR* 1.16), which reads like a discourse on childbearing, identified two dates as definitive moments. These were also the two moments that formulated Mary's history, namely her pregnancy as commemorated 15 August/the 9th of Av, and the birth of Jesus, as later commemorated in December, the period of Hanukkah.[8] Within a late ancient ritualistic context narratives served as symbolic reminders of the opposition and apposition of Judaism vis-à-vis Christianity, and especially vis-à-vis Jerusalemite practices.

Stories like those included in *Lamentations Rabbah* responded to acts of erasure which the Church applied by grafting celebrations with overwhelming significance for Christians onto the Jewish commemorative calendar. The biblical exegesis of *Lamentations Rabbah* projected metaphors of calendrical mobility that expressed, symbolically and concretely, simultaneous claims. Whether the text asserted that the Bethlehem wind blew away the messiah or that a single bereaved mother could usher disasters on a national scale, this subversive presentation of Christian (and Roman) traditions counterbalanced memory with contemporary Jewish customs.

Paradoxically, the figure of Mary, a mother, a companion, a woman of surpassing merit, played a pivotal role in the formulation of messianic figures in Jewish apocalyptic visions which accompanied the transition from Roman to Persian and thence to Muslim rule. By the beginning of the seventh century, a culminating point in the history of the cult of Mary,[9] Jewish apocalyptic visions (like *Sefer*

and Vespasian, both emperors suppressors of Jewish revolts, in *Tanhuma*, Lublin, 221, with S. Krauss, 'The Emperor Hadrian', *HaShiloah* 39 (1920), 536 (Heb.).

[8] Perhaps the 'imperial' narrative of *LamR* on Lam. 1: 16 reflected the shifting of the feast of the Nativity from August to December, a transition that occurred in the middle of the 6th cent. Verhelst, 'Le 15 Août', 173 expresses astonishment at the link between the two Jewish feasts and concludes that the rabbis erred since they intended to refer to the feast of the Nativity of 6 Jan. which preceded that of December. My explanation suggests that there is no reason to hypothesize a rabbinic error. The same narrative, this time enlisted in an exegesis of Lam. 4: 19 (*our pursuers were swifter than the eagles of heaven*), is used to illustrate the swift progress of the Roman army within the context of the strained relations between the dwellers of Betar, Bar Kokhba's last bastion, and of Jerusalem.

[9] See above, Ch. 6, n. 32.

Zerubbabel quoted above) generated a messiah with a fierce mother, Hepheiba or Hephziba, who was cast as a perfect foil of Mary.[10] The Jewish Mother was to lead an army against the king of Persia. She was a woman who would confront kings fearlessly, even to the point of slaying them. Mother of Menahem, the appointed messiah, she was the appointed recipient of the rod once given to Adam, Moses, Aaron, Joshua, and David.[11] The metamorphosis of a gentle virginal-maternal figure into a female warrior-protector suggests that calendrical ceremonies activated rather than concealed contacts. Perhaps Mary's phenomenal success in saving Constantinople and the power of her maternity mobilized new Jewish perceptions of the shape and ancestry of a Jewish Messiah.[12]

As each creed weighed its respective values, rabbinic preoccupation with the pre-eminence of the Hebrew Bible extolled the valour of orality and of the exclusive transmission of biblical interpretation:

Rabbi Judah b. Shalom said: When the Holy One told Moses 'Write down' (Exod. 34: 27), the latter wanted the Mishnah (also) to be in writing. However, the Holy One [refused], anticipating a time when the nations of the world would translate the Torah, read it in Greek and then say 'We are Israel'. [Until now the scales have been balanced.] The Holy One will then address the nations, saying: 'You contend that you are my children. That may be so, yet, only those who possess my secret (*mysterion*; *mastirin*) are my children.' 'And what is this "secret"?', they asked. 'It is the Mishnah that is given orally.'[13]

At the heart of this exegesis of the Exodus pericope on the giving of the Torah tablets stood a syllogism of paternity, an acknowledgement that the Hebrew Bible had been a universal gift but that the biblical myth of the chosen people hinged not only on written Scripture

---

[10] See above, Ch. 6, n. 33.

[11] *Sefer Zerubbabel*, above, n. 1.

[12] By then, the location of the nativity cave in Bethlehem, and not on the road to town, had been firmly established, Taylor, *Christians and the Holy Places*, 112, completing the displacement of date and location for the memorialization of the Theotokos.

[13] *Tanhuma, Ki Tisa* 34, see S. Lieberman, *Hellenism in Jewish Palestine* (New York 1950) for text and translation (slightly modified), p. 207. The dates of the Tanhumas have not been established although the words are ascribed to a 4th-cent. *amora*. Nor is it clear what midrashic layers contributed to their formation. There is a new English translation of Buber's edition, *Midrash Tanhuma* (S. Buber's recension),

but also, and vitally, on orally transmitted Torah learning.[14] This was one of the claims which Christianity vigorously combated from the very beginning, insisting on its own identity as *verus Israel*, the true Israel.[15] Matthew 15: 2, 3, 6 criticized Jewish dependence on the 'traditions of the elders', thereby rejecting rabbinic reliance on oral law. In the second century Justin of Palestinian Flavia Neapolis (Shechem) contended that the *mysterium* which the Midrash presents as the Oral Torah or the Mishnah was the cross.[16] Herein emerged a fundamental and unbridgeable difference between Judaism and Christianity, in spite of the commonality of Sacred Scripture.[17]

trans. J. T. Townsend (Hoboken 1997). Cf. *Pesiqta Rabbati* 5 (ed. Friedmann); *Tanhuma Va-Year* 5, with the comments of M. Bregman, 'Mishnah and LXX as "Mystery": An Example of Jewish–Christian Polemic in the Byzantine Period', in L. I. Levine (ed.), *Continuity and Renewal: Jews and Judaism in Byzantine-Christian Palestine* (Jerusalem 2004), 333–42.

[14] For rabbinic debates regarding the universality of the Torah, M. Hirshman, *Torah for the Entire World* (Tel Aviv 1999) (Heb.) where the author argues that such universal trends characterize tannaitic attitudes, as they do the NT (esp. Paul's famous dictum in Gal. 3: 23–8). On rabbinic dialogues with Roman dignitaries regarding the nature of the divinity and Torah law, M.-D. Herr, 'The Historical Significance of the Dialogues between Jewish Sages and Roman Dignitaries', *Scripta Hierosolymitana* 22 (1971), 123–50.

[15] See the famed study of Marcel Simon, *Verus Israel* (Paris), Eng. trans.

[16] *Trypho* 94.2. The term, *mysterion* or *misterin*, in the sense of secret or divine knowledge given only to Jews appears in several midrashic contexts, see S. Krauss, *Griechische und lateinische Lehnwörter im Talmud, Midrash und Targum* (Berlin 1898), s.v., and the electronic database of *The Hebrew Academy of Language. The Historical Dictionary of the Hebrew Language. Section of Ancient Literature*, s.v. Justin's dramatically different conclusion is based on his interpretation of Num. 21: 4–10, an episode that has nothing to do with the Torah but which had given rise to a debate regarding the ostensible violation of the Second Commandment. In the course of the wilderness wandering of the Israelites, scarcity of water prompts complaints followed by a demonstration of divine wrath in the shape of poisonous snakes. Many die. A confession of sin induces a change of the divine mind, and God orders Moses to fashion a serpent which, like the cross for Justin, becomes a source of life. Whoever is bitten by a real snake, gazes at the artificial one and is immediately cured. On anti-Jewish apologetics, Simon, *Verus Israel*, 87–123, 165–213. On Justin, W. A. Shotwell, *The Biblical Exegesis of Justine Martyr* (London, 1965).

[17] *PT Pe'ah* 2.6 (17a) and *Hag.* 1.8 (76d) anticipate the claim of equality, based on the same Scripture, with the Christians producing the Septuagint. For text and interpretation, Lieberman, *Hellenism*, 207–8, who also compares the physical shape of Christian and Jewish books, with the Bible universally accessible but the Jewish oral law recorded only in private (secret) rolls and codices.

The example of Midrash, Justin, and the 'secret' of the True Israel highlights the negations and affirmations that informed the Jewish–Christian debate in late antiquity, as well as the self-definition of Judaism, Christianity, Samaritanism, and later of Islam. The Bible had spawned interpretations that were structured around the problem of imitation and of the obscurities inherent in the text. Because such writing, with its deceptive encoding, was also sacred, it permitted a ceaseless quarrel of interpretations, primary against secondary. Confronting Judaism's greater claim to antiquity, and hence to respectability, Augustine presented Jews as blind men holding a torch and illuminating the way for others while themselves blundering blindly.[18] This vision countered Jewish claims to be the bearers of the only knowledge that God conferred on a specific group and that separated Israel from the peoples of the world.[19]

To appropriate authority over a work whose denotation had shifted from the Hebrew Bible to the Christian Scripture, categories of interpretation privileged meanings to the detriment of the 'other'. In this agonistic struggle the multiplicity of interpretations did not put an end to difficulties or to doubts.[20] For Eusebius of Caesarea the

---

[18] B. Blumenkranz, *Juifs et chrétiens dans le monde occidental 430–1096* (Paris 1960).

[19] *Tanhuma, Ki Tisa* 34 (Townsend, II, p. 161), above. One notes that Augustine's own way to the heart of the divine, as recounted in his *Confessions*, bore an uncanny (and unintentional) resemblance to rabbinic experiences. As he was lounging in a garden Augustine overheard a child rehearsing the words 'pick up and read' (*Conf.* 8.12.29), a voice that he took to heart as a message directly from God. The Palestinian Talmud contains a tale of two rabbis who apprehended the truth through a *bat kol*, a message from God conveyed through the mouth of an innocent infant (on *bat kol* (voice, echo, reverberating sound), Lieberman, *Hellenism*, 194–9). As the two embarked on a long and potentially hazardous journey from Palestine to Babylon to pay homage to a famed Babylonian sage, they happened to pass by a synagogue whence came the voice of a child reciting the verse 'And Samuel died' (I Sam. 28: 3), *PT Shab.* 6.9 (8c); cf. *BT Meg.* 32a. The name, hardly a rarity, was synonymous with that of the sage they had hoped to visit. They took it to signify the death of the rabbi they intended to visit and consequently decided to stay at home.

[20] In general, see the various articles in C. Brekelmans and M. Haran (eds.), *Hebrew Bible/Old Testament: The History of its Interpretation*, i (Göttingen 1996). See also E. Z. Melamed, *Bible Commentators*, 2nd edn. (Jerusalem 1978), i, on biblical interpretation of the sages, in the Targums, esp. Onkelos, Jonathan, and to the Latter Prophets (Heb.). For Christian exegesis, R. P. C. Hanson, 'Biblical Exegesis in the Early Church', in P. R. Ackroyd and C. F. Evans (eds.), *The Cambridge History of the Bible* (Cambridge 1970), I. 412–53, and other articles in same collection. See also

Church alone was 'the godly polity' (*to theosebes politeuma*), a phrase that encapsulated the new Christian universal monotheism.[21] The altered horizons of imperial religiosity from Constantine onward required further clarification of the boundaries between the two religious communities.[22] Rabbinic writings continuously if obliquely contested the very concept of 'the godly policy' in a variety of ways. After the redaction of the Palestinian Talmud (*c.*400), exegetical activities were channelled into midrashic compilations and into public sermons.[23] Imaginative poets further enriched the liturgy of

R. M. Grant, *A Short History of Biblical Interpretation* (New York 1948). W. Horbury, 'Jews and Christians on the Bible, Demarcation and Convergence (325–451)', in idem, *Jews and Christians in Contact and Controversy* (Edinburgh 1998), 200–25.

[21] Hollerich, *Eusebius' Isaiah*, 14, and in general, E. Peterson, *Der Monotheismus als politisches Problem: Ein Beitrag zur Geschichte der politischen Theologie im Imperium Romanum* (Leipzig 1935, repr. 1951), 45–147.

[22] Hollerich, *Eusebius' Isaiah*, 104.

[23] Stemberger, *Introduction to the Talmud and Midrash*; L. Zunz, *Die gottesdienstlichen Vorträge der Juden, historisch entwickelt* (repr. Piscataway, NJ, 2003). While direct contacts among biblical interpreters are rarely attested the intellectual fermentation on Palestinian soil suggests an ongoing exchange, both amicable and mostly antagonistic. The presence of the library of Origen in Caesarea was an important factor in stimulating the activities of Christian scholars and of Jewish–Christian polemics, E. Urbach, 'Rabbinic Exegesis on Origen and Jewish–Christian Polemics', *Scripta Hierosolymitana* 22 (1971), 247–75. Jerome's contacts with Jews and Judaism have become a subject of some controversy, H. I. Newman, 'Jerome's Judaizers', *JECS* 9 (2001), 421–52; W. Kinzig, 'Jewish and "Judaizing" Eschatologies in Jerome', in R. Kalmin and S. Schwartz (eds.), *Jewish Culture and Society under the Christian Roman Empire* (Leuven 2003), 409–29, the latter suggesting that Jerome's attacks were aimed at philo-semitic exegetical tradition advocating an eschatology that cast Jerusalem as the Jewish capital of a restored Israel. On Eusebius' rather slight Hebrew, Hollerich, *Eusebius of Caesarea's Commentary on Isaiah*, 81 and *passim*. On exegetical contacts see G. Stemberger, 'Exegetical Contacts between Christians and Jews in the Roman Empire', in Brekelmans and Haran, *Hebrew Bible/Old Testament*, 569–86, esp. 577–83 on Palestine. See also L. M. Barth, 'Reading Rabbinic Bible Exegesis', *Approaches to Ancient Judaism* 4 (1983), 81–93; J. R. Baskin, 'Rabbinic–Patristic Exegetical Contacts in Late Antiquity: A Bibliographical Reappraisal', *Approaches in Ancient Judaism* 5 (1985), 53–80. On polemical allusions to Christianity in late ancient rabbinic compilations in general, R. T. Herford, *Christianity in Talmud and Midrasch* (1903; repr. 1975), and in the *Pesiqta de Rab Kahana* in particular, L. M. Barth, 'The "Three Rebukes" and the "Seven of Consolation": Sermons in *Pesikta de Rav Kahana*', *JJS* 33 (1982), 503–15; L. H. Silberman, 'Challenge and Response: Pesiqta de Rab Kahana Chapter 26 as an Oblique Reply to Christian Claims', *HTR* 79 (1986), 247–53. For sober remarks on the perennial Franciscan ascription of rabbinic disparaging comments to contemporary Jewish-Christians, Shoemaker, *Ancient Traditions* 212–56; and B. L. Visotzky, *Fathers of the World: Essays in Rabbinic and Patristic Literature* (Tübingen 1995), *passim*.

the synagogue with thousands of poems (*piyyutim*) composed for every occasion listed in the calendar.[24] As a centre of Jewish, Samaritan, pagan, and Christian learning, the province of Palestine in late antiquity had a fair if not substantial share. The precise circumstances that shaped a specific interpretation and its reinterpretation are beyond recovery. But the texts registered voices vying to record their claim to the exclusivity and genuineness of the structures that supported each creed. Rituals and ceremonies harmonized the official/scholarly interpretation with practices which assigned time and place to the creed's self-celebration. The stakes were high because they touched the very possibility of reading Scripture.

The presence of Islam in Palestine-Syria redrew the lines of argumentation. The ninth-century 'Account of the Disputation of the Priest' (*Qissat Mujadalat al Usquf*), an example of Jewish–Christian polemics under Islam, allegedly written by a priest who converted to Judaism, exemplified the permutations of polemics.[25] While resorting to arguments familiar from late ancient disputations, the author also employed themes which had been incorporated in Muslim anti-Christian polemics via Judaism.[26] As yet another paradox: Jewish anti-Christian polemicists resorted to Muslim writings to derive what Muslim authors had borrowed from Judaism in order to combat Christianity. So intricate were the links which Islam had to forge with the two major Palestinian creeds that one tradition depicted Umar, the conqueror of Jerusalem, bowing to the will of the city's patriarch on the question of whether or not to allow Jews to live in Jerusalem.

'Tell of the Sons of Israel for there is no fault in it', quotes a *hadit* which reflected both respect and reserve for Jewish and Christian Scripture.[27] A Muslim was not forbidden to read the Torah, Psalms,

---

[24] In general, I. Elbogen, *Jewish Liturgy: A Comprehensive History*, trans. R. P. Scheindlin (Philadelphia 1993); and Yahalom, *Poetry and Society*.

[25] D. L. Lasker and S. Stroumsa, *The Polemic of Nestor the Priest*, 2 vols. (Jerusalem 1996), who ascribed a Syrian provenance to the work.

[26] Ibid. 22. See also D. Thomas, *Anti-Christian Polemic in Early Islam: Abu Isa al Warraq's Against the Trinity* (Cambridge 1992). See also C. Adang, *Muslim Writers on Judaism and the Hebrew Bible: From Ibn Rabban to Ibn Hazm* (Leiden 1996).

[27] M. J. Kister, *Studies on the Emergence of Islam* (Jerusalem 1998), *passim*.

and the Gospels but the Quran was all by itself more than sufficient for believers. Proximity bred imitation. To what extend could a Muslim resemble a Christian or a Jew? As little as possible would have been the answer during the early centuries of Islam. Both were heretics. Rituals were important signifiers. The Prophet forbade his followers to sway while praying, as Jews did, or to pray with raised arms and voice.[28] Muslims were not to chat with each other during prayers, as Jews and Christians did.

Shoes became an arena of ritual polemics. Shoes reflected status and were the apparel of prophets. Shoes were an ornament of prayer and Muslims were ordered to pray wearing shoes because this was the opposite of what the Jews did.[29] Perhaps the Jews in the Hijaz prayed in this posture. There are no Jewish sources which either confirm or refute this custom. When Palestinian Jews approached the Temple Mount in Jerusalem they had to take off their shoes (*M Ber.* 9.5). In the synagogues some wore shoes during prayer while others prayed barefoot (*M Meg.* 4.8). The Sepphoris synagogue mosaic prominently placed two pairs of sandals, without their owners, in a scene devoted to the sacrifice of Isaac.[30] The Palestinian Talmud preserved a narrative that lent support to the custom of praying without shoes:

Yehudah son of R. Hiya, used to leave his sandals [outside] when he entered the synagogue. They disappeared. He said: Had I not gone to the synagogue my sandals would not have gone either (*PT BM* 2.8, 8c).[31]

At some point Muslims, too, started to pray barefoot. With the assistance of scriptural exegesis the Prophet was said to have been once seen taking off his shoes while praying. The saying, coupled with the emergence of luxurious mosques decorated with marble floors and covered with priceless rugs, reinforced separation between feet and shoes during prayer.

Opposition to Judaism and to Christianity meant that Muslim believers could commit a gross error by sharing the liturgy of these

---

[28] Ibid. 179–92 (Heb. trans.).   [29] Ibid.

[30] Above, Ch. 6, 272. But the scene allegedly took place on Mount Moriah, later identified with the Temple Mount, and hence an area which fell under the prohibition of wearing shoes.

[31] Evidence discussed by M. Kister in an appendix to the articles gathered in the Hebrew translation of Kister's *Studies*, 193–200.

'errors' or heresies. Such mistakes were not uncommon under the
turbulent skies of Palestine. Around 500, a woman from Pamphylia
who had settled on the Mount of Olives in Jerusalem realized,
while attending service in the church of the Ascension, that she was
in the middle of a gathering of Chalcedonians.[32] A Monophysite, the
woman turned to flee but found the church's gates closed. She then
hid behind a pillar throughout the liturgy. Later she fell ill and heard
on her death-bed a voice telling her that she was about to face severe
charges regarding the purity of her 'orthodoxy'. The narrator, fully
aware of the irresistible attraction of the sanctuaries of Jerusalem,
intended the story to illustrate the perils and pitfalls of pilgrimage
and of life in Jerusalem, above all the potential and perennial exposure to heresy.[33] In Jerusalem, more than anywhere in Palestine, the
allure of other creeds, of other sects, other rituals, and of other
memories, proved the strongest. Whether or not Jerusalem and
Palestine endowed Islam with limbs and flesh, as has been recently
argued, remains an intriguing if controversial prospect.[34]

  In the wars of words conducted in late ancient Palestine strategies of
remembering became narratives that could wound and kill. Whether
these were imperial laws, sermons delivered in church, speeches made
in public places, poems recited in sanctuaries, the danger was the
same. Beyond remembering (and forgetting) lurked conflicts which
were congenital to Palestinian existence. Thus the remembrance of a
long ago and how it ended in violence, either when the Jews ruled
Judaea or the Christians were a persecuted minority, or pagans the
dominating majority, was calculated to rescue the present by uncovering conflict as a cement of the community. It was therefore necessary
to construct scenarios in which remembering was valued in terms of
the violence and anger which must not be forgotten.

  The effort to bring to light a dynamics of conflict is sure to
encounter resistance because in a struggle to have the upper hand

---

[32] John Rufus, *Pleroph.* 80.
[33] Jan-Eric Steppa, 'Heresy and Orthodoxy: The Anti-Chalcedonian Hagiography
of John Rufus', in *Christian Gaza in Late Antiquity*, 103–4; Biton-Ashkelony, *Encountering the Sacred.*
[34] P. Crone and M. Cook, *Hagarism: The Making of the Islamic World* (Cambridge
1977); M. Sharon, 'The Cities of Eretz Israel under Islamic Rule', *Cathedra* 40 (1986),
83–120 (Heb.).

'victory' meant to have power over others. In the case of the Samaritans it was a triumph which expressed superiority in fighting an 'external' war. In the case of the war over biblical interpretation the victory was scored by an opinion and by the advantage gained by one faction when, and if, its opponent conceded, tacitly, a defeat. To ratify the victory of one group and idea over another also meant to acknowledge the absence of the unitary and to admit the divisibility of society. Since institutional power was often seen to favour unity and indivisibility, the exercise of power, be it by the government over recalcitrant elements, by one religious party over another, by bishops over rebellious clergy and monks, by men over women, by the centre over the periphery, by dreams over reality, implicitly admitted the fragility of its commonwealth vision. The conflicts surveyed here denoted the absence of a sense of rallying and gathering together which had been characteristic of the polytheistic pre-Christian Roman world. Rather than take on the partisan meaning of being a 'Roman', the Christian-'Roman' government named its regime and issued laws which increased stratification and differentiation.

None of the religions which coexisted under Palestinian horizons in late antiquity was singular or interchangeable. Recurrent claims made religion the cement of concord and of conflict. They stifled the voice of strife that would be the strongest bond of the community. There were several bonds, all forming a tight network that connected citizens throughout the territory. One was the ostensibly uniting bond which linked all the inhabitants of Palestine through the administrative structures of the 'superpower'. The others were the divisive bonds of ethnicity and religion which had to be kept tight because they joined the group and prevented its collapse. Thus the rabbis found it necessary to regulate, knot, and bind Jews to each other every day because the threat of a tear was always looming. Monastic manuals and activities linked monks on a daily basis to prevent break-ups so that neither hate nor strife would arise.

The language of discord began with the social bond. It paraded an assembly or a custom that could be broken or destroyed. Strife led to dissolution. The vocabulary of hate which marked Christian anti-Jewish discourse purported to re-establish communications after years of dispute if only one party understood the 'positive' message of the other. Legal speeches, basically the fundamental denial of the rights of non-Christians from the fourth century onward, intended to extol the socially positive and to establish bonds in terms of unbinding. Such modes of speech uncovered the lineaments of violence that the official discourse covered over and even repressed.

Between Constantine and Abd al-Malik a threat of conflict always loomed. What kept rival parties at bay was also, in itself, a harbinger of violence. It was, however, impossible to devise laws for future conflicts, predictable as these might be. Yet, a single description can sometimes suffice for both camps to the point of making adversaries into abstractions. In late ancient Palestine opposing parties used the same language and the same words as though in the midst of division there was only one possible language to indicate the reciprocity of violent exchange. Jewish, Christian, Samaritan, and pagan writings, poetic, philosophical, historical, didactic, used words that established antagonistic poles by repetition, imitation, and borrowing.

In a classic analysis of the Mediterranean world after the two great waves of late ancient invasions, the Germanic in the fifth century, and the Muslim in the seventh, Henri Pirenne concluded that the Arabs were able to face Rome without being absorbed by its civilization because 'the Germans had nothing with which to oppose the Christianity of the Empire'.[35] By contrast Islam infused the Arabs with a sense of superiority which prevented assimilation. Huntington, hence, may indeed be correct in his assessment that faith, then as now, is the driving force behind monumental clashes of civilizations. Yet, such confrontations are sharpened not within a global context but in specifically contested territories. Palestine in late antiquity provides an uncontroversial case in point. The insurmountable divisions which Palestinian creeds erected in late antiquity showed that it was possible to live side by side in self-created cocoons. Islam perfected what the Christian establishment in Palestine and Constantinople had formulated. Winning creeds acted like conquerors, demanding submission, treating the other as a heretic (or infidel), advocating their own superiority.

From the seventh century onwards, argues Pirenne, two different and hostile civilizations existed on the shores of the Mediterranean,

---

[35] H. Pirenne, *Mohammed and Charlemagne*, Eng. trans. B. Miall (London 1939), 150.

shattering its unity and transforming a sea which had once been the centre of Christianity into a frontier.[36] *Mutatis mutandis*, would Huntington argue, such dichotomy now applies worldwide. It could hardly be otherwise. Palestinian creeds and Palestinian-shaped faiths, although preaching peace, promoted dissension. The presence of so many religions in so crowded a space, each vying to destroy the ideological basis of the other, while contributing to the circulation of ideas and of merchandise, also bred disorder and competition. Imperial attempts to impose unity by decree throughout the provinces failed. Muslim attempts to wean the peoples of Palestine of their respective beliefs, rooted not in panic but in unshakeable conviction, proved on the whole more effective.

[36] Ibid. 152–3.

APPENDIX

A Note on Jewish Sources

Of the sources used in this study the Jewish and Samaritans texts raise a host of difficulties. The Samaritan chronicles are late medieval compilations which preserve earlier material that can be used, with extreme caution, to complement the information provided by other sources. The chronicles are crucially important since they reflect the way in which the Samaritans themselves viewed their history. I refer to current debates regarding their reliability in the third chapter.

Even more difficult and demanding for historians of late antiquity are the Jewish sources. A large body of material is contained in the so-called *piyyut* or synagogal liturgical poetry, a genre which is still practised.[1] The corpus of Palestinian *piyyut*, numbering many thousands, has been transmitted via several channels including European poetic traditions, medieval and early modern, stemming from the Cairo Genizah, Ashkenaz, Italy, and Romania. Their importance cannot be overstated. Piyyutim accompanied and enlivened synagogue service in late ancient Palestine. Their language marked the metamorphosis of Hebrew from a language used on a daily basis as a tool of talking into a sacred language and an instrument of poetry par excellence.[2] Hebrew-Palestinian piyyutim are ornate, archaic, and allusive, and are curiously reminiscent of the styles which dominated late ancient Greek and Latin poetry.[3] There are also piyyutim in Aramaic, the daily language

---

[1] For a good introduction see Elbogen, *Jewish Liturgy: A Comprehensive History*, trans. with notes Scheindlin.

[2] The transition is nicely captured by Rabbi Yonathan of Eleutheropolis (Beth Govrin) (early 4th cent.?), who divided Palestinian linguistic horizons into four, assigning poetry or cultural matters to Greek, battle or military and administrative matters to Latin, dirge to Aramaic, and daily matters to Hebrew, thereby demonstrating the continuing attachment to the land via the language of the Bible (*PT Meg.* 1.11). J. Yahalom, *Poetic Language in the Early Piyyut* (Jerusalem 1985), 162–81, esp. 178 (Heb.), and idem, *Poetry and Society*, 46–50. On the earliest (?) known *paytan* see Horbury, 'Suffering and Messianism in Yose ben Yose', 143–82. One major problem is that numerous publications on piyyut in the last three decades have appeared in Hebrew, a language inaccessible to the majority of scholars dealing with late antiquity. Only a handful of the piyyutim themselves have been translated into a modern language.

[3] Roberts, *The Jeweled Style: Poetry and Poetics in Late Antiquity*.

of the Jews in late ancient Palestine. Aramaic piyyutim were used to express sorrow in public, both genuine and mock.[4] Scholarly consensus has placed the provenance of the *piyyutim* in Palestine and has assigned their *floruit* to the fifth–sixth century, rendering these poems a crucial corollary of both the written evidence, like inscriptions and rabbinic texts, and the archaeological and artistic evidence, such as the synagogues and their mosaics.

By their nature *piyyutim* were not conceived as a tool of chronology but they provide a complement to contemporary sources especially where they serve as the sole voice of the Jewish community. I have briefly discussed elsewhere the potential contribution of *piyyut* to history, specifically as a reflection of moods prevailing in the Jewish community during the crucial period of transition from Roman to Persian and later to Islamic rule.[5] In those studies I emphasized the difficulty of reconstructing history out of elusive poetic references which nevertheless historians cannot afford to ignore. Thus the *piyyutim* which seem to echo the euphoria which had settled on Palestinian Jewry at the dawn of the Persian period and the ensuing disappointment are especially important since they provide a single documentary counterbalance to the plethora of well-documented Christian responses to events of the same era. Like no other Jewish source of late antiquity, *piyyut* provides a sense of what synagogue audiences heard and/or wanted to hear.

The Passover *Haggadah* provides another example of a potential confusion between 'late ancient' and 'medieval' Jewish sources. A compilation of uncertain date the *Haggadah* is possibly the single most important text with which practically every Jew is familiar. It has a troubled history. 'The origins of the Passover *Haggadah* and the seder service are to be sought in transforming a biblical ritual tied to the temple sacrifice into a domestic celebration with liturgical and pedagogic elements...', a transformation that commenced even before the destruction of the Temple in CE 70![6] Whether the *Haggadah*, as a whole, already existed prior to CE 70, and this seems doubtful, has been a hotly contested topic with no consensus in sight.[7] What seems clear is that several elements of the *Haggadah* belong to a late ancient

---

[4] Yahalom, *Poetry and Society*, 50–60.

[5] Sivan, 'From Byzantine to Persian Jerusalem' (2000); 'Palestine between Byzantium and Persia' (2004).

[6] Bokser, *The Origins of the Seder: The Passover Rite and Early Rabbinic Judaism.* Quote is from S. C. Reif, 'The Early Liturgy of the Synagogue', in W. Horbury *et al.* (eds.), *The Cambridge History of Judaism*, iii (Cambridge 1999), 339.

[7] L. Finkelstein, 'The Oldest Midrash: Pre-Rabbinic Ideals and Teachings in the Passover Haggadah', *HTR* 31 (1939), 291–317 (placing the Haggadah in the 2nd cent. BCE); S. Zeitlin, 'The First Night of Passover', *JQR* 38 (1948), 431–60 (dating the Haggadah to a period not before the 3rd cent. CE).

stage of compilation. Especially noteworthy here is Yuval's methodology which attempts to date several strands in conjunction with the development of the Christian theology of Easter.[8] Following him my own presentation and analysis of late ancient Haggadic tales is done within a context of Jewish–Christian relations in Palestine.

Without doubt the most troublesome sources remain the huge and vague category usually labelled 'rabbinic'.[9] These include the Mishnah (redacted *c*. CE 200), the Tosefta (redacted between 250 and 300), the Talmuds, of which the so-called Yerushalmi or Palestinian Talmud is a compilation produced around CE 400 and the Bavli or Babylonian Talmud *c*. CE 600, as well as *midrashim* or exegetical works of law and lore of varying redactional dates. Four matters hamper the use of these sources by historians: (1) the lack of critical editions for most of these, (2) the uncertainty of the dates of individual components and of the entire enterprise, (3) the relationship between these compilations and the authorities to whom pronouncements are attributed, and (4) sharply contrasting scholarly views regarding the historicity or lack of it of all these sources. Are rabbinic texts a pure literary construct with little or no relation to the reality in which they were composed, circulated, or redacted? Is there no relation between named rabbis and the opinions attributed to them? Notwithstanding, the volume of scholarly work on rabbinic texts is overwhelming and much of it has been published in Hebrew.

It is hardly surprising, therefore, that historians of late antiquity have in general shied away from Jewish sources or have used them rather rarely. In this book I have used nearly exclusively Palestinian sources whose redaction can be assigned to 'late antiquity', in other words, to somewhere between CE 200 and 650, as well as texts which contain layers which likewise can be reasonably assigned to late antiquity. Rarely I resort to the Babylonian Talmud, particularly when it cites Palestinian sources. When using sources whose redactional date has been considered 'medieval' (i.e. post-seventh century) I selected only the material which seemed to belong to a late ancient layer. I have not dealt with variant readings. The rabbinic opinions which I quote, even while they might or might not directly represent what had actually been uttered by a specific rabbi at a specific time, are nevertheless best understood within the historical context of the late ancient redaction of the text. In general I have endeavoured to select passages which were

---

[8] Yuval, *'Two Nations in Your Womb': Perceptions of Jews and Christians*, 71–107 (Heb.).

[9] For a brief overview see C. Hezser, 'Classical Rabbinic Literature', in M. Goodman (ed.), *The Oxford Handbook of Jewish Studies* (Oxford 2002), 115–40.

formulated not in a vacuum of a literary cosmos existing solely in the fertile imagination of the rabbis but in close conjunction with the Palestinian environment and contemporary conflicts.

The rest of the sources used in this study are familiar to any student of the Roman empire in late antiquity. Many are available in critical editions and many have benefited from erudite commentaries, although the *Patrologia* still contains a host of texts which await scholarly scrutiny and some authors like those produced by members of the rhetorical school of Gaza, have been 'discovered' only in recent years.[10] Many texts are now available in translation. Their date, even when not established with minute precision, is on the whole known with reasonable accuracy.

[10] See Ch 8.

Bibliography

Aaron, D. H., 'Judaism's Holy Language', *Approaches to Ancient Judaism* 16 (1990), 49–107.

Abel, F.-M., 'Gaza au VI siècle d'après le rhéteur Chorikios', *RB* 40 (1931), 5–31.

—— 'L'Église du baptême du Christ', *RB* 41 (1932), 245–8.

—— 'L'Île de Jotabe', *RB* 47 (1938), 510–38.

—— *Géographie de la Palestine* (repr. Paris 1967).

—— See also under Vincent.

Abrams, P., *Historical Sociology* (Ithaca, NY, 1982).

Adang, C., *Muslim Writers on Judaism and the Hebrew Bible: From Ibn Rabban to Ibn Hazm* (Leiden 1996).

Adler, E. N., and Seligsohn, M., 'Une nouvelle chronique samaritaine', *REJ* 44 (1902), 188–222; 45 (1902), 70–98, 223–54; 46 (1903), 123–46.

Adler, M., 'The Emperor Julian and the Jews', *JQR* 5 (1893), 591–51.

Alexander, P. S., 'Bavli Berakhot 55a–57b: The Talmudic Dreambook in Context', *JJS* 46 (1995), 230–48.

—— 'Jerusalem and the Omphalos of the World: On the History of a Geographical Concept', in L. I. Levine (ed.), *Jerusalem: Its Sanctity and Centrality to Judaism, Christianity, and Islam* (New York 1999), 104–19.

Alliata, E., 'The Pilgrimage Routes during the Byzantine Period in Transjordan', in M. Piccirillo and E. Alliata (eds.), *The Madaba Map Centenary 1897–1997* (Jerusalem 1999), 122–6 (also via Franciscan Cyberspot).

—— See also under Piccirillo.

Alon, G., *The Jews in their Land in the Talmudic Age, CE 70–640*, trans. G. Levi (Cambridge, Mass., 1989).

Amit, D., 'Priests and the Memory of the Temple in the Synagogues of Southern Judaea', in Levine (ed.), *Continuity and Renewal* (Jerusalem 2004), 143–54 (Heb.).

Anderson, R. T., and Giles, T., *The Keepers: An Introduction to the History and Culture of the Samaritans* (Peabody, Mass. 2002).

Arce, P. A., 'Culte islamique au Tombeau de la Vierge', *Atti del congresso assunzionistico orientale* (Jerusalem 1951), 177–93.

Archaeological Survey of Israel (Jerusalem 1990) (Heb. and Eng.).

Arjava, A., *Women and Roman Law in Late Antiquity* (Oxford 1996).

Arnold, D., *The Early Episcopal Career of Athanasius of Alexandria* (Notre Dame 1991).

Ashkenazi, Y., 'Paganism in Gaza in the Fifth and Sixth Centuries', *Cathedra* 60 (1991), 106–15 (Heb.).

Aubineau, M., *Les Homélies Festales d'Hésychius de Jérusalem*, 2 vols. (Subsidia Hagiographica 59; Brussels 1978–80).

Avemarie, See under Henten.

Aviam, M., 'The Ancient Synagogue at Bar'am', in Levine (ed.), *Continuity and Renewal* (Jerusalem 2004), 544–53 (Heb.).

—— See also under Frankel.

Avigad, N., *Discovering Jerusalem* (Jerusalem 1980).

Avi Yonah, M., 'The Economics of Byzantine Palestine', *IEJ* 8 (1958), 35–51.

—— 'On the Date of the Limes Palestinae', *Eretz Israel* 5 (1959), 135–7 (Heb.).

—— 'A Sixth Century Inscription from Sepphoris', *IEJ* 11 (1961), 184–7.

—— *The Jews of Palestine: A Political History from the Bar Kokhba War to the Arab Conquest* (Eng. trans. of 1946 Hebrew original) (New York 1976).

—— *Art in Ancient Palestine* (Jerusalem 1981).

—— *The Holy Land: A Historical Geography from the Persian to the Arab Conquest* (rev. version Jerusalem 2002).

Avner, R., 'The Recovery of the Kathisma Church and its Influence on Octagonal Buildings', in *One Land—Many Cultures: Archaeological Studies in Honor of Stanislau Loffreda* (Jerusalem 2003), 173–86.

—— 'The Kathisma Church on the Road from Jerusalem to Bethlehem', *Qadmoniot* 130 (2005), 117–21 (Heb.).

—— See also under Tzaferis.

Avni, G., 'Christian Secondary Use of Jewish Burial Caves in Jerusalem in Light of New Excavations at the Aceldama Tombs', in F. Manns and E. Alliata (eds.), *Early Christianity in Context: Monuments and Documents* (Jerusalem 1993), 265–76.

—— *Nomads, Farmers, and Town Dwellers: Pastoralist–Sedentist Interaction in the Negev Highlands, Sixth–Eighth Centuries* CE (Supplement to the Archaeological Survey of Israel; Jerusalem: Israel Antiquities Authority, 1996).

—— 'The Necropoleis of Jerusalem and Beth Govrin in the Fourth to the Seventh Centuries: An Example of Urban Cemeteries in Palestine in the Roman and Byzantine Periods' (Ph.D., the Hebrew University, 1997).

—— See also under Rosen.

Ayalon, E., 'Horbat Migdal (Tsur Natan): An Ancient Samaritan Village', in E. Stern and H. Eshel (eds.), *The Samaritans* (Jerusalem 2002), 272–88 (Heb.).

Bacher, W., 'Die Jahrmarkt an der Terebinte bei Hebron', _ZAW_ 29 (1909), 294–311.

Bacht, H., 'Die Rolle des orientalischen Mönchtums in den kirchenpolitischen Auseinandersetzungen um Chalkedon (431–519)', in A. Grillmeier and H. Bacht (eds.), _Das Konzil von Chalkedon_ (Würzburg 1953), ii. 193–314.

Bagatti, B., _The Church from the Gentiles in Palestine: History and Archaeology_, trans. E. Hoade (Jerusalem 1971).

——— _Antichi villaggi cristiani della Guidea e del Neghev_ (Jerusalem 1983) (Eng. trans. P. Rotondi, _Ancient Christian Villages of Judaea and Negev_, Jerusalem 2002).

Baker, C. M., _Rebuilding the House of Israel: Architectures of Gender in Jewish Antiquity_ (Stanford 2002).

Baldovin, J. F., _The Urban Character of Christian Worship: The Origins, Development and Meaning of Stational Liturgy_ (Rome 1987).

Baly, C., 'Shivta', _PEFQS_ 68 (1935), 171–81.

Bar, D., 'Settlement and Economy in Eretz-Israel during the Late Roman and Byzantine Periods (70–641 CE)', _Cathedra_ 107 (2003), 24–46 (Heb.).

Barag, D., 'The Kingdom of Heaven in a Christian Epitaph of 474 CE from Gaza', _Eretz Israel_ 19 (1987), 242–5 (Heb.).

——— 'The Dated Jewish Inscription from Binyamina Reconsidered', _Atiqot_ 25 (1994), 179–81.

——— _et al._, 'The Synagogue at En-Gedi', in Levine (ed.), _Ancient Synagogues Revealed_ (Jerusalem 1981), 116–19.

Baras, Z. _et al._ (eds.), _Eretz Israel the Destruction of the Temple to the Muslim Conquest_ (Jerusalem 1982) (Heb.).

Bar Ilan, M., 'Why did the Tannaim discuss the Borders of Eretz Israel', _Teudah_ 7 (1991), 95–110.

——— Review of Sokoloff–Yahalom, _Jewish Palestinian Aramaic Poetry_, _Mahut_ 23 (2001), 167–88 (Heb.).

Barker, G., and Mattingly, D. (eds.), _The Archaeology of Mediterranean Landscapes_ (Oxford 2000).

Barnes, T. D., _Constantine and Eusebius_ (Cambridge, Mass., 1981).

Barth, L. M., 'The "Three Rebukes" and the "Seven of Consolation": Sermons in the _Pesikta de Rav Kahana_', _JJS_ 33 (1982), 503–15.

——— 'Reading Rabbinic Bible Exegesis', _Approaches to Ancient Judaism_ 4 (1983), 81–93.

Baskin, J. R., 'Rabbinic–Patristic Exegetical Contacts in Late Antiquity: A Bibliographical Reappraisal', _Approaches to Ancient Judaism_ 5 (1985), 53–80.

—— *Midrashic Women: Formations of the Feminine in Rabbinic Literature* (Hanover, NH, 2002).

Bastiaensen, A. A. R., 'Jérôme hagiographe', in G. Freyburger and L. Pernot (eds.), *Du héros païen au saint chrétien* (Collection REA 14; Paris 1997), 97–123.

Baynes, N. H., 'The Finding of the Virgin's Robe', *Annuaire de l'Institut de philologie et d'histoire orientales et slaves* 9 (1949), 87–97.

—— 'The Icons before Iconoclasm', *HTR* 44 (1951), 93–106.

—— See also under Dawes.

Beaucamp, J., *et al.*, 'La Persécution des chrétiens de Nagran et la chronologie himyarite', *Aram* 11–12 (1999–2000), 15–83.

Beck, H. G., *Kirche und theologische Literatur im byzantinischen Reich* (Munich 1959).

Belayche, N., 'Pagan Festivals in Fourth Century Gaza', in B. Biton-Ashkelony and A. Kofsky (eds.), *Christian Gaza in Late Antiquity* (Leiden 2004), 5–22.

Ben David, H., 'Oil Presses and Oil Production in the Golan in the Mishnaic and Talmudic Periods', *Atiqot* 34 (1998), 1–61.

—— 'The Lower Golan in the Late Second Temple, Mishnah and Talmud Periods' (Ph.D., Bar Ilan University, 2000) (Heb.).

Ben Dov, M., *The Dig at Temple Mount* (Jerusalem 1982) (Heb.).

Beneševic, V., 'Sur la date de la mosaïque de la Transfiguration au Mont Sinaï', *Byzantion* 1 (1924), 145–72.

Ben-Hayyim, A., *Tevat Marka: A Collection of Samaritan Midrashim* (Jerusalem 1988) (Heb.).

Berger, D., 'Three Typological Themes in Early Jewish Messianism', *AJS Review* 10 (1985), 141–64.

Berliner (Landau), R., 'What do Daniel and the Lions do on the Ark in Naaran's Ancient Synagogue', *Judea and Samaria Research Studies (Mehkarei Yehuda VeShomron)*, 3 (1993), 213–19 (Heb.; Eng. abstract on p. xxii).

Bernardi, J., *Grégoire de Nazienze: Discours 4–5 contre Julien* (Paris 1983).

Bichovsky, G., 'Numismatic Finds from Synagogues as Evidence of the Gallus Revolt', lecture given at the conference on *New Studies on the Ancient Synagogue and its World* (Bar Ilan University, 10 June 2004), abstract pp. 22–4.

Biddle, M., *The Tomb of Christ* (Stroud 1999).

Bieberstein, K., 'Die Porta Neapolitana, die Nea Maria und die Nea Sophia in der Neapolis von Jerusalem', *ZDPV* 105 (1989), 110–22.

—— and Bloedhorn, H., *Jerusalem: Grundzüge der Baugeschichte vom Chalkolithikum bis zur Frühzeit der osmanischen Herrschaft*, 3 vols. (Wiesbaden 1994).

Bihain, E., 'L'Épître de Cyrille de Jérusalem à Constance sur la vision de la croix (BHG3 413)', *Byz.* 43 (1973), 264–96.

Binns, John, *Ascetics and Ambassadors of Christ: The Monasteries of Palestine 341–631* (Oxford 1994).

Birger-Calderon, R. See under Hirschfeld.

Biton-Ashkelony, B., 'Imitatio Mosis and Pilgrimage in the Life of Peter the Iberian', in eadem and A. Kofsky (eds.), *Christian Gaza in Late Antiquity* (2004), 107–29.

—— *Encountering the Sacred: The Debate on Christian Pilgrimage in Late Antiquity* (Berkeley 2005).

—— and Kofsky, A., 'Gazan Monasticism in the Byzantine Period', *Cathedra* 96 (2000), 69–110 (Heb.).

—— —— (eds.), *Christian Gaza in Late Antiquity* (Leiden 2004).

Black, M., 'The Festival of Encaenia Ecclesiae in the Ancient Church with special Reference to Palestine and Syria', *JEH* 5 (1954), 78–86.

Blakely, J. A., *The Joint Expedition to Caesarea Maritima Excavation Reports*, vol. 4: *The Pottery and the Dating of Vault I. Horeum, Mithraeum, and Later Uses* (Lewiston, NY, 1987).

Blanchetiere, F., 'Julien. Philhellène, philosémite, antichrétien: L'Affaire du temple de Jérusalem', *JJS* 31 (1980), 61–81.

Blasi, A., 'Symbolic Interactionism as Theory', *Sociology and Social Research* 56 (1972), 453–65.

Bloedhorn. See under Bieberstein.

Blumenkranz, B., *Juifs et chrétiens dans le monde occidental 430–1096* (Paris 1960).

Bokser, B. M., *The Origins of the Seder: The Passover Rite and Early Rabbinic J* (Berkeley 1984).

—— 'Ritualizing the Seder', *Journal of the American Academy of Religion* 56 (1988), 443–71.

Bonner, G., 'The Extinction of Paganism and the Church Historian', *JEH* 35 (1984), 339–57.

Borgehammar, S., *How the Holy Cross was Found: From Event to Medieval Legend* (Stockholm 1991).

Bottini, G. C., *et al.* (eds.), *Christian Archaeology in the Holy Land: New Discoveries* (Jerusalem 1990).

—— *et al.* (eds.), *One Land—Many Cultures: Archaeological Studies in Honor of Stanislau Loffreda* (Jerusalem 2003).

Bowersock. G. W., 'The Greek Moses: Confusion of Ethnic and Cultural Components in Late Roman and Early Byzantine Palestine', in H. Lapin (ed.), *Religious and Ethnic Communities in Later Roman Palestine* (Bethesda 1998), 31–48.

—— 'Inscriptions in the Nile Festival Building at Sepphoris: The House of the Daughter of the Governor (AD 517–18?) and her Husband Asbolius Patricius', *JRA* 17 (2004), 764–6.

Bowman, G., ' "Mapping History's Redemption": Eschatology and Topography in the *Itinerarium Burdigalense*', in L. I. Levine (ed.), *Jerusalem* (1999), 163–87.

Bowman, J., *Samaritan Documents relating to their History, Religion, and Life* (Pittsburgh 1977).

Boyarin, D., *Dying for God: Martyrdom and the Making of Christianity and Judaism* (Stanford 1999).

Bradbury, S., *Severus of Minorca. Letter on the Conversion of the Jews* (Oxford 1996).

Bradshaw, P. F., and Hoffman, L. A. (eds.), *Passover and Easter: Origin and History to Modern Times* (Notre Dame, Ind., 1999).

—— —— (eds.), *Passover and Easter: The Symbolic Structuring of Sacred Seasons* (Notre Dame 1999).

Brandes, W., 'Heraclius between Restoration and Reform. Some Remarks on Recent Research', in G. J. Reinink and B. H. Stolte (eds), *The Reign of Heraclius. Crisis and Confrontation* (Leuven 2002), 17–40.

Bregman, M., 'Mishnah and LXX as "Mystery": An Example of Jewish–Christian Polemic in the Byzantine Period', in L. I. Levine (ed.), *Continuity and Renewal* (Jerusalem 2004), 333–42.

Brekelmans, C., and Haran, M. (eds.), *Hebrew Bible/Old Testament: The History of its Interpretation*, i (Göttingen 1996).

Brock, S. P., 'An Early Syriac Life of Maximus the Confessor', *AB* 91 (1973), 299–346.

—— 'The Rebuilding of the Temple', *PEQ* 108 (1976), 103–7.

—— 'A Letter Attributed to Cyril of Jerusalem on the Rebuilding of the Temple', *BSOAS* 40 (1977), 267–86.

—— 'Syriac Dispute Poems: The Various Types', in G. J. Reinink and H. L. J. Vanstiphout (eds.), *Dispute Poems and Dialogues in the Ancient and Medieval Near East* (Leiden 1991), 109–19.

Broshi, M., 'The Population of Western Palestine in the Roman-Byzantine Period', *BASOR* 236 (1980), 1–10.

Brown, P., *The World of Late Antiquity* (London 1971).

—— *The Body and Society* (New York 1988).

—— *Poverty and Leadership in the Later Roman Empire* (Hanover, NH, 2002).

Brown, R. E., *The Birth of the Messiah: A Commentary on the Infancy Narratives in Matthew and Luke* (Garden City, NY, 1977).

Brubacker, L., 'Memories of Helena: Patterns in Female Imperial Matronage in the Fourth and Fifth Centuries', in L. James (ed.), *Women, Men and Eunuchs: Gender in Byzantium* (London 1997), 52–75.

Büchler, A., *The Political and Social Leaders of the Jewish Community of Sepphoris in the Second and Third Centuries* (London 1909).

Büchler, A.,'The Patriarch R. Judah I and the Graeco-Roman Cities of Palestine', *Studies in Jewish History* (London 1954), 179–244.

Burman, J., 'The Christian Empress Eudocia', in J. W. Perreault (ed.), *Les Femmes et le monachisme byzantine* (Athens 1991), 51–9.

Cameron, Al., 'Wandering Poets: A Literary Movement in Byzantine Egypt', *Historia* 14 (1965), 470–509.

—— *Porphyrius the Charioteer* (Oxford 1973).

—— *Circus Factions* (Oxford 1976).

—— 'Flavius: A Nicety of Protocol', *Latomus* 47 (1988), 26–33.

Cameron, Av., 'The Virgin's Robe: An Episode in the History of Early Seventh Century Constantinople', *Byz.* 49 (1979), 42–59.

—— 'The Language of Images: The Rise of Icons and Christian Representations', *Studies in Church History* 28 (1992), 1–42.

—— and Hall, S. G., *Eusebius' Life of Constantine* (Oxford 1999).

Caner, D., 'Sinai Pilgrimage and Ascetic Romance: Pseudo-Nilus *Narrationes* in Context', in L. Ellis and F. Kidner (eds.), *Travel, Communications, and Geography in Late Antiquity: Sacred and Profane*. Proceedings of the IV Shifting Frontiers in Late Antiquity Conference (San Francisco 2001) (Aldershot 2004), 135–47.

Capelle, D. B., 'La Fête de la Vierge à Jérusalem', *Le Muséon* 56 (1943), 1–33.

Carmichael, C. M., *The Laws of Deuteronomy* (Ithaca 1974).

Caseau, B., 'Sacred Landscapes', in G. W. Bowersock *et al.* (eds.), *Interpreting Late Antiquity* (Cambridge, Mass., 1999, 2001), 21–59.

—— '*Polemein Lithois*: La Désacralisation des espaces et des objets religieux païens durant l'Antiquité tardive', in M. Kaplan (ed.), *Le Sacré et son inscription dans l'espace à Byzance et en Occident* (Paris 2001), 61–123.

Casson, L., and Hettich, E. L. (eds.), *Excavations at Nessana: Literary Papyri* (Princeton 1950).

Chantraine, H., 'Die Kreuzesvision von 351: Fakten und Probleme', *BZ* 86–7 (1993–4), 430–41.

Chapman, R., in G. S. P. Freeman-Grenville *et al.* (eds.), *The Onomasticon of Eusebius* (2003), gazetteer.

Chauvot, A. (trans. and comm.) *Procope de Gaza, Priscien de Césarée. Panégyriques de l'empereur Anastase* (Bonn 1986).

Chen, D., 'The Design of the Ancient Synagogues in Galilee', *LA* 28 (1978), 193–202.

—— 'Dating the Cardo Maximus in Jerusalem', *PEQ* 114 (1982), 43–5.

—— 'Byzantine Architects at Work in Oboda, Nessana and Rehovot, Palaestina Tertia: A Study in Paleo-Christian Architectural Design', *LA* 35 (1985), 291–6.

Chitty, D. J., 'Jerusalem after Chalcedon, AD 451–519', *The Christian East* 2 (1952–3), 22–32.

—— *The Desert a City* (Oxford 1966).

—— 'Abba Isaiah', *JTS* 22 (1971), 47–72.

Chuvin, P., 'Christianisation et résistance des cultes traditionnels', in *Hellénisme et christianisme* (Villeneuve d'Ascq 2004), 15–34.

Ciccolella, 'Phaedra's Shining Roses: Reading Euripides in Sixth-Century Gaza', *Scripta Classica Israelica* 26 (2007), 181–204.

—— *Cinque poeti bizantini. Anacreontee dal Barberiniano Greco 310* (Alessandria 2000).

Clark, E. A., *Jerome, Chrysostom and Friends* (New York 1979).

—— 'Claims on the Bones of St Stephen: The Partisans of Melania and Eudocia', *Church History* 51 (1982), 141–56.

—— *The Life of Melania the Younger* (New York 1984).

—— *Ascetic Piety and Women's Faith* (Lewiston, NY, 1986).

—— *The Origenist Controversy: The Cultural Construction of an Early Christian Debate* (Princeton 1992).

—— 'Ideology, History and the Construction of "Woman" in Late Antique Christianity', *JECS* 2 (1994), 155–84.

Clark, G., *Women in Late Antiquity* (Oxford 1993).

Cohen, G. D., 'Esau as Symbol in Early Medieval Thought', in A. Altmann (ed.), *Jewish Medieval and Renaissance Studies* (Cambridge, Mass., 1967), 19–48.

Cohen, J. M., *A Samaritan Chronicle: A Source-Critical Analysis of the Life and Times of the Great Samaritan Reformer Baba Rabbah* (Leiden 1981).

Cohen, N. G., 'Earliest Evidence of the Haftarah Cycle for the Sabbaths between 17 Be-Tamuz and Sukkot in Philo', *JJS* 48 (1997), 225–49.

Cohen, R., 'The Marvelous Mosaics of Kissufim', *Biblical Archaeology Review* 6 (1980), 16–23.

Cohn, E. W., 'Second Thoughts about the Perforated Stone on the Haram of Jerusalem', *PEQ* 114 (1982), 143–6.

Colt, H. D. (ed.), *Excavations at Nessana*, i (London 1962).

Conybeare, F. C., *Rituale Armenorum* (Oxford 1905).

Corrigan, K., *Visual Polemics in the Ninth Century Psalter* (Cambridge 1992).

Coser, L. A., *The Functions of Social Conflicts* (New York 1956).

Cotton, H. M., *et al.*, 'The Papyrology of the Roman Near East: A Survey', *JRS* 85 (1995), 214–35.

Cotton, H., and Price, J., 'A Bi-Lingual Epitaph from Zoar in the Hecht Museum: The Greek Inscription', *Michmanim* 15 (2001), 10–12.

Covolo, F. dal, *et al.* (eds.), *Eusebio di Vercelli e il suo tempo* (Rome 1997).

Cowley, A., *Aramaic Papyri of the Fifth Century BC* (Oxford 1923).

Cox Miller, P., *Dreams in Late Antiquity: Studies in the Imagination of a Culture* (Princeton 1994).

Cranfield, C. E. B., 'Some Reflections on the Subject of the Virgin Birth', *Scottish Journal of Theology* 41 (1988), 177–89.

Crowfoot, J. W. *et al.*, *Samaria-Sebaste*, i (London 1942).

Crown, A. D., 'The Samaritans in the Byzantine Orbit', *BJRL* 69 (1986–7), 96–138.

Crown, A. D., and Pummer, R., *A Bibliography of the Samaritans. Revised, Expanded and Annotated*, 3rd edn. (ATLA Bibliography Series 51; Lanham, Md., 2005).

—— —— and Tal, A. (eds.), *A Companion to Samaritan Studies* (Tübingen 1993).

Curran, J., *Pagan City and Christian Capital: Rome in the Fourth Century* (Oxford 2000).

Dagron, G., *Constantinople imaginaire* (Paris 1984).

—— and Déroche, V. (eds.), *Doctrina Jacobi nuper baptizati*, *TM* 11 (1991), 47 ff.

Dahari, Uzi, *Monastic Settlements in South Sinai* (Israel Antiquities Authority, Reports 9; Jerusalem 2000).

Daley, B. E., *On the Dormition of Mary* (Crestwood, NY, 1998).

—— ' "At the Hour of our Death": Mary's Dormition and Christian Dying in Late Patristic and Early Byzantine Literature', *DOP* 55 (2001), 71–89.

Damascelli, A., 'Croce, maledizione e redenzioni: Un'eco di Purim in Galati 3.13', *Henoch* 23 (2001), 227–41.

Dan, Y., 'The Circus and its Factions in Eretz Israel during the Byzantine Period', *Cathedra* 4 (1977), 133–46 (Heb.).

—— 'Jews and Sea Trade in the Indian Ocean before the Islamic Period', *Studies in the History of the Jewish People and the Land of Israel* 5 (1980), 153–8.

—— 'Jewish–Samaritan Relations in Eretz Israel in the Late Byzantine Period (6–7th centuries)', *Zion* 46 (1981), 67–76 (Heb.).

—— 'Palaestina Salutaris (Tertia) and its Capital', *IEJ* 32 (1982), 134–7.

—— *The City in Eretz Israel during the Late Roman and Byzantine Periods* (Jerusalem 1984) (Heb.).

Dar, S., 'Sanctuaries of the Hermon', in A. Kasher *et al.* (eds.), *Greece and Rome in Eretz Israel* (Jerusalem 1989), 296–316 (Heb.).

—— *The History of Hermon: Settlement and Temples of the Itureans* (Tel Aviv 1994) (Heb.) (Eng. abstract pp. 375–6).

—— *Sumaqa: A Jewish Village on the Carmel* (Tel Aviv 1998) (Heb.).

—— 'Samaritan Rebellions in the Byzantine Period: The Archaeological Evidence', in E. Stern and H. Eshel, *The Samaritans* (Jerusalem 2002), 444–53 (Heb.).

—— et al., Raqit: Marinus' Estate on the Carmel, Israel (Jerusalem: Israel Exploration Society, 2003).

Dauphin, C. M., 'Jewish and Christian Communities in the Roman and Byzantine Gaulinitis: A Study of Evidence from Archaeological Surveys', PEQ 11 (1982), 129–42.

—— 'Brothels, Baths and Babes: Prostitution in the Byzantine Holy Land', Classics Ireland 3 (1996), 47–72.

—— 'Leprosy, Lust and Lice: Health and Hygiene in Byzantine Palestine', Bulletin of the Anglo-Israel Archaeological Society 15 (1996–7), 55–80.

—— La Palestine byzantine, 3 vols. (Oxford 1998).

—— 'Interdits alimentaires et territorialité en Palestine byzantine', in Mélanges Gilbert Dagron, TM 14 (2002), 147–66.

—— and Gibson, S., 'Landscape Archaeology at er-Ramthaniyye in the Golan Heights', in J.-L. Fiches and S. van de Leeuw (eds.), Archéologie et espaces: Actes des Xe rencontres internationales d'archéologie et d'histoire, Antibes (Juan les Pins 1990), 435–65.

—— —— 'Ancient Settlements in their Landscapes: The Results of Ten Years of Survey on the Golan Heights (1978–1988)', Bulletin of the Anglo-Israel Archaeological Society 12 (1992–3), 7–31.

—— —— 'Pèlerinage ghassanide au sanctuaire byzantin de Saint Jean-Baptiste à er-Ramthaniyye en Gaulanitide', in Akten des XII internationalen Kongresses für christliche Archäologie (Münster 1995), 667–73.

—— et al., 'Farj en Gaulanitide: Refuge judéo-chrétien?', POC 34 (1984), 233–45.

—— et al., 'Païens, juifs, judéo-chrétiens, chrétiens et musulmans en Gaulanitide: Les Inscriptions de Na'aran, Kafr Naffakh, Farj et Er-Ramthaniyye', POC 46 (1996), 305–40.

Davidson, I., Parody in Jewish Literature (New York 1907).

—— (ed.), Genizah Studies in Memory of Solomon Schechter (New York 1928).

Davies, P. R., 'Passover and the Dating of the Aqedah', JJS 30 (1979), 59–67.

—— 'Martyrdom and Redemption: On the Development of Isaac Typology in the Early Church', SP 17 (1982), 652–8.

Davis, N. Z., Society and Culture in Early Modern France (Stanford 1975); now available in electronic form.

Dawes, E., and Baynes, N. H., Three Byzantine Saints (London and Oxford 1948).

Delehaye, H., Vita Danielis Stylitae, AB. 32 (1913), 121–216.

—— 'Une vie inédite de Saint Jean l'Aumonier', AB 45 (1927), 1–74.

Demsky, A., 'The Permitted Villages of Sebaste in the Rehov Mosaic', IEJ 29 (1979), 182–93.

Demsky, A., 'Holy City and Holy Land as Viewed by Jews and Christians in the Byzantine Period', in A. Houtman, M. Poorthuis, and J. Schwartz (eds.), *Sanctity of Time and Space in Tradition and Modernity* (Leiden 1998), 285–96.

Déroche. See under Dagron.

Devos, P., 'La Servante de Dieu Poemenia d'après Pallade, la tradition copte et Jean Rufus', *AB* 87 (1969), 189–212.

Devreesse, R., 'La Vie de S Maxime le Confesseur et ses recensions', *AB* 46 (1928), 5–49.

—— 'Le Christianisme dans la péninsule sinaïtique dès origines à l'arrivée des Musulmans', *RB* 49 (1940), 205–23.

De Vries, B., *Umm el Jimal: A Frontier Town and its Landscape in Northern Jordan* (JRA Suppl. 26; Portsmouth, RI, 1998).

Dexinger, F., 'The Beliefs of the Samaritans in the Byzantine Period', in E. Stern and H. Eshel, *The Samaritans* Jerusalem, 2002), 496–518 (Heb.).

Di Segni, L., 'Scythopolis (Beth Shean) during the Samaritan Rebellion of 529 CE', in D. Jacoby and Y. Tsafrir (eds.), *Jews, Samaritans and Christians in Byzantine Palestine* (Jerusalem 1988), 217–27 (Heb.).

—— 'The Life of Chariton', in V. L. Wimbush (ed.), *Ascetic Behavior in Greco-Roman Antiquity: A Sourcebook* (Minneapolis 1990), 393–421.

—— 'A Jewish Greek Inscription from the Vicinity of Caesarea Maritima', *Atiqot* 22 (1993), 133–6.

—— 'The Date of the Binyamina Inscription and the Question of Byzantine Dora', *Atiqot* 25 (1994), 183–6.

—— '*Eis theos* in Palestinian Inscriptions', *SCI* 13 (1994), 94–115.

—— 'The Involvement of Local, Municipal, and Provincial Authorities in Urban Building in Late Antiquity', in J. Humphrey (ed.), *The Roman and Byzantine Near East* (Ann Arbor 1995), 312–32.

—— 'Mutual Relations between Samaritans, Jews and Christians in Byzantine Palestine', *New Samaritan Studies* (1995), 185–94.

—— 'A Dated Inscription from Beth Shean and the Cult of Dionysos Ktistes in Roman Scythopolis', *SCI* 16 (1997), 139–61.

—— 'Dated Greek Inscriptions from Palestine from the Roman and Byzantine Period' (Ph.D., the Hebrew University, 1997) (Eng.).

—— 'The Samaritans in Roman-Byzantine Palestine', in H. Lapin (ed.), *Religious and Ethnic Communities* (Bethesda 1998), 51–66.

—— 'A Chapel of St Paul at Caesarea Maritima? The Inscriptions', *LA* 50 (2000), 383–400.

—— 'Samaritan Revolts in Byzantine Palestine', in E. Stern and H. Eshel (eds.), *The Samaritans* (Jerusalem 2002), 454–80 (Heb.).

—— 'The Beer Sheva Edict Reconsidered', *SCI* 23 (2004), 131–58.

—— 'The Territory of Gaza: Notes of Historical Geography', in B. Biton-Ashkelony and A. Kofsky (eds.), *Christian Gaza* (Leiden 2004), 41–58.

—— and Tsafrir, Y., 'Ethnic Compositions of the Population of Jerusalem in the Byzantine Period', in Y. Tsafrir and S. Safrai (eds.), *The History of Jerusalem* (Jerusalem 1999), 261–80.

Diels, H., 'Über die von Prokop beschreibene Kunstuhr von Gaza', *Abhandlungen der königlich preussischen Akademie der Wissenschaft, Philosophisch-Historische Klasse* 7 (1917), 1–39.

Donner, H., 'Die Palästinabeschreibung des Epiphanius Monachus Hagiopolita', *ZDPV* 87 (1971), 42–92.

—— 'The Uniqueness of the Madaba Map and its Restoration in 1965', in *Madaba Map Centenary* (Franciscan Cyberspace).

Douval, A. J., *Cyril of Jerusalem, Mystagogue: The Authorship of the 'Mystagogal Catecheses'* (Washington, DC, 2001).

Downey, G., 'John of Gaza and the Mosaic of Ge and Karpoi', in R. Stielwell (ed.), *Antioch on the Orontes*, ii (Princeton 1938), 205–12.

—— 'The Christian Schools of Palestine: A Chapter of Literary History', *Harvard Library Bulletin* 12 (1958), 310–11.

—— *Gaza in the Early Sixth Century* (Norman, Okla., 1963).

Drake, H. A., *Constantine and the Bishops: The Politics of Intolerance* (Baltimore 2000).

Drijvers, J. W., *Helena Augusta: The Mother of Constantine the Great and the Legend of her Finding of the True Cross* (Leiden 1992).

—— 'Ammianus Marcellinus 23.1.2.3: The Rebuilding of the Temple in Jerusalem', in J. den Boeft and H. C. Teitler (eds.), *Cognitio Gestorum: The Historiographic Art of Ammianus* (Amsterdam 1992), 19–26.

—— 'Helena Augusta: Exemplary Christian Empress', *SP* 24 (1993), 85–90.

—— 'Promoting Jerusalem: Cyril and the True Cross', in idem and J. W. Watt (eds.), *Portraits of Spiritual Authority: Religious Power in Early Christianity, Byzantium and the Christian Orient* (Leiden 1999), 79–95.

—— 'The Syriac Julian Romance: Aspects of the Jewish–Christian Controversy in Late Antiquity', in H. L. J. Vanstiphout *et al.* (eds.), *All Those Nations—Cultural Encounters within and with the Near East: Studies presented to H. Drijvers* (Groningen 1999), 31–42.

—— 'Heraclius and the *restitutio crusis*. Notes on Symbolism and Ideology' in G. J. Reinink and B. H. Stolte (eds), *The Reign of Heraclius. Crisis and Confrontation* (Leuven 2002), 175–90.

—— *Cyril of Jerusalem, Bishop and City* (Leiden 2004).

—— and Drijvers, H. J. W., *The Finding of the True Cross: The Judas Kyriakos Legend in Syriac* (Louvain 1997).

Duchesne, L., *Liber Pontificalis*, i (Paris 1955).

Durkheim, E., *The Rules of Sociological Methods*, trans. W. D. Halls (New York 1982).

Duval, N., 'Essai sur la signification des vignettes topographiques', in M. Piccirillo and E. Alliata, *The Madaba Map Centenary*, available via the Internet under Franciscan Cyberspot.

Dvorjetski, E., and Segal, A., 'The "Nile Festival" Mosaic and its Relation to the Cultural Life in Eretz Israel in the Roman and Byzantine Periods', *Bamah Dramah Quarterly* 141–2 (1995), 100–5 (Heb.).

Dyson, S. L., 'Native Revolt Patterns in the Roman Empire', *ANRW* II.3 (1975), 138–75.

Edwards, D. R., *Religion and Power: Pagans, Jews, and Christians in the Greek East* (New York 1996).

Ehrlich, M., and Bar, D., 'Jerusalem according to the Description of the Bordeaux Pilgrim: Geography and Theological Aspects', *Cathedra* 113 (2004), 35–52 (Heb.).

Eck, W., 'Zur Neulesung der Julian-Inschrift von Ma'ayan Barukh', *Chiron* 30 (2000), 857–9.

Elad, A., *Medieval Jerusalem and Islamic Worship* (Leiden 1995).

Elbogen, I., *Jewish Liturgy: A Comprehensive History*, trans. with notes R. P. Scheindlin (Philadelphia 1993).

Elert, E., 'Theodore von Pharan und Theodor von Raithu', *Theologische Literaturzeitung* 76 (1951), 67–76.

Eliav, Y. Z., 'Hadrian's Actions in the Jerusalem Temple Mount according to Cassius Dio and Xiphilini Manus', *Jewish Studies Quarterly* 4 (1997), 125–44.

—— 'Temple Mount as a Cult Place and as a Political Center in Judaism and Christianity: A Re-Appraisal', in Y. Reiter (ed.), *Sovereignty of God and Man: Sanctity and Political Centrality on Temple Mount* (Jerusalem 2001), 25–56 (Heb.).

—— *God's Mountain: The Temple Mount in Time, Place and Memory* (Baltimore 2005).

Elior, R., 'From Earthly Temple to Heavenly Shrines: Prayer and Sacred Liturgy in the Hekhalot Literature and its Relation to Temple Traditions', *Tarbiz* 64 (1995), 341–80 (Heb.).

—— 'Hekhalot and Merkavah Literature: Its Relation to Temple, the Heavenly Temple, and the Diminished Temple', in L. I. Levine (ed.), *Continuity and Renewal* (Jerusalem 2004), 107–42 (Heb.).

Elizur, V. (Noam), 'A Glimpse into the World of a Golanide Tanna: Rabbi Eliezer the Qappar', *At Atar* 4–5 (1999), 59–66 (Heb.).

—— See also under Noam-Elizur.

Elliot, J. D., 'The Elusa Oikoumene' (Ph.D., Mississipi State University, 1981).

Elliott, J. K., *The Apocryphal New Testament* (Oxford 1993).

Elm. S., 'Marking the Self in Late Antiquity: Inscriptions, Baptism, and the Conversion of Mimes', in B. Vinken and B. Menken (eds.), *Stigmata* (Weimar 2003), 47–68.

Elsner, J., *Art and the Roman Viewer: The Transformation of Art from the Pagan World to Christianity* (Cambridge 1995).

Elter, R., and Hassoune, A., 'Le Monastère de saint Hilarion: Les Vestiges archéologiques du site de Umm el-Amr', in C. Saliou (ed.), *Gaza dans l'Antiquité Tardive* (Salerno 2005), 13–40.

Epstein, C., and Tzaferis, V., 'The Baptistery at Sussita-Hippos', *Atiqot* 20 (1991), 89–94.

Erikson, K. T., *Wayward Puritans: A Study in the Sociology of Deviance* (New York 1966).

Erickson-Gini, T., 'Nabatean or Roman? Reconsidering the Date of the Camp at Avdat in Light of Recent Excavations', in P. W. M. Freeman *et al.* (eds.), *Limes XVIII: Proceedings of the XVIIIth International Congress of Roman Frontier Studies held in Amman, Jordan* (Sept. 2000) (BAR Int. Ser.; Oxford 2002), 113–30.

—— 'Crisis and Renewal: Settlement in the Central Negev in the Third and Fourth Centuries, with an Emphasis on the Finds from Recent Excavations in Mampsis, Oboda and Mezad 'En Hazeva'' (Ph.D., the Hebrew University of Jerusalem, 2004).

Esbroeck, See under Van Esbroeck.

Eshel, H., 'A Note on "Miqvaot" at Sepphoris', in D. R. Edwards and C. T. McCullough (eds.), *Archaeology and the Galilee* (Atlanta 1997), 131–3.

—— 'The Development of the Attribution of Sanctity to Mount Gerizim', in E. Stern and H. Eshel, *The Samaritans* (Jerusalem 2002), 192–209.

Evans Grubbs, J., *Law and Family in Late Antiquity: The Emperor Constantine's Marriage Legislation* (Oxford 1995).

Evenari, M., *et al.*, *The Negev: The Challenge of a Desert* (Cambridge, Mass., 1971).

Everman, D., 'Survey of the Coastal Area North of Caesarea and of the Aqueducts: Preliminary Report', in R. L. Vann (ed.), *Caesarea Papers* (JRA Suppl. Series 5; Ann Arbor 1992), 181–93.

Fabian, P., 'The Late Roman Military Camp at Beer Sheva: A New Discovery', in *The Roman and Byzantine Near East* (JRA Suppl. 14; Ann Arbor 1995), 235–40.

—— 'Evidence of Earthquake Destruction in the Archaeological Record: The Case of Ancient Avdat', in *Big Cities World Conference on Natural Disaster Mitigation in Conjunction with the Tenth International Seminar on Earthquake Prognostics. Abstracts* (Jan. 1996, Cairo), p. 25.

Febvre, L., *A New Kind of History*, trans. K. Folca (New York 1973).

Federlin, J. L., 'Recherches sur les laures et monastères de la plaine de Jordanie et du désert de Jerusalem', *La Terre Sainte* 20 (1903), 117–331.

Fedwick, E. J., *The Church and the Charisma of Leadership in Basil of Caesarea* (Toronto 1979).

Festugière, A. J. *La Vie de Théodore de Sykéon* (Brussels 1970).

Feuchtwanger, N., 'Late Sixth Century Metal Ampoules', in D. Jacoby and Y. Tsafrir (eds.), *Jews, Samaritans and Christians in Byzantine Palestine* (Jerusalem (1988), 27–52 (Heb.).

Fiema, Z. T., 'Late Antique Petra and its Hinterland: Recent Research and New Interpretations', in J. H. Humphrey (ed.), *The Roman and Byzantine Near East*, 3 (JRA suppl. 49; Portsmouth 2002), 191–252.

—— and Frösén, J., *Petra: A City Forgotten and Rediscovered* (Helsinki 2002).

Figueras, P., 'Monks and Monasteries in the Negev Desert', *LA* 45 (1995), 401–50.

—— *From Gaza to Pelusium: Materials for the Historical Geography of North Sinai and South-West Palestine 332 BCE–640 CE* (=*Beer Sheva* 14; Beer Sheva: Ben Gurion University, 2000).

—— 'Mythological Themes in Palestinian Mosaics from the Byzantine Period', *Aram* 15 (2003), 49–69.

Fine, S., *This Holy Place: On the Sanctity of the Synagogue during the Greco-Roman Period* (Notre Dame 1997).

Finkelstein, L., 'The Oldest Midrash: Pre-Rabbinic Ideals and Teachings in the Passover Haggadah', *HTR* 31 (1939), 291–317.

Fischer, M., *et al.*, *En Boqeq, ii: The Officina—An Early Roman Building on the Dead Sea Shore* (Mainz 2000).

Fishbane, M., 'Oral Tradition in Judaism', in *Scripture beyond the Written Word*, workshop (June 2002, Istanbul) (downloaded from the internet).

Fitzgerald, G. M., *Beth-Shan Excavations 1921–1923. The Arab and Byzantine Levels* (Philadelphia 1931) 18–30.

Fleischer, E., 'Lament on the Killing of Jews in the Land of Israel during Heraclius' Time', *Shalem* 5 (1977), 209–27.

—— 'On Solving the Date and the Provenance of R. Eleazar Birabbi Kilir', *Tarbiz* 54 (1985), 383–427 (Heb.).

Flesher, See under Urman.

Flusin, B., *Miracle et histoire dans l'œuvre de Cyrille de Scythopolis* (Paris 1983).

—— 'Démons et Sarrasins: L'Auteur et le propos des *Diègèmata stèriktika* d'Anastase le Sinaïte', *TM* 11 (1991), 380–409.

—— 'L'Esplanade du Temple à l'arrivée des Arabes d'après deux recits byzantins', in J. Raby and J. Johns (eds.), *Bayt Al-Makdis: Abd al-Malik's Jerusalem* (Oxford 1992), 17–31.

—— *Saint Anastase le Perse et l'histoire de la Palestine au debut du VII s.*, 2 vols. (Paris 1992).

Foerster, G., 'Allegorical and Symbolic Motifs with Christian Significance from Mosaic Pavements of Sixth-Century Palestinian Synagogues', in G. C. Bottini *et al.* (eds.), *Christian Archaeology in the Holy Land: New Discoveries* (Jerusalem 1990), 545–52.

—— 'The Ancient Synagogues of the Galilee', in L. I. Levine (ed.), *The Galilee in Late Antiquity* (New York 1992), 289–319.

—— 'Has there indeed been a Revolution in the Dating of Galilean Synagogues?', in L. I. Levine (ed.), *Continuity and Renewal: Jews and Judaism in Byzantine-Christian Palestine* (Jerusalem 2004), 526–9.

—— and Tsafrir, Y., 'City Center (North): Excavations of the Hebrew University Expedition', in *The Beth Shean Excavation Project (1989–1991), Excavations and Surveys in Israel* 11 (1992), 3–32.

—— See also under Tsafrir.

Fonrobert, C. E., *Menstrual Purity: Rabbinic and Christian Reconstructions of Biblical Gender* (Stanford 2000).

Forsyth, G. K., and Weitzman, K., *The Monastery of St Catherine at Mount Sinai: The Church and the Fortress of Justinian* (Ann Arbor 1973).

Foss, C., 'The Near Eastern Countryside in Late Antiquity: A Review Article', in *The Roman and Byzantine Near East* (1995), 213–34.

Fowden, E. Key, *The Barbarian Plain: Saint Sergius between Rome and Iran* (Berkeley 1999).

Fowden, G., 'Bishops and Temples in the Eastern Roman Empire', *JTS* 29 (1978), 53–78.

—— *Empire to Commonwealth: Consequences of Monotheism in Late Antiquity* (Princeton 1993).

Fradkin, E., 'Jewish Ascalon in the Mishnaic Period', *Cathedra* 19 (1981), 3–10 (Heb.).

Frank, G., *The Memory of the Eyes: Pilgrims to Living Saints in Christian Late Antiquity* (Berkeley 2000).

Frankel, R., and Finkelstein, I., 'The Northeastern Corner of Eretz Israel in the Baraita "Boundaries of Eretz Israel"', *Cathedra* 27 (1983), 39–46 (Heb.).

—— Getzov, N., Aviam, M., and Degani, A., *Settlement Dynamics and Regional Diversity in Ancient Upper Galilee* (Archaeological Survey of Upper Galilee) (Jerusalem 2001).

Fraser, M. A., 'The Feast of the Encaenia in the Fourth Century and in the Ancient Liturgical Sources of Jerusalem' (Ph.D. diss., University of Durham 1995; available through the internet).

Freeman-Grenville, G. S. P., *et al.*, *Palestine in the Fourth Century: The Onomasticon by Eusebius of Caesarea* (Jerusalem 2003).

Friedlander, G. (ed. and trans.), *Pirke de Rabbi Eliezer* (London 1916; repr. New York 1981).

Friedlander, P., *Spätantiker Gemäldezyklus in Gaza, Studi e Testi* 89. (Città del Vaticano 1939).

Friedman, M. A., *Jewish Marriage in Palestine: A Cairo Geniza Study,* 2 vols. (Tel Aviv and New York 1981).

Fritz, V., and Kempinski, A., *Ergebnisse der Ausgrabungen auf Hirbet al-Msas-Tel Masos 1972–1975,* 2 vols. (Wiesbaden 1983).

Frolow, A., 'La Vrai Croix et les expéditions d'Héraclius en Perse', *REB* 11 (1953), 88–105.

Frösén, J., Arjava, A., and Lehtinen, M. (eds.), *The Petra Papyri,* i (ACORP 4; Amman 2002).

—— See also under Fiema.

Frymer-Kensky, T., 'Philosophy and the Case of Sex in the Bible', *Semeia* 45 (1989), 89–102.

Gaddis, M., *There is no Crime for those who have Christ: Religious Violence in the Christian Roman Empire* (Berkeley 2005).

—— See also under Price.

Gafni, I. (ed.), *Land, Center and Diaspora: Jewish Constructs in Late Antiquity* (Sheffield 1997).

—— 'Jerusalem in Rabbinic Literature', in Y. Tsafrir and S. Safrai (eds.), *The History of Jerusalem* (Jerusalem 1999), 35–60.

Gardner, J. F., *Women in Roman Law and Society* (London 1986).

Garitte, G., 'La Vie prémétaphrastique de Saint Chariton', *Bulletin de l'Institut historique belge de Rome* 21 (1941), 16–46.

—— *Le Calendrier Palestino-Géorgien de Sinaiticus 34* (Subsidia Hagiographica 30 Brussels 1958).

—— (ed.), *Expugnatio Hierosolymae AD 614* (Arabic versions and Latin translation) (CSCO 340; Louvain 1973).

Garzya, A., and Loenertz, R.-J. (eds.), *Procopii Gazae Epistolae et Declamationes* (Studia Patristica et Byzantina 9; Rome 1963).

Gatier, P.-L., 'Villages du Proche-Orient protobyzantin (4ème–7ème siècle): Étude régionale', in G. R. D. King and Av. Cameron (eds.), *The Byzantine and Early Islamic Near East,* ii: *Land Use and Settlement Patterns* (Princeton 1994), 17–48.

—— 'Des Girafes pour l'empereur', *Topoi* 6 (1996), 903–41.

—— 'Les Girafes de Gaza', in C. Saliou (ed.), *Gaza dans l'Antiquité Tardive* (Salerno 2005), 75–92.

Geiger, J., 'The Latin Language in Roman Palestine', *Cathedra* 74 (1994), 3–21 (Heb.).

——'How much Latin in Greek Palestine?' in Hannah Rosen (ed.), *Aspects of Latin: Papers from the Seventh International Colloquium on Latin Linguistics*, Jerusalem 1993 (Innsbruck 1996), 39–57.

——'Some Latin Authors from the Greek East', *CQ* 49 (1999), 606–17, esp. 606–12.

——'Language, Culture and Identity in Ancient Palestine', in E. N. Ostenfeld (ed.), *Greek Romans and Roman Greeks: Studies in Cultural Interaction* (Aarhus Studies in Mediterranean Antiquity III; Aarhus 2002), 233–46.

Gersht, R., 'Roman Statuary used in Byzantine Caesarea', in K. G. Holum *et al.* (eds.), *Caesarea Papers*, 2 (Portsmouth 1999), 389–98.

Geva, Hillel (ed.), *Ancient Jerusalem Revealed* (Jerusalem 2000).

Giardina, A., 'Melania the Saint', in A. Fraschetti (ed.), *Roman Women*, trans. L. Lappin (Chicago 2001), 190–207.

Gibson, See under Dauphin.

Gichon, M., *En Boqeq: Ausgrabungen in einer Oase am Toten Meer*, i (Mainz 1993).

Giddens, A., *Studies in Social and Political Theory* (London 1977).

——*Central Problems in Social Theory* (London 1979).

Gil, M., *A History of Palestine 634–1099* (Cambridge 1992).

Giles. See under Anderson.

Ginzberg, L., *The Legends of the Jews*, 7 vols. (Philadelphia 1909–38, repr. 1968).

Girard, R., *Violence and the Sacred* (Baltimore 1977).

——*Des choses cachées depuis la fondation du Monde* (Paris 1978).

Glazier-McDonald. See under McCollough.

Glucker, C. A. M., *The City of Gaza in the Roman and Byzantine Periods* (BAR IS 325; Oxford 1987).

Goldschmidt, E. D., *The Passover Haggadah: Its Sources and History* (Jerusalem 1960), 73–84 (Heb.).

Golinkin, D., 'Jerusalem in Jewish Law and Custom: A Preliminary Typology', in L. I. Levine (ed.), *Jerusalem* (1999), 408–23.

Gonen, R. (ed.), *Contested Holiness: Jewish, Muslim and Christian Perspectives on the Temple Mount in Jerusalem* (Jersey City 2003).

Goodblat, D. M., *The Monarchic Principle: Studies in Jewish Self Governing in Antiquity* (Tübingen 1994).

Goodman, M., 'Palestinian Rabbis and the Conversion of Constantine to Christianity', in P. Schäfer and C. Hezser (eds.), *The Talmud Yerushalmi and Graeco-Roman Culture*, ii (Tübingen 2000), 1–9.

Goranson, S. C., 'Joseph of Tiberias Revisited: Orthodoxies and Heresies in Fourth Century Galilee', in E. M. Meyers (ed.), *Galilee through the Centuries: Confluence of Cultures* (Winona Lake, Ind. 1999), 335–43.

Grant, R. M., *A Short History of Biblical Interpretation* (New York 1948).

Gray, P. T. R., 'Palestine and Justinian's Legislation on Non-Christian Religions', in B. Halpern and D. W. Hobson (eds.), *Law, Politics and Society in the Ancient Mediterranean World* (Sheffield 1993), 241–70.

Greatrex, G., 'Stephanus, the Father of Procopius of Caesarea?', *Medieval Prosopography* 17 (1996), 125–45.

Gregg, R. C., and Urman, D., *Jews, Pagans and Christians in the Golan Heights: Greek and Other Inscriptions of the Roman and Byzantine Eras* (Atlanta 1996).

Grégoire, H., and Kugener M.-A. (eds. and trans.), *Marc le Diacre: Vie de Porphyre, évêque de Gaza* (Paris 1930).

Griffith, S. H., 'From Aramaic to Arabic: The Languages of the Monasteries of Palestine in the Byzantine and Early Islamic Period', *DOP* 51 (1997), 11–31.

Grillmeier, A., *Christ in Christian Tradition, i: From the Apostolic Age to the Council of Chalcedon*, trans. J. Bowden (Atlanta 1975).

Grillmeier, A., and Bacht, H. (eds.), *Das Konzil von Chalkedon: Geschichte und Gegenwart*, 2 (4th edn., Würzburg 1973).

Groh, D., 'The *Onomasticon* of Eusebius and the Rise of Christian Palestine', *SP* 18 (1983), 23–31.

Grossi, V., 'Cross', in *Encyclopedia of the Early Church*, 2 vols. (ed. A. Di Berardino, trans. A. Walford) (New York 1992).

Gutwein, K. C., *Third Palestine: A Regional Study in Byzantine Urbanism* (Washington, DC, 1981).

Haarer, F. K., *Anastasius I. Politics and Empire in the Late Roman World* (Cambridge 2006), 115–62.

Habas, E., 'The Nawa-Der'a Road', *SCI* 14 (1995), 138–42.

—— 'The Halachic Status of Caesarea as Reflected in Talmudic Literature', in A. Raban and K. Holum (eds.), *Caesare Maritima: Retrospective* (Leiden 1996), 454–68.

Hachlili, R., 'Aspects of Similarity and Diversity in the Architecture and Art of Ancient Synagogues and Churches in the Land of Israel', *ZDPV* 113 (1977), 92–122.

—— 'The Zodiac in Ancient Jewish Art: Representation and Significance', *BASOR* 228 (1977), 61–77.

—— *Ancient Jewish Art and Archaeology in the Land of Israel* (Leiden 1988).

—— 'Late Antique Jewish Art from the Golan', in *The Roman and Byzantine Near East: Some Recent Archaeological Research* (JRA Suppl. 14; Ann Arbor 1995), 183–212.

—— 'The Zodiac in Ancient Jewish Synagogal Art', *Jerusalem and Eretz Israel* 1 (2003), 87–122 (Heb.).

HaCohen, D., 'Kadesh and Rekem, Kadesh Barnea and Rekem Geah', *Judea and Samaria Research Studies* 11 (2002), 25–40 (Heb.).

Haiman, M., *Map of Har Hamran Southeast* (199) (Jerusalem: Israel Antiquities Authority, 1993).

—— 'Agriculture and Nomad–State Relations in the Negev Desert in the Byzantine and Early Islamic Periods', *BASOR* 297 (1995), 29–53.

Halbwachs, M., *On Collective Memory* (trans.), L. Coser (Chicago 1992).

Hall, S. G., 'The Origins of Easter', *SP* 15 (1984), 554–67.

—— See also under Cameron.

Halloun, M., and Sharon, M., *Supplement to the Map of Har Nafha: Ancient Rock Inscriptions* (Jerusalem: Israel Antiquities Authority, 1990).

Hamilton, A., 'Jerusalem', in P. Allen *et al.* (eds.), *Prayer and Spirituality in the Early Church* (Everton Park, Qld. Australia, 1998), 291–9.

Hamilton, R. W., 'Two Churches at Gaza as Described by Choricius of Gaza', *PEQ* (1930), 178–91.

Hammond, P. C., 'New Evidence for the Fourth Century Destruction of Petra', *BASOR* 238 (1980), 65–7.

Hanson, R. P. C., 'Biblical Exegesis in the Early Church', in P. R. Ackroyd and C. F. Evans (eds.), *The Cambridge History of the Bible* (Cambridge 1970), I. 412–53.

Haran. See under Brekelmans.

Harkavy, A., 'Me'asef Nidahim', 13, *Ha'meliz* 15 (1879), 640 (Heb.).

Harland, P. A., *Associations, Synagogues, and Congregations: Claiming a Place in Ancient Mediterranean Society* (Minneapolis 2003).

Hartal, M., 'Khirbet Zemel: Northern Golan: An Iturean Settlement', in Zvi Gal (ed.), *Eretz Zafon: Studies in Galilean Archaeology* (Jerusalem: IAA, 2002), 75*–117*.

Hartley, E., *et al.* (eds.), *Constantine the Great: York's Roman Emperor. Catalogue of an Exhibit* (York 2006).

Hassoune. See under Elter.

Hay, K. M., 'Evolution of Resistance: Peter the Iberian, Itinerant Bishop', in P. Allen *et al.* (eds.), *Prayer and Spirituality in the Early Church* (Everton Park, Qld. Australia, 1998), 159–68.

Hefele, C. H., and Leclercq, H. *Histoire des conciles* (Paris 1907–52).

Heinemann, J., 'Remnants of Ancient *Piyyutim* in the Palestinian *Targum* Tradition', *Hasifrut* 4 (1973), 362–75 (Heb.).

Henten, J. W. van, and Avemarie, F., *Martyrdom and Noble Death: Selected Texts from Graeco-Roman, Jewish and Christian Antiquity* (London 2002).

Herford, R. T., *Christianity in Talmud and Midrasch* (1903; repr. 1975).

Herr, M.-D., 'Hellenistic Influences within the Jewish City in Eretz Israel from the Fourth to the Sixth Centuries', *Cathedra* 8 (1978), 90–4 (Heb.).

Herrin, J., *The Formation of Christendom* (Oxford 1987).

—— 'Public and Private Forms of Religious Commitment among Byzantine Women', in L. Archer, S. Fischler, and M. Wyke (eds.), *Women in Ancient Societies: An Illusion of Night* (Basingstoke 1994), 181–223.

Hevelone-Harper, J., *Letters to the Great Old Man: Monks, Laity and Spiritual Authority in Sixth Century Gaza* (Baltimore 2005).

Hezser, C., *The Social Structure of the Rabbinic Movement in Roman Palestine* (Tübingen 1997).

—— 'The (In)Significance of Jerusalem in the Talmud Yerushalmi', in P. Schäfer and C. Hezser (eds.), *The Talmud Yerushalmi and Greco-Roman Culture*, ii (Tübingen 2000), 11–49.

—— *Jewish Literacy in Roman Palestine* (Tübingen 2001).

—— 'Classical Rabbinic Literature', in M. Goodman (ed.), *The Oxford Handbook of Jewish Studies* (Oxford 2002), 115–40.

—— (ed.), *Rabbinic Law in its Roman and Near Eastern Context* (Tübingen 2003).

Hildesheimer, H., and Klein, S., *Studies in the Geography of Eretz Israel*, trans. from German by H. Bar Darom (Jerusalem 1965).

Himmelfarb, M., 'Sefer Zerubbabel', in D. Stern and M. J. Mirsky (eds.), *Rabbinic Fantasies* (Philadelphia 1990), 67–90.

—— 'The Messiah in the Talmud Yerushalmi and Sefer Zerubbabel', in P. Schäfer (ed.), *The Talmud Yerushalmi and Graeco-Roman Culture*, iii (Tübingen 2002), 369–89.

Hirschfeld, Y., 'A Church and Water Reservoir Built by Empress Eudocia', *LA* 40 (1990), 339–71.

—— *The Judean Desert Monasteries in the Byzantine Period* (New Haven 1992).

—— *The Desert of the Holy City: The Judaean Desert Monasteries in the Byzantine Period* (Jerusalem 2002) (Heb.) (an earlier version appeared in English in 1992).

—— (ed.), *Ramat Hanadiv Excavations* (Jerusalem 2000).

—— 'Man and Society in Byzantine Shivta', *Qadmoniot* 125 (2003), 2–17 (Heb.).

—— 'Social Aspects of the Late Antique Village of Shivta', *JRA* 16 (2003), 395–408.

—— 'The Monasteries of Gaza: An Archaeological Review', in B. Biton-Ashkelony and A. Kofsky (eds.), *Christian Gaza* (Leiden 2004), 61–88.

—— and Birger-Calderon, R., 'Early Roman and Byzantine Estates near Caesarea', *IEJ* 41 (1991), 81–111.

Hirshman, M., *Torah for the Entire World* (Tel Aviv 1999) (Heb.).

Hoffman, L. A., *Beyond the Text: A Holistic Approach to Liturgy* (Bloomington 1987) (now available as an electronic book).

—— See also under Bradshaw.

Hohlfelder, R. L., 'A Twilight of Paganism in the Holy Land: Numismatic Evidence from the Excavations at Tell Er Ras', in idem (ed.), *City, Town and Countryside in the Early Byzantine Era* (New York 1982), 77–9.

—— 'Caesarea's Master Harbor Builders: Lessons Learned, Lessons Applied?' in A. Raban and K. G. Holum (eds.), *Caesarea Maritima: Retrospective* (Leiden 1996), 77–101.

Hollerich, M. J., *Eusebius of Caesarea's Commentary on Isaiah* (Oxford 1999).

Holum, K. G., *Theodosian Empresses: Women and Imperial Dominion in Late Antiquity* (Berkeley 1982).

—— *King Herod's Dream: Caesarea on the Sea* (New York 1988).

—— 'Identity and the Late Antique City: The Case of Caesarea', in H. Lapin (ed.), *Religious and Ethnic Communities in Later Roman Palestine* (Bethesda 1998), 159–77.

—— 'The Excavations of the Combined Caesarea Expedition: The Warehouse near the Harbor and Temple Mount', *Qadmoniot* 128 (2004), 102–12 (Heb.).

—— See also under Lehmann.

Hombergen, D., *The Second Origenist Controversy: A New Perspective on Cyril of Scythopolis; Monastic Biographies as Historical Sources for Sixth Century Origenism* (Rome 2001).

—— 'Barsanuphius and John of Gaza and the Origenist Controversy', in B. Biton-Ashkelony and A. Kofsky (eds.), *Christian Gaza in Late Antiquity* (Leiden 2004), 173–81.

Honigmann, E., 'Juvenal of Jerusalem', *DOP* 5 (1950), 209–79.

—— *Le Couvent de Barsum et le Patriarchat Jacobit d'Antioche et de la Syrie* (Louvain 1954).

Horbury, W., 'Suffering and Messianism in Yose ben Yose', in B. McNeil and W. Horbury (eds.), *Suffering and Martyrdom in the New Testament* (Cambridge 1981), 143–82.

—— 'A Proselyte's heis theos Inscription near Caesarea', *PEQ* 129 (1997), 133–7.

—— 'Jews and Christians on the Bible, Demarcation and Convergence (325–451)', in idem, *Jews and Christians in Contact and Controversy* (Edinburgh 1998), 200–25.

Horn, C. B., Review of J.-E. Steppa, *John Rufus and the World Vision of Anti-Chalcedonian Culture* (2002), in *Hugoye: Journal of Syriac Studies* 6 (2003), downloaded from *www.syrcom.cua.edu/Hugoye*.

Horowitz, E., 'The Rite to be Reckless: On the Perpetration and Interpretation of Purim Violence', *Poetics Today* 15 (1994), 9–54.

—— *Reckless Rites: Purim as the Legacy of Jewish Violence* (Princeton 2006).

Hoyland, R., 'Language and Identity: The Twin Histories of Arabic and Aramaic—Why did Aramaic Succeed where Greek Failed?', *SCI* 23 (2004), 183–99.

—— 'History, Fiction and Authorship in the First Centuries of Islam', in J. Bray (ed.), *Writing and Representation in Medieval Islam* (London 2006), 16–46.

Humphrey, J. H., 'Prolegomena to the Study of the Hippodrome at Caesarea Maritima', *BASOR* 213 (1974), 2–45.

—— 'Summary of the 1974 Excavations in the Caesarea Hippodrome', *BASOR* 218 (1975), 1–24.

Hunt, E. D., *Holy Land Pilgrimage in the Later Roman Empire AD 312–460* (Oxford 1982).

—— 'Constantine and Jerusalem', *JEH* 48 (1997), 405–24.

Hunt, E. D., 'Imperial Building at Rome: The Role of Constantine', in K. Lomas and T. Cornell (eds.), *Bread and Circuses: Evergetism and Municipal Patronage in Roman Italy* (London 2003), 105–24.

Huntington, S. P., *The Clash of Civilizations and the Remaking of World Order* (New York 1996).

Huttenmeister, F., and Reeg, G., *Die antike Synagogen in Israel*, i (Wiesbaden 1977).

Ilan, T., *Mine and Yours are Hers: Revealing Women's History from Rabbinic Literature* (Leiden 1997).

Ilan, Z., *Ancient Synagogues in Israel* (Tel Aviv: Ministry of Defense, 1991) (Heb.).

Irshai, O., 'The Christianization of Palestine (Review of Walker)', *Cathedra* 74 (1994), 39–47 (Heb.).

—— 'Constantine and the Jews: The Prohibition against Entering Jerusalem—History and Hagiography', *Zion* 60 (1995), 129–78 (Heb.).

—— 'Cyril of Jerusalem: The Apparition of the Cross and the Jews', in O. Limor and G. G. Stroumsa (eds.), *Contra Iudaeos* (Tübingen 1996), 85–104.

—— 'The Jerusalem Bishopric and the Jews in the Fourth Century: History and Eschatology', in L. I. Levine (ed.), *Jerusalem* (1999), 204–20.

—— 'The Priesthood in Jewish Society of Late Antiquity', in L. I. Levine (ed.), *Continuity and Renewal* (Jerusalem 2004), 67–106 (Heb.).

Isaac, B., *The Limits of Empire* (Oxford 1990).

—— 'Eusebius and the Geography of the Roman Provinces', in D. L. Kennedy (ed.), *The Roman Army in the East* (1996), repr. in B. Isaac, *The Near East under Roman Rule* (Leiden 1998), 284–309.

—— *The Near East under Roman Rule* (Leiden 1998).

—— 'Inscriptions and Religious Identity on the Golan', in *The Roman and Byzantine Near East* 2 (1999), 179–88.

—— 'Epigraphic Remains from the Byzantine Period', in Y. Tsafrir and S. Safrai (eds.), *The History of Jerusalem* (1999), 384–5.

Israel, Y., 'Survey of Pottery Workshops, Nahal Lakish-Nahal Besor', *Excavations and Surveys in Israel* 13 (1993 [1995]), 106–7.

Issar, A. S., and Zohar, M., *Climate Change: Environment and Civilization in the Middle East* (Berlin 2004).

Jacobs, A., *Remains of the Jews: The Holy Land and Christian Empire in Late Antiquity* (Stanford 2004).

Jacobs, M., *Die Institution des jüdischen Patriarchen* (Tübingen 1995).

Jacoby, D., and Tsafrir, Y. (eds.), *Jews, Samaritans and Christians in Byzantine Palestine* (Jerusalem 1988).

Janvier, Y., *La Législation du Bas-Empire romain sur les édifices publics* (Aix-en-Provence 1969).

Japhet, S., 'From the King's Sanctuary to the Chosen City', in L. I. Levine (ed.), *Jerusalem* (New York 1999), 3–15.

Jeremias, J., *Heiligengraber in Jesu Umwelt* (Göttingen 1958).

Jones, A. H. M., 'The Urbanization of the Iturean Principality', *JRS* 21 (1931), 265–75.

—— *The Greek City from Alexander to Justinian* (Oxford 1940).

—— 'The Cloth Industry under the Roman Empire', *Economic History Review* 2 (1960).

—— *The Later Roman Empire*, 2 vols. (Norman, Okla., 1964).

Jüssen, K., *Die dogmatischen Anschauungen des Hesychius von Jerusalem*, 2 vols. (Münster 1931–4).

Juster, J., *Les Juits dans l'empire romain*, 2 vols. (Paris 1914).

Kaegi, W. E., *Byzantium and the Decline of Rome* (Princeton 1968).

—— *Byzantium and the Early Islamic Conquest* (Cambridge 1992).

—— *Heraclius: Emperor of Byzantium* (Cambridge 2003).

Kalimi, I., and Purvis, J. D., 'The Hiding of the Temple Vessels in Jewish and Samaritan Literature', *CBQ* 56 (1994), 679–85.

Kalmin, R., 'Dreams and Dream Interpreters', in idem, *Sages, Stories, Authors and Editors in Rabbinic Babylonia* (Atlanta 1994), 61–80.

Kaplan, M., *Les Propriétés de la couronne et de l'église dans l'empire byzantin (V–Ve S.)* (Byzantina Sorbonensia 2; Paris 1976).

Kasher, M., *Torah Shlema: Megilat Esther* (Jerusalem 1994) (Heb.).

Kasher, R., The Mythological Figure of Moses in Light of Some Unpublished Midrashic Fragments', *JQR* 88 (1998), 19–42.

—— 'The Beliefs of Synagogue *Meturgemanim* and their Audience' in L. I. Levine (ed.), *Continuity and Renewal* (Jerusalem 2004), 420–42.

Kaster, R. A., *Guardians of Language: The Grammarian and Society in Late Antiquity* (Berkeley 1988).

Kedar, B. Z., 'A Dangerous Baptism at Khisfin in the Late 6ᵗʰ Century', in D. Jacoby and Y. Tsafrir (eds.), *Jews, Samaritans and Christians in Byzantine Palestine* (Jerusalem 1988), 238–41 (Heb.).

Kedar, Y., *The Ancient Agriculture in the Negev Mountains* (Jerusalem 1967) (Heb.).

Keenan, J. G., 'The Names Flavius and Aurelius as Status Designations in Late Roman Egypt', *ZPE* 11 (1973), 33–63.

—— 'An Afterthought on the Names Flavius and Aurelius', *ZPE* 53 (1983), 245–50.

Kehoe, P. H., 'The Adultery Mime Reconsidered', in D. F. Bright and E. S. Ramage, *Classical Texts and their Traditions: Studies in Honor of C. R. Trahman* (Chico, Calif., 1984), 89–106.

Kennedy, D., *The Roman Army in Jordan* (London 2004).

Kennedy, G. A., *Greek Rhetoric under the Christian Emperors* (Princeton 1983).

Kessler, E., *Bound by the Bible: Jews, Christians and the Sacrifice of Isaac* (Cambridge 2004).

Khoperia, L., 'Old Georgian Sources concerning Maximus the Confessor's Life', *Le Muséon* 116 (2003), 395–414.

Kimelman, R., '*Birkat Ha-Minim* and the Lack of Evidence for an Anti-Christian Jewish Prayer in Late Antiquity', in E. P. Sanders, A. I. Baumgarten, A. Mendelson (eds.), *Jewish and Christian Self-Definition*, 3 vols. (Philadelphia 1981), ii. 226–44.

Kinzig, W., 'Jewish and "Judaizing" Eschatologies in Jerome', in R. Kalmin and S. Schwartz (eds.), *Jewish Culture and Society under the Christian Roman Empire* (Leuven 2003), 409–29.

Kippenberg, H.-G., *Garizim und Synagoge: Traditionsgeschichtliche Untersuchungen zur Samaritan Religion der aramäischen Period* (Berlin 1971).

Kirk, G. E., and Welles, C. B., 'The Inscriptions', in H. D. Colt (ed.), *Excavations at Nessana*, i (London 1962), 131–97.

Kister, M. J., *Studies on the Emergence of Islam* (Jerusalem 1998).

Klausner, J., *Jesus, his Life, Times and Teaching*, trans. H. Danby (New York 1979).

Klein, M. L., *The Fragments of Targums of the Pentateuch* (Rome 1980).

—— *Genizah Manuscripts of Palestinian Targum to the Pentateuch I–II* (Cincinnati 1986).

Klein, S., *Studies in the Geography of Eretz Israel*, trans. from the German by H. Bar Darom (Jerusalam 1965) (Heb.).

Kleinbauer, W. E., 'Antioch, Jerusalem, and Rome: The Patronage of Emperor Constantius II and Architectural Invention', *Gesta* 45 (2006), 125–45.

Klingenberg, E., 'Roman Imperial Legislation Prohibiting Jews from Owning Gentile Slaves', *Jewish Law Association Studies* 4 (1990), 89–98.

—— 'Justinians Novellen zur Judengesetzgebung', *Aschkenas* 8 (1998), 7–27.

Koet, B. J., ' "Sag lieber, dass er diesen Traum positiv deuten soll": Über die Traumdeutung nach einem rabbinischen Traumbuch (Babylonischer Talmud Berachot 55–57)', *Kirche und Israel* 17 (2002), 133–49.

Kofsky, A., 'Peter the Iberian: Pilgrimage, Monasticism and Ecclesiastical Politics in Byzantine Palestine', *LA* 47 (1997), 209–22.

—— 'Mamre: A Case of a Regional Cult?', in idem and G. G. Stroumsa (eds.), *Sharing the Sacred* (Jerusalem 1998), 19–30.

—— 'What Happened to the Monophysite Monasticism of Gaza', in B. Biton-Ashkelony and A. Kofsky (eds.), *Christian Gaza in Late Antiquity* (Leiden 2004), 183–94.

—— See also under Biton-Ashkelony.

Korjenkov, A. M., and Mazor, E., 'Earthquake Characteristics Reconstructed from Archaeological Damage Patterns: Shivta, the Negev, Israel', *Israel Journal of Earth Sciences* 48 (1999), 265–82.

—— —— 'Seismogenic Origin of Ancient Avdat Ruins, Negev Desert, Israel', *Natural Hazards* 18 (1999), 193–226.

Kraemer, C. J. (ed.), *Excavations in Nessana*, iii: *The Non-Literary Papyri* (Princeton 1958).

Krauss, S., *Griechische und lateinische Lehnwörter im Talmud, Midrasch und Targum* (Berlin 1898; repr. 1964).

—— 'Der Jahrmarkt von Batnan', *ZAW* 29 (1909), 148–52.

—— 'The Emperor Hadrian', *HaShiloah* 39 (1920) (Heb.).

—— 'The Metropolis (*kerach*), City (*ir*) and Village (*kefar*) in the Talmud', *He-Atid* 3 (1923), 50–61 (Heb.).

Kriesberg, L., *The Sociology of Social Conflicts* (Englewood Chiffs, NJ, 1973).

Kristianpoller, A., *Traum und Traumdeutung* (Monumenta Talmudica 2; Vienna and Berlin 1923).

Kruk, R., 'Timotheus of Gaza's On animals in the Arabic Tradition', *Le Muséon* 114 (2001), 355–87.

Kühnel, B., 'Jerusalem in Christian Art from the Fourth to the Seventh Centuries', in Y. Tsafrir and S. Safrai (eds.), *The History of Jerusalem: The Roman and Byzantine Periods 70–638* (Jerusalem 1999), 441–75 (Heb.).

Kuhnen, H.-P., *Studien zur Chronologie und Siedlungsarchäologie des Carmel (Israel) zwischen Hellenismus und Spätantike* (Wiesbaden 1989).

Kundert, L., *Die Opferung/Bindung Isaaks*, 2 vols. (Neukirchen-Vluyn 1998).

Lachs, S. T., 'A Polemical Element in Mishnah Berakot', *JQR* 56 (1965), 81–4.

Lagrange, M. J., 'Le Sanctuaire de la lapidation de saint Étienne à Jérusalem', *ROC* 12 (1907), 412–28.

Lampinen, P., 'The Gold Hoard of 4th-c. Solidi found in 1993', in K. Holum, A. Raban, and J. Patrick (eds.), *Caesarea Papers* 2 (JRA Suppl. Sef. 35; Portsmouth 1999), 368–88.

Lane Fox, R. J., 'The Life of Daniel', in M. J. Edwards and S. Swain (eds.), *Portraits: Biographical Representation in the Greek and Latin Literature of the Roman Empire* (Oxford 1997), 175–225.

Langer, R., 'The Birkat Betulim: A Study of the Jewish Celebration of Bridal Virginity', *Proceedings of the American Academy for Jewish Research* 61 (1995), 59–94.

Lapin, H., 'Rabbis and Cities: Some Aspects of the Rabbinic Movement in its Graeco-Roman Environment', in P. Schäfer and C. Hezser (eds.), *The Talmud Yerushalmi and Graeco-Roman Culture*, ii (Tübingen 2000), 51–80.

Lasker, D. L., and Stroumsa, S., *The Polemic of Nestor the Priest*, 2 vols. (Jerusalem 1996).

Lattimore, R., *Themes in Greek and Roman Epitaphs* (Urbana 1962).

Lawrence, See under Woolley.

Le Déaut, R., *La Nuit pascale: Essai sur la signification de la Pâque juive à partir du Targum d'Exode* (Rome 1963).

Leeb, H., *Die Gesänge im Gemeingottesdienst von Jerusalem (vom 5 bis 8 J.)* (Vienna 1970).

Lehmann, C. M., and Holum, K. G., *The Greek and Latin Inscriptions of Caesarea Maritima: Joint Expedition to Caesarea Maritima Excavation Reports*, 5 (Boston 2000).

Leiman, Z. S., *The Canonization of Hebrew Scriptures: The Talmudic and Midrashic Evidence* (Hamden, Conn., 1976).

Lender, Y., *Map of Har Nafha (196): Archaeological Survey of Israel* (Jerusalem 1990).

Lenski, N., 'Empresses in the Holy Land: The Creation of a Christian Utopia in Late Antique Palestine', in L. Ellis and F. Kindner (eds.), *Travel, Communications and Geography in Late Antiquity* (Aldershot 2004), 113–24.

LeStrange, G., *Palestine under the Moslems: A Description of Syria and the Holy Land from AD 650–1500* (London 1890).

Levenson, D. B., 'Julian's Attempt to Rebuild the Temple: An Inventory of Ancient and Medieval Sources', in H. W. Attridge *et al.* (eds.), *Of Scribes and Scrolls: Studies on the Hebrew Bible, Intertestamental Judaism, and Christian Origins presented to John Strugnell on the occasion of his 60th birthday* (Lanham and New York, 1990), 261–79.

—— 'The Ancient and Medieval Sources for the Emperor Julian's Attempt to Rebuild the Jerusalem Temple', *JSJ* 35 (2004), 408–50.

Levenson, J. D., *The Death and Resurrection of the Beloved Son: The Trans-formation of Child Sacrifice in Judaism and Christianity* (New Haven 1993).

Levey, S. H., *The Messiah: An Aramaic Interpretation—The Messianic Exegesis of the Targum* (Cincinnati 1974).

Lévi, I., 'L'Apocalypse de Zorobabel et le roi de Perse Siroès', *REJ* 68 (1914) and 69 (1919), 108–15.

Levine, L. I., *Roman Caesarea* (Qedem Monographs 2; Jerusalem 1975).

—— 'R. Abbahu of Caesarea', in J. Neusner (ed.), *Christianity, Judaism and Other Graeco-Roman Cults: Studies for Morton Smith at Sixty* (Leiden 1975), 56–76.

—— 'The Inscription in the 'En Gedi Synagogue', in idem (ed.), *Ancient Synagogues Revealed* (Jerusalem 1982), 140–5.

—— *The Rabbinic Class in Roman Palestine in Late Antiquity* (Jerusalem 1989).

—— 'The Sages and the Synagogue in Late Antiquity', in idem (ed.), *The Galilee in Late Antiquity* (New York 1992).

—— 'The Status of the Patriarch in the Third and Fourth Centuries', *JJS* 47 (1996), 1–32.

—— 'Synagogue Officials: The Evidence from Caesarea and its Implications for Palestine and the Diaspora', in A. Raban and K. G. Holum (eds.), *Caesarea Maritima: Retrospective* (Leiden 1996), 392–400.

—— (ed.), *Jerusalem: Its Sanctity and Centrality to Judaism, Christianity and Islam* (New York 1999).

—— *The Ancient Synagogue* (New Haven 2000).

—— 'The History and Significance of the Menorah in Antiquity', in idem and Z. Weiss (eds.), *From Dura to Sepphoris* (JRA Suppl. 20; Portsmouth, RI, 2000), 131–53.

—— 'Contextualizing Jewish Art: The Synagogues at Hammat Tiberias and Sepphoris', in R. Kalmin and S. Schwartz (eds.), *Jewish Culture and Society under the Christian Roman Empire* (Leuven 2003), 91–131.

—— (ed.), *Continuity and Renewal: Jews and Judaism in Byzantine-Christian Palestine* (Jerusalem 2004).

—— 'Between Rome and Byzantium in Jewish History: Documentations, Reality, and the Issue of Periodization', in idem (ed.), *Continuity and Renewal*, 7–48 (Heb.).

Levinson, J., 'Mother of Nations: Literary Identities in a Changing World', in L. I. Levine (ed.), *Continuity and Renewal* (Jerusalem 2004), 465–85 (Heb.).

Levy, M., 'The Struggle of Orthodoxy over the Control of the Jerusalemite Patriarchate in the Seventh Century', *Cathedra* 64 (1992), 31–58 (Heb.).

Levy-Rubin, M., *The Continuatio of the Samaritan Chronicle of Abu L-Fath Al-Samiri Al-Danafi: Text, Translation and Annotation* (Princeton 2002).

Lewy, H., 'Zu dem Traumbuche des Artemidorus', *Rheinisches Museum* 48 (1893), 398–419.

Lewy, Y., 'Julian the Apostate and the Building of the Temple', *The Jerusalem Cathedra* 3 (1983), 70–96.

Lieberman, S., 'The Martyrs of Caesarea', *Annuaire de l'Institut de Philologie et d'Histoire Orientales et Slaves* 7 (1939–44), 395–446.

—— *Hellenism in Jewish Palestine* (New York 1950; 2nd edn., New York 1962).

Lieu, J., 'Melito of Sardis: The *Peri Pascha*', in eadem, *Image and Reality: The Jews in the World of the Christians in the Second Century* (Edinburgh: Clark, 1996), 199–240.

Lieu, S. N. C. (ed.), *The Emperor Julian: Panegyric and Polemic* (Liverpool 1986).

Lifshitz, B., 'Une inscription byzantine de Césarée en Israël', *REG* 70 (1957), 118–32.

—— 'Césarée de Palestine, son histoire et ses institutions', *ANRW* II. 8 (Berlin 1977), 490–518.

—— *Donateurs et fondateurs dans les synagogues juives* (Paris 1967).

Lim, R., *Public Disputation, Power and Social Order in Late Antiquity* (Berkeley 1995).

—— 'Converting the Un-Christianizable: The Baptism of Stage Peformers in Late Antiquity', in K. Mills and A. Grafton (eds.), *Conversion in Late Antiquity and the Early Middle Ages: Seeing and Believing* (Rochester 2003), 84–126.

Limberis, V., *Divine Heiress: The Virgin Mary and the Creation of Christian Constantinople* (New York 1994).

Limor, O., and Stroumsa, G. G. (eds.), *Contra Iudaeos: Ancient and Medieval Polemics between Christians and Jews* (Tübingen 1996).

Linder, A., 'Jerusalem as a Focal Point in the Conflict between Judaism and Christianity', in B. Z. Kedar and Z. Baras (eds.), *Jerusalem in the Middle Ages: Selected Papers* (Jerusalem 1979), 5–26 (Heb.).

—— *The Jews in Roman Imperial Legislation* (Detroit 1987).

Litsas, F. K., 'Choricius' (Ph.D., University of Chicago 1980) (available via the internet).

—— 'Choricius of Gaza and his Descriptions of Festivals at Gaza', *Jahrbuch des österreichischen Byzantinistik* 32 (1982), 427–36.

Littman, E., Magie, D., and Stuart, D. R., *Princeton University Archaeological Expedition to Syria*, III A (Princeton 1921).

Longo, O., 'The Theater of the Polis', in J. J. Winkler and F. I. Zeitlin (eds.), *Nothing to do with Dionysos?* (Princeton 1990), 12–19.

Lozovsky, N., *The Earth is Our Book* (Ann Arbor 2000).

Lurie, B.-Z., *Megillath Taanith* (Jerusalem 1964) (Heb.).

McCollough, C. T., and Glazier-McDonald, B., 'An Aramaic Bronze Amulet', *Atiqot* 28 (1996), 161–5.

—— —— 'Magic and Medicine in Byzantine Galilee: A Bronze Amulet from Sepphoris', in D. R. Edwards and C. T. McCollough (eds.), *Archaeology and the Galilee* (Atlanta 1997), 143–9.

MacDonald, J. (ed.), *Memar Marqah: The Teaching of Marqah*, 2 vols. (Berlin 1963).

McKay, H. A., 'Ancient Synagogues: The Continuing Dialectic between Two Major Views', *Currents in Research: Biblical Studies* 6 (1998), 103–42.

MacMullen, R., 'The Epigraphical Habit in the Roman Empire', *American Journal of Philology* 103 (1982), 233–46.

—— *Christianizing the Roman Empire AD 100–400* (New Haven 1984).

—— 'Judicial Savagery in the Roman Empire', *Chiron* 16 (1986), 147–66; repr. in idem, *Changes in the Roman Empire: Essays in the Ordinary* (Princeton 1990), 67–77.

Mader, E., *Mambre*, 2 vols. (Freiburg 1957).

Magen, Y., 'The Roman Theater of Shechem', in E. Schiller (ed.), *Zeev Vilnay's Jubilee Volume* (Jerusalem 1984), i. 269–77 (Heb.).

—— 'The Church of Mary Theotokos on Mount Gerizim', in G. C. Borrini, L. di Segni, and E. Alliata (eds.), *Christian Archaeology in the Holy Land: New Discoveries. Essay in Honor of Virgilio C. Corbo* (Jerusalem 1990), 333–42.

—— Mount Gerizim—A Temple-City', *Qadmoniot* 23 (1990), 70–96 (Heb.).

—— 'Mount Gerizim and the Samaritans', in F. Manns and E. Alliata (eds.), *Early Christianity in Context: Monuments and Documents* (Jerusalem 1993), 91–148.

—— 'Samaritan Synagogues', in F. Manns and E. Alliata (eds.), *Early Christianity in Context: Monuments and Documents* (Jerusalem 1993), 193–230.

—— 'Samaritan Synagogues', *Judea and Samaria: Research Studies* 2 (1993), 229–64 (Heb.).

—— 'Mount Gerizim during the Roman and Byzantine Periods', *Qadmoniot* 120 (2000), 133–43 (Heb.).

—— 'The Areas of Samaritan Settlement in the Roman-Byzantine Period', in E. Stern and H. Eshel (eds.), *The Samaritans* (Jerusalem 2002), 245–71 (Heb.).

—— 'Samaritan Synagogues', in E. Stern and H. Eshel (eds.), *The Samaritans* (Jerusalem 2002), 382–443 (Heb.).

—— 'The Samaritans in the Roman-Byzantine Period', in E. Stern and H. Eshel (eds.), *The Samaritans* (Jerusalem 2002), 213–44.

—— et al., 'The Church at 'Anab el-Kebir', *Qadmoniot* 36 (2003), 47–54 (Heb.).

—— *Flavia Neapolis: Shechem in the Roman Period* (Jerusalem 2005) (Heb.).

Magness, J., *Jerusalem Ceramic Chronology, circa 200–800* CE (Sheffield 1993).

Magness, J., 'When were the Galilean Synagogues Built?', *Cathedra* 101 (2002), 19–38 (Heb.).

—— *The Archaeology of the Early Islamic Settlement in Palestine* (Winona Lake, Ind., 2003).

—— 'Helios and the Zodiac Cycle in Ancient Palestinian Synagogues', in W. G. Dever and S. G. Gitin (eds.), *Symbiosis, Symbolism and the Power of the Past* (Winona Lake, Ind., 2003), 363–89.

Magness, J., 'Synagogues in Ancient Palestine: Problems of Typology and Chronology', in L. I. Levine (ed.), *Continuity and Renewal* (Jerusalem 2004), 507–25 (Heb.).

—— and Avni, G., 'Jews and Christians in a Late Roman Cemetery at Beth Guvrin', in H. Lapin (ed.), *Religious and Ethnic Communities in Later Roman Palestine* (Bethesda 1998), 87–114.

Maguire, H., 'Truth and Convention in Byzantine Descriptions of Works of Art', *DOP* 28 (1974), 111–40.

—— 'The Good Life', in G. W. Bowersock *et al.* (eds.), *Interpreting Late Antiquity* (Cambridge, Mass., 1999, 2001), 238–57.

Malineau, V., 'L'Apport de l'*Apologie de mimes* de Chorikios de Gaza à la connaissance du théâtre du VIe siècle', in C. Saliou (ed.), *Gaza dans l'Antiquité Tardive* (Salerno 2005), 149–69.

Manfredi, M., *Inno cristiano al Nilo*, in P. J. Parsons and J. R. Rea (eds.), *Papyri: Greek and Egyptian edited by Various Hands in Honor of E. G. Turner* (London 1981), no. 10, pp. 49–62.

Mango, C., *The Art of the Byzantine Empire 312–1453: Sources and Documents* (1972; repr. Toronto 1986).

—— 'Héraclius, Sahrvaraz et la vrai croix', TM 9 (1985), 105–17.

—— 'The Temple Mount AD 614–638', in J. Johns and J. Raby (eds.), *Bayt al Maqdies: Abd al Malik's Jerusalem* (Oxford 1992), 1–16.

Manns, F., 'Un centre Judéo-chrétien important: Sepphoris', in idem, *Essais sur le Judéo-Christianisme* (Studium Biblicum Franciscanum 12; Jerusalem 1977), 165–93.

Maoz, Z., *Jewish Settlements and Synagogues in the Golan* (Kazrin 1980) (Heb.).

—— 'Comments on Jewish and Christian Communities in Byzantine Palestine', *PEQ* 117 (1985), 59–68.

—— 'Hispin', in E. Stern (ed.), *The New Encyclopedia of Archaeological Excavations in the Holy Land*, 4 vols. (New York and Jerusalem 1993).

—— 'The Synagogue at Capernaum: A Radical Solution', in J. Humphrey (ed.), *The Roman and Byzantine Near East*, ii (Portsmouth 1999), 137–48.

Maraval, P., *Lieux saints et pèlerinage d'Orient: histoire et géographie des origines à la conquête arabe* (Paris 1985).

——— 'The Earliest Phase of Christian Pilgrimage in the Near East', *DOP* 56 (2002), 63–74.

Margalit, N., ' "Not by Her Mouth Do We Live": A Literary/Anthropological Reading of Gender in Mishnah Ketubbot Chapter 1', *Prooftext* (2000), 61–86.

Margulies, M., *Midrash Vayyikra Rabbah* (Jerusalem 1960).

Marinescu, C. A., 'Transformations: Classical Objects and their Re-Use during Late Antiquity', in R. W. Mathisen and H. S. Sivan (eds.), *Shifting Frontiers in Late Antiquity* (Aldershot 1996), 285–98.

Markus, R., *The End of Ancient Christianity* (Cambridge 1991).

——— 'How on Earth could Places Become Holy? Origins of the Christian Idea of Holy Places', *JECS* 2/3 (1994), 257–71.

Matthews, J., *Western Aristocracies and Imperial Court* (Oxford 1975).

Mayerson, P., *The Ancient Agriculture Regime of Nessana and the Central Negev* (London: British School of Archaeology in Jerusalem, 1960).

——— 'The First Muslim Attacks on Southern Palestine', *Transactions and Proceedings of the American Philological Association* 95 (1964), 155–99, repr. in idem, *Monks, Martyrs* (1994), 53–98.

——— 'Observations on the "Nilus" Narrationes: Evidence for an Unknown Christian Sect?', *Journal of the American Research Center in Egypt* 12 (1975), 51–74.

——— 'The Ammonius Narrative: Bedouin and Blemmye Attacks in Sinai', in *The Bible World: Essays in Honor of Cyrus H. Gordon* (New York 1980), 133–48.

——— 'The Pilgrim Routes to Mount Sinai and the Armenians', *IEJ* 32 (1982), 44–57.

——— 'The City of Elusa in the Literary Sources of the 4th–6th Centuries', *IEJ* 33 (1983), 247–53.

——— 'Palaestina versus Arabia in Byzantine Sources', *ZPE* 56 (1984), 223–30, repr. in idem, *Monks, Martyrs* (1994), 224–31.

——— 'Antiochus Monachus' on Dreams: An Historical Note', *JJS* 35 (1984), 51–6.

——— 'The Wine and Vineyards of Gaza in the Byzantine Period', *BASOR* 257 (1985), 75–80.

——— 'Choricius of Gaza on the Water Supply System of Caesarea', *IEJ* 36 (1986), 269–72.

——— 'The Saracens and the Limes', *BASOR* 262 (1986), 35–47.

——— 'Libanius and the Administration of Palestine', *ZPE* 69 (1987), 251–60.

——— 'Urbanization in Palaestina Tertia: Pilgrims and Paradoxes', *Cathedra* 45 (1987), 19–40 (Heb.), repr. in Eng. in idem, *Monks, Martyrs* (1994), 232–45.

Mayerson, P., 'Justinian's Novel 103 and the Reorganization of Palestine', *BASOR* 209 (1988), 65–71.

—— 'P. Ness. 58 and two Vaticinia ex Eventu in Hebrew', *ZPE* 77 (1989), 283–6.

—— 'Saracens and Romans: Micro–Macro Relationships', *BASOR* 274 (1989), 71–9.

—— 'The Island of Iotabe in Byzantine Sources', *BASOR* 287 (1992), 1–4, repr. in idem, *Monks, Martyrs* (1994), 352–5.

—— *Monks, Martyrs, Soldiers and Saracens* (Jerusalem 1994).

Mayerson, P., 'A Note on Iotabe and Several Other Islands in the Red Sea', *BASOR* 298 (1995), 33–6.

Mazar, B., *The Mountain of the Lord* (New York 1975).

Mazar, E., *The Temple Mount Excavations in Jerusalem 1968–78*, ii: *The Byzantine and Early Islamic Period* (Jerusalem 2003).

Mazor, G., and Bar Nathan, R., 'Scythopolis: Capital of Palestina Secunda', *Qadmoniot* 27 (1994), 117–37 (Heb.).

Meimaris, Y. E., *Sacred Names, Saints, Martyrs and Church Officials in the Greek Inscriptions and Papyri pertaining to the Christian Church of Palestine* (Athens 1986).

—— and Kritikakou-Nikolarupoulou, K. F., *Inscriptions from Palaestina Tertia*, Ia: *The Greek Inscriptions from Ghor es Safi (Byzantine Zoora)* (Athens 2005).

Melamed, E. Z., 'The *Onomasticon* of Eusebius', *Tarbiz* 3 (1932), 314–27, 393–409; 4 (1933), 78–96, 249–84 (Heb.).

—— *Bible Commentators*, 2nd edn. (Jerusalem 1978).

Mendham, J., *The Seventh General Council, the Second of Nicea, in which the Worship of Images was Established* (London 1849).

Meyers, C., '"Women of the Neighborhood" (Ruth 4.17): Informal Female Networks in Ancient Israel', in A. Brenner (ed.), *Feminist Companion to the Bible: Ruth and Esther*, 2nd seri. (Sheffield 1999), 110 ff.

Michel, A., *Les Églises d'époque byzantine et umayyade de la Jordanie (Provinces d'Arabie et de Palestine), V–VIIIs: Typologie architecturale et aménagements liturgiques* (Turnhout 2001).

Millar, F., *The Emperor in the Roman World* (Ithaca 1977).

—— *The Roman Near East 31 BC–AD 337* (Cambridge, Mass., 1993).

—— 'Ethnic Identity in the Roman Near East 325–450: Language, Religion and Culture', *Mediterranean Archaeology* 11 (1998), 159–76.

—— 'The Theodosian Dynasty and the Arabs: Saracens or Ishmaelites?' in E. Gruen (ed.), *Cultural Borrowings and Ethnic Appropriations in Antiquity* (Stuttgart 2005), 297 f.

—— *A Greek Roman Empire* (Berkeley 2006).

—— 'Libanius and the Near East', *Scripta Classica Israelica* 26 (2007), 155–80.

Miller, S. S., *Studies in the History and Traditions of Sepphoris* (Leiden 1984).

—— 'R. Hanina bar Hama at Sepphoris', in L. I. Levine (ed.), *The Galilee in Late Antiquity* (New York 1992), 175–200.

—— 'The Minim of Sepphoris Reconsidered', *HTR* 86 (1993), 377–402.

—— 'Further Thoughts on the Minim of Sepphoris', in *Proceedings of the Eleventh World Congress of Jewish Studies*, B1 (Jerusalem 1994), 1–8.

—— 'New Perspectives on the History of Sepphoris', in E. M. Meyers (ed.), *Galilee through the Centuries: Confluence of Cultures* (Winona Lake, Ind., 1999), 145–59.

—— 'Those Cantankerous Sepphoreans Revisited', in R. Chazan *et al.* (eds.), *Ki Baruch Hu: Ancient Near Eastern, Biblical and Judaic Studies in Honor of Baruch A. Levine* (Winona Lake, Ind., 1999), 543–73.

—— ' "Epigraphical" Rabbis, Helios, and Psalm 19', *JQR* 91 (2004), 27–76.

Milner, C., 'The Image of the Rightful Ruler: Anicia Juliana's Constantine Mosaic in the Church of Hagios Poleuktos', in P. Magdalino (ed.), *New Constantines: The Rhythm of Imperial Renewal in Byzantium* (Aldershot 1994), 73–81.

Mills, K., and Grafton, A. (eds.), *Conversion in Late Antiquity and the Early Middle Ages: Seeing and Believing* (Rochester 2003).

Mimouni, S. C., *Dormition et assomption de Marie: Histoire des traditions anciennes* (Théologie Historique 98; Paris 1995).

Mirkovic, A. *Prelude to Constantine. The Abgar Tradition in Early Christianity* (Frankfurt 2004).

Misgav, H., 'Development of Jewish Memorial Customs in the Roman-Byzantine Period based on Burial Inscriptions', *Judea and Samaria Research Studies* 11 (2002), 123–36 (Heb.).

Montgomery, J. A., *The Samaritans: The Earliest Jewish Sect, their History, Theology and Literature* (Philadelphia 1907; repr. New York 1968).

Moore, C. A., *Esther* (The Anchor Bible Commentaries; Garden City 1971).

Mor, M., *From Samaria to Shechem: The Samaritans in Antiquity* (Jerusalem 2003).

Moran, O., and Palmach, D., *The Water Cisterns on Negev Mount* (Sde Boker, 1985) (Heb.).

Morony, M. G., 'Economic Boundaries? Late Antiquity and Early Islam', *Journal of the Economic and Social History of the Orient* 47 (2004), 166–94.

Morrisson, C., and Sodini, J.-P., 'The Sixth Century Economy', in A. E. Laiou (ed.), *The Economic History of Byzantium* (Washington, DC, 2002), 171–220.

Moss, C., 'Jacob of Serugh's Homilies on the Spectacles', *Le Muséon* 48 (1935), 87–112.

Moulton, W., 'Gleanings in Archaeology and Epigraphy: A Caesarean Inscription', *Annual of the American School of Oriental Research in Jerusalem* 1 (1919–20), 86–90.

Mouterde, R., 'Antiquités de l'Hermon et de la Beqa', *Mélanges de l'Université Saint Joseph*, Beirut 29 (1951–2), 21–39.

Müller. W., *Die Heilige Stadt: Roma quadrata, himmlisches Jerusalem und die Mythe vom Weltnabel* (Stuttgart 1961).

Münz-Manor, O., 'Carnivalesque Ambivalence and the Christian *Other* in Aramaic Poems from Byzantine Palestine', in G. Stroumsa and R. Barfil (eds.) *Jews in Byzantium* (forthcoming).

Murphy, F. X., 'Melania the Elder: A Biographical Note', *Traditio* 5 (1947), 59–77.

Musil, A., *Arabia Petraea*, 3 vols. (Vienna 1907–8).

Nagy, R. M., *et al.* (eds.), *Sepphoris in Galilee: Crosscurrents of Culture* (North Carolina Museum of Art) (Raleigh 1996).

Nathanson B. Geller, 'The Fourth Century Jewish "Revolt" during the Reign of Gallus' (Ph.D., Duke University 1981).

Nau, F., 'Le Texte grec des récits du moine Anastase sur les saints pères du Sinai', *OC* 2 (1902), 60–89.

—— 'Sur les mots *politikos* et *politeumenos* et sur plusiers textes grecs rélatifs à saint Étienne', *ROC* 11 (1906), 199–219.

—— 'Résumé de monographies syriaques: Histoire de BarSauma de Nisibis', *ROC* 8 (1913), 270–6, 378–89, and *ROC* 9 (1914), 113–34, 278–89, 414–19.

—— 'Deux épisodes de l'histoire juive sous Théodose II d'après la vie de Barsauma le Syrien', *REJ* 83 (1927), 184–206.

Naveh, J., *On Mosaic and Stone* (Jerusalem 1978) (Heb.).

—— 'A Greek Dedication in Samaritan Letters', *IEJ* 31 (1981), 220–2.

—— 'Ancient Synagogue Inscriptions', in L. I. Levine (ed.), *Ancient Synagogues Revealed* (Jerusalem 1982), 133–9.

—— *On Sherd and Papyrus* (Jerusalem 1992) (Heb.).

—— 'The Zoar Tombstones', *Tarbiz* 64 (1995), 476–97 (Heb.).

—— 'Seven New Tombstones from Zoar', *Tarbiz* 69 (2000), 619–35.

Negev, A., 'Nabatean Inscriptions from Avdat', *IEJ* 13 (1963), 113–24.

—— 'The Churches in the Central Negev: An Archaeological Survey', *RB* 81 (1974), 400–22.

—— 'Inscriptions on Rock no. 5 in Wadi Haggag, Sinai', *Eretz Israel* 12 (1975), 134–6 (Heb.).

—— 'The Nabataeans and the Provincia Arabia', in *ANRW* II.6 (1977), 520–686.

—— *The Greek Inscriptions from the Negev* (Jerusalem 1981).

—— *Masters of the Desert: The Story of the Nabataeans* (Jerusalem 1983) (Heb.).

—— *Nabatean Archaeology Today* (New York 1986).

—— *The Architecture of Mampsis: Final Report* (Jerusalem 1988).

—— 'The Cathedral of Elusa and the New Typology and Chronology of the Byzantine Churches in the Negev', *LA* 39 (1989), 129–42.

—— *Personal Names in the Nabatean Realm* (Qedem monographs 32; Jerusalem 1991).

Nelson, B., *On the Roads to Modernity*, ed. T. Hoff (Totowa, NJ, 1981).

Netzer. See also under Weiss.

Netzer, E., and Weiss, Z., 'New Evidence for Late Roman and Byzantine Sepphoris', in J. Humphrey (ed.), *The Roman and Byzantine Near East: Some Recent Archaeological Research* (JRA Suppl. 14; Ann Arbor 1995), 164–76.

Neusner, J., 'The City as Useless Symbol in Late Antique Judaism', in *Major Trends in Formative Judaism*, i: *Society and Symbol in Political Crisis* (Chico, Calif. 1983), 29–40.

—— *Judaism in Society: The Evidence of the Yerushalmi* (Chicago 1983).

—— *Judaism and Christianity in the Age of Constantine* (Chicago 1987).

Nevo, Y., *Pagans and Herders: A Re-Examination of the Negev Runoff Cultivation Systems in the Byzantine and Early Arab Periods* (Sde Boqer 1991).

—— *Ancient Arabic Inscriptions of the Negev* (Jerusalem 1993).

Newman, H. I., 'Jerome and the Jews' (Ph.D., Hebrew University 1997) (Heb.).

—— 'Jerome's Judaizers', *JECS* 9 (2001), 421–52.

Neyt, F., 'A Form of Charismatic Authority', *Eastern Churches Review* 6 (1974), 52–65.

—— *et al.* (eds. and trans.), *Barsanuphe et Jean de Gaza: Correspondance* (SC 426, 427, 450, 451, 469; Paris 1998–2002).

Niehoff, M., 'A Dream which is not Interpreted is like a Letter which is not Read', *JJS* 43 (1992), 58–84.

Nielsen, E. A., *Three Faces of God: Society and the Categories of Totality in the Philosophy of Emile Durkheim* (New York 1999).

Nixon, C. E. V., and Saylor Rodgers, B., *In Praise of Later Roman Emperors: The Panegyrici Latini* (Berkeley 1994).

Noam-Elizur, V., *Megilat Taanit* (Jerusalem 2003) (Heb.).

Norman, A. F., *Libanius' Autobiography: Oration I* (Oxford 1965).

North, J., 'Religious Toleration in Republican Rome', *Proceedings of the Cambridge Philosophical Society* 205 (1979), 85–103.

—— 'The Development of Religious Pluralism', in J. Lieu, J. North, and T. Rajak (eds.), *The Jews among Pagans and Christians in the Roman Empire* (London 1992), 174–93.

Oleson, J. P., 'Artifactual Evidence for the History of the Harbors of Caesarea', in A. Raban and K. G. Holum (eds.), *Caesarea Maritima: Retrospective* (Leiden 1996), 350–77.

Ousterhout, R. G., 'The Church of Santo Stefano: A "Jerusalem" in Bologna', *Gesta* 20 (1981), 311–21.

—— (ed.), *The Blessings of Pilgrimage* (Urbana 1990).

Ovadiah, A., *Corpus of the Byzantine Churches in the Holy Land* (Bonn 1970).

—— 'The Synagogue at Gaza', in L. I. Levine (ed.), *Ancient Synagogues Revealed* (Jerusalem 1982), 129–32.

—— 'Art of the Ancient Synagogues in Israel', in D. Urman and P. V. M. Flesher (eds.), *Ancient Synagogues* (Leiden 1995), 301–18.

—— 'The Mosaic Workshop of Gaza in Christian Antiquity', in D. Urman and P. V. M. Flesher (eds.), *Ancient Synagogues* (Leiden 1995), ii. 367–72.

Panayotakis, C., 'Baptism and Crucifixion on the Mimic Stage', *Mnemosyne* 50 (1997), 302–19.

Panayotov, A., 'The Synagogue in the Copper Market of Constantinople: A Note on the Christian Attitudes towards Jews in the Fifth Century', *OCP* 68 (2002), 319–34.

Parkes, J., *The Conflict of the Church and the Synagogue: A Study in the Rise of Antisemitism* (London 1934).

Parmentier, M., ' "No Stone Upon Another?" Reactions of Church Fathers against the Emperor Julian's Attempt to Rebuild the Temple', in Marcel Poorthuis and Chana Safrai (eds.), *The Centrality of Jerusalem: Historical Perspectives* (Kampen 1996), 143–59.

Patlagean, E., *Pauvreté économique et pauvreté sociale à Byzance* (Paris 1977).

Patrich, J., *Sabas, Leader of Palestinian Monasticism: A Comparative Study in Eastern Monasticism* (Dumbarton Oaks Studies 32; Washington, DC, 1994).

—— 'Warehouses and Granaries in Caesarea Maritima', in A. Raban and K. G. Holum (eds.) *Caesarea Maritima: Retrospective* (Leiden 1996), 146–73.

—— 'The Church of the Holy Sepulchre: History and Architecture', in Y. Tsafrir and S. Safrai (eds.), *The History of Jerusalem* (Jerusalem 1999), 353–81.

—— 'A Chapel of St Paul at Caesarea Maritima?' *LA* 50 (2000), 363–82.

—— 'The Martyrs of Caesarea: The Urban Context', *LA* 52 (2002), 321–46.

Peeters, P., 'Le Sanctuaire de la lapidation de saint Étienne, à propos d'une controverse', *AB* 27 (1906), 359–68.

—— 'La Vie géorgienne de Saint Porphyre de Gaza', *AB* 59 (1941), 65–216.

Pereira, A. S. Rodrigues, *Studies in Aramaic Poetry, c. 100 BCE–c. 600 CE: Selected Jewish, Christian and Samaritan Poems* (Assen 1997).

Perrone, L., Review of Bagatti, *Antichi villagi*, in *Cristianesimo nella storia* 5 (1984), 602–7.

—— 'Dissenso dottrinale e propaganda visionaria: Le Pleroforie di Giovanni di Maiuma', *Augustinianum* 29 (1989), 451–95.

—— 'Monasticism as a Factor of Religious Interaction in the Holy Land during the Byzantine Period', in A. Kofsky and G. Stroumsa (eds.), *Sharing the Sacred: Religious Contacts and Conflicts in the Holy Land* (Jerusalem 1998), 67–98.

—— '"The Mystery of Judaea" (Jerome Ep. 46): The Holy City of Jerusalem between History and Symbol in Early Christian Thought', in L. I. Levine (ed.), *Jerusalem* (1999), 221–39.

—— 'The Necessity of Advice: Spiritual Direction as a School of Christianity in the Correspondence of Barsanuphius and John of Gaza', in B. Biton-Ashkelony and A. Kofsky (eds.), *Christian Gaza in Late Antiquity* (Leiden 2004), 131–49.

Peters. F. E., 'Who built the Dome of the Rock?', *Graeco-Arabica* 1 (1983), 119–38.

—— *Jerusalem* (Princeton 1985).

Peterson, E., *Eis Theos: Epigraphische, formgeschichte und religionsgeschichtliche Untersuchungen.* (Göttingen 1926).

—— *Der Monotheismus als politisches Problem: Ein Beitrag zur Geschichte der politischen Theologie im Imperium Romanum* (Leipzig 1935; repr. 1951).

Peterson, W., 'Eusebius and the Paschal Controversy', in H. Attridge and G. Hata (eds.), *Eusebius, Christianity and Judaism* (Detroit 1992), 311–29.

Petuchowski, J., '"Do This in Remembrance of Me" (I Cor 11:24)', *JBL* 76 (1957), 293–8.

Piccirillo, M., 'Le iscrizioni di Umm er-Rasas-Kastron Mefaa in Giordania I (1986–1987)', *LA* 32 (1987).

—— 'The Jerusalem–Esbous Road', *Studies in the History and Archaeology of Jordan* 3 (1987), 165–72.

—— 'La strada', *LA* 46 (1996), 285–300.

—— 'La chiesa di San Paolo a Umm al-Rasas', *LA* 47 (1997), 389–90.

—— 'Aenon Sapsaphas and Bethabara', in *The Madaba Map Centenary 1897–1997* (Jerusalem 1999), 219–20 (also via Franciscan Cyberspot).

—— and Alliata, E., *Mount Nebo: New Archaeological Excavations 1967–1997* (Jerusalem 1998).

—— —— (eds.), *The Madaba Map Centenary, 1897–1997. Travelling through the Byzantine–Umayyad Period.* Proceedings of the International

Conference held in Amman (Jerusalem 1999). Articles now available via Franciscan cyberspot.

Pieri, D., *Le Commerce du vin oriental à Pépoque Byzantine (V–VII s.). Le Témoignage des amphores en Gaule* (Beirut 2005).

Piganiol, A., 'L'Hémispherion et l'omphalos des lieux saints', *Cahiers archéologiques* 1 (1945), 7–14.

Pirenne, H., *Mohammed and Charlemagne,* Eng. trans. B. Miall (London 1939).

Pixner, B., 'Nazoreans on Mount Zion', in S. Mimouni and F. Stanley Jones (eds.), *Le Judéo-Christianisme dans tous ses états. Actes du Colloque de Jérusalem 1998* (Paris 2001), 289–316.

Politis, C., 'The Sanctuary of Agios Lot, the City of Zoara and the Zared River', in *The Madaba Map Centenary 1897–1997* (Jerusalem 1999), 225–7.

—— 'Ancient Arabs, Jews and Greeks on the Shores of the Dead Sea', *Studies in the History and Archaeology of Jordan* 8 (2004), 361–70.

Porath, Y., 'Pipelines of the Caesarea Water Supply System', *Atiqot* 10 (1990), 100–10 (Heb.).

Porten, B., *Jews of Elephantine and Aramaeans of Syrene* (Jerusalem 1974).

Pressler, C., *The View of Women found in the Deuteronomic Family Laws* (Berlin 1993).

Price, R. M. (trans.), *A History of the Monks of Syria by Theodoret of Cyrrhus* (Cistercian Studies 88; Kalamazoo 1985).

—— (trans.), *Lives of the Monks of Palestine by Cyril of Scythopolis* (Kalamazoo 1991).

—— and Gaddis, M., *The Acts of the Council of Chalcedon,* 3 vols. (TTH; Liverpool 2005).

Primus, C., 'The Borders of Judaism: The Land of Israel in Early Rabbinic Judaism', in L. A. Hoffman (ed.), *The Land of Israel: Jewish Perspectives* (Notre Dame 1986), 97–108.

Pullan, W., 'Jerusalem from Alpha to Omega in the Santa Pudenziana Mosaic', *Jewish Art* 23/24 (1997–8), 405–17.

Pummer, R., *Early Christian Authors on Samaritans and Samaritanism* (Tübingen 2002).

—— See also under Crown.

Purvis, J., 'Joseph in the Samaritan Tradition', in *Studies on the Testament of Moses* (Missoula, Mont. 1975), 147–53.

Quarles, C., 'Jesus as Mamzer. Review Essay', *Bulletin for Biblical Research* 14 (2004), 243–55.

Raban, A., 'The History of Caesarea's Harbors', *Qadmoniot* 37 (2004), 2–22 (Heb.).

—— and Holum, K. G. (eds.), *Caesarea Maritima: Retrospective after Two Millennia* (Leiden 1996).

Rabello, A. M., *Giustiniano, Ebrei e Samaritani alla luce delle fonti storico-litterarie, ecclesiastiche e giuridiche*, 2 vols. (Milan 1987–8).

—— 'The Samaritans in Justinian's Code 1.5', in A. Tal and M. Florentin (eds.), *Proceedings of the First International Congress of the Société d'Études Samaritaines, Tel Aviv, 1988* (Tel Aviv 1991), 139–46.

—— 'The Ban on Circumcision as a Cause of Bar Kokhba Rebellion', *Israel Law Review* 29 (1995), 176–214.

—— 'The Samaritans in Justinian's Corpus Iuris Civilis', *Israel Law Review* 31 (1997), 724 f., repr. in idem, *The Jews in the Roman Empire: Legal Problems from Herod to Justinian* (Aldershot 2000), no. XI.

—— 'The Samaritans in Roman Law', in E. Stern and H. Eshel (eds.), *The Samaritans* (Jerusalem 2002), 481–95 (Heb.).

Ray, W. D., 'August 15 and the Development of the Jerusalem Calendar' (unpub. Ph.D., University of Notre Dame 2000).

Raynor, J. T., 'Social and Cultural Relationships in Scythopolis/Beth Shean in the Roman and Byzantine Periods' (unpub. Ph.D., Duke University 1982).

Reeg, G., *Die Ortsnamen Israels nach der rabbinischen Literatur* (Wiesbaden 1989).

Reeves, J. C., *Trajectories in Near Eastern Apocalyptic: A Postrabbinic Jewish Apocalypse Reader* (Leiden 2005).

Regnault, L., 'Les Apophtegmes en Palestine aux Ve–VIe siècles', *Irénikon* 54 (1981), 320–30.

Rehaut, D., 'Le Récitation d'ekphraseis: une réalité vivante à Gaza au VIe siècle', in C. Saliou (ed.), *Gaza dans l'Antiquité Tardive* (Salerno 2005), 197–220.

Reif, S. C., 'The Early Liturgy of the Synagogue', in W. Horbury *et al.* (eds.), *The Cambridge History of Judaism*, iii (Cambridge 1999), 326–57.

Reijners, G. Q., *The Terminology of the Holy Cross in Early Christian Literature* (Nijmegen 1965).

Reiner, E., 'Joseph the Comes of Tiberias and the Jewish–Christian Dialogue in Fourth Century Galilee', in L. I. Levine (ed.), *Continuity and Renewal* (Jerusalem 2004), 355–86 (Heb.).

Renoux, A., *Le Codex Arménien Jérusalem 121* (PO 36; Turnhout 1971).

Renoux, C., 'Hierosolymitana: Aperçu bibliographique de publications depuis 1960', *Archiv für Liturgiewissenschaft* 23 (1981), 1–29 and 149–75.

Retsö, J., *The Arabs in Antiquity* (London, 2003).

Reynolds, P., 'Levantine Amphorae from Cilicia to Gaza: A Typology and Analysis of Regional Production Trends from the 2nd to the 6th Cent.', in J. M. Gurt, J. Buxed, and M. A. Cau (eds.), *Late Roman Coarse Wares*, i: *Cooking Ware and Amphorae* (BAR IS 1340; Oxford 2005), 563–611.

Reynolds, R. W., 'The Adultery Mine', *CQ* 40 (1946), 77–84.

Richardson, P., 'Archaeological Evidence for Religion and Urbanism in Caesarea Maritima', in T. L. Donaldson (ed.), *Religious Rivalries and the Struggle for Success in Caesarea Maritima* (Waterloo, Ont., 2000), 11–34.

Riskin, S., *Women and Jewish Divorce: The Rebellious Wife, the Agunah and the Right of Women to Initiate Divorce in Jewish Law. A Halakhic Solution* (Hoboken, NJ, 1989).

Robert, L., and Robert, J., 'Bulletin épigraphique', *REG* 71 (1958), 344.

Roberts, M. J., *The Jeweled Style: Poetry and Poetics in Late Antiquity* (Ithaca 1989).

Rokeah, D., 'Ben Stara who is Ben Pantera: Towards the Clarification of a Philological Historical Problem', *Tarbiz* 39 (1970), 9–18 (Heb.).

Rosen, S. A., and Avni, G., *The Oded Sites: Investigations of Two Early Islamic Pastoral Camps South of the Ramon Crater* (Beer Sheva 11; Beer Sheva: Ben Gurion University, 1997).

Rosenfeld, B.-Z., 'The Crisis of the Jewish Patriarchate in the Fourth Century', *Zion* 53 (1988), 239–57.

Rosenfeld, B.-Z., 'Nawa: Capital of the Bashan from Herod to the Muslim Conquest', *Al Atar* 4–5 (1999), 83–93 (Heb.).

Rosenthal-Heginbottom, R. (ed.), T*he Nabataeans in the Negev* (Haifa 2003).

Roth, C., 'The Feast of Purim and the Origins of Blood Accusations', *Speculum* 8 (1933), 520–6.

Roth, M. T., ' "She Will Die by the Iron Dagger": Adultery and Neo-Babylonian Marriage', *Journal of the Economic and Social History of the Orient* 31 (1988), 186–206.

Rothaus, R., 'Christianization and De-Paganization: The Late Antique Creation of a Conceptual Frontier', in R. Mathisen and H. S. Sivan (eds.), *Shifting Frontiers in Late Antiquity* (Aldershot 1996), 299–308.

Roth-Gerson, L., *The Greek Inscriptions from the Synagogues of Eretz Israel* (Jerusalem 1987) (Heb.).

Rousseau, P., *Ascetics, Authority and the Church in the Age of Jerome and Cassian* (Oxford 1978).

Rousselle, A., *Porneia: On Desire and the Body in Antiquity*, trans. F. Pheasant (New York 1996).

Roussin, L., 'A Group of Early Christian Capitals from the Temple Platform', in R. L. Vann (ed.), *Caesarea Papers* (JRA Suppl. Ser. 5; Ann Arbor 1992), 173–7.

—— 'The Zodiac in Synagogue Decoration', in D. R. Edwards (ed.), *Archaeology and the Galilee: Texts and Contexts in the Graeco-Roman and Byzantine Periods* (Atlanta 1997), 83–96.

Rubin, R., *The Negev as a Settled Land: Urbanization and Settlement in the Desert in the Byzantine Period* (Jerusalem 1990) (Heb.).

—— 'Urbanization, Settlement and Agriculture in the Negev Desert: The Impact of the Roman-Byzantine Empire on the Frontier', *ZDPV* 112 (1996), 49–60.

Rubin, Z., 'The Church of the Holy Sepulchre and the Conflict between the Sees of Caesarea and Jerusalem', *Jerusalem Cathedra* 2 (1982), 79–105.

—— 'The Spread of Christianity', in Z. Baras *et al.* (eds.), *Eretz Israel* (Jerusalem 1982), 234–51 (Heb.).

—— 'Christianity in Byzantine Palestine: Missionary Activity and Religious Coercion', *Jerusalem Cathedra* 3 (1983), 97–113.

—— 'Byzantium and Southern Arabia—the policy of Anastasius', in D. H. French and C. S. Lightfoot (eds.), *The Eastern Frontier of the Roman Empire*, ii (Oxford 1989), 383–420.

—— 'The See of Caesarea in Conflict with Jerusalem from Nicaea to Chalcedon', in A. Raban and K. G. Holum (eds.), *Caesarea Maritima: Retrospective* (Leiden 1996), 562–7.

—— 'Porphyrius of Gaza and the Conflict between Christianity and Paganism in Southern Palestine', in G. G. Stroumsa and A. Kofsky (eds.), *Sharing the Sacred* (Jerusalem 1998), 31–66.

—— 'The Cult of the Holy Places and Christian Politics in Byzantine Jerusalem', in L. I. Levine (ed.), *Jerusalem* (New York 1999), 151–62.

—— 'Jerusalem in the Byzantine Period', in Y. Tsafrir and S. Safrai (eds.), *The History of Jerusalem* (Jerusalem 1999), 199–237.

Russell, K. W., 'The Earthquake of May 19, AD 363', *BASOR* 238 (1980), 51.

Rutgers, L., 'Justinian's Novella 146 between Jews and Christians', in R. Kalmin and S. Schwartz, *Jewish Culture and Society* (Leuven 2003), 385–407.

Sadek, M.-M., 'Gaza', *Dossiers d'archéologie* 240 (Jan.–Feb. 1999), 46–67.

Safrai, S., 'The Practical Implementation of the Sabbatical Year after the Destruction of the Second Temple', *Tarbiz* 36 (1967), 1–21 (Heb.).

—— 'The Synagogues south of Mt Judah', *Immanuel* 3 (1973–4), 44–50.

—— 'Jerusalem Pilgrimage after the Destruction of the Second Temple', in A. Oppenheimer *et al.* (eds.), *Jerusalem in the Second Temple Period: Abraham Schalit Memorial Volume* (Jerusalem 1980), 376–93 (Heb.).

—— and Stern, M. (eds.), *The Jewish People in the First Century*, i–ii (Assen 1974–6).

Safrai, Z., 'Samaritan Synagogues in the Roman-Byzantine Period', *Cathedra* 4 (1977), 84–112 (Heb.).

—— 'The Fairs in Eretz Israel during the Period of Mishna and Talmud', *Zion* 49 (1984), 139–58.

—— 'Marginal Notes on the Rehov Inscription', *Zion* 42 (1987), 1–23 (Heb.).

Šahid, I., *The Martyrs of Najran: New Documents* (Subsidia Hagiographia 49; Brussels 1971).

Šahid, I., *Byzantium and the Arabs in the Fifth Century* (Washington, DC, 1989).

—— *Byzantium and the Arabs in the Sixth Century,* i (Washington, DC, 1995).

Saidel, B. A., 'On the Periphery of an Agricultural Hinterland in the Negev Highlands: Rekhes Nafha 396 in the Sixth through the Eighth Centuries CE', *JANES* 64 (2005), 241–55.

Saliou, C. (ed.), 'L'Archéologie palestinienne', *Dossiers d'archéologie* 240 (Jan.–Feb. 1999).

—— 'Gaza dans l'antiquité tardive: nouveaux documents épigraphiques', *RB* 107 (2000), 390–411.

—— (ed.), *Gaza dans l'Antiquité tardive: Archéologie, rhétorique et histoire* (Salerno 2005).

—— 'L'Orateur et la ville: réflexions sur l'apport de Chorikios à la connaissance de l'histoire de l'espace de Gaza', in eadem (ed.), *Gaza dans l'Antiquité tardive* (Salerno 2005), 171–195.

Saller, S. J., *The Memorial of Moses on Mt Nebo,* 3 vols. (1941–50).

Saradi Mendelovici, H., 'The Dissolution of the Urban Space in the Early Byzantine Centuries: The Evidence of the Imperial Legislation', *Symmeikta* 9 (1994), 295–308.

Sarte, M. L., *Trois études sur l'Arabie romaine et byzantine* (Brussels 1982).

Sartre, M., *L'Orient romain* (Paris 1991).

Satlow, M. L., *Jewish Marriage in Antiquity* (Princeton 2001).

Satran, D., *Biblical Prophets in Byzantine Palestine: Reassessing the Lives of the Prophets* (Leiden 1995).

Schick, C., 'Die Stephankirche der Kaiserin Eudokia bei Jerusalem', *ZDPV* 11 (1888), 249–57.

Schick, R., *The Christian Communities of Palestine from Byzantine to Islamic Rule* (Studies in Late Antiquity and Early Islam 2; Princeton 1995).

Schirmann, J., 'The Battle between Behemoth and Leviathan according to an Ancient Hebrew *Piyyut*', *Proceedings of the Israel Academy of Sciences and Humanities* 4.13 (1970), 1–43.

—— 'Yannai the Paytan, his Poetry and his Worldview', in idem, *Studies in the History of Hebrew Poetry and Drama* (Jerusalem 1979), 41–65 (Heb.).

Schwabe, M., 'Eudaimon and the School of Rhetoric at Elusa', *Zion* 2 (1937), 106–20 (Heb.).

Schwartz, E., *Johanness Rufus, ein monophysitischer Schriftsteller* (Sitzungsbericht der Heidelberger Akad. D. Wiss., phil.-hist. Kl.; Heidelberg 1912).

—— *Kyrillos von Skythopolis* (Leipzig 1939).

Schwartz, J., *The Jewish Settlements in Judea after the Bar Kockba War until the Arab Conquest* (Jerusalem 1986) (Heb.).

—— 'The Encaenia of the Church of the Holy Sepulchre, the Temple of Solomon and the Jews', *TZ* 43 (1987), 265–81.

—— 'Gallus, Julian and Anti-Christian Polemic in Pesikta Rabbati', *TZ* 46 (1990), 1–19.

Schwartz, S., *Imperialism and Jewish Society 200 BCE–640 CE* (Princeton 2001).

—— 'Historiography on the Jews in the "Talmudic Period": 70–640 CE', in M. Goodman (ed.), *The Oxford Handbook of Jewish Studies* (Oxford 2002), 79–114.

Scopello, M., 'Julie, manichéenne d'Antioche', *Antiquité tardive* 5 (1997), 187–209.

Seeck, O., *Die Briefe des Libanius* (Leipzig 1906; repr. Hildesheim 1966).

Segal, Al., *Two Powers in Heaven* (Leiden 1977).

Segal, Ar., *The Byzantine City of Shivta, Negev Desert, Israel* (BAR IS 179; Oxford 1983).

—— *Architectural Decoration in Byzantine Shivta, Negev Desert, Israel* (Oxford 1988).

—— *The Theatres in Eretz Israel in Antiquity* (Jerusalem 2000) (Heb.).

—— and Eisenberg, M., 'Hippos-Sussita of the Decapolis: First Five Years of Excavation' [sic], *Qadmoniot* 38 (2005), 15–29.

—— *et al.*, *Hippos-Sussita: Fifth Season of Excavations (2004) and Summary of all Five Seasons (2000–2004)* (Haifa 2005).

—— See also under Dvorjetski.

Seligsohn. See under Adler.

Sellers, R. V., *The Council of Chalcedon: A Historical and Doctrinal Survey* (London 1953).

Sharon, M., 'The Cities of Eretz Israel under Islamic Rule', *Cathedra* 40 (1986), 83–120 (Heb.).

—— *Corpus Inscriptionum Arabicarum Palaestinae*, i (Leiden 1997).

Shaw, B. D., 'The Camel in Roman North Africa and the Sahara; History, Ideology and the Human Economy', *Bulletin de l'Institut fondamental d'afrique noire*, Dakar 4 (1979), 663–721; repr. in idem, *Environment and Society in Roman North Africa* (Aldershot 1995).

Shereshevski, Y., *Byzantine Urban Settlements in the Negev Desert* (Beer Sheva 5; Beer Sheva: Ben Gurion University, 1991).

Shnan, A., *One Bible and Multiple Translations: Torah Tales in Light of Aramaic Targumim* (Tel Aviv 1993).

Shoemaker, S. J., ' "Let Us Go and Burn Her Body": The Image of the Jews in Early Dormition Traditions', *JECS* 68 (1999), 775–823.

—— 'The (Re?)Discovery of the Kathisma Church and the Cult of the Virgin in Late Antique Palestine', *Maria: A Journal of Marian Studies* 2 (2001), 21–72.

Shoemaker, S. J., *Ancient Traditions of the Virgin Mary's Dormition and Assumption* (Oxford 2002).

—— 'Christmas in the Qur'an: The Qu'ranic Account of Jesus' Nativity and Palestinian Local Tradition', *Jerusalem Studies in Arabic and Islam* 28 (2003), 24–7.

Shotwell, W. A., *The Biblical Exegesis of Justin Martyr* (London 1965).

Silberman, L. H., 'Challenge and Response: Pesiqta de Rab Kahana Chapter 26 as an Oblique Reply to Christian Claims', *HTR* 79 (1986), 247–53.

Simmel, G., *Conflict and the Web of Group Affiliations*, trans. K. H Wolff and R. Bendix (Glencoe, Ill., 1955).

Simon, M., 'Remarques sur l'angélolatrie juive au début de l'ère chrétienne', *Comptes rendues de l'Académie des Inscriptions et Belles Lettres* (1971), 120–34.

—— 'Anti-Jewish Polemic: The Arguments Employed' in idem, *Verus Israel*, 156–78.

—— *Verus Israel*, trans H. McKeating (Oxford 1986).

Sion, O., 'Jordan Desert Asceticism', *Qadmoniot* 29 (1996), 25–32 (Heb.).

—— 'The Monasteries of the "Desert of the Jordan"', *LA* 46 (1996), 245–64.

Sivan, H., *Biblical Images: The Dura Europos Synagogue*. Guide to the exhibit (New Haven 1978).

—— 'Holy Land Pilgrimage and Western Audience: Egeria and her Circle', *CQ* 38 (1988), 528–35.

—— 'Who was Egeria? Pilgrimage and Piety in the Age of Gratian' *HTR* 81 (1988), 59–71.

—— 'Pilgrimage, Monasticism, and the Emergence of Christian Palestine in the Fourth Century', in R. Ousterhout (ed.), *The Blessings of Pilgrimage* (Urbana 1990), 54–65.

—— 'Anician Women, The Cento of Proba, and Aristocratic Conversion in the Fourth Century', *VC* 47 (1993), 140–57.

—— 'On Hymen and Holiness in Late Antiquity: Opposition to Aristocratic Female Asceticism at Rome', *Jahrbuch für Antike und Christentum* 36 (1993), 81–93.

—— 'Rabbinics and Roman Law: Jewish–Gentile (Christian) Marriage in Late Antiquity', *REJ* 156 (1997), 59–100.

—— 'The Body of a Sinner. The Price of Piety: The Politics of Adultery in Late Antiquity', *Annales* 53 (1998), 231–53.

—— 'Revealing the Concealed: Rabbinic and Roman Legal Perspectives on the Crime of Adultery', *ZSS.RA* 116 (1999), 112–46.

—— 'From Byzantine to Persian Jerusalem: Jewish Perspectives and Jewish–Christian Polemics', *GRBS* 41 (2000), 277–306.

—— 'The Silent Women of Yehud: Notes on Ezra 9', *JJS* 51 (2000), 3–18.

—— 'Canonizing Law in Late Antiquity: Legal Constructs of Judaism in the Theodosian Code', in M. Finkelberg and G. G. Stroumsa (eds.), *Homer, the Bible and Beyond: Literary and Religious Canons in the Ancient World* (Leiden 2002), 213–25.

—— *Dinah's Daughters: Gender and Judaism from the Hebrew Bible to Late Antiquity* (Philadelphia 2002) (as H. Zlotnick).

—— 'From Athanaric to Ataulf: The Shifting Horizons of "Gothicness" in Late Antiquity', in J.-M. Carrié and R. Lizzi Testa (eds.), *Humana Sapit: Études d'antiquité tardive offertes à Lellia Cracco Ruggini* (Turnhout and Paris 2002), 55–62.

—— *Between Woman, Man and God: A New Interpretation of the Ten Commandments* (New York 2004).

—— 'Palestine between Byzantium and Persia (CE 614–619', in *La Persia e Bisanzio. Atti dei Convegni Lincei* (Rome 2004), 77–92.

—— 'Contesting Calendars: The 9th of Av and the Feast of the Theotokos', in B. Caseau *et al.* (eds.), *Pèlerinages et lieux saints dans l'antiquité et le Moyen Âge* (Paris 2006), 443–56.

Slotki, J. J., *Midrash Rabbah: Leviticus* (London 1939; repr. 1961).

Smith Lewis, A., *The Forty Martyrs of the Sinai Desert and the Story of Eulogios* (Hora Semiticae 9; Cambridge 1912).

Smith, J. Z., 'Towards Interpreting Demonic Powers in Hellenistic and Roman Antiquity', in *ANRW* II. Principat 16.1 (Berlin 1978), 425–39.

Smith, M., 'Helios in Palestine', *Eretz Israel* 16 (1982), 199–214.

Smith, P., 'People of the Holy Land from Prehistory to the Recent Past', in T. Levy (ed.), *The Archaeology of Society in the Holy Land* (Leicester 1995).

Smith, R. B. E., *Julian's Gods: Religion and Philosophy in the Thought and Action of Julian the Apostate* (London 1996).

Sokoloff, M., and Yahalom, J., *Jewish Palestinian Aramaic Poetry from Late Antiquity. Critical Edition with Introduction and Commentary* (Jerusalem 1999) (Heb.).

Solzbacher, R., *Mönche, Pilgrer und Sarazen: Studien zum Frühchristentum auf der südlichen Sinaihalbinsel von den Anfangen bis zum Beginn islamischer Herrschaft* (Altenberge 1989).

Spain Alexander, S., 'Heraclius, Byzantine Imperial Ideology and the David Plates', *Speculum* 52 (1977), 217–37.

Starr, J., 'Byzantine Jewry on the Eve of the Arab Conquest (565–638)', *JPOS* 15 (1935).

Stemberger, B., 'Der Traum in der rabbinischen Literatur', *Kairos* 18 (1976), 1–42.

Stemberger, G., *Introduction to the Talmud and Midrash*, trans. M. Bock-muehl (Edinburgh 1991).

—— 'Exegetical Contacts between Christians and Jews in the Roman Em-pire', in C. Brekelmans and M. Haran (eds.), *Hebrew Bible/Old Testament* (Göttingen 1996), 569–86.

—— *Jews and Christians in the Holy Land: Palestine in the Fourth Century*, trans. R. Tuschling (Edinburgh 2000).

Stenhouse, P., *The Kitab al-Tarikh of Abu'l Fath* (Sydney 1985).

Stenhouse, P., 'Samaritan Chronicles', in A. D. Crown (ed.), *The Samaritans* (Tübingen 1989), 218–65.

Steppa, J.-E., *John Rufus and the World Vision of Anti-Chalcedonian Culture* (Piscataway, NY, 2002).

—— 'Heresy and Orthodoxy: The Anti-Chalcedonian Hagiography of John Rufus', in B. Biton-Ashkelony and A. Kofsky (eds.), *Christian Gaza in Late Antiquity* (Leiden 2004), 89–106.

Stern, D., 'Midrash and the Language of Exegesis: A Study of Vayikra Rabbah, Chapter 1', in G. H. Hartman and S. Budick (eds.), *Midrash and Literature* (New Haven 1986), 105–24.

Stern, E., 'Transforming Comfort: Hermeneutics and Theology: The Haftarot of Consolation', *Prooftexts* 23 (2003), 150–81.

—— and Eshel, H. (eds.), *The Samaritans* (Jerusalem 2002) (Heb.).

Stern, I., 'The Art of the Image in the Halakha during the Mishna and Talmud Periods', *Zion* 61 (1996), 397–419 (Heb.).

Stern, M., *Greek and Latin Authors on Jews and Judaism*, 2 vols. (Jerusalem 1980).

Stern, S., *Jewish Identity in Early Rabbinic Writings* (Leiden 1994).

—— *Calendar and Community* (Oxford 2001).

—— See also under Stern, I.

Sternberg, A. G., *The Zodiac of Tiberias* (Tiberias 1972) (Heb.).

Stevenson, K. W., 'The Ceremonies of Light: Their Shape and Function in the Paschal Vigil Liturgy', *Ephemerides Liturgicae* 99 (1985), 175 ff.

Stone, Michael E., *Armenian Inscriptions from Sinai: An Intermediate Report* (Sydney 1979).

—— *The Armenian Inscriptions of the Sinai* (Cambridge, Mass., 1982).

Strange, J., 'Some Remarks on the Synagogues of Capernaum and Khirbet Shema', in L. I. Levine (ed.), *Continuity and Renewal* (Jerusalem 2004), 530–43.

Stroumsa, G. G, 'Whose Jerusalem'? *Cathedra* 11 (1989), 119–24 (Heb.).

—— 'From Anti-Judaism to Antisemitism in Early Christianity', in O. Limor and G. G. Stroumsa (eds.), *Contra Iudaeos: Ancient and Medieval Polemics between Christians and Jews* (Tübingen 1996), 1–26.

—— 'Mystical Jerusalems', in L. I. Levine (ed.), *Jerusalem* (New York 1999), 349–70.

—— See also under Limor.

Stroumsa, S. See under Lasker.

Strus, A., *Khirbet Fattir-Bet Gemal: Two Ancient Jewish and Christian Sites in Israel* (Rome 2003).

Stulman, L., 'Sex and Familial Crimes in the D Code: A Witness to Mores in Transition', *Journal for the Study of the Old Testament* 53 (1992).

Sussman, Y., 'A Halakhic Inscription from the Beth Shean Valley', *Tarbiz* 43 (1973–4), 88–158 (Heb.).

—— 'The Boundaries of Eretz Israel', *Tarbiz* 45 (1976), 213–57 (Heb.).

—— 'The Inscription in the Synagogue at Rehov', in L. I. Levine (ed.), *Ancient Synagogues Revealed* (Jerusalem 1981), 146–53.

Swartz, M., 'Sage, Priest, and Poet: Typologies of Religious Leadership in the Ancient Synagogue', in S. Fine (ed.), *Jews, Christians, and Polytheists in the Ancient Synagogue* (London 1999), 101–17.

Tabory, J., *Jewish Festivals in the Time of the Mishnah and Talmud* (Jerusalem 1995), 323–67 (Heb.).

—— *The Passover Ritual throughout the Generations* (Tel Aviv 1996) (Heb.).

Tajfel, H., *Human Groups and Social Categories* (Cambridge 1981).

Tal, A., 'The Hebrew and Aramaic Literature of the Samaritans', in E. Stern and H. Eshel (eds.), *The Samaritans* (Jerusalem 2002), 519–36 (Heb.).

Tal, A. See also under Crown.

Talgam, R., 'Similarities and Differences between Synagogue and Church Mosaics in Palestine during the Byzantine and Umayyad Periods', in L. I. Levine and Z. Weiss (eds.), *From Dura to Sepphoris* (Portsmouth 2000), 93–110.

—— See also under Weiss.

—— 'Measuring Time in Sixth-Century Gaza: The Clock Ekphrasis of Procopius', in J. Patrich, L. Di Segni, and R. Talgam (eds.), *Festschrift in Honor of Yoram Tsafrir* (forthcoming).

—— 'The Ekphrasis Eikonos of Procopius of Gaza: The Depiction of Mythological Themes in Palestine and Arabic during the Fifth and Sixth Centuries', in B. Bitton Ashkelony and A. Kofsky (eds), *Christian Gaza in Late Antiquity* (Leiden 2004), 209–34.

Talmon, S., 'Biblical Traditions on Samaritan History', in E. Stern and H. Eshel, *The Samaritans* (Jerusalem 2002), 7–27.

Tampellini, S., 'Aspetti di polemica anti giudaica nell'opera di Esichio', *Annali di Storia dell'Esegesi* 16 (1999), 353–8.

Taylor, J. E., *Christians and the Holy Places: The Myth of Jewish-Christian Origins* (Oxford 1993).

Taylor, J. E., 'Introduction' in eadem *et al.*, *Palestine in the Fourth Century: The Onomasticon of Eusebius of Caesarea* (Jerusalem 2003).

Taylor, M. S., *Anti-Judaism and Early Christian Identity: A Critique of Scholarly Consensus* (Leiden 1994).

Thomas, D., *Anti-Christian Polemic in Early Islam: Abu Isa al Warraq's Against the Trinity* (Cambridge 1992).

Thomsen, P., 'Palästina nach dem Onomasticon des Eusebius', *ZDPV* 26 (1903), 97–198.

—— 'Die lateinischen und griechischen Inschriften der Stadt Jerusalem', *ZDPV* 44 (1921).

Thornton, T. C. G., 'The Crucifixion of Haman and the Scandal of the Cross', *JTS* 37 (1986), 419–26.

Thunberg, L., 'Early Christian Interpretations of the Three Angels in Gen 18', *SP* 8 (1966), 560–70.

Treggiari, S., *Roman Marriage: Iusti Coniugi from the Time of Cicero to the Time of Ulpian* (Oxford 1991).

Trendall, A. D., *The Shellal Mosaic* (Canberra 1957).

Trexler, R., 'From the Mouths of Babes: Christianization by Children in Sixteenth Century New Spain', in *Church and Community, 1200–1600* (Rome 1987), 549–73.

Trifon, D., 'Did the Priestly Courses Move from Judah to Galilee after the Bar Kokhba Revolt?', *Tarbiz* 59 (1990), 77–93 (Heb.).

Trombley, F., 'Brumalia', *Oxford Dictionary of Byzantium* 1 (New York 1991), 327–8.

—— *Hellenic Religion and Christianization, c. 370–529*, 2 vols. (Leiden 1993–5).

Tsafrir, Y., 'Jerusalem', *Reallexicon zur byzantinischen Kunst* 3 (1975), 525–615.

Tsafrir, Y., 'The Provinces in Eretz-Israel: Names, Limits and Administrative Zones', in Z. Baras *et al.* (eds.), *Eretz Israel from the Destruction of the Second Temple to the Muslim Conquest* (Jerusalem 1982), 350–86 (Heb.).

—— 'Why were the Negev, the Southern Transjordan and the Sinai transferred from the Provincia Arabia to Provincia Palestina at the end of the Third Century?' *Cathedra* 30 (1983), 35–56 (Heb.).

—— *Eretz Israel from the Destruction of the Second Temple to the Muslim Conquest*, ii: *Archaeology and Art* (Jerusalem 1984) (Heb.).

—— *Ancient Churches Revealed* (Jerusalem 1993).

—— 'The Synagogues at Capernaum and Meroth and the Dating of the Galilean Synagogue', in J. Humphrey (ed.), *The Roman and Byzantine Near East* (Ann Arbor 1995), 151–61.

—— 'The Fate of Pagan Cult Places in Palestine: The Archaeological Evidence with emphasis on Beth Shean', in H. Lapin (ed.), *Religious and Ethnic Communities in Later Roman Palestine* (Bethesda 1998), 197–218.

—— 'Byzantine Jerusalem: The Configuration of a Christian City', in L. I. Levine (ed.), *Jerusalem* (New York 1999), 133–50.

—— 'The Topography and Archaeology of Aelia Capitolina', in idem and S. Safrai (eds.), *The History of Jerusalem: The Roman and Byzantine Periods (70–638 CE)* (Jerusalem 1999) (Heb.), 115–66.

—— and Foerster, G., 'From Byzantine Scythopolis to Arab Baysan: Changing Urban Concepts', *Cathedra* 64 (1992), 3–30 (Heb.).

—— —— 'From Scythopolis to Baysan: Changing Concepts of Urbanism', in G. R. D. King and Av. Cameron (eds.), *The Byzantine and Early Islamic Near East*, ii (Princeton 1994), 95–115.

—— —— 'Urbanism at Scythopolis-Beth Shean in the Fourth to the Seventh Centuries', *DOP* 51 (1997), 85–146.

—— *et al.*, *Excavations at Rehovot in the Negev*, i: *The North Church* (Qedem Monographs 25; Jerusalem 1988).

—— See also under Di Segni.

Turner, J. H., *The Structure of Sociological Theory* (Homewood, Ill., 1974).

Turner, V., *Dramas, Fields and Metaphors: Symbolic Action in Human Society* (Ithaca, NY, 1975).

Twomey, V., *Apostolikos Thronos: The Primacy of Rome as reflected in the Church History of Eusebius and the Historico-Apologetic Writings of Saint Athanasius* (Münsterische Beiträge zur Theologie; Münster 1982).

Tzaferis, V., and Avner, R., 'The Excavations at Banias', *Qadmoniot* 23 (1990), 110–14 (Heb.).

—— and Bar Lev, S., 'A Byzantine Inscription from Khisfin', *Atiqot* 11 (1976), 114–15.

—— and Urman, D., 'Excavations at Kursi', *Qadmoniot* 6 (1973), 62–4 (Heb.).

—— See also under Epstein.

Ulmer, R., 'The Semiotics of the Dream Sequence in Talmud Yerushalmi Ma'aser Sheni', *Henoch* 23 (2001), 305–23.

Urbach, E. E., 'Homilies of the Rabbis on the Prophets of the Nations and the Balaam Stories', *Tarbiz* 25 (1956), 272–89 (Heb.).

—— 'Rabbinic Exegesis on Origen and Jewish–Christian Polemics', *Scripta Hierosolymitana* 22 (1971), 247–75.

—— *The Sages: Their Concepts and Beliefs*, trans. I. Abrahams, 2 vols. (Jerusalem 1979; repr. 1987).

Urman, D., 'Jewish Inscriptions from Dabbura in the Golan', *IEJ* 22 (1972), 16–23.

—— *The Golan: A Profile of a Region during the Roman and Byzantine Periods* (BAR IS 269; Oxford 1985).

Urman, D., 'Public Structures and Jewish Communities in the Golan Heights', in idem and Flesher, P. V. M., (eds.), *Ancient Synagogues: Historical Analysis and Archaeological Discovery* (Leiden 1995), 373–617.

——— 'Nessana Excavations 1987–1995', in idem (ed.), *Nessana. Excavations and Studies*, i (Beer Sheva 2004), 1*–118*.

——— See also under Gregg.

Vailhé, S., 'Les Monastères et les églises St Étienne à Jérusalem', *EO* 8 (1905), 78–86.

Valbelle, D., and Bonnet, C. (eds.), *Le Sinaï durant l'antiquité et le Moyen Âge: 4000 ans d'histoire* (Paris 1998).

Valler, S., *Women and Womanhood in the Stories of the Babylonian Talmud* (Tel Aviv 1993) (Heb.).

Van Dam, R., 'From Paganism to Christianity at Late Antique Gaza', *Viator* 16 (1985), 1–20.

Van den Ven, P., 'Les Écrits de S. Syméon Stylite le Jeune avec trois sermons inédits', *Le Muséon* 70 (1957).

Van der Horst, P., *Japheth in the Tents of Shem: Studies on Jewish Hellenism in Antiquity* (Leuven 2002).

——— and Parmentier, M. F. G., 'A New Early Christian Poem on the Sacrifice of Isaac', in *Le Codex de Vision* (2002), 155–72.

Van Esbroeck, M., 'The Georgian Inscriptions', in M. E. Stone, *The Armenian Inscriptions of the Sinai* (Cambridge, Mass., 1982), 171–9.

——— 'Jean II de Jérusalem et les cultes de S Étienne, de la Sainte Sion et de la Croix', *AB* 102 (1984), 99–134.

——— 'Le soi-disant Roman de Julien l'Apostat', *OCA* 229 (1987), 191–202.

——— 'Un canon liturgique géorgien pour l'assomption de la Vierge', repr. in idem, *Aux origines de la Dormition de la Vierge: Études historiques sur les traditions orientales* (Variorum 1995), xiv. 1–18.

Van Nuffelen, P., 'Deux fausses lettres de Julien l'Apostat', *VC* 55 (2001), 131–50.

Van Parys, M., 'Abba Silvain et ses disciples: Une famille monastique entre Scété et la Palestine à la fin du IVe et dans la première moitié du Ve siècles', *Irenikon* 61 (1988), 315–31.

Vasiliev, A. A., 'Notes on Some Episodes concerning the Relations between the Arabs and the Byzantine Empire from the Fourth to the Sixth Century', *DOP* 9–10 (1956), 306–16.

Verhelst, S., 'Une homélie de Jean de Bolnisi et la durée du carême en Syrie-Palestine', *Questions Liturgiques* 78 (1997), 201–20.

——— 'Trois remarques sur la *Pesiqta de-rav Kahana* et le christianisme', in S. Mimouni and F. Stanley Jones (eds.), *Le Judéo-Christianisme dans tous ses états*. Actes du colloque de Jérusalem 1998 (Paris 2001), 367–80.

——— 'Le 15 août, le 9 Av et le Kathisme', *Questions Liturgiques* 82 (2001), 161–91.

—— 'Les Lieux de station du lectionnaire de Jérusalem', *POC* 54 (2004), 13–70.

Vilnay, Z., *Legends of Jerusalem* (Philadelphia 1987).

Vincent, H.-L., 'Le Sanctuaire juif d'Ayn Duq', *RB* 28 (1919), 532–63.

—— and Abel, F.-M., *Jerusalem nouvelle*, II.2 (Paris 1925).

—— and Benoit, B., 'Un sanctuaire dans la région de Jéricho: La Synagogue de Naarah', *RB* 68 (1961), 163–77.

—— and Carriere, B., 'La synagoga de Noaarah', *RB* 30 (1921), 579–601.

Visotzky, B. L., 'Anti-Christian Polemic in Leviticus Rabbah', *PAAJR* 56 (1990), 83–100; repr. in idem, *Fathers of the World: Essays in Rabbinic and Patristic Literature* (Tübingen 1995).

Vitto, F., 'The Interior Decoration of Palestinian Churches and Synagogues', *BF* 21 (1995), 283–300.

Vogt, J., *Kaiser Julian und das Judentum* (Leipzig 1939).

Von Erffa, H. M., *Ikonologie der Genesis*, 2 vols. (Munich 1995).

Von Schonborn, C., *Sophrone de Jérusalem: Vie monastique et confession dogmatique* (Paris 1972).

Wainwright, P., 'The Authenticity of the Recently Discovered Letter Attributed to Cyril of Jerusalem', *VC* 40 (1986), 286–93.

Walfish, B. D., *Esther in Medieval Garb: Jewish Interpretation of the Book of Esther in the Middle Ages* (Albany, NY, 1993).

Walker, P., *Holy City, Holy Places? Christian Attitudes to Jerusalem and the Holy Land in the Fourth Century* (Oxford 1990).

—— 'Cyril of Jerusalem: The Apparition of the Cross and the Jews', in O. Limor and G. G. Stroumsa (eds.), *Contra Iudaeos* (Tübingen 1996), 85–104.

Warner, M., and Safrai, Z., 'Hoards and Revolts: The Chronological Distribution of Coin Hoards in Eretz Israel during the Roman and Byzantine Periods', *Cathedra* 101 (2001), 71–90.

Wasserfall, R. K. (ed.), *Women and Water: Menstruation in Jewish Life and Law* (Hanover, NH, 1999).

Wasserstein, D. J., 'Why did Arabic Succeed where Greek Failed? Language Change in the Near East after Muhammad', *SCI* 22 (2003), 257–72.

Weber, M., *From Max Weber: Essays in Sociology*, trans. H. H. Gerth and C. Wright Mills (New York 1946).

Wechsler, M. G., 'The Purim-Passover Connection: A Reflection of Jewish Exegetical Tradition in the Peshitta Book of Esther', *JBL* 117 (1998), 321–7.

Wegner, A., 'Aux origines de la croyance en l'Assomption: L'Homélie de Théoteknos de Livias en Palestine (fin du VI–début du VII siècle)', in *De Primordiis Cultus Mariani*, vol. iv (Rome 1970), 327–39.

Wegner, J. R., *Chattel or Person? The Status of Women in the Mishnah* (New York 1988).

Weingarten, S., ' "And This Shall Be A Token To Thee" (EX 3: 12): *Lapis Sinaiticus* in Jewish and Christian Traditions', *JJS* 54 (2003), 1–20.

Weippert, M., 'Archäologischer Jahresbericht', *ZDPV* 82 (1966), 274–330.

Weiss, Z., 'Greco-Roman Influences on the Art and Architecture of the Jewish City in Roman Palestine', in H. Lapin (ed.), *Religious and Ethnic Communities* (Bethesda 1998), 219–46.

—— 'The Sepphoris Synagogue Mosaic and the Role of Talmudic Literature in its Iconographical Study' in L. I. Levine and Z. Weiss (eds.), *From Dura to Sepphoris* (JRA Suppl. 20; Portsmouth, RI, 2000), 15–30.

—— 'Biblical Stories in Early Jewish Art: Jewish–Christian Polemic or Intracommunal Dialogue', in Lee I. Levine (ed.), *Continuity and Renewal* (Jerusalem 2004), 245–69 (Heb.).

—— *The Sepphoris Synagogue: Deciphering an Ancient Message through its Archaeological and Socio-Historical Contexts* (Jerusalem 2005).

Weiss, Z., and Netzer, E., *Promise and Redemption: A Synagogue Mosaic from Sepphoris* (Jerusalem 1996).

—— —— 'Sepphoris during the Byzantine Period', in R. M. Nagy *et al.* (eds.), *Sepphoris in Galilee: Crosscurrents of Culture* (Winona Lake, Ind., 1996), 81–8.

—— —— 'Architectural Development of Sepphoris during the Roman and Byzantine Periods', in D. R. Edwards and C. T. McCollough *Archaeology and the Galilee: Texts and Contexts in the Graeco-Roman and Byzantine Periods* (Atlanta 1997), 117–30.

—— —— 'The Excavations of the Hebrew University Expedition in Sepphoris 1992–1996', *Qadmoniot* 30 (1997), 3–21 (Heb.).

—— and Talgam, R., 'The Nile Festival Building and its Mosaics: Mythological Representations in Early Byzantine Sepphoris', in J. H. Humphrey (ed.), *The Roman and Byzantine Near East* (JRS Suppl. 49; Portsmouth, RI, 2002), 55–90.

Weitzman. See under Forsyth.

Wenham, G. T., 'Betulah: A Girl of Marriageable Age', *Vetus Testamentum* 22 (1972), 326–48.

Wharton, A., *Refiguring the Post Classical City: Dura Europos, Jerash, Jerusalem and Ravenna* (Cambridge 1995).

—— 'Erasure: Eliminating the Space of Late Ancient Judaism', in L. I. Levine and Z. Weiss (eds.), *From Dura to Sepphoris* (JRA Suppl. 40; Portsmouth, RI, 2000), 195–214.

Whitcomb, D., Review of Avni, *Nomads*, and of Rosen and Avni, *The Oded Sites*, *BASOR* 311 (1998), 100–2.

White, M. L., *Building God's House in the Roman World* (Baltimore 1990).

Wiedemann, T. E. J. *Emperors and Gladiators* (London 1992).

Wilken, R. L., *Chrysostom on the Jews: Rhetoric and Reality in the Late Fourth Century* (Berkeley 1985).

—— 'The Restoration of Israel in Biblical Prophecy: Christian and Jewish Responses in the Early Byzantine Period', in J. Neusner and S. Frerichs (eds.), *To See Ourselves as Others See Us* (Chico, Calif., 1985), 443–72.

—— *The Land Called Holy: Palestine in Christian History and Thought* (New Haven 1992).

—— 'Loving the Jerusalem Below: The Monks of Palestine', in L. I. Levine (ed.), *Jerusalem* (New York 1999), 240–50.

Wilkinson, J., 'Christian Pilgrims in Jerusalem during the Byzantine Period', *PEQ* 108 (1976), 75–101.

—— *Egeria's Travels in the Holy Land* (Jerusalem and Warminster 1981).

—— *Jerusalem Pilgrims before the Crusades*, rev. edn. (Warminster 2002).

Wind, W., 'The Crucifixion of Haman', *Journal of the Warburg Institute* 1 (1937), 245–8.

Winkler, J. J., and Zeitlin F. I. (eds.), 'Introduction', in *Nothing to do with Dionysos? Athenian Drama in its Social Context* (Princeton 1990).

Wolf, C. U., 'Eusebius of Caesarea and the *Onomasticon*', *BA* 27 (1964), 66–96.

Woolley, C. L., and Lawrence, T. E., *The Wilderness of Zin* (London 1936).

Wutz, F., *Onomastica Sacra: Untersuchungen zum Liber Interpretationis Hebraicorum Nominum des Hl Hieronymus* (TU 41; Leipzig 1914).

Yahalom, J., 'On the Validity of Literary Composition as a Historical Source', *Cathedra* 11 (1979), 125–33 (Heb.).

—— 'Angels do not Understand Aramaic. On the Literary Use of Jewish Palestinian Aramaic in Late Antiquity', *JJS* 47 (1996), 33–44.

—— *Poetry and Society in Jewish Galilee of Late Antiquity* (Tel Aviv 1999) (Heb.).

—— 'The Temple and the City in Liturgical Hebrew Poetry', in J. Prawer and H. Ben-Shammai (eds.), *The History of Jerusalem* (Jerusalem and New York 1999), 270–94.

Yankelevitch, R., 'The Proportion between the Size of the Jewish and Gentile Population in Eretz Israel in the Era of the Mishnah and the Talmud', *Cathedra* 61 (1991), 156–75 (Heb.).

Yarnold, E., *Cyril of Jerusalem* (London 2000).

Yeivin, Z., 'On the Medium Size City', *Eretz Israel* 19 (1987), 59–71 (Heb.).

Youtie, H. C., 'Ostraca from Sbeita', *American Journal of Archaeology* 40 (1936), 452–7.

Yuval, I. J., 'Those who skip: The Passover Haggadah and Christian Easter', *Tarbiz* 65 (1995), 5–28 (Heb.).

—— 'Easter and Passover as Early Jewish–Christian Dialogue' in P. F. Bradshaw and L. A. Hoffman, *Passover and Easter: Origin and History to Modern Times* (Notre Dame 1999), 98–124.

Yuval, I. J., *'Two Nations in Your Womb'*: *Perceptions of Jews and Christians* (Tel Aviv 2000) (Heb.).

Zadok, R., 'The Ethno-Linguistic Character of the Semitic-Speaking Population (excluding Jews and Samaritans) of Lebanon, Palestine and Adjacent Regions during the Hellenistic, Roman and Byzantine Periods: A Preliminary Survey of the Onomastic Evidence', *Michmanim* 12 (1998), 5*–36*.

Zertal, A., 'The Samaritans in the District of Caesarea', *Ariel* 48 (1979), 98–116.

Zigelman, A., 'Castra or Porphyrion?', *Michmanim* 15 (2001), 32–6 (Heb.).

Zlotnick, H. See under Sivan.

Zohar. See under Issar.

Zori, N., 'An Archaeological Survey of the Beth Shean Valley', in *The Beth Shean Valley. The 17th Archaeological Convention* (Jerusalem 1962), 124–98 (Heb.).

—— 'The House of Kyrios Leontius at Beth Shean', *IEJ* 16 (1966), 123–34.

Index